AF324859

# Cases on
# International Business
# and Finance in
# Japanese Corporations

Second Edition

# Cases on International Business and Finance in Japanese Corporations

**Mitsuru Misawa**
*University of Hawai'i at Mānoa, USA*

**World Scientific**

NEW JERSEY • LONDON • SINGAPORE • BEIJING • SHANGHAI • HONG KONG • TAIPEI • CHENNAI

*Published by*

World Scientific Publishing Co. Pte. Ltd.

5 Toh Tuck Link, Singapore 596224

*USA office:* 27 Warren Street, Suite 401-402, Hackensack, NJ 07601

*UK office:* 57 Shelton Street, Covent Garden, London WC2H 9HE

**Library of Congress Cataloging-in-Publication Data**
Misawa, Mitsuru, 1936–
   Cases on international business and finance in Japanese corporations / Mitsuru Misawa. --
2nd edition.
     pages cm
  Includes index.
  ISBN 978-9814663090 (alk. paper)
  1. Corporations--Japan--Finance.  2. International business enterprises--Japan.  I. Title.
  HG4245.M47  2015
  332'.0410952--dc23

                          2015001530

**British Library Cataloguing-in-Publication Data**
A catalogue record for this book is available from the British Library.



In-house Editors: Qi Xiao/Sandhya Venkatesh

Typeset by Stallion Press
Email: enquiries@stallionpress.com

Printed in Singapore by B & Jo Enterprise Pte Ltd

**Dedications**

To my two daughters,
Anne Megumi Misawa and Marie Lei Misawa
And to my two grandchildren,
Madelyn Kimie Wong and Dylan Minghui Misawa Wong

# Preface to the Second Edition

Since the release of the first edition, it has been widely used as both a professional reference and an academic text suitable for upper-level undergraduate or graduate courses at business schools. The objective of this book is to provide relevant and in-depth information on the current state of business in Japan.

I recently conducted additional case constructions of 10 Japanese companies from field studies, consisting of numerous visits to and interviews with managers of those corporations. The second edition contains these 10 new cases added to reflect the most current changes in the economy that have taken place in Japan since the release of the first edition.

When the world economy is facing serious difficulties, the management of Japanese corporations is attracting attention from all over the world. Many of these corporations have been successful in the marketing, production, financing, and allocation of their resources in today's borderless environment. However, these success stories are only partially known in the world.

As shown in this casebook, Japanese businesses have already entered a new era in which they must modify major traditional management practices, such as corporate solidarity, homogeneity, and commitment, in order to succeed. They must introduce the concepts of individualism and the merit system into their management practices. They must also maintain the advantages of their present legal and regulatory system while at the same time discarding its weak points. They have realized the necessity of shifting away from their conventional system and adopting some new practices. Japanese businesses are aware that the economy can take new steps toward progress only when a new style of Japanese business and legal system is established. Today, Japanese businesses feel the necessity of maintaining their positive assets while at the same time nurturing management techniques oriented towards entrepreneurship and high-technology industries.

In coping with rapid changes in the environment, Japanese management techniques and legal practices continue to change. In the era of internationalization, Japan and foreign countries have followed a path of convergence, despite differing in traditions. By following this course, businesses both in Japan and abroad are expected to achieve greater progress in productivity, cost efficiency, and profit maximization, while maintaining good quality control. Professionals must be open-minded in evaluating these techniques and practices, regardless of the source country, and must try to be both flexible and aggressive in experimenting with innovations, in order to refine and polish the traditional techniques and practices of their own styles of business. An analysis of these techniques and practices, based on a wide range of actual case studies, would be invaluable for anyone seeking to improve their business practices. The efficacy and practicality of any management technique is put to the test only when transplanted from the soil in which it was nurtured to a new and different environment.

There is a great deal to be learned from such a study by both Japanese and foreign professionals. In this sense, the management techniques and legal practices newly adopted by Japan, and the Japanese management techniques and legal practices adopted by foreign countries, are an area of research that fully deserves the attention of scholars and experts both in Japan and foreign countries. These studies should serve as valuable test cases for the theory and practice of modern business. It is hoped that this casebook will be used as a starting point for such studies.

Reflecting these problem consciousness, my endeavor of case writing for Japanese companies and industries as teaching material has been very successful. My 20 cases are listed on Harvard Business Publishing (HBS) for sale in the US, on the Asian Case Research Center (ACRC), University of Hong Kong (http://www.acrc.org.hk/) for sale in Asia and on ECCH (the European Case Clearing House) (http://www.ecch.com/) for sale in Europe. For a list of my 20 cases on HBS, please visit:

http://cb.hbsp.harvard.edu/cb/web/search_results.seam?Ntt=misawa&N=0&searchButton.x=20&searchButton.y=11.

In 2013, 2,575 copies of my cases were sold through Harvard Business Publishing (2,219 copies), ECCH (162 copies) and University of Hong

Kong (194 copies). The total number of my cases sold in the past seven years is now 13,526 copies (for details, see the tables in the Appendix).

Top business schools of the world such as Harvard Business School, MIT Sloan School of Management and Wharton School are constantly using my cases as shown in the Appendix. Taking this opportunity, I decided to publish my second edition of the casebook containing my 20 cases for better serving the needs of worldwide users of my cases.

As Appendix shows, as constant big users, you will find notable names such as Harvard, MIT, Northwestern, University of Washington, USC, Wharton, and Cornell in the US, and SDA Bacconi School of Management (Italy), which is ranked 5th MBA in Europe and 15th in the world by the *Financial Times,* and Instituto De Empresa, Business (Spain), which *Financial Times*, 2013, European Business School Ranking, ranked 1st in Europe. It also shows all the big users' names and the large and prestigious users in the past five years (2009–2013).

Finally, I would like to express my deep appreciation to my two daughters, Anne Megumi Misawa and Marie Lei Misawa, who have provided me with continued support and encouragement during the writing of this casebook.

Mitsuru Misawa
Honolulu, Hawaii

# Preface to the First Edition

*Now Japan continues to drive change. We've learned much over the past years from companies in Japan. The best practices that we've learned on how to develop new products or how to work better in teams, many of those have come from Japanese companies.*[1]

> — Jeffrey R. Immelt, chairman and CEO,
> General Electric Company, US

Japan is a country that is extremely difficult for outsiders to understand. Language plays the most basic barrier to understanding the culture: the only language used to communicate among inhabitants is Japanese; English is used to a limited degree for education and in daily life. Moreover, Japanese people are extremely cautious in disclosing their thoughts to outsiders. The basis of this attitude lies in the traditional character of the Japanese people, which is expressed in various mottos and proverbs, such as "Silence is golden" and "Speaking less makes one look more graceful." Corporations are no exception and are run essentially on the same principles.

Japan has the second largest gross national product in the world. It exports an enormous number of excellent quality products, such as automobiles, home appliances, and electronic components that are closely integrated into the daily lives of people the world over. Thus, corporations and consumers around the world are interested in better understanding Japan's economy, how its corporations are run, and how decisions about its products are made.

---

[1] Nikkei Global Management Forum (October 20, 2003) "GE's Strategy for Building Corporate Value", http://www.nni.nikkei.co.jp/FR/NIKKEI/ngmf/ngmf2003/2003ngmf_sp_immelt.html.

However, case studies of Japanese corporations written in English are not readily available. There are two reasons behind this:

1.  It is partly due to the attitudes of Japanese corporations. They do not wish to have their case studies published unless authored by someone with whom they have a close relationship and whom they can trust.
2.  While there are quite a few foreign scholars who claim to be well versed on Japanese matters, a very limited number are capable of communicating in Japanese, and so their information is limited to secondhand sources, i.e., articles and books already written in English. This language deficiency makes it difficult for foreign scholars to write about the Japanese economy and corporations and, similarly, difficult for Japanese scholars to write case studies in English because of their limited English language abilities.

Meanwhile, the demand for cases written about Japanese corporations as teaching materials is accelerating. This is due to the following factors:

1.  The number of business schools in the US that focus on Asia-Pacific studies is increasing. The Shidler College of Business at the University of Hawai'i at Mānoa, where I am a professor, is one of those schools. A thorough education focusing on the Asia-Pacific region requires case studies of Japanese corporations.
2.  The trend shows that an increasing number of universities in the US are teaching courses about Japanese corporations and their peculiarities. The re-emergence of Japanese corporations, after experiencing a period of negative growth for 15 years, known as the "lost age", is attracting worldwide attention. The number of US corporations and students who wish to study the revival process is increasing.
3.  The internationalization of the Japanese economy prompted the internationalization of Japanese education as well. Most of the leading Japanese universities are now offering MBA courses in English. Side by side, Japanese and foreign students are studying to be future international business professionals.

The lack of case studies written in English and the growing demand for such case studies are the reasons I have written this casebook. After visiting a number of corporations and meeting with their top executives, I have developed field case studies from 10 corporations that I believe will provide outsiders with an understanding of the Japanese economy and Japanese corporations. These case studies contain abundant information and data that could be collected only by a Japanese person and are quite unique in that they are written from an insider's perspective. It is my hope that this casebook will be used by universities in the US, as well as in Japan and other Asian countries.

Over the years I have gained much insight into both Japanese and American issues of finance, law, and international business. I have had first-hand involvement and extensive dealings with various projects for many companies. I have had considerable access to relevant information and also have a broad-based familiarity with the issues discussed in the cases. It is because of my own long experience in the fields of international finance and business that the top management of these corporations allowed me to write their case studies.

This casebook is meant for use as a textbook in business schools for their graduate or undergraduate International Business and International Finance courses. My students of International Finance, both graduate and undergraduate, at Shidler College of Business at the University of Hawai'i at Mānoa, have given me positive feedback about these cases.

This casebook may also be useful for business people interested in Japanese corporations and the Japanese economy. Foreign companies dealing with Japanese companies may achieve smoother business transactions with a better understanding of their counterparts, and those companies intending to do business with Japanese companies will be better prepared by reading this casebook.

The cases in this book deal with international business and finance. Each case presented is a real story. These cases were selected to depict, as accurately as possible, the issues that the Japanese economy and Japanese corporations are facing today. Each case contains a fair amount of previously undisclosed information used by the executive to make actual decisions. A case study relying solely on published information will limit the skills and the insights that the reader can obtain through analytical exercises. By including this previously undisclosed information, the reader will be able to realistically place himself/herself in the shoes of the executive who made the decision.

Each case presents multiple decisions that could be made, and all of those decisions might be correct. There is no way to ascertain which decision is best. Therefore, it is not a question of whether the actual decision made by the executive was correct. The reader is supposed to identify the issues first, then analyze the various problems that exist, and, finally, decide on the course of action. Necessary and sufficient information for this process is included in each case. The aim of these cases is to learn about the decision-making process and the techniques used in making an "intelligent" decision, based on the given information. It, therefore, is far more convincing, and the student can face the case more sincerely, if the case is based on an actual incident rather than a fictitious one.

Although it is not possible to completely understand the Japanese economy or Japanese corporations merely through these cases, the reader should be able to get a good grasp of them. I trust my selection will fulfill this purpose.

Mitsuru Misawa

# Acknowledgments

I am grateful to the following people who helped me publish this casebook.

First of all, I wish to thank the Asia Case Research Center (ACRC), the University of Hong Kong who has copyright for all my 20 cases and who allowed publishing this casebook, the second edition, by World Scientific. It is a tremendous benefit for students to be able to purchase one book containing all of my 20 cases, rather than having to buy each case individually.

In my research for the 20 cases, I had to visit companies, arrange interviews, and obtain reference materials. I am therefore indebted to the executives of these companies for their kind understanding and cooperation.

It was necessary for me to make several trips to Japan to complete my work. This would not have been possible without the research fund provided by Shidler College of Business, the University of Hawai'i at Mānoa. I wish to sincerely thank all these helps.

Above all, I wish to express my love and gratitude to my family, especially my two daughters, Anne Megumi Misawa and Marie Lei Misawa, for their support of this book and their contribution to my research.

My hometown is in Nagano Prefecture, Japan, an area known for its beautiful mountains and rivers. My parents rest there. The University of Hawai'i at Mānoa, where my office is located, is in Blue Hawai'i, an island paradise full of beautiful hibiscus flowers in the southern Pacific. As I worked on this casebook, I thought of my hometown thousands of miles away, and admired the gentle undulation of Diamond Head through the window of my office.

Mitsuru Misawa

# About the Author

Dr. Misawa received his LLB from Tokyo University Law School in 1960, LLM from Harvard Law School in 1964, MBA from the University of Hawai'i as an East–West Center grantee in 1965 and PhD from the University of Michigan (International Finance) in 1967.

He is a professor of finance (International Finance and International Banking) and the director of the Center for Japanese Global Investment and Finance at the University of Hawai'i, which was established in 1997 under the sponsorship of the Council for Better Corporate Citizenship of Japanese Keidanren (Japanese Federation of Economic Organizations). He was granted tenure at the University of Hawai'i in June 1998.

Before he joined the University of Hawai'i in August 1996, he had been with the Industrial Bank of Japan (IBJ), the most prestigious investment bank in Japan, (now Mizuho Financial Group), for 30 years. His career included assignments as an investment banker in New York and Tokyo, for 15 years each. During his career at IBJ, he served as the executive vice president, IBJ Trust Bank (NY), deputy general manager, Loan Department, IBJ (Tokyo), in charge of large scale companies such as Nissan, Sony, Komatsu, etc., the general manager, International Headquarter, IBJ (Tokyo), and the president, IBJ Leasing (NY) as well as a member of the board of directors, IBJ Leasing (Tokyo). One of the financial arrangements he conducted as an investment banker at IBJ was the Nissan Motor's direct investment to manufacture trucks and cars in Smyrna, Tennessee in 1983. For a total financing of $400 million, he employed "global financial engineering" techniques. Since then, these techniques have been widely used by other Japanese investment to the US.

His researches have been published in numerous academic and professional journals, including *Sloan Management Review, Financial Management, The Columbia Journal of World Business, Vanderbilt Journal of Transnational Law, The Banking Law Journal, Temple International and Comparative Law Journal, Columbia Journal of Asian Law, Journal of International Law and Business of Northwestern University School of Law*, and *Penn State International Law Review* (the Dickinson School of Law).

In the US, his 20 Cases are listed on Harvard Business Online (http://cb.hbsp.harvard.edu/cb/search/misawa?Ntk=HEMainSearch&N=0) under Misawa. They are also listed on the European Case Clearing House (http:/www.ecch.com/) in Europe and on the Asian Case Research Center (ACRC) at University of Hong Kong (http:/www.acrc.org.hk/) in Asia. Through them, he sold 2,060 copies of his cases in 2007, 1,555 copies in 2008, 1,895 copies in 2009, 2,327 copies in 2010, 1,492 copies in 2011, 1,798 copies in 2012, 2,575 copies in 2013 and 2,778 copies in 2014. The total number sold to universities and companies worldwide in the past eight years is 16,304 copies. Harvard Business School (MBA) purchased 1,063 copies of his cases for their own use in 2010. Other major universities and business schools such as MIT, USC, Wharton School and Cornell are also constant users of his case (for the details, see Appendix).

From 1989 to 1996, he served as the US Counselor on the Keidanren's "Council for Better Corporate Citizenship". From 1993 to 1996, he had served as a member of the Business School's Visiting Committee of the University of Michigan, which was composed of global business executives. Dr. Misawa was appointed "Colonel of the State of Kentucky" in 1984 and "Arkansas Traveler" in 1985 by the two states in recognition of his achievements in soliciting Japanese investments for them.

In September 2011, Dr. Misawa published a book entitled *Current Business and Legal Issues in Japan's Banking and Finance Industry*, Second Edition (five new chapters added to the first edition) by World Scientific.

His current address:

**Mitsuru Misawa, PhD**
Professor of Finance
Director of the Center for Japanese Global
    Investment and Finance
Shidler College of Business
University of Hawaiʻi at Mānoa
2404 Maile Way, E-601E
Honolulu, HI 96822-2282, USA
Tel: (808) 956-9713
Fax: (808) 956-9713
E-mail: misawa@hawaii.edu
Webpage: http://www2.hawaii.edu/~misawa/

# Contents



**1 Tokyo Disneyland: Licensing vs. Joint Venture**     **33**

Tokyo Disneyland was the result of a licensing agreement between Walt Disney (WD) of the US and Oriental Land Corporation (OL) of Japan. The agreement stated that WD would receive a license fee of 7% of sales in exchange for WD providing OL its managerial and technological know-how, and assuming small risks in the venture. When WD proposed a second project with OL, OL's senior executives tried to find a way to make WD a risk-taking partner through investment in the business as a precondition to venturing into the project. To prepare for the negotiations, OL's management asked the finance team to calculate the project's net present value as seen from WD's standpoint using two methods, i.e., using the existing licensing method and using a joint venture method in which WD would share appropriate risks.

**2 Tokyo Disneyland and the DisneySea Park: Corporate**
**Governance and Differences in Capital Budgeting Concepts**
**and Methods between American and Japanese Companies**     **61**

In 1997, Japan's Oriental Land Corporation and the Walt Disney Company, its licenser for Tokyo Disneyland, had intense discussions about the possibility of building an additional theme park called Tokyo DisneySea Park. The difference in the economic and political assessment of the project between the American and Japanese firm was the root cause of disagreement. Japan and USA use significantly different capital budgeting techniques. The difference in decision making between Japanese and American firms also reflects the difference in corporate governance techniques between the two countries. For example, the principles of discounted cash flow, such as the net present value (NPV) and the internal rate of return (IRR), are widely used outside the realm of Japanese corporate finance. Although familiar with these tools, Japanese executives rarely use them and often consider them invalid tools for the decision-making process. Instead, Japanese corporations have come to rely on the average accounting return method for their financial analyses. The reason behind Japanese businesses rejecting NPV and IRR lies in Japan's socioeconomic conventions and the nation's history.

## 3  A Rogue Trader at Daiwa Bank (A): Management Responsibility under Different Jurisprudential Systems, Practices and Cultures                     93

Sumio Abekawa, Daiwa Bank's president, received a letter on July 18, 1995 from Toshihide Iguchi, vice-president of the bank's New York branch. In that letter, Iguchi confessed to losing about US$1.1 billion (approximately ¥123 billion) by selling the bank's securities in order to cover up the loss from his unauthorized trading of US Treasury Bonds over 11 years. The senior management at the bank reported the loss two months later on September 18 to the Federal Reserve Bank of New York and the New York State Banking Department. The bank directors faced a number of challenging questions: Had the bank complied with the reporting requirements? What would be the potential liability of the directors? Would the Japanese bank directors be held liable for violating the law of a foreign country? How could the Japanese Ministry of Finance help?

## 4  A Rogue Trader at Daiwa Bank (B): The Board Meeting on September 25, 1995 in Japan                     111

This case raises many basic legal and economic issues regarding directors' responsibilities for the activities of their employees, which were not discussed in the main case, "A Rogue Trader at Daiwa Bank: Management Responsibility under Different Jurisprudential Systems, Practices and Cultures." According to an official at Japan's Ministry of Finance, the individuals involved in this case may not have directly contributed to the incident at hand as they were not only trustworthy but also very capable professionals. Could they be held responsible for responsibilities delegated to others? Irrespective of this fact, were they liable and responsible for this situation? What about the bank's responsibility as an institution? The additional questions were: (1) Was there any non-feasance regarding duties in establishing an internal control system? (2) Could the directors claim principle of trusting right? (3) Was Daiwa Bank also responsible under the principle of *respondeat superior?*



In February 2005, the top management of Fuji Television Network, Inc. (Fuji TV), one of Japan's leading media conglomerates, was informed by its main brokerage that a small IT services firm, Livedoor Co. (Livedoor), had succeeded in buying 35% of the shares in Nippon Broadcasting System Inc. (NBS), of which Fuji TV owned 12.39% and which it was in the process of acquiring through a takeover bid, to make NBS its subsidiary. What made the issue even more complicated was that NBS's main asset was its 22.5% stake in Fuji TV. The news that a relatively unknown company had managed to buy 35% of NBS's shares thus came as a great shock to the top management of Fuji TV, which had to study and determine effective tactics to counter Livedoor's planned acquisition of NBS. They immediately instructed legal counselors to conduct a study on what would be the most effective and legal actions Fuji TV could undertake against Livedoor. At the same time, they asked the planning department to calculate the corporate value of NBS using both American and Japanese methods. This involved forming judgments about the price Fuji TV should be prepared to pay if it went through with acquiring NBS completely. The case addresses issues of strategic fit between the bidder and the target, target performance, valuation, financing decisions, and whether and how the target's anti-takeover moves might affect outcomes in the battle for corporate control.



Internet service firm Livedoor allegedly took advantage of loopholes in the securities trading laws to swell the amount of assets held by the firm and its president, Takafumi Horie (Horie), who led the Livedoor group.

Livedoor was established in April 1996 with ¥6 million in capital. It made its stock market debut in April 2000, with a stock market value of ¥57.2 billion. Its market capitalization surged to ¥830 billion in December 2005, a 15-fold spike, caused by a series of highly tactical moves intended to boost the stock prices of the parent and group firms. Livedoor's strategy essentially focused on how to attract speculative investments from individual investors, largely ignoring institutional players. A 100-for-1 stock split in December 2003 sent the price of Livedoor's shares soaring to the ¥18,000 mark at once, although the ex-split price should theoretically have been just ¥2,220. Livedoor's operations turned out to be a kind of "money game" under the guise of efforts to challenge the establishment. Where did Livedoor deviate from the path of fair business, and what kind of illegality was involved in its activities? Shedding light on these questions should help both companies and investors make more constructive use of the securities and capital markets.

## 7  Nireco Japan: Introduction of the Poison Pill                167

A big factor behind the looming threat of hostile takeovers in Japan was the rapid dissolution of cross-shareholdings, which began in the 1990s, between creditor banks and corporate borrowers in particular. At the same time, foreign ownership of Japanese companies, which used to account for only a small percent of all outstanding shares, had now risen to approximately 20%. The proportion of free-floating shares had thus risen significantly. This also meant that buying out a company through a takeover bid (TOB) in Japan had become far easier. Recognizing the trend, and driven by the fear of Japanese companies being swallowed up by foreign investors, Hidemaru Yamada, president of Nireco Corp. (Nireco) — a high-tech measuring-device manufacturer — thought that his company needed to introduce a "poison pill" defense to counter possible hostile TOBs. With this thought, Yamada diverged from Japan's traditional way of thinking, which assumed that hostile takeovers had little chance of success in Japan. Nireco assessed the situation, taking into account Japan's institutional infrastructure, its law and its economic conditions. In March 2005, Nireco announced what it called a "security plan," which included an issue of subscription warrants to existing shareholders in the event of an unfriendly takeover bid.

## 8  Ina Food Industry: A New Management Philosophy for Japanese Businesses                                        197

Ina Food Industry Co. Ltd. (Ina Foods) was led by Hiroshi Tsukakoshi, Ina Food's 68-year-old chairman, who had been with the company through an incredible 48 years of continuous revenue and profit growth. The company was a leading manufacturer of powdered agar, a traditional gelatine product derived from seaweed. Tsukakoshi's cautionary attitude about quick growth was quite unique in current times when return on investment and total market value were considered key management indices. His belief was that if management were not preoccupied purely with revenue, and focused instead on establishing steady growth, the company would continue to exist for a long time. This would, in turn, make happier everybody who was directly or indirectly associated with the company. He believed that his role as president was to make employees happy at work. In the summer of 2006, he felt he had done a good job so far. The business had prospered and did not pose any urgent problems. But he also felt that he should not simply sit back and savor his success. There were tremendous growth opportunities and he knew operations had to be improved before those opportunities could be targeted. He had been thinking that real joy came from change and from going to the next level. His long-time belief had been that no company could get to the future by standing still.

## 9  OSG Corporation: Hedging Transaction Exposure                215

On Monday, April 24, 2006, the US dollar fell to a new three-month low against the yen to ¥114.30 = US$1, carrying over its weakness from Friday's trading in New York where it fell more than ¥2 (1.75%). Teruhide Osawa, president of OSG Corporation, Japan (OSG), a multinational cutting-tool producer, was following the foreign exchange market on his computer screen that Monday. Faced with big fluctuations in the yen–dollar exchange rate, he summoned the manager of the Support Center Finance Group, Koji Sonobe. He asked Sonobe to analyze and report on how OSG's exposure to foreign currency transactions was currently being measured and how it could be managed in the future. He asked the manager specifically how the company was currently hedging its foreign currency exposures. The board's consensus was that the amount of currency risk exposure that should remain covered depended on the management's philosophy and decision. OSG's policy in the past did not intend to hedge transaction exposure perfectly and intended to leave it partially open to the market. The board would need to decide how much hedging was required as a policy.

## 10  Bank of Japan's Meeting in March 2006: An End to the Quantitative Easing Policy?                241

The policy board of the Bank of Japan (BOJ) convened for a two-day meeting starting March 8, 2006. It was expected that the board would decide to end its five-year, extremely loose monetary policy, which was designed to combat persistent deflation, and to set forth the quantitative easing approach. A decision to end the policy meant Japan would return to a normal monetary stance, targeting interest rates after five years of pursuing an unorthodox policy. The BOJ's decision was not easy. Although the law established the BOJ's independence, there was considerable opposition from the government, including Prime Minister Koizumi, to an early end to the quantitative monetary easing approach. Politicians were concerned that a "premature" monetary policy change could hamper the economic recovery from deflation. Because no major central bank had ever had such a loose monetary policy, no one knew for sure how to end it smoothly. In the end, the BOJ did as expected and lifted its quantitative easing policy, replacing it with a more standard inflation targeting policy. The bank now had to avoid sending shock waves through the country's recovering economy and through world markets, to which end the BOJ drew up a set of measures aimed at averting possible market turmoil.

## 11  World Co. Ltd., Japan: Why Go Private?                267

Early 2005 saw the first hostile takeover in Japan when Livedoor, an upstart internet company, took on Fuji TV in a battle that shook Japan. Financed by foreign capital, this first takeover scared Japan's traditional business establishment who now feared that the threat of hostile takeovers had finally become a reality in Japan. In response, many companies scrambled to introduce anti-takeover defenses. This however posed a challenge as the US institutional infrastructure supporting poison pills differed considerably from that of Japan. At the same time Japan had gone through numerous public company accounting scandals and was in the midst of dramatic changes in disclosure and corporate governance rules and regulations governing issuers of publicly traded securities and their officers and directors. Mr. Hidezo Terai, president of World Co. Ltd., Japan (hereafter World), a publicly traded company in the Tokyo and Osaka Stock Exchanges, contemplated whether it would be advisable and possible to seek relief from these rules and regulations and protect World from possible hostile takeovers by terminating World's status as a publicly traded company, or "going private." However, there are business as well as legal considerations that must be thoroughly evaluated before the decision to go private or stay public can be taken. The top executives of World immediately instructed its planning and legal departments to conduct a study on these points.

## 12  J-COM: Share-Trade Irregularities on the Day of IPO                                287

December 8, 2005 was a very special day for J-COM Co. Ltd. (J-Com) president Yasuhiko Okamoto as this was the day his company would be listed on the Tokyo Stock Exchange (TSE). After the market opened, he had been watching J-Com's stock price go up in bid-only mode, along with officials from Nikko Citigroup Ltd., the lead manager for the listing, when a sell order for more than 40 times the firm's outstanding shares was placed by Mizuho Securities (Mizuho Sec). Before the end of the day, Okamoto found that Mizuho Sec suffered losses of at least ¥27 billion following an input order for the sale of one share for ¥610,000 which was accidentally entered as 610,000 shares for ¥1 each. The error threw the exchange into turmoil, and Mizuho Sec's president, Makoto Fukuda, apologized for the error. The new J-Com shares had a starting price of ¥672,000, but after the misplaced order they fell to the day's bottom trading limit of ¥572,000 each. After Mizuho Sec bought back the shares, they rose to the maximum allowable single day gain of ¥700,000. Mizuho Sec bought back about 514,000 shares, but since the number of sold shares exceeded the number of existing shares which stood at 14,500, there was a possibility that Mizuho Sec would not be able to hand shares over to the investors who bought them. Mizuho Sec planned to discuss with the TSE and its clearing organization whether it would be allowed to make cash payments in lieu of delivering J-Com shares. President Yasuhiko Okamoto of J-Com wanted the market to value his company properly and under normal conditions. He was not happy to know that some brokerages had taken advantage of the mistake by Mizuho Sec and had started speculating with J-Com shares, while other investors, who bought shares that they underwrote, were losing money, since on December 8 the low price was ¥572,000, which was lower than the initial public offering (IPO) price of ¥672,000. Should these transactions, made on the back of a clear error, be honored? What steps should the players, such as J-Com, TSE, the regulator and Mizuho Sec take? What do they stand to lose from the market turmoil involving the J-Com stock?

## 13  Softbank's New Strategy: The Largest LBO in Japan    307

Softbank Corp. (Softbank) has announced the final agreement with British cellular phone giant Vodafone Group Plc (Vodafone) to buy its Japanese unit, Vodafone KK, for ¥1.75 trillion. Under the agreement, Softbank will gain 97.7% of stocks in Vodafone KK and acquire about ¥200 billion in its interest-bearing debts. To pay for the deal, which is the largest business acquisition ever undergone by a Japanese firm, Softbank plans to raise between 1.1 trillion to 1.2 trillion yen through leveraged-buyout arrangement, by using Vodafone KK's assets as collateral. Softbank president Masayoshi Son feels satisfied that he has successfully accomplished a big deal, laying the foundation for a business that will continue to expand. But he knows that some key questions have to be answered in order to meet the future proactively. First, in what direction should he take Softbank from here? Can Softbank maintain its culture, structure, and ability to respond quickly and effectively to client needs throughout the period of anticipated rapid growth? Second, should antitrust considerations preclude the deal? Can Softbank in fact raise the necessary funds to effect this acquisition? Is Softbank's claim of "synergy" no more than an opportunity to lop off overlapping operations? Third, and perhaps the biggest question of all, can this acquisition work as a serious and positive strategy, or is it merely a defensive tactic to eliminate Softbank's most troublesome and dangerous competitors? The top management of Softbank must answer these questions clearly to outsiders, including its shareholders. The immediate concern for the top management of Softbank is the borrowing of about ¥1.3 trillion to finance its purchase. The sum is the largest ever to be raised for a buyout by a single Japanese company. The top management has instructed the planning department to conduct a study on financing alternatives and the all-in cost of these alternatives (yen, US dollars and British pounds) in terms of yen.

## 14  Keidanren: Foreign Political Contributions in Japan    335

In Japan, there has been increased scrutiny of companies' general participation in the political process, in particular political campaign contributions. Over the past decade, Japan has placed new restrictions on companies' political giving and has required greater disclosure of campaign contributions. Increasingly, shareholders are seeking to hold companies accountable for their campaign contributions. On May 23, 2006 Canon Inc.'s chairman Fujio Mitarai was appointed chairman of Nippon Keidanren, Japan's influential corporate sector champion. In terms of concrete policy demands, Keidanren was approaching a turning point. Among the themes that would be given priority, establishing corporate ethics would be vital. The senior management of Keidanren was quite busy in preparing the new policy statements. Among others, whether Keidanren should express its policy for promoting voluntary political donations by foreign corporations in Japan was the issue. Canon was one of the excellent companies in Japan but foreign corporations like Canon couldn't make political donations at that time.

## 15  Tokyo Disneyland (3): New Strategies Needed
###    for Sluggish Demand    363

On May 9, 2005, Oriental Land Co. Ltd. (OL) has announced the changes in the company's top management. The early summer of 2005 was a real sizzler for the new management. They were feeling the heat not only from the humid weather in Tokyo in the rainy season but also from the visitors' numbers that had just come in. The total combined attendance at Tokyo Disneyland Park and Tokyo DisneySea Park for this fiscal year (April 1, 2004 to March 31, 2005) amounted to 25.021 million guests, 98.2% of last year's attendance. The top management was concerned that this decrease in attendance might be an alarming warning of tough times ahead and that a prime example of a successful foreign investment in Japan was now caught in a completely new structural change — the factors that had been critical to its past success were now diminishing. The top management considered that amusement park and leisure land industry continue to provide little cause for optimism, due to factors such as slackening consumer spending and demographic changes. Under these conditions, the Oriental Land Group decided to focus on the two long-term strategies aimed at further growth: developing Tokyo Disney Resort into a "Destination Resort" and expanding businesses outside Maihama area (where Tokyo Disney Resort is located). In addition to the long-term strategies, the top management considers that a study is needed to know whether they can diversify the operating base. They would specifically like to know whether current pricing policy is right or not under deflation which Japanese economy has been suffering for long time and how changes in the pricing to visitors, if necessary, will influence on the company's cash flows in the future. The strategy taken depends to a large measure on management's opinion about the price elasticity of demand by the visitors to the company's services. The top management asked the planning department to study the possible price changes and use net present value (NPV) methods to evaluate these alternatives on the basis of the future cash flows, incorporating the company's long-term strategies already established.

## 16  Licensing Arrangement or Joint Venture (4): An *Ex Post* Case Study of Tokyo Disneyland     385

In the late 1970s, Walt Disney corporation sought to expand its enterprise to Japan. Oriental Land Corp., which represented the Japanese side of the negotiations, and Walt Disney, had to decide on a licensing arrangement or a joint venture. The objective of this study is to examine the actual determinants, models, and data of that investment choice. This case study is of value to governments and multinational enterprises that want to explore an optimal alliance with a foreign partner. Based on the law, the Japanese government intervened in the negotiations between the Oriental Land Corp. and Walt Disney as to the form of the arrangement for Tokyo Disneyland. Thirty years later, it is worthwhile to examine the validity of their decisions and which arrangement benefited the project and the partners most. This paper presents ex post empirical evidence for this discussion. The efficacy and effectiveness of the law that allows the Japanese government to intervene are also questioned.

**17  Ina Food Industry (2): Marketing
Strategies in a Deflationary Environment**                    **409**

Ina Food Industry Co. Ltd. (Ina Food) is situated in the city of Ina, Nagano
Prefecture, and surrounded by the soaring mountains of the Japanese
Alps. Hiroshi Tsukakoshi, Ina Food's 75-year-old chairman, has led the
company through an incredible 55 years of continuous revenue and profit
growth. The company is a leading manufacturer of powdered agar, a traditional gelatine product derived from seaweed. In the summer of 2012,
Tsukakoshi is looking through the windows of his office in Ina City. He is
thinking about how he aims for his company to be a corporation that is
conscious of the global environment. He feels he has done a good job so
far. The business has prospered and does not present any urgent problems.
However, he also feels that he should not simply sit back and savor his
success. He is facing his retirement and has concerns about the long-term
growth of the company. He is thinking it might be the right time to introduce some new marketing strategies for the company. There is also
another reason for concern: Japan's deflationary environment, persistent
for 20 years now. He is interested in increasing sales volume and profit by
raising prices when most other companies are lowering theirs under deflation. In this environment, even keeping prices constant means a relative
increase of price. Tsukakoshi believes that, in essence, as long as a company is confident in the competitiveness of its products, there are always
methods to raise prices and increase profits. The key is raising the prices
of merchandise and services in a way that the customers can accept.
Raising prices in a difficult economic climate is a risky decision.
Nevertheless, the company is successful in raising the price under deflation. While the Japanese economy faces serious difficulties, the company
has obtained successful results thanks to marketing, producing, financing,
and allocating resources.


**18  Bank of Japan (2): The Meeting on April 4, 2013
(Doubling Japan's Monetary Base via Government
Bond Purchases)**                                          **427**

Shinzõ Abe, the current prime minister of Japan, has been promoting various economic stimulus measures — dubbed "Abenomics" — since taking

office in December 2012. So far, his relentless pressure on the Bank of Japan (BOJ) to further ease its monetary policy has had some impact on the markets. It is a combination of monetary relaxation, heavy fiscal spending, and targeted growth strategies. The detailed policies include inflation targeting at a 2% annual rate, correction of the excessive yen appreciation, radical quantitative easing, expansion of public investment, buying operations of Japanese government bonds (JGBs) by the BOJ, and revision of the BOJ Act. On April 4, 2013, the Japanese parliament approved Haruhiko Kuroda for a full, five-year term as the BOJ's governor. He officially replaced his predecessor, Masaaski Shirakawa, who stepped down on March 19 before his official term was expected to end on April 8. The new BOJ launched an aggressive easing program in what markets said are surprisingly bold first steps by Kuroda as he begins his campaign to rid the economy of over 20 years of deflation. By taking every currently conceivable measure at once, he is driving home the point that the central bank's monetary easing has entered a new dimension. The BOJ policy board has thus agreed to a 2% price-rise target at the earliest possible time, with a time horizon of about two years. With this, the BOJ has cut off its own retreat. The markets have taken the BOJ's recent decision to set a 2% inflation target as the last big step in the first round of Abe's policy push. The markets are concerned that government interference and pressure on the BOJ endangers its independence. Also, concerns are being raised that even if these new economic policies being implemented by Abe and the BOJ lift Japan out of deflation, an even more formidable challenge might await the government. The concerns are: higher interest rates, currency war fears, and the appearance of an economic bubble. It is too early to determine the actual efficacy and validity of the BOJ's new monetary policy, which is a brave experiment. History will evaluate it later on an ex post basis. But we can study now the details of the BOJ's decision.



The economic policies advocated by Prime Minister Shinzō Abe of Japan, dubbed Abenomics, have weakened the yen and given new life to Japan's stock market. Abe calls for the "three arrows" to conquer Japan's more-than-a-decade-long deflation, along with aggressive monetary easing and large-scale public works projects. There are three components of Abenomics: monetary easing, fiscal spending, and growth strategies. But the third component, growth strategies, is among the key policies. The economy-boosting effects of Abenomics and the Bank of Japan's (BOJ) bold monetary easing policy are stirring up considerable global interest in Japan. Without plans for keeping the growth momentum alive, however, the current excitement may all be for nothing. This sudden interest in Japan is being driven by three main factors: (1) the extraordinary size of the BOJ's easing has caught many overseas investors by surprise. The central bank plans to double the monetary base to 270 trillion yen in two years, a far cry from the previous policy of incremental easing; (2) corporate profits are rising more quickly than expected; and (3) Japan's Abenomics stands out as a bright spot amid the global economic gloom. But these expectations can be lofty. Of the three components of Abenomics, monetary easing and fiscal spending are unlikely to inflict much pain on the public, apart from the fact that younger generations will be forced to pay back the debt the government is rapidly incurring. But the third component, growth strategies, can only be effective when addressing regulatory issues that have long been left untouched. What Japan needs most is regulatory and structural reform. These painful, drastic reforms will shuffle the deck for protected businesses. While structural reforms almost always inflict pain on vested interests protected by regulatory walls, creative initiatives by newcomers benefit consumers and help to revitalize the economy.

## 20  Saizeriya and the Use of Foreign Currency Coupon Swaps: Was This for Hedging or Speculation?                     477

Saizeriya Co. Ltd. (Saizeriya), a company involved in the restaurant business, had aimed to provide healthy and tasty Italian meals at affordable prices to everyone since its establishment. On December 9, 2008, Yasuhiko Shogaki, Saizeriya's president, made a public announcement as to the loss of ¥15 billion caused by the use of foreign currency coupon swaps. On the same day, Shogaki further announced that because of such transactions as derivatives meant to hedge against foreign exchange risks, this Italian-restaurant chain operator might fall into the red in terms of group net earnings that fiscal year through August 2009. He said Saizeriya had signed derivatives deals with BNP Paribas Securities (Japan) Ltd. in October 2007 to procure Australian dollars (A\$), needed to import food from that country. Following the disclosure, Saizeriya's stock price went limit-down on December 10, 2008 as investors rushed to dump the stock. Some directors and shareholders questioned this disclosure. But Shogaki had to decide whether the company should continue hedging, such as with swaps, despite the fact that Saizeriya suffered huge losses this time. If Saizeriya did not arrange any hedging, the company could enjoy yen appreciation merits for the payments in A\$.

# Introduction

The history of Japan's economy during the 60 years after the Second World War followed a trend of internationalization. Many corporations switched from doing business domestically to doing business internationally. Because Japan is geographically small with limited natural resources, economic growth and a higher per capita income became viable only through the export of products to overseas markets. As a result, every company concentrated on producing inexpensive goods of better quality in a cost-effective manner. Internationalization was the goal for every company.

While globalization of the Japanese economy has been advancing with astounding speed, significant differences remain between the management philosophy and techniques used within Japanese companies and those used in the West. These include the significant differences in the use of capital budgeting techniques, economic and political assessment of projects, decision-making styles, and techniques of corporate governance. Furthermore, Keiretsu (interlocking shareholdings) still plays an important role in the financing of companies in Japan. Such differences have a momentous impact on the decision-making processes within companies, and this book illustrates many of the key differences that exist in the realm of corporate governance and finance.

September 1985 marked a change in the progression of the Japanese economy. Six industrialized countries of the world signed the Plaza Accord, increasing the value of the yen until it reached its peak in August 1995 of ¥79/$, more than four times stronger than it had been during the fixed exchange rate period, i.e., ¥360/$. Encouraged by the yen's appreciation and super fluidity of currency in the domestic market, many Japanese companies rushed to buy real estate overseas, including the famous Plaza Hotel, where the abovementioned Plaza Accord was signed. However, contrary to the expectation of Japanese industries, this strong yen introduced a long-term economic downturn and a substantial deterioration of the economy.

The export industry, which was the foundation of the Japanese economy, was hit hard by the sharp yen appreciation. The Japanese economy went into the most serious recession in 70 years since the Great Depression in 1930, during the early Showa period. Financial uncertainty and plunging prices added to the recession, creating a severe deflation spiral. Industrial companies, tormented by excess product supplies due to the lack of demand for exports, sought relief through employment adjustments, which, in turn, caused further weakening of consumption and demand. The economic growth rate was –0.7% in 1997 and –2.8% in 1998 — an unbelievable downturn for the Japanese economy that had been growing continuously since the end of the Second World War. The Nikkei average, which reached its historical peak of ¥38,916 in December 1998, started to drop. The land price index, which is based on the price in 1983 as 100, reached its peak at 488 in 1990, but dropped sharply to 144 in 1995.

The Japanese economy suffered from the aftermath of this recession for a long time. Reduction of personal and business financial assets caused severe shrinkage in personal spending and business capital investments. Banks had to cope with huge bad debts and place borrowing companies under a credit crunch in order to reduce assets. Starting in 1995, the economy entered a period that is now referred to as "the lost age", a period of compound depression in which prices dropped and the net gross national product growth rate was negative. To combat the situation, the Bank of Japan introduced a zero-interest policy, i.e., a super money-easing policy, which had not been seen in the world's economic history for many years. However, its effect was dubious, to say the least. It is a common belief that, although inflation can be cured by a mix of monetary and fiscal policies, there is no cure for deflation. Consumers are wise and will not spend money today if they know that prices will drop tomorrow. Moreover, the per capita income level of the Japanese was high, and they already owned everything they wanted. There was no reason for them to spend money hastily. Japanese companies' executives used various hard and soft policies in order to survive this "lost age".

Japan is currently in an up phase. In fact, the economy has continued expanding for 58 months since February 2002, beating the 57 months of the Izanagi boom, from November 1965 to July 1970. However, the Japanese economy has a basic structural problem — the domestic economy is shrinking, and competition is becoming harsher due to the reduction and aging of the total population. Essentially, the Japanese economy has no alternative but to pursue the world market by adapting itself to globalization. Restructuring of its industrial formation through corporate buyouts and reorganization is an unavoidable task for Japanese corporations.

With the backdrop of this brief recent history of the Japanese economy, these case studies were chosen from a broad range of Japanese corporations. The 10 cases, briefly described, can be classified into the following categories:

1. Internationalization. Examples of internationalization of the Japanese economy are described in two cases: a successful foreign investment in Japan — Tokyo Disneyland — and a failed Japanese investment in New York — Daiwa Bank.
2. Mergers and Acquisitions. Japanese corporations are busy dealing with mergers and acquisitions (M&As). Fuji TV vs. Livedoor and Nireco are two cases that have been included to discuss hostile takeovers and countermeasures against them.
3. Small companies. When discussing the Japanese economy, small companies cannot be disregarded. The case of Ina Food is an excellent example of a thriving small company.
4. Parts manufacturing. OSG is included as a case representing the parts manufacturing industry of Japan. This company, although not fashionable, is the world's leader in the industry and sustains the Japanese economy.
5. Macro economy. The decision-making process of the Bank of Japan that steers the macro economy is described in another case. A description is given of how the breadth and depth of the decision-making process of a governing body differs from that of an individual company.

## *Case 1 — Tokyo Disneyland: Licensing vs. Joint Venture*

The biggest obstacle in establishing Tokyo Disneyland was the amount of risk that the US side (Walt Disney) was willing to take in the particular project. The issue hinged on the question of whether Walt Disney wanted to license the project or participate in a joint venture; this has always been an issue of negotiation in any project involving Japanese and US corporations. In this particular case, a sharp difference of opinion existed from each side at the start of the negotiations, probably because of the size and nature of the project, i.e., a project in the leisure industry, which is essentially part of an intangible service industry. Although the Japanese side took a strong stance, claiming that "the US side should take half of the risk", the negotiation was finally settled as a licensing deal in which Walt Disney would not take any risk at all. On first impression, this looked as if Walt Disney had won.

However, reality sometimes turns out to be stranger than fiction, and Walt Disney later realized that the deal was not as good as originally thought. Initially, Walt Disney had asked for 7% of the sales as a fee without taking any risk — purely a protection against the project's potential failure. What happened in reality was that the project turned out to be a big hit, and Walt Disney recognized that it could have acquired a far larger return if agreement had been made to assume some risk with a joint venture format. This mistake must have served as a big lesson to Walt Disney's management because it adopted the joint venture format for subsequent projects in France and Hong Kong. From this case, the reader can learn about the strategies and delicate techniques of negotiation between international parties, as well as their consequences.

## *Case 2 — Tokyo Disneyland and the DisneySea Park: Corporate Governance and Differences in Capital Budgeting Concepts and Methods between American and Japanese Companies*

This case is based on another Tokyo Disneyland project, similar to Case 1. The difference between the Japanese and US sides, in terms of capital budgeting concepts and methods, is always one of the important themes in US–Japan negotiations concerning investments. In the negotiation of the Tokyo DisneySea Park, which is Tokyo Disneyland's second project, the two sides went head-to-head once again about cost/profit estimation. "Capital budgeting" is an extremely important calculation for estimating profitability in order to determine whether to go ahead with a project or to abandon it. In some cases, differences in the method of calculating this profitability and differences in opinion have led to abandoning the investment, which had been based on international cooperation.

What lay at the heart of the dispute was not merely a question of which capital budgeting methodology to use, but also a fundamental difference in the purpose of a corporation. While in the US a business exists simply for its shareholders, in Japan, a business exists for all stakeholders, i.e., not only shareholders but also employees, banks, and clients. This is the root cause for the generally negative view that Japanese companies hold against the internal rate of return (IRR) and net present value (NPV) accounting techniques that are commonly used in the US as methods for calculating how to maximize shareholders' assets.

Although the discounted cash flow concept is well accepted among corporations in the US, Japanese corporations do not appreciate it for the following reasons. In the Japanese economy, which has experienced deflation for a long time, future cash flow has higher purchasing power. The short-term deposit interest rate is nearly zero in Japan, where the zero-interest-rate policy has been adopted for a long time. In fact, the net interest rate is negative if one deposits money in a bank after deducting various handling charges. Under this condition, Japanese corporations think it correct not to discount any future cash flow. They think that a negative number should be applied to the opportunity cost if any discount is to be executed. Thus, as a result of their calculation method, future cash has a higher value than current cash. In order to understand the difference between capital budgeting techniques in the US and Japan and to make a fair judgment on which method should be used, one must also keep in mind the differences in the macro-economic status of the corporations of the two countries.

The case shows not only the different capital budgeting techniques used in the two countries but also how to adapt in a joint project across borders. The case introduces a new method, "average cash flow return method", as a popular capital budgeting technique among Japanese banks. One of the outstanding features of Japan's business culture is that the main bank of a Japanese corporation often participates in its major decision-making processes and provides various management advice. This major difference in the investment profitability calculation techniques between the US and Japan is an extremely important issue, one that can determine whether a joint venture project is to go ahead or not. In those cases, it often happens that the main bank functions as a go-between at the Japanese company's request to provide a third technique to which both sides can agree. This case study is a perfect example for illustrating the relationship between the main bank and its client in Japan.

## Case 3 — A Rogue Trader at Daiwa Bank (A): Management Responsibility under Different Jurisprudential Systems, Practices and Cultures

## Case 4 — A Rogue Trader at Daiwa Bank (B): The Board Meeting on September 25, 1995 in Japan

The events described in both cases occurred in 1995 at Daiwa Bank, which existed in New York City when the incident occurred. The aftershock of this incident continued to be felt in the Japanese financial market for more than 10 years. As a result of this incident, Daiwa Bank, then one of Japan's leading banks, weakened substantially and eventually was absorbed into the newly established Resona Bank in Japan. All of this was caused by the actions of one trader at the bank's New York branch. During 10 years of unauthorized dealings of US Treasury bonds, this trader lost US\$1.1 billion. This dire incident came to light when the person responsible for the huge loss reported the entire matter in a letter to the president of the Bank in Japan. The news stunned the entire Japanese business community. The size of the loss and the length of time for which it stayed undiscovered were well beyond the precedent.

There was no question that the bank's manager should have been held responsible for failing to adequately supervise subordinates and for the lack of an internal monitoring mechanism, but the more significant mistake was a basic error in handling the problem after it was discovered.

It was this error that decided the fate of the bank. I know of no other case that better teaches how grave the consequences of an executive's decision can be. The dealer responsible had put in more than 10 years of indescribable effort to recover the loss on his own, but had finally given up. This abnormal turn of events was impossible for members of Japanese corporations to comprehend because their philosophy is that respect for the organization overrides everything else.

The executives at Daiwa Bank's head office first tried to grasp the situation before anything else, then dispatched a group of inspectors and confided everything to the Ministry of Finance, the responsible government agency, and asked for its guidance in handling the matter. However, all these activities took more time than they expected. That was the management's critical mistake. The executives never realized that they were required by New York law to report this illegal action to the Federal Reserve Board within 30 days of learning about it. This inaction caused them to lose the Federal Reserve Board's trust and, hence, to lose their banking license; eventually, they had to withdraw from New York.

This incident was reported worldwide, teaching the international financial market several lessons:

1. The necessity of internationalization and the risks behind it. This incident would not have occurred if Daiwa Bank had remained a local bank in Osaka, Japan. Perhaps its attempt at being an international bank exceeded its human resource capabilities. The lesson is: Internationalization should not be an automatic choice for growth.
2. The requirement for Daiwa Bank to construct an operating system suited for its international location. If it wanted to operate in New York, it should have paid more attention to the proverb "When in Rome, do as the Romans do." It tried to operate the way it operated in Japan. In the Japanese corporate environment, a strong sense of trust exists among staff members because of Japan's system of lifetime employment. This system, imported to the New York branch, may be the reason why the offender, a locally hired person, was blindly trusted by his supervisors, consequently, allowing the illegal act to be hidden for as long as 10 years.
3. The need to be fully aware of differences in culture and laws. For example, disclosure responsibility differs between the US and Japan.

According to the US Securities and Exchange Law, it is management's responsibility to disclose any major incident that can affect the stock price as soon as it becomes aware of the incident. Under the guidelines of the Commercial Law of Japan, however, management is required to be extremely careful in confirming the accuracy of any incidents before disclosure, considering possible grave consequences. In other words, management is allowed to take ample time to investigate the incident. There is, however, no excuse for ignorance of the law on the part of management.

A derivative lawsuit was brought by shareholders against Daiwa Bank's 32 managers, alleging failure of management responsibility and asking for damages in the amount of US$1.1 billion. Many Japanese managers were amazed by this enormous amount and reacted by rejecting internationalization, afraid that the trade-off was too large. The Keidanren (Japan Federation of Economic Organizations) reviewed the shareholders' litigation system triggered by this case and succeeded in reducing the responsibilities of the members of the board of directors by the enactment of the revised Commerce Law in December 2001. As a consequence, the experience from this incident put the breaks on internationalization.

## *Case 5 — Hostile Takeover Battle in Japan: Fuji TV vs. Livedoor for NBS*

## *Case 6 — Livedoor: The Rise and Fall of a Market Maverick*

These two case studies are about a hostile takeover that occurred in Japan in 2005. Various US economic systems were introduced into Japan after the end of the Second World War. These included the Securities Exchange Law and corporate takeovers by tender offers specified by that law. Although there have been several successful examples of corporate takeovers, this system has never really been popular in Japan.

The idea of corporate M&As seems outlandish to the Japanese mind because its economy is based on lifetime employment and seniority, and appreciating and honoring the harmony of the society. However, things have started to change. Many Japanese business people have come to realize that M&A is an unavoidable path in order for the Japanese economy to assure sustainable corporate growth, even in a low growth period.

One young man, Takafumi Horie, quickly sensed this change in the wind. Horie was nicknamed "Horiemon" after a comic book character and quickly became a sort of idol for young people. He started with nothing in 1969, but the startup company he created, Livedoor, became a leading company in the IT industry within a few years. One technique he used to make his company grow was splitting one stock into 100 new stocks, which, although not illegal, was highly irregular in the traditional corporate world of Japan. In order to keep expanding his company, the only viable way left to him was buying existing companies. Believing that the IT industry could grow further by merging with the TV news/media industry, he targeted Fuji TV, a leading media company. Fuji TV and its subsidiary, Nippon Broadcasting System (NBS), owned each other's shares. Therefore, since NBS owned 22.5% of Fuji TV's shares, and shares of NBS were also traded on the stock market, Horie thought he could automatically control Fuji TV if he could acquire NBS through a takeover bid.

On detecting Livedoor's scheme, Fuji TV embarked on a takeover bid of NBS in order to make it a 50% subsidiary by January 2005; at that point, it owned only 12.39% of the NBS shares. To counter this move, Livedoor acquired a 30% stake in NBS shares through an unexpected attack using off-market trading. From then on, Livedoor and Fuji TV went to war using all kinds of strategies, including a court battle, to take over NBS.

The battle between these two companies became a symbol of a new age in corporate Japan in the following two ways:

1. The battle was being fought between a solid establishment in the Japanese business circle, Fuji TV, and a venture company, Livedoor, a comparative fledgling whose history went back no more than 10 years. The president of Fuji TV, Hisashi Hieda, characterized his opponent's behavior by saying it was "like stepping onto another person's tatami

floor with shoes on".[1] The president of Livedoor, Takafumi Horie, bluntly countered by saying, "if you've got money, there's nothing you cannot do".[2] As a result of this incident, polemicists of the Japanese financial world sternly discussed the question: What should be the ethical rule for corporations in the new era?

2. Livedoor obtained the US$765 million required for the acquisition through Lehman Brothers, a leading US investment bank, using moving strike convertible bonds (MSCBs), a technique rather new to Japan. The Japanese market considered it an attack of American culture and values on Japan's traditional corporations. This elevated its sense of vigilance against acquisitions of Japanese corporations by US giant multinationals that are assumed to exist in the background.

This acquisition drama attracted the attention of the general public who thought it closely related to their own daily life. Unfortunately, this acquisition came to an end as Takafumi Horie was arrested for allegedly violating the Securities Exchange Law. The general public saw the harsh rise and fall of IT industry companies first hand through this incident.

Japanese companies have come to a unanimous conclusion that corporate acquisitions are a reality now in Japanese society and that US multinationals have to be watched most carefully. Frequent discussion among Japanese executives was: What is the corporate value? As the Japanese business world became acclimatized to the idea that a hostile takeover may be beneficial if it increased the corporate value, Japanese corporate executives were stunned, realizing how vulnerable their positions really were. They started seriously examining defenses that could be used against corporate acquisitions.

## *Case 7 — Nireco Japan: Introduction of the Poison Pill*

Nireco was the first Japanese company to officially adopt a defensive plan against corporate acquisition. The argument between the company and its

---

[1] See press release, February 2, 2005, www.c-direct.ne.jp/japanese/uj/pdf/10104676/00030906. pdf.

[2] *Nihon Keizai Shinbun*, January 22, 2006, http://markets.nikkei.co.jp/special/sp020.cfm?i d=dxka034122&date=20060122. Original source: Horie, T., *Kaseguga Kachi* (*Money is Almighty*), Kobunsha Publishing Company, August 2004.

shareholders as to the appropriateness of the plan developed into a court battle. The court determined that the buyout prevention plan interfered with the selling of shares and that its implementation would act against the interest of shareholders. Therefore, the takeover prevention plan must not be excessive and must be appropriate. Since then, this has become the consensus of Japan's business world.

Although our attention tends to be distracted by who is the winner or loser in a hostile takeover, the key point is whether the shareholders, who hold the right to decide, are given an opportunity to make a judgment, as well as sufficient information on which to base their judgment. For this, management must make sure that the shareholders' rights have not been encroached upon. Parallel to this, a trend has begun of publicly traded companies delisting in fear of a takeover by an overseas multinational. However, to be listed or not listed is a big question that should not be discussed from the viewpoint of a takeover prevention plan alone.

## *Case 8 — Ina Food Industry: A New Management Philosophy for Japanese Businesses*

This case study describes a unique, relatively small company that has always sought moderate growth despite its being a highly profitable company. Because of this approach, it has never needed to obtain large funds by being listed on the stock market. While most firms tend to operate in major cities such as Tokyo, Osaka, and Nagoya, this company has always been located in Ina City, Nagano Prefecture, and focused on the manufacturing and marketing of foodstuffs. Ina Food is currently trying to venture into the biotech and pharmaceutical fields by providing products based on agar, produced from seaweed.

The company has maintained an increase in sales and profit for 48 years consecutively, through a delicately controlled growth optimization plan. This record is related to the management's belief that "the company exists for the society and the employees"[3] and makes it a top priority

---

[3] *Nihon Keizai Shinbun,* May 23–27, 2006, p. 8. Also see, Tsukakoshi, H., "Iikaisha wo Tsukurimashou (Let Us Build a Good Company)," *Bunya,* Seventh Edition, 2005, pp. 11–213.

to return its profits to those two parties. While we tend to look only at the glamorous successes of large corporations such as Toyota, Sony, and Matsushita (Panasonic) when talking about Japanese companies, we should not forget that these minor and unglamorous companies support the national economy. It is extremely important to analyze the performances of these small- and medium-sized enterprises to understand the future of the Japanese economy.

For some time, people have talked about the manufacturing of goods as the key strength of the Japanese economy. The products of Ina Food are of superior quality, as are many other Japanese products. The best proof of that is the Japanese car industry, which maintains an awesome share in the world market. When a group of US automobile delegates visited a Japanese automobile component manufacturer, one of the delegates asked after the plant tour: "What is the product defect ratio here?" The expected answer was 1% to 2%, which is reasonable for even a top-notch plant that produces some faulty products from time to time. The Japanese plant manager flatly answered, "It is 0%," to the amazement of the visitors. This is a true anecdote that describes the quality level of Japanese products.

## Case 9 — OSG Corporation: Hedging Transaction Exposure

OSG is the world's top manufacturer of cutting tools that are used for manufacturing fastening devices, i.e., male and female threaded components such as bolts and nuts, which are indispensable basic components of all industrial products. In the course of its growth, from a leading Japanese company to a leading world company, OSG was prey to a large amount of transaction exposure in terms of accounts receivables and payables. The value of the yen versus the value of foreign currencies moved radically under the floating currency market, so the risk due to the transaction exposure reached a level that could not be overlooked by top management.

Until recently, it has been the general understanding among Japanese corporations that the foreign exchange risk stays within a reasonable level because the gain and loss stays within a reasonable range. This is because of the netting principle, which explains gains and losses as offsetting each other in either a yen appreciation or depreciation stage. However, the overwhelming attitude now among leading corporations in Japan is to hedge the risk at the point of transaction. This is based on the view that it is preferable to fix every earning status accurately in its infant stage and not leave it exposed to market movements. Driving this new trend is the corporate governance concept of protecting shareholders' interests by protecting, as much as possible, the corporation's profit and loss from risk.

OSG's top executives' policy was to decide whether to hedge against the foreign exchange risk and to what degree, that is, proportionate hedging. They were to decide on this at the board of directors' meeting and were to give specific instructions to appropriate departments, rather than leave them to the operating departments for decision. The number of Japanese corporations cognizant of such market risks is increasing. Through this case, the reader can learn about the prevailing status of the use of finance technology in management among Japanese corporations.

## Case 10 — Bank of Japan's Meeting in March 2006: An End to the Quantitative Easing Policy?

The tenth case is about the Bank of Japan, which is in charge of Japan's monetary policy. The Bank of Japan is also a corporation whose stocks are traded on the stock market. What differentiates it from other corporations is that its decisions control the macro economy of Japan and substantially affect the international markets as well. Therefore, its decisions must be made with ample prudence and strict decisiveness. Since its decisions also will be judged in retrospect, the responsibility of the decision-maker is great.

A historical decision that terminated the ultra-easy monetary policy that had existed since March 2001 was made at the Bank of Japan's policy meeting on March 8, 2006. The decision was made on a judgment about whether the increase in the consumer price index was a sign of permanent improvement, a departure from the deflation that existed for so long, or whether it was just a temporary improvement. The government has always been cautious in changing the easy monetary policy because it is concerned about the economy. Although the Bank of Japan Law guarantees the independence of the Bank of Japan from the government, it also asks for cooperation between the two parties so that the Bank of Japan cannot totally disregard the government's wishes.

There was concern about the decision's effect on the international market. If the Japanese interest rate were raised, yen that had been moving out of Japan because of its extremely low interest rate would return. This would trigger the selling of US government bonds, which would, in turn, push up the long-term US interest rate and affect the US economy. The relative selling and buying of US dollars vs. Japanese yen would cause the yen to appreciate. The yen's appreciation would, in turn, reduce the profits of Japanese exporting industries. Contemplating this chain of events must have frustrated the decision-maker at the Bank of Japan, since this decision might have triggered a world recession.

The reader is reminded that all decisions eventually are made by human beings, and, therefore, it is impossible to completely eliminate the possibility of a misunderstanding of data or an error in judgment. That is why the decision maker makes every effort to arrive at a correct decision. This case also shows that the decision-making process of the Bank of Japan, which has been hidden behind a thick veil until now, is, in fact, quite democratic and no different from that of European and US banking systems.

## *Case 11 — World Co. Ltd., Japan: Why Go Private?*

After weighing the benefits of going private against the burdens of remaining a public company, as well as considering the risks associated with going private, the top management of World Co. concluded that returning a public company to private status was the appropriate course of action for it. On July 25, 2005, World announced to the public that the company planned to go private through a management buyout.

This decision was criticized by some. Going private would jeopardize the company because it would be less transparent and it would escape the obligation of information disclosure to the public. One opinion was that this was a strategy for the management to protect itself from any takeover. If we assume that that was not its intention, then what they intend to do should be explained to the shareholder and society. In any case, it is important for future managers to continue evaluating what is best for the company, staying public or going private.

In the US, it is said that more small public companies are going private because of the stringent accounting and auditing standards required by law. At the same time, however, on witnessing the collapse of big public companies like Enron because of accounting skullduggery, small public companies are seeing that increased corporate governance resulting from compliance can enhance their reputations and growth opportunities in the US.

A private or unlisted company is one that is not listed on any stock market; in other words, it is privately held. These companies are owned by founders, managers or private investors. A publicly traded company is a company whose stocks — all or a majority — are traded on an open market so that general stockholders have claims on the company's assets and profits. Corporations whose stock is traded in the US stock market are required to file quarterly earnings reports with the Securities and Exchange Commission (SEC), while similar reports are required in Japan by the Ministry of Finance (MOF) if they are listed on the Japanese markets. These reports are intended to be disclosed to the public for use by current and future shareholders. On the other hand, for corporations whose stock is not traded on the stock market, it is not possible for the general public to participate in trading shares and no financial information is available to non-shareholders.

The greatest merit of a listed company is being able to obtain long-term funds, either through stocks or bonds, for growth and expansion purposes. Since it is possible to acquire a large sum of funds in one shot through the securities market, the issuing cost per share is lower. While unlisted companies are not required to disclose corporate information, they cannot obtain funds through securities markets and are limited to borrowing money from banks.

One of the most prevalent misunderstandings is the belief that all large companies are listed on exchange markets, which implies that unlisted companies are therefore small firms. Both in the US and Japan, there are many large corporations that are not listed. In 2004, there were 305 US privately-held corporations which had sales of more than US$1 billion, qualifying for the list of America's largest private companies as below. In Japan, Suntry, Takenaka Construction and YKK are the top three largest private companies.

US Top 10 Private Companies:

1. Cargill; 2. Koch Industries; 3. Mars; 4. Publix Super Markets; 5. Bechtel; 6. Pricewaterhouse Coopers; 7. Ernst & Young; 8. C&S Wholesale; 9. Meijer; 10. HE Butt Grocery.

This case will teach the concept of going private and provide readers with a background on Japanese corporate behavior and practice. The readers can examine the cultivation of American and Japanese corporate business, and the impact of contrasting American and Japanese cultures, customs and values in the decision-making process.

## Case 12 — J-COM: Share-Trade Irregularities on the Day of IPO

There are many managerial questions in this case. Who was responsible for this unprecedented case? Comment on this old saying: "To err is human, but to really screw things up, you needed a computerized system without proper controls." Isn't it true that typing is an underappreciated skill? Should the specific trader involved be allowed to continue trading on the exchange after this incident?

Could J-Com, the issuer, sue someone for damages? The company has to show evidence of the damages caused by this incident and it will be difficult to show the relationship between cause and effect. It could even be argued that the company might have gained from the event since its stock prices was higher due to the increased name recognition. Moreover, J-Com's president Yasuhiko Okamoto publicly announced on the day of the IPO, "We aren't considering taking any legal action against the broker at this time."[4]

It is commonly said: "Excessive computerization makes bourses much more vulnerable to technical glitches and basic human error." It might have been an innocuous mistake in any other industry. But a single mistake in what should have been a straightforward sell order by a broker

---

[4]Nikkei (December 8, 2005) http://markets.nikkei.co.jp/special/sp014.cfm?id=d2e0801108&date=20051208 (accessed April 11, 2007).

led the Japanese stock market to tumble on December 8, 2005, heightening fears that excessive computerization makes bourses much more vulnerable to technical glitches and basic human error even as global bourses strive to become faster and more integrated than ever. Japanese brokerage giant Mizuho Sec admitted that the wrong order was initially placed due to a basic input error by one of its dealers. Yet that simple mistake quickly ballooned into some of the year's biggest losses on what had been a bullish year for the Tokyo bourse, leading to an investigation into how and if similar mistakes could be stopped from here on out.

This debacle by Mizuho Sec should make traders more cautious about each order they put through, especially as they now have proof about just how quickly a single input error can escalate into a problem for the entire stock trading system. To blame computers for the upheaval in the Tokyo Stock Exchange is misguided. Computerization is inevitable. It just means there will need to be more mechanisms to make sure orders are executed correctly.

One factor that aggravated the problem was the large population of stock investors who deliberately cancelled or changed their orders to roil the market. Another was the explosive growth of online trading by individual investors who conduct transactions dozens of times a day, frequently cancelling and changing their orders. Haphazard adjustments to the system in response to surging trading volume have created the potential for many glitches to occur in the future. It is clear that the trading system has not caught up with the rapid changes occurring in the stock market; and the problem is not purely technological in nature. It is a challenge demanding a comprehensive response from the securities industry based on whole scale examinations not just of computer systems but of the exchange's monitoring regime and trading.

This case is most powerful when the readers are put in the position of J-Com's president, the issuer of the IPO. The real crux of this case is managerial decision-making and the value of good leadership when something unexpected happens. The readers could discuss the steps the president took in the wake of the wrong order and what they think the president should have done. The case is a lesson in thinking about whether the best interests of the company were looked after and whether the president did the right thing.

## *Case 13 — Softbank's New Strategy: The Largest LBO in Japan*

On March 17, 2006, Japanese Internet Company Softbank Corp. (Softbank) announced that it had reached a final agreement with British cellular phone giant Vodafone Group Plc. (Vodafone) to buy its Japanese unit, Vodafone K.K. for ¥1.75 trillion. Under the agreement, Softbank would acquire a 97.7% stake in Vodafone K.K. through a wholly owned subsidiary. Markets said that, as part of the acquisition, Softbank would take over roughly ¥200 billion of the unit's interest-bearing debts. To finance the largest business acquisition ever by a Japanese firm, Softbank intended to raise between ¥1.1 trillion and ¥1.2 trillion through leveraged-buyout (LBO) financing, using Vodafone K.K.'s assets as collateral.

Founded by Masayoshi Son in 1981, Softbank was the second-largest broadband internet access provider in Japan, after Nippon Telegraph and Telephone Corp. (NTT). Its subsidiary, Yahoo, Japan Corp. (Yahoo Japan), operated the most popular web portal in the nation. With 15 million customers, Vodafone K.K. was Japan's third-largest mobile operator.

Son's primary drive for acquiring Vodafone K.K. was for Softbank to become larger and to reap the benefits of size in competition and negotiation. In other words, he desired for his company to gain market power and dominance. He also hoped to further diversify and spread his company's risks. Because Softbank and Vodafone K.K. operated in different industries, he apparently intended to achieve synergies between these operations and across different industries. Softbank sought to gain access to the strategic proprietary assets that Vodafone K.K. possessed. The acquisition of Vodafone K.K. also made it easier for Softbank to tap into the global (non-Japanese) capital markets. In essence, Softbank aimed to build a multilateral communications business, integrating news, video and other online content with Vodafone's cellular and fixed-line services.

There are several reasons for a company to buy out another firm: Some takeovers are opportunistic; the target company will be attractively priced for one reason or another. In such cases, the acquiring company thinks that it can make substantial profits in the long run. Other takeovers are strategic. Emphasis is put on the secondary effects of the acquisition. For example, an acquiring company thinks the target company's good distribution capabilities can be applied to marketing of its own products. A corporate acquisition is also attractive for the acquiring company as it can enter new markets and expand its business portfolio by acquiring established businesses. Such an acquisition is generally less risky and could also be cheaper than entering new markets and expanding its business portfolio from scratch. In the case of a green field investment doing everything from scratch and taking two to three years for its starting operations, the market might have disappeared by the time it actually starts. Sometimes, when an acquiring company buys a competitor, it does so not only because the acquisition provides a direct benefit if the competitor is conducting a profitable operation, but also because it provides the indirect benefit of eliminating competition and possibly enables the acquiring company to raise the price of its products in the long run. Acquisitions are also conducted to produce synergies. The combined companies might be worth more than the sum of the two separate companies. The most conspicuous effect of a merger of two companies is typically the labor cost reduction.

However, a large company's acquisition of a smaller company often invites criticism. It is not rare that a large company's acquisition is mainly aimed at increasing sales and market share rather than to improve profitability. Such an acquisition is generally not appreciated by stockholders. Society also frowns upon such acquisitions as it sees them as monopolistic or oligopolistic. These acquisitions often take place because the acquiring company can execute the acquisition without incurring a financial burden because it can use the assets of the acquired company to finance the acquisition.

The pros and cons of takeovers differ from case to case. This case analyzes the pros and cons of this deal for Softbank. This case introduces various negotiation techniques applicable to international ventures, particularly those related to investment and joint ventures in Japan. Also this case examines the cultures, customs and values of Japanese corporate business and their impact on decision-making processes.

## *Case 14 — Keidanren: Foreign Political Contributions in Japan*

The objective of this case is to study and review business ethics issues in connection with political donations by corporations in Japan. There has been a spate of political corruption cases in Japan over the past two decades, some of which have involved senior politicians and the top management of large corporations. This has led to increased scrutiny of companies' participation in the political process in general, and of their political campaign contributions in particular. Increasingly, shareholders are seeking to hold companies accountable for their campaign contributions. The lack of transparency to shareholders and the ineffectiveness of the government's enforcement mechanisms have led to many lawsuits brought by shareholders in Japan.

However, political activities generally require substantial funds, and the situation in Japan is no different. Consequently, politicians solicit donations from corporations that tend to influence politics to their benefit. A continuing question in Japan is whether a company is entitled to freely undertake political activities. Is donation of political funds one aspect of this freedom, even if such actions will exert influence over political trends? As long as the powerful mix of money and politics remains loosely regulated, democracy will continue to be undermined because the potential for corrupt or undesirable influences in politics will continue.

Regarding corporate political donations, there are differing views on what is legal and what types of corporate donations to politicians and political parties are acceptable; even court decisions are divided in Japan. These questions were raised in this case in such a way that the managerial dimensions of the problem are discussed.

Fujio Mitarai has been the appointed chairman of the Japanese Federation of Economic Organizations (Keidanren) since May 23, 2006. Keidanren is regarded by many as the strongest interest group in Japan. By law, foreigners, foreign companies and companies with foreign capital affiliations of over 30% of total capital are barred from making political donations. Although there have been a number of high-profile scandals involving political donations by Japanese companies and their executives, Keidanren has continued supporting the system of political donations. As the new chairman, should Mitarai press for a change in the law so that foreign companies will be allowed to make political donations?

# Case 15 — Tokyo Disneyland (3): New Strategies Needed for Sluggish Demand

# Case 16 — Licensing Arrangement or Joint Venture (4): An Ex Post Case Study of Tokyo Disneyland

There are two other cases on the same company: *Case 1 — Tokyo Disneyland: Licensing vs. Joint Venture* and *Case 2 — Tokyo Disneyland and the DisneySea Park: Corporate Governance and Difference in Capital Budgeting Concepts and Methods between American and Japanese Companies*.

These four cases may be read or taught on a stand-alone basis or combined with the other cases to create a joint-negotiation exercise.

## Case 15:

On May 9, 2005, Oriental Land Co. Ltd. (OL) had announced the changes in the company's top management that Toshio Kagami, president, would be chairman and CEO, and Yoshio Fukushima, senior executive management director would be the new president and COO. The company also announced that this organizational change was intended to strengthen the company's business management. The top management considered that amusement park and leisure land industry continue to provide little cause for optimism in Japan, due to factors such as slackening consumer spending and demographic changes. Under these conditions, the OL Group decided to focus on the two long-term strategies aimed at further growth.

Since September 2000, OL had never made a decision for changing the pricing. The top management must have considered the changing the price at that time was not attractive, although the long-term investment plan had been executed as schedule. The management looked taking a "wait and see" attitude for the pricing up until Japanese economy will be recovering fully so that it can escape from deflation. But on May 9, 2006 the ticket price hike of 5% was announced by OL. As to the reason for increasing the prices, the director and executive officer, Mr. Teruo Mitsui explained that the value of the theme park as a whole rose due to introductions of several new attractions.

For this decision, the question was how to get more visitors. The top management would specifically like to know whether current pricing policy was right or not under deflation which Japanese economy had been suffering for a long time and how changes in the pricing to visitors, if necessary, would influence on the company's cash flows in the future. The study was made by the planning department, which finally presented the results of the study, after carefully examining all the relevant data and analyses to the top management of OL. Then, they underwent intense soul searching in order to arrive at the most viable strategic decision on how best to cope with the new structural problems.

OL's top management had much to contemplate and consider. To address the issues more articulately, the top management asked the planning department to conduct a sensitivity analysis, based on different projections of visitors' growth and decrease, price increase and decrease, cost structures, profitability ratios and interest rate levels for both and more alternatives.

Was OL up to the task of overcoming the sluggish demand and remaining a leisure industry leader in Asia? The top management is now so confident that OL is a legend to carry forward and the foundation for that is to be laid down for the success.

## Case 16:

In the late 1970s, Walt Disney (WD) corporation sought to expand its enterprise to Japan. Oriental Land Corp. (OL), which represented the Japanese side, and Walt Disney, had to decide on a licensing arrangement or a joint venture. When a multinational enterprise is expanding its business with a local firm in a foreign country, how do they decide whether to select a licensing arrangement or a joint venture? Which of these choices would give them the most benefits?

The negotiations to bring Disneyland to Japan, which started in December of 1974, took four years and five months to complete. Both companies finally came to an agreement on April 30, 1979. According to the agreement, OL would pay a license fee equivalent to 10% of the gate receipts and 5% of other sales (this averaged to about 7% of the total annual revenue). Licensing is a popular method for companies to profit from foreign markets without the need to commit sizable funds. A license fee is a way to spread the research and development costs with the licensee and also a means of repatriating profits in a form more acceptable to host countries than dividends. The main disadvantages of licensing are: possible loss of quality control, and possible loss of opportunity to enter the foreign market with direct investment later. A joint venture, on the other hand, is defined as shared ownership in a foreign business. It is a mode to share risks and profits. Potential difficulties may arise if the partners have different views or objectives in certain critical decision areas.

Although deciding whether to enter into a licensing or joint venture agreement depends on various parameters, generally it can be said that when the project is very promising, the foreign investor should push for a joint venture and the host company should push for a licensing arrangement. Conversely, when the project's prospects are not assured of success, the foreign investor should push for a licensing arrangement and the host company should push for a joint venture.

WD as the foreign investor studied from the Japanese case that joint venture arrangement could offer higher combined returns/value as the project. This did not escape WD's notice and when similar situations arose in the development of Euro Disney and Hong Kong Disneyland, WD strove to obtain maximum profits through joint ventures. It seems WD decided it is necessary to take certain risk in foreign investment. For Hong Kong Disneyland, at the start, the Hong Kong government held a 57% stake, while The Walt Disney Company had 43%. But after the expansion plans were announced in 2009, when WD invested HK$3.63 billion (US$465 million), Hong Kong government's holdings were reduced to 52% while WD's shares increased to 48%. For Euro Disney, Disneyland Paris is operated by French company Euro Disney S.C.A., a public company of which 39.78% of its stock is held by WD, 10% by the Saudi Prince Alwaleed and 50.22% by other shareholders.

The objective of this study is to examine the actual determinants, models, and data of that investment choice. The model provided in this case will be of use to MNEs in evaluating whether their past investment decisions — specifically joint venture vs. licensing agreement, were shrewd. Based on their findings, they have options to abandon current modes in favor of alternatives. Investments have long lives and cash flow returns in later years may change from expected schedules. The competitive situation may be different later. Decision-makers will learn from both active and passive information gathering and can use it to make better decisions for the future. On this basis, this study can proceed to real option analysis.

## Case 17 — Ina Food Industry (2): Marketing Strategies in a Deflationary Environment

There is another case on the same company: *Case 8 — Ina Food Industry: A New Management Philosophy for Japanese Businesses*.

These two cases may be read or taught on a stand-alone basis or combined with the other case to create a joint-negotiation exercise.

This is a case study of a Japanese company that has achieved sales growth in Japan's current deflationary economy. Ina Food is a medium-sized, domestic, closely held manufacturer of powdered agar, a traditional gelatin product derived from seaweed. The success of this particular company is in large part due to powdered agar's meteoric popularity increase in Japan.

In 2005, it was discovered that oligosaccharides in agar have cancer-resistant properties. It was also discovered that agar deters constipation, making it a sought after ingredient to use in meals for the aged, especially. As its range of uses grew, so did its demand. Sales in 2011 amounted to ¥17.398 billion ($173.98 million at ¥100/$) with ordinary income for the same period at ¥2.4 billion ($24 million at ¥100/$). This was an increase in both sales and profits of approximately 1.5–2.0% from the previous year.

The company's policy is not quick growth, but stable growth. With this policy, the company has been enjoying an incredible 53 years of continuous sales and profit growth. The company's constant price increase has been very successful. The company employs its own original price strategy, which is investigated and discussed in this case.

Since December 29, 1989 when the Japanese stock market reached a historical all-time high (¥38,915), the Japanese economy lost two decades to economic stagnation. To counter these alarming deflationary trends, Japan enacted a zero-interest-rate policy, but so far it has not fostered sufficient expansion to induce recovery. Neither has the most recent expansion of the monetary base. Changing expectations of deflation to expectations of inflation in consumers is not easy.

During a deflationary period, consumers are reluctant to spend. Companies selling a good or service must make adjustments in order to continue earning profits, attempt to break even, or sometimes even lose as little money as possible in the hopes of staying afloat until the deflationary period ends. With any decision as drastic as this, it is important to carefully judge how it will affect every facet of the company such as brand, customers' perceptions, and anticipated position once the deflationary period ends. A common first move by companies navigating this difficult situation is to explore changing their pricing strategy. Price decreases, including predatory-pricing strategies to combat decreased market share and insufficient demand are popular choices.

Resource-abundant, or more established companies, however, are more likely to have a choice. Common rationale dictates that resource-rich companies will have the infrastructure and holdings to survive a drought. But overuse of price as a promotional tool might damage the prestige of a brand. Consumers may perceive such price cuts as an admission of product quality reduction, reducing previously high brand associations and awareness. Preferences for a certain brand are easily damaged, or forgotten, after price promotion. In sustainable pricing strategies, companies have to consider both internal and external influences.

This is the path that Japanese economy has walked in the past 20 years and it looks that US economy is now walking on the same path. This study explores how Japanese companies assess the effects of pricing strategy on company performance under deflation, and identifies those strategies that may help other companies to maintain successful performance despite deflation.

### *Case 18 — Bank of Japan (2): The Meeting on April 4, 2013 (Doubling Japan's Monetary Base via Government Bond Purchases)*

### *Case 19 — Abenomics of Japan: What Was It? Could This Conquer Japan's Decade-Long Deflation?*

These two cases may be read or taught on a stand-alone basis or combined with the other case to create a joint-negotiation exercise.

Two cases are on a review of Abenomics, which is the bold plan to end deflationary recession in Japan. In order to catalyze economic activity and pull Japan from its two-decade period of deflationary recession, new Prime Minister Shinzo Abe has enacted a bold recovery strategy focusing on three core areas. Referred to as Abenomics, it combines monetary relaxation, heavy short-term fiscal spending, and social and regulatory reform to spur growth. A main marker put forth by Abe is a 2% annual inflation rate. Thus far, his programs, which have been running for about a year, have had some successes, but have not yet yielded the dramatic shift that he has hoped for. The two cases explore the projects and rate them, as well as outline possible future courses.

For nearly the past two decades, Japan has suffered from deflationary spiral. It began with deflation caused by a fall in overall demand. Consumers, noticing the continuing trend of decreasing prices, reasoned that future prices would be lower than current prices, therefore electing to postpone their purchases in an effort to get the best prices. On the production side, consumers' lack of involvement led to idle capacity. When the market failed to absorb producers' output, investment sources also dried up, compounding the dearth of aggregate demand. In an effort to rectify these alarming trends and jump-start the economy, the extreme measure of a zero-interest-rate policy was enacted by Japan in February 1999. However, 10 years elapsed and still the policy did not yield sufficient economic expansion. The next tactic used to stimulate the economy was that of expanding the monetary base, enacted by former governor Shirakawa of the BOJ for the period of August 2008 to March 2013. Changing expectations of deflation to expectations of inflation in consumers was not easy. This was the path that the Japanese economy had walked in the previous 20 years before Abenomics was initiated in April 2013.

Abenomics, initiated in April 2013, has so far yielded positive returns, and has the potential to surpass the previous, ineffectual programs. After the April enactment, the yen sharply decreased in value, crossing the ¥100/$ boundary. It has since hovered in that area, and currently sits at ¥102.27/$ (as of January 24, 2014). This depreciation in value has promoted export profitability, which in turn has led to rising stock prices. While these gains are certainly welcome, critical concerns nonetheless remain. For one, exports account for only roughly 15% of the Japanese

GDP. Despite success in this sector, the collective power of the Japanese economy is decreasing, indicated by the rapidly shrinking total monetary value in dollars. Another issue on the horizon that must be addressed is the long-term projection of interest rates. While devising strategies to combat these problems is certainly necessary, the real end to Japanese national deflation and economic resurgence will come with a restoration of confidence and spending domestically.

The first thrust of Prime Minister Abe's revitalization campaign sought to raise expectations with a bold declaration: double the monetary base and double the purchase of JGB and exchange-traded funds. Haruhiko Kuroda, who had been confirmed on April 4, 2013 as the BOJ's governor, announced this intention in a new BOJ program called "Quantitative and Qualitative Monetary Easing". The plan would create a bolder central bank that would be more active in the marketplace in the hopes of buoying corporate investment and fostering consumer spending. Specifically, the central bank would effect the monetary base doubling plan by dramatically increasing its holdings of JGB bonds over two years. A critical parameter of this policy's success rests on the degree to which the BOJ can reverse inflation expectations. Currently, the population of Japan on the whole expects continuing deflation, an assumption buttressed by a consumer price index that has been often negative since 1994, as well as persistently negative expectations of future inflation.

The first two components of Abenomics, monetary easing and increased fiscal spending, are likely to be met with public support. The third component, growth strategies, will be seen as a shuffling of the deck for entrenched, so-called protected businesses, and thus will be more difficult. However, it is imperative that these regulatory and structural reforms happen because they are undeniably what Japan needs most. The opportunities for newcomers to the market will present consumers with more options and in the process revitalize the economy.

History has shown time and again that reflationary tactics carry with them large risks. Of special concern to Japan is the appearance of a bubble, which is what occurred in the 1980s. To protect against this possibility, the Abe government is monetizing debt. By printing money to buy government bonds, they are in effect leveraging future income to protect the present. This has long been eschewed by the Japanese government, as there are two severe dangers looming if the policies are not employed effectively. The first danger is that too aggressive a push might steer the Japanese bond market to fear inflation, sparking a hike in long-term borrowing costs and slowing recovery. The second danger is a phenomenon that would specifically target households. If jobs commanding higher incomes are not created, the forced inflation will serve only to erode purchasing power and diminish consumer confidence, perpetuating the status quo of consumer spending as a negative force on the economy.

Another cause for concern is Japan's falling national economic power. Though the depreciation of the yen has promoted indirect foreign investments, it has also had the effect of significantly shrinking national GDP. The IMF global economic outlook of April 2013 reported that Japan's GDP in terms of dollars fell from $5.96 trillion in 2012 to $5.14 trillion in 2013, a nearly 14% drop. This number will place Japan's national worth at roughly half of China's. In order to buttress the economy as the yen depreciates, Japan needs to make direct investment more accessible to foreign firms. Currently, foreign investment is exceedingly low in terms of both flow and stock. It is in Japan's best interests to open its market to the outside. This tactic, aimed at the third of Abe's three pillars, is the most important because it has the best chance to ensure growth in the future.

### Case 20 — Saizeriya and the Use of Foreign Currency Coupon Swaps: Was This for Hedging or Speculation?

Saizeriya was a company involved in the restaurant business. It focused on providing healthy and tasty Italian meals at affordable prices to its customers. Aiming to achieve higher quality at lower prices, the company established a uniform production and sales system that covered everything from the procurement of ingredients to service at its 775 chain restaurants throughout Japan. Hoping to offer richer and more varied food to more customers around the world, the company opened its first overseas restaurant in China in 2003, and by 2013 it operated a total of 24 restaurants in Shanghai, Guangzhou, Beijing and Taiwan. The company was established in 1973 and employed 2,200 employees throughout Asia in 2013. Its annual sales totaled ¥84,949 million (US$791.84 million).

On December 9, 2008, Yasuhiko Shogaki, president of Saizeriya made a public announcement as to losses caused by the use of foreign currency coupon swaps. Saizeriya announced that on December 10, 2008 it terminated its Forex reference-type Australian dollars currency coupon swap contracts with BNP Paribas Securities (Japan) Ltd., which caused a substantial potential valuation loss. A survey by the Financial Services Agency (FSA), the Japanese government in January 2011 showed the number of small and midsize companies holding currency derivatives contracts, which inflicted huge losses following the yen's sharp appreciation against the dollar, totaled some 19,000. Banks have sold around 64,000 of these contracts to smaller businesses since fiscal year 2004. After surveying about 120 banks, the FSA found that roughly 40,000 contracts, or around 60% of the total, were still outstanding as of the end of September, 2010. Smaller firms exposed to these products are estimated to have lost tens of millions of yen a month. And terminating their contracts could cost 200–300 million yen.

The present case is analyzing the risk of a product that became clear through the disclosure of the contents of the foreign currency coupon swap of a Japanese company. The same product was sold to many companies in Japan and many of the buyers are having difficulties in disposing them. Similar cases have also abundant in South Korea and India, and are becoming an international problem. There has been no report of a company disclosing the contents of such a foreign currency coupon swap trading. This case conducts professional analyses of the contents of the disclosure of the trade by the Subject Company and points out the inherent exceptionally high risk of the deal. Managers of companies will be able to read this case in order to avoid similar incidents. This is not a simple case study but an analysis of high universal validity and internationality that is applicable to many similar cases and should be valuable to a wide range of readers as similar products can be found on the market worldwide.

Business has become increasingly international, and companies cannot ignore the impact of currency changes on cash flows, profitability, and their asset and liability position. Many companies try to manage their currency exposures through hedging. It is a risk management strategy used in limiting or offsetting probability of loss from fluctuations in the prices of currencies. It also eliminates any gain from an increase in the value of the asset hedged against. The question is whether the risk should or should not be managed. Or what is to be gained by the companies from hedging? The gain must compensate the cost of hedging.

Companies practicing international trade often seek to hedge risk. Banks offer various derivatives to these companies, using high-powered computers capable of developing sophisticated mathematical programs to create hosts of new "synthetics" that can identify hundreds of never-before-imagined trades in currencies. SWAP is one of them. These derivatives are associated with high risk and so it is very close to speculation rather than just hedging.

For the company like Saizeriya in this article, there was an explicit intent in buying and selling the SWAP contract to perform the socially beneficial function of hedging risks stemming from exchange rate fluctuations between the yen and the Australian dollars. However, as we have studied, the SWAP trading has three main problems: (1) The product contents are very complex and difficult to understand; (2) they have high market risk and liquidity risk; (3) they are often misunderstood as safe products because they are typically handled by respectable financial institutions, such as major banks. These problems are highlighted more specifically in this case.

The FSA, Japan had called on banks to take steps to address the issue, which it feared could force companies into financial difficulty even if their core operations were sound. The FSA should have continued to be an effective prudential policymaker, but there should be some data-gathering mechanism to throw early warning signals about such wholesale defaults before the same gets out of proportion. These companies should also act with caution, rather than blindly believing the words of anybody and thereby getting into trouble. They should resort only to normal contractual hedge instruments such as simple forward contracts and plain vanilla options which they understand fully.

Presently, most of these companies have filed civil suits against their respective banks seeking a declaration that the contract is void. Saizeriya filed civil suits against BNP Paribas Securities that sought damages of ¥16.8 billion at Tokyo District Court on July 3, 2012. Now, the banks' legal responsibility is questioned in the courts. A few banks have also rushed for settlements, sharing a substantial portion of the loss on their own account.

## Teaching Notes

If this casebook is to be used as course text, teaching notes have been prepared to assist course instructors. Faculty members of recognized academic institutions may apply for access to the teaching notes at:

Asian Case Research Centre, University of Hong Kong (www.acrc.org.hk).

Multiple copies of individual cases may be ordered online at the same website or at:

Harvard Business School Publishing, Harvard University (www.hbsp.com);
European Case Clearing House (www.ecch.com).

# 1

# Tokyo Disneyland: Licensing vs. Joint Venture

*A theme park that materializes the "Kingdom Never Ending Dream and Magic".*

— Walt Disney[1]

In 1997, the senior executives of the Japanese Oriental Land Corporation (OL), known to many as the Japanese version of Disneyland,[2] were on a roller-coaster ride. They were at once anxious to grow their existing company through a new project as well as make Walt Disney Productions (WD) a risk-taking partner through direct investment in Japan's second theme park. This was to be a precondition to participating in the new project being proposed.[3] Although the partnership between OL and WD was a prominent success story of foreign investments in Japan by a US company, the partnership (see **Exhibit 1**) floundered as differences between the two companies about management philosophies and decision-making techniques had created tensions, resulting in mixed feelings towards the new project. In preparation for the negotiation, the net present value (NPV) of the two potential partnership models, i.e., the existing licensing method and a joint venture (JV) method in which WD would share some risks, were compared and evaluated. With both companies holding on to

---

[1] OL website on Tokyo DisneySea, http://www.olc.co.jp/company/resort/tokyodisneysea/index.html (accessed June 30, 2005).

[2] Tokyo Disneyland, http://www.olc.co.jp/en/company/resort/tokyodisneyland/index.html (accessed June 30, 2005).

[3] In the past, negotiations with WD were almost on the brink of disruption more than once, and appeared to be irreparable. It was the president, Takahashi, who resolved the situation each time. For Mr. Takahashi's works, see Kagami, T., an excerpt from "Umi wo Koeru Souzouryoku" (Imagination Extending across Seas), *Kodansha*, May 26, 2003, p. 50.

**Exhibit 1**  Basic Data of OL (1997)

| Name | OL Group | |
|---|---|---|
| Date of Establishment | July 11, 1960 | |
| Paid-in Capital | US$534 million | |
| Sales | US$1.5 billion | |
| Income before Tax | US$237 million | |
| President | Toshio Kagami | |
| Directors and Officers | 28 | |
| Employees | 2,493 (full time) | |
| | 6,355 (part time) | |
| Address | 1-1, Maihama, Urayasushi, Chiba-ken, Japan | |
| Main Banks | Industrial Bank of Japan | |
| | Mitsui Trust Bank | |
| Major Shareholders | Mitsui Real Estate Corp. | 20.48% |
| | Keisei Electric Railway Corp. | 11.20% |
| Tie-up Company | Disney Enterprises Inc. (USA) | |

*Source*: Yukashoken Houkokusho (Annual Reports), Oriental Land Corp. 1996–2001, http://www.olc.co.jp/en/company/profile/index.html (accessed June 30, 2005).

their own agenda, it was a tough job for senior executives on both sides to resolve the differences and clear the obstacles in order to arrive at a mutually beneficial agreement.

## OL's Diversification Plan

Since 1983, OL has operated Tokyo Disneyland under a license (at a fee of 7%) with WD.[4] It took both companies four and a half years to arrive

---

[4] In the initial negotiation, the Japanese side requested a reduction of the license fee from 10% to 5% and required WD to bear a certain percentage of the risk, which infuriated WD so much that it interrupted the negotiations. For details, see Takahashi, M. (OL's first president), an excerpt from "Watakushi no Rirekisho (My Personal History)" series, *Nikkei* (*Japan Economic Journal*), WD, no. 20, July 20, 1999, p. 36. The % figure of the license fee for WD was not publicly disclosed by OL. The figure could be calculated from what OL actually paid WD in the past. See details in Yukashoken Houkokusho. (Annual

at the agreement. The prime reason for the delay was the ongoing negotiations for the reduction of the license fee and contract term.[5] In the spring of 1997, 37 years after OL had been established (1960), senior executives, who until then were enjoying the success of this stable and grounded company, began to ponder the timeliness of embarking on a new business endeavor to fuel growth and enhance OL's earning capability.

Although senior executives of OL were uneasy about the risks in initiating new ventures when the general economy was not faring well, they also recognized the need for new investments to maintain visitors' interests.[6] Their initial enthusiasm was, however, tempered by two factors: (i) the amount of investment needed would be large, and (ii) the number of visitors would eventually diminish. They knew that approximately 75% of OL's customers were repeat visitors.[7] The question was whether, after two or three visits, they would come back for a fourth time? They were concerned that customers would eventually get bored with the existing attractions and facilities, resulting in a decline in the number of visitors.

OL's staff forecasted that the number of visitors in 1998 would drop by 4% compared to that in 1997 (see **Exhibit 2** for the actual attendance from 1983 to 1997).[8] Furthermore, the number of shareholders had

---

Reports), Oriental Land Corp. 1996–2001, http://www.olc.co.jp/en/company/profile/index.html (accessed June 30, 2005).

[5] WD wanted 50 years while OL insisted on 20 years. In the end, they agreed on a basic term of 20 years, which was extendable five times, for five years each time, to a maximum extension of 25 years, so that the total possible term would be 45 years. The Japanese side must have thought that 45 years was too long, and that it was humiliating to accept it. For details, see Kagami, T., an excerpt from "Umi wo Koeru Souzouryoku (Imagination Extending across Seas)", *Kodansha*, May 26, 2003, pp. 52–53.

[6] The need for a new theme park was justified by the fact that with the opening of the Maihama Station of the Keiyo Line, the number of visitors increased tremendously, such that it would soon reach its capacity. Also, Chiba Prefecture requested the use of unused parkland. For the new investment plan, see Takahashi, M., an excerpt from "Watakushi no Rirekisho (My Personal History)" series, *Nikkei* (*Japan Economic Journal*), no. 29, July 30, 1999, p. 40.

[7] For the ratio of repeat visitors in the total number of entrants, see Arima, T., "Disneyland Story", *Nikkei Business Bunko*, July 1, 2001, pp. 170–171.

[8] See Takahashi, M., an excerpt from "Watakushi no Rirekisho (My Personal History)" series for the positive attitude of OL towards additional investments, *Nikkei* (*Japan Economic Journal*), no. 28, July 29, 1999, p. 40.

**Exhibit 2**   Tokyo Disneyland Attendance (1983–1997)

| Year | Attendance |
|------|------------|
| 1983 | 9,933,000 |
| 1984 | 10,013,000 |
| 1985 | 10,675,000 |
| 1986 | 10,665,000 |
| 1987 | 11,975,000 |
| 1988 | 13,382,000 |
| 1989 | 14,752,000 |
| 1990 | 15,876,000 |
| 1991 | 16,139,000 |
| 1992 | 15,815,000 |
| 1993 | 16,030,000 |
| 1994 | 15,509,000 |
| 1995 | 16,986,000 |
| 1996 | 17,368,000 |
| 1997 | 16,686,000 |

*Source:* Yukashoken Houkokusho (Annual Reports), Oriental Land Corp. 1996–2001. See also http://www.olc.co.jp/en/company/guest/index.html.

increased after the company had been listed on the Tokyo Stock Exchange in 1996, and they would expect higher stock prices and dividends. Thus, the senior executives felt a greater sense of responsibility to provide assurance of the company's future to shareholders.

In June 1988, after celebrating its fifth anniversary, OL embarked on a thorough study of the second theme park.[9] Initially, WD, the licenser,

---

[9] In the meanwhile, Mitsuaki Mori, who was sent from The Industrial Bank of Japan succeeded Takahashi as the president. WD witnessed a management changeover in 1984 as well, creating a powerful team with Michael Eisner, the chairman, and Frank Wells, the president. For further details, see Kagami, T., an excerpt from "Umi wo Koeru Souzouryoku (Imagination Extending across Seas)", *Kodansha*, May 26, 2003, pp. 98–99.

proposed construction of Disney Hollywood Magic, based on the concept of a movie studio. OL however, was not convinced, as the Disney Hollywood Magic concept had not been used in the US Disneyland. The senior executives of OL told WD, "We would like to make up our minds after seeing it in the US."[10]

OL thought that,

*[T]he second theme park should have a marketability independent from the Tokyo Disneyland. It should not be the second park simply to catch the guests overflowing from the Tokyo Disneyland. Unless it provides an experience entirely different from that offered by the Tokyo Disneyland, there is little meaning for building it.*[11]

A meeting was held in September 1991 in Tokyo, and was attended by WD and OL's top brass. At this meeting, OL officially announced that it had to object to the Disney Hollywood Magic idea, since OL believed that the "Studio Tour" concept proposed by WD was unfit for the Japanese market (the movie industry in Japan was not as popular as Hollywood was in the US) and difficult to reach profitability (it was hard to attract repeat customers).[12] The top executives of WD seemed considerably disappointed. WD's president, Frank Wells, lamented, "Was our effort the Myth of Sisyphus[13] after all?"[14]

---

[10] Statement made by OL's president, Takahashi, to WD's president, Wells. For further details, see Kagami, T., an excerpt from "Umi wo Koeru Souzouryoku (Imagination Extending across Seas)", *Kodansha*, May 26, 2003, p. 98.

[11] See Kagami, T., an excerpt from "Umi wo Koeru Souzouryoku (Imagination Extending across Seas)", *Kodansha*, May 26, 2003, p. 105.

[12] There was a harsh exchange of words. For details, see Takahashi, M., an excerpt from "Watakushi no Rirekisho (My Personal History)" series, *Nikkei* (*Japan Economic Journal*), no. 29, July 30, 1999, p. 40.

[13] Sisyphus was a character in Greek mythology who angered Zeus and was sentenced to roll a boulder to the top of a mountain. The minute he got to the top though, it would roll back down so that he had to repeat the task forever, signifying a useless work of grand order. For details, http://homepage.mac.com/cparada/GML/Sisyphus.html (accessed June 30, 2005).

[14] Statement made by president Wells of WD. For details, see Kagami, T., an excerpt from "Umi wo Koeru Souzouryoku (Imagination Extending across Seas)", *Kodansha*, May 26, 2003, pp. 105–106.

After the meeting, OL had to work hard to reinstate WD's trust in the project and to renew the study of the second theme park.[15] It was then that WD proposed a new venture, the DisneySea Park Project,[16] which they guaranteed to backup completely.[17] The initial plan was to build seven seas in the theme park. Although some differences of opinion still existed, OL saw that the timing was good. As they had started their own study for a second theme park, and the offer was in line with their plans to increase visitors,[18] the senior executives of OL immediately instructed the planning department to conduct a feasibility study on WD's offer.

> *The reason that it took as long as 10 years for the second project is because it needed a lot of work to adjust the concept between us and WD. WD wanted us to build something like an MGM studio in Florida. However, there is a difference between what Americans feel and Japanese people feel about movies. We also had a strong attachment to the theme concerning the sea. The reason was that Maihama in Chiba Prefecture, where the Tokyo Disneyland and the Tokyo DisneySea are located, is a landfill. Japan is an island country surrounded by seas. Historically speaking, cultures were brought to Japan across the seas. The Japanese have a strong love of the sea; you may call it our home.*

> — Kagami, president of OL[19]

---

[15] Kagami, T., an excerpt from "Umi wo Koeru Souzouryoku (Imagination Extending across Seas)", *Kodansha*, May 26, 2003, p. 106.

[16] Takahashi and Kagami flew to the US to meet WD on July 21, 1992. See Kagami, T., an excerpt from "Umi wo Koeru Souzouryoku (Imagination Extending across Seas), *Kodansha*, May 26, 2003, pp. 110–111.

[17] Takahashi, M., an excerpt from "Watakushi no Rirekisho (My Personal History)" series, *Nikkei (Japan Economic Journal)*, no. 29, July 30, 1999, p. 40.

[18] See Kagami, T., "Konna Shiawasena Shigoto wa Nai (There Is No Such Enjoyable Work as This)", from "Ningen Hakken, Watakushi no Keiei Tetsugaku (Finding Human Beings — My Management Philosophy)", *Nikkei Business Bunko*, August 1, 2004, pp. 164–165.

[19] Statement made by president Toshio Kagami of OL. For details, see note 18, *op. cit. supra*.

OL's planning department consisted of a group of corporate elites who had studied at American business schools. The specific instruction given by the senior executives to the planning department was as follows:

"WD's participation in the Japanese projects has been the licensing method, in which it is to be compensated by a fixed 7% fee of the total annual revenue regardless of the profits ... I believe the new project gives us an opportunity to propose a joint venture to WD. My idea is to issue preferred stock (annual dividend: 5%) in an amount equivalent to 20% of the total funds of US$3.4 billion required for the new project,[20] 30% of which, i.e., US$203 million, is to be purchased by WD.[21]

I want you to calculate the NPV for the next seven years for the following two cases. It is obvious that WD will want the case with a higher NPV. Your NPV calculation should be based on the assumption that the new project is added to the existing project. In any case, I would assume that WD's current participation method is very difficult to change for the time being.

Case 1 (License Method):

A 7% license fee will be paid for the entire project: the new project and the existing project.[22] This is WD's preferred method of participation. Please calculate the NPV for the period 1998–2004.

---

[20] The total investment to the Tokyo DisneySea project reached US$2.8 billion. In particular, the investment made over four years in the entire Maihama district was US$4.2 billion. In order to collect these funds, OL strived to be listed on the big board (the 1st section) of the Tokyo Stock Exchange Market. The company invested all the money collected on the open market and its internal withholding reserves in the Tokyo DisneySea. Corporate bonds (rated as AA plus) and loans contributed to the remainder. The enormous investment was supported by a bountiful cash flow. For details, see Kagami, T., an excerpt from "Umi wo Koeru Souzouryoku (Imagination Extending across Seas)", *Kodansha*, May 26, 2003, pp. 148–149.

[21] WD's position in the contract (that it would not take any risk, and collect only the license fee) had caused a lot of commotion in Japan. The president of the Industrial Bank of Japan called this policy a "strange one" and one that was "never heard of in Japan". See Arima, T., "Disneyland Story", *Nikkei Business Bunko*, July 1, 2001, pp. 136–138.

[22] WD strongly requested a 10% license fee, which OL's board members shot down. For details, see Takahashi, M., an excerpt from "Watakushi no Rirekisho (My Personal History)" series, *Nikkei (Japan Economic Journal)*, July 1–31, 1999, No. 22, July 23, 1999, p. 40.

Case 2 (JV Method):

I would like to know how the NPV for the total project for the same period would be affected if WD subscribed to US$203 million of preferred stock, based on the assumption that the license method is still in place. This large sum will lower the NPV; the question is by how much. This is OL's preferred method of partnership — we don't know if WD will agree to the scheme."

## Tokyo Disneyland

In April 1979, 19 years after its establishment, OL executed a license agreement with WD,[23] involving the design, construction and operation of Tokyo Disneyland. In December 1980, the construction of Tokyo Disneyland began at Maihama District,[24] in what is now the city of Urayasu.[25] In April 1983, Tokyo Disneyland opened its doors for business. In December 1996, the company's stock was listed on the First Section of the Tokyo Stock Exchange.

When Tokyo Disneyland opened, it started with an initial investment of approximately US$1.53 billion,[26] and was injected with a similar amount over the next 18 years.[27] This long-term commitment of funds

---

[23] The US–Japan negotiation of bringing Disneyland to Japan took four years and five months to conclude after WD's management team first visited Japan in December 1974. Initially, OL's parent company (owned 48% share), Mitsui Real Estate Corp., objected in particular to the agreement conditions. Despite this, OL and WD finally came to an agreement on April 30, 1979. For details, see Takahashi, M., an excerpt from "Watakushi no Rirekisho (My Personal History)" series, *Nikkei* (*Japan Economic Journal*), July 1–31, 1999, no. 25, July 26, 1999, p. 40.

[24] Mr. Kawasaki, then president of Keisei Electric Railway Co., managed to obtain a large plot of land from the Chiba Prefecture government, in anticipation of revenue from hotels that could be built adjacent to the theme park. OL did not want to secure the land in advance to avoid it being lost to other developers. Takahashi, M., an excerpt from "Watakushi no Rirekisho (My Personal History)" series, *Nikkei* (*Japan Economic Journal*), July 1–31, 1999, no. 13, July 14, 1999, p. 40.

[25] OL's chronology, http://www.olc.co.jp/en/company/history/index.html (accessed June 30, 2005).

[26] US$1 = ¥118.02 in 1997.

[27] OL invested US$237 million in the first five years and another US$593 million in the next five years. In other words, it made additional investments of US$847 million after the

resulted in the addition of new features, including "Star Tours", "Splash Mountain" and "Winnie the Pooh".[28] As a result of these new attractions, Tokyo Disneyland boasted 17 million visitors in 1997, the world's largest visitor volume.[29] The opening of hotels nearby, directly run by OL, factored in additional contributions to revenues. Cost control measures like curbing personnel costs were showing results. At the same time, however, profits were relatively low as a result of heavy depreciation, opening costs and interest burden (see **Exhibit 3**).

## Walt Disney Productions

As OL's primary licenser, WD held a very small amount of OL's equity in exchange for its significant contribution of expertise and support. Initially, WD invested US$3.5 million in the project, which was only 0.42% of the total initial investment. According to the agreement, OL had to pay a license fee equivalent to 10% of the gate receipts and 5% of other sales (this averaged to about 7% of the total annual revenue).[30]

Since WD only owned a small share, the dividend payments were nominal. In addition, there were no interest payments or any principal repayments to WD, as there was no outstanding loan. Generally speaking, WD had almost no cash investment in OL, and as a result, there was

---

opening. For details, see Takahashi, M., an excerpt from "Watakushi no Rirekisho (My Personal History)" series, *Nihon Keizai Shimbun*, no. 29, July 30, 1999, p. 40.

[28] For details on additional attractions, see Kagami, T., an excerpt from "Umi wo Koeru Souzouryoku (Imagination Extending across Seas)", *Kodansha*, May 26, 2003, pp. 72–73.

[29] After seeing that the total construction cost exceeded the budgeted amount by US$678 million, president Takahashi sent a message to the staff to continue building so that the theme park would be better than the one in Los Angeles or Florida. Kagami, T., an excerpt from "Umi wo Koeru Souzouryoku (Imagination Extending across Seas)", *Kodansha*, May 26, 2003, p. 61.

[30] WD originally demanded a 10% license fee, to which OL's parent company Mitsui Real Estate Corp. strongly objected. OL's management group requested WD to lower the royalty to 5% in accordance with the intention of Mr. Tsuboi (president of Mitsui Real Estate Corp.), which infuriated WD and caused mistrust. For details, see Takahashi, M., an excerpt from "Watakushi no Rirekisho (My Personal History)" series, *Nikkei* (*Japan Economic Journal*), July 1–31, 1999, no. 19, July 20, 1999, p. 36.

**Exhibit 3**  OL's Past Financial Data as of 1997

(US$ million)

| Year | No. of Visitors (thou-sands) | Sales Revenue | Operating Costs | (Depre-ciation) | Adminis-trative Expenses | Interest Paid | Other Extra-ordinary Expenses | Income Before Tax | Taxes (47%) | Income after Tax | Invest-ment | Fixed Assets | Total Assets |
|---|---|---|---|---|---|---|---|---|---|---|---|---|---|
| | | | | | | — Past — | | | | | | | |
| 1996 | 16,986 | 1,453.2 | 1,095.0 | 87.5 | 107.6 | 10.6 | 0.0169 | 237.9 | 113.4 | 124.5 | 1,331.8 | 1,164.6 | 1,770.2 |
| 1997 | 17,368 | 1,533.3 | 1,125.5 | 93.9 | 104.5 | 8.5 | 0.56 | 238.4 | 103.6 | 134.7 | 258.3 | 1,218.9 | 3,011.7 |

*Source*: Yukashoken Houkokusho (Annual Reports), Oriental Land Corp. 1996–2001, http://www.olc.co.jp/en/ir/ir.html (accessed June 30, 2005).

almost zero negative cash flow, with positive cash flow coming from the receipt of the license fee.

Under normal circumstances, when a Japanese manufacturing company entered into a license agreement with an overseas company, it would commonly cause negative side effects on account of exports to an overseas market. In contrast, in the leisure industry, there were few or no negative side effects because products were neither imported nor exported. As a result, the new Disney project appeared to be an ideal, risk free arrangement for WD.[31] Nevertheless, WD wished to maximize revenue from Japan through the license fees paid by OL.[32,33] It had a substantial interest in the new DisneySea Park project being planned, and behaved as if it were a primary and lead investor.

## The Theme Park Industry in Japan

OL had built a reputation as the unchallenged leader in the Japanese theme park industry (see **Exhibit 4**). In the early years, OL's annual visitor count neared 17 million, approximately 4 times more than that at their direct competitor, Yokohama Sea Paradise.[34] However, the total number of visitors had since been declining with each passing year, even though the theme park industry was at its peak in the early 1990s, ahead of all other leisure industries in Japan. According to a survey, the market size of

---

[31] OL thought that 45 years was too long. OL's president Kagami believed a long-term agreement in the engineering world where technology becomes obsolete so quickly could certainly be called an "unfair agreement". For details, see Kagami, T., an excerpt from "Umi wo Koeru Souzouryoku (Imagination Extending across Seas)", *Kodansha*, May 26, 2003, pp. 52–53.

[32] From the very beginning in 1978, OL had been trying their best to make WD bear some risks, but their efforts were in vain. Mitsui Real Estate Corp., which was OL's parent company, held a firm position that it could guaranty the project borrowing up to 48% of its investment and not more, and that the balance should be borne by the American side. For details, see Takahashi, M., an excerpt from "Watakushi no Rirekisho (My Personal History)" series, *Nikkei* (*Japan Economic Journal*), no. 23, July 24, 1999, p. 40.

[33] Behind this tough contract condition was the problem of WD's management. See Arima, T., "Disneyland Story", *Nikkei Business Bunko*, July 1, 2001, pp. 146–147.

[34] See Prince Hotels and Resorts, http://www.seaparadise.co.jp/ (accessed June 30, 2005).

**Exhibit 4**   Ten Largest Theme Parks in Japan (1997)

(Unit = 10 Thousands)

|  |  | Number of Visitors |
|---|---|---|
| 1 | Tokyo Disneyland | 1,730 |
| 2 | Yokohama Sea Paradise | 479 |
| 3 | Nagashima Hot Springs | 384 |
| 4 | House Tempos, Nagasaki Holland Village | 376 |
| 5 | Aso Farm Land | 349 |
| 6 | Yokohama Cosmo World | 335 |
| 7 | Suzuka Circuit | 282 |
| 8 | Takarazuka Family Land | 206 |
| 9 | Space World | 200 |
| 10 | Baruke Espania | 192 |

*Source*: *Nikkei* (*Japan Economic Journal*), February 17, 2000, p. 30, http://www.olc.co.jp/ir/ir.html (accessed June 30, 2005).

amusement parks and leisure attractions in Japan would diminish from US$5.20 billion in 1997 to US$4.27 billion in 2000.[35]

The reasons for such decline included: (1) receding customer interest as the varying establishments began offering similar services and activities; (2) the inability to reduce the entrance fees to entice customers because of the companies' burden of recovering the high initial investment; and (3) a prolonged recession and growing deflation.

## New Project: Tokyo DisneySea Park

*As long as there is an imagination, the Park will never be completed.*

— Walt Disney[36]

---

[35] *Nihon Keizai Shimbun* (*Japan Economic Journal*), February 17, 2000, p. 30.

[36] OL's website on Tokyo DisneySea, http://www.olc.co.jp/company/resort/tokyodisneysea/index.html (accessed June 30, 2005).

Given that economic conditions in 1997 were weak, OL had to decide whether it should undertake a project as large as the Tokyo DisneySea Park.[37] The initial investment of US$3.39 billion was a significant amount. On receiving the proposal, OL's senior executives consulted with all the parties concerned. Many questioned the undertaking as the project was a tall order in the midst of a poor economic climate. The sheer size of the project fazed all stakeholders, the management as well as many major shareholders and lenders.[38]

OL adopted a cautious stance at first as the project appeared too colossal, was extremely risky and its profitability was uncertain.[39] WD believed that the Sea Park project had a high potential for success, and recommended that OL aggressively increase its investment if it was determined to expand its business.[40,41] The Tokyo DisneySea Park focused on offering

---

[37] Tokyo DisneySea Park, http://www.olc.co.jp/en/company/resort/tokyodisneysea/index.html (accessed June 30, 2005).

[38] Mr. Kagami, OL's president, said that the biggest rationale for the name "Tokyo DisneySea" lay in its location: within a radius of 100 km, there lived over 300 million people with high disposable incomes. For details, see Kagami, T., "Challenge of Second Venture: DisneySea", *Shukan Toyo Keizai*, May 12, 2001, pp. 52–53.

[39] OL strongly resisted WD's traditional licensing fee format. OL believed it was unfair for it to pay royalties of approximately US$51 million each year, when WD did not have to take any risks, and used the land for free with no financial burden. For details on the fierce exchanges between the two companies, see Takahashi, M., an excerpt from "Watakushi no Rirekisho (My Personal History)" series, *Nikkei* (*Japan Economic Journal*), no. 29, July 30, 1999, p. 40.

[40] WD implemented stringent conditions for the Japanese side for the joint project in Japan, but the success in Tokyo helped WD to revive OL's royalty payments to WD increased to approximately US$68 million in 1988. WD made use of the income to invest in hotels in Disney World. For details, see Arima, T., "Disneyland Story", *Nikkei Business Bunko*, July 1, 2001, p. 174.

[41] The majority of revenue from the theme park was generated by sales of novelty goods, foods and beverages, which totaled US$482 million, and not from entrance fees, which totaled US$399 million. The license fee was 10% for the entrance fee and novelty goods, and only 5% on foods and beverages. As a result, WD was earning a limited profit since it charged a lower license fee in the category with higher sales. The lesson that WD learned in Tokyo Disneyland was applied to Euro Disney, where it strived to obtain the maximum profit possible. See Arima, T., "Disneyland Story", *Nikkei Business Bunko*, July 1, 2001, pp. 172–173.

memorable adventures and romantic settings in its seven major theme areas: Mysterious Island's Prometheus Volcano, Indy Jones Adventure, Aquatopia Loading Zone for Port Discovery, "20,000 Leagues Under the Sea" Mysterious Island, Mystic Rhythm, Transit Steamer Line and Disney Symphony.[42] The theme park had a total of 23 attractions and storylines, strung together through the feature show, "DisneySea Symphony", with its sparkling dances of lights and water fountains topped off with wondrous fantasy effects. The planners believed that the attendance would surge if visitors perceived added value in staying at a hotel located at the theme park; the result was Tokyo DisneySea's hotel, "Miracosta".[43] The Sea Park and Miracosta were to be thrown open to the public simultaneously, the synergy of the two new facilities attracting droves of visitors from all over the world.

## *Project Profitability*

OL's planning department reported the following analysis to the senior executives: future income and expenses were estimated for up to seven years based on 1997 data, with certain financial assumptions (see **Exhibit 5**).

The planning department was able to project financial data for 1998–2004 based on data from 1996 to 1997 (see **Exhibit 3**) and the assumptions presented in **Exhibit 5**. Since the new project represented an expansion to the existing company, the marginal contribution of the new investment had to be projected. As it was extremely difficult to separate the expansion project from the existing company, two projections of cash flow were drafted, one with the expansion to OL and one without. The difference of the two projections would then represent the anticipated cash flow of the new project. This step-by-step process followed by the planning department is shown in **Exhibits 6–8**.

---

[42] OL website, http://www.olc.co.jp/company/resort/index.html (accessed June 30, 2005).

[43] Kagami, T., "Japanese People Have Imagination Abilities", "Japanese Economy Will Come Back", edited by Eisuke Kashiwabara and Nobuhiko Shima, *Askie Communications*, 2003, pp. 36–41.

**Exhibit 5**   Assumptions for Projection of OL's Financial Data

1. An initial capital investment in Tokyo DisneySea Park of US$3.4 billion was made in 2000.
2. The number of visitors would remain the same during the next four years, and would increase by 30% in 2002 when Tokyo DisneySea Park would be opened. They would increase by 10% in 2003 and 2004. In 1997, the average admission fee per person was US$84.70. Given the deflationary climate, admission fees would increase by 2% during the four years after 1997, and would increase by 15% in 2002 at the opening of Tokyo DisneySea Park, and would again increase by 10% in 2003. In 2004, admission fees would remain at the same rate as in 2003. If the new project was not undertaken, the number of visitors would remain the same during the seven-year period, and admission fees would increase by 2% over those seven years.[44]
3. Operating costs other than depreciation (67% of the sales, 1997 data), administrative expenses (7%), and other expenses (4%) would increase proportionately with the increase in sales. These projections would be applied irrespective of OL's decision on the investment.
4. Depreciation of the US$3.4 billion investment in 2000 would be conducted using the straight-line method over 20 years.
5. Funds borrowed as of 1997 totaled US$195 million, for which interest payments in 1997 amounted to US$8.5 million (interest rate on debt is 4.34%). It was assumed that the cost of future borrowing would be 4.34% (the same as that of 1997). It was also assumed that for the future investments, two-thirds would be financed by the internal withholding reserves and capital increases (including the issuance of preferred stocks) and one-third would be financed by borrowings. This assumption was made based on the past performance of the company.[45]
6. The Japanese rate of taxation was 47%.

## *An Opportunity*

Using the above analysis, OL's planning department reported the estimated profit of the new project to the senior executives. Specifically, the new theme park would not be profitable during the first three years, but would be thereafter; and the cash flow, including amortization, would stay positive from the start. The top brass at OL were unperturbed at being in

---

[44] OL's website (Business Growth, Comparative Advantage, Management Message, etc.), http://www.olc.co.jp/en/ir/ir.html (accessed June 30, 2005).

[45] OL's website, http://olc.netir-wsp.com/FaqU,locale,en_US.html (accessed June 30, 2005).

**Exhibit 6**    OL's Projected Financial Data without the New Project in 1998–2004

(US$ million)

| | No. of Visitors (Thousands) | Admission Fee (US$) | Sales | Operating Cost (Excluding Depreciation) (67% of Sales) | Depreciation | Administrative Expenses (7% of Sales) | Interest Paid |
|---|---|---|---|---|---|---|---|
| 1997 (Actual) | 17,368 | 84.7 | 1,533.3 | 1,027.3 | 93.9 | 107.3 | 8.5 |
| 1998 | 17,368 | 86.4 | 1,501.1 | 1,005.7 | 93.9 | 105.1 | 7.6 |
| 1999 | 17,368 | 88.2 | 1,531.1 | 1,025.8 | 93.9 | 107.2 | 6.9 |
| 2000 | 17,368 | 90.0 | 1,561.7 | 1,046.3 | 93.9 | 109.3 | 6.2 |
| 2001 | 17,368 | 91.7 | 1,592.9 | 1,067.2 | 93.9 | 111.5 | 5.5 |
| 2002 | 17,368 | 93.5 | 1,624.7 | 1,088.5 | 93.9 | 113.7 | 5.0 |
| 2003 | 17,368 | 95.4 | 1,657.2 | 1,110.3 | 93.9 | 116.0 | 4.5 |
| 2004 | 17,368 | 97.3 | 1,690.3 | 1,132.5 | 93.9 | 118.3 | 4.1 |

| | Other Expenses (4% of Sales) | Income before Tax | Taxes (47%) | Income after Tax | Fixed Assets |
|---|---|---|---|---|---|
| 1997 (Actual) | 61.3 | 238.4 | 112.0 | 134.7 | 1,125.1 |
| 1998 | 60.0 | 228.7 | 107.5 | 121.2 | 1,031.3 |
| 1999 | 61.2 | 235.6 | 111.0 | 125.1 | 937.5 |
| 2000 | 62.5 | 243.5 | 114.5 | 129.1 | 843.7 |
| 2001 | 63.7 | 251.0 | 118.0 | 133.0 | 749.9 |
| 2002 | 65.0 | 258.4 | 121.4 | 136.9 | 656.0 |
| 2003 | 66.3 | 264.3 | 124.2 | 140.1 | 562.3 |
| 2004 | 67.6 | 273.9 | 128.7 | 145.2 | 468.5 |

*Note:* Trial calculations based upon certain assumptions.

*Source*: OL's Annual Reports, http://www.olc.co.jp/en/ir/ir.html (accessed June 30, 2005).

**Exhibit 7**  OL's Projected Financial Data with the New Project in 1998–2004

(US$ million)

| | No. of Visitors (Thousands) | Admission Fee (US$) | Sales | Operating Cost (Excluding Depreciation) (67% of Sales) | Depreciation | Administrative Expenses (7% of Sales) | Interest Paid |
|---|---|---|---|---|---|---|---|
| 1997 (Actual) | 17,368 | 84.7 | 1,533.3 | 1,027.3 | 93.9 | 107.3 | 8.5 |
| 1998 | 17,368 | 86.4 | 1,501.1 | 1,005.7 | 93.9 | 105.1 | 7.6 |
| 1999 | 17,368 | 88.2 | 1,531.1 | 1,025.8 | 93.9 | 107.2 | 6.9 |
| 2000 | 17,368 | 90.0 | 1,561.7 | 1,046.3 | 263.3 | 109.3 | 55.2 |
| 2001 | 17,368 | 91.7 | 1,592.9 | 1,067.2 | 263.3 | 111.5 | 49.7 |
| 2002 | 22,578 | 105.5 | 2,381.3 | 1,595.5 | 263.3 | 166.7 | 46.7 |
| 2003 | 24,836 | 110.9 | 2,881.3 | 1,930.5 | 263.3 | 202.0 | 43.7 |
| 2004 | 27,319 | 116.0 | 3,169.4 | 2,123.5 | 263.3 | 221.9 | 40.8 |

| | Other Expenses (4% of Sales) | Income before Tax | Taxes (47%) | Income after Tax | Fixed Assets |
|---|---|---|---|---|---|
| 1997 (Actual) | 61.3 | 238.4 | 112.0 | 134.7 | 1,125.1 |
| 1998 | 60.0 | 228.7 | 107.5 | 121.2 | 1,031.3 |
| 1999 | 61.2 | 235.6 | 111.0 | 125.1 | 937.5 |
| 2000 | 62.5 | 25.1 | 11.8 | 13.3 | 4,232.9 |
| 2001 | 63.7 | 37.4 | 17.6 | 19.8 | 3,969.7 |
| 2002 | 95.3 | 213.9 | 100.5 | 113.4 | 3,536.9 |
| 2003 | 115.3 | 326.9 | 153.5 | 173.2 | 3,273.7 |
| 2004 | 126.8 | 393.2 | 184.8 | 208.4 | 3,010.4 |

*Note:* Trial calculations based upon certain financial assumptions.

*Source*: OL's Annual Reports, http://www.olc.co.jp/en/ir/ir.html (accessed June 30, 2005).

**Exhibit 8**   Income and Cash Flows from the New Project, 1998–2004

(US$ million)

| | Without the Project | | | With the Project | | | The New Project | | | |
|---|---|---|---|---|---|---|---|---|---|---|
| | Depre-ciation | Income | Cash Flow | Depre-ciation | Income | Cash Flow | Depre-ciation | Income | Cash Flow | Fixed Assets |
| 1997 (Actual) | 93.9 | 134.7 | 228.6 | 93.9 | 134.7 | 228.6 | 0 | 0 | 0 | |
| 1998 | 93.9 | 121.2 | 215.1 | 93.9 | 121.2 | 215.1 | 0 | 0 | 0 | |
| 1999 | 93.9 | 125.1 | 219.0 | 93.9 | 125.1 | 219.0 | 0 | 0 | 0 | |
| 2000 | 93.9 | 129.1 | 223.0 | 263.3 | 13.3 | 276.6 | 169.4 | Δ115.8 | 53.6 | 3,219.8 |
| 2001 | 93.9 | 133.0 | 226.9 | 263.3 | 19.8 | 283.1 | 169.4 | Δ113.2 | 56.2 | 3,050.0 |
| 2002 | 93.9 | 136.9 | 230.8 | 263.3 | 113.4 | 376.7 | 169.4 | Δ23.5 | 145.9 | 2,880.9 |
| 2003 | 93.9 | 140.1 | 234.0 | 263.3 | 173.2 | 436.5 | 169.4 | 33.1 | 202.5 | 2,711.4 |
| 2004 | 93.9 | 145.2 | 239.1 | 263.3 | 208.4 | 471.70 | 169.4 | 63.2 | 232.6 | 2,541.9 |

*Note:* Trial calculations based upon certain financial assumptions.

*Source*: OL's Annual Reports, http://www.olc.co.jp/en/ir/ir.html (accessed June 30, 2005).

the red for the first few years as they considered it normal when dealing with such a large project. Moreover, they said that the positive cash flow from the start meant that the new project was good.

In order to determine whether the project deserved the go-ahead, they wanted to further examine the potential collaboration with WD. As a second part to the study, the planning department of OL calculated the NPV as seen from WD's standpoint for the two potential methods mentioned above: (1) to proceed with the existing licensing method, or (2) a JV method in which WD would share some of the risks. The senior executives' strategy was based on an assumption that WD would choose the option that had a higher estimated NPV. They planned to guide WD towards the JV method, allowing shared risk.

OL's senior executives realized that there was still a yawning gap between the views the two companies held about this project, one that could not be bridged easily. While WD's goal when negotiating was to maximize its right, OL desired to break free of intervention from WD and develop the project as freely as possible. Since their first venture proved to be mutually beneficial, OL wanted to execute the second project as an equal partner, i.e., with a 50/50 relationship. WD would not be amenable to this position, perpetuating an impasse for a while.[46]

OL's senior executives believed in the Japanese philosophy of medieval times, "know your enemy to win the war" and "moving first wins the war". They saw an opportunity ahead, and needed to make a wise first move to assure future success of the project.

## *Project Valuation (Licensing vs. Joint Venture)*

The planning department had to prepare the calculations of NPV based on the two scenarios as instructed by their superiors at OL. The calculations were based on certain assumptions, as shown in **Exhibit 9**.

---

[46] Kagami, T., an excerpt from "Umi wo Koeru Souzouryoku (Imagination Extending across Seas)", *Kodansha*, May 26, 2003, p. 102.

**Exhibit 9**  Assumptions of NPV Trial Calculations

1. OL pays 7% of sales as a licensing fee to WD.
2. The future ¥/US$ value over the seven year investment period can be forecasted, based upon purchasing power parity.
   The following data was provided in January 1997:
     (1)  spot = ¥118.02/US$
     (2)  $\pi^¥ = 0.9\%$ p.a. (Japanese inflation rate)[47]
     (3)  $\pi^\$ = 4.56\%$ p.a. (US inflation rate)
3. All incremental earnings to WD from the prospective investment project in Japan are collected as repatriating cash flows to WD. A foreign investor's assessment of a project's returns depends on the actual cash flows that are returned to it, in its own currency. Dividends will be charged withholding tax at 15%, and license fees at 5%.
4. OL proposes issuance of preferred stocks to WD. Amount: US$203 million (6% of the total needed funds of US$3.4 billion), Dividend Payment: 5% p.a.
5. Assume the cash flows generated from WD use a weighted average cost of capital of 8% to discount prospective investment cash flows. Also assume that the Japanese investment poses a variety of risks, and WD additionally requires a hurdle rate of about 2%.

# Decision Time

After carefully examining the relevant data and analyses, the planning department finally presented the results of the study to OL's senior executives. They underwent intense discussion in order to arrive at the most viable strategic decision on how best to handle negotiations with WD. They had to get past overwhelming criticism of WD's one-sided business practice and its refusal to assume any risks by the company directors, lenders and major shareholders.[48,49]

---

[47] Based on 1997 data, an assumption was made for future inflation rates: for Japan at 0.9% p.a. and for the US at 4.56% p.a., IMF Country Data, http://www.fedstats.gov/imf/ (accessed June 30, 2005).

[48] OL's main banks were the Industrial Bank of Japan and Mitsui Trust Bank. The cooperative bank group approved a loan of US$551 million to OL in the interim. See Arima, T., "Disneyland Story", *Nikkei Business Bunko*, July 1, 2001, pp. 164–166.

[49] From the initial negotiation, which was held in 1979, the period of the contract had been another bone of contention between WD and OL. While WD insisted on a

The board members, representing the major shareholders and banks, had differing opinions, and the senior executives of OL had to get their consent. The concerns represented by the main banks were always very important, particularly in Japan, since the banks not only provided financial support, but also contributed much needed management advice (see **Exhibits 10** and **11**). The main bank explained that OL's profit structure had reached a level of stability, and that the timing was optimal for correcting the lopsided agreement with WD. The bank also agreed that the new project was risky, not only because it required a huge investment but also because it would be difficult to succeed without WD's aggressive support and participation. The main bank further advised OL to seek capital from WD to share the risk, and to arrange WD's loan guaranty with the *pari passu* clause in accordance with the investment ratio as a part of its financing conditions.[50] Another bank, which was also OL's regular business partner, warned the company to be careful about WD's final decision. OL was concerned that its competitors were working on proposals that could be put forth in the event that it forfeited the new project.[51,52]

It was no secret that WD had been a real partner to OL, not simply a licenser, as seen in the quasi-JV in the Tokyo Disney project. Without

---

50-year duration, OL would not accept such a long duration. When WD offered to reduce the duration to 45 years, OL felt that this was too small a reduction. For details, see Takahashi, M., an excerpt from "Watakushi no Rirekisho (My Personal History)" series, *Nikkei (Japan Economic Journal)*, July 1–31, 1999, no. 22, July 23, 1999, p. 40. See also footnote 29.

[50] See footnote 20.

[51] OL had an initial competitor. It was Mitsubishi Estate Group, which was trying to bring Disney to the foothills of Mt. Fuji. The company offered a plot of land of 3 million tsubo (2,450 acre) that it owned at the foothill of Mt. Fuji, but it did not want to pay for the construction fee or royalty. As a result, Urayasu was chosen as the ultimate site. For details, see Takahashi, M., an excerpt from "Watakushi no Rirekisho (My Personal History)" series, *Nikkei (Japan Economic Journal)*, July 1–31, 1999, no. 16, July 17, 1999, p. 40.

[52] When WD's management team came to Japan in 1974, they met with Mitsubishi Estate Group immediately after the meeting with OL with the obvious intention of creating a competitive atmosphere between them. The Japanese people involved did not appreciate the way WD handled the situation. Arima, T., "Disneyland Story", *Nikkei Business Bunko*, July 1, 2001, p. 147.

**Exhibit 10**  Tokyo Disneyland Top Management (1997)

| Name | Position | Age | Years of Service | Former Affiliation | Share Holdings (Thousand Shares) |
| --- | --- | --- | --- | --- | --- |
| Kohzo Kato | Chairman | 70 | 13 | Chiba Prefecture Office (Major shareholder and Landlord) | 65 |
| Toshio Kagami | President | 62 | 26 | Keisei Railroad Corp. (Major shareholder) | 47 |
| Noboru Kamizawa | Executive Vice-President | 64 | 26 | Asahi Tochi Kogyo Corp. | 47 |
| Yasuo Okuyama | Managing Director | 57 | 33 | — | 24 |
| Tetsu Nakayama | same as above | 59 | 36 | Japan Airline Corp. | 14 |
| Kazuo Kato | same as above | 60 | 5 | IBJ (Major shareholder and Main Bank) | 12 |
| Teruo Mitsui | same as above | 58 | 5 | Mitsui Trust Bank (Major shareholder and Main Bank) | 12 |
| Yu Kojima | same as above | 60 | 39 | Keisei Railroad Corp. (Major shareholder) | 8 |
| Takeshi Okamura | same as above | 65 | 1 | National Police Agency | 0 |
| Yoshiro Fukushima | same as above | 52 | 29 | — | 3 |
| Fumio Tsuchiya | same as above | 56 | 19 | Keisei Railroad Corp. (Major shareholder) | 3 |
| Shigeru Matsuki | same as above | 55 | 22 | Same | 3 |
| Seiwa Takahashi | Director and Advisor | 83 | 35 | Founder | 403 |
| Kurawo Murata | same as above | 75 | 4 | IBJ (Major shareholder and Main Bank) | 0 |
| Junichiro Tanaka | Outside Director | 66 | 1 | President, Mitsui Real Estate Corp. (Major shareholder) | 0 |

*Source:* OL's Annual Report, Yukashoken Houkokusho (Annual Reports), Oriental Land Corp. 1996–2001, http://www.olc.co.jp/en/company/profile/board.html (accessed June 30, 2005).

**Exhibit 11**  Major Shareholders of OL (1997)

|  | No. of Shareholders | No. of Shares (1,000) | % |
|---|---|---|---|
| Government and Municipality | 3 | 39,601 | 3.96 |
| Banks | 184 | 283,804 | 28.35 |
| Securities Companies | 42 | 4,665 | 0.46 |
| Corporations | 653 | 452,178 | 45.16 |
| Foreigners | 283 | 59,898 | 5.98 |
| Individuals | 75,617 | 161,073 | 16.09 |
| Total | 76,782 | 1,001,219 | 100.00 |

*Source:* OL's Annual Report, Yukashoken Houkokusho (Annual Report), Oriental Land Corp. 1996.

their insightful advice and support, OL would not have achieved the success it enjoyed. On acknowledging this, the question arose as to whether it was necessary for WD to partake of the risk in the new project as well.

OL's senior executives had much to contemplate and consider. Never before had they felt such pressure as they did during that summer of 1997. They knew they had to weigh all the facts, carefully examine the data and consider all possible angles of the deal, as it was no secret that WD would play hard-ball in its negotiation efforts. To address the issues, senior executives asked the planning department to conduct a sensitivity analysis, based on different projections of sales growth, cost structures, profitability ratios and interest rate levels for both, case 1 and case 2. Usually, Japanese companies did not rely solely on numbers and figures as final determinants for such a weighted decision. Rather, the argument that was presented had to be based on convincing financial analyses, in addition to all other relevant non-financial factors.

## Conclusion

*We are often asked about the cause of success of this project that brought a revolution into the leisure industry in Japan. We believe that it is because it was a combination of Walt Disney's genius idea, i.e., family entertainment that makes 'families and friends unite across age, sex and nationality', with the delicate service of Japanese people. It was also fueled by an economic factor: the project was synchronized with an increase in income levels and an increase in spare time for the Japanese. The late Mr. Frank Wells, WD's president, once said, 'The Japanese operation is doing better than ours. There's nothing more we can teach them. Rather, we are learning from them.'*

— Takahashi, OL's first president[53]

In 1997, the two parties engaged in intense negotiations. Both teams struggled to find ways of reaching an agreement.[54] Key points to consider in the senior executives' decision-making were:

1. Should WD share the concern about the idea of JV and the risks involved? Given the possible negative reaction by WD, perhaps an issue should not be created. In contrast, if the issue is not put the issue on the table, it is almost certain that everyone, including board members, major shareholders and the main banks, might raise questions about the deal not being examined from all angles.
2. What would the alternative plan be if WD, as was expected, refused the idea of a JV? Should OL just: (a) give up right away; or (b) negotiate tenaciously. Feeling snubbed, WD could possibly take the project to one of OL's competitors, which was a significant risk.

---

[53] OL's management explained why this project became a hit. For details, see Takahashi, M., an excerpt from "Watakushi no Rirekisho (My Personal History)" series, *Nikkei* (*Japan Economic Journal*), no. 30, July 31, 1999, p. 40.

[54] In July 1990, OL had a business negotiation with WD on the kind of attractions that should be included in the second park. In addition to the issue of the license fee, there was a difference of opinion concerning essential issues such as success fees. OL received a letter from WD in 1992, saying that the latter wanted to shelve the planning as it was disappointed with the fact that OL could not offer any improvement in the license fee. For details, see of Kagami, T., an excerpt from "Umi wo Koeru Souzouryoku (Imagination Extending across Seas)", *Kodansha*, May 26, 2003, p. 102.

In the end, OL's senior executives agreed to undertake the new project, as they had done with previous projects, via the licensing mode. The board of directors supported this decision.

*WD, a prestigious licensor with great know-how, and OL, a licensee with a huge plot of land having great potential, were united. The success of investments as large as ¥500 billion (US$4.2 billion) in four years in the Tokyo Disney Sea Park would have been impossible if either of the factors did not exist. The two companies' relation changed from confrontational to one of the indispensable partners. Our relation with Disney was originally that of a master and a servant, but it changed to one of equality as OL grew, and also with the growth of OL's capabilities and experiences, so that we were able to discuss more freely. A continuation of hard-edged negotiations changed to more agreeable discussions as we mutually grew to realize that both sides are indispensable partners to the other side. We came to have a common understanding that 'disrupting negotiation is the worst kind of negotiation.'*

— Kagami, President of OL[55]

At a news conference held on September 4, 2001, at the opening of Tokyo DisneySea Park (Urayasu, Chiba), OL's top executive declared, "According to our plan, the initial investment of US$3.4 billion would be recovered in five to six years" (see **Exhibit 12** for the stock price performance of OL during 1997–2001).[56,57]

---

[55] Kagami, T., an excerpt from "Umi wo Koeru Souzouryoku (Imagination Extending across Seas)", *Kodansha*, May 26, 2003, pp. 210–211.

[56] Remark made by president Toshio Kagami at the time of the opening of Tokyo DisneySea on September 4, 2000. For more details, see *Nikkei* (*Japan Economic Journal*), November 7, 2002, p. 11.

[57] The park was completed in 2001, but not without difficulties. Several contractors refused to bid for the construction work of Tokyo DisneySea after seeing the specifications. They claimed that it was technically too difficult. This meant that much high-tech engineering was involved in the construction hidden under the stage. See Kagami, T., an excerpt from "Umi wo Koeru Souzouryoku (Imagination Extending across Seas)", *Kodansha*, May 26, 2003, pp. 131–135.

**Exhibit 12**   Common Stock Price Range and Distribution of Stockholders, 1998–2004

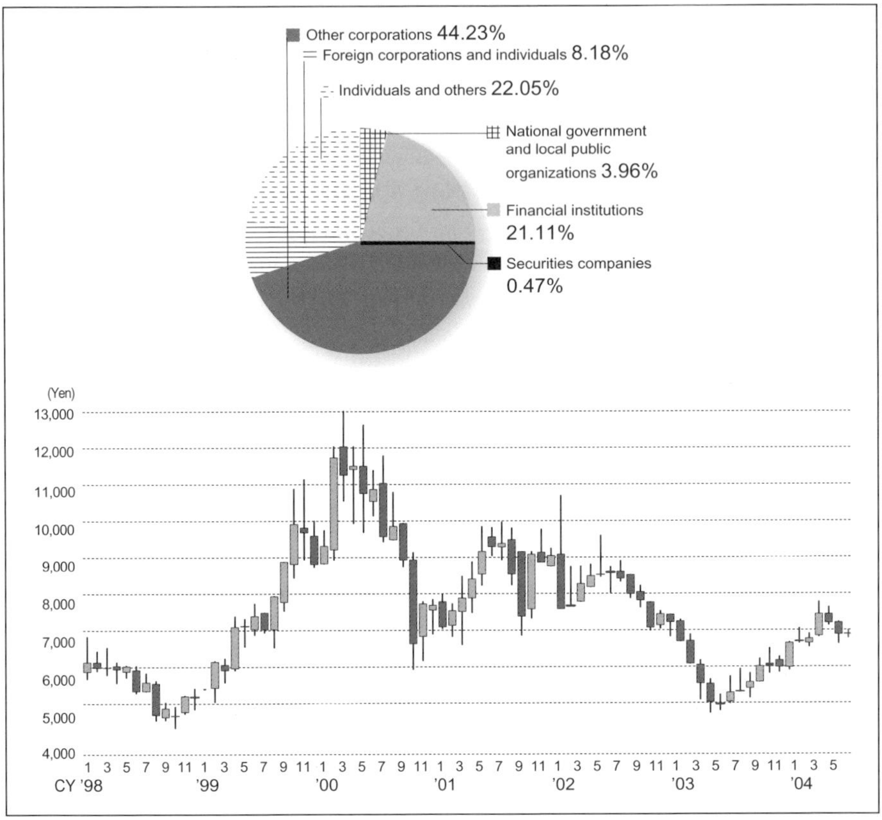

*Source*: OL's Annual Reports, http://www.olc.co.jp/en/ir/ir.html (accessed February 20, 2015).

WD's top executive, who attended the meeting, praised OL and stated that, "There is no third park plan in Japan yet, but we would work with OL if there would be one."[58–60]

---

[58] Remark made by Mr. Michael Eisner, Chairman of WD, at the opening of Tokyo DisneySea Park. For more details, see note 53, *op. cit. supra.*

[59] The Tokyo Disneyland was recognized for its contribution to the advancement of US–Japan relations by the Japan Society of Northern California in October 2002. The management teams of both, WD and OL, expressed their profound joy over the recognition. See Kagami, T., An excerpt from "Umi wo Koeru Souzouryoku (Imagination Extending across Seas)", *Kodansha*, May 26, 2003, pp. 268–269.

[60] However, Tokyo DisneySea is not attracting as many people as anticipated. See Komatsuda, M., "Tokyo Disneyland, Secret of Continuing Success", *Shogyokai*, p. 197.

# For Further Discussion

For questions 1 to 4, use the work done by the planning department in the case as reference.

1.  Prepare OL's *pro forma* future financial data (using a spreadsheet program) for the new project for the years 1998–2004. The format for the past data of the company is shown in **Exhibit 3**. Use the assumptions given in **Exhibit 5** of the case.
2.  Estimate the future exchange rate between the US dollar and the yen, using the assumptions in **Exhibit 9** in the case and the formula below.

$$\frac{F}{S} = \frac{1 + \pi^{\yen}}{1 + \pi^{\$}}$$

where:
$\quad$ F $=$ Future spot rates
$\quad$ S $=$ Current spot rates
$\quad$ $\pi^{\yen} =$ Yen's inflation rate
$\quad$ $\pi^{\$} =$ Dollar's inflation rate

3.  Prepare the Case 1 projections of the repatriation of the license fee and the incremental earnings for WD with the new expansion in 2000 (1998–2004), based on certain assumptions in **Exhibit 9** and **Exhibit 5** of the case, and the formula shown above.
4.  Prepare the Case 2 projections of the repatriation of the license fee plus dividend, and the incremental earnings for WD with the new expansion in 2000 (1998–2004), based on certain assumptions in **Exhibit 9** and **Exhibit 5** of the case, and the formula shown above.
5.  OL's senior executives decided to undertake this project under the Case 1 method (licensing only) in 1997 and their decision was supported by the board of directors. Why did the company decide to invest such huge amounts for the sea park in 2000 with the method they disliked?
6.  In what ways do you think Tokyo DisneySea Park can sustain growth in the future?

**2**

# Tokyo Disneyland and the DisneySea Park: Corporate Governance and Differences in Capital Budgeting Concepts and Methods between American and Japanese Companies

In the spring of 1997, it had been 14 years since Tokyo Disneyland opened its doors for business. Company executives at Japanese Oriental Land Corporation (OL), known to many as the company that brought Disneyland to Japan (see **Exhibit 1**) were enjoying the success of their well-established company, and began looking at new business endeavors that would allow for further growth and enhance OL's earning capability.

While there was an undoubted need for growth and expansion, the timing and approach of any new endeavor would be critical. Management knew that most of OL's customers were repeat visitors. However, while customers were expected to return two or three times, it was not clear if they would come back for a fourth visit. There was concern that customers would eventually get bored with the existing attractions and facilities, resulting in a severe shortage of customers. The company forecasted that the number of visitors in 1998 would be 4% lower than the year before.

Some years before, OL had received an inquiry from their licenser, the Walt Disney Company (WD), to consider the idea of constructing a new entertainment park, the DisneySea Park Project. The conditions of this new joint project would be similar to the conditions of the original — OL

61

**Exhibit 1**   Basic Data of Oriental Land Corp. (1997)

| | |
|---|---|
| Name | Oriental Land Co. Ltd. |
| Date of Establishment | July 11, 1960 |
| Paid-in Capital | ¥63 billion (US$0.53 billion) |
| Sales | ¥180 billion (US$1.53 billion) |
| Income before tax | ¥28 billion (US$0.24 billion) |
| President | Toshio Kagami |
| Members of Board | 28 |
| Employees | 2,493 (full time) |
| | 6,355 (part time) |
| Address | 1-1, Maihama, Urayasushi, Chiba-ken, Japan |
| Main Banks | Industrial Bank of Japan |
| | Mitsui Trust Bank |
| Major Shareholders | Mitsui Real Estate Corp. (20.48%) |
| | Keisei Electric Railway Corp. (11.20%) |
| Tie-up Company | Disney Enterprises Inc. (USA) |

*Source:* Yukashoken Houkokusho (Annual Reports), Oriental Land Corp. 1996–2001. For the company profile, see http://www.olc.co.jp/en/company/profile/index.html.

would pay WD a licensing fee for the continuous use of the name "Disney", and in return, WD would provide OL with valuable technical advice and management support for the new project.

OL's directors had to make a tough decision. As a licensee, WD had its own agenda and negotiations with them had been hard in the past. Meanwhile, OL had a number of stakeholders it had to please including: the parent company, the main bank, landlords, and shareholders, all of whom had their own representatives on OL's board of directors. The relationship among these parties determined and controlled the firm's strategic direction. OL's management had to incorporate all of these various interests in their decision-making process to come up with an optimal decision. The first step would be a thorough financial analysis of the new project, which could be presented to the various parties.

# The Original Tokyo Disneyland

In April 1979, 19 years after OL's establishment, the company signed a license agreement with WD, involving the design, construction, and operation of Tokyo Disneyland.[1] In December 1980, the construction of Tokyo Disneyland began in Maihama district, in the village of Urayasu (currently Maihama, in the city of Urayasu). Less than three years after construction had begun, Tokyo Disneyland opened its doors for business in April 1983.

Tokyo Disneyland was a smashing hit. The first year it drew 10.3 million visitors, in line with WD's expectations. After the opening year, the number of visitors never went below 10 million, reaching 13.38 million by the fifth year. The number of visitors peaked in 1998, at 17.45 million and the park's attendance figures never dropped below 16 million in the years that followed. A prediction that the initial enthusiasm would wear off was proven wrong (see **Exhibit 2**).

According to a visitor analysis conducted by OL in 1988, the percentage of repeat customers was 75%,[2] far above US Disney's 50%. Geographically speaking, about 70% of the park's visitors were from the neighboring Kanto area, near Tokyo. A large number of repeat visitors from other regions also contributed to the park's success. Visitors spent an average of ¥7,000 (US$59.31)[3] on admission fee, foods, beverages and novelty goods exceeding the original estimate of ¥5,000 (US$42.37), resulting in total sales of ¥80 billion (US$0.88 billion).[4]

On revisiting, people had new experiences because the park kept adding new attractions. Some of those new attractions were: Tokyo Disneyland Electrical Parade (1985), Big Thunder Mountain (1987), and Splash Mountain (1992).[5]

---

[1] For OL's chronology, see http://www.olc.co.jp/en/company/history/index.html.

[2] For the ratio of repeat customers as a percentage of the total number of entrants, see Arima, T., "Disneyland Story", *Nikkei Business Bunko*, July 1, 2001, pp. 170–171.

[3] This case uses the following rate for all currency conversions: US$1 = ¥118.02 in 1997.

[4] See Takahashi, M. (OL's first president), an excerpt from "Watakushi no Rirekisho (My Personal History)" series, *Nikkei (Japan Economic Journal)*, no. 28, July 29, 1999, p. 40.

[5] As to the additional attractions, see Kagami, T., an excerpt from "Umi wo Koeru Souzouryoku (Imagination Extending across Seas)", *Kodansha*, May 26, 2003, pp. 72–73.

**Exhibit 2**   Oriental Land's Past Financial Data as of 1997

Unit: US$1 million

| Year | No. of visitors (thou-sands) | Sales Revenue | Operating Costs (exc. dep.) | Depre-ciation | Adminis-trative Expenses | Interest Paid | Other Expenses | Income Before Tax | Taxes | Income After Tax | Invest-ment | Fixed Assets | Total Assets |
|---|---|---|---|---|---|---|---|---|---|---|---|---|---|
| | | | | | — Past — | | | | | | | | |
| '96 | 16,986 | 1,453.2 | 1,007.5 | 87.5 | 107.6 | 10.6 | 2.1 | 237.9 | 113.4 | 124.5 | 1,331.8 | 1,164.6 | 3,007.1 |
| '97 | 17,368 | 1,533.3 | 1,027.3 | 93.9 | 107.3 | 8.5 | 57.9 | 238.4 | 103.6 | 134.7 | 258.3 | 1,215.0 | 3,011.7 |

*Source*: Compiled from Yukashoken Houkokusho (Annual Reports), Oriental Land Corp. 1996–2001. See http://www.olc.co.jp/en/ir/ir.html.

# Negotiations Involving Tokyo Disneyland

## *Walt Disney's Position*

In January 1979, OL received a stern letter from WD saying,

*If you cannot accept the terms, we have to stop this project.*[6]

— Donn Tatum, chairman of WD

Walt Disney had proven to be a tough negotiator when it negotiated the terms for Tokyo Disneyland. Although WD liked the location of Urayasu, its offer in 1979 was to provide only the know-how without shouldering any risk.[7] It was not willing to pay anything for the construction of the park, but it wanted 10% royalty on the admission fee and sales of foods and beverages.[8] OL strongly objected to this proposal, with its board of directors saying that "We have never seen such a lopsided contract condition and high royalty."[9] Finally, an agreement was signed which stipulated a license fee of 10% on admission fees and 5% on food, beverages and novelty goods. OL was able to make the project profitable in four years, despite hefty licensing fees that were an average 7% of sales. The reason was not an increase in the number of entrants, but rather an increase in customer spending on food and beverages as well as on novelty goods.

At the time of the negotiations, Walt Disney's financial position was weak.[10] Disneyland and Walt Disney World were attracting approximately 10 million entrants each year, and WD could not raise the entrance fee to increase income. Also, the movie and TV production division was doing poorly. Under these conditions, collecting a fixed amount of money from their overseas partner, regardless of the theme park's success, was an attractive proposition for WD. This was a tough condition for the Japanese partner, but if Disney could find a partner who would want to do the

---

[6] For the details, see Takahashi, M., an excerpt from "Watakushi no Rirekisho (My Personal History)" series, *Nikkei (Japan Economic Journal)*, July 23, 1999, p. 40.

[7] For the details, see Takahashi, M., an excerpt from "Watakushi no Rirekisho (My Personal History)" series, *Nikkei (Japan Economic Journal)*, no. 16, July 17, 1999, p. 40.

[8] Ibid.

[9] Ibid.

[10] See Arima, T., "Disneyland Story", *Nikkei Business Bunko*, July 1, 2001, pp. 146–147.

project under these terms, they would draft a contract, assuming the partner could build a Disneyland to their stringent quality standards.[11]

In 1984, a management change at Walt Disney created a powerful team, with Michael Eisner as the company's chairman and Frank Wells as its president. With the help of the license income from Tokyo Disneyland, Eisner's management team built hotels in Disney World. In turn, the income from the hotels helped to revive WD, whose performance had been at an all time low under the leadership of E. Cardon Walker as chairman (1980–1983) and Ron W. Miller as president (1980–1984).[12]

## *Competitor*

For the development of Tokyo Disneyland, OL initially had a competitor, the Mitsubishi Estate Group, which was trying to bring Disney to the foothills of Mt. Fuji.[13] WD had received more than 20 offers from Japan and one of them was Mitsubishi Estate Group. WD sent six top management people to Japan in December 1974. After visiting the site at the foothill of Mt. Fuji, they came to Urayasu, where Tokyo Disneyland was later built.[14]

Mitsubishi Estate Group offered WD 3 million tsubo (2,450 acres),[15] which it owned at the foothill of Mt. Fuji, in exchange for WD constructing Disneyland. So although the Group offered the land, they would not construct the park and had no way of reaching an agreement with WD which, according to Masatomo Takahashi, "wanted the royalty but [wanted to] pay nothing".[16] Thus Urayasu, owned by OL and across the River Edogawa from Tokyo's population of 33 million, was chosen as the site for Japan's Disneyland.[17]

---

[11] Ibid.

[12] See Arima, T., "Disneyland Story", *Nikkei Business Bunko*, July 1, 2001, p. 174.

[13] Takahashi, M., an excerpt from "Watakushi no Rirekisho (My Personal History)" series, *Nikkei (Japan Economic Journal)*, no. 13, July 14, 1999, p. 40.

[14] Ibid.

[15] 1 acre = 4,047 m$^2$ or 1,226.36 tsubo.

[16] Takahashi, M., an excerpt from "Watakushi no Rirekisho (My Personal History)" series, *Nikkei (Japan Economic Journal)*, no. 13, July 14, 1999, p. 40.

[17] Ibid.

In fact, Mitsubishi Estate Group refused to accept WD's proposal as it thought it would hardly be possible to operate profitably under such a condition. OL, on the other hand, accepted the condition knowing that it would be hard for them to overcome.[18]

## The Position of Various Stakeholders

### *Mitsui Real Estate Group*

The Mitsui Real Estate Group (MREG), OL's parent company, owned 20.48% of OL's shares. Since the initial negotiations in 1979, MREG had been very critical of all the deals with WD. The first issue was the period of the contract. During a meeting between the American and Japanese sides in November 1978, Azuma Tsuboi, the MREG's president, objected to the terms of the contract. He said:

*While it is such a violently moving time that we have no way of knowing what is going to happen 10 years ahead, how come we can have a contract for as long as 50 years. Doing so makes it something similar to the US–Japan Trade Agreement of the Edo Period [some 100 years ago]. We will never be able to accept such a servile agreement.*[19]

— Azuma Tsuboi, president of Mitsui Real Estate Corp.

The second problem involved the license fees. WD originally demanded a 10% license fee, to which MREG strongly objected.

*Disneyland is a remnant of the previous century. The Japanese would soon be bored of it. There is no way to be profitable if we paid 10% royalty to the US side.*[20]

— Azuma Tsuboi, president of Mitsui Real Estate Corp.

---

[18] Arima, T. "Disneyland Story", *Nikkei Business Bunko*, July 1, 2001, p. 147.

[19] For details, see Takahashi, M., an excerpt from "Watakushi no Rirekisho (My Personal History)" series, *Nikkei (Japan Economic Journal)*, no. 29, July 30, 1999, p. 40.

[20] For details, see Takahashi, M., an excerpt from "Watakushi no Rirekisho (My Personal History)" series, *Nikkei (Japan Economic Journal)*, no. 19, July 20, 1999, p. 36.

WD was infuriated when OL's management requested a lower royalty of 5%, in accordance with Azuma Tsuboi's demands. WD's fury in turn caused the Japanese parties to mistrust it.[21]

The third issue was risk-sharing. From the start of the project in 1978, MREG had guaranteed the project borrowing up to 48% of its investment but no more, in which case the remaining balance would have to be borne by WD. Azuma Tsuboi had the following to say about this issue.

*The matter is decided by our board meeting, [it is] not my personal decision. This is such a humiliating contract and we, as a company of the proud Mitsui Group, cannot accept it. If you really wish to do it, do it on your own.*[22]

— Azuma Tsuboi, president of Mitsui Real Estate Corp.

## The Main Bank

Tokyo Disneyland was financed by a group of 22 banks. The group was headed by the Industrial Bank of Japan (IBJ), and Mitsui Trust Bank was the second largest partner. WD's position in the Tokyo Disneyland contract — take no risk, just collect the fee — caused a lot of commotion amongst the Japanese banks. Kisaburo Ikeura, IBJ's president, called this policy "a very strange one" and stated:

*WD's position was that they don't offer any land or money, take no risk; you must construct as we tell you to do, and we collect 10% license fee for entrance fees and 5% license fee for beverages and novelty goods; such a policy was never heard of in Japan.*[23]

— Kisaburo Ikeura, president of IBJ

IBJ was a successful bank and was often referred to as the "Morgan Guaranty Trust Bank" of Japan. It dealt with many large Japanese

---

[21] Ibid.

[22] Ibid.

[23] For details, see Takahashi, M., an excerpt from "Watakushi no Rirekisho (My Personal History)" series, *Nikkei (Japan Economic Journal)*, no. 19, July 20, 1999, pp. 136–138.

corporations in many complex and delicate transactions. But because it used to be a government-owned bank, its borrowers were chosen in accordance with current government policies, or were traditional companies in the heavy industries sector, such as steel, ships and machinery, which supported the recovery of the Japanese economy after the Second World War. IBJ's top management, however, believed that the future of Japanese industries would shift toward the service industries, based on software and technology, and become much more internationalised, with joint ventures and export industries becoming popular.[24] So IBJ shifted its lending targets accordingly and was quite willing to lend to OL, as it considered OL to be a potential future leader.[25] The group of banks decided to lend ¥65 billion (US$0.55 billion) in August 1979 to OL. By 1997, when the DisneySea Park was being discussed, total bank loans amounted to ¥195 billion (US$1.65 billion), indicating the group's strong commitment to the project.

The main banks in Japan were closely involved in companies' internal affairs, both in cross-ownership and as a prime lender (see **Exhibit 3**). The relation between OL and the IBJ was close. Mitsuaki Mori, who was sent from IBJ, succeeded Masatomo Takahashi as the second president of OL. Mituaki Mori (1988–1992) passed away suddenly in 1992 and Masatomo Takahashi (1992–1995) returned as the third president.

## *Landlord*

OL was granted a vast plot of reclaimed land by the government, which could be taken back if not used for its agreed upon purpose within a certain time frame.[26] In March 1962, Chiharu Kawasaki, president of Keisei Electric Railway Co., one of OL's largest shareholders, asked Masatomo Takahashi to approach the prefecture to negotiate a grant of 1 million tsubo of reclaimed land to OL.[27]

---

[24] Takahashi, M., an excerpt from "Watakushi no Rirekisho (My Personal History)" series, *Nikkei (Japan Economic Journal)*, no. 24, July 25, 1999, p. 40.

[25] Ibid.

[26] Takahashi, M., an excerpt from "Watakushi no Rirekisho (My Personal History)" series, *Nikkei (Japan Economic Journal)*, no. 13, July 14, 1999, p. 40.

[27] Ibid.

**Exhibit 3**   Major Shareholders of Oriental Land (1997)

| | No. of Shareholders | No. of Shares (1,000) | % |
|---|---|---|---|
| Government & Municipality | 3 | 39,601 | 3.96 |
| Banks | 184 | 283,804 | 28.35 |
| Securities Companies | 42 | 4,665 | 0.46 |
| Corporations | 653 | 452,178 | 45.16 |
| Foreigners | 283 | 59,898 | 5.98 |
| Individuals | 75,617 | 161,073 | 16.09 |
| Total | 76,782 | 1,001,219 | 100.00 |

*Source*: OL's Annual Report, Yukashoken Houkokusho (Annual Reports), Oriental Land Corp. 1996–2001.

When Masatomo Takahashi went to the Chiba Prefecture to negotiate the land grant, they said:

*We hear that even the Disneyland in Los Angeles is only 90,000 tsubo (73 acres). We've never heard of an amusement park as large as 1 million tsubo, which is 10 times that.*[28]

— Chiba government office

Eventually OL got 750,000 tsubo. Kawasaki later told Takahashi the reason he wanted a large piece of land.

*If you go to Disneyland in Los Angeles, you will learn that by the time the company wanted to build a few hotels close to the park as the business was booming, all the adjacent lands had been bought up by others. I didn't want to see the same thing happen to us.*[29]

— Chiharu Kawasaki, former president of Keisei Electric Railway Co.

---

[28] Takahashi, M., an excerpt from "Watakushi no Rirekisho (My Personal History)" series, *Nikkei (Japan Economic Journal)*, no. 13, July 14, 1999, p. 40.
[29] Ibid.

In his autobiography, Takahashi wrote that he later found that Kawasaki had shown foresight when suggesting the acquisition of a large piece of real estate to accommodate any future expansion.[30]

With the opening of Maihama station on the Keiyo line in 1988 — a 43-km railroad between Tokyo and Soga — the number of entrants to Disneyland increased tremendously, topping 13 million that year.[31] Then, there was a request from the Chiba Prefecture, where Tokyo Disneyland was located, prompting the use of unused park land measuring around 300,000 tsubo. Since the land was public property, OL wanted to use it for something the public could enjoy.[32] Moreover, OL's top management was also mindful of the fact that the plot of land was reclaimed from the sea, causing many fishermen to loose their jobs and way of life; they felt a social responsibility to help these people.[33]

## Oriental Land's Listing on the Tokyo Stock Exchange

OL's listing on the Tokyo Stock Exchange in 1996 resulted in an increase in the number of shareholders. The company's initial public offering (IPO) was welcomed by investors: the closing price on the first day was ¥8,850 (US$74.99) a share, exceeding its offer price by 9%. In the same year, OL reported total sales of ¥171.5 billion (US$1.45 billion), and income before tax of ¥28 billion (US$0.24 billion), with Tokyo Disneyland's visitor numbers a shade below 17 million.

The company's market evaluation after the initial enthusiasm had, however, been disappointing. The stock price in 1997 was about ¥8,000 (US$67.79), lower than its IPO price of ¥8,055 (US$68.26) in December 1996. The original investors were not compensated at all. The negative evaluation of this investment put pressure on OL's senior management to perform (see **Exhibit 3**).

---

[30] Ibid.

[31] Ibid.

[32] Ibid.

[33] Takahashi, M., an excerpt from "Watakushi no Rirekisho (My Personal History)" series, *Nikkei (Japan Economic Journal)*, no. 12, July 13, 1999, p. 40.

# A New Capital Investment: DisneySea Park

Tokyo DisneySea was to be a unique institution, a first of its kind in the world. Japan was an island country surrounded by seas and as such the Japanese had a strong attachment to a theme concerning the sea. The target audience was those adults who had been children when Tokyo Disneyland had been introduced. Although economic conditions in 1997 were weak, OL had to decide whether to undertake a project as large as the Tokyo DisneySea Park. The initial investment alone would be ¥400 billion (US$3.4 billion); the companies' total assets were valued at ¥355.18 billion (US$1.77 billion) and annual profits before tax were ¥28.32 billion (US$0.24 billion) in fiscal year 1997.[34]

On receiving WD's proposal to build this new amusement park, OL's directors ordered its planning department to conduct a financial feasibility study. The senior management wanted to know how long it would take for the DisneySea Park to start generating profits, and if the company's current profit earning capability would be able to sustain the investment period, assuming construction would start in 2000.

The company's senior executives also consulted the stakeholders. This gargantuan investment in the midst of a poor economic climate led many to question the undertaking, creating doubt in the minds of not only the management but also parent company, shareholders and lenders.[35]

## *Tough Negotiations*

WD wished to maximize revenue from Japan through license fees. It therefore had a substantial interest in the new DisneySea Park project. WD expected income similar to that received for Tokyo Disneyland, and behaved as if it were a primary and lead investor.[36] The two companies

---

[34] The Japanese fiscal year runs from April 1 to March 31.

[35] Kagami, T., an excerpt from "Umi wo Koeru Souzouryoku (Imagination Extending across Seas)", *Kodansha*, May 26, 2003, pp. 99–114.

[36] From the very start of the project in 1978 OL had been trying its best, in vain, to make WD bear some risks. For details, see Takahashi, M., an excerpt from "Watakushi no Rirekisho (My Personal History)" series, *Nikkei (Japan Economic Journal)*, no. 23, July 24, 1999, p. 40.

could not agree on the next course of action and the relationship between the two was unharmonious. OL's top management went to the USA in August 1997 to smooth ruffled feathers. As OL's troop sat down to a dinner hosted by WD, a WD side spokesman said, "Mr. Chairman, our president is furious. There is no point in any discussions. We have to ask you to go back to Tokyo."[37] OL's top management, strongly opposed to the licensing fee format for the second park, responded on the spot:

*Since we are paying a royalty in excess of ¥6 billion (US$50.84M) each year, we can hardly agree with a plan to do it under the same condition. It is quite unfair if the US side is to take no risk, use the land free with no financial burden, but collect the royalty. We don't want that.*[38]

— Masatomo Takahashi, former president of OL

Takahashi wrote extensively about his experiences as president of OL in his autobiography. Engaged in the landfill work, he developed a strong love for the land and strongly desired to use the land for the Japanese. He fought fiercely against those who resisted his ideas and was determined to push through the business he was entrusted with. He crossed the Pacific Ocean innumerable times for the sake of negotiations, often returning thoroughly fatigued.[39]

WD, on the other hand, had believed it had made a gross error in judgment by placing OL under such tough conditions. However, once it realized what a big success Tokyo Disneyland was, WD's top management claimed the earlier agreement with OL had been a big mistake. WD believed it had chosen a conservative route with its no-risk policy and had ended up with the short end of the stick, earning only a limited profit

---

[37] Arima, T., "Disneyland Story", *Nikkei Business Bunko*, July 1, 2001, p. 36.

[38] For details, see Takahashi, M., an excerpt from "Watakushi no Rirekisho (My Personal History)" series, *Nikkei (Japan Economic Journal)*, no. 29, July 30, 1999, p. 40.

[39] Masatomo Takahashi expressed his feelings in his autobiography. See Takahashi, M., an excerpt from "Watakushi no Rirekisho (My Personal History)" series, *Nikkei (Japan Economic Journal)*, no. 20, July 21, 1999, p. 40. Also see Kagami, T., an excerpt from "Umi wo Koeru Souzouryoku (Imagination Extending across Seas)", *Kodansha*, May 26, 2003, p. 50.

while being used by OL.[40] Consequently, WD changed its policy after its experience with Tokyo Disneyland and DisneySea to aggressively expand into overseas markets, with a motto of "Never repeat the mistake of Tokyo Disneyland!"[41]

## *The Board of Directors*

There were 28 members on OL's board of directors and their average age was over 60, reflecting Japan's traditional promotion system based on seniority (see **Exhibit 4**). While, on average, American boards had fewer than 15 members many Japanese companies had more than 30 directors. Directors in Japan were often senior employees chosen by the president. Thus, in many Japanese firms they were also corporate officers. Promotion to the board was a means of rewarding senior officers.

Since OL was a new company, very few of the board members were from within the organization and most of them were members representing main banks, shareholders, and property owners. They basically voiced the opinions of the organizations they represented.

## *Financial Projections*

To overcome the deadlock in negotiations with WD, OL's senior executives asked the planning department for a financial analysis as top priority. Because DisneySea Park represented a key part of OL's strategic vision, a convincing financial analysis demonstrating a high rate of future profitability would help convince WD and all OL's stakeholders to commit to this new venture.

A seven-year projection with sensitivity analysis was computed by OL's planning department. Financial data for 1998–2004 was projected based on historical data (see **Exhibit 2**) and a specific set of financial assumptions (see **Appendix 1**). Since the new project would be an

---

[40] This was a comment by WD's president Eisner. For details, see Arima, T., "Disneyland Story", *Nikkei Business Bunko*, July 1, 2001, pp. 172–173.

[41] For details, see Arima, T., "Disneyland Story", *Nikkei Business Bunko*, July 1, 2001, pp. 172–173.

**Exhibit 4**   Members of Oriental Land's Board of Directors (1997)

| Name | Position | Age | Years of Service | Former Affiliation | Share Holdings (thousand shares) |
|---|---|---|---|---|---|
| Kohzo Kato | Chairman | 70 | 13 | Chiba Prefecture Office (Major shareholder and landlord) | 65 |
| Toshio Kagami | President | 62 | 26 | Keisei Railroad Corp. (Major shareholder) | 47 |
| Noboru Kamizawa | Executive Vice President | 64 | 26 | Asahi Tochi Kogyo Corp | 47 |
| Yasuo Okuyama | Managing Director | 57 | 33 | — | 24 |
| Toru Nakayama | same as above | 59 | 36 | Japan Airline Corp. | 14 |
| Kazuo Kato | same as above | 60 | 5 | IBJ (Major shareholder and main bank) | 12 |
| Teruo Mitsui | same as above | 58 | 5 | Mitsui Trust Bank (Major shareholder and main bank) | 12 |
| Yutaka Kojima | same as above | 60 | 39 | Keisei Railroad Corp. (Major shareholder) | 8 |
| Takeshi Okamura | same as above | 65 | 1 | National Police Agency | 0 |
| Yoshiro Fukushima | same as above | 52 | 29 | — | 3 |
| Fumio Tsuchiya | same as above | 56 | 19 | Keisei Railroad Corp. (Major shareholder) | 3 |
| Shigeru Matsuki | same as above | 55 | 22 | Same | 3 |
| Masatomo Takahashi | Director & Advisor | 83 | 35 | Founder | 403 |
| Kurao Murata | same as above | 75 | 4 | IBJ (Major shareholder and main bank) | 0 |
| Junichiro Tanaka | Outside Director | 66 | 1 | President, Mitsui Real Estate Corp. (Major shareholder) | 0 |

*Note*: There were 13 other officer-directors. The total number of the board members was 28.
*Source*: OL's Annual Report, Yukashoken Houkokusho (Annual Reports), Oriental Land Corp. 1996–2001. For OL's Directors, see http://www.olc.co.jp/en/company/profile/board.html.

expansion of the existing company, the marginal contribution of the new investment had to be projected. As it was extremely difficult to separate the expanding project from the existing company, two projections of cash flow were drafted, one with the expansion and one without. The difference of the two projections would then represent the anticipated cash flow of the new project. The planning department projected the following exhibits step-by-step.

- Projected depreciation scheduling for OL, 1998–2004 (20 years straight line) (**Exhibit 5**)
- Projected debt costs for OL, 1998–2004 (10-year loans) (**Exhibit 6**)
- OL's projected financial data without the new project, 1998–2004 (**Exhibit 7**)
- OL's projected financial data with the new project, 1998–2004 (**Exhibit 8**)
- Income and cash flow from the new project (**Exhibit 9**)

## *The Capital Budgeting Exercise*

The planning department believed they had enough information to build a US model using net present value (NPV) on the project as well as a Japanese model using the average accounting return (AAR) (see **Appendix 2** for the pros and cons of these techniques). For hurdle rate and terminal value, OL had been using 5% as its weighted average cost of capital. OL decided to use a hurdle rate of 5.65% for this project due to the huge anticipated risks. OL considered that a reasonable estimate of the terminal value of the project beyond the 5-year projection period could be calculated with a commonly used capitalisation formula:

$$\text{Terminal value} = \text{Cash flow of the fifth year/discount rate}$$

OL used a model based on the assumptions shown in **Appendix 1** to conduct a sensitivity analysis using different projections of sales growth, the profitability ratio and interest rates. Interest rates were kept very low in Japan to counter deflation.

**Exhibit 5**   Projected Depreciation Scheduling for Oriental Land 1998–2004 (at 20 Years Straight Line)

Unit: US$1 million

| | Fixed Assets (Before Depreciation) | Depr. | Book Value | New Invest. (2000) | Depr. | Book Value | Fixed Assets After New Investment | Total Depr. After New Investment |
|---|---|---|---|---|---|---|---|---|
| 1997 (Actual) | 1,218.86 | 93.9 | 1,124.96 | | | | 1,124.96 | 93.9 |
| 1998 | | 93.9 | 1,031.06 | | | | 1,031.06 | 93.9 |
| 1999 | | 93.9 | 937.16 | | | | 937.16 | 93.9 |
| 2000 | | 93.9 | 843.26 | 3,389.30 | 169.46 | 3,219.84 | 4,063.10 | 263.36 |
| 2001 | | 93.9 | 749.36 | | 169.46 | 3,050.38 | 3,799.74 | 263.36 |
| 2002 | | 93.9 | 655.46 | | 169.46 | 2,880.92 | 3,536.38 | 263.36 |
| 2003 | | 93.9 | 561.56 | | 169.46 | 2,711.46 | 3,273.02 | 263.36 |
| 2004 | | 93.9 | 467.66 | | 169.46 | 2,542.07 | 3,009.66 | 263.36 |

*Note*: Trial calculations based upon certain assumptions.

*Source*: OL's Annual Reports, http://www.olc.co.jp/en/ir/ir.html.

**Exhibit 6**　Projected Debt Costs for Oriental Land, 1998–2004 (at 4.34%, 10-Year Loans)

Unit: US$1 million

| | Existing Debt | Interest Payments | Outstanding for New Borrowings in 2000 | Total Debt Outstanding After New Borrowings in 2000 | Total Interest Payments |
|---|---|---|---|---|---|
| 1997 (Actual) | 195 | 8.46 | | 195 | 8.46 |
| 1998 | 175 | 7.60 | | 175 | 7.60 |
| 1999 | 157 | 6.81 | | 157 | 6.81 |
| 2000 | 142 | 6.16 | 1,129 | 1,271 | 55.16 |
| 2001 | 128 | 5.56 | 1,016 | 1,144 | 49.65 |
| 2002 | 115 | 4.99 | 960 | 1,076 | 46.66 |
| 2003 | 103 | 4.47 | 903 | 1,006 | 43.66 |
| 2004 | 93 | 4.04 | 847 | 940 | 40.80 |

*Note*: Trial calculations based upon certain assumptions.
*Source*: OL's Annual Reports, http://www.olc.co.jp/en/ir/ir.html.

Based on the incomes and cash flows from the new project 1999–2004, Tokyo DisneySea Park, the planning department calculated:

1. American NPV and internal rate of return IRR
2. Japanese AAR

American corporate financiers differed greatly from their Japanese counterparts in their evaluation of the ¥400 billion investment for the development of the DisneySea Park in 2000. Using the American method, a positive NPV was calculated and the IRR was higher than the hurdle rate of OL. This suggested that the DisneySea Project was an appropriate and feasible investment.

Conversely, from the perspective of the traditional Japanese AAR method, the rate of return was very low and even reflected negative figures. Using this method, the DisneySea Park seemed neither attractive nor sensible.

**Exhibit 7**   Oriental Land's Projected Financial Data Without the New Project in 1998–2004

Unit: US$1 million

| | No. of Visitors (thousands) | Admission Fee (US$) | Sales | Operating Cost (excluding depreciation) (67% of Sales) | Depreciation | Administrative Expenses (7% of Sales) | Interest Paid |
|---|---|---|---|---|---|---|---|
| 1997 (Actual) | 17,368 | 88.3 | 1,533.3 | 1,027.3 | 93.9 | 107.3 | 8.5 |
| 1998 | 17,368 | 90.1 | 1,564.9 | 1,048.4 | 93.9 | 109.5 | 7.6 |
| 1999 | 17,368 | 91.9 | 1,596.1 | 1,069.4 | 93.9 | 111.7 | 6.8 |
| 2000 | 17,368 | 93.7 | 1,627.4 | 1,090.4 | 93.9 | 113.9 | 6.2 |
| 2001 | 17,368 | 95.6 | 1,660.4 | 1,112.5 | 93.9 | 116.2 | 5.6 |
| 2002 | 17,368 | 97.5 | 1,693.4 | 1,134.6 | 93.9 | 118.5 | 5.0 |
| 2003 | 17,368 | 99.5 | 1,728.1 | 1,157.8 | 93.9 | 121.0 | 4.5 |
| 2004 | 17,368 | 101.5 | 1,762.9 | 1,181.1 | 93.9 | 123.4 | 4.1 |

Unit: US$ million

| | Other Expenses (4% of Sales) | Income Before Tax | Taxes (43%) | Income After Tax | Fixed Assets |
|---|---|---|---|---|---|
| 1997 (Actual) | 57.9 | 238.4 | 103.6 | 134.7 | 1,125.0 |
| 1998 | 62.6 | 242.9 | 104.4 | 138.5 | 1,031.1 |
| 1999 | 63.8 | 250.5 | 107.7 | 142.8 | 937.2 |
| 2000 | 65.1 | 257.9 | 110.9 | 147.0 | 843.3 |
| 2001 | 66.4 | 265.8 | 114.3 | 151.5 | 749.4 |
| 2002 | 67.7 | 273.7 | 117.7 | 156.0 | 655.5 |
| 2003 | 69.1 | 281.8 | 121.2 | 160.6 | 561.6 |
| 2004 | 70.5 | 289.9 | 124.7 | 165.2 | 467.7 |

*Note*: Trial calculations based upon certain assumptions.
*Source*: OL's Annual Reports, http://www.olc.co.jp/en/ir/ir.html.

**Exhibit 8**   Oriental Land's Projected Financial Data with the New Project in 1998–2004

Unit: US$1 million

| | No. of Visitors (thousands) | Admission Fee (US$) | Sales | Operating Cost (excluding depreciation) (67% of Sales) | Depreciation | Administrative Expenses (7% of Sales) | Interest Paid |
|---|---|---|---|---|---|---|---|
| 1997 (Actual) | 17,368 | 88.3 | 1,533.3 | 1,027.3 | 93.9 | 107.3 | 8.5 |
| 1998 | 17,368 | 90.1 | 1,564.9 | 1,048.4 | 93.9 | 109.5 | 7.6 |
| 1999 | 17,368 | 91.9 | 1,596.1 | 1,069.4 | 93.9 | 111.7 | 6.8 |
| 2000 | 17,368 | 93.7 | 1,627.4 | 1,090.4 | 263.4 | 113.9 | 55.2 |
| 2001 | 17,368 | 95.6 | 1,660.4 | 1,112.5 | 263.4 | 116.2 | 49.7 |
| 2002 | 22,578 | 109.9 | 2,481.3 | 1,662.5 | 263.4 | 173.7 | 46.7 |
| 2003 | 24,836 | 120.9 | 3,002.7 | 2,011.8 | 263.4 | 210.1 | 43.7 |
| 2004 | 27,319 | 120.9 | 3,302.9 | 2,212.9 | 263.4 | 231.1 | 40.8 |

Unit: US$1 million

| | Other Expenses (4% of Sales) | Income Before Tax | Taxes (43%) | Income After Tax | Fixed Assets |
|---|---|---|---|---|---|
| 1997 (Actual) | 57.9 | 238.4 | 103.6 | 134.7 | 1,125.0 |
| 1998 | 62.6 | 242.9 | 104.4 | 138.5 | 1,031.1 |
| 1999 | 63.8 | 250.5 | 107.7 | 142.8 | 937.2 |
| 2000 | 65.1 | 39.4 | 16.9 | 22.5 | 4,063.1 |
| 2001 | 66.4 | 52.4 | 22.5 | 29.9 | 3,799.7 |
| 2002 | 99.2 | 235.8 | 101.4 | 134.4 | 3,536.4 |
| 2003 | 120.0 | 353.7 | 152.1 | 201.6 | 3,273.0 |
| 2004 | 132.1 | 422.6 | 181.7 | 240.9 | 3,009.7 |

*Note*: Trial calculations based upon certain assumptions.

*Source*: OL's Annual Reports, http://www.olc.co.jp/en/ir/ir.html.

**Exhibit 9**   Incomes and Cash Flows from the New Project, 1998–2004

Unit: US$1 million

| | Without the Project | | | With the Project | | | The New Project | | | |
|---|---|---|---|---|---|---|---|---|---|---|
| | Depre-ciation | Income | Cash Flow | Depre-ciation | Income | Cash Flow | Depre-ciation | Income | Cash Flow | Fixed Assets |
| 1997 (Actual) | 93.9 | 134.7 | 228.6 | 93.9 | 134.7 | 228.6 | 0 | 0 | 0 | |
| 1998 | 93.9 | 138.7 | 222.6 | 93.9 | 138.5 | 215.1 | 0 | 0 | 0 | |
| 1999 | 93.9 | 142.8 | 226.7 | 93.9 | 142.8 | 219.0 | 0 | 0 | 0 | |
| 2000 | 93.9 | 147.0 | 230.6 | 263.3 | 22.5 | 284.2 | 169.4 | (124.5) | 44.9 | 3,219.8 |
| 2001 | 93.9 | 151.5 | 234.8 | 263.3 | 29.9 | 291.2 | 169.4 | (121.6) | 47.8 | 3,050.3 |
| 2002 | 93.9 | 156.0 | 239.1 | 263.3 | 134.4 | 388.3 | 169.4 | (21.6) | 147.8 | 2,880.9 |
| 2003 | 93.9 | 160.6 | 243.2 | 263.3 | 201.6 | 450.8 | 169.4 | 41.0 | 210.4 | 2,711.4 |
| 2004 | 93.9 | 165.6 | 247.5 | 263.3 | 240.9 | 487.7 | 169.4 | 75.3 | 244.7 | 2,541.9 |

*Note*: Trial calculations based upon certain assumptions.

*Source*: OL's Annual Reports, http://www.olc.co.jp/en/ir/ir.html.

The conflicting results caused a dilemma for OL's senior executives. As was common in such cases, they took the results of the two analyses to IBJ, OL's main bank.[42]

IBJ tried to mediate between the diverging projections. IBJ told OL that, upon successful conclusion of the mediation between OL and WD, they would be interested in financing the project if the project analysis appropriately combined both the American and Japanese methods.[43] With regard to the analyses, IBJ presented a third method as follows:

*New capital budgeting was based on a new concept, responding to the difference in opinions of the two parties, the US and Japan, called the average cash flow return method (ACFR) for the purpose of this discussion. The difference between this and the conventional average return method is that (1) the depreciation is added to the after tax income (therefore the numerator is not income but cash flow); (2) the denominator is the initial investment (not the average figure of the book values at the end of each year); (3) the book value of the fixed asset at the end of the final year is added to the cash flow of the final year (the sales value); and (4) discounted cash flow methods are not used. The average return (%) is then calculated.[44]*

— Industrial Bank of Japan

The planning department calculated the return based on IBJ's suggestion. Their new calculations showed a return on the investment higher than that calculated under the traditional AAR method.

## Corporate Governance

OL's senior executives realized that the following differences in the Japanese and Anglo/American theories of corporate governance were relevant to the decision making process in the case of Tokyo DisneySea Park (see **Table 1**).

---

[42] For details, see Takahashi, M., an excerpt from "Watakushi no Rirekisho (My Personal History)" series, *Nikkei (Japan Economic Journal)*, no. 26, July 27, 1999, p. 40.

[43] Ibid.

[44] Ibid.

**Table 1**   Theories of Corporate Governance

1. The idea of maximizing shareholder wealth was realistic both in theory and in practice in the Anglo-American markets. The firm had to strive to maximize the return to shareholders, as measured by the sum of cash flows, capital gains and dividends, for a given level of risk.

   In contrast, Japanese markets worked on the theory that a firm's objective was to maximize corporate wealth. A firm had to treat shareholders on a par with other stakeholders, such as management, labor, suppliers, creditors, the local community and the government. The goal was to earn as much as possible, but to retain enough of the corporate wealth for the benefit of all stakeholders. The definition of corporate wealth was broader than financial wealth. It included the firm's technical, market and human resources.

2. The difference in capital budgeting between Japanese and Anglo-American firms reflected the difference in their corporate governance. The NPV rule was most compatible with Anglo-American firms. Implementing the NPV rule on an investment, and deriving a positive NPV, allowed the NPV to then belong to its shareholders. This line of reasoning held true with Anglo-American corporate governance. However, this theory would adversely impact Japanese corporate governance, since maximizing shareholders' wealth was not the primary goal of management in Japan.

3. The study of agency theory examines the principal–agent relationship within a company. Agents (managers) are likely to have their own goals that do not directly accord with those of the principals. In Anglo-American firms, the principals' (shareholders') goal is to maximize shareholder wealth. In order to reach this goal they can use positive or negative incentives to get agents on the same line as the principals. For example, liberal use of stock options in Anglo-American firms can get management to think like shareholders. In Japanese firms, the principals (stakeholders) themselves can have different goals. The principal–agent relationship is therefore far more complex.

4. Instead of seeking long-term value maximization, Anglo-American firms tended to seek short term value maximization to meet the market's expected quarterly earnings. In contrast, Japanese firms tended to be patient and focus on long term stakeholder wealth maximization.

5. Employees were important stakeholders in any firm. Although the permanent employment system in Japan was gradually changing, the traditional system was still used by many Japanese firms with little expectation of change (see **Exhibit 10**). It was therefore natural for management to be more concerned with long term success instead of considering the interest of stockholders. The American NPV concept, which analysed investment success and profitability of stockholders, did not fit within this viewpoint.

**Exhibit 10**  Lifetime Employment System

Traditional lifetime employment in Japan is a system designed to reduce outflow of employees from the firm; those with knowledge acquired through training and experience in the firm are given special opportunities for promotion and offered premium remunerations when there is a large value placed on such human capital. This system in Japan is an economic as well as social institution, characterized by an implicit contract and reciprocal exchange of trust, goodwill and commitment between employers and workers. This institution emerged as an equilibrium outcome of the dynamic interactions among management, labor and government, and became an integral part of Japan's employment system over the past hundred years. It was reinforced by complementary institutions such as state welfare policies, labor laws, corporate governance, social norms, family values and the education system.

For details, see Moriguchi, C. and Ono, H., *Japan's Lifetime Employment: A Century's Perspective*, http://ideas.repec.org/p/hhs/eijswp/0205.html.

## *Decision Time*

After the financial analysis was presented to OL's senior management, OL went through several rounds of negotiations with WD and also consulted with all their other stakeholders. It was time to make a decision. They had to make a choice between the results of their internal study or the opinion of their various stakeholders. The decision was tough as they could not decide simply based on personal preference. All the numbers had to be based on a convincing financial analysis projecting a final high rate of profitability for the company to commit to the new venture. But Japanese firms typically did not rely on the numbers and figures alone as the final determinants in such a weighted decision. The decision maker had to consider all relevant non-financial factors as well.

## Conclusion: Success for Both?

OL senior executives made a decision keeping in mind the vast differences in culture and principles that existed between the Japanese and the American methods of evaluating projects and various different positions of stakeholders. The DisneySea Park was given the go-ahead.

It was 6 a.m. on September 4, 2001. It was the day of the grand opening of the Tokyo DisneySea. The only concern was the weather.[45] The management teams of both WD and OL expressed their profound joy for the success of the project.

*I feel I am honoured. I feel especially touched when I know that the Tokyo Disneyland and the Tokyo DisneySea, which resulted from the cooperation between OL and WD, proves the success of collaboration between a US company and a Japanese company and that it is possible to sustain the success. Japan will continue to be one of the centers in the fields of movies, theme parks, fashions, games and technologies as long as the world maintains its peace. I wish our success continues.* [46]

— Michael Eisner, president of WD

*I have a hope of jointly developing entirely different business, other than theme parks, in Japan and other areas of Asia together with your company.*

— Toshio Kagami, president of OL[47]

*I feel that people are the same all around the world, joining the grand opening ceremony of the Tokyo DisneySea. Everybody will have smiles on their faces if we provide really wonderful entertainment, so that I see no national boundary in our business.*

— Michael Eisner, president of WD[48]

---

[45] Kagami, T., an excerpt from "Umi wo Koeru Souzouryoku (Imagination Extending across Seas)", *Kodansha*, May 26, 2003, p. 8.

[46] Tokyo Disneyland was recognized for contributing to the advancement of US–Japan relations by the Japan Society of Northern California in October 2002. See Kagami, T., an excerpt from "Umi wo Koeru Souzouryoku (Imagination Extending across Seas)", *Kodansha*, May 26, 2003, pp. 268–269.

[47] See ibid.

[48] See Kagami, T., an excerpt from "Umi wo Koeru Souzouryoku (Imagination Extending across Seas)", *Kodansha*, May 26, 2003, pp. 268–269.

## For Further Discussion

1. Is Japanese corporate governance changing?
2. How do Japanese cultural, historical, and institutional variables make Japanese corporate governance different from Anglo-American counterparts?
3. Explore the differences in the Japanese and Western investment decision-making process and the conflicts that arise therein.
4. The way agency theory is interpreted in Japan differs from the way it is applied to Western companies. Why so?
5. Prepare OL's *pro forma* future financial data for the new project for 1998–2004. The company's past data is shown in **Exhibit 2**. Use the assumptions in Appendix 1 given in the case.
6. Calculate the new project valuation using the Japanese capital budgeting technique — the AAR method.
7. Calculate the terminal value for DisneySea Park to be used for the American methods.
8. Using the data from **Exhibit 9**, calculate NPV and IRR for the Tokyo DisneySea Park.
9. Calculate the capital budgeting based on the ACFR method.
10. OL's senior executives decided to undertake this project in 1997. Why did the executives make this major investment despite the fact that the decision could not be supported by their own capital budgeting (or AAR method)?

## Appendix 1  Assumptions for Financial Projections

A seven-year projection with sensitivities was computed by OL's planning department. Future income and expenses were estimated for up to seven years based on 1996–1997 historical data (see **Exhibit 2**). The following financial assumptions were made:

1. An initial capital investment in Tokyo DisneySea Park of ¥400 billion (US$3.4 billion) will be made in 2000.
2. The number of visitors will remain the same during the next four years and will increase 30% in 2002 when Tokyo DisneySea Park will be opened. They will increase 10% in 2003 and 2004. In 1997, the average admission fee per person was ¥10,421 (US$88.30). Given the deflationary

climate, admission fees will increase by 2% annually during the four years after 1997, and will increase by 15% in 2002 at the opening of Tokyo DisneySea Park and will again increase by 10% in 2003. In 2004, admission fees will remain at the same rate as in 2003.

    If the new project is not undertaken, the number of visitors will remain the same during the seven-year period and admission fees will increase by 2% annually over those seven years.[49]

3.  Operating costs other than depreciation (67% of the sales, the ratio of 1997 data), administrative expenses (7%), and other expenses (4%) will increase proportionately with the increase in sales. These projections will be applied despite OL's decision to invest or not.

4.  Depreciation of the ¥400 billion (US$3.4 billion) investment in 2000 will be conducted using the straight-line method over 20 years.

5.  Funds borrowed as of 1997 totaled ¥23 billion (US$195 million), for which interest payments in 1997 were ¥1 billion (US$8.5 million) (the debt interest rate is 4.34%). It was assumed that the cost of future borrowing would be 4.34% (the same as that in 1997). It was also assumed that for future investments, two-thirds would be financed by the internal withholding reserves and capital increases (including the issuance of preferred stocks) and one-third would be financed by borrowings. This assumption was made based on the past performance of the company.[50]

6.  The Japanese rate of taxation was 43%.


# Appendix 2  Pros and Cons of Different Capital Budgeting Techniques (US and Japan)

1.  Japanese Method (Average Accounting Return) Formula:

$$\text{Average Accounting Return} = \frac{\text{Average Net Income}}{\text{Average Investment}}$$

---

[49] For the basis of this data, see OL's website (Business Growth, Comparative Advantage, Management Message, etc.), http://www.olc.co.jp/en/ir/ir.html.

[50] See OL's website, http://olc.netir-wsp.com/FaqU,locale,en_US.html. (Frequently asked questions:

How does the company plan to use cash flow in the future?
What is the repayment schedule on the company's interest-bearing loans?
What are the company's upcoming capital investment plans?)

Features:

(1)  Use "average net income". Sum net income/T years.
(2)  No time factor, future values are not discounted.
(3)  Terminal value is not taken into consideration.
(4)  "Investment" is the average of the fixed assets (book value). Sum fixed assets (book value)/T years.

Pros:

(1)  This conventional method has long been a common method of evaluating capital investment projects in Japan.
(2)  This method fits into Japanese management; for Japanese executives, the concept of opportunity cost is very difficult to comprehend. The concept of selling a corporation or its facilities to other parties is foreign to the Japanese. They have traditionally discarded the value of plants and facilities when a project is over.
(3)  It is easy to understand and is based on Japanese "consensus" decision making processes.
(4)  Japanese banks like this method since the refund period is calculated in the same way.

Cons:

(1)  It does not take into account the matter of timing. It would have been the same if the net income in the first year had occurred in the last year. It does not discount the future income.
(2)  It does not have any guidance on what the right-targeted rate of return should be. It does not pay attention to the discount rate of the market.
(3)  It ignores all cash flow occurring after the operation period. Therefore it does not pay attention to the salvage value.
(4)  Depreciation is not added to the refunding resources since the investment amount is calculated on the basis of the book value after depreciation.

2. US Method (NVP and IRR) Formula:

NPV is defined as follows:

$$\text{NPV} = -C_0 + \sum_{t=1}^{T} \frac{\text{CF}_t(1-\tau)}{(1+\bar{r})^t}$$

$C_0$ = initial investment
$CF_t$ = expected before-tax cash flow in year $t$
$\tau$ = tax rate
$\bar{r}$ = weighted average cost of capital
$T$ = life of the project

The internal rate of return is defined as the value of IRR in the following equation:

$$C_0 = \sum_{t=1}^{T} \frac{\text{CF}_t(1-\tau)}{(1+\text{IRR})^t}$$

Features:

(1)  Use the "cash flow".
(2)  Time factor (DCF method).
(3)  Terminal value is added.

Pros:

(1)  These are theoretically the best approaches established in the US.
(2)  "Cash flow" is used.
(3)  The time value of money is accounted for by discounting cash flow.
(4)  Implementing the NPV rule on an investment and deriving a positive NPV allows the NPV to then belong to its shareholders.
(5)  It holds true with US corporate governance.
(6)  Open to new theories such as options approach.

Cons:

(1) It is more difficult to understand than the average accounting return method.

(2) No popularity in Japan since managers in Japan are much less "number driven".

3. A New Method (Average Cash Flow Return Method) Formula:

$$\text{Average Cash Flow Return} = \frac{A + B}{C}$$

A = Average Cash Flow (Sum cash flow/T years)

B = Book value of the fixed asset at the end of the project

C = Initial Investment

Features:

(1) Use "cash flow".

(2) No time factor.

(3) Book value of the investment's fixed asset is added as terminal value.

(4) Use initial investments as the "investment".

Pros:

(1) Compromise between Japanese and US methods without being radically different from either.

(2) This method employs the concept of cash flow and uses the initial investment as the denominator. In this way, the numerator and denominator stand on the same basis, using both figures before deduction of depreciation.

(3) Not only should this method win over Japanese managers but it would also become invaluable to American managers who strive to maintain alignment with the accounting methods implemented.

(4)  Aggressive Japanese banks like this method since their loan periods can be reduced as compared to the traditional method.

Cons:

(1)  DCF is not used.
(2)  Eventually the US method will replace this method even in Japan.

**3**

# A Rogue Trader at Daiwa Bank (A): Management Responsibility under Different Jurisprudential Systems, Practices and Cultures

July 18, 1995 was a day that Sumio Abekawa, president of the Japan-based Daiwa Bank (the bank), would never forget. On that day, Abekawa received a letter from Toshihide Iguchi, vice-president of the bank's New York branch in charge of securities trading and control. In his letter, Iguchi explained that he had been selling securities that the bank had in custody to cover up for a loss he had caused by unauthorized and unlisted trading of US Treasury bonds. He reported that his trading had resulted in the bank losing approximately US$1.1 billion[1] and that he covered up his trading by concealing the trading certificates.[2]

On September 18, the senior management at the bank reported the loss to the Federal Reserve Bank (FRB) of New York and New York State Banking Department (NYSBD). The bank's directors faced a number of challenging questions: Had the bank complied with the reporting requirements? What would the potential liability of the directors be? Would the Japanese bank directors be held liable for violating the law of a foreign country? How could the Japanese Ministry of Finance (MOF) help?

## Keep it Strictly Confidential

Upon receiving the letter, Abekawa immediately showed it to six other directors at the bank — two vice-presidents, the board chairman, the

---

[1] US$1 = ¥111.83 on July 14, 2005.

[2] For details of the concealment of this financial catastrophe by Daiwa bank, see Watanabe, Y. (1995) "Daiwa Bank Conceals Wrongdoings", *Bungei Shunju*, December.

93

general affairs/human resources director, the international department manager (former New York branch manager) and the planning, accounting and securities director.

Meanwhile, Abekawa instructed the two vice-presidents and international department manager to investigate this incident clandestinely. The investigators found that the practice of multiple reviews of transactions, a common custom for all financial institutions, had not worked in this situation. The unauthorized trading, as mentioned in Iguchi's letter, had remained undetected for years. There was an indication that the criminal conduct of one individual had caused a huge financial loss. Based on this, the investigators believed that what Iguchi had written was true. Abekawa advised them to keep this matter confidential.

With the knowledge of Abekawa and the international department manager, the bank then filed a false call report with the US Treasury Department on July 31, stating that the Treasury bills it had sold without authorization were the property of its New York branch.

On August 8, Abekawa, the international department manager and a few other senior personnel met with the Banking Bureau director-general and Commercial Banks Division director of the Japanese MOF. They reported the incident to the ministry officials and asked for their advice on how to handle the situation and how to disclose it to the public. The Banking Bureau director-general thought that given Japan's financial situation, the following month of September would be the worst time to disclose the huge loss. He requested the bank officials to keep this calamity in strict confidence.[3]

## Share Placement

On July 27, the bank issued 50 million shares of preferred stock without publicly disclosing the huge financial loss that Iguchi had reported. Asahi Mutual Life Insurance (Asahi Seimei), a major life insurance company in Japan owning 2.7 million shares in the bank, bought 5 million common shares of the bank's common stock in six installments between late August and late September 1995.

---

[3] "Daiwa Bank Scandal", *Shukan Toyo Keizai* (*Weekly Oriental Economist*), December 2, 1995.

Asahi Seimei commented later that it had made the stock purchase on Daiwa's request. It decided that its purchase of additional stock in the bank would help enhance its business in the Kansai District, where the bank had its head office in Japan.[4]

## It's Time to Tell

In late August 1995, Abekawa instructed the international department manager to consult a US lawyer after the department in charge of the bank's US operations advised that there were stringent securities regulations in the US. The international department manager followed suit and told Abekawa and other senior personnel that under US law, the bank was obliged to report the incident to the FRB of New York and the NYSBD (see **Exhibit 1**).

Abekawa then informed the commercial banks division director of the Japanese MOF that he had decided to report this matter to the FRB in mid-September. On September 18, the bank reported this financial fiasco

**Exhibit 1**   US Regulation H

FRB Rule on Reports of Crimes and Suspected Crimes, 12 C.F.R. §208.20 (1996).

A state member bank shall file a criminal referral report … in every situation where the state member bank suspects one of its directors, officers, employees, agents, or other institution-affiliated parties of having committed or aided in the commission of a crime … A state member bank shall file the report … no later than 30 calendar days after the date of detection of the loss or the known or suspected criminal violation or activity. If no suspect has been identified within 30 calendar days after the date of detection of the loss, or the known, attempted, or suspected criminal violation or activity, reporting may be delayed an additional 30 calendar days or until a suspect has been identified; but in no case shall reporting of known or suspected crimes be delayed more than 60 calendar days after the date of detection of the loss or known, attempted, or suspected criminal violation or activity. When a report requirement is triggered by the identification of a suspect or group of suspects, the reporting period commences with the identification of each suspect or group of suspects.

---

[4] "Daiwa Bank's Huge Loss Case, Disclosure Tardiness Undeniable: Finding of Stock Issuance after Former Bank Employee's Confession Causes Mistrust in Domestic and Overseas Markets", *Nihon Keizai Shimbun*, November 29, 1995.

to the FRB vice-chairman and the NYSBD superintendent. The FRB and NYSBD wondered why the bank had not reported this incident earlier.

It was embarrassing for Abekawa that such a scandal happened at the bank during his tenure, but as the bank's president, he had to tell the directors and auditors. On September 7, three representative directors learned about this incident in a management meeting. Thirteen other directors heard about this unfortunate occurrence during a board meeting on September 25. Three standing auditors and two non-standing/external auditors learned about this debacle on September 26 — the same day that Abekawa publicly announced this matter at a news conference, and the US Federal Bureau of Investigation arrested Iguchi.[5]

## Directors' Meeting at the Headquarters

The bank directors were puzzled and tried to discern what had gone wrong. On September 25, they had a board meeting at the bank's headquarters in Osaka, Japan. There was a heated discussion. They talked about the potential responsibilities of the bank directors and officers.

One of the issues that the directors discussed was: Had the bank complied with the reporting requirements in both the US and Japan? With regard to the US requirements, they looked closely at the US Regulation H. For Japanese regulations on banks' reporting, they knew the details (see **Exhibit 2**).

The directors also turned to Article 266 of the Japanese Commercial Law which stated, among other things, that directors who committed an act violating any law would have to be jointly and severally liable (see **Exhibit 3**). The point of debate was whether "any law" would include foreign laws. This brought them to another crucial point: they honestly admitted that they had been quite unaware of the specifics of the laws and regulations governing US banks. The reality was that many Japanese financial institutions were also unaware of US laws.[6] It was pointed out

---

[5] "Daiwa Bank's Huge Loss, 30,000 Unauthorized Transactions: FBI Announces Arrest of Daiwa Bank's Former Employee", *Nihon Keizai Shimbun*, September 27, 1995.

[6] Volkman, B.P. (1998) "The Global Convergence of Bank Regulations and Standards for Compliance", *Banking Law Journal*, 115: 550–554.

**Exhibit 2**   Japanese Regulations on a Bank's Reporting

The code of ethics of the Japanese Federation Banking Association[7] defines the importance of disclosure by its member banks as follows:

> A bank, in consideration of its social responsibility and public mission, is required to obtain a broad understanding and trust from the society, and in particular, from its shareholders and investors.
>
> Fair disclosure of management information for being selected and judged by the market and users should contribute to not only the promotion of the society's understanding of and trust on the bank, but also to its own self-cleaning capability in order to achieve healthier management.
>
> Such management information disclosures should be geared toward timely and appropriate provisions of various types of information required for rational judgments by shareholders, investors and users.[8]

As a publicly held company, a bank is required to make timely and appropriate disclosures of corporate information to the public, including investors. Far more important to a bank than the general regulations of the Commercial Law and the Securities Exchange Law is the disclosure duty defined in the Banking Law. For a bank which is engaged in the special business of handling another person's asset, the contents of information to be disclosed to the MOF and its method of disclosure are more specifically defined in the Banking Law.[9]

that even American bankers were only vaguely aware of the requirements about banking and the related penalty.[10]

Moreover, the directors knew of a general theory known as "management decision". According to this theory, a director's responsibility was pursuable only when either a material or negligent error existed in the recognition of a fact which then became the premise of the director's judgment when taking the particular business measure, or the decision making

---

[7] See The Japanese Federation Banking Association, "The Code of Ethics", September 1997, http://www.zenginkyo.or.jp/en/index.html (accessed July 8, 2005).

[8] See Federation of Bankers Association, "The Code of Ethics", September 1997, http://www009.upp.so-net.ne.jp/juka/zenginkyo_code.htm (accessed July 8, 2005).

[9] Ministry of Internal Affairs and Communications, "Law Data Providing System", The Banking Law of Japan, Law No. 59 of 1981, Article 24, available at http://law.e-gov.go.jp/cgi-bin/idxsearch.cg, updated on August 4, 2005 (accessed July 8, 2005).

[10] Miller, S.A. (1996) "How Daiwa Self-Destructed", *Banking Law Journal*, 113: 560–565.

**Exhibit 3**   Japanese Commercial Law — Article 266

1. In the following cases, directors who have committed any one of the acts mentioned below shall be jointly and severally liable in effecting performance, or in damages to the company, (1) for the amount which has been distributed or divided legally, (2) for the amount of loans not yet repaid, or (3)–(5) inclusive for the amount of any damage caused to the company:

   (1) where they have submitted to a general meeting the proposal for the distribution of profits in contravention of the provision in Article 290, Paragraph 1, or they have distributed money in contravention of the provision in Articles 293–295, Paragraph 3.
   (2) where they have loaned money to another director.
   (3) where they have effected any transaction in contravention of the provision in Article 264, Paragraph 1.
   (4) where they have effected any transaction mentioned in the preceding article.
   (5) where they have committed any act which violates any law or ordinance or the articles of incorporation.

2. In cases where any act mentioned in the preceding paragraph has been committed in accordance with the resolution of the board of directors, the directors who have assented to such resolution shall be deemed to have committed such an act.
3. The directors who have participated in the resolution mentioned in the preceding paragraph, and who have not expressed their dissent in the minutes, shall be presumed to have assented to such resolution.
4. The liability of directors mentioned in Paragraph 1 cannot be released except by the unanimous consent of all the shareholders.
5. The liability of directors in respect of the transaction mentioned in item (4) of Paragraph 1 may be released by majority of two-thirds or more of the votes of the total number of the issued shares, notwithstanding the provisions of the preceding paragraph. In this case, the directors shall show all material facts as to such transaction at a general meeting of shareholders.

processes or its contents were particularly unreasonable or inappropriate. This had to be considered in light of the fact that a director was given a wide range of discretionary power in making a management decision.

The question in this case was whether the directors should have been granted any discretionary power to judge if a decision abided by a foreign law or not since they were neither American citizens nor lived in the US.

The directors thought that it had been adequate to report the incident to the Japanese MOF and simply to obey its guidance. Except having advised the bank not to disclose the scandal, the Ministry did not tell the bank what to do. Therefore, the directors felt that there was no expectation to report the financial debacle to the US authorities against the Ministry's instructions.

## Disclosure Responsibility to the Shareholders: US and Japan

The directors also examined the bank's potential liability, if any, when it issued 50 million shares of preferred stock to Asahi Seimei on July 27 without making known the financial disaster that Iguchi's trading had caused. At the time, companies were not allowed to own stocks in the form of Treasury bonds in Japan. Therefore, when a company wanted to ask a third party to obtain the company's stock or increase the number of stocks the third party owned, it was common practice in Japan to ask the third party to purchase the company's stocks through the stock market. Since the shares were issued in Japan, the placement fell under the Japanese Securities Exchange Law of Japan which was modelled after the US Securities Act of 1933 and Securities Exchange Act of 1934 (see **Exhibits 4–6**).

The Securities and Exchange Law of Japan contained a detailed rule on disclosures by corporations, and directors could be indicted for criminal and civil responsibilities under this law. However, the Commercial Law of Japan, which was based on German law,[11] did not provide a similar level of protection. Even though it had provisions to protect the investors, it failed to sufficiently cover the situation of corporate information disclosure.[12]

Due to this legal difference, Daiwa's directors noticed that there was a marked difference between the US and Japan regarding strictness in the pursuit of disclosure duties of corporations. The average Japanese company had not felt a need to immediately disclose important information.

---

[11] The Commercial Law of Japan, Law No. 48 (March 9, 1899) (amended 18 times) (hereinafter "Commercial Law"). For details, see Ministry of Internal Affairs and Communications, "Law Data Providing System", updated on August 4, 2005, http://www.ron.gr.jp/law/law/syouhou1.htm (accessed July 8, 2005).

[12] Commercial Law, Article 210.

**Exhibit 4**  US Securities Act 1933

The Securities Act of 1933[13] is concerned with the initial distribution of securities rather than subsequent trading. Securities which are offered to the public through mail or the channels of interstate commerce must be registered with the Securities and Exchange Commission (SEC) by the issuer. The registration statement must contain specified information about the security, the issuer and the underwriters. It becomes effective in 20 days, unless the SEC declares it effective sooner, or institutes an administrative proceeding to prevent or suspend its effectiveness. The SEC has no authority to approve any security or to pass on its merits. Its sole function is to assure that the registration statement is accurate and complete. A prospectus containing the basic information in the registration statement must be given to the buyer. Civil and criminal liabilities are imposed for material misstatements or omissions in the registration statement or prospectus. There is also a general anti-fraud provision — enforceable by injunctive and criminal sanctions — which applies whenever a security is sold by use of mail or the channels of interstate commerce, whether in the course of a distribution pursuant to a registration statement or in the course of ordinary market trading. Certain types of securities and transactions are exempt from the registration and prospectus requirements, but not from the anti-fraud provision.

# The Aftermath

## *Shareholders' Lawsuit*

Certain bank shareholders[14] requested the bank's auditor to initiate a legal action against the bank managers within 30 days, but the auditor refused to do so. The shareholders then decided to sue the bank themselves. In November 1995, they filed a suit against 32 defendants in the district court of Osaka, claiming US$1.1 billion in damages caused by the loss at the New York branch of Daiwa Bank.[15] The defendants included Daiwa's former chairman of the board and former officers, as well as its current president and officers.

In September 2000, the district court of Osaka delivered judgment on the shareholders' representative action (see **Exhibit 7**). The court ordered

---

[13] 15 U.S.C. §§77a–77mm (1934), as amended, 15 U.S.C. §§77a–77mm (1970).

[14] Two individual shareholders and one corporate shareholder.

[15] "Stockholders Representative Action to be Filed Tomorrow Asking 1.1 Billion Dollars in Damages", *Nihon Keizai Shimbun*, November 16, 1995.

**Exhibit 5**    US Securities Exchange Act 1934

The Securities Exchange Act of 1934[16] is concerned primarily with the distribution process and has to do with post-distribution trading. It has four basic purposes: to afford a measure of disclosure to people who buy and sell securities; to prevent and afford remedies for fraud in securities trading and manipulation of the markets; to regulate the securities markets; and to control the amount of the nation's credit which goes into those markets. All stock exchanges must register unless exempted by the SEC, which has certain supervisory functions with respect to their rules and authority to suspend or expel exchange members who violate the Act. The SEC also has certain authority with respect to various exchange practices such as short-selling, the specialist system, floor trading and hypothecation by brokers of customers' securities. No security may be listed on an exchange unless its issuer files an application for registration with both the exchange and the SEC, containing the same information as is required for new issues by the 1933 Act. This information must be kept current by the filing of annual and other reports with the exchange and the SEC. The solicitation of proxies in respect of listed and registered securities is subject to SEC control, and there are certain provisions governing the trading in such securities by the issuer's officer, directors and principal stockholders.

There are general provisions outlawing fraud and manipulation in both the exchange and over-the-counter markets, and the SEC has a considerable amount of rule-making authority. The credit provisions of the Act give the board of governors of the Federal Reserve System authority to promulgate margin rules, and the SEC the task of enforcing them.

As to what must be disclosed, the US court held:

Under any reasonably liberal construction, these anti-fraud provisions [§10(b) and Rule 10b-5] apply to directors and officers who, in purchasing the stock of the corporation from others, fail to disclose a fact coming to their knowledge by reason of their position, which would materially affect the judgment of the other party to the transaction.[17]

12 bank directors to pay a combined US$775 million in compensation. The penalties ranged from US$70 million to US$530 million per director. The unprecedented amount of the judgment was an enormous shock to Japan and the international community.

---

[16] 15 U.S.C. §§78a–78jj (1934), as amended, 15 U.S.C. §§78a–78hh (1).

[17] Kardon v. National Gypsum Co., 73 F. Supp. 798, 800 (E. D. Pa. 1947).

**Exhibit 6**   Japanese Securities Exchange Law 1948

After the Second World War, Japan enacted the Securities Exchange Law[18] (based on two American statutes: (1) the Securities Act of 1933 and (2) the Securities Exchange Act of 1934), which called for detailed disclosure to ensure the protection of investors.

Prior to the enactment of the Securities Exchange Law in 1948, the Commercial Law[19] served as the only law regulating security issues in Japan. Under the Commercial Law, the corporate promoters had to disclose the required information at the time of incorporation by publishing the articles of incorporation in the official gazette, or in a daily newspaper.[20] The disclosure requirements of the Commercial Law therefore provided insufficient investor protection. In contrast to the Commercial Law, the Securities Exchange Law was a great advancement, requiring publicity and the supply of detailed information concerning publicly held companies whose securities did not meet the requirements of "exempt securities" or "exempt transactions".

Commercial Law was modelled after German laws, while the Securities and Exchange Law was copied from the US laws. Germany is a civil law country, while the US is a country of the common law. Any confusion in the concepts of disclosure in Japan may be attributed to the slight difference in the disclosure rules of the two source countries.

The Securities Exchange Law[21] defines a disclosure system concerning securities exchange reports to provide judicious investment information to investors concerning the issuing market and the secondary market that constitute the securities market for the proper management of the national economy and the protection of investors.[22]

There are three distinct types of regulatory devices in the Securities Exchange Law: (1) anti-fraud provisions[23]; (2) provisions requiring the registration or licensing of certain persons engaging in the securities business[24]; and (3) provisions requiring the registration of securities.[25]

Anti-fraud provisions are intended to enable the administrator to issue public warnings, to investigate suspected fraudulent activities, to take injunctive or other steps

(*Continued*)

---

[18] The Securities Exchange Law of Japan, Law No. 25 of 1948, Article 127, no. 4 (hereinafter Securities Exchange Law), available at http://www.japanlaw.info/f_statements/ PARENT/DX.htm (last visited July 8, 2004).

[19] Commercial Law, Law No. 48 (March 9, 1899) (amended 18 times). For details, see Ministry of Internal Affairs and Communications, "Law Data Providing System", updated on August 4, 2005, http://www.ron.gr.jp/law/law/syouhou1.htm (accessed July 8, 2005).

[20] Commercial Law, Articles 166, 173, 175, 183, 184 and 188.

[21] Securities Exchange Law, Law No. 25 of 1948, Article 127, no. 4, available at http:// www.japanlaw.info/f_statements/ PARENT/DX.htm (last visited July 8, 2004).

[22] Securities Exchange Law, Article 1.

[23] Securities Exchange Law, Articles 157–171.

[24] Securities Exchange Law, Articles 28–66-5.

[25] Securities Exchange Law, Articles 3–27-30.

**Exhibit 6**   (*Continued*)

to stop them, and as a last resort, to punish them. Registration of brokers, dealers, agents and investment advisers is intended to prevent fraudulent or unqualified persons from entering the securities business, to supervise their activities within the state once registered, and to remove them from registration if they fall below any of the statutory standards. Registration of securities is intended to give the investor a "run for his money" by excluding from the market those securities which do not satisfy the statutory standards.

The Commercial Law[26] obligates corporations to submit various statements (operating statement, balance sheet, profit and loss statement, profit disposal plan, and schedules of financial statements) to reconciliate the interests of shareholders and creditors.[27]

The Commercial Law, which governs all companies involved in commercial activities, also sets forth rules concerning information disclosure. It defines, specifically, the rules concerning: publication of items related to corporate registration[28]; efficacies of registrations and publications[29]; submission of financial statements and schedules for financial statements to auditors[30]; maintaining and publicly reporting financial statements etc.[31]; and reporting, approving, and publicly reporting financial statements.[32]

The corporate information disclosure system under the Commercial Law differs from the disclosure system under the Securities Exchange Law in the following ways:

1. A disclosure under the Commercial Law is aimed primarily at shareholders and creditors, but a disclosure under the Securities Exchange Law is aimed at the general public including those who are not the shareholders of the particular company.
2. A disclosure under the Commercial Law is aimed at primarily reporting dividend generating profits and the collateral capability of a corporation, while a disclosure under the Securities Exchange Law is aimed at providing information for making investment judgments, thus the disclosures are more detailed and cover a wider scope.
3. The protection of shareholders and creditors under the Commercial Law falls in the category of protection of private interests so that it relies on an autonomous control under the private law, while the protection of investors under the Securities Exchange Law is based on a national objective aimed at the proper management of the national economy through fair issuing and trading of securities.

---

[26] Commercial Law, Law No. 48 (March 9, 1899) (amended 18 times). For details, see Ministry of Internal Affairs and Communications, "Law Data Providing System", updated on August 4, 2005, http://www.ron.gr.jp/law/law/syouhou1.htm (accessed July 8, 2005).

[27] Commercial Law, Articles 11 and 188.

[28] Commercial Law, Article 12.

[29] Commercial Law, Article 12.

[30] Commercial Law Articles 281–282.

[31] Commercial Law, Article 282.

[32] Commercial Law, Article 283.

**Exhibit 7**  Japanese Court Ruling

The Japanese court ruled that[33]:

(1)  The general manager of the New York branch failed to report to the US authorities despite having full knowledge of the unauthorized trading. He also committed the crimes of filing a report of fraudulent contents with the FBI and made false entries into the books and records of the New York branch, both of which were violations of the United States Code. In November 1995, the general manager of the New York branch was arrested and indicted in the federal district court of the Southern District of New York for misprision of felony and obstruction of the examination of the financial institutions by the authorities. Also the allegations were made against the bank as a corporation of the crimes.[34] He was then considered to have violated the director's duties of care and loyalty as a good manager.

(2)  The general manager of the American operations at the main office did not commit these acts, but he could have prevented them from being executed. Therefore, he was considered to have violated the director's duties of care and loyalty as a good manager.

(3)  The president, executive vice-president in charge of international operations and representative director, and the general manager of the international department at the main office failed to report to the US authorities while knowing about the unauthorized transactions. As to the filing of the report of the fraudulent contents, it can only be assumed that they either gave explicit instructions for or approved the fraudulent call, but it is surely known that they failed to prevent it, thus constituting violations of supervising duties as superiors in the chain of command. This kind of conduct was clearly a violation of the United States Code and is considered a violation of a director's duties of care and loyalty as a good manager.

(4)  Other executive vice-presidents, representative directors and directors who are not in international operations, were aware of the unauthorized trading of this case. They failed to report to the US authorities. They could at least have prevented such an act. Therefore, they were considered to have violated the directors' duties of care and loyalty as good managers.

(5)  For the directors who came to know about the unauthorized dealings after the fact, circumstances have not proven that they could have previously known the facts of the crime. Therefore, they could not be accused of any violations of the directors' duties of care and loyalty as good managers.

The five auditors received the report about the case on the day it was made public. All those defendants who were informed of the case after the fact could not be held liable for any violations of the directors' duties of care and loyalty as good managers.

---

[33] For the details of the court decision, see Osaka District Court, September 20, 2000, *Shoji Homu*, No. 1573, at 4–51.

[34] For details, see Commercial Law, Law No. 48 (March 9, 1899) (amended 18 times). For details, see Ministry of Internal Affairs and Communications, "Law Data Providing System", updated on August 4, 2005, http://www.ron.gr.jp/law/law/syouhou1.htm (accessed July 8, 2005).

## *The Response of US Regulators*

On November 2, 1995, the FRB ordered the bank to close its branches and terminate all its operations in the US within 90 days.[35] FRB had also ordered that in the next three years, the bank was obliged to submit a written petition if either the bank or its affiliates would like to reopen its operations in the US. This petition would then be subject to the US authorities' discretion.

According to the International Banking Act (IBA),[36] there were two grounds on which the FRB could possibly base its decision of ordering the bank to leave the US (see **Exhibit 8**). The first possible reason was that the bank had not been subject to the Japanese MOF's regulation.

**Exhibit 8**   US International Banking Act

See Sections 7(e) and 10(b) of the IBA, added in 1991 as amendments.

The board may order a foreign bank to terminate the activities of such branch, agency, or subsidiary, if the board finds that:

(A)  the foreign bank is not subject to comprehensive supervision or regulation on a consolidated basis by the appropriate authorities in its home country

(B)  there is reasonable cause to believe that such a foreign bank, or any affiliate of such a foreign bank, has committed a violation of law or engaged in an unsafe or unsound banking practice in the US; and as a result of such violation or practice, the continued operation of the foreign bank's branch, agency, or commercial lending company subsidiary in the US would not be consistent with the public interest or with the purposes of this Act, the Bank Holding Company Act of 1956, or the Federal Deposit Insurance Act. 12 U.S.C. §3107(b) (1994).

And in case of termination of a federal branch of agency:

The board may transmit to the comptroller of the currency a recommendation that the license of any federal branch or federal agency of a foreign bank be terminated in accordance with Section 4(1)[12 U.S.C. §3102(I)] if the board has reasonable cause to believe that such foreign bank, or any affiliate of such foreign bank, has engaged in conduct for which the activities of any state branch or agency may be terminated. 12 U.S.C. §3105(e)(5) (1994).

---

[35] Kishi, S. (1995) "Fault of the Ministry of Finance which Betrayed the World and Japan: Japan's Financial Administration Far Apart from Anglo-Saxon Logic", *Economist* (Japan), December 5, 1995, pp. 40–42.

[36] 12 U.S.C. §611 (1994).

The second was that the bank's operations included those activities that could be considered unsafe and unsound banking practices.

The order to terminate operations that was given to the bank was the first action of its kind that the FRB had taken since the IBA revision in 1991. While some people thought that this action was too severe, it was neither unusual nor unduly harsh if one understood the trend toward increased supervision by US authorities over foreign banks.

## *Japan's Regulatory Body under Fire*

It was August 8, 1995 when the president, an executive vice-president in charge of international operations and a managing director of Daiwa Bank met with the director general of the Banking Bureau of MOF at the bank's club to report the incident. In response, the director general of the Banking Bureau told the representatives of the bank, "It [is] bad timing," as disclosure might trigger instability in financial circles.[37] On September 18, 40 days after being informed of the incident, the MOF finally notified US authorities.

Aside from focusing on the attempts by the bank to hide its losses, US criticism quickly targeted the closed-room administrative practices of the MOF itself. Critics said that it was the MOF that was really at fault in the matter rather than the bank, since it failed to follow necessary procedures after receiving the report from the bank. John Bussey, foreign editor of the *Wall Street Journal* and former Tokyo bureau chief, had this to say about the MOF:

*The real rogue is Japan's [MOF]. In the Daiwa affair and in its handling of Japan's banking crisis, the [MOF] has shown its remarkable overconfidence and its willingness to bamboozle U.S. bank regulators, the Japanese public and even itself … So maybe it wasn't surprising that the [MOF] thought it could flout US banking regulations this summer by failing to report — for six weeks — what it had learned about Daiwa's illegal trades in the US The trades cost Daiwa $1.1 billion. But they cost the [MOF] its reputation.[38]*

— J. Bussey, *Wall Street Journal*

---

[37] "MOF's Confusion at its Peak: Distrust of Japan's Financial Administration Heightens Regarding Daiwa Bank Scandal: Disbanding of MOF is Suggested", *Shukan Toyo Keizai* (*Weekly Oriental Economist*), December 2, 1995.

[38] Bussey, J. "Japan's Bungling Ministry of Finance", *Wall Street Journal*, November 10, 1995.

As mentioned before, the bank was "obligated to report to the FRB within 30 days after the criminal case was suspected", according to Regulation H.[39] While the MOF's reporting duty was not answerable to this law, it should have advised the bank to report to the FRB.[40] The MOF was accused of being morally responsible for this nonfeasance.

As for this implicit responsibility for the nonfeasance of the MOF,[41] there was a strong view among informed sources in the Japanese financial world that the MOF did not know about this 30-day disclosure duty under the US IBA.[42] However, the FRB and US prosecutors did not think that this was true.[43] In the Senate Banking Committee's hearing on the Daiwa Bank incident, Alan Greenspan, chairman of the FRB said about MOF's delay in reporting to the US authorities that "It is regretful that MOF made this error," while chairman of the Banking Committee, Senator D'Amato, criticized the MOF saying, "MOF, which prevented the speedy report to the US authorities in a collusion with Daiwa, severely damaged the trust between the two governments."

The characteristics of MOF's response to the bank incident were described as obfuscation and delay,[44] which was MOF's traditional technique based on their governing principle: "Never let them know; let them rely on us."[45] This secrecy-prone administrative technique by the MOF severely damaged the international credibility of Japan. Nevertheless, the MOF insisted that this problem was created by the "difference of culture

---

[39] See **Exhibit 1**.

[40] "Suggestion for Disbanding of MOF Surfaced Abruptly with Daiwa Bank Sandal", *Shukan Toyo Keizai* (*Weekly Oriental Economist*), December 2, 1995.

[41] The attitude taken by MOF in this case is a violation of the agreement among the banking supervisory agencies of various national governments established to control international banking transactions. (Basle Committee on Banking Supervision, Minimum Standards for the Supervision of International Banking Groups and their Cross-Border Establishments, July 1992.) See the website of bank for International Settlements, http://www.bis.org/bcbs/.

[42] See Resona Holdings Inc. (2004) "Message from the Management: Message from the Chairman", http://www.resona-hd.co.jp/e-group/g_01a.htm (accessed July 11, 2005).

[43] Ibid.

[44] "Daiwa Bank Scandal", *Shukan Toyo Keizai* (*Weekly Oriental Economist*), December 2, 1995.

[45] Ibid.

between Japan and the United States",[46] and did not accept its fault, which was really the crux of the problem.

## Looking Forward: "Reborn" as Resona Bank

On March 1, 2002, Daiwa Bank merged with Asahi Bank resulting in the creation of a new bank — Resona. Resona Bank's parent company was Resona Holdings Inc., a company listed on the Tokyo Stock Exchange. Resona Holdings Inc.'s major business included "managing and supervising banking and other subsidiaries as well as other related activities".

The name Resona was derived from the Latin word *resonus*, meaning "to resonate" or "to resound". Having learned its lessons from the Iguchi fiasco, and possibly other financial debacles, Resona Bank appreciated the importance of corporate governance and of an open and forward-looking organizational culture. The chairman of Resona Holdings Inc., Eiji Hosoya, stated in his message to the shareholders on March 1, 2004:

> *The second major issue we are addressing in implementing internal reforms to revitalize our corporate culture ... We are conducting activities to address this issue in two principle areas. The first is renovating the mindset of our personnel, and the second is strengthening our corporate governance systems to provide for proper management ... Specifically, in June 2003, Resona Holdings, Inc. became the first major financial group to form corporate governance committees. As a result, we now have a strong framework for the surveillance of management ... Our efforts are particularly focused on changing the mind-set of staff, which tends to be inward-looking.*
>
> — Eiji Hosoya, chairman of Resona Holdings Inc.[47]

---

[46] "Suggestions of Splitting MOF Surfaced Abruptly with Daiwa Bank Scandal: MOF Campaign of Bureaucracy Shows Sign of Fatigue", *Shukan Toyo Kezai* (*Weekly Oriental Economist*), December 2, 1995.

[47] Resona Holdings Inc. (2004) "Message from the Management: Message from the Chairman", http://www.resona-hd.co.jp/e-group/g_01a.htm (accessed July 11, 2005).

# For Further Discussion

1. What were the regulatory requirements that Daiwa Bank and/or its officers had to comply with? Did the bank and/or the officers comply with them?
2. What would be the potential liability of the bank's directors? Should the bank's directors be held liable for violating the law of a foreign country such as the US?
3. The bank's directors claimed that they were not aware of the specifics of US laws and regulations. Could they use this as a good defense?
4. The bank's directors thought of the possible argument of "management decision" (i.e., directors should be given the discretionary power to judge) to defend themselves. Do you think this argument would work to their advantage?
5. The bank's directors thought that it was adequate to report the Iguchi fiasco to the Japanese MOF and to simply obey the ministry's advice in keeping this matter confidential. The ministry did not give further advice. On such a basis, the bank's directors did not feel the need to report to the US regulatory or related authorities. What do you think about this argument?
6. On July 27, 1995, the bank issued 50 million shares of preferred stock without disclosing the financial disaster that Iguchi's unauthorized trading had caused. Do you think the bank's directors had any disclosure responsibilities under US and/or Japanese laws?

# 4

# A Rogue Trader at Daiwa Bank (B): The Board Meeting on September 25, 1995 in Japan*

On July 18, 1995, Sumino Abewaka, president of Daiwa Bank, received a letter informing him of illegal trades at the New York branch which had resulted in a loss of approximately US$1.1 billion. Over two months later, on September 25, a board meeting took place. In their main headquarters in Osaka, directors in charge discussed the (possible) outcome and their responsibilities in relation to the incident. Heated discussion followed in an attempt to outline the responsibilities of officers and the directors.

## Toshihide Iguchi's Cover-Up

When a bank traded US Treasury bonds, securities companies — the bank's counterpart in the transactions — normally sent transaction confirmation statements to the transaction control section of the bank. However, Toshihide Iguchi, the "rogue trader" who was vice-president of the New York branch, instructed the securities companies to send those statements directly to him. He also hid the true securities balance statements sent from custodial banks, which held the traded Treasury bonds, and delivered forged statements to the custodial control section of the bank.

How could this happen? First, Iguchi was in charge of both securities trading and securities control. Second, he held these positions in the section that traded Treasury bonds for 11 years. It was quite unusual, even among Japanese banks, for an employee to remain essentially in one

---

*This case requires students to be familiar with Case 3 "A Rogue Trader at Daiwa Bank (A): Management Responsibility under Different Jurisprudential Systems, Practices and Cultures", in this book.

position for such a long period. Third, although it is customary for bank employees in the US and Europe to take a long vacation once a year while another employee handles his or her job, Iguchi never took any long vacations during the 11-year period. Finally, with regard to market risk management, it was customary for Japanese banks to set up a trading limit for each trader. In this case, however, the bank failed to detect the loss, which substantially exceeded the capacity of its New York branch. Although it was true that the loss was covered up by unlisted or out-of-book transactions, the management's responsibility for the lack of more effective and stringent control was indisputable.

## The Internal Control System and Management Responsibility

One issue addressed in the September 25 board meeting was the adequacy of Daiwa Bank's internal control system. In particular, the directors asked themselves if they had failed to establish and maintain sufficient internal control. Two issues were discussed: "responsibility of care" and the "principle of trusting rights" on the condition that directors are responsible for establishing an internal control system (see **Exhibit 1** for definitions of relevant legal principles).

**Exhibit 1**   Definitions of Relevant Legal Principles

Directors have various responsibilities towards their companies, and the breach of these responsibilities may not only be detrimental to those companies and their shareholders, but may also lead to civil and criminal liability of the individual director concerned.

US common law recognizes that directors have fiduciary responsibilities to the corporation and its shareholders consisting of the responsibilities of care, loyalty and good faith.[1]

The responsibility of care requires directors to act on an informed basis, and the responsibility of loyalty requires directors to serve the company and its shareholders to the exclusion of all other interests. The responsibility of good faith is an overarching

*(Continued)*

---

[1] Block, D.J., Barton, N.E. and Radin, S.A. (1998) *The Business Judgment Rule: Fiduciary Duties of Corporate Directors*, Fifth Edition, Chapter 2, "Fiduciary Duties of Corporate Directors", New York: Aspen Law & Business.

**Exhibit 1**   (*Continued*)

responsibility incorporating principles underlying the responsibilities of care and loyalty.

The following three principles are relevant to this case.

### (1) Director's Responsibility of Care

A director's responsibility of care refers to the duty to exercise appropriate diligence in overseeing the management of the company, making decisions and taking other actions. In meeting the responsibility of care, directors are expected to:

1. Attend and participate in board and committee meetings. Personal participation is required.
2. Remain properly informed about the company's business and affairs. Directors should devote appropriate time to reviewing periodic updates provided by management, as well as studying board materials prior to each meeting.
3. Rely on others. Directors are entitled to rely on information provided by other sources (management, officers, counsel, experts, etc.) who they reasonably believe to be competent. If a director has knowledge of incompetence or relies on someone he or she unreasonably believes to be competent, a director may be liable.
4. Make inquiries. Directors should make inquiries about potential problems that come to their attention and follow up until they are reasonably satisfied that management is addressing them appropriately.

### (2) Principle of Trusting Right[2]

Directors must exercise their powers collectively, and the majority decision will prevail. The articles of association will govern how the directors are to proceed and will often authorize directors to delegate the exercise of their powers to a committee consisting of one or more directors, or to a managing director.

Using principles drawn from the law of agency, the following guidelines can be laid down:

1. Full time executive directors should devote as far as possible their whole time and energies to company matters during office hours. This does not preclude them from acting as non-executive directors of other companies with the corresponding responsibilities that such appointments bring, subject to the provisions of their contract with the company.
2. If employed as having particular skills, for example, as being a professional accountant, a director should display the skill or ability expected from a person of

(*Continued*)

---

[2]This principle is a derivative of responsibility Cof care.

**Exhibit 1**   (*Continued*)

> that profession. A professional accountant may, depending on the circumstances, be held professionally responsible if he should be found negligent in the discharge of his duties as a director.
> 3. Having regard to the articles of association and the demands of business, certain responsibilities may properly be left to some other official, and directors are justified in trusting that official to perform such responsibilities honestly in the absence of grounds for suspicion.
>
> This principle is as an acceptable notion in the US, and the US Court established a principle that a director is not allowed to rely on the reports and analyses provided by other directors and subordinates if "abnormal facts" exist.[3]
>
> **(3) Respondeat Superior**
>
> The meaning of the Latin phrase *respondeat superior* is "let the master answer". *Respondeat Superior* is a key doctrine in the law of agency which provides that an employer (principal) is responsible for any of his/her/its employees' (agents') actions during the "course of employment". Therefore, an agent who signs an agreement to purchase goods for his/her employer can establish a binding contract between the seller and the employer. For example: if a delivery truck driver negligently hits a child in the street, the company for which the driver works will be liable for the injuries.[4]

Regarding "responsibility of care", the question was whether there had been a lack of sufficient separation between the securities trading department and the fund settlement/administration department. Directors also looked at the bank's holiday system as a possible reason for the risk management problems in its New York office.

Regarding the "principle of trusting right", the question was whether there had been job-related negligence in the establishment and regulation of the internal control system. In the meeting, the executives discussed three groups of people who could be held liable for the failure of the internal control system. First, the three directors who successively served as New York branch manager within the 11-year period in question might be held liable for inadequacies in the system used to confirm the storage

---

[3] Block, D.J., Barton, N.E. and Radin, S.A. (1998), *op. cit.*

[4] *Black's Law Dictionary*, 1951, Fourth Edition, West Publishing Co., p. 1475.

balance of T-bills. Second, the internal auditor, who visited the New York branch in September 1993, could be held liable for failing to detect the flaws in the system. This auditor, who was appointed by the president under the Japanese Commercial Code and was stationed at the headquarters in Japan, had a responsibility to check the operations of the New York branch once every three years. And finally, the president's and executive vice-president's responsibility was questioned. There was a chance the president and executive vice-president might not be accused of neglecting their supervisory duties on the grounds that they were allowed to delegate responsibility to branch directors (in this case, the New York branch director) and also directors in charge of the inspection department which monitored the storage balance of T-bills. The corporate organization was structured in such a way that the president and the executive vice-president did not have supervisory responsibilities unless special circumstances raised doubts about the job performance of any director with frontline responsibilities.

## Daiwa Bank's Responsibility

Besides looking at the responsibility of the individual directors, the management was also concerned that the bank as an institution could be held liable, under *respondeat superior*, for the damages its customers and the US financial authorities suffered as a result of the illegal trades by Iguchi (see **Exhibit 1** for definitions of relevant legal principles). It was clear Iguchi had committed a felony. The larger question was whether the bank was guilty of misprision; in other words, did the bank neglect to prevent and/or to report the felony? Or could Daiwa Bank allege that the case was a personal wrongdoing committed by Iguchi, and that the bank was a victim and was not responsible for the misconduct?

## For Further Discussion

1. Was there any nonfeasance regarding duties in establishing an internal control system?
2. Can directors claim principle of trusting right?
3. Is Daiwa Bank also responsible under the principle of *respondeat superior*?

# 5

# Hostile Takeover Battle in Japan: Fuji TV vs. Livedoor for NBS

On January 17, 2005 Fuji Television Network Inc.[1] (Fuji TV), the centerpiece of the giant Fujisankei Communications Group (FCG),[2] made a takeover bid for Nippon Broadcasting System Inc.[3] (NBS).[4] The move intended to make NBS, an AM radio station that owned 22.5% of Fuji TV, a consolidated subsidiary. Their plans were thwarted, however, by maverick CEO Takafumi Horie and his rapacious internet company, Livedoor Co. (Livedoor).[5] Livedoor had purchased more than a third of the NBS stock through off-floor trading (see **Exhibit 1**), a move that violated Japan's unspoken yet accustomed rule against this type of backdoor business practice common in other parts of the world. The news that Livedoor, an internet company operating on the fringes of Japan's corporate establishment, had bought such a large number of NBS shares came as a shock to Fuji TV's management, many of whom were not even familiar with the company.

Following the news of Livedoor's hostile takeover bid on February 8, Fuji TV was informed on that day that Livedoor received ¥80 billion[6] in financing from Lehman Brothers,[7] a well-known US investment bank. Lehman Brothers used a special financing scheme consisting of MSCBs

---

[1] For the company profile, see http://www.fujitv.co.jp/index.html.

[2] For the company profile, see http://www.fujisankei-g.co.jp/

[3] For the company profile, see http://www.jolf.co.jp/company/.

[4] See the press release, http://www.c-direct.ne.jp/japanese/uj/pdf/10104676/00029546.pdf.

[5] For the company profile, see http://corp.livedoor.com/company/outline.html.

[6] At the end of February 2005, the exchange rate was ¥104.58 = US$1.

[7] For the company profile, see http://www.rikunabi2006.com/RN/06/KDBG/R/0296329005. htm.

**Exhibit 1**   Timeline of the Battle Between Fuji TV, NBS and Livedoor

| | |
|---|---|
| January 17, 2005 | Fuji TV announces its plan of a takeover bid for NBS. |
| February 8, 2005 | Livedoor acquires more than one-third of NBS's outstanding shares in **off-floor trading**, etc. |
| February 23, 2005 | NBS decides to issue new **share warrants**. |
| February 24, 2005 | Livedoor requests the Tokyo District Court to issue an injunction order against the issue of **share warrants**. |
| March 8, 2005 | Fuji TV announces that it has acquired approximately 37% of NBS's shares. |
| March 11, 2005 | Tokyo District Court issues an injunction order against the issue of share warrants by NBS. |
| March 12, 2005 | Livedoor warns NBS's directors that the removal of **crown jewels** is illegal. |
| March 15, 2005 | Fuji TV announces that it will increase annual dividends five-fold. |
| March 16, 2005 | Livedoor announces that it has acquired more than 50% of NBS's shares on the voting right base. <br> Tokyo District Court rejects NBS's appeal. |
| March 22, 2005 | Fuji TV establishes a new issue frame of ¥50 billion. |
| March 23, 2005 | Tokyo High Court also decides against new share warrants. It decides that a discussion on corporate value is not proper for the court. |
| March 24, 2005 | NBS decides to loan its Fuji TV shares to SBI Holdings, which suddenly appears as a **white knight**. |
| March 31, 2005 | Three outside board members of NBS quit. |
| April 18, 2005 | Fuji TV and Livedoor reach settlement. |

(moving strike convertible bonds) to fund the bid.[8] The company was further informed that Livedoor's purchase of NBS shares was the first step towards its ultimate acquisition target, Fuji TV.[9]

---

[8] At the time most Japanese companies and their management were unfamiliar with MSCBs. These financial instruments are bonds with share warrants (convertible bonds). Due to the amendment of the Commercial Law in 2002, bonds are defined as: (1) common bonds and (2) bonds with share warrants. See http://www.nomura.co.jp/terms/japan/te/sinkabuyoyakus.html and http://www.nomura.co.jp/terms./english/m/mscb.html.

[9] See the press release of February 2, 2005, http://www.c-direct.ne.jp/japanese/uj/pdf/10104676/00030906.pdf.

For a long time, takeovers of Japanese companies financed by US funds had been anticipated, and now those expectations had been realized. Executives at Fuji TV understood this was a battle between US and Japanese financing strategies. But this fight was not solely between the US and Japan, it was also a public challenge by an upstart internet company and its flamboyant CEO to the old media establishment and Japan's traditional corporate culture. As such, it drew unprecedented attention from both the Japanese press and the Japanese public who were eager to see which company, and more importantly, which culture, would prevail.

## Company Profiles[10]

FCG (the Group) had around 10,000 employees and 100 companies in the media and entertainment industry.[11] The Group claimed to be one of the world's largest media groups. It was a loose keiretsu founded by the Shikanai family, who saw its management control dissipate in the early 1990s. The Group's flagship business was the *Sankei Shimbun*, Japan's leading national daily with a circulation of around 2 million.

NBS, a national AM radio station located in Tokyo, was a core company in the Group's portfolio. Incorporated in 1953, the company was led by its president, Akinobu Kamebuchi,[12] a former DJ at NBS. Its first radio broadcast took place in 1954, and by 1959 it was on the air for 24 hours a day. The company went public in 1996, and by 2005 it had become one of the dominant players in Japan's radio industry, operating 37 stations and managing one of the world's largest radio broadcasting networks (see **Exhibit 2** for basic data on Fuji, Livedoor and NBS).

Fuji TV, a major commercial TV network, was established as a subsidiary of NBS in 1957. Since 1993, when a boardroom coup ousted the founding Shikanai family[13], Hisashi Hieda[14] had controlled the company, becoming the face of old-guard corporate Japan through this saga. As a

---

[10] For details, see "Mainichishinbunsha", *Economist* (Japan), April 5, 2005, pp. 111–113.

[11] See the website, http://www.fujisankei-g.co.jp/.

[12] For Akinobu Kamabuchi, see http://search.jp.aol.com/advhandler.adp.

[13] For Shikanai, see http://www.tfcc.or.jp/economy/.

[14] For Hisashi Hieda, see http://www.yomiuri.co.jp/atmoney/mnews/20050309mh06.htm.

**Exhibit 2**   Basic Data of Three Companies (2005)

| Name | Fuji TV | Livedoor | NBS |
|---|---|---|---|
| **Address** | Minatoku, Tokyo | Shinjuku, Tokyo | Chiyodaku, Tokyo |
| **Established** | November 18, 1957 | August 1997 | April 23, 1954 |
| **Capital** | ¥114.75 billion | ¥64 billion | ¥4.2 billion |
| **Chairman & CEO** | Hisashi Hieda | Takafumi Horie | |
| **President** | Koichi Murakami | Takafumi Horie | Akinobu Kamebuchi |
| **Employees** | 1,367 | 1,798 | 240 |
| **Business** | TV Broadcasting Operation | Internet Related Operation | Radio Broadcasting Operation |

*Source*: For Fuji TV, see http://www.fujitv.co.jp. For Livedoor, see http://corp.livedoor.com/company/outline.html. For NBS, see http://www.jolf.co.jp/company/annai.html.

member of Keidanren,[15] the company was already a representative of Japan's old-guard corporate establishment. By 2005, the company had 28 domestic stations, 20 overseas offices and a 30% stake in interactive broadcasting venture "Satellite Service". Fuji TV claimed to broadcast to around 98% of the Japanese population. The success of the company had reversed the parent–subsidiary relationship with NBS, but no action was taken to remedy the situation until Fuji's takeover bid for NBS was announced on January 17, 2005.

Livedoor, an internet service provider based in Tokyo, was established in April 1996 with ¥6 million[16] in capital. It made its stock market debut in April 2000. When many IT companies stumbled with the collapse of the internet bubble, Livedoor, led by Takafumi Horie, a high-profile 33-year-old leader known as "Horiemon", weathered the hard times and

---

[15] The Japanese Federation of Economic Organizations (Keidanren) is a general economic organization consisting of 1,623 companies and other organizations, which include 91 companies with foreign capital affiliations and 1,306 major representatives of Japanese companies. It is the strongest lobby in Japan that applies pressure on the government as well as overseas organizations by collecting business opinions from business communities on many important issues ranging from economic and industrial issues to labor issues urging speedy solutions. See the Federation's website at http://www.keidanren.or.jp/Japanese/profile/pro001.htm.

[16] On April 1, 1996, the exchange rate was ¥107.53=US$1. See Bank of Japan's homepage, http://www.boj.or.jp/stat/stat_f.htm.

continued to expand its business. Under Horie's control, the corporate group of which Livedoor was the center grew rapidly through the acquisitions of as many as 40 firms. Its growth could be illustrated through Livedoor's market capitalization which grew more than nine-fold in two months from about ¥100 billion in November 2003 to over ¥900 billion in January 2004. As this growth was largely fuelled by the Livedoor group's frequent use of acquisitions and stock splits, many of the old-guard business elite regarded Horie with suspicion and disdain for his un-Japanese ways of doing business. Meanwhile, Horie's controversial way of doing business and his public criticism of the country's business establishment made him a popular figure amongst young Japanese.

## The Takeover

On January 17, 2005, Fuji TV made a tender offer of ¥5,950[17] per NBS share that would be valid from January 18 till February 21 of the same year. At the time of the offer, Fuji TV owned 12.39% of outstanding NBS shares and planned to purchase enough shares to own a minimum of 50% of NBS's outstanding common stock. As there was no maximum target ownership share set for the offer, Fuji TV had not ruled out the possibility of delisting NBS if they were offered enough shares, or exploring the possibility to delist NBS in the future. The takeover would revert the subsidiary–parent relationship which existed between Fuji TV and NBS. Moreover, Fuji TV considered that in view of global developments in the Information Technology and Communication industry and the transition to an era marked by integration of broadcasting and other forms of communications, it should actively promote alliances with the Group's companies to profit from synergy effects on business know-how, technological development capabilities, marketing infrastructures and human resources.[18]

The unexpected hostile takeover bid by Livedoor threw a monkey wrench in Fuji TV's plans. Livedoor amassed approximately 30% of NBS

---

[17] The purchase price was approximately 21% higher than the average closing price of NBS on the Tokyo Stock Exchange during the three-month period ending January 14, 2005.

[18] See press release ("Notice of Tender Offer Terms") of January 17, 2005 by Fuji TV, http://www.fujitv.co.jp/index.html.

shares through ToSTNeT-1,[19] the off-hour trading system run by the Tokyo Stock Exchange to effect block trades which, due to a loophole, allowed the company to not file disclosure reports about significant shareholders.[20] Having surpassed the mandatory threshold for takeover bids, on February 8, 2005 Livedoor announced a takeover bid for NBS.

## Internal Studies Commissioned by Fuji TV's Top Management

After being informed of Livedoor's purchase of NBS stock, the top management at Fuji TV immediately instructed their legal counselors and planning department to conduct studies on Livedoor's activities. The specific instructions given by the top executives to the two departments were as follows.[21]

The legal counselors:

1. Study and report on the tactics undertaken by Livedoor, and their legality.[22] In particular, the top executives were interested in Livedoor's acquisition of a large amount of NBS's share via off-floor trading (ToSTNeT-1).

2. The executives also wanted to know more about the MSCBs used by Livedoor to fund their takeover attempt. Moreover, it was rumored in the market that Lehman Brothers of the US had worked out the

---

[19] The tidings are executed from 8:20 a.m. to 9:00 a.m., from 11:00 a.m. to 12:30 p.m. and from 3:00 p.m. to 4:30 p.m. through ToSTNet at the Tokyo Stock Exchange. For details, see Tokyo Stock Exchange, http://www.tse.or.jp/gloassary/gloss_t/tachiaigai.html.

[20] The Securities Exchange Law prohibited the trading of a large amount of shares that could affect the management right of a company through off-floor transactions other than for a takeover bid. (Securities Exchange Law, Article 27-2) Off-floor trading was a quasi rule-breaking technique based on a perfunctory understanding of in-market trading, but off-floor trading was essentially an off-market trading in that it was a negotiated transaction. It was contrary to the intent of the law — to provide information to all investors so that they can trade fairly.

[21] See the press release of February 2, 2005, http://www.c-direct.ne.jp/japanese/uj/pdf/10104676/00030906.pdf.

[22] Ibid.

takeover scheme. This method of using MSCBs seemed to be dubious, if not actually illegal. The top executives wanted the legal department to find out if this was the case.[23]

3. List all the possible tactics Fuji TV could undertake to thwart Livedoor and report on the legality and effectiveness of these possible methods.[24]

At the same time, the planning department was asked the following:

1. Report on the corporate value of NBS. Due to the takeover battle, the stock price of NBS was rising and the executives needed to know what price they could be expected to pay for NBS as a result of the takeover battle and the resulting rise in the NBS share price. For the estimation, both the American and Japanese methods had to be used as Fuji TV had to know at what price their opponents and the American financier valued NBS.

## The Legal Counselors' Response

The legal counselors labored night and day to devise a strategic response to Livedoor's acquisition of NBS shares. This resulted in the following analysis which was presented to Fuji TVs top management.

1. A large amount of NBS's shares was acquired by Livedoor in an off-floor trade. According to the Securities Exchange Law, a stock purchase that might cause a change in the management right of a company had to be executed either (1) on market or (2) as a takeover bid, if it

---

[23] MSCBs, which Livedoor used to obtain ¥80 billion from Lehman Brothers, Tokyo, to finance the purchase of Nippon Broadcasting System's shares, was criticized as "very likely a betrayal of shareholders' trust", because "it is obvious that Horie, Livedoor's president, had lent his shares, which were put to short sell, resulting in stock price drops, thus hurting shareholders" ("Mainichishinbunsha", *Economist* [*Japanese Economic Journal*] November 4, 2005, p. 9).

[24] See the press release of February 2, 2005, http://www.c-direct.ne.jp/japanese/uj/pdf/10104676/00030906.pdf.

was to be executed off-market.[25] Although off-floor trading was technically "on-market trading", it was no different from "off-market trading" in that general investors had difficulty in accessing information and had a problem in terms of information disclosure. The legal department therefore had to conclude that acquiring such a large share of NBS shares through off-floor trading was illegal.[26]

2. The MSCBs used by Livedoor to fund their takeover attempt could be regarded as unduly beneficial to current subscribers. This was certainly the case when the MSCBs were combined with loaned stocks (see **Exhibit 3**). If so, Livedoor's use of them would be illegal as this was prohibited by the Commercial Law.[27] In the end, Fuji TVs legal counselors had to conclude it was not possible to make a definitive statement on the legality of financing a takeover with MSCBs, as it was a new method which had not been tested in the market and its effect on existing shareholders was thus unknown.

3. The legal counselors also presented a list of possible countermeasures, described below.[28]

- **Share Warrants**

   One preventive measure against hostile takeover was to issue share warrants to third parties (not restricted to existing shareholders)[29] in advance, forcing the company to buy back its own shares at a later time, possibly at higher prices. This method was especially useful when the bidder was expected to use such tactics as "GreenMailer" (see **Exhibit 4** for an overview of a lexicon of mergers and acquisitions, and **Exhibits 5–7** for more information on share warrants).[30]

---

[25] Securities Exchange Law, Article 27-2.

[26] See the press release of February 2, 2005, http://www.c-direct.ne.jp/japanese/uj/pdf/10104676/00030906.pdf.

[27] Commercial Law, Article 241.

[28] See the press release of February 2, 2005, http://www.c-direct.ne.jp/japanese/uj/pdf/10104676/00030906.pdf.

[29] Commercial Law, Article 280-2.

[30] In Japan it is considered a hostile takeover to buy the shares in the market and ask the company to buy them at higher prices. For details, see http://learning.xrea.jp/%A5%B0%A5%EA%A1%BC%A5%F3%A5%E1%A1%BC%A5%E9%A1%BC.html.

**Exhibit 3**  Moving Strike Convertible Bonds

MSCBs are also revered to as "death spiral" financing and they are the latest big thing in Japan's investment banking world.[31] MSCBs are used in a controversial financing method that delivers fat profits but carries big risks. The technique can raise money for cash-hungry companies but is also susceptible to abuse.

MSCB means "convertible bond with conversion price downward revision term". The underwriter tries to lower the company's share price by short selling as much as it can manage borrowing shares from large shareholders in order to collect the fund. When the conversion price drops due to the conversion price downward revision term, the underwriter converts the convertible bonds to more shares than the shares the underwriter owes and to be returned to the large shareholders. This makes the underwriter to earn the profit by the difference between the average short sale price and the conversion price for each share. Since the underwriter converts the convertible bonds without fail in order to collect the invested fund, this is also beneficial to the issuing company as well as it does not have to redeem the bond in the future. In other words, it provides an effect similar to capital increase for the issuing company.

The further the stock falls, the more shares the investment bank gets. Existing investors suffer because the company issues more shares, diluting their stake. The risk is that the stock price drop triggers a spiral of declines followed by ever more share issues, hence the term death spiral financing.

The losers in an MSCB issue are existing shareholders:

(1)  The issuance of MSCB will certainly result in short selling by the underwriter so that the share price drops.

(2)  The number of outstanding shares increases enormously due to the underwriters' conversion of the convertible bonds to shares. This causes a slowdown of share price movement and the share price stagnates.

In the present case, the conversion bond underwriter was Lehman Brothers, a US investment bank, and president Horie, who is a major shareholder of Livedoor, was lending his own shares to Lehman.[32]

(see the following example)

*(Continued)*

---

[31] US regulators clamped down on the practice after finding shark financiers drove dozens of small companies out of business by shorting their shares and triggering ever more share issues at progressively lower prices.

[32] "Mainichishinbunsha", *Economist* (Japan), April 11, 2005, p. 9.

**Exhibit 3**    (*Continued*)

Let us take a closer look at MSCBs with the help of a model:

| | |
|---|---|
| Issuer: | A |
| Underwriter: | B |
| Major shareholder (e.g., president): | C |
| Issuing amount: | ¥10 billion |
| Share price: | ¥500 |
| Conversion price: | ¥600 per share (20% above the market price) |
| Downward revision term: | The conversion price when the share price drops to ¥300 shall be ¥360 (20% above the market price) |

B borrows shares equivalent to ¥10 billion (20 million shares) from C and sells them on the market. The number of borrowed shares is normally very large so that the selling causes a share price drop. Let us assume that the price drops from ¥500 to ¥300. Since the conversion price at that point is ¥360, B converts MSCB to shares. As a consequence, B obtains 27.78 million shares, of which 20 million shares will be returned to C. B ends up acquiring 7.78 million shares as the profit: ¥2.3 billion (= 7.78 million shares × ¥300). As a consequence, A succeeds in financing ¥10 billion and B obtains a profit of ¥2.3 billion, while C gets a certain share lending fee (see the following flowchart).

## MSCB'S FLOWCHART

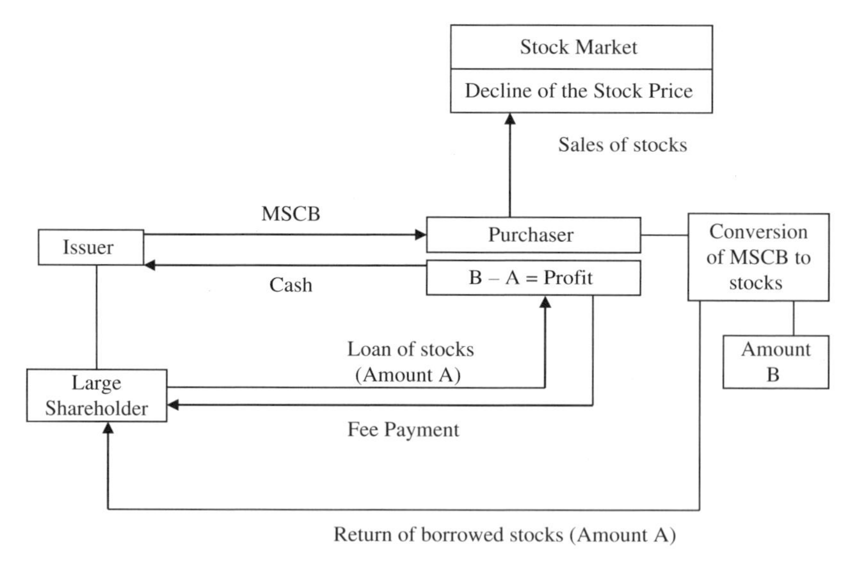

**Exhibit 4**    Mergers and Acquisitions Lexicon

When a company's board and management tries to resist a buyer's overtures, colorful merger and acquisition terms come up. Here are some terms and tactics being used in connection with mergers and acquisitions in the US.

**Greenmail** — A play on blackmail, greenmail is sent when an unfriendly bidder buys a large block of stock and then demands that the target company buys back the stock at a higher price if it does not want to be taken over. A greenmailer usually has no plan for an actual takeover, and only wants to make money. Greenmail is also called a "goodbye kiss" or a "bon voyage bonus".

**Pac Man** — A target firm turns around and tries to take over the company that made the hostile bid.

**Poison pill** — A target company tries to make its own stock less attractive to the buyer, usually by issuing a huge number of new shares to existing shareholders at a low price to dilute the voting rights of the bidder and make a takeover more difficult and expensive.

**Scorched earth policy** — A firm sells off its valuable and desired assets — called "crown jewels" — or assumes liabilities to make a takeover unattractive. If taken too far, this tactic can destroy the company.

**White knight** — A white knight is a company that saves the day by making a friendly takeover offer to a company that is threatened by a hostile takeover from a "black knight".

**Lady Macbeth strategy** — A company poses as a white knight to gain trust, but then joins an unfriendly bidder.

*Source*: *Japan Times*, March 26, 2005, http://search.japantimes.co.jp/print/business/nb03-2005/nb20050326a3.htm.

- **Capital Increase**

  NBS could also increase the number of outstanding shares up to 2.4 times[33] by allocating new issues to Fuji TV. Using this method, Fuji TV would be able make NBS its subsidiary regardless of the outcome of their takeover bid. In this scenario, existing shareholders would have no choice but to accept their takeover bid because a drop in share price was inevitable as a result of large-scale dilution. Increasing capital on a large scale by getting directors to arbitrarily

---

[33] This number is based on the company's treasury and unissued share capital.

**Exhibit 5**  Share Warrants

There were no restrictions when issuing share warrants on such things as the subscribers targeted by the issue or the subscription right exercising period; the conversion price was set in advance. Issuing share warrants was recognized as a means of friendly takeover in Japan, ever since the US company Wal-Mart,[34] for all practical purposes, placed Seiyu[35] under its umbrella in 2002 by obtaining its share warrants.[36]

As an instrument in defending against hostile takeovers, the function of share warrants was to lower the ratio of voting rights of the party who was attempting the hostile takeover. This was realized by providing share warrants to its existing shareholders in advance and then making them exercise their rights when the hostile takeover became a reality, thus increasing the number of outstanding shares. In the case of Fuji TV vs. Livedoor, the main question was the legality of a new issue by NBS with Fuji TV as an exclusive subscriber.[37]

If NBS intended to use this technique as a defensive measure against the hostile takeover after it happened, there was a chance it would not be accepted by the court.[38]

select only major shareholders they liked was against the basic principles of a corporation, which was that shareholders were entitled to be treated equally.

- **Crown Jewels**

  NBS's "crown jewel" (see **Exhibit 4** and **8**) was its 22.5% share in Fuji TV, which was worth approximately ¥140 billion, or roughly 70% of the total market value (¥200 billion) of NBS's outstanding stocks in February 2005. This meant that if Livedoor bought over 50% of outstanding NBS stock for ¥100 billion, they would gain

---

[34] See Wal-Mart homepage, http://www.walmart.com/.

[35] See Seiyu homepage, http://www.seiyu.co.jp/.

[36] For details of the friendly takeover of Seiyu by Wal-Mart, see http://www.cool-knowledge.com/020411wal-mart-toiu-vision.htm.

[37] For details, see press releases by Nippon Broadcasting "Notice Regarding Issuance of Stock Acquisition Rights through Third-Party Allocation", on February 23, 2005 and "Approval of Issuance of Stock Acquisition Rights", on February 24, 2005, http://www.jolf.co.jp/company/IR1242/index.html.

[38] A corporate law amendment which was expected to be introduced in 2006 would have enabled the use of share warrants as a "poison pill" by coercing shareholders to exercise warrants when needed for a company having modified the articles of incorporation in advance. "Mainichishinbunsha", *Economist* (Japan), April 11, 2005, p. 18.

**Exhibit 6**   Court's Decision on Examples of Justifiable Issuance of Share Warrants

What is notable is that the Tokyo High Court clearly indicated the examples of a justifiable issuance of share warrants. In other words, although it judged that NBS's countermeasure using share warrants was an excessive defense in this situation, it did indicate that defenses against certain takeover acts were lawful. One can say that an "infrastructure," i.e., a standard, is now in place by a court for facing the great age of mergers and acquisitions to come in Japan. This court decision is viewed as a "monumental decision to be remembered in the M&A history of Japanese companies".[39] Although the concept of share warrants was introduced in the last amended Commercial Law,[40] it was never used as a defensive measure against a hostile takeover because it was thought that "the outcome is unpredictable as there is no court's judgment standard".

The court decision provided examples of improper acquisitions of shares:

1. *Greenmailer* — When the buyer is merely interested in selling shares by artificially raising stock price without any sincere intention of participating in the company's management.
2. *Scorched earth operation* — If the buyer's intention is a scorched earth operation in which the buyer transfers the company's intellectual property, know-how, confidential information, clients, etc. to itself or its affiliate companies.
3. *Company's assets are used for wrong purposes, such as in a leveraged buyout (LBO)* — When the buyer intends to use the company's assets as collateral to raise funds to pay off the buyer's or its affiliate company's debts or obligations.
4. *High dividend payments or selling shares at high prices is intended* — When the buyer intends to dispose of the company's large assets such as real estate and negotiable instruments to make it possible to offer high dividends temporarily or to sell the shares when the stock price rises sharply.

The court stated that a person or entity waging such a hostile takeover does not deserve protection as a shareholder, and that the board of directors is justified in issuing share warrants with the principal objective of maintaining and securing management rights as a countermeasure. However, the management is responsible for proving that such an extraordinary circumstance exists.

Issuing share warrants will not be approved as a defensive measure in the US simply because it is an LBO-type takeover, in which the buyer is expected to acquire

*(Continued)*

---

[39] *Nikkei (Japan Economic Journal)*, March 24, 2005, p. 11.
[40] Amendment of Commercial Law in April 1, 2002. For details, see http://members. at.infoseek.co.jp/barexam/note/history_sh.htm.

**Exhibit 6**  (*Continued*)

funds using the target company's assets as collateral.[41] Compared with US courts' decisions, the decision in this case is favorable to the management of the target company. It is not necessarily a bad thing for a hostile buyer to try and use the poorly managed assets and know-how of a company more efficiently. The present decision can be appreciated because it clarifies the rule for defensive measures.[42] It makes it easier for a company, which is the target of a hostile takeover, to introduce defensive poison pills, as long as they can show that the buyer is motivated by one of these four types of improper acquisition of shares. Poison pills have generally been criticized in Japan by shareholders as tools for securing managers' jobs or a response to the risk of a drop in share price; therefore, Japanese companies thinking about introducing poison pills are happy with this court decision.[43]

control of approximately ¥140 billion worth of Fuji TV. Another jewel in the NBS crown was the stocks it owned of Pony Canyon, a major music label.[44] NBS owned more than 56% of Pony Canyon's outstanding stock. In the year ending in March 2004, Pony Canyon contributed 54% to NBS's ¥110 billion in consolidated sales. At that time, NBS had 56% of Pony Canyon's 800,000 outstanding shares, while Fuji TV held 27%.[45] In order for NBC to sell such an important

---

[41] When triggered, this poison pill allows shareholders to acquire additional shares below market price, thereby increasing the number of shares outstanding and making the takeover prohibitively expensive. Such plans are the subject of some controversy in the United States, a corporate provision to combat hostile takeover. The vast majority of pills were instituted after November 1985, when the Delaware Supreme Court upheld a company's right to adopt a poison pill without shareholder approval in Moran v. Household International, Inc., Del. Ch., 490 A.2d 1059 (1985). For the case, see http://www.law.unlv.edu/faculty/rlawless/mergers/moran.htm.

[42] *Nikkei* (*Japan Economic Journal*), March 24, 2005, p. 11.

[43] Ibid

[44] Pony Canyon Inc. is a major music label, a key subsidiary of NBS's. It was established on October 1, 1966 as a record label under the name of NBS and renamed Pony Inc. in 1970. On October 21, 1987, it merged with the record company Canyon to form Pony Canyon. Pony started publishing computer games software in 1982, and published game titles for many computer platforms and consoles. For their homepage, see http://music.ponycanyon.co.jp/.

[45] For details, see *Japan Times*, April 7, 2005 (http://search.japantimes.co.jp/print/business/nb04-2005/nb20050407a2.htm).

**Exhibit 7**   Court Decision on the Share Warrants

Livedoor requested a temporary injunction on the share warrants to be issued to Fuji TV which NBS had tried as a countermeasure against Livedoor's hostile takeover attempt.[46] The Tokyo High Court rejected NBS's appeal for a temporary injunction at Livedoor's request.[47] What could be the reasons for the court's decision?

The Tokyo High Court ruled that when a conflict exists between the managing right of a company and an attempt to maintain and secure the managing right of the existing manager or a specific shareholder, an issue of share warrants with which to reduce the shareholding ratio of a party who is attempting a hostile takeover, is considered to be an "extremely unfair method" in accordance with Article 280, Section 39-4 and Article 280, Section 10 of the Commercial Law.[48]

The court judged that the issuance of share warrants in the present case was expected to reduce the share ratio of Livedoor, support the incumbent management, and influence the takeover matter. The court also judged that, because the issuance of share warrants was intended for securing the managing right of NBS by Fuji TV, the issuance was extremely unfair as it was against the shareholders' benefit. The court further stated:

1. There is no concrete evidence that Livedoor is attempting a hostile takeover primarily as a money game.
2. The judgment on whether Livedoor's control of the company may damage the corporate value of the company is a management decision that should be made based on the judgments and evaluations of the shareholders and securities markets, and it was not proper for the court to make.

*(Continued)*

---

[46] For the decision of the Tokyo Lower Court, see press releases by Nippon Broadcasting, "Notice of Regarding Ruling on Request for Court Injunction Blocking Issuance of Stock Acquisition Rights and Appeal against the Ruling", March 11, 2005; and "Notification Regarding Rejection of Objection to Temporary Court Injunction Blocking Issuance of Stock Acquisition Rights and of Appeal against the Ruling", March 16, 2005. For both, see http://www.jolf.co.jp/company/IR1242/index.html.

[47] Tokyo High Court, the 16th Civil Section, March 23, 2005. For details, see press release by Nippon Broadcasting "Notification Regarding Dismissal of Appeal against Lower Court of Temporary Injunction to Block Issuance of Stock Acquisition Rights", March 23, 2005, http://www.jolf.co.jp/company/IR1242/index.html (accessed July 13, 2005).

[48] Tokyo High Court, the 16th Civil Section, March 23, 2005. For details, see press release by Nippon Broadcasting "Notification Regarding Dismissal of Appeal against Lower Court of Temporary Injunction to Block Issuance of Stock Acquisition Rights", March 23, 2005, http://www.jolf.co.jp/company/IR1242/index.html (accessed July 13, 2005). Also, for details of the court decision, see *Nikkei* (*Japan Economic Journal*), March 24, 2005, p. 12.

**Exhibit 7**   (*Continued*)

3. Because ToSNet-1 trading (off-floor trading) is trading on the securities exchange market owned and operated by the Tokyo Stock Exchange under the Securities Exchange Law, it does not violate the Securities Exchange Law,[49] and the use of this system by Livedoor does not constitute any particular circumstance that justifies the issue warrants of the present case by NBS.

Based on this, the Tokyo High Court ruled that the issuance of share warrants in such a large amount in this case constituted a misuse of rights provided to the board of directors of NBS. Upon hearing this decision, NBS withdrew the issuance of share warrants on the day of the court judgment.

**Exhibit 8**   Crown Jewels

If we are to analogize a target company in a takeover bid to a king's crown, the company's important assets and major businesses are jewels on the crown. Without the jewels, the crown is just a cap. Similarly, if the valuable assets of a company are transferred to a third party, the company becomes less attractive to the party who is trying to take it over. Thus, transfer of crown jewels is a scorched earth defense.[50]

asset as Pony Canyon as part of a takeover defense against Livedoor, a logical explanation other than just for a defense against a takeover was necessary. Otherwise, the management had to be fully prepared for the possibility of a derivatives suit filed by existing shareholders against them when they sold NBS's interest in Pony Canyon.

- **Stock Loan**

  NBS could transfer ownership of its Fuji TV shares to a third party by lending the shares to them. If the shareholders' re-coding date[51] occurred while the stocks were lent to a third party, the borrower's name, and not NBS's, would be recorded on the shareholders list. It

---

[49] Securities Exchange Law, Article 27-2.

[50] According to *Japan Times*, March 26, 2005, a firm that sells off its valuable and desired assets, called "crown jewels", is undertaking a scorched earth policy. For details, see http://search.japantimes.co.jp/print/business/nb03-,2005/nb20050326a3.htm.

[51] The date is fixed by the company in accordance with the Tokyo Stock Exchange rules to determine who the shareholders are on the register. For details, see the Tokyo Stock Exchange's website: http://www.tse.or.jp/.

would then be the borrower's right to exercise the voting rights and receive dividends.

Using a stock loan as a defensive measure against Livedoor would be equivalent to taking away NBS's voting rights as a Fuji TV shareholder and giving them to a third party. This was a so-called "scorched earth defense operation" and the third party was a "white knight".

However, if the period of loan was long, such as five years, there was the possibility that the loan would be recognized as a selling transaction if the case got to court. Additionally, if the loan was recognized as "an important part of NBS's operations", the situation would require a special decision by a stockholder's meeting.[52] Livedoor might try to claim damages in court, but this required a number of legal processes and proof, so claiming damages was not a feasible option for Livedoor[53] (see **Exhibit 9**).

- **New Issue Frame**

  Fuji TV could establish a new issue frame of approximately ¥50 billion with the underlying goal of fending off an attack on Fuji TV by Livedoor, which appeared to consider Fuji TV its real target in the battle for NBS. The idea was that even if Livedoor tried to execute a takeover bid aiming to capture as much as 50% of Fuji TV's outstanding shares (1.27 million shares), Fuji TV could increase the number of shares up to 6 million by using its newly established issue frame before the takeover bid period ended. In other words, even if Livedoor succeeded in acquiring 50% of outstanding Fuji TV shares, Fuji TV could issue additional shares thereby lowering

**Exhibit 9**   Stock Loan

A loaned stock is a stock that is loaned for a certain period of time by a contract called a "stock loan agreement", in which the loan period can be arbitrarily established and the ownership is transferred to the borrower for that period. The borrower returns the stocks to the lender on completion of the agreed period and pays rent for the same.

---

[52] Commercial Law, Article 245.

[53] Civil Law, Law No. 899 (April 27, 1896), Article 709. For the law, see http://law.e-gov. go.jp/cgi-bin/idxsearch.cgi.

**Exhibit 10**   New Issue Frame

> A new issue frame is a mechanism to determine the number of shares to be issued for a company issuing stocks. By reporting the issuing frame to the Ministry of Finance[54] in advance, a company can issue new shares at any time within a predetermined period and within the predetermined frame without having to report each instance to the Ministry of Finance. While it normally takes about a month or so, the issuing process can be simplified by establishing the issuing frame in advance, and the whole process can be shortened to approximately two weeks.

Livedoor's shareholding ratio to a mere 21%, effectively making it impossible for them to control Fuji TV (see **Exhibit 10**).

- **Substantially Increase Annual Dividends**

  Fuji TV and NBS could announce a four- to five-fold increase in annual dividends. As a result of this announcement, the price of Fuji TV and NBS stocks would rise so that acquisitions of these shares through a takeover bid by Livedoor would become more expensive, and thus more difficult.

- **Modification of the Takeover Bid Condition**

  The takeover bid condition could be modified by lowering the number of buyout shares after the takeover bid was initiated. These tactics may, however, be against the Securities Exchange Law,[55] and such an act might confuse investors and affect the stock price.

---

[54] The Ministry of Finance was reorganized on January 6, 2001. The name was changed from "Okurasho" to "Zaimusho" in Japanese, but the English name still remains the same. For more information about the reorganization, see the Ministry's website: http://www.mof.go.jp.

[55] Securities Exchange Law Ordinance, Law No. 321, September 30, 1964, Article 13-1 provides: "No reduction of the price of the purchase, reduction of the number of share certificates to be purchased, curtailment of the period of the purchase, or other changes in the purchase conditions may be made." It is not clear from this article, for example, whether the company could reduce the target number of shares to be purchased, if the company still declares to the market that it will purchase all the shares possible regardless the target numbers. This declaration could be considered that it didn't reduce the number of shares to be purchased, as so specified in the law.

# Planning Department's Response

The planning department's study, after a careful examination of all the relevant data and analyses, was presented to the top management of Fuji TV.[56] It has already studied the corporate value of NBS as a part of its due diligence process in connection with Fuji TV's takeover bid for NBS.[57]

1. The best tactic the target company could follow was to increase its corporate value[58] (see **Exhibit 11**).

**Exhibit 11**　Corporate Value

In the US, corporate value was considered to be the "net present value (NPV) of all the cash flows of the particular corporation which generate in the future and are discounted by the opportunity cost".[59] Because cash flow was difficult to calculate, corporate value was normally regarded in Japan as the "value obtained by subtracting the current cash and deposit from the sum of the aggregate market value of its stocks plus the interest generating liabilities".[60] Because the aggregate market value is the amount the shareholders can collect in the market, the phrase can be substituted for "shareholders' value". Therefore, when corporate managers say "increasing the corporate value as the most efficient countermeasure against a hostile takeover attempt", they normally mean raising the value of the company in the market to make the buyout more difficult.

In Japan, corporate value also includes providing employment opportunities, contribution to the local society and relations with stakeholders.[61] Although these factors seem to be unrelated to shareholders' value, they do not contradict the shareholders' value in the long run. For example, assume a company reduced the number of employees and R&D costs artificially in order to temporarily raise the profit. The stock price may have gone up because of the increase of profit. However, loss of workforce and delay in development of new products would weaken the company's competitive capability, resulting in a reduced cash flow, and causing its stock price to go down, thus reducing the shareholders' value. Japanese managers believe that it is indispensable to obtain the stakeholders' favorable evaluation on a long-term basis and not just focus on the short term pursuit of profit, in order to increase the shareholders' value on a long-term basis.[62]

---

[56] See the press release of February 2, 2005, http://www.c-direct.ne.jp/japanese/uj/pdf/10104676/00030906.pdf.

[57] Ibid.

[58] Ibid.

[59] For the definition, see Bank of Japan's homepage, http://www.boj.or.jp/stat/stat_f.htm.

[60] For the Japanese definition, see http://music.ponycanyon.co.jp/.

[61] Ibid.

[62] Ibid.

2.   The corporate value of NBS as of February 28, 2005 was:

Calculated using the US Method          ¥176,031 million
Calculated using the Japanese Method    ¥193,800 million

The value varied based upon the daily stock price of the company, the weighted average cost of capital and the cash flow growth rate (see **Exhibits 12–14**). At most, the value was ¥200,000 million.

# NBS and Fuji TV Hit Back

Various tactics were used in the battle between Livedoor and Fuji TV for controlling interest in NBS. Alarmed at Livedoor's move, NBS and Fuji TV staged a frantic defense against Livedoor, with NBS deciding to issue a large number of share warrants to Fuji TV on February 23, 2005

**Exhibit 12**   Corporate Value Calculations

Calculation formulas (US vs. Japan) are as follows:

US Method

The corporate value of the company represents the continuing value of the operations. This value, like all asset values according to financial theory (perpetuity), is the present value of all future free cash flows that the company is expected to yield. The value is calculated by the following formula as the present value of a perpetual net operating cash flow (PNOCF) generated in the most current year by the company. The growth rate ($g$) assumed for PNOCF and the company's weighted average cost of capital (WACC) are given.

$$\text{The Corporate Value} = \text{PNOCF} \times (1 + g)/(\text{WACC} - g)\text{[63]}$$

Japanese Method

The Japanese calculate the corporate value based upon the net asset value. The formula is all that the company can get from the market by selling all the shares, minus the borrowed money the company should repay, and plus the cash in hand.[64]

$$\text{The Corporate Value} = (\text{The stock price} \times \text{The number of shares issued})$$
$$- \text{borrowed money} + \text{cash in hand.}$$

---

[63] David K. Eiteman, Arthur I. Stonehill and Michael H. Moffett (2004) *Multinational Business Finance*, 10th Edition, Pearson, pp. 545–546.

[64] Mainichishinbunsha", *Economist* (Japan), April 5, 2005, p. 48.

**Exhibit 13**    Data on Corporate Value for NBS (as of February 28, 2005)

| 1 | No. of Stocks Issued | 32,800,000 shares |
|---|---|---|
| 2 | Stock Price | ¥6,000 per share |
| 3 | Borrowed Funds | ¥22.0 billion |
| 4 | Cash in Hand | ¥1.3 billion |
| 5 | Weighted Average Cost of Capital (WACC) | 10% p.a. |
| 6 | Growth Rate of the Cash Flow | 2% p.a. |

*Source:* NBS, http://www.jolf.co.jp/company/annai.html.

**Exhibit 14**    Past Financial Highlights

Unit: Millions of Yen

| | Fuji TV | | Livedoor | | NBS | |
|---|---|---|---|---|---|---|
| **Year ended March 31** | 2003 | 2004 | 2003 | 2004 | 2003 | 2004 |
| **Operating Revenue** | 429,004 | 455,945 | 10,825 | 30,869 | 33,724 | 30,843 |
| **Ordinary Income** | 37,744 | 45,564 | 1,314 | 5,034 | 895 | 1,100 |
| **Net Income** | 14,816 | 24,714 | 489 | 3,577 | 4,352 | 15,020 |
| **Depreciation** | 10,329 | 11,312 | 372 | 622 | 219 | 206 |
| **Earnings per Share (yen)** | 13,617 | 22,765 | 1,131 | 6.40 | 132 | 458 |
| **Total Assets** | 480,913 | 625,786 | 16,639 | 100,220 | 51,318 | 79,131 |

*Source*: For Fuji TV, see website of Fuji TV (http://www.fujitv.co.jp/jp/). For Livedoor, see website of Livedoor (http://finance.livedoor.com/quote/financial?k=con&c=4753). For NBS, see website of NBS (http://www.jolf.co.jp/company/IR1242/index.html).

(see **Exhibits 1** and **15**). These warrants would give Fuji TV the option to dilute Livedoor's shareholding ratio in NBS if Livedoor acquired a majority ownership in NBS. Livedoor's share, as of February 23, 2005, could drop from more than 40% to 16% once the share warrants were used.

The legality of this issuance by NBS was tested in court, where Livedoor requested a temporary injunction against the issuance.[65] The specific issue was whether NBS's claim, that "becoming a subsidiary of Fuji TV (as opposed to a subsidiary of Livedoor) increased the corporate value of NBS", could be allowed at the expense of the existing

---

[65] "Mainichishinbunsha", *Economist* (Japan), April 1, 2005, p. 9.

**Exhibit 15**   Tactics Fuji TV Undertook

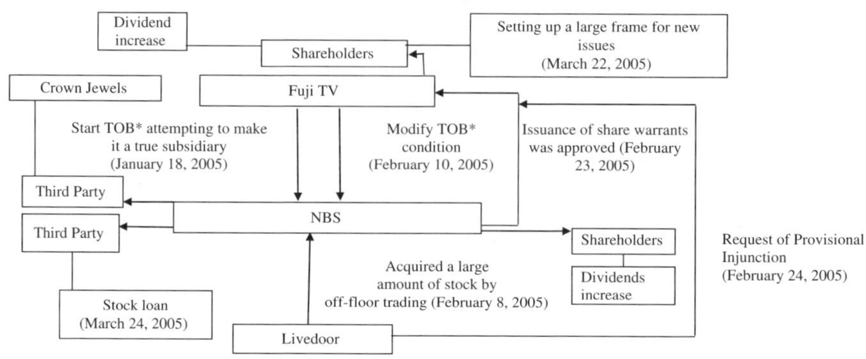


*TOB=Takeover Bid

shareholders.[66] On March 11, 2005, the warrant issue was ruled by the Tokyo District and High Courts to be unjustifiable. After being shelved as a result of the court case, the issuance was cancelled after the ruling.

Furthermore, Fuji TV announced that they would increase dividends five-fold compared to the previous year. This was intended to boost the stock price of Fuji TV to protect it from the Livedoor's attack. Moreover, Fuji TV lowered its takeover bid target parameters during the offer period, whilst maintaining a takeover bid price for NBS significantly below the market price. By these two methods, Fuji TV endeavored to accomplish the takeover bid at the earliest possible time. Fuji TV also tried to pour cold water on Livedoor's enthusiasm by using the crown jewel tactics (e.g., the sale of Pony Canyon, an important subsidiary of NBS, could be executed by NBS by Fuji TV's instructions).[67] Lastly, Fuji TV set up a large "frame for new issues" to prevent Livedoor from taking it over. Meanwhile, NBS took another defensive measure by loaning stocks to a

---

[66] Ibid.

[67] See *Nikkei* (*Japan Economic Journal*), March 16, 2005, http://it.nikkei.co.jp/business/special/fuji_livedoor.aspx?ichiran=True&i=2005031606961ra&page=14. It was reported that Fuji TV was threatening Livedoor by indicating the possibility of the sale of Pony Canyon. For this, Livedoor strongly requested Fuji TV to maintain the corporate value of NBS as it was.

third party (SBI Holdings),[68] a new player who suddenly appeared on the stage as Fuji TV's white knight (see **Exhibit 2**).

## Decision Time

In early April 2005, the top management of Fuji TV had much to contemplate and consider. Never before had they felt such pressure as they did during the weeks since they first heard of Livedoor's acquisition of NBS shares. All tactics suggested by Fuji TV's legal and planning departments were undertaken. Yet, there seemed to be no sign of success.

Fuji TVs top management knew they had to weigh all the facts and possibilities, carefully examine the data and information, and consider all possible angles of the battle. Key points they had to consider with regard to the decision making process were:

1. Were there any other tactics they could undertake to improve the situation? If so, were they legal and effective?
2. How much money would be needed for Fuji TV to buy all the remaining NBS stocks to make NBS a full subsidiary (100%)?
3. What about the possibility of undertaking a Pac Man defense: Fuji TV could turn around and try to take over Livedoor. The top management knew that Livedoor was actively looking for an opportunity to take over Fuji TV. For initiating a Pac Man defense, huge funds would be needed.
4. A friendly settlement.

The top management had to get the consent of a majority of shareholders for all the major tactics it undertook. For this, ample justification had to be prepared. The main bank showed it was concerned about the way the top management would handle the battle. This was very important, especially in Japan, since the main banks not only provided financial support but also provided valuable management advice.

---

[68] SBI Holdings is an investment fund in Japan, whose total assets are $3.755 billion (¥392.70 billion) as of March 31, 2004. For details on SBI Holdings, see http://www.sbigroup.co.jp/.

## What the Bosses Said

Hisashi Hieda, Chairman of the board of Fuji TV said:

> *The technique employed by Livedoor is close to circumvention of the law. An international acceptable rule is needed in Japan as well. No sneak attack should be the rule that every party must abide by. Even in M&A [mergers and acquisitions] activities, adjustments with stakeholders must be honoured in order to aim for a long term growth of a corporation.*

Takafumi Horie, president of Livedoor, countered that:

> *I don't think it is a breach of the rules that Livedoor acquired NBS's shares on off-floor trading. If prior adjustments with employees and shareholders are needed, M&A activities cannot make any advance.*[69]

## Conclusion

The controversial takeover battle between Livedoor and Fuji TV over NBS transfixed Japan for more than three months and ended in an amicable settlement on April 18, 2005, when both companies reached a basic agreement to form a capital and business alliance.[70] In order to make NBS its subsidiary, Fuji TV bought 50% of outstanding NBS shares owned by Livedoor for the sum of ¥147.3 billion. Since Fuji TV's planning department had estimated that the corporate value of NBS was ¥200 billion at most, Fuji TV paid Livedoor 47.3% more for NBS than what they had earlier estimated it was worth. It was said in the market that NBS's shares

---

[69] Hisashi Hieda, chairman of the board of Fuji TV and Takafumi Horie, president of Livedoor, who had been in a battle over NBS's stocks, were invited together to appear on a hearing of the "Corporate Ruling Committee" of the Liberal Democratic Party held on June 16, 2005. The above were their comments made at the committee hearing. For details, see *Nikkei Company News*, June 16, 2005, http://it.nikkei.co.jp/business/special/fuji_livedoor.aspx?ichiran=True&i=2005061603876ra&page=1.

[70] For details, see press release by Nippon Broadcasting on April 18, 2005 on "Notification of Basic Agreement Making Nippon Broadcasting System a Wholly Owned Subsidiary", http://www.jolf.co.jp/company/IR1242/index.html.

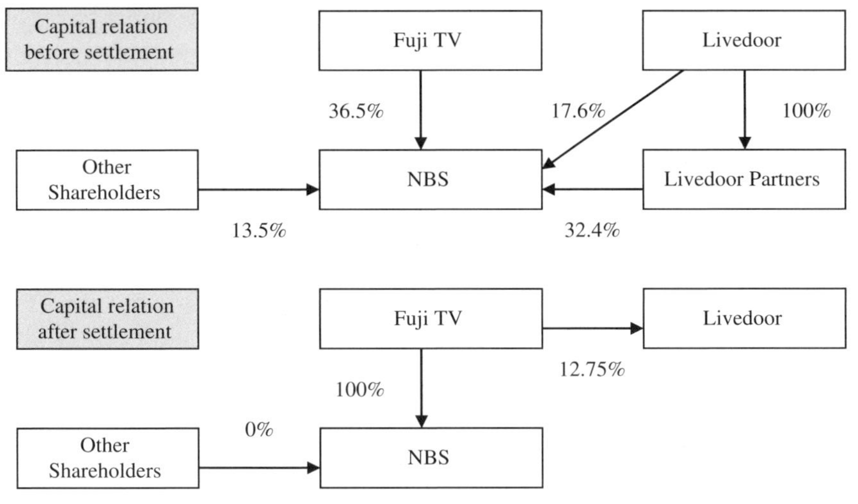
**Exhibit 16**   Structure of Settlement between Fuji TV and Livedoor



were acquired by Livedoor for a total cost of about ¥100 billion and therefore Livedoor turned out to be a winner, earning about ¥47.3 billion when it sold its NBS shares to Fuji TV. In addition, Fuji TV agreed to invest up to 12.75% in Livedoor by accepting its allocation of new shares to a third party (Fuji TV was a third party as it didn't hold any Livedoor shares at the time[71]). In the end, the hostile takeover battle that shook Japan found reconciliation in a monetary exchange (see **Exhibits 16** and **17**).

Many questions, however, still remained: Was Livedoor a mere "greenmailer" and could the top management of Fuji TV justify their additional ¥47.3 billion investment? Who really won one of Japan's most visible takeover battles and what would be the end result were not yet known.

Although the challenge by Fuji TV and Livedoor may have ended more in drama than in substance, it would at least be remembered for its strong impact on Japanese corporate culture and practices and the complacency of the media establishment. In Japan, it was epoch-making that business, academia and politics were involved in the great debate on "who owns a company?" At the time this case unfolded, Japanese companies

---

[71] It was customary in Japan to allocate new shares to a third party when the company tried to create a new major shareholder.

**Exhibit 17**    Stock Price and Turnover of NBS

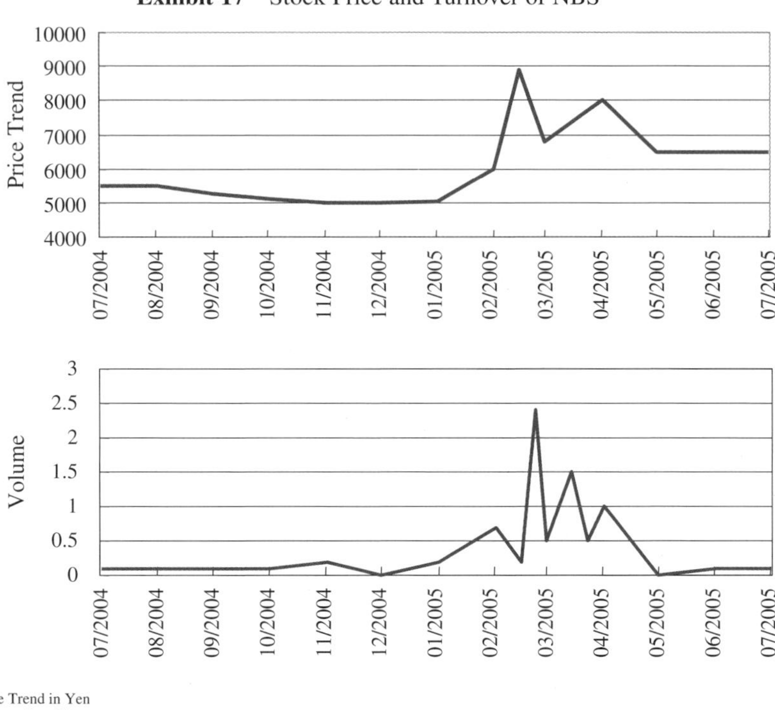

Price Trend in Yen
Volume in million

*Source*: http://quote.yahoo.co.jp/q?s=4660.t&d=b.

disregarded the interests of the shareholders and also other stakeholders, including employees. By the end of 2005, the debate looked likely to go on as Japanese corporate culture and practices, which had hitherto paid insufficient attention to the shareholders' interests, were being brought into question. However, at the same time, the American way of shareholder supremacy also tended to be looked at askance. In the end, the issues addressed in this case will undoubtedly play a role of blowing a fresh wind of the times into Japan's corporate society.

## For Further Discussion

1. Calculate the corporate value of NBS as of February 28, 2005, using both the Japanese and US methods.

2.  The battle between Fuji TV and Livedoor was settled on April 18, 2005, with both parties agreeing on capital and business development cooperation. Why did Fuji TV eventually decide not to engage Livedoor in a hostile takeover battle, rather paying a hefty premium to Livedoor for the NBS shares Livedoor had acquired?
3.  What did Livedoor want to accomplish by attempting a hostile takeover of NBS?
4.  In this battle between the establishment and the young iconoclast, both sides have engaged in actions that are questionable from a governance perspective. List all these issues and comment on them.
5.  What about the rules and regulations on M&As in Japan? Are they well established?

## Appendix  Statistical Observation of Mergers and Acquisitons (M&A) in Japan

The arrival of the age of hostile takeovers in Japan has been anticipated for a long time, although a large amount of friendly M&A activity has already been occurring in Japan. The total number of friendly M&A cases in Japan in 2004 was 2,133 (an increase of 1.1% from the previous year) still maintaining a high level[72] (see **Appendix Exhibit 1**). From the viewpoint of M&A styles, the number of stock buyouts (an increase of 13% from the previous year) in 2004 was 590 cases, the highest ever. In particular, there were 99 cases of stock exchange, which was an increase of 45.6% from the previous year. The number of stock acquisition cases, primarily consisting of cases involving new share issues and cases in which the buyers are buyout funds, increased 9.8% as well. Cases in which business units were the targets of acquisition — a parent company typically converting its business units into separate entities and selling off the shares of these spun-off companies — also contributed to the record increase of stock buyouts.

The number of mergers in 2004 was 350 (a 9.8% drop from the previous year). In addition to mergers among financial companies and

---

[72] For details, see Nomura Securities, http://www.nomura.co.jp/terms/japan/ki/m_and_a.html.

**Appendix Exhibit 1**   M&A in Japan

(Number, %)

| Year | Between Japanese Companies | | Japanese Companies →Foreign Companies | | Foreign Companies →Japanese Companies | | Total | |
|---|---|---|---|---|---|---|---|---|
| | Number | % increase | Number | % increase | Number | % increase | Number | % increase |
| 1986 | 68 | — | 146 | — | 5 | — | 219 | — |
| 1987 | 98 | 44.1 | 199 | 36.3 | 1 | −80.0 | 298 | 36.1 |
| 1988 | 161 | 64.3 | 270 | 35.7 | 7 | 600.0 | 438 | 47.0 |
| 1989 | 172 | 6.8 | 408 | 51.1 | 10 | 42.9 | 590 | 34.7 |
| 1990 | 341 | 98.3 | 450 | 10.3 | 9 | −10.0 | 800 | 35.6 |
| 1991 | 385 | 12.9 | 246 | −45.3 | 12 | 20.0 | 64 | −19.7 |
| 1992 | 417 | 8.3 | 174 | −29.3 | 33 | 175.0 | 624 | −3.0 |
| 1993 | 486 | 16.5 | 112 | −35.6 | 36 | 9.1 | 634 | 1.6 |
| 1994 | 421 | −13.4 | 159 | 42.0 | 38 | 5.6 | 618 | −2.5 |
| 1995 | 381 | −9.5 | 179 | 12.6 | 42 | 10.5 | 602 | −2.6 |
| 1996 | 433 | 13.6 | 203 | 13.4 | 38 | −9.5 | 674 | 12.0 |
| 1997 | 567 | 30.9 | 182 | −10.3 | 60 | 57.9 | 809 | 20.0 |
| 1998 | 703 | 24.0 | 192 | 5.5 | 97 | 61.7 | 992 | 22.6 |
| 1999 | 1,057 | 50.4 | 194 | 1.0 | 115 | 18.6 | 1,366 | 37.7 |
| 2000 | 1,436 | 35.9 | 298 | 53.6 | 146 | 27.0 | 1,880 | 37.6 |
| 2001 | 1,545 | 7.6 | 239 | −19.8 | 125 | −14.4 | 1,909 | 1.5 |
| 2002 | 1,993 | 29.0 | 260 | 8.8 | 121 | −3.2 | 2,374 | 24.4 |
| 2003 | 1,799 | −9.7 | 209 | −19.6 | 102 | −15.7 | 2,110 | −11.1 |
| 2004 | 1,752 | −2.6 | 286 | 36.8 | 95 | −6.9 | 2,133 | 1.1 |

*Source*: Nomura Securities Co., "Trend of Japanese M&A", p. 4, http://www.nomuraholdings.com/jp/press/securities/050111/050111_a.pdf.

pharmaceutical companies, mergers among subsidiaries due to reorganization of a group were also notable. There were 337 cases of capital participations (a 6.3% increase from the previous year). A rise in cases involving capital increase, particularly in information/telecommunication and fund businesses, was observed. The following is an analysis of these trends for the year 2004, classifying them according to whether participants were Japanese or foreign companies (see also **Appendix Exhibit 2**).

(1) IN–IN (M&A between Japanese companies) amounted to 1,752 cases (2.6% drop from the previous year) with a marked trend for large scale M&A for enhancement of existing businesses and aggressive business expansion plans.

(2) IN–OUT (M&A of offshore companies by Japanese companies) amounted to 286 cases (36.8% increase from the previous year) and it was close to a high of 298 cases reached in 2000. In terms of geographical areas, 126 cases of M&A were recorded for the Asia–Oceania region, in particular, China. Cases involving operations located in North America increased substantially to 91 cases (a 35.8% increase from the previous year), and the same in Europe also increased to 64 cases (a 12.3% increase from the previous year). In terms of types of businesses, there is no specific field more frequently represented than others, although there is an increasing trend in such fields as electrical machinery, chemical, financial and pharmaceutical industries in Asian countries, especially, China, as well as in US corporations' participations in buyouts and in supplying capital.

(3) OUT–IN (M&A of Japanese companies by offshore companies) amounted to only 95 cases (see **Appendix Exhibit 2**). M&A by US companies reached 47 cases (20.5% increase from the previous year) and the increase was mainly due to acquisitions of Japanese companies by buyout funds, particularly acquisitions of fixed assets such as golf courses. In most other areas, the tendency was down with 29 cases by Asia–Oceania-based companies (a 2 case drop from the previous year), 19 M&A cases by European companies (an 11 case drop from the previous year), and 0 cases by companies based in

**Appendix Exhibit 2**   Trend of M&A of Japanese Companies by Foreign Companies

(Unit: Number)

| Year | Area | | | | Methods | | | | Total | |
|---|---|---|---|---|---|---|---|---|---|---|
| | North America | Asia Oceania | Europe | Others | Consolidation | Stock Purchase | Asset Purchase | Capital Participation | | % increase |
| 1993 | 23 | 6 | 7 | 0 | 1 | 18 | 4 | 13 | 36 | — |
| 1994 | 22 | 4 | 12 | 0 | 1 | 21 | 4 | 12 | 38 | 5.6 |
| 1995 | 19 | 11 | 12 | 0 | 1 | 20 | 7 | 14 | 42 | 10.5 |
| 1996 | 15 | 11 | 11 | 1 | 0 | 20 | 7 | 11 | 38 | −9.5 |
| 1997 | 35 | 14 | 11 | 0 | 0 | 28 | 12 | 20 | 60 | 57.9 |
| 1998 | 54 | 16 | 22 | 5 | 4 | 52 | 22 | 19 | 97 | 61.7 |
| 1999 | 60 | 11 | 41 | 3 | 2 | 52 | 24 | 37 | 115 | 18.6 |
| 2000 | 81 | 24 | 40 | 1 | 3 | 58 | 35 | 50 | 146 | 27.0 |
| 2001 | 54 | 22 | 49 | 0 | 2 | 53 | 30 | 40 | 125 | −14.4 |
| 2002 | 59 | 25 | 35 | 2 | 2 | 45 | 40 | 34 | 121 | −3.2 |
| 2003 | 39 | 27 | 30 | 6 | 3 | 39 | 32 | 28 | 102 | −15.7 |
| 2004 | 47 | 29 | 19 | 0 | 2 | 35 | 34 | 24 | | |

*Source*: Nomura Securities Co., "Trend of Japanese M&A", p. 4, http://www.nomuraholdings.com/jp/press/securities/050111/050111_a.pdf.

other areas (a 6 case drop from the previous year). In terms of styles, asset acquisition only increased to 34 cases (a 2 case increase from the previous year), while stock purchase fell to 35 cases (a 4 case drop from the previous year) and capital participation fell to 24 cases (a 4 case drop from the previous year).

# 6

# Livedoor: The Rise and Fall
# of a Market Maverick[1]

Livedoor Co. (Livedoor) was founded in 1996 by Takafumi Horie (Horie). A high-profile 33-year-old leader in the internet business, Horie had been leading his e-baby through a series of mergers and acquisitions (M&As) to expand its portfolio of businesses and secure growth. His strategies, which were based on US-style M&As unconventional in Japan, shifted into a higher gear in 2005 when he launched a hostile battle against Fuji Television Network Inc. (Fuji TV). Horie tried to take over control for Nippon Broadcasting System Inc. (NBS), a radio broadcaster in the media group led by Fuji TV.[2] The contest between Fuji TV and Livedoor to take control of NBS was headline-grabbing, and it heralded a surging wave of takeover bids and brought some serious shortcomings in the country's M&A rules to public notice.

In the months that followed the takeover, Horie became a business celebrity and was viewed as the incarnation of a growing new business culture in Japan (see **Exhibit 1**). However, his rise to the top came to an abrupt end when, on January 16, 2006, Tokyo district's public prosecutors and the Securities and Exchange Surveillance Commission (SESC)[3] raided Livedoor's headquarters and its president's private residence, i.e., Horie's home. They suspected that the internet services company had violated the Securities and Exchange Law when it acquired the publisher MoneyLife in October 2004 (see **Exhibits 1** and **2**). When news of the

---

[1] For maximum benefit from this case, it is recommended that students read Case 5 "Hostile Takeover in Japan: Fuji TV vs. Livedoor for NBS" in this book. The current case can be used on its own or in conjunction with the Fuji case.

[2] See Case 5 in this book.

[3] The Securities and Exchange Surveillance Commission is Japan's securities watchdog. See its website for details: http://www.fsa.go.jp/sesc/english/index.htm.

**Exhibit 1**   Chronology of Events

| | |
|---|---|
| April 1996 | Takafumi Horie set up Livin' on the EDGE, a website design firm, in Tokyo. |
| April 2000 | Livin' on the EDGE listed its shares on the Tokyo Stock Exchange's Mothers market for start-ups. |
| November 2002 | Livin' on the EDGE took over operations of internet service provider Livedoor. |
| April 2003 | Livin' on the EDGE changed its name to Edge. |
| February 2004 | Edge changed its name to Livedoor. |
| March 2004 | Livedoor bought a majority stake in Nippon Global Securities through a tender-offer bid. |
| June 2004 | Livedoor sought to purchase Kintetsu Buffaloes, a professional baseball team, but was rejected. |
| July 2004 | Nippon Global Securities changed its name to Livedoor Securities. |
| February 2005 | Livedoor acquired 35% stake in Nippon Broadcasting System to become its biggest shareholder. |
| March 2005 | Tokyo District Court barred NBS from issuing share warrants to Fuji TV as a way of defending itself against Livedoor's hostile takeover bid. Livedoor boosted its NBS stake to more than 50%. Tokyo High Court upheld ruling in favor of Livedoor. |
| April 2005 | Livedoor, Fuji TV ended battle for control of NBS. |
| September 2005 | Horie run in Hiroshima's No. 6 district in the general elections but failed to win seat. |
| January 16, 2006 | Prosecutors searched Livedoor's headquarters and Horie's home. |

*Source: Nihon Keizai Shinbun*, January 17, 2006, http://markets.nikkei.co.jp/special/sp020.cfm?id=d1d1609216&date=20060116.

raids broke, Livedoor's high stock price immediately plummeted as panicked investors started dumping their stock, with trade reaching volumes high enough to overload the Tokyo Stock Exchange's computer system. The probe would put his internet empire under rigorous legal scrutiny, and could reveal some of the hidden, possibly ugly, aspects of the phenomenon that had kept the business community buzzing for the past two years.[4]

---

[4]*Nihon Keizai Shinbun*, January 16, 2006, http://markets.nikkei.co.jp/special/sp020.cfm?id=d1c1600m16&date=20060116.

**Exhibit 2**  Securities Fraud

Fraud is commonly understood as dishonesty calculated for advantage. A person who is dishonest may be called a fraud. In the US legal system, fraud is a specific offense with certain features. Securities Fraud is defined to be a false representation of a matter of fact — whether by words or by conduct, by false or misleading allegations, or by concealment of what should have been disclosed — that deceives and is intended to deceive another so that the individual will act upon it to her or his legal injury.

Civil securities fraud, also known as investment fraud, is a practice where investors are deceived and manipulated, resulting in theft. This is a form of white-collar crime which has been on the rise as the internet and the world wide web have brought white-collar criminals and their victims closer together, resulting in an upsurge in global economic crime. The trading volume in the US and Japanese securities markets has grown dramatically over the last decade. This growth has led to an increase in fraud and misconduct by investors, executives, shareholders and other market participants. Fraudulent schemes perpetrated in the securities markets can ultimately have a devastating impact on the viability and operation of these markets.

Securities fraud is becoming more complex as the industry develops more complicated investment vehicles in an effort to obtain higher rates of return. In addition, white-collar criminals are expanding the scope of their fraud and are looking outside the US for new markets, new investors to defraud and banking secrecy havens to hide their unjust enrichment. The securities industry is one of the most critical and influential industries in the US and Japan, and is regulated by the Securities and Exchange Commission in the US, and the Ministry of Finance in Japan.

These financial markets provide the opportunity for wealth to be obtained and the opportunity for white-collar criminals to take advantage of unwary investors. Recovering assets from the proceeds of securities fraud is an expensive undertaking.

Potential victims of this crime are those who have invested money in the company; typically people aged 50 years or older are the most victimized by securities fraud. Potential perpetrators of securities frauds are any high-ranking official within the company who might have access to the financial reports that can be manipulated.

Recent examples of securities frauds in the US are the Enron and WorldCom scandals. Both companies were guilty of theft from investors and defrauding the federal government with fraudulent tax reports. The elements of the crime are theft of capital from investors and defrauding the accounting companies about the financial reports.

*Source:* Tokyo Stock Exchange, http://www.tse.or.jp/beginner/online/online08.html.

# Livedoor: The Company

Although Livedoor was categorized as an internet company, the majority of its earnings were generated by its financial businesses. The financial segment accounted for about 60% of sales and more than half of the operating profit.[5] The company was run by Takafumi Horie, its founder, and although his high profile gave the impression that Livedoor was a one-man operation, the firm's directors were heavily involved in corporate management decisions. Directors Ryoji Miyauchi and Fumito Kumagai — an accountant and a former brokerage employee, respectively — played major roles in important business decisions such as acquisitions.

## President Horie, Who?

At 33, Horie, the CEO and founder of Livedoor, was at the center of a storm. The gleeful atmosphere among the staid suits of Tokyo came from what Horie had come to represent. Over the past few years, he had become the chieftain of a tribe of internet entrepreneurs who hung out in the shiningly chic Roppongi Hills complex. To this Hills Tribe, the future of business was the internet, in sharp contrast to the long-established Square Tribe of neckties and suits, members of which still considered manufacturing the only respectable industry. To the Squares, Horie and the Hills were playing a speculative "money game" with no tangible products.

Except for Horie, the Tokyo University dropout, who started what became Livedoor in 1997, was the author of no fewer than 17 books celebrating his moneymaking, cash-grabbing ethos, and had titles like *Earning Money is Everything: From Zero to 10 Billion Yen My Way.* He appeared to be living proof of his boast. In the past five fiscal years Livedoor had acquired 27 companies, increasing revenue 22-fold to nearly ¥85 billion. He had also been an aggressive financial democrat, constantly splitting his stock so that younger and less well-off Japanese could afford to become shareholders. A single share of Livedoor bought in early 2003 had multiplied into 10,000 shares today. The stock became hugely popular — even schoolchildren became stockholders. And since Horie retained a 17% stake in his company, the cash influx from the horde of new but small investors made him even richer on paper.

---

[5] *Nihon Keizai Shinbun*, January 16, 2006, http://markets.nikkei.co.jp/special/sp020.cfm?id=e003y00516&date=20060116.

In the self-deprecating world of Japanese business, Horie was a loud sign that screamed "love me, love my money". The chubby, self-described geek eschewed business suits for designer t-shirts and jeans worth US$400. He drove a Ferrari and dated models and actresses. One day he bought a racehorse; on another he announced a private space tourism venture; on another he said he was recording a music album. "I don't think I'm going to die," he wrote in one of his books. "At the current rate of scientific research, isn't it possible that they'll come up with a way to do away with death, if you pump enough money into it?" He had many enemies and he loved identifying them in public. "All evils come from aged business managers," he often declared. And the more they called his deal-making style into question, the more daring he made them, straying into territory that was exclusive to the big boys, like trying to buy a professional baseball team, thus invoking the ire of Japan's powerful media conglomerates, who owned some of the richest teams; and politics — running, unsuccessfully, against a machine politician but scoring new points with his young and fervent stockholder fan base.

The following was a list of remarks by Horie about money, corporate acquisitions and other topics since his emergence in 2004 as what many saw as a young, confident mold-breaker in Japan's hidebound corporate world.

- "Money can completely change one's personality, and the moment when the change takes place is interesting ... What can move human beings is money." (From his book *One Who Earns Wins* in 2004.)[6]
- "I can buy any company if I borrow money." (On a TV program in March 2005.)[7]
- "I've been saying, '(Livedoor) is sure to overtake Yahoo.' Now I think we can say we topped Yahoo in terms of public awareness." (In a speech at Tokyo University in April 2005.)[8]

---

[6] *Nihon Keizai Shinbun*, January 22, 2006, http://markets.nikkei.co.jp/special/sp020.cfm?id=dxka034122&date=20060122, from Horie, Takafumi (2004) *Kaseguga Kachi* (*Money is almighty*), Kobunsha Publishing Company.

[7] *Nihon Keizai Shinbun*, January 22, 2006, http://markets.nikkei.co.jp/special/sp020.cfm?id=dxka034122&date=20060122.

[8] Ibid.

- "Becoming a leader is the easiest way if I am to change Japan." (At a press conference at the Foreign Correspondents' Club of Japan in September 2005.)[9]
- "Why am I running in an election? Because there is a chance I could become a prime minister." (In September 2005 after filing his candidacy for a seat for the House of Representative.)[10]
- "In the next House of Representatives election, I will return to this Hiroshima No. 6 constituency." (In September 2005, after he failed to win a lower house seat.)[11]

## Livedoor Engineered Higher Stock Prices

Over a period of about a year, starting in August 2003, Livedoor essentially split each of its stocks into 10,000 shares through multiple stock splits. While a stock split was legal and did not raise corporate value in itself, a large stock split often caused a temporary rise in stock price because the stock split procedures led to a shortage in stocks (see **Exhibit 3**). Livedoor's market capitalization, which was about ¥100 billion in November 2003, surpassed ¥900 billion in January 2004, growing nine-fold. Behind the steep jump in the corporate value were a series of highly tactical moves intended to boost the stock prices of the parent and group firms. Livedoor's strategy focused on attracting speculative investment from individual investors, and largely ignoring institutional players. A 100-for-1 stock split in December 2003 sent the price of Livedoor shares soaring to the ¥18,000 mark at once, although the ex-split price should theoretically have been just ¥2,220.

Since then, Livedoor began gaining wider recognition among retail investors hunting for issues that might let them make quick capital gains. To cash in on the trend, Horie began taking actions to grab the spotlight in an apparent effort to lure more individual investors. The rapid increase in individual investors using online trading in recent years also served as a tail wind for the firm.

---

[9] Ibid.

[10] Ibid.

[11] Ibid.

**Exhibit 3**   Stock Splits

Stock-splits simply involve a company altering the number of its outstanding shares and proportionally adjusting the share price to compensate. This in no way affects the intrinsic value of shares that are split. When a company declares a stock-split, the price of the stock will decrease, but the number of shares will increase proportionately. For example, if you own 100 shares of a company that trades at $100 a share and it declares a 2-for-1 stock split, you will own a total of 200 shares at $50 a share after the split. A stock split has no effect on the value of what shareholders own. If the company pays a dividend, your dividends paid per share will also fall proportionately.

Companies often split their stock when they believe the price of their stock exceeds the amount smaller individual investors would be willing to pay for the stock. By reducing the price of the stock, companies try to make their stock more affordable to these investors. Although most stock-splits are done as 2-for-1, companies can split their stock in any number of ways, including 3-for-1, 3-for-2, and so forth.

Stock-splits work differently in Japan. The new shares are not distributed for several months. During this time, investors can buy or sell their "old" shares, but are unable to sell the shares they are about to receive. Investors will hold on to the old share during the split but will not receive the new share for several months, at which point they can sell it. This system is the result of ownership being tracked on paper rather than electronically. It takes time to print out new share certificates. Because investors do not have access to the new shares, a significant fraction of the company cannot trade. When investors cannot sell, prices tend to rise.

*Source:* The website of Tokyo Securities Exchange: http://www.tse.or.Jp/Glossary/Gloss_K/Bunkatu. Html.

Armed with higher stock prices that were inflated through stock splits, Livedoor went on an acquisition spree starting in 2004, taking over about 20 firms with cash and through stock-swap arrangements. It spent more than ¥50 billion to acquire firms, including a brokerage, an accounting software developer and the predecessor to Livedoor Marketing.[12] It effectively expanded the user base of its services by covering a broader area through takeovers — from finance to retail operations — and putting itself in the headlines. However, some criticized the firm for practices that seemed to make use of loopholes in regulations, such as its use of stock splits to raise stock prices and the way it acquired shares in the NBS.[13]

---

[12] *Nihon Keizai Shinbun*, January 18, 2006, http://markets.nikkei.co.jp/special/sp020.cfm?id=d1g1803z18&date=20060118.

[13] Ibid.

# Tokyo Prosecutors Raid Livedoor's Headquarters

On January 16, 2006, Tokyo district's public prosecutors and the SESC[14] raided Livedoor's headquarters and its president's private residence, i.e., Horie's home. The prosecutor's office had been examining the process under which Livedoor Marketing crafted its acquisition strategy, and how it issued instructions within the company. It was questioning Horie and other senior executives about their management decisions.[15]

They suspected that the internet services company had violated the Securities and Exchange Law when their subsidiary, Livedoor Marketing, acquired a privately held publishing company called MoneyLife back in October 2004.[16] Livedoor Marketing was also under suspicion for leaking information with regard to strong third-quarter sales and pre-tax profit figures the company released in November 2004.[17]

## *Under Investigation: The Takeover of MoneyLife*

Livedoor had continued to grow by leveraging its rising stock price to take over other companies, but it was now being accused of manipulating the stock price of a subsidiary in order to make a profit on the sale of the subsidiary's shares (see **Exhibit 4**).[18]

One of the focal points of the investigation was the way that Livedoor Marketing[19] — itself a subsidiary of Livedoor Ltd. — turned publisher MoneyLife into a subsidiary in a deal that was announced on October 25, 2004. In this stock-swap deal, Livedoor Marketing was to exchange one

---

[14] The Securities and Exchange Surveillance Commission is Japan's securities watchdog. See its website for details: http://www.fsa.go.jp/sesc/english/index.htm.

[15] *Nihon Keizai Shinbun*, January 16, 2006,, http://markets.nikkei.co.jp/special/sp020.cfm?id=d3l1606816&date=20060116.

[16] Ibid.

[17] Ibid.

[18] *Nihon Keizai Shinbun*, January 18, 2006, http://markets.nikkei.co.jp/special/sp020.cfm?id=d1g1803z18&date=20060118.

[19] Livedoor Marketing Co. was a Livedoor subsidiary listed on the Tokyo Stock Exchange's Mothers market and was previously named Value Click Japan Inc. See *Nihon Keizai Shinbun*, January 18, 2006, http://markets.nikkei.co.jp/special/sp020.cfm?id=d1g1803z18&date.

**Exhibit 4**   Livedoor's Stock Price

*Source: Nihon Keizai Shinbun*, http://company.nikkei.co.jp/index.cfm?scode=4753.

of its shares for each share in MoneyLife. However, unbeknownst to the market, all of MoneyLife's shares were already held by an investment partnership fund, which was essentially controlled by Livedoor. So MoneyLife had, in fact, already been acquired when the fund bought the shares in exchange for cash from former shareholders.[20]

Prosecutors were believed to suspect that the fund arranged Livedoor Marketing's acquisition of MoneyLife through a stock swap in order to enjoy profits from the sale of Livedoor Marketing shares.[21] On the day before the takeover plan was announced, Livedoor Marketing's shares closed at ¥1750.[22, 23] The fund was to receive 160,000 shares, which meant that at this price, the takeover would have cost slightly more than ¥280 million. On November 8, 2004, Livedoor Marketing's stock price jumped as soon as the firm announced that it would conduct a 100-for-1 stock

---

[20] *Nihon Keizai Shinbun*, January 18, 2006, http://markets.nikkei.co.jp/special/sp020.cfm?id=d1g1803z18&date=20060118.

[21] Ibid.

[22] US$1= ¥105.57 on November 8, 2004.

[23] Share prices and amounts in this chapter are based on the total number of outstanding shares in January 2006.

split. By December 16, 2004, the firm's stock had skyrocketed to ¥80,500, more than 45 times the stock price before the announcement of the MoneyLife takeover.[24]

The stock-split was executed on January 20, 2005, the same day that the takeover was completed, and Livedoor Marketing's stock closed at ¥27,900. Although it is unclear when the fund sold its Livedoor Marketing shares, the fact is that if it had sold all the shares that it acquired through the stock-swap at this point, it would have raked in almost ¥4.5 billion. This type of move, in which stock prices rose because of stock-splits, and then this higher stock price was leveraged to take over other firms through stock-swaps, had been the standard acquisition strategy for parent firm Livedoor.[25]

## Testing the Market System: Ignoring Unwritten Rules and Etiquette

Livedoor, led by Horie, had high visibility in the securities markets because of such deals as its acquisition of NBS shares through off-hour transactions instead of through a tender offer bid.[26] The company's issuance of ¥80 billion in moving-strike convertible bonds,[27] and the group's 100-for-1 stock-splits[28] had also grabbed the market's attention. Livedoor had been a Japanese pioneer in large stock-splits, with Horie sounding like a modern day alchemist when he said: "The 1:100 stock-split will undoubtedly come into fashion."[29]

These transactions that ignored standard practice raised eyebrows and irked financial authorities, which were powerless to take action because the moves themselves did not violate the Securities and Exchange Law. "We didn't approve of these transactions, but there was nothing we could

---

[24] *Nihon Keizai Shinbun*, January 18, 2006, http://markets.nikkei.co.jp/special/sp020.cfm?id=d1g1803z18&date=20060118.

[25] Ibid.

[26] See Case 5 in this book.

[27] Ibid.

[28] Ibid.

[29] *Nihon Keizai Shinbun*, January 16, 2006, http://markets.nikkei.co.jp/special/sp020.cfm?id=d1d1609216&date=20060116.

do," a senior official from the Financial Services Agency noted.[30] With revisions on the Securities and Exchange Law on the back burner, the Tokyo Stock Exchange took steps that included putting in place rules concerning large-scale stock-splits.[31]

An official at a European brokerage asserted that traditionally, market participants had self-regulated their actions even when following the rules.[32] "This way, a certain level of order and discipline is maintained by all," said the official.[33]

## Related Developments

1. Fuji TV would likely reconsider its business cooperation with Livedoor if alleged violations of the securities law by an affiliate of Livedoor proved to be true. "We can only monitor how the investigation unfolds, but we will need to review our business co-operation if the Livedoor group is found to have violated the law systemically," a Fuji TV executive said on January 16, 2006.[34] In February 2005, Fuji TV and Livedoor vied for control of NBS, a core member of the Fujisankei Communications Group. In a deal reached in April 2005, Fuji TV agreed to acquire a 12.75% stake in Livedoor for ¥44 billion, thus making Fuji TV the second-largest shareholder in Livedoor, behind Horie. As part of a business tie-up, the two firms also agreed to work together to bolster Livedoor's public wireless LAN business.[35] Despite pledging not to sell its Livedoor shares until September 30, 2007, Fuji TV would likely ask for the agreement to be revised if the Livedoor group was found to have violated the law.[36]

---

[30] Ibid.

[31] *Nihon Keizai Shinbun*, January 17, 2006, http://it.nikkei.co.jp/business/special/fuji_livedoor.aspx?ichiran=True&i=2006011611034ra&page=4.

[32] See Case 5 in this book.

[33] Ibid.

[34] *Nihon Keizai Shinbun*, January 17, 2006, http://markets.nikkei.co.jp/special/sp020.cfm?id=e003y17818&date=20060118.

[35] See Case 5 in this book.

[36] *Nihon Keizai Shinbun*, January 17, 2006, http://markets.nikkei.co.jp/special/sp020.cfm?id=d311701617&date=20060117.

2. The Japan Business Federation, or Nippon Keidanren, might act against Livedoor if the firm was found to have engaged in illicit activity, a senior official at the nation's most powerful business lobby said on January 16, 2006.[37] Nippon Keidanren might impose such sanctions as a suspension of Livedoor's activity with the lobby. When Livedoor became a Nippon Keidanren member in the December 2005, Okuda, chairman of Keidanren, expressed hope that its joining would "provide a good opportunity for the company to learn about corporate ethics. Horie's past saying that one can do anything as long as they have money was the worst type of thinking in Japan."[38]

3. Livedoor and Livedoor Marketing were both listed on the Mothers market of the Tokyo Stock Exchange for start-ups. The Tokyo Stock Exchange demanded that both firms disclose information to investors. If the case against them grew, the exchange would consider placing Livedoor and Livedoor Marketing stock on the supervision post. It would even consider delisting them if it was convinced that they had acted maliciously to deceive investors.[39]

4. Horie ran in the general election held in September 2005 after he accepted the Prime Minister Junichiro Koizumi's request to run against a Liberal Democratic Party (LDP) rebel. But Horie declined and ran in the 6th District of Hiroshima against Shizuka Kamei, who was then spearheading the movement against Koizumi's controversial plans to privatize the postal services. LDP lawmakers showed their support for Horie by giving speeches on his behalf, but Horie failed to win a seat. When the news about Livedoor's possibly illegal activities broke, LDP lawmakers scrambled to respond to prosecutors' raid on Livedoor's offices. The latest events involving Livedoor "are very unfortunate and regrettable", said a senior LDP official.[40]

---

[37] *Nihon Keizai Shinbun*, January 18, 2006, http://markets.nikkei.co.jp/special/sp020.cfm?id=dxkd028218&date=20060118.

[38] Ibid.

[39] *Nihon Keizai Shinbun*, January 18, 2006, http://markets.nikkei.co.jp/special/sp020.cfm?id=d2d1801r18&date=20060118.

[40] *Nihon Keizai Shinbun*, January 16, 2006, http://markets.nikkei.co.jp/special/sp020.cfm?id=d3l1605x16&date=20060116.

# Growth Strategy Threatened

Livedoor group's stocks nosedived on January 17, 2006, with shares in all seven firms[41] going limit-down[42] and reducing the group's market capitalization by about ¥150 billion[43] in a development sure to impact its growth strategy. Livedoor had leveraged its high stock price to grow rapidly through acquisitions. Its market capitalization had been about ¥5 billion when was first listed, but had ballooned to ¥700 billion right before the prosecutors raided its headquarters. High stock prices and a large market capitalization were seen as signs of credibility, enabling businesses to procure funds more easily from the capital markets.[44]

Livedoor's cash revenue from its core operations for the year ended September 30, 2005 was just over ¥2 billion. But it had spent ¥66.4 billion on investments, including share purchases. These activities were funded by the more than ¥100 billion in cash that the company raised by issuing moving-strike convertible bonds, among other measures. Through stock-swaps, Livedoor's ability to take over others rose, along with its market capitalization. An acquisition-driven earnings growth sent its stock price even higher (see **Exhibit 4**).[45]

---

[41] They are; Cecile, MEX, LD Auto, TLinux, Dynacity, Medix Exchange and Livedoor Auto. For these companies, see the homepage of Livedoor, http://blog.livedoor.jp/ldmatome/archives/50088521.html.

[42] Regulatory bodies are generally wary when stock prices rise or fall too fast. For this, a circuit breaker is a tool to control trading of shares by setting a limit on price movement. In order to give time to the markets to recover their poise, stocks that rise or fall above a certain percentage are stopped from trading. The Tokyo Stock Exchange has upper and two lower limits according to the price levels of the stocks. For example, 10% limit a day is set for the stock of which market price is ¥1,000 a share. The circuit is thus the band between the lower and upper limits. Circuits are built to check the volatility in the market, to arrest panic and to keep the market under some control. For details, see the website of TSE, http://search.jp.aol.com/advhandler.adp.

[43] US$1 = ¥115.83 on January 17, 2006.

[44] *Nihon Keizai Shinbun*, January 18, 2006, http://markets.nikkei.co.jp/special/sp020.cfm?id=d1d1907b19&date=20060119.

[45] Ibid.

## The New Management

At an emergency press conference held at 7 a.m. on January 17, 2006, after prosecutors ended their all-night raid on Livedoor, Horie said the firm would make public the results of an internal probe as soon as possible. Moreover, according to Horie, the raids would not have a negative impact on Livedoor's operations.[46] He said: "We will continue normal operations. There is no particular problem with our business, we want to make business expansion efforts."[47]

However, Tokyo district's prosecutor's office arrested Horie and three other executives on January 23, 2006 for allegedly violating the Securities and Exchange Law by spreading false information to deceive investors.[48] Following this arrest, Horie stepped down as president of Livedoor on January 24, 2006.

The company subsequently appointed its 60-year-old senior vice-president Kozo Hiramatsu as president. Hiramatsu was an experienced manager and well respected.[49] A former Sony Corp. employee, he had worked in several foreign firms, including AOL Japan Inc., before joining the firm that later became Yayoi Co., a business software firm. He was president of this firm when it became part of the Livedoor group in 2004.[50]

Hiramatsu denied any involvement in the alleged illegal acts of Livedoor's executives, telling reporters that he did not work at the company at the time the deals in question were made.[51] Livedoor said that it established a management committee headed by Hiramatsu. The committee was to manage day-to-day operations while the board of directors supervised the executives.[52]

---

[46] *Nihon Keizai Shinbun*, January 17, 2006, http://markets.nikkei.co.jp/special/sp020.cfm?id=dxkc002417&date=20060117.

[47] Ibid.

[48] *Nihon Keizai Shinbun*, January 23, 2006, http://markets.nikkei.co.jp/special/sp020.cfm?id=d1g2302023&date=20060123.

[49] *Nihon Keizai Shinbun*, January 24, 2006, http://it.nikkei.co.jp/business/special/fuji_livedoor.aspx?ichiran=True&i=2006012406162ra&page=5.

[50] *Nihon Keizai Shinbun*, January 24, 2006, http://markets.nikkei.co.jp/special/sp020.cfm?id=d2e2401124&date=20060124.

[51] Ibid.

[52] Ibid.

# More Problems: Tokyo Stock Exchange Delists Livedoor

The Tokyo Stock Exchange decided on March 13, 2006 to delist Livedoor, expelling the business community's new bête noire from the trading floor.[53] The decision came after the SESC filed a criminal complaint against Livedoor and its president, Takafumi Horie, over accounts falsification. Livedoor's stock was removed from the exchange's Mothers market for start-ups on April 14, 2006 a move that would naturally hurt the company's shareholders, who had already been battered by the stock's crash. Livedoor's downfall had far-reaching repercussions on the fastest-growing segment of the investor community: individual investors. Because it was once the darling of the stock market, the company had an exceptionally broad shareholder base. The number of Livedoor shareholders totaled 220,000 at the end of September 2005, outstripping the figures for such corporate giants as NEC Corp. and Fujitsu Ltd. of Japan. Some Livedoor shareholders were contemplating damages suits against the company.[54]

# A Company in Crisis: What to Do?

Since revelations in mid-January 2006 that the company was being investigated for violations of the securities law, Livedoor officials had been busy cooperating with authorities to uncover the alleged manipulation of financial statements, crafting safeguards to prevent a recurrence, apologizing to business associates, and negotiating with affiliates seeking to leave the group. Plans to rehabilitate business operations had been neglected as a result.

Amid such concerns, the company now also faced the prospect of being cut off from the capital markets that had fuelled its financing operations.

Livedoor's stock closed at ¥66 on March 13, 2006; the group's collective market capitalization had plunged to ¥192 billion, 19% of the level

---

[53] *Nihon Keizai Shinbun*, March 13, 2006, http://it.nikkei.co.jp/business/special/fuji_livedoor.aspx?ichiran=True&i=2006031309537ra&page=1.
[54] Ibid.

prior to the scandal. Advertising income from Livedoor's web portal site was down 70% since the scandal came to light. And the company's financing segment, including the mainline investment operations, had not generated new business.[55]

As part of the efforts to bolster creditworthiness and to turn around its fortunes, Livedoor could attempt to rebuild with the backing of an information technology firm or investment fund, to seek a sponsor after conducting a management buyout, or to operate on a reduced scale by letting go of group firms. Where should the firm focus efforts?

## Conclusion

With its business being affected by the arrests of its top executives, such as clients cancelling internet advertising deals, Livedoor's new management faced the task of quickly restoring normal operations and reviving the company. How could they do that?

The delisting in particular would hamper rebuilding efforts of the new management. The embattled internet services firm's task of restoring credibility and regaining its business footing had become even more daunting. While maintaining its image as an internet company, Livedoor generated growth through its investment activities. As such, the lack of access to the capital markets would hurt it more than it would a conventional publicly traded firm.

If its market capitalization continued to take a hit, the Livedoor group's profit growth might come to a screeching halt. And if the plunge in share price led to paper losses on holdings in group firms, Livedoor's profits would be eroded and it would push the stocks down further. Livedoor's cash and deposits totaled roughly ¥95 billion on September 30, 2005, an amount that exceeded its annual sales. But the investigation was sure to create internal confusion, and might bring its growth strategy to a dead end.[56]

---

[55] *Nihon Keizai Shinbun*, March 13, 2006, http://it.nikkei.co.jp/business/special/fuji_livedoor.aspx?ichiran=True&i=2006031309537ra&page=1.

[56] *Nihon Keizai Shinbun*, January 18, 2006, http://markets.nikkei.co.jp/special/sp020.cfm?id=d1d1907b19&date=20060119.

# For Further Discussion

1. This is a company in crisis. What immediate actions should the top management take to stabilize the company?
2. How should the top management lead a company through a crisis in the long term?
3. Can Livedoor survive by itself? If not, what is the next step? What about a possible alliance with a big company who can afford to support it?
4. Where did Horie go wrong?
5. Why is this incident so significant? Why was Livedoor targeted for investigation?
6. Can any company seek compensation over the fall in Livedoor's share price?
7. How would you comment on Livedoor's rise and fall? Does this symbolize an era of deregulation?
8. Who should share responsibility for Livedoor's scam? Livedoor's top management used a raft of fraudulent securities schemes. Is the management the only party that should be blamed for this?
9. What kind of partner should be selected by Livedoor if it really needs a sponsor for its survival?

# 7

# Nireco Japan: Introduction of the Poison Pill

It has long been believed that hostile takeover bids had little chance of succeeding in Japan. This perception changed in early 2005 with the takeover battle for Nippon Broadcasting System Inc. (NBS), fought between Livedoor Co. Ltd. (Livedoor) and Fuji Television Network Inc. (Fuji TV).[1] It was a high-profile case which attracted a lot of media attention because it was the first domestic takeover bid (TOB) to use American style mergers and acquisitions (M&A) tactics in Japan. With the battle for NBS, the threat of hostile takeovers had become a reality in Japan.

In February 2005, Hidemaru Yamada, president of Nireco Corporation (Nireco)[2] thought this incident would trigger hostile takeovers of Japanese companies, particularly by American firms[3] (see **Exhibits 1–4** for information on Nireco). Fearing that Japanese companies would be swallowed by foreign investors, Yamada thought his company needed to introduce "poison pill" defenses as a means to counter hostile takeover bids (see **Exhibit 5**).[4]

---

[1] For details, see Case 5 "Hostile Takeover in Japan: Fuji TV vs. Livedoor for NBS" in this book.

[2] Nireco provides a wide range of control and measuring systems for the printing, iron, steel and agriculture industries. The product line includes an array of tension-control systems for web printing and steel strip manufacturing, automatic-register control, print-quality inspection, gluing, near-infrared analyzing, image analysis, hydraulic/pneumatic control, and automatic marking and storing systems, all which are designed to give total support to various production processes. For more details on the company and its products, see http://www.nireco.co.jp/jap/#.

[3] See Nireco's press release, "Our Security Plan to Maximize Corporate Value", March 14, 2005, http://www.nireco.co.jp/jap/info/050315.html.

[4] See the company's announcement, "For the Plan to Improve Corporate Value", March 14, 2005, http://www.nireco.co.jp/jap/#.

**Exhibit 1**   Basic Data of Nireco Corp.

| Location | 2951-4, Ishikawa-machi, Hachioji, Tokyo 192-8522 Japan |
|---|---|
| Telephone | 0426-42-3111 |
| Industry | Electric Appliance |
| Established | November 4, 1950 |
| President | Hidemaru Yamada |
| Number of Employees | 225 |
| Avg. Age of Employees | 40.7 years |
| Listed | JASDAQ |
| Listed Since | October 27, 1989 |
| Capital | ¥3,072,350,000 |

*Source*: "Nireco (6863)", Yahoo! Japan, http://profile.yahoo.co.jp/biz/fundamental/9893.html.

**Exhibit 2**   Nireco's History

The company currently known as Nireco made its start in 1921 when a German enter-prise under the name Askania Werke AG established a Japanese subsidiary called Askania.

Five years after its founding, Askania reorganized to become a joint-stock corpo-ration, at the same time redirecting its business activity from importing to domestic production of hydraulic-jet-pipe automatic control systems.

Eventually, Askania was renamed Nippon Regulator; at this point, based on manufacturing experience and technological know-how gained during the second world war, the company became a developer and manufacturer of process automation systems, carving a name for itself as a pioneer in automatic control systems. In 1984, the name was changed to Nireco, and till today the company has been actively involved in the development of industry in Japan. Today, factors such as the effective use of resources, energy conservation, automation and standardization are indispen-sable for industries, and Nireco has been able to effectively implement automatic control.

Nireco had long provided a wide range of control and measuring systems for the printing, iron, steel and agriculture industries. The product lines boasted an array of tension-control systems for web printing and steel strip manufacturing, and also included automatic-register control, print-quality inspection, gluing, near-infrared

*(Continued)*

**Exhibit 2**   (*Continued*)

---

analysing, image-analysis, hydraulic/pneumatic control, automatic marking and storing systems. All were designed to give total support to various production processes.

**Timeline**

1950   Nippon Regulator Co. Ltd. established in Chuo-ku, Tokyo
1961   Subsidiary Chiyoda Seiki Co. Ltd. established
1972   Subsidiary Nireco Service Co. Ltd. (currently Nireco Keiso Co., Ltd.) established
1979   Head office opened in Hachioji, Tokyo
1984   Corporate name changed to Nireco Co. Ltd.
1989   Registered as an OTC company with Japan Securities Dealers Association
1994   French company Calgraph Co. Ltd. acquired and made a subsidiary
1998   Acquired Chinese company Jinriki Kakkobun following application for capital increase
2000   Nireco America Corporation established

---

*Source*: Nireco Company Outline, http://www.nireco.com/english/company/top_comp.html.

**Exhibit 3**   Nireco's Global Network

---

Nireco has been a company with international roots and a global perspective. It has pursued a consistent global strategy with two strands. First, Nireco expanded abroad based on close relationships with overseas companies that understood its technology and businesses. Second, overseas growth has been characterized by technology transfers to its longstanding overseas sales companies, which present opportunities for profitable localized production.

For example, Calgraph S.A., a French supplier of color register control systems, began working with Nireco in the early 1990s to adapt its systems to a wider range of presses. Based on a relationship of trust and complementing technologies, Nireco acquired an equity stake in the company. Today, Calgraph is a wholly owned subsidiary, operating as both a manufacturing facility and a sales company for the European market. Nireco's partner companies share the conviction that progress

---

(*Continued*)

**Exhibit 3**   (*Continued*)

begins with people — a notion that has sustained Nireco through five decades of globalization.

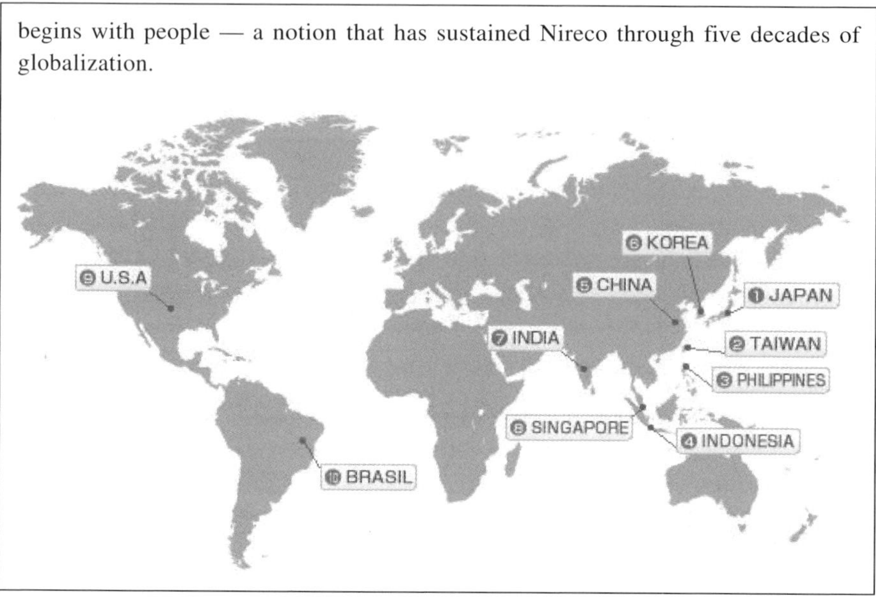


*Source*: "A Global Outlook: A Tradition at Nireco", http://www.nireco.com/english/network/top_net.html.

**Exhibit 4**   Nireco's Financial Data

(US$ million)[5]

| Year | Sales Revenue | Operating Income | Income before Tax | Income after Tax | Total Assets |
|---|---|---|---|---|---|
| 2002 | 54.08 | (3.28) | (6.06) | (5.43) | 120.13 (As of March 31, 2003 |
| 2003 | 60.23 | 1.21 | 2.66 | 2.80 | 125.81 (As of March 31, 2004) |
| 2004 | 64.90 | 1.14 | 1.80 | 1.06 | 125.04 (As of March 31, 2005) |

*Source*: "Nireco (6863)", Yahoo! Japan, http://profile.yahoo.co.jp/biz/fundamental/9893.html.

---

[5] US$1 = ¥107.08 on April 19, 2005.

**Exhibit 5**   Poison Pill

"Poison pill" is a reference to literal poison pills carried by various spies throughout history, and by the Nazi leaders in the Second World War. Spies could take such pills when discovered, eliminating any possibility of being interrogated for the enemy's gain. It has since become a term referring to any strategy in business or politics which attempts to avoid a negative outcome by increasing the costs of the negative outcome to those who seek it.

In business, poison pills, usually known by their more formal name "shareholder rights plans", are often used to avoid takeover bids. These are attempts by a potential acquirer to obtain and control a block of shares in a target company, and thereby gain control of the board and, through it, the company's management. There are several types of "poison pills" that can be used by a company that thinks it is the target of a takeover:

- The target issues a large number of new securities, often preferred stock, to existing shareholders. These new securities usually have severe redemption provisions, such as allowing holders (other than the acquirer) to convert the security into a large number of common shares if a takeover occurs. This immediately dilutes the percentage of the target owned by the acquirer, and makes it more expensive to acquire 50% of the target's stock. This form of poison pill is sometimes called a shareholder rights plan because it is intended to give management (and possibly shareholders) the right to approve an acquisition, potentially requiring the acquirer to pay a premium for control of the target.
- The target adds to its charter a provision which gives the current shareholders the right to sell their shares to the acquirer at an increased price (usually 100% above the recent average share price), if the acquirer's share of the company reaches a critical limit (usually one-third). This kind of poison pill cannot stop a determined acquirer but ensures a high price for the company.
- The target takes on large debts in an effort to make the debt load too high to be attractive — the acquirer would eventually have to pay the debts.
- The company buys a number of smaller companies using a stock swap, diluting the value of the target's stock.
- The target grants its employees stock options that are immediately exercisable if the company is taken over. This is intended to give employees an incentive to continue working for the target company, at least until a merger is completed, instead of looking for a new job as soon as takeover discussions begin. However, with the release of the "golden handcuffs", many discontent employees may quit immediately after they've cashed in their stock options. This poison pill may create an exodus of talented employees. In many high-tech businesses, attrition of talented human resources often means an empty shell is left behind for the new owner.

*Source*: *Wikipedia*, http://en.wikipedia.org/wiki/Poison_pill.

# Hidemaru Yamada: Imperatives for Introducing Takeover Defenses

President Yamada saw the Fuji vs. Livedoor saga as an opportunity for his company to rethink the relationship between companies and their shareholders.[6] He believed that a big factor behind the looming threat of hostile takeovers was the dissolution of cross-shareholdings that began in the 1990s, particularly between main banks and corporate borrowers. As a result of this uncoupling, Nireco's share of stable shareholders[7] fell from 62% to about 58% between 1999 and 2005 (see **Exhibit 6**). On the other hand, foreign ownership of Nireco, which used to account for only nil of all outstanding shares, had risen to 8.91% (see **Exhibit 7**). The increase in the proportion of free-floating shares, including foreign ownership not yet

**Exhibit 6**   Nireco's Major Shareholders

As of March 31, 2005

| Company | No. of Shares Held (1,000 Shares) | % |
|---|---|---|
| Nireco | 1,016 | 10.16 |
| Mizuho Trust Bank | 790 | 7.90 |
| Hakushin Kikaku Printing Co. | 586 | 5.86 |
| JFE Steel Corp. | 468 | 4.68 |
| Tokyo Tomin Bank | 444 | 4.44 |
| Nireco Customers' Stock Holding Group | 423 | 4.23 |
| Mizuho Bank | 419 | 4.19 |
| CSFB Euro BB Client SFPVL (Agent: Citibank N.A. Tokyo Branch) | 377 | 3.77 |
| SOMPO Japan | 319 | 3.19 |
| SFP Value Realization Master Fund Ltd. (Agent: Credit Swiss First Boston) | 285 | 2.85 |
| **Total** | 5,129 | 51.27 |

*Source*: Nireco's Annual Report (Yakushikei Honkokosho), 2004.

---

[6] See Nireco's press release, "Our Security Plan to Maximize Corporate Value", *op. cit.*

[7] Stable shareholders refer to those holding shares for long-term business relationships.

**Exhibit 7**   Nireco's Major Shareholders

As of March 31, 2005

| | Banks | Securities Firms | Corporations | Foreign | | Domestic Individual | Total | Odd Lot Shares |
|---|---|---|---|---|---|---|---|---|
| | | | | Corporations | Individual | | | |
| No. of Shares (1,000 Shares) | 2,355 | 284 | 2,607 | 888 | — | 3,834 | 9,968 | 37.249 |
| % | 23.63 | 2.85 | 26.15 | 8.91 | | 38.46 | 100 | |

*Source*: Nireco's Annual Report (Yakushikei Honkokosho), 2004.

**Exhibit 8**   Nireco's Stock Prices

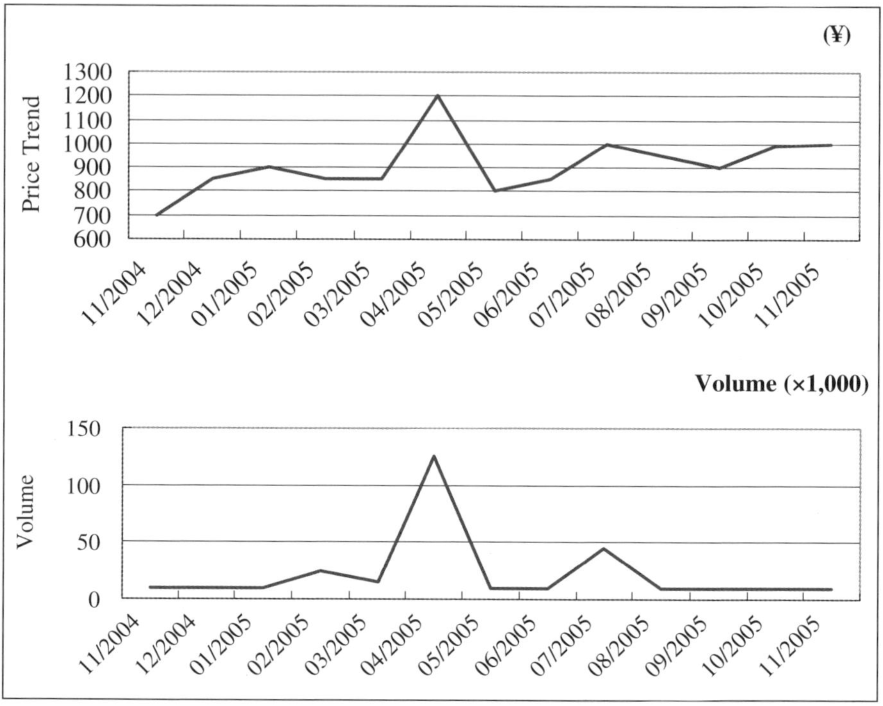

*Source*: Yahoo! Japan Corporation, http://quote.yahoo.co.jp/q?s=6863&d=1y.

registered,[8] meant that buying out Nireco through TOBs had become easier.

Another fact which bothered him was that shares of Japanese companies were relatively inexpensive, making it an opportune time for foreign parties to buy Japanese companies.[9] On February 1, 2005, the average stock price in Japan was ¥11,330,[10] just 29.11% of its peak price of ¥38,915.87 in 1989 (see **Exhibit 8**). On February 1, 2005, Nireco's stock

---

[8] Foreign shareholders tend to hold shares without registering their name.

[9] See Nireco's press release, "Our Security Plan to Maximize Corporate Value", *op. cit.*

[10] US$1 = ¥103.93 on February 1, 2005.

price was ¥832, a mere 39.6% of its 10 year peak of ¥2,100, which it reached on June 26, 1996.

Yamada had much to contemplate and consider. He realized that Japanese companies faced a big hurdle in setting up poison pill defenses,[11] since the US institutional infrastructure supporting poison pills differed considerably from that of Japan. US companies also had the benefit of a significant number of legal suits on poison pill defenses while companies in Japan had no experience of this kind. Yamada was also of the opinion that Nireco's stock price had been undervalued by the market for some time, making it an opportune takeover target, especially for foreign companies.[12]

In taking the first steps to erect strong defenses against a possible hostile takeover, Yamada asked the legal counselor and outside consulting firm to conduct a study and report the findings to the board of directors. Questions he wanted answered were: Was it legal to introduce defense measures against hostile takeovers? What kind of defensive tactics were other Japanese companies, particularly those feeling threatened, introducing? What defense tactics could Nireco introduce? Answers had to address the legality and effectiveness of these tactics.

A few weeks later, both departments reported their studies to the board.

## The Legal Counselor's Report

The legal department's report covered the positions of the Japanese government and the Tokyo Stock Exchange (TSE) on the introduction of the poison pill in Japanese corporations. It also introduced US court decisions on various takeover defense tactics.[13,14]

---

[11] Ibid.

[12] The PBR (Price Bookvalue Ratio; stock price/bookvalue of the asset) of the company had been less than 1 for some years, which showed that the stock price was relatively low in terms of the net asset value. See *Nihon Keizai Shinbun*, October 11, 2005, http://www.nikkei.co.jp/china/special2/20050609cc869000_09.html.

[13] American M&A laws and court cases were good reference material for Japanese companies, since Japanese laws and cases were not yet well developed.

[14] See Nireco's press release, "Our Security Plan to Maximize Corporate Value", *op. cit.*

## *Ministry of Justice — Revision of Commercial Law*

The Commercial Law was scheduled to be revised in April 2006. This revised Commercial Law was expected to make provisions for poison pills that would bring down the voting right ratios of those attempting a take-over, and allow for "golden shares" that gave vetoing powers to friendly shareholders.[15]

A poison pill in the form of the right plan considered under the new Commercial Law, gave existing shareholders share warrants in advance with which they could acquire common shares. When a hostile buyer bought shares up to a predetermined number, the warrants were exercised automatically to issue common shares.[16] A method of forcefully converting the shares of a party who was recognized as a hostile buyer into shares without voting rights would also be made possible.[17] The objective was to nullify the voting rights of the takeover buyer.

The task of recognizing hostile activity would be given to management, and the conditions for taking action would be defined in the articles of incorporation. If a company were armed with these measures, it was less likely to be the target of a hostile takeover. Thus, these types of defensive measures were warning type measures.

Preferred and subordinate shares that provided special rights to shareholders would become easier to use with the revision of the law.[18] "Golden shares" that provided vetoes to shareholders were a defensive measure. Under the revised Commercial Law, a company listed on the stock market could have transfer limitation only for golden shares.[19] The transfer limitation prevented the golden shares from being transferred to the hostile shareholders. It provided an almighty veto power to friendly shareholders while preventing double-crossing.[20]

Lastly, under the current law, a director could be dismissed only by a special resolution, approved by two-third votes at the shareholders

---

[15] *Economist* (Japan), April 1, 2005, p. 18.

[16] Ibid.

[17] Ibid.

[18] Ibid.

[19] Ibid.

[20] Ibid.

meeting;[21] the revised Commercial Law would relax it to an approval by majority.[22] However, if the article of incorporation could be modified by the shareholders' meeting to say that the dismissal required a special resolution, the same condition could be continued.[23]

## *Ministry of Economy, Trade and Industry on Defensive Measures against Hostile Takeovers*

In May 2005, the Ministry of Economy, Trade and Industry, together with the Ministry of Justice, jointly released a directive for companies using defensive measures to protect themselves against a hostile takeover. It was a guideline for whether a defensive measure was legal or reasonable from the market's point of view. The guidelines could not be legally enforced, but prompted companies to obey the rules when introducing defensive measures. The directive requested companies to disclose a defensive measure prior to its implementation and following the wishes of shareholders, thereby providing a hedge against managers' wanton use of the defensive measure to secure their own jobs. The directive also suggested that the introduction of a poison pill for lowering the buyer's voting right ratio should be approved at the shareholders' meeting.[24] The intent was to stop excessively defensive plans that might interfere with proper takeovers which would help raise the value of the corporation. On top of voting for defensive measures at the shareholders' meeting, a rule was to be established beforehand stipulating that a defensive measure would be cancelled if the purchase proposal benefited the shareholders. It further stated that even after share warrants were issued, shareholders' meetings should be held periodically to revisit whether the defensive measure should be sustained.[25]

---

[21] Japanese Corporate Law, Article 257.

[22] For details, see http://www.meinan.net/h17zeiseikaisei/10syouho1.htm.

[23] Ibid.

[24] *Nihon Keizai Shinbun*, May 28, 2005, pp. 2–5.

[25] Ministry of Economy, Trade and Industry, Minutes of Third Meeting, Corporate Value Study Group, October 20, 2004, http://www.meti.go.jp/policy/economic_industrial/gather/0000624/index.html.

The difficulty of organizing a shareholders' meeting on short notice meant that defensive measures could be taken based on a decision by the directors. In that case, certain conditions had to be met, such as "objective conditions for cancelling the defensive measure had to be determined in advance" or that "checks by outside members such as outside board members had to be mandated."[26] The objective was to make sure that the board of directors did not make a purely self-motivated decision. This procedure also allowed the shareholders, to cancel a defensive measure if they so desired.

The directive listed instances in which a defensive measure was appropriate: (1) a "greenmail" situation, i.e., the buyer's intention was to ask the company to buy back shares at peak price; (2) "scorched earth tactics", i.e., the buyer's intention was to sell the company's assets; (3) an "oppressive two-step buyout", i.e., the buyer essentially forced shareholders to sell shares, etc. The directive requested that companies be careful not to reject proper purchase offers, and be mindful of shareholders' interests. The instruction warned against "golden shares" in particular as they "treated shareholders discriminately". It generally indicated a negative opinion about golden shares by stating "a listed company should be cautious about issuing golden shares without having a mechanism to cancel them".

# Financial Services Agency

The Financial Services Agency (FSA) was responsible for ensuring the stability of the financial system in Japan. The FSA protected depositors, insurance policy holders and securities investors. It also ensured the financial system ran smoothly through the inspection and supervision of private sector financial institutions and the surveillance of securities transactions. Moreover, the FSA played a role in the planning and policy making process forging the financial system, performing important roles for the sound development of the national economy.[27]

---

[26] Ibid.

[27] For details, see FSA's homepage, http://www.fsa.go.jp/.

The takeover battle for NBS exposed various loopholes in the government's policy concerning the financial market. For example, there was the acquisition of shares through a niche in the TOB system,[28] and the deficiencies of the "Large Ownership Report"[29] system. The latter obligated those shareholders who owned more than 5% of outstanding shares in a listed company to report this fact to the FSA. Strict compliance with this rule, however, had never been enforced. The limitations of the existing administrative control were made obvious as well. For example, Livedoor had purchased more than a third of NBS's outstanding stock through off-floor trading, a move that violated Japan's unspoken rule against backdoor business practices common in other parts of the world. The current administrative controls couldn't prevent this kind of move from happening in Japan.

Exceptions to rules made the financial environment more fragile. For example, investment funds that traded shares daily were not required by the Large Ownership Report to report changes in their share ownership ratios. This special treatment was for the convenience of institutional investors who traded shares in large quantities. However, such a lopsided treatment was sure to cause trouble in the future. In the US, the Securities and Exchange Commission vigilantly monitored the market for any problems, and established rules almost monthly based on court precedents.[30] In Japan, issuing a rule normally required a change of law, thus the FSA dealt with problems on a case by case basis, responding to questions concerning interpretations of the law.

As M&As became more versatile as a result of new venture businesses and foreign capital, keeping grey zones would increase the risk of confusion. At the same time, narrowing the rule would stifle transactions. Whether transparency could be achieved without excessive control would depend on how the government handled this situation.

---

[28] The TOB procedures are specified in Article 27-2 of the Japanese Securities Exchange Law, Law No. 25 of 1948. See http://law.e-gov.go.jp/cgi-bin/idxsearch.cgi.

[29] Japanese companies are required to report 10 major shareholders annually to the Ministry of Finance. For details of the requirements, see http://www.smrj.go.jp/isif/series/okabunushi_y24.html.

[30] The US's SEC proposes to update and simplify the rules and regulations constantly. See the SEC's homepage, http://www.sec.gov/.

## Tokyo Stock Exchange

The TSE, as Japan's premier stock trading market, strived to strike a balance between its public responsibility in providing financial infrastructure and its own profitability. The TSE's basic corporate governance philosophy sought to: reflect a wide variety of opinions in its management and market operations; increase the transparency of its management by clarifying the authorities and responsibilities of its corporate divisions; increase its accountability; and ensure reliable operations as a self-regulatory organization, thereby gaining investor and shareholder confidence. According to its charter, the TSE intended to provide an efficient, convenient, fair and reliable marketplace.[31]

The TSE was concerned that in the aftermath of the takeover battle for NBS "a substantial number of companies may try to adopt defensive measures neglecting general investors as a result". As such, it prepared a directive asking companies to practice voluntary restraint against excessively defensive measures that violated investors' rights — such as golden shares that provided vetoes to certain shareholders at shareholders' meetings — and issued a notice on April 21, 2005 requesting compliance.[32] At the time, it was said that the TSE intended to turn the directive into official policy by the fall of 2005 and that it would severely punish companies that disobeyed.

The new Commercial Law, to be introduced in 2006, would make easier and legal the use of classified shares, such as golden shares and share warrants.[33] The TSE, however, seemed to believe that any defensive measures that lead to violations of investors' rights and unexpected damages to investors were improper, even if they were allowed under the law; the TSE sought a higher standard as a controller of the market.[34]

While the New York Stock Exchange prohibited the issuance of golden shares once a company was listed,[35] the TSE would not allow an

---

[31] See the TSE's homepage, http://www.tse.or.jp/english/about/history.html.

[32] *Nihon Keizai Shinbun*, June 30, 2005, p. 3.

[33] *Nikkei* (*Japanese Economic Journal*), June 30, 2005, p. 3.

[34] Ibid.

[35] The New York Stock Exchange allows US companies to list dual-class voting shares. Once shares are listed, however, companies cannot reduce the voting rights of the existing

issuance of golden shares even before a company was listed. Even when a listed holding company was to provide golden shares to a non-listed subsidiary, the TSE advised against it if the subsidiary could dictate the corporate value of the entire group. It also asked for voluntary restraint against issuance of shares with multiple voting rights, such as a share with 100 voting rights attached. Concerning the issuance of share warrants, the TSE was requesting not to only provide them to shareholders at the time of introduction, but rather to provide them to all shareholders when a buyer appeared.

The TSE also asked for enhancement of disclosure of information to shareholders: companies should clearly indicate the purpose of defensive countermeasures and their possible influence on shareholders. It also obligated companies to disclose the procedures and standards of implementation of the countermeasures. If the articles of incorporation were to be modified with future introduction of countermeasures in mind, this intention should be disclosed (see **Exhibit 9**).

## Decisions by the US Court

Despite their seemingly obvious advantages,[36] poison pills had become the target of increasingly potent shareholder activism in the US. The primary complaints against poison pills were that they entrenched management and the board and discouraged legitimate tender offers.

Corporate boards in the US faced a wave of unsolicited or hostile takeovers during the 1980s. In response to these threats, corporate boards felt compelled to formulate defensive measures. For example, measures such as the poison pill, white knights, pac man, charter amendments and other assorted tools were deployed either to thwart a hostile bid, or to make a bid more expensive.

But because a board could be acting in its own interest rather than that of the corporation and its shareholders, they had an enhanced duty of care.

---

shares or issue a new class of superior voting shares. For details, see Golden Share, http://www.investopedia.com/terms/g/goldenshare.asp.

[36] A shareholders rights plan can protect the shareholder from coercive or abusive takeover tactics, and ensures shareholders receive a fair price once the company is sold.

**Exhibit 9**   History of Tokyo Stock Exchange

In the 1870s, a securities system was introduced in Japan and public bond negotiation began. This resulted in the request for a public trading institution, and the "Stock Exchange Ordinance" was enacted in May 1878. Based on this ordinance, the "Tokyo Stock Exchange Co. Ltd." was established on May 15, 1878, and trading began on June 1.

In March 1943, the Japan Securities Exchange Law was enacted to reorganize the Stock Exchange as a war-time controlled institution. On June 30, 1943, 11 stock exchanges throughout Japan were unified and a quasi-public corporation, the Japan Securities Exchange, was established (dissolved in April 1947).

With worsening war conditions and air-raids on the main island of Japan, the securities market was forced to suspend trading in all securities markets from August 10, 1945. It was difficult to re-open the Stock Exchange by a Memorandum of Supreme Commander of Allied Powers (SCAP) in September 1945; however, trading resumed with unofficial group transactions in December 1945.

The Securities and Exchange Law was enacted in March 1947, and entirely revised in April 1948. On April 1, 1949, stock exchanges were established in Tokyo, Osaka and Nagoya. Trading on these exchanges began on May 16. In July of that same year, five additional stock exchanges were established: in Kyoto (merged into Osaka Securities Exchange in March 2001), Kobe (dissolved in October 1967), Hiroshima (merged into Tokyo Stock Exchange in March 2000), Fukuoka and Niigata (merged with Tokyo Stock Exchange in March 2000). In addition, the Sapporo Securities Exchange was established in April 1950. Consequently, Japan now has five stock exchanges.

*Source*: Tokyo Stock Exchange's website, http://www.tse.or.jp/english/about/history.html.

Because of the greater responsibility they bore, there was a need for judicial examination before the protections of the business judgment rule[37]

---

[37] The business judgment rule is a general theory that a director's responsibility is pursuable only when either a material or negligent error exists in the recognition of a fact which formed the basis for the director's judgment, or the decision-making processes or its contents were particularly unreasonable or inappropriate, considering the fact that a director is given a wide range of discretionary power in making a management decision. For details, see Misawa, Mitsuru (2005) "Bank Directors' Decision on Bad Loans: A Comparative Study of US and Japanese Standards of Required Care", *Banking Law Journal*, 122(5): 444.

could be conferred.[38] The first case that departed from the traditional business judgment rule presumption and which held directors to a higher level of responsibility involved protectionist measures taken by Unocal,[39] an American oil and gas company, to fend off a hostile TOB by Mesa Petroleum Co., an independent oil company led by T. Boone Pickens, a famous corporate raider.

The Delaware Supreme Court in Unocal developed an enhanced scrutiny test because it saw that a potential conflict of interest by the board of director's was real in the context of a takeover bid; namely, a board of directors could attempt to thwart a takeover bid to protect or entrench themselves rather than respond objectively to a bid on its merits. "The directors are of necessity confronted with a conflict of interest, and an objective decision is difficult."[40]

In the Unocal case, the Supreme Court outlined a two-step test that a board of directors had to pass in order to receive the protection of the business judgment rule. The Unocal two-tier test required a board of directors to show that:

- It "had reasonable grounds for believing that a danger to corporate policy and effectiveness existed because of another person's stock ownership".[41]
- Any defensive measure was "reasonable in relation to the threat posed".[42]

The court did also outlined a broad limitation to the proportionality of a board's defensive response by saying that "Such powers are not absolute. A corporation does not have unbridled discretion to defeat any perceived threat by any means available."[43]

---

[38] Unocal Corp. v. Mesa Petroleum Co., Del. Supr., 493 A.2d 954 (1985).

[39] Unocal Corp. v. Mesa Petroleum Co., Del. Supr., 493 A.2d 946 (1985).

[40] Unocal Corp. v. Mesa Petroleum Co., Del. Supr., 493 A.2d 954–955 (1985).

[41] Unocal Corp. v. Mesa Petroleum Co., Del. Supr., 493 A.2d 955 (1985).

[42] Ibid.

[43] Ibid.

# The Consulting Firm's Report

The consulting firm's report presented various anti-takeover tactics being considered by Japanese companies.[44]

According to a survey of 100 company presidents conducted by *Nikkei* in April 2005, more than 40% of respondents had started studying defensive countermeasures against hostile takeovers, partly as a result of the high-profile TOB between Fuji TV and Livedoor.[45] Those considering introducing countermeasures against hostile takeovers numbered 41.5%, and a total of 61.5% answered positively to the needs for defensive countermeasures — combining those who had already "introduced" and those who "were not yet studying but felt needs for [defensive counter-measures]". Only 12.3% of respondents said "there was no need for [defensive countermeasures]".[46]

The specific plans of Japanese companies included:[47]

- **Maintenance of stable management by a higher stock price:** For example, the stock price could be raised to increase the aggregate market price of the company and shareholders could benefit from increasing dividends.
- **Revised articles of incorporation:** The articles of incorporation could be revised to expand the stock issuing frame and increase the number of stipulated directors.
- **Cross-shareholding:** Cross-shareholding, a phenomenon unique to Japan, had been waning but was now regaining popularity. According to the *Nikkei* survey, approximately 70% of the surveyed companies said that cross-shareholding was necessary for business co-operation and was a useful defensive measure.[48]
- **Use of US type techniques:** The poison pill was the most popular technique, followed by the white knight, the crown jewel (disposing important assets), the scorched earth defense (selling off everything to

---

[44] See Nireco's press release, "Our Security Plan to Maximize Corporate Value", *op. cit.*
[45] *Nihon Keizai Shinbun*, April 23, 2005, p. 11.
[46] Ibid.
[47] See Nireco's press release, "Our Security Plan to Maximize Corporate Value", *op. cit.*
[48] *Nihon Keizai Shinbun*, April 23, 2005, p. 11.

**Exhibit 10**   Use of US Type Techniques by Japanese Companies

58.5%   Poison pill

17.4   White knight

7.3   Crown jewel

4.0   Pac man defense

2.4   Golden parachute

9.8   Others

*Source*: *Nihon Keizai Shinbun*, April 23, 2005, p. 11.

create a hollow company). The pac man defense[49] and golden parachute[50] were also being studied (see **Exhibits 10** and **11**).

The consulting firm singled out three typical defensive measures that Japanese companies were already considering:[51]

- **Not lowering the hurdles for dismissing directors:** The current Commercial Law laid down that the dismissal of a director required a special resolution approved by two-third votes at the shareholders'

---

[49] The acquiree may take an offensive, proactive stand. For details, see http://media.wiley.com/product_data/excerpt/51/04713277/0471327751.pdf.

[50] This manoeuvre results in significant compensation to the acquiree's top executives if there is a change in control of the acquiree and the executive is terminated from the position currently held. For details, see http://media.wiley.com/product_data/excerpt/51/04713277/0471327751.pdf.

[51] See Nireco's press release, "Our Security Plan to Maximize Corporate Value", *op. cit.*

**Exhibit 11**    M&As Have Their Own Lexicon

When a company's board and management try to resist a buyer's overtures, colorful merger and acquisition terms come up. Here are some terms and tactics being used in connection with M&As in the US.

**Greenmail:** A play on blackmail, greenmail is sent when an unfriendly bidder buys a large block of stock and then demands the target company buy back the stock at a higher price if it does not want to be taken over. A greenmailer usually has no plan for an actual takeover, and only wants to make money. Greenmail is also called a "goodbye kiss" or a "bon voyage bonus".

**Pac man:** A target firm turns around and tries to take over the company that made the hostile bid.

**Poison pill:** A target company tries to make its own stock less attractive to the buyer, usually by issuing a huge number of new shares to existing shareholders at a low price to dilute the voting rights of the bidder and make a takeover more difficult and expensive.

**Scorched earth policy:** A firm sells off its valuable and desired assets — called "crown jewels" — or assumes liabilities to make a takeover unattractive. If taken too far, this tactic can destroy the company.

**White knight:** A white knight is a company that saves the day by making a friendly takeover offer to a company threatened by a hostile one from a "black knight".

**Lady Macbeth strategy:** A company poses as a white knight to gain trust, but then joins an unfriendly bidder, this strategy is named after the character in William Shakespeare's "Macbeth" who acts noble and virtuous as a way to take advantage of others.

*Source: Japan Times*, March 26, 2005, http://search.japantimes.co.jp/print/business/nb03-2005/nb20050326a3.htm.

meeting.[52] The revised Commercial Law would however relax this mandate to an approval by a majority of the votes.[53] However, if the article of incorporation could be modified by the shareholders to say that it required a special resolution, the same condition could be continued.[54]

---

[52] Japanese Corporate Law, Article 257.

[53] For details, see http://www.meinan.net/h17zeiseikaisei/10syouho1.htm.

[54] Ibid.

While it was not uncommon to find an article of incorporation which stated that the number of directors had to be more than three, it was a risky arrangement from the point of view of preventing a takeover. If company A acquired a majority share in company B, it could send in 15 new directors in addition to the 14 existing ones, and succeed in replacing the representative director, thereby easily taking over company B. An effective way to prevent such a takeover was to introduce a limit for the total number of directors, e.g., "no more than 15". This could be done by passing a resolution at the shareholders' meeting and by always filling out the ranks. If the frame was only half filled, the buyer would be able to control the board just by acquiring the majority voting rights.

Although this tactic did not work for a company where the term of the director was one year, it was useful for controlling the company until the next election as long as the term was two years and the company taking over had not bought out more than two-thirds of the entire shares.[55]

- **Make your friendly trading partners part of the defense plan:** It was possible to have an agreement with a major trading partner which stated that the partner could cancel any contract unilaterally if the controlling shareholder changed.

  While the basic objective of such an agreement was to maintain a stable relation with a trading partner on the premise of a certain management policy, it could be used as a defense mechanism against a hostile takeover by hinting to the other side about the possible loss of a major trading partner. NBS had used such tactics when defending itself from a hostile TOB by Livedoor. Besides issuing share warrants to Fuji TV, NBS had added a cancellation clause to its agreement with a trading partner, a professional baseball team. The Tokyo High Court noted that this clause was an action "intended to benefit their battle", and did not approve it. The court's decision may have been different if such an agreement had existed prior to the battle.[56]

---

[55] *Nihon Keizai Shinbun*, June 30, 2005, p. 3.

[56] Kinyu Zaisei Homu Jijyo (Banking and Financial Legal Issues), Kinyu Zaisei Jijyo Kenkyuukai, No. 1733, March 15, 2005, pp. 10–17.

- **Always have a comprehensive business plan ready:** Issuing new shares to a third party in order to reduce the hostile buyer's voting right ratio was a viable alternative defense in an emergency, especially if the new shares were issued to a friendly company. However, authorized capital should not be forgotten as an alternative: A company could issue new shares so long as the total number of shares was within the frame authorized by the shareholders' meeting.[57] If there was no room left within the frame, expanding it beforehand through the shareholders' meeting might be necessary. If the main objective of the expansion was related to a change in the shareholders' composition, the shareholders would be unlikely to pass the resolution. In order for a defense against a hostile buyer not to be recognized as the main objective, a bona fide business plan had to be prepared in advance.

  The Tokyo District Court delivered an injunction against the issuance of share warrants by NBS.[58] The Tokyo High Court, in support of the lower court's decision, judged that the main objective of the share warrants was in fact to maintain the existing control of the company. It stated that the purpose of issuing the share warrants (raising funds) was "difficult to believe as it is more likely devised as an excuse after the conflict occurred".[59]

  Last but not least, the consulting firm presented an example of the "right plan" which Chrysler Corp., a US automotive manufacturer, implemented in February 1998 (see **Exhibit 12**).[60] It announced that it was extending a poison pill plan until February 23, 2008, under which the rights become exercisable if anyone announced a tender offer for

---

[57] Japanese Commercial Law, Article 166.

[58] For the decision of the Toyo Lower Court, see press releases by Nippon Broadcasting, "Notice Regarding Ruling on Request for Court Injunction Blocking Issuance of Stock Acquisition Rights and Appeal Against the Ruling", March 11, 2005; and "Notification Regarding Rejection of Objection to Temporary Court Injunction Blocking Issuance of Stock Acquisition Rights and of Appeal Against the Ruling", March 16, 2005. For both, see http://www.jolf.co.jp/company/IR1242/index.html.

[59] Tokyo High Court, 16th Civil Section, March 23, 2005. For details, see the press release by Nippon Broadcasting on "Notification Regarding Dismissal of Appeal Against Lower Court of Temporary Injunction to Block Issuance of Stock Acquisition Rights", March 23, 2005, http://www.jolf.co.jp/company/IR1242/index.html.

[60] See Nireco's press release, "Our Security Plan to Maximize Corporate Value", *op. cit.*

**Exhibit 12**   Chrysler's "Right Plan"

On February 5, 1998 Chrysler Corporation announced that its board of directors had adopted a new stockholder rights plan to replace the plan it had, which would expire on February 23, 1998.

Under the new plan, one right would be distributed for each share of Chrysler common stock outstanding at the close of business on February 23, 1998. Initially, the rights were attached to the common stock and were not exercisable. The rights would become exercisable and would trade separately from the common stock 10 days after any person or group acquired 15% or more of Chrysler's outstanding common stock, or 10 business days after, or on such later date as the board of directors may designate, any person or group commenced or announced their intent to commence a tender offer for 15% or more of Chrysler's outstanding common stock. Each right would entitle the holder to purchase one two-hundredth of a preferred share at an exercise price of US$145.

If any person or group acquired 15% or more of Chrysler's common stock, the rights not held by the 15% stockholder would become exercisable to purchase Chrysler common stock at a 50% discount. If a person or group acquired at least 15% but less than 50% of Chrysler's common stock, the board could elect to exchange each right not held by the 15% stockholder for one share of Chrysler common stock.

The new rights would expire on February 23, 2008. The board directed its corporate governance committee to review the plan during its fifth year to determine whether it continued to be in the best interests of the company and its stockholders. The board could elect to redeem the rights at US$0.01 per right. The rights agreement was not adopted in response to any specific takeover bid, nor was the company aware of any such effort.

*Source*: See Chrysler's press release on February 5, 1998, http://www.prnewswire.com/cgi-bin/ stories.pl?ACCT=104&STORY=/www/story/2-5-98/409704&EDATE=.

15% or more, or acquired 15% of Chrysler's outstanding common shares (for the "right plan", see **Exhibits 12** and **13**).

# Decision Time

Hidemaru Yamada wondered how certain takeover defenses would operate in Japan, should they be deployed.[61] Another question was whether such defenses were ultimately beneficial to shareholders. Shareholders

---

[61] Ibid.

**Exhibit 13**   Rights Plans

Shareholder rights plans have existed in the US since the early 1980s, and provide a defense against unwelcome takeover offers. A shareholder rights plan is designed to give negotiating leverage to the target company's board of directors and to give the board more control over the timing of the response to an unsolicited bid. A shareholder rights plan is also designed to protect the company's shareholders from coercive or abusive takeover tactics, and to ensure that shareholders receive a fair price if the company is sold. Shareholder rights plans seek to accomplish these goals by threatening to inflict a substantial economic loss, in the form of an unacceptable level of dilution, on a bidder that takes action without the approval of the target's board. Under a typical shareholder rights plan, shareholders are issued rights to buy stock at a significant discount (generally 50%) from the market price. The rights become exercisable when a hostile bidder buys a specified percentage of the target company's stock (generally between 10% and 20%). Due to the potential significant dilution, the bidder is more likely to negotiate with the board, which has the ability to eliminate the rights plan or to exempt the bidder from the rights plan's dilutive effect.

would certainly exercise vigilance to make sure defenses were not simply used as entrenchment devices by boards.

The consulting firm informed the board that academic research in the US examining the price reaction to defensive actions had shown mixed results, suggesting that the defense measures were good for stockholders in some cases and bad in others.[62] Yamada expected a certain amount of controversy to surround the effectiveness of the poison pills,[63] as well as the ultimate benefits of the defensive moves. But he thought that the company could be a fore runner in the introduction of takeover defenses in Japan.

The next question was whether the company should proceed with a poison pill directly,[64] or take less radical steps to defend itself. For example, Nireco might propose increases in authorized capital ceilings, possibly stating that such an increase was meant to "prepare for future expansion in the scale of the business", or was to be used to "flexibly implement future capital strategies". Companies with sufficient

---

[62] Ibid.

[63] Ibid.

[64] Ibid.

authorized capital could issue shares or warrants as part of a takeover defense, and that issuance did not always require a shareholder vote.

Among the various tactics that the legal counselor and consulting firm had studied, Yamada considered the poison pill to be the most appropriate for the company.[65] The chosen defense came in the form of stock rights which would be issued to existing shareholders, enabling them to purchase additional shares at a price below market value; and these rights could only be exercised in the event of a potential takeover. Yamada believed this tactic would be effective in Japan.[66] However, he was concerned that some shareholders would take Nireco to court and eliminate this defense. Also, Nireco's board of directors might have differing opinions and he had to get their consent. This was perhaps overly cautious, as by global standards, Nireco's board was insider-dominated, and had only two outside directors (see **Exhibit 14**). The main bank's position was also important in Japan, since it provided financial support and also management advice. It was therefore critical for Yamada to consider how important it was for Nireco to have a poison pill in place before there was a specific takeover threat.

Yamada must have felt the weight of responsibility on his shoulders on March 14, 2005[67] as he and his management team come up with a defensive plan to position the company against possible TOBs.[68,69] Modeled after Chrysler's plan, Nireco introduced the following blueprint to protect itself against hostile TOBs:

- All shareholders as of March 31, 2005 would be given two subscription warrants for every share owned. Each warrant would entitle the holder to buy a new share in Nireco.
- The warrants were not transferable and a holder could use their warrants to purchase new shares if a hostile takeover led to a shareholder acquiring more than 20% of Nireco's outstanding shares.

---

[65] Ibid.

[66] Ibid.

[67] Ibid.

[68] Ibid.

[69] For details, see the company's press release, May 20, 2005. See the company's website, http://www.nireco.co.jp/jap/ir/secu.html

**Exhibit 14**   Nireco's Board of Directors

| Position | Name | Birth Data | Background | Shares Held (1,000 shares) |
|---|---|---|---|---|
| Chairman | Yoshihiko Ota | December 24, 1935 | Entered Nireco in 1959 | 62 |
| President | Hidemaru Yamada | January 27, 1945 | Entered Nireco in 1965 | 40 |
| Director | Kenichi Kawaji | January 18, 1948 | Entered Nireco in 1973 | 17 |
| Director | Yoshihiro Tsuboya | March 23, 1943 | Entered Nireco in 1961 | 11 |
| Director | Noboru Kaneko | November 17, 1945 | Entered Nireco in 1984 | 13 |
| Director | Atsushi Iwama | March 25, 1951 | Entered Nireco in 1972 | 12 |
| Standing Auditor | Junichi Onozawa | January 25, 1944 | Entered Nireco in 1968 | 11 |
| Auditor | Mitsuhiko Hayashi | November 17, 1942 | Joined Nireco in June 2003 from Toppan Printing Co. (a major customer) | 0 |
| Auditor | Minoru Uchida | May 31, 1935 | Joined Nireco in June 2003 (Certified Tax Accountant) | 1 |
| TOTAL | | | | 167 |

*Source*: Nireco's Annual Report (Yakushikei Honkokosho), 2004.


# Conclusion

Japan's first corporate poison pill met its demise on June 2, 2005 when Nireco received an injunction from the Tokyo District Court.[70] The action struck a blow against companies considering similar schemes to combat hostile TOBs.

---

[70] For details, see Court Judgment, Tokyo District Court, Heisei 17 (Yo) No. 20050, http://www.courts.go.jp/app/files/hanrei_jp/486/005486_hanrei.pdf.

SFP Value Realization Master Fund Ltd. (SFP), a major Nireco shareholder with a stake of about 6.8%, filed a lawsuit seeking a court injunction against the proposed poison pill on May 9, 2005. It argued that the implementation of the scheme would adversely affect Nireco's shareholders. SFP owned 3.19% shares as of March 31, 2005, but later increased its holdings significantly (see **Exhibit 6**). In response to SFP's lawsuit, the Tokyo District Court delivered an injunction against the issuance of the share warrants on June 2, 2005 on the grounds that "it corresponded to an extremely unfair issuance that the Commercial Law prohibited."[71]

The Tokyo District Court indicated three conditions for a share warrant issuance to be allowed as a defensive measure "in peace time", i.e., when no battle existed for management rights. The court pointed out that an issuance of share warrants as a defense against a hostile takeover required "basically a decision of the shareholders' meeting". However, this requirement could be replaced with a decision of the board meeting if (1) there was a mechanism to reflect the opinion of the shareholders' meeting; (2) a willful activation of the defensive measure by the board meeting could be prevented; and (3) it did not cause any unexpected damages to shareholders.

The court judged that Nireco had not set up a mechanism to incorporate the opinion of the shareholders at the shareholders' meeting to be held at the end of June 2005, and that the board of directors might not obey the recommendation of the special committee regarding the exercise of share warrants. Thus, the court concluded that Nireco's introduction of the poison pill "lacked justifiability as a premeditated countermeasure against a hostile takeover", considering the fact that "there was a risk of existing shareholders incurring unexpected damages because of dilution of stocks".

Nireco's case, in which the Tokyo District Court served an injunction order against the issuance of share warrants, was a poison pill of a special nature: share warrants were issued to shareholders prior to any announcement of a hostile TOB. The court questioned two points, which were related to securing and confirming the third party's positions by the board

---

[71] This position was confirmed at Court Judgment, Tokyo Higher Court, Heisei 17 (Ra) No. 942, http://www.tkclex.ne.jp/saishin/0507b.html.

members. One was whether there were any measures by which the defensive measure could be suitably judged by highly independent, outside members. Although Nireco claimed that it would "observe the (third party) special committee's recommendations to the fullest extent", the district court pointed out that "there was room for the board of directors to not obey the recommendations".

The other point questioned under what circumstance the defensive measure would be activated. In the Livedoor case, the Tokyo High Court gave examples of cases where the issuance of share warrants was considered appropriate, such as when the buyer asked the company to buy back shares at high prices or was about to dispose of the company's assets in order to obtain temporary profits. Nireco claimed that a defensive measure was justifiable for a case where the takeover was contrary to the benefits of stakeholders, e.g., employees, customers and suppliers, in addition to the conditions that the Tokyo High Court indicated. In response to this claim, the Tokyo District Court ruled that "such a judgment standard was too broad and lacked clarity to be used as a means of preventing willful judgments of the board of directors".

Based on the court's decision, Nireco decided to suspend the introduction of the poison pill. This decision was announced to the public on June 15, 2005.[72]

> *Nireco's distinction and reputation increased as a result of the recent turmoil related to our effort in introducing defense tactics. In the past, we could not get orders easily for the survey instrument for the semiconductor, but recently business for Nireco has been good. It is regrettable that Nireco is unable to introduce the poison pill, but there were a few customers who considered that a company that tries to introduce defense tactics must be of good standing, and they evaluated our effort favorably. As a matter of fact, Nireco succeeded in advancing quite a few new contracts with customers.*
>
> — Hidemaru Yamada, president, Nireco[73]

---

[72] For the company's announcement of June 15, 2005, see the its website, http://www.nireco.co.jp/jap/ir/chushi.html.

[73] For his comment for the press, see Nikkei Net, August 30, 2005, http://company.nikkei.co.jp/news/news.cfm?Nik_Code=0015108&Page=1&Back_sid=IR_CT&KIJIID=20050830NKM0045&DATE_FORSEARCH=2005/08/30.

# For Further Discussion

1. What are the pros and cons of takeovers?
2. How can the increase in hostile takeovers in Japan be explained in terms of the country's economic, social, and legal background?
3. In the face of possible takeover attempts, executive boards of Japanese corporations are currently involved in heated discussions regarding the introduction of poison pills to defend the management of listed corporations. What kind of measures can be introduced in what timeframe?
4. The most effective defense against hostile takeovers is the maximization of corporate value. However, many companies, particularly those feeling a greater sense of threat, are hoping to introduce takeover defenses. It was against this backdrop that the Ministry of Economy, Trade, and Industry and the Ministry of Justice issued in May 2005 the "Guidelines Regarding Takeover Defense for the Purpose of Protection and Enhancement of Corporate Value and Shareholder's Common Interests," a document aimed at creating rules for takeover defenses. Japan's corporate law has been reformed with one eye kept on US law, which laid the groundwork for the introduction of poison pill (rights plan) defenses, like those available in the US, to guard against takeovers. How can these developments be assessed?
5. What, if any, are the differences in institutional infrastructure between the US and Japan with regard to the introduction of a poison pill?
6. What effect could the appointment of outside directors in Japan have in addressing the concerns of shareholders?
7. Japanese business management has already expressed its concern that the introduction of excessive poison pills will cause confusion in the stock market. What kinds of concerns are they?

**8**

# Ina Food Industry:
# A New Management Philosophy
# for Japanese Businesses

Ina Food Industry Co. Ltd. was situated in the city of Ina, Nagano Prefecture, and surrounded by the soaring mountains of the Japanese Alps. Hiroshi Tsukakoshi, Ina Food's 68-year-old chairman (see **Exhibit 1**), had led the company through an incredible 48 years of continuous revenue and profit growth (see **Exhibit 2**). The company was a leading manufacturer of powdered agar,[1] a traditional gelatine product derived from seaweed. In 2005, news about the medicinal benefits of their product led to a boom in demand. As a result, Ina Food experienced phenomenal growth in sales. Revenues for the six-month period ending in December 2005 amounted to 20 billion yen[2] with ordinary income for the same period at 3.8 billion yen. This was an increase in both sales and profits of approximately 40–50% from the previous year.

Instead of celebrating, however, Tsukakoshi felt that this rapid growth was an unfortunate event. He would rather have had a 7% increase in both sales and profit.[3] This was because Tsukakoshi believed that if a business grew too fast, there would always be a backlash. A sudden increase in business presented a problem for a small firm such as Ina Food, which had approximately 400 employees, since it had limited in-house talent to handle sudden change. This in turn could result in the hollowing out of efficient operations maintained by in-house talent due to vast outsourcing.

---

[1] Agar was originally a product of a cottage industry by farmers, who utilized the three coldest months of the year to produce the product. As a result, both quality and quantity had historically been unstable.

[2] US$1=¥117.62 on December 28, 2005.

[3] *Nihon Keizai Shinbun*, May 23–27, 2006, p. 8. Also, see Tsukakoshi, H. (2005) "Iikaisha wo Tsukurimashou (Let Us Build a Good Company)", in *Bunya*, Seventh Edition, pp. 11–213.

**Exhibit 1**   Company Profile

| | |
|---|---|
| Company name | Ina Food Industry Co. Ltd. |
| Chairman and CEO | Hiroshi Tsukakoshi |
| President and COO | Osamu Inoue |
| Date established | June 18, 1958 |
| Capital | ¥96.8 million |
| Annual sales | ¥20,074 million (2005) |
| Operating income | ¥3,819 million (2005) |
| Head office address | 5074 Nishiharuchika, Ina-City, Nagano, Japan |
| Plants | Sawando Plant, Kitaoka Plant, Fujisawa Plant, Inosawa Plant |
| Branches | Tokyo, Nagoya, Osaka |
| Business offices | Sapporo, Sendai, Nagano, Fukuoka, Okayama |
| Number of employees | 346 (in 2005) |

Ina Food Industry Co. Ltd. was established in 1958 to produce agar. This natural gelatine was originally developed as an important ingredient and used in traditional Japanese confectionery. Its manufacture was the product of a cottage industry by farmers, who used the natural cold during the coldest three months of the year for its production. As a consequence of (a) production being confined to only the three winter months of the year when the farmers were free, (b) the quantity and quality not being stable or reliable, (c) it appearing in both bars and a fibrous state, and (d) it being the victim of a seasonally fluctuating market, use of the product was avoided by large industry.

Ina Food therefore concentrated on producing powdered agar, developed sources from which the raw material could be imported and stored throughout the year, and through the consolidation of production into a highly efficient process, achieved a stable market that eliminated fluctuating prices to develop a stronger demand. The history of the company was actually the history of the development of powdered agar in Japan.

Recently, with the discovery of the cancer-resistant properties of oligosaccharides in agar, agar's effectiveness as a deterrent of constipation, its use in meals for the aged etc., distinctively effective uses of agar had been on the increase.

It had therefore been his strong belief that sudden growth should always be avoided.

*A company exists for its employees. Happiness and steady growth makes it possible for the company to grow forever.*

— Hiroshi Tsukakoshi, chairman of Ina Food[4]

---

[4] Ibid.

**Exhibit 2**   Sales, Operating Income and Number of Employees for Ina Food for the Past 10 Years

INA FOOD INDUSTRY Co. Ltd.

| | 1997 | 1998 | 1999 | 2000 | 2001 | 2002 | 2003 | 2004 | 2005 | 2006 | 2007 | 2008 | 2009 | 2010 | 2011 | 2012 |
|---|---|---|---|---|---|---|---|---|---|---|---|---|---|---|---|---|
| sales | 9,757 | 9,843 | 10,630 | 10,910 | 11,787 | 12,422 | 13,317 | 14,411 | 20,074 | 17,468 | 16,522 | 15,937 | 15,906 | 17,135 | 17,398 | 17,449 |
| Operating Income | 705 | 834 | 1,123 | 1,085 | 1,325 | 1,603 | 2,025 | 2,373 | 3,819 | 2,602 | 1,857 | 1,597 | 1,885 | 2,356 | 2,404 | 2,291 |
| Number of Employees | 249 | 259 | 264 | 277 | 286 | 302 | 304 | 329 | 345 | 378 | 385 | 385 | 387 | 393 | 409 | 423 |

# 2005: A Special Year

The business boom for Ina Food was caused by a notion promoted on national TV that agar contains lots of vegetable fibers and is effective in preventing obesity, high blood pressure, hyperlipidemia and diabetes. In response to this broadcast, Ina Food began receiving a flood of orders for agar.

At first, Tsukakoshi felt that it should not fulfil the orders.[5] This rather counter-intuitive decision came from his motto "Those who plan for the distant future will be rich and those who plan for the near future will be poor" taken from Sontoku Ninomiya (1787–1856), who was highly respected in Japan for his work ethics and benevolence.[6]

---

[5] Ibid.

[6] Ninomiya Sontoku was a farm technologist and the leading agricultural philosopher of the late Edo period (1600–1868). His practical and moral teachings, which urged cultivators to raise output and pay their taxes, helped strengthen the economic basis of Tokugawa rule. For this he was later praised as a paragon of virtue in the national ethics textbooks of the 1930s. Ninomiya taught farmers to improve themselves through *hotoku* ("repaying virtue"), the idea that benefits received from heaven, man, and earth should be repaid, and that doing so would create a "true society" of peacefulness and prosperity. To the familiar

However, it soon received many letters from consumers writing about their illnesses and seeking Ina Food's help in curing them. "I have diabetes," they wrote, or "I am plagued with various illnesses; I must improve my health."[7] When Tsukakoshi told his employees about these letters, they agreed to help. To fulfil the orders, the company had to operate its plant 24 hours a day, seven days a week, for the first time in its history.[8]

After a few months of operating at full capacity, the employees started showing signs of strain. Tsukakoshi believed they could not continue production at this breakneck pace and he decided instead to cut down production and allocate a limited amount of products to current customers proportionally to their orders. He also anticipated that the order level would return to normal once the hype died down. He was proven right. The boom disappeared as quickly as it had come, and some of the distributors even asked the company to take back excess inventories.

## Tsukakoshi's Management Philosophy

During his time at Ina Food over nearly half a century, Tsukakoshi had developed his own unique philosophy on business and an answer to the question "What is a company?" (see **Exhibit 3**).

His cautious attitude towards quick growth was unique at a time when a company's return on sales and total market value were considered a management's key performance indices. Since the day he took over the management reins at Ina Food in 1958, he had experienced many tough situations in which all the employees had worked together to support the company and push it through the rough patch. Consequently, he began to think that the company did not exist for the management or even for itself; rather, it existed for the happiness of the employees. If all the employees

---

Confucian virtues of sincerity, diligence, and thrift, Ninomiya added cooperation with others to his code of ethics. See Kodansha (1983) *Kodansha Encyclopedia of Japan*, Tokyo: Kodansha, Vol. 6, p. 7.

[7] *Nihon Keizai Shinbun*, May 23–27, 2006, p. 8. Also, see Tsukakoshi, H. (2005) "Iikaisha wo Tsukurimashou (Let us Build a Good Company)", in *Bunya*, 7th Edition, pp. 11–213.

[8] Ibid.

**Exhibit 3**  Main Business

**1. Agar for professional use (Sawando plant)**

A stable quality and supply of agar were assured by an abundant supply of quality cold groundwater. Enormous amounts of water go into the production of agar from seaweed. The Sawando plant is favored with a plentiful supply of groundwater that remains at 12°C the year round. This natural environment ensures a stable supply and quality of its agar products.

**2. Compound of water soluble gums (Fujisawa plant)**

The modern and hygienic Fujisawa plant produces Inagel, a compound of agar and water-soluble gums. Inagel is a medicinal product produced in a completely dust-free environment.

**3. Products for households (Kitaoka plant)**

A healthy product that helps in cooking, Kanten Papa is easy to use and made by hand. This is the very basis that mothers use in cooking at home and preparing family meals. Today, as Japanese people worry about preserving their family life, easy-to-use ingredients become all the more significant in preparing family meals.

**4. Agarose business**

Ina Food is pushing the frontier of biotechnology. This attitude assures their task of exploring new possibilities for agar. By upgrading their refining process, they have found a new application for agar in the field of fine chemicals. Research at Ina Food is not only for making profits, but also allows exited young researchers to pursue their dreams.

**5. Processing machines department**

The company develops unique machinery for agar users. Their know-how of agar production is used to best advantage for agar users.

**6. Restaurant business (Kanten Papa Gardens)**

Bountiful greenery contributes to the beauty of the town. The head office and the Kitaoka plant were built on a site surrounded by a forest of evergreens. The company has tried to preserve as many trees as possible. In 1988, it developed a corporate garden of over 60,000 square meters where wild flowers and grasses abound with mountain azaleas and hydrangeas which are voluntarily cared for by the employees who treasure their beauty.

*Himawari-Tei "The restaurant of delicious cuisine"*

Visitors enjoy the unique and distinctive menu of Himawari-Tei which has been specifically prepared for young groups and for family dining. Local beer is served

*(Continued)*

**Exhibit 3**   (*Continued*)

at this restaurant, whose theme is fun and friendship. It has a "Spanish" patio and a shop of imported interior goods.

*Satsuki-Tei "Agar restaurant"*

This is an agar restaurant for the health conscious. It is located in a wooded (Japanese red pine) corner on the premises belonging to the Kitaoka plant. The dishes featuring agar and seaweed satisfy the health conscious customers of these days.

### 7. Research and development

The survival of an enterprise rests on its R&D capabilities. R&D is the mainstay of an enterprise. Based on this conviction, Ina Food made it a rule to always engage 10% of its workforce in the R&D of materials and production technologies. Agar, which is mostly dietary fibers of very low calorific value, presents limitless possibilities of development.

Presentation of the proposed uses of agar determines demand. New types of agar developed from basic R&D for new uses of agar increase benefits for their customers. The company is fully equipped with the necessary facilities to conduct conclusive experiments.

### 8. Agarlite (Inosawa plant)

Recycling of waste created from agar production produces this product. Corporations in the 21st century are becoming increasingly inseparable from their respective localities. The cleaning of the plants and work sites, and the cleansing of the adjacent river beds are all undertaken by the employees. The seaweed waste that is generated from the agar manufacturing process is also recycled and effectively used for growing-beds which produce edible mushrooms.

### 9. Inashoku (Food material for business use)

Brand new agar products for the food service industry are produced by Ina Food. Good health is always important to all people, and eating healthy food is one of the key factors in achieving it. There is a vast demand for healthy, tasty and easy-to-prepare products in the food service industry. "Inashoku" club is the new brand to serve such needs; all the products are mainly made from agar.

### 10. Kanten-Papa Garden

The head office and the Kitaoka plant were built on a site surrounded by a forest of evergreens. They are also surrounded by red pine forest, wild flowers, grasses and seasonal flowers. Ina Food has also tried to preserve as many trees as possible.

*(Continued)*

**Exhibit 3**   (*Continued*)

> In 1988, the company developed a corporate garden over 100,000 square meters where wild flowers and grasses abound with mountain azaleas and hydrangeas which are voluntarily cared for by the employees who treasure their beauty.
>
> Kanten Papa Hall is meant for cultural activities of the community in the area. The facilities have been taken over for multi-purpose uses such as presentations, training sessions, study sessions and exhibitions. The audio equipment and the floor-heating equipment used in winter provide a comfortable life throughout the year.
>
> Katsurakoba is a tea room, the ideal place for visitors to relax, with a great view from the window.

were happy and had a high morale, the communities they lived in would improve, thus making a contribution to society.[9]

What Tsukakoshi strived for was the perpetual existence of the company; it was not quick growth that he wanted, but stable growth. He believed that history showed how rapid growth was always followed by quick decline. Decline, and the resultant restructuring, forced employees and suppliers out onto the streets, seriously damaging the community. His belief was that if management were not preoccupied purely with revenue, and focused instead on establishing steady growth, the company would continue to exist for a long time. This would, in turn, make happier everybody who was directly or indirectly associated with the company. He believed that his role as top management was to make employees happy at work.

*Let us build a good company. I hope to make it a company not just with good management indices, but a company that people would call a good company.*

— Hiroshi Tsukakoshi, chairman of Ina Food[10]

Every Ina Food employee carried a card printed with the company's credo: "Let us build a good company."

---

[9] Ibid.

[10] *Nihon Keizai Shinbun*, 2006, *op. cit.* Also, see Tsukakoshi, H. (2005), *op. cit.*

# **Tsukakoshi's Personal History**[11]

Hiroshi Tsukakoshi was born in 1937 in Japan's Komagane City in the southern part of Nagano Prefecture. His father, an artist of European style paintings, passed away when he was eight years old and so he had very few memories of his father. His mother had a day job, and also worked at growing rice and potatoes at home. Although he had to help his mother with the farming after school, he got passing grades; this taught him that where there was a will, there was a way.

When he was 17 years old he came down with tuberculosis, the very disease that had been the cause of his father's death. Caused primarily by overwork and malnutrition, the disease forced him to drop out of high school. As he was the only student amongst the 250 in his year who contracted tuberculosis, Hiroshi was upset: "Why am I the only one to get tuberculosis, especially when I worked the hardest?"[12] He spent three years in a hospital followed by a long period of recovery in which he lost the best years of his youth.

His disease and hospitalization confined him to a dark hospital room where he realized how precious good health was and how it was irreplaceable. After he was cured, he was fortunate enough to be hired by a local lumber company. Despite the tough employment conditions, Hiroshi worked hard because he was glad to work again.

Tsukakoshi's decision-making agility and business acumen did not go unnoticed. One day, he had driven a truck for more than 40 kilometers only to find that, because of a communication error, there was no lumber to bring back. Not wanting to go back empty handed, he bought a pile of timber lying nearby, returning to the company with a loaded truck. This kind of managerial prowess must have caught the eye of the president, for, after having been with the company for only one and a half years, at the age of 21, he was asked to help rebuild an agar producing company which belonged to the president's friend. Ina Food was deep in the red, and it seemed that the agar producer did not have much to offer.

---

[11] Ibid.

[12] Ibid.

Tsukakoshi joined Ina Food in 1958 as "acting president". The company employed just 17 temporary people then. Although it had annual sales of ¥10 million, it was also losing millions of yen every year. It had no unique technology, no credibility, no stable employees and no particular major clients. Tsukakoshi had no knowledge about agar or manufacturing and relied on chemistry reference books for information, and learned production engineering and accounting on his own. Not only did he have to overcome his own ignorance of the field, he also found that because of a lack of funds, the company could not buy new machines. In this case, he found that the only thing he could do was to improve the employees' morale to increase productivity.

Tsukakoshi and the president of Ina Food did everything they could do to improve the morale of the employees. When a machine broke down, the two would work all night to fix it. They also often chose to defer their salary payments, preferring rather to pay the employees on time.

One thing they learned from these tough experiences was that unexpected work and difficult jobs were better done by all employees working together as a group. When they had to replace the kettle used for boiling seaweed, they worked around the clock for four days in a row. During this time, the female employees cooked food for the male employees so that they could eat in the plant and continue their work; this gave them a sense of solidarity. As a result of these experiences, Tsukakoshi formed a solid belief that he would manage the company for the employees' happiness, to pay them back for their dedication.


## The Company's Growth[13]

Although Ina Food made fewer losses every year, it was not making profits. In those days, the demand for agar came primarily from industry, i.e., for the production of traditional Japanese sweet cakes such as *yokan* (a sweet cake made of agar and beans), or jelly, made by confectionary companies. The profit margin in these areas was very thin.

In order to become profitable, Ina Food tried producing imitation powdered juice, a highly popular item those days. Although the technique

---

[13] Ibid.

they used to make artificially flavored juices was incredibly labor-intensive in nature, they were able to generate more profit from it than from selling agar.

After ten years of struggle, Ina Food finally began reporting profits. Just then, many factors came together to change the face of the agar industry. First, the price of agar swung violently up and down depending on the weather. For example, a warm winter caused agar to foul and no serious attempt was made to improve the situation as agar was only a secondary source of income for farmers. This meant that agar would sometimes be in short supply, and its prices in the market would soar. Another problem that Ina Food faced was that the women who collected seaweeds from which agar was extracted were getting old, and it was becoming difficult to recruit young women divers, and this caused the material price to go up. Agar producers and middlemen thus began using these unfortunate situations to their benefit by simply increasing the price while supplying less agar, which upset confectioners.

The Oil Crisis of 1973 brought out the problems of the agar industry in the extreme and agar prices tripled within a mere 12 months. Ina Food tried to keep its price low in the beginning, but with a barrage of orders from all over the country, they eventually raised their prices, following the market. As a consequence, they made a fortune. The high prices infuriated confectioners, however, and they cried that they would stop making *yokan* and switch to producing other cakes that did not contain agar. Hence agar producers lost credit overall. Tsukakoshi found the entire situation very stressful as he worried about the impact it would have on the industry and Ina Food in particular.

Tsukakoshi believed that their business would have no future if they continued to aggravate their clients by allowing the price to swing up and down violently. Consequently, he set out to find ways to stabilize the price, quality and supply of agar. In order to store more agar, Tsukakoshi built four additional bays of storage buildings using the profit earned from the price hike. At the same time, the production facilities and the factory were enlarged to increase production capacity. Furthermore, he visited various countries to secure suppliers for raw materials needed in the production of agar in order to stabilize the flow inputs. He visited approximately 20 countries, including Chile, the Portuguese Azores Islands in the

Atlantic Ocean, Morocco, China, South Korea and Vietnam in search of partner companies.

His objective was not to find cheap supply sources based on cheap labor but to nurture local companies. He did not, however, want to invest in local companies or even establish resident representatives; his plan was to provide local firms with technology only. Local companies were often in need of technology, but did not want to be controlled by outsiders. He aimed for mutual benefits: the local companies could improve their raw material qualities while Ina Food could secure an exclusive source of supplies. As a result of his travels, the company signed partnership agreements with suppliers from four countries, including Chile, Morocco and South Korea. He believed any localization attempt that was simply seeking cheap labor costs in developing countries could not achieve the trust of the suppliers, and such an attempt would simply make the investor a deracinated wanderer, which would never grow in that country.

As a result of its new and stable supplies and its increased storage capacity, the company was able to release a large amount of agar to stabilize the price when market demand started to soar. On August 16, 1977, the company published an opinion advertisement in an industry paper (Japan Food Newspaper) declaring "Agar is no longer a market-driven flamboyant merchandise."[14]

## Product Image[15]

Agar was made from seaweeds such as tengusa and ogonori that were originally harvested from the seas around the Izu peninsula in Japan. Traditionally, agar production was a popular second source of income for farmers in Nagano Prefecture. They extracted juice from the seaweeds which was then boiled down. The resulting concentrate was frozen by exposing it to the cold winter air during the night, after which it was allowed to thaw during the warmth of the daytime. Repeating this freezing and thawing cycle removed the water content and allowed for the production of agar in various shapes such as rods, strings and powders.

---

[14] Ibid.
[15] Ibid.

Immediately after he joined Ina Food, Tsukakoshi created an agar product branded "Pickel" (a German word for a rock climbing tool; an ice axe). He named it after his father who was nicknamed "Pickel" because of his sharply protruding chin. The product didn't sell at all. This made Tsukakoshi realize that perhaps it was necessary to increase consumer awareness of the very word "agar" (*kanten*)[16] to make the product more popular. This led to the brand name "Kanten Papa", which he developed with the help of his employees in 1980. Kanten Papa was aimed at families and the domestic use of agar, which until then had primarily been used in industrial scale food manufacturing. The brand name was inspired by a popular TV program on NHK[17] called Sweet Papa, in which celebrity fathers and their children appeared as couples. The name Kanten Papa thus aimed to invoke the popularity of the program with families when they bought agar. The company also created a product named "Kanten Cook" named after Captain Cook. The products were a big hit with consumers.

Kanten Papa was sold through stores in Nagano Prefecture, where the company was located, and in Yamanashi Prefecture nearby. The product made it easy for everyone to produce fruit jelly, and owing to its success, the following year Ina Food was approached by a nationwide supermarket store wanting to offer Kanten Papa through its network. Tsukakoshi, however, turned them down because he thought a small local company like itself would not be able to follow up easily if something unexpected were to happen. For one thing, the company didn't even have a department to handle claims. If Ina Food had allowed the supermarket chain to handle the product, it could have been a big hit as it would have been made available all over the country. Tsukakoshi felt that a product that shot to popularity would be quickly forgotten and that supplying Kanten Papa to a major, national, supermarket chain would deviate from the his "Annual Growth Ring" management policy that sought a slow steady growth.[18]

---

[16] "Kanten" is phonetic Japanese for agar.

[17] This word stands for Nippon Hosou Kyoukai (Japan Broadcasting Association), the largest TV network in Japan.

[18] Annual growth ring is the layer of wood growth put on a tree during a single growing season. It is readily distinguished because of differences in the cells formed during the early and late parts of the season. In Japan this word is commonly used to show the "slow but steady" type of management style, philosophy and principle.

However, the company soon started getting letters and phone calls from consumers living all over Japan asking for Kanten Papa. To serve these customers, Tsukakoshi set up a mail order department, which by 2005 had 250,000 regular customers. This allowed for an ideal relationship with their clients. As soon as Ina Food received a complaint or a thank you letter, they sent back a hand-written letter to the client. Although they sold the products through the internet, relationships with their clients were such that when an employee handling client communications got married, he or she received numerous gifts from the client congratulating him or her on the marriage. Had the company sold its product in large quantities to distributors, such a relation with the end-users of its products would not have been possible. By 2005, the company also had sales offices throughout the nation and was selling some of its merchandise through supermarkets. Moreover, Ina Food had opened nine direct outlet stores and hoped to gradually increase them in a modest manner.

## Research and Development[19]

The company's research laboratory was set up in the 1960s, initially employing one researcher. Ina Food later made it company policy to employ research staff equivalent to 10% of the total amount of employees. By 2005, it had 40 staff in the research and development (R&D) department as it had approximately 400 employees.

Initially, research focused on agar production technology. Since then, the R&D department's focus had shifted to researching possible uses of agar, i.e., application development. Tsukakoshi believed in and encouraged research, as many new products were found in that way. This was illustrated by a plaque displayed at the research laboratory for 25 years which read "Serendipity".

In one discovery, the research department noted that they sometimes created agar which could not be solidified. Such a product, while obviously unsuitable for normal usage, could have some use if they could develop a technology to produce it in a stable manner. A use was found: a

---

[19]*Nihon Keizai Shinbun*, 2006, *op. cit.* Also see, Tsukakoshi, H. (2005), *op. cit.*

soft agar for elderly patients who had difficulty swallowing. The company then produced soft foods made of agar by adding water and cooked food chopped into small pieces which made it easier to swallow for elderly people. The technology to produce unsolidified agar was patented and was also used to produce agar juices, lipsticks and cosmetic foundations. The research department also regularly took newly developed materials to exhibitions of other industries such as high-tech materials and showed them around, asking, "Can you use these for your products or processes?"

## Contribution to the Community[20]

Ina Food's headquarters were surrounded by nature. Originally built to provide a good working environment, it had since become an asset to the local community. The plot on which the headquarters stood measured approximately 100,000 square meters. Development of the plot started in 1987 with only the factory. Then when it came to building a parking lot for the employees, Tsukakoshi thought it would be nice if employees could park their cars in the middle of the woods, so he built one in the middle of red pine woods.

Subsequently, Tsukakoshi heard locals and visitors alike make comments such as "it would be nice to have a place to eat here". In response to this, he opened a health food restaurant serving agar and seaweed. The restaurant proved to be hugely popular, and soon he added a wild grass garden and a flower bed, as well as another restaurant. These developments were followed by relocating the headquarters there, and the building of a multipurpose hall to serve the community. The company called it Kanten Papa Garden, and the plot became a sightseeing spot for the community. Almost every year they organized a Kanten Festival where they served *tokoroten* (a sort of noodle made from agar) free of charge at food stands operated by Ina Food employees.

The company built a pedestrian bridge in front of the factory because Tsukakoshi thought it was dangerous for employees and visitors to cross the busy road on foot. The company also planted cherry trees along the

---

[20] Ibid.

road. It built a fountain using underground water that came to be favored by so many people that they had to stand in queue to get water, and so the company built another fountain. The area was cleaned every morning by the employees voluntarily. Tsukakoshi thought it was in people's nature to be attracted to a beautiful area. He believed that making their workplace beautiful contributed to a beautification of the community.

Moreover, employees parked their cars far from the store when they parked in the parking lot of a supermarket for the convenience of pregnant women and elderly people. The company also prohibited its employees from making a right turn when commuting[21] to prevent traffic congestions caused by waiting to make a right turn. They were told to make left turns when coming to work even if it meant they drove further.

He believed the employees' morale and morals went hand in hand. If a company's management thought about its employees' welfare first, the employees' morale improved and they ended up acting with high morals. That resulted in the company's contribution to the community.


# IPO: Not Interested[22]

Small- and medium-sized companies were going public one after the other during the Japanese bubble economy from the late 1980s to the early 1990s. However, Tsukakoshi kept away from such a trend. Toward the end of the 1990s, many securities brokerage companies came to visit Ina Food urging them to go public. Tsukakoshi was in favor of the idea at one point, but as soon as he heard about maximization of profits, total market value management, and an achievement-oriented policy in the IT boom that followed, he rejected the idea.

He felt that he would not be able to manage the company for the employees and for its contributions to the community if the company was listed. Tsukakoshi felt that if the stock market appreciated Ina Food's current management style and a rise in stock price was a result of that, he would not mind going public, but he suspected the stock market was only interested in how much profit the company made. He believed

---

[21] In Japan, like in the UK, they drive on the left.

[22] *Nihon Keizai Shinbun*, 2006, *op. cit.* Also see, Tsukakoshi, H. (2005), *op. cit.*

that the purpose of the company was the happiness of its employees. The market, however, seemed to reward companies who fired employees during restructuring rounds with higher stock prices. To Tsukakoshi, it seemed that the market was confusing the means with the object. His motto was for profit to be the means to make employees happier, and not the object.

Tsukakoshi believed that there was "an axis of progress" and "an axis of trend" in human society. The axis of progress was a straight line that led to an ideal society. The axis of trend was a movement of the society that swung constantly to the left and right, perpendicular to the axis of progress. He felt people should pay attention to the axis of trend, but not misunderstand it as the path to follow. American-style management that paid heavy attention to shareholders' profit was a trend in his eyes. If one wanted stability and long-term existence of the company, one should not be influenced by it. To move steadily along the axis of progress with a thorough understanding of the optimum growth rate while keeping an eye on the trend was the kind of management he was aiming at.

## Decision Time for the Future

In the summer of 2006, Tsukakoshi was looking through the windows of his office in Ina City, Japan. The head office and Kitaoka plant which he was looking at were designed as part of the landscape. They had built their workplace with their own hands. The corporate garden, developed in 1988, displayed over 60,000 square meters of wild flowers and grasses containing mountain azaleas and hydrangeas which were voluntarily cared for by the employees who treasured their beauty.

He aimed for his company to be a corporation that was conscious of the global environment. It had been his strong belief that no good company could exist independently of the surrounding communities. Employees tending flowers was no different from them wishing their town to be beautiful and the surrounding nature to be preserved.

He felt he had done a good job so far. The business had prospered and did not pose any urgent problems. But he also felt that he should not simply sit back and savor his success. There were tremendous growth opportunities and he knew operations should be improved before those opportunities could be targeted.

He had been thinking that real joy came from change and from going to the next level. His long-time belief had been that no company could get to the future by standing still. His vivacious personality, intelligence and "can do" attitude had set the tone for the company.

Based on this, his attention had been directed towards various operational as well as management issues to identify any pressing matters that needed change. He was questioning himself about what changes needed to be made. He thought of the following possibilities, although he did not believe they would happen soon.

1. The company had not explored the possibility of exporting its products. Bearing various risks in foreign markets in mind, should the company export its products? What about production overseas?
2. Growth eventually would need financing. Small- and medium-sized companies were going public one after the other. Although Ina Food had managed to stay away from an IPO thus far, could it grow without going public?
3. Good quality agar products could not be manufactured without good materials, high quality water and a good production process. It had been the company's practice to import high-quality materials from overseas suppliers. It also ensured a large stock of materials, thus contributing to the stability of agar markets around the world. However, Tsukakoshi wondered how long the company could enjoy an overseas supply of materials. Should it try to make extra efforts to secure longer term material supply contracts from foreign sources?
4. R&D had always aimed at further improving the company by seeking new possible uses for agar. They promoted their developments to customers for use in their corporate applications and actively proposed new products to meet predicted requirements in advance. To be able to do this, the company had made it a policy to have research staff that was equal to 10% of the total number of employees. Tsukakoshi wondered whether this investment in R&D would be sufficient in the future.

5. Tsukakoshi considered that in its quest to seek better profits and efficiency, the company must be wary of: not inconveniencing its suppliers, not discarding its regard for the environment and not resorting to forcing sacrifices upon its employees. He thought the company had to maintain a meaningful presence, and had to constantly strive to be a corporate entity with an endeavor that was lauded and appreciated by the stakeholders — all those around it. He was concerned that there might have been areas that had been overlooked and which had not been given adequate attention. If so, the company had to find them and improve in these areas.

6. He believed that the true corporate objective rested in seeking various ways in which the corporation might serve society while it ensured the livelihood of its employees. He also firmly believed that the pursuit of growth and profit were merely a means for attaining these objectives. He had done a lot in these areas, but wondered what else could be done for employees and society in the future.

## For Further Discussion

1. List the major contributions that Hiroshi Tsukakoshi made to Ina Food?
2. Study the possibility of exporting Ina Food's products to the overseas market. Are the products suitable for the export market? The company is currently not so enthusiastic on exports. Why?
3. The top management at Ina Food does not plan to go public at the moment. If you were the owner of the company, what would you do? It is not uncommon now, in Japan and the US, for companies that once became public to become private again. Why are they doing so?
4. Define corporate social responsibility: profit seeking versus treating employees well.

**9**

# OSG Corporation:
# Hedging Transaction Exposure

On Monday, April 24, 2006, the US dollar fell to a new three-month low against the yen of ¥114.30/$ in Tokyo's foreign exchange market, the lowest rate since January 16, 2006. This was a reflection of trading in New York three days earlier, on Friday, where the dollar had fallen more than 1.75% against the yen. The depreciation of the dollar against the yen was a direct result of a meeting of the G7 in Washington DC on April 21, 2006. In that meeting, G7 leaders voiced dissatisfaction over the slow speed of China's currency reforms since the renminbi's revaluation in July 2005. They called for greater currency flexibility, particularly in China, sparking speculation that a stronger renminbi would boost other Asian currencies, including the yen.[1] At the same time, the G7 called for more dialogue between oil-producing and oil-consuming countries, and further improvement in oil market transparency with "more complete and timely data on production, consumption and inventories, and for clear reporting of oil reserves", while reaffirming the need to promote greater energy efficiency.[2] The benchmark crude-oil contract had reached yet another record high in New York at US$75.35 a barrel on April 21, 2006. With prices forecast to top US$80 in the near future, higher volatility in the yen–dollar exchange rate was expected (see **Exhibit 1**).

On that same Monday, Teruhide Osawa, president of OSG Corporation (OSG), was following the foreign exchange market from his office in Toyokawa, Japan. He looked at his computer screen and was very surprised to see that the yen had appreciated 1.75% against the dollar in one day. It made him wonder about the effect such a volatile exchange rate would have on OSG, a manufacturer of cutting tools used by industries

---

[1] Nikkei Net, April 25, 2006, http://www.nikkei.co.jp/news/market/20060425m2ds0imf0625.html.
[2] Ibid.

**Exhibit 1**   Gist of Statement Issued by G-7 Financial Leaders on April 21, 2006

The following is the gist of a statement and an annex issued on April 21, 2006 by finance ministers and central bank governors of the Group of Seven major industrialized nations after their meeting in Washington.

- The world economic outlook remains favorable.
- Inflation remains contained despite high oil prices and global trade growth being buoyant.
- Risks remain from oil market developments, global imbalances and growing protectionism.
- The G-7 calls for greater investment from oil-producing nations in exploration, production, energy infrastructure and refinery capacity.
- Greater exchange rate flexibility is desirable in emerging economies with large current account surpluses, especially China.
- Excess volatility and disorderly movements in exchange rates are undesirable for economic growth.
- Further action is needed in Japan to ensure the economic recovery with fiscal soundness and structural reforms.
- Further action is needed in the United States to boost national savings.
- Further action is needed in Europe to implement structural reforms for labor market.
- Greater exchange rate flexibility is critical for China to allow necessary appreciations of the renminbi to address global imbalances.

*Source*: Nikkei Net, April 22, 2006, http://www.nikkei.co.jp/news/past/honbun.cfm?i=AT3S2200D %2022042006&g=MH&d=20060422.

worldwide. Although business had been prospering and did not pose any urgent problems, Osawa felt that he should not sit back and savor his success. The business continued to have global opportunities for growth and he knew that any improvement in operations should be undertaken before further growth.

Faced with the big fluctuation in the yen–dollar exchange rate on that day, Osawa asked Koji Sonobe, director and general manager of the Support Center Finance Group[3] to analyze and report how OSG's foreign currency transaction exposure was measured and how it could be managed. Osawa specifically wanted to know more about how the company was currently hedging its foreign currency exposures. Sonobe was asked

---

[3] This is a department within OSG, whose mission is to provide technical and accounting advice and help to other departments and to affiliated companies in the same group. See OSG's Annual Report (2005), http://www.ofg-ir.com/english2/annual/.

to give a presentation a month later at the board of directors' meeting on this issue and possible future currency hedging strategies for OSG.

## The Thoughts of OSG's President

Teruhide Osawa, president of OSG (see **Exhibit 2**), had been thinking that real joy came from change and from going to the next level. His long time belief had been that no company could get to the future by standing still. His vivacious personality, intelligence and "can do" attitude had set the tone for the company. Given his belief for scanning the status quo for areas of potential improvement, his attention had been drawn to various operational and management issues that needed change.

Exhibit 2   Profile of OSG

| | |
|---|---|
| Corporate Name | OSG CORPORATION |
| Headquarters | 3-22 Honnogahara, Toyokawa City, Aichi Prefecture, Japan |
| E-mail | cs-info@osg.co.jp |
| Established | March 26, 1938 |
| Capital | ¥10,404 million |
| Number of Employees | 4,012 |
| Sales Amount | ¥65,975 million (in 2005) |
| Stock Market | First Section of Tokyo and Nagoya Stock Exchange |

**OSG Trademark**

OSG is an initialism derived from the company's full name, Osawa Screw Grinding Co., Ltd.

**Business Profile**

OSG manufactures and sells cutting tools, forming dies, measuring tools, machine tools and parts. It imports tools for sale; acquires, leases and transfers patent rights; and provides instruction in engineering.

**Customers and Market Share**

More than 3,000 screws are used in the production of a single automobile. Each hole drilled for a screw requires precise threading cut with a tap. Noted for their accuracy and speed, OSG taps are used extensively by manufacturers, especially of automobiles and aircraft, making OSG the number one tap producer globally. All of Japan's top automotive companies purchase 50% or more of their taps from OSG. With this, OSG's domestic market share for a tap was 49.3% in 2005.

*Source*: OSG Annual Report (2005), http://www.osg-ir.com/english2/welcome.

Foreign exchange transaction exposure[4] (see **Exhibit 3**) was one such subject that had caught his attention. Exposure to foreign currencies changed the value of outstanding import and export contracts which had been entered into prior to a change in exchange rates, but which were not due to be settled until after the exchange rates changed. This could change the value of existing contractual obligations, for example, the values of an account receivable or an account payable. Osawa was fully aware that currency-related gains and losses could have a destructive impact on reporting earnings.

## OSG's History and the Opportunity for Growth

OSG had a history that stretched over 65 years. In 1938, the company was founded by Hideo Osawa, Teruhide Osawa's father, as the Osawa Screw Grinding Co., Ltd. in Musashino, Tokyo, for the manufacture of taps and dies.[5] OSG expanded its product line over time, and by 2006 it manufactured and sold cutting tools, forming dies, measuring tools, and machine tools and parts. The company also imported tools for sale; acquired, leased and transferred patent rights; and provided instruction in engineering. OSG's customers were the automotive and aerospace industry, as well as producers of a wide range of products such as heavy electrical machinery and precision metals.

*OSG will continue to focus its efforts on markets with potential for growth and develop its business on a global scale by carving out a niche in the new global marketplace.*

— Teruhide Osawa, president, OSG[6]

---

[4]Transaction exposure is defined as the potential risk for change in the home currency value of import and export contracts because of constantly changing foreign exchange rates. For details of the definition and operations, see Eiteman, D.K., Stonehill, A.I. and Moffett, M.H. (2007). *Multinational Business Finance*, 11th Edition, Massachusetts: Pearson, pp. 205–234.

[5]Taps are tools for cutting an internal screw thread. Dies are tools for cutting/forming an external screw thread.

[6]IR Info, OSG, http://www.osg-ir.com/english2/annual/.

**Exhibit 3**    The Foreign Exchange Market

In the foreign exchange market, currencies are traded to facilitate execution of commercial or investment transactions. The exchange rate is the value of a currency in terms of another currency. Market participants are individuals, businesses and governments. Some of them use the foreign exchange market to hedge foreign exchange risk.

The foreign exchange market comprises spot transactions, outright forward transactions and swap transactions. A spot transaction is the purchase and sale of foreign exchange with delivery and payment to take place on the following day. For forward transaction, delivery and payment are required on the second business day after the anniversary date[7], although the forward rates are quoted at the time of agreement. A swap transaction is the simultaneous execution of sale and purchase of foreign exchange for two different value dates; a spot against forward and a forward–forward swap. According to the Bank of International Settlements (BIS), daily global net turnover of the foreign exchange market was estimated to be US$1.880 trillion in April 2004.[8] Swap transactions and outright forwards together made up 57% of foreign exchange market transactions at that time (see following table).

| **Global foreign exchange market turnover**[9] | | | | | | |
| Daily averages in April, in billions of US$ | | | | | | |
| | 1989 | 1992 | 1995 | 1998 | 2001 | 2004 |
| --- | --- | --- | --- | --- | --- | --- |
| Spot transactions | 317 | 394 | 494 | 568 | 387 | 621 |
| Outright forwards | 27 | 58 | 97 | 128 | 131 | 208 |
| Foreign exchange swaps | 190 | 324 | 546 | 734 | 656 | 944 |
| Estimated gaps in reporting | 56 | 44 | 53 | 60 | 26 | 107 |
| Total "traditional" turnover | 590 | 820 | 1,190 | 1,490 | 1,200 | 1,880 |
| *Memo: Turnover at April 2004 exchange rates*[10] | 650 | 840 | 1,120 | 1,590 | 1,380 | 1,880 |

*Source*: Bank for International Settlement (2005), "Triennial Central Bank Survey: Foreign Exchange and Derivatives Market Activity in 2004", p. 5.

---

[7] Forward exchange rates are quoted for one, two, three, six and twelve months. Payment is on the second business day after the even-month anniversary of the trade.

[8] Bank for International Settlement (2005). "Triennial Central Bank Survey: Foreign Exchange and Derivatives Market Activity in 2004", p. 5.

[9] Adjusted for local and cross-border double counting.

[10] Non-US dollar legs of foreign currency transactions were converted from current US dollar amounts into original currency amounts at average exchange rates for April of each survey year, and then reconverted into US dollar amounts at average April 2004 exchange rates.

> *Our long-term goal is to increase our overseas sales ratio to 50%, from its current 37.7%.*
>
> — Teruhide Osawa, president, OSG[11]

OSG was able to expand beyond Japan into North America, South America, Asia and Europe because of its expertise in the field of cutting tools and related technologies, which it had accumulated since its establishment, and because of the sales and marketing data which served as the base for its operations.[12] The company's expansion into overseas markets began in 1968, with the establishment of OSG Tap and Die Inc. in Chicago; a plant in Brazil had been in operation for more than 30 years. In 1995, the company stepped up the pace of building overseas networks against the backdrop of the continued expansion of the global automotive industry. Subsequently, a headquarter was established in Europe in 1997, which was expanding rapidly as a marketing base.

OSG's business expansion was associated with Japan's automotive industry, which had enjoyed much success at home and abroad. By 2006, OSG was using its experience to increase its market share among major automakers in Europe and the US, and to take part in the emerging automotive markets in Asia. The company continued to focus its efforts on markets with a potential for growth and developed its business on a global scale by carving out a tap market niche in the global marketplace. In the Americas, its business was firmly established and growing of its own accord. OSG planned to expand its share in the tap market supplying major US automotive manufacturers, which was less than 20% in 2006.

The company originally established a foothold in Europe with the help of sales agents and was able to quickly position itself, despite its lack of resources and the complexity of the market. This indirect sales system, however, became a hindrance when the company decided to aggressively penetrate and further develop the European market. Hence it regrouped and established local subsidiaries throughout Europe that were steadily developing their business areas. It was also focusing on the high-growth markets of China and other Asian countries, including India. OSG had already positioned itself strongly with a production and sales network in China. Its

---

[11] OSG Annual Report (2005), http://www.osg-ir.com/english2/welcome.
[12] Ibid.

sales team of approximately 70 local sales people, built in a period of only three years, was a source of pride for the company. Achievements like this symbolized OSG's commitment to localization (see **Exhibit 4**).

**Exhibit 4**    History of OSG

| | |
|---|---|
| March 1938 | Hideo Osawa established Osawa Screw Grinding Co., Ltd. in Musashino, Tokyo. |
| May 1943 | Completed Aichi plant in Ichinomiya, Aichi. |
| August 1956 | Began manufacturing thread-rolling cylindrical dies. |
| May 1957 | Began manufacturing screw thread gauges. |
| April 1961 | Completed Toyokawa plant in Toyokawa, Aichi. |
| June 1963 | Changed name to OSG Manufacturing Company. |
| December 1963 | Separation of sales and manufacturing operations; the sales division was named OSG Corporation. |
| December 1964 | Listed with Class 2 of Nagoya Stock Exchange Market. |
| March 1967 | Completed Oike plant in Ichinomiya, Aichi. |
| February 1968 | OSG Tap and Die Inc. established in Chicago, US. |
| April 1970 | Established a joint company, Taiho Tool Mfg. Co., Ltd. in Kaohsiung, Taiwan. |
| August 1970 | Began manufacturing end mills. |
| December 1970 | Listed with Class 2 of Tokyo Stock Exchange Market. |
| December 1971 | Completed Toyohashi plant in Toyohashi, Aichi. |
| August 1973 | Acquired Sossner Corp., a tap manufacturer in US. |
| November 1974 | OSG Ferramentas de Precisao Ltda. established in Sao Paulo, Brazil. |
| September 1980 | Began manufacturing carbide end mills. |
| June 1981 | Listed with Class 1 of both Tokyo and Nagoya Stock Exchange Market. |
| January 1982 | Completed Shinshiro plant in Shinshiro, Aichi. |
| March 1984 | Began production of EX-Gold Drills. |
| October 1985 | Established OSG Korea Corporation in Taegu, Korea. |
| January 1988 | Established OSG Canada Ltd. in Toronto, Canada. |
| November 1990 | Completed Yana plant in Shinshiro, Aichi. |
| December 1990 | Established OSG Asia Pte. Ltd. in Singapore. |
| April 1992 | Became a majority stock holder of Nihon Hard Metal Co., Ltd. |
| December 1992 | Merged with OSG Corporation. |
| February 1993 | Moved the head office to Toyokawa, Aichi. |
| January 1994 | Acquired Hermecor, a tap manufacturing company in Mexico, and renamed it OSG Royco. |
| October 1995 | Shinshiro plant won TPM grand prix award. |

(*Continued*)

**Exhibit 4**   (*Continued*)

| | |
|---|---|
| November 1995 | Became majority stock holder of Norman Tap and Die in UK and plan to fully acquire company by 1999. |
| October 1996 | Yana and Toyohashi plants won TPM grand prix award. |
| November 1996 | Established OSG Thailand Co., Ltd. in Bangkok, Thailand. |
| October 1997 | Established Dabao (Dongguan) Molding and Cutting Tool Co., Ltd. in Guangzhou, China. |
| December 1997 | Completed CS Center within the head office in Toyokawa. |
| December 1997 | Acquired A.I.M.O., SA trading company (active in Belgium, France and the Netherlands). |
| January 1998 | Opened Hongu Center, warehousing facility in Ichinomiya, Aichi. |
| April 1999 | Established OSG Europe S.A. in Belgium to supervise group companies in Europe. |
| April 1999 | Renamed Norman Tap and Die, UK to OSG UK Limited, and A.I.M.O. to OSG A.I.M.O. S.A. respectively. |
| September 1999 | Involved in business co-operation with the Nastec Corporation. |
| October 1999 | Shinshiro plant successively won TPM grand prix award. |
| May 2000 | Acquired Thrane Tool A/S, a tool wholesale company in Denmark, and renamed to OSG Scandinavia A/S. |
| November 2000 | Nine major plants simultaneously received ISO 14001 certification. |
| December 2000 | Acquired Kamiya Seikoh Inc., reorganized and renamed it Kamiya Seikoh Corporation. |
| April 2001 | Involved in business co-operation with Toyota Caelum, Inc. |
| September 2001 | Established OSG (Shanghai) Corporation in Shanghai, China. |
| October 2001 | QCT in Illinois, US and CCT in India acquired. |
| December 2001 | Coating division became separate as OSG Coating Service Co., Ltd. |
| July 2002 | OSG TI S/L established jointly with Trans Inter, general distributor in Spain. |
| September 2002 | Georgia Plant closed (production transferred to OSG/Royco, S.A. de C.V. in Mexico and OSG Ferramentas de Precisao Ltda. in Brazil). |
| January 2003 | OSG GmbH established in Germany. |
| November 2003 | Established Cutting Tool Innovations Inc., US. |
| December 2003 | Acquired Vumat Ltd., distributor in Italy, and established OSG Italia. |
| June 2004 | Acquired Sterling Die Inc., US. |
| June 2004 | Completed OSG (Shanghai) Precision Tool Co., Ltd. in Songjiang Industrial Zone, Shanghai, China. |
| December 2004 | Completed Design Center. |

*Source*: OSG Annual Report (2005), http://www.osg-ir.com/english2/welcome.

# Strong Overseas Sales — Results for Fiscal Year 2005[13]

In the fiscal year ending on November 30, 2005, the global economy had been robust. Most economies around the world grew spurred by significant growth in several key regions, notably Asia, and despite rising prices for crude oil and raw materials.[14]

Buoyed by the strong performance of Japan's main trading partners, the Japanese economy was steadily recovering from 15 years of recession. Growth was driven mainly by exports and private capital investment, but personal consumption was providing an increased contribution.

OSG's consolidated results, which included figures for the Company and 44 of its significant subsidiaries — three more than in the previous year — reflected the favorable economic climate. Sales performance was up across the board in all the company's major product categories and operating regions. As a result, OSG's consolidated net sales in fiscal 2005 climbed to ¥78,131[15] million, a year-on-year increase of 18.4% to reach a record high for the sixth consecutive year.[16]

## *The Americas*

Sales in the Americas amounted to ¥12,587 million, an increase of 25.5% from fiscal 2004. Operating income increased to ¥1,816 million, advancing 54.9% from 2004. Sales were up because of strong performances by Japanese automotive and related auto part manufacturers and because of the resurgence of the North American aerospace industry.[17]

---

[13] Ibid.

[14] Ibid.

[15] US$1 = ¥120.00 on November 30, 2005.

[16] OSG Annual Report (2005), http://www.osg-ir.com/english2/welcome.

[17] Ibid.

## *Europe*

OSG's European operations recorded sales of ¥4,634 million, an 18.5% year-on-year increase from 2004, and an operating income of ¥594 million, up 13.5% from 2004. The company had been localizing its operations in Europe in recent years. It was shifting from a network of sales agencies to subsidiaries under the guidance of its headquarters in the region, OSG Europe S.A., which was established in 1997. Over the past six years, the company had constructed a regional network that covered the UK, Belgium, the Netherlands, France, Denmark, Spain, Germany and Italy. This network, the largest of its kind among Japanese tool manufacturers in Europe, supported the company's aggressive targeting of the automotive, aerospace, and metal mould industry markets in those nations. Steadily expanding the territory, the company was busy positioning itself in Eastern Europe.[18]

## *Asia, Excluding Japan*

OSG's sales in Asia totaled ¥13,045 million, jumping 38.9% from 2004 to make Asia its second largest sales region. Operating income rose 60.7% from 2004 to ¥2,073 million.

The Asian market was experiencing high growth rates in general, and OSG was achieving even higher sales growth there because of its continued aggressive investment in expanding its Asian network. Strong sales were supported by vigorous demand from major tool users in each nation: the industry for heavy electric machinery, precision metal die, and automotives in China; the automobile and motorbike industries in Singapore, Thailand, and other countries in South-East Asia; the screw production industry in Taiwan; and the automobile and metal die industries in Korea. To meet burgeoning demand from the digital consumer electronics, IT, automotive, and screw production industries in Taiwan, OSG increased local production capacity in that country in fiscal 2005.[19]

---

[18] Ibid.

[19] Ibid.

# Hedging Against Transaction Exposure

The increase in overseas sales and purchases led to a rise in OSG's foreign exchange transaction exposure which exists when firms have outstanding import and export contracts denominated in a foreign currency, due to be settled in foreign currencies. All short or long term receivables and payables in foreign currencies were converted into Japanese yen before they were entered into the balance sheet of the firm. This conversion to Japanese yen is a standard procedure for any Japanese company. If any profit or loss arose later due to a variation of foreign currency value because of a no-hedging provision, such a profit or loss was recognized in the profit/loss statement of the particular fiscal term.

If OSG was to be paid for a particular export in a foreign currency by the foreign buyer 90 days later, it was necessary for them to convert the payment into Japanese yen when the payment was received. If the value of the yen had appreciated relative to the foreign currency during the said 90 days, the yen value that OSG would receive would decrease from the originally anticipated amount. Depending on the degree of the yen appreciation during this period, OSG's risk could be substantial. Such a foreign exchange exposure risk could be minimized by various means.

The best policy to avoid exposure was by invoicing the buyer in yen, thereby shifting the transaction risk to the foreign buyer. However, it was generally difficult for an exporter to insist on the home currency transaction except in the case of a US exporter using his/her home currency, US dollars, which was the key currency for international trade. Demanding foreign buyers to pay OSG in yen would make OSG less competitive. The effect of such a demand was thus dependent on the international competitiveness of the merchandise.

If OSG could not avoid foreign exchange exposure by billing in yen, it could minimize its exposure using the following hedging methods:

1. Internal Hedging
   This was a method called "leads and lags", i.e., OSG could reduce transaction exposure by accelerating or decelerating the timing of payments that was to be made or received in foreign currencies.

2.  External Hedging

    This was a method that used forward contracts, money market hedges and option contracts, which necessarily meant the use of both foreign exchange and money markets. Many firms used forward contracts since it was the simplest way to hedge foreign exchange exposure. Once the transaction period was defined, the necessary data for such a contract, such as the forward rate and transaction fee, could be provided by the market.

Osawa was fully aware that there were three basic strategies for managing foreign exchange exposure. These strategies were:

1.  Never hedge.
2.  Hedge every exposure.
3.  Hedge on selective occasions.

Osawa knew that his company was applying the selective hedging method and that the decision whether to hedge or not depended on the future forecasted spot exchange rate. He considered this to be a good time for the company to study and re-examine the way it was managing its foreign exchange exposure.

He considered that selective hedging strategies that were implemented as a result of forecasts of the future spot rate were passive. In order to use the selective hedging method, it was necessary to make a decision whether to hedge for each individual transaction. More specifically, OSG's exports would not be hedged for foreign exchange exposure if the company thought that Japanese yen would depreciate. On the other hand, the company would hedge its exposure when it thought that the yen would appreciate. In light of the magnitude of risk, Osawa believed that this decision had to be made by the company's top management. He asked the Support Center Finance Group to study whether the company could add value by hedging more because of market imperfections and economies of scale and to investigate what methods or instruments were to be used to hedge.

# Current Policy on Transaction Exposure

*Foreign exchange forward contracts and foreign currency option contracts are utilized to hedge foreign exchange exposures in export sales and procurement from overseas suppliers.*

— OSG Annual Report, 2005[20]


Koji Sonobe, director and general manager of the Support Center Finance Group, explained the following at the board meeting on April 27, 2006.

1. At the end of November 2005, the accounts receivables were ¥12,378 million (a) and the accounts payables were ¥5,270 million (b) respectively. The transaction exposure in terms of foreign currencies was equivalent to ¥3,252 million (26.27% of (a)) for the accounts receivables and ¥395 million equivalent (7.50% of (b)) for the accounts payables (see **Exhibits 5–8**).

2. The company was currently not fully hedging against transactions exposure. At the end of November 2005, the hedging coverage ratio was 40% for the account receivables (in US dollars and euros), and accounts payables were not hedged at all (see **Exhibits 7** and **8**). For 40% of the hedges, the most direct method of eliminating transaction exposure was used, which was to hedge the risk with a forward exchange contract through associated banks (see **Exhibit 9**).[21]

   a. The reason for using this policy was that the company believed that transaction risk could be minimized by netting it out. OSG made frequent and sizable foreign currency transactions. Unexpected exchange rate charges netted out over many different transactions.

   b. The transactions hedged were the ones for which profitability was secured after hedging, using forward exchange contracts quoted by the associated banks.

---

[20] OSG Annual Report (2005), http://www.osg-ir.com/english2/annual/ p. 25.

[21] Only one of the subsidiaries was using foreign currency option contracts to manage the exposure to fluctuations in foreign exchange but the parent was not using them. See OSG Annual Report (2005), http://www.osg ir.com/english2/annual/, p. 25.

**Exhibit 5**   Consolidated Balance Sheets for OSG: November 30, 2005 and 2004

Yen in millions; US dollar in thousands

**ASSETS**

| | ¥ in 2005 | ¥ in 2004 | US$ in 2005 |
|---|---|---|---|
| **Current assets:** | | | |
| Cash and cash equivalents | 6,075 | 6,112 | 50,625 |
| Time deposits | 144 | 157 | 1,200 |
| Marketable securities | 1 | 1 | 8 |
| **Notes and accounts receivable:** | | | |
| Trade notes | 4,212 | 3,798 | 35,100 |
| Trade accounts | 11,924 | 9,975 | 99,367 |
| Other | 454 | 148 | 3,783 |
| Allowance for doubtful accounts | (206) | (177) | (1,717) |
| Total | 16,384 | 13,744 | 136,533 |
| Inventories | 19,524 | 15,070 | 162,700 |
| Deferred tax assets | 1,554 | 1,318 | 12,950 |
| Prepaid expenses and other current assets | 1,612 | 1,053 | 13,434 |
| Total current assets | 45,294 | 37,455 | 377,450 |
| **Property, plant and equipment:** | | | |
| Land | 9,788 | 9,614 | 81,567 |
| Buildings and structures | 25,295 | 23,001 | 210,792 |
| Machinery and equipment | 63,590 | 58,434 | 529,916 |
| Tools, furniture and fixtures | 4,367 | 3,999 | 36,392 |
| Construction in progress | 1,846 | 1,333 | 15,383 |
| Other | 325 | 296 | 2,708 |
| Total | 105,211 | 96,677 | 876,758 |
| Accumulated depreciation | (65,165) | (60,276) | (543,041) |
| Net property, plant and equipment | 40,046 | 36,401 | 333,717 |
| **Investments and other assets:** | | | |
| Investment securities | 2,520 | 2,594 | 21,000 |
| Investments in unconsolidated subsidiaries and associated companies | 1,284 | 928 | 10,700 |
| Goodwill | 959 | 753 | 7,992 |
| Deferred tax assets | 1,370 | 1,197 | 11,416 |
| Other assets | 2,125 | 1,822 | 17,708 |
| Total investments and other assets | 8,258 | 7,294 | 68,816 |
| **TOTAL** | ¥93,598 | ¥81,150 | $779,983 |

(*Continued*)

**Exhibit 5**   (*Continued*)

| LIABILITIES AND SHAREHOLDERS' EQUITY | ¥ in 2005 | ¥ in 2004 | US$ in 2005 |
|---|---|---|---|
| **Current liabilities:** | | | |
| Short term borrowings | 5,697 | 3,267 | 47,475 |
| Current portion of long-term debt | 571 | 1,200 | 4,758 |
| **Notes and accounts payable:** | | | |
| Trade notes | 1,209 | 2,037 | 10,075 |
| Trade accounts | 4,061 | 2,712 | 33,842 |
| Other | 899 | 553 | 7,492 |
| Total | 6,169 | 5,302 | 51,409 |
| Accrued expenses | 5,215 | 4,642 | 43,458 |
| Income taxes payable | 2,983 | 3,006 | 24,858 |
| Other current liabilities | 716 | 604 | 5,967 |
| Total current liabilities | 21,351 | 18,021 | 177,925 |
| **Long term liabilities:** | | | |
| Long term debt | 7,902 | 13,836 | 65,850 |
| Liability for employees' retirement benefits | 3,055 | 2,987 | 5,458 |
| Retirement allowances for directors and corporate auditors | 68 | 307 | 567 |
| Deferred tax liabilities | 349 | 404 | 2,908 |
| Other long-term liabilities | 488 | 475 | 4,067 |
| Total long-term liabilities | 11,862 | 18,009 | 98,850 |
| **Minority interest in consolidated subsidiaries** | 5,737 | 4,655 | 39,856 |
| **Shareholders' equity:** | | | |
| Common stock: | | | |
| Authorized: 194,050 thousand shares on November 30, 2005 and 2004 | | | |
| Issued: 98,955 thousand shares at November 30, 2005 and 2004 | 10,404 | 10,404 | 86,700 |
| Capital surplus | 14,381 | 12,334 | 119,842 |
| Retained earnings | 32,357 | 25,636 | 269,642 |
| Unrealized gain on available-for-sale securities | 1,027 | 738 | 8,558 |
| Foreign currency translation adjustments | (2,670) | (3,843) | (22,250) |
| **Treasury stock — at cost:** | | | |
| 876 thousand shares and 7,721 thousand shares on November 30, 2005 and 2004, respectively | (851) | (4,804) | (7,092) |
| Total shareholder's equity | 54,648 | 40,465 | 455,400 |
| **TOTAL** | ¥93,598 | ¥81,150 | $779,983 |

*Source:* OSG Annual Report (2005), http://www.osg-ii.com/cnglish2/welcome.

**Exhibit 6**   Consolidated Statements of Income for OSG in Years Ended November 30, 2005 and 2004

|  | Yen in millions; US dollar in thousands | | |
|---|---|---|---|
|  | **¥ in 2005** | **¥ in 2004** | **US$ in 2005** |
| Net sales | 78,131 | 65,976 | 651,092 |
| Cost of sales | 47,784 | 40,807 | 398,200 |
| Gross profit | 30,347 | 25,169 | 252,892 |
| Selling, general and administrative expenses | 16,221 | 14,139 | 135,175 |
| Operating income | 14,126 | 11,030 | 117,717 |
| **Other income (expenses):** | | | |
| Interest and dividend income | 107 | 83 | 892 |
| Interest expense | (205) | (200) | (1,708) |
| Foreign exchange gain (loss) | 176 | (114) | 1,466 |
| Sales discounts | (656) | (576) | (5,467) |
| Gain on sales of property, plant and equipment — net | 125 | 6 | 1,042 |
| Loss on disposals of property, plant and equipment | (129) | (149) | (1,075) |
| Gain on sales of securities — net | 598 | 4 | 4,983 |
| Equity in earnings of associated companies | 152 | 138 | 1,267 |
| Other — net | 183 | 90 | 1,525 |
| Total | 351 | (718) | 2,925 |
| Income before income taxes and minority interests | 14,477 | 10,312 | 120,642 |
| **Income taxes:** | | | |
| Current | 5,507 | 4,474 | 45,891 |
| Deferred | (625) | (405) | (5,208) |
| Total income taxes | 4,882 | 4,069 | 40,683 |
| Minority interests in net income | 836 | 595 | 6,967 |
| Net income | 8,759 | 5,648 | 72,992 |
| **Per share of common stock:** | | | |
| Net income | 89.10 | 60.32 | 0.74 |
| Diluted net income | 86.90 | 55.66 | 0.72 |
| Cash dividends applicable to the year | 26.00 | 18.00 | 0.22 |

*Source:* OSG Annual Report (2005), http://www.osg-ir.com/english2/welcome.

**Exhibit 7**   OSG's Accounting on Derivatives

OSG and certain subsidiaries used derivative financial instruments to manage their exposure to fluctuations in foreign exchange. OSG did not enter into derivatives for trading or speculative purposes.

Derivative financial instruments and foreign currency transactions were classified and accounted for as follows:

All derivatives were recognized as either assets or liabilities and measured at fair value, and gains or losses on derivative transactions were recognized in the statements of income.

1. If derivatives used for hedging purposes qualified for hedge accounting because of a high correlation and effectiveness between the hedging instruments and the hedged items, gains or losses on derivatives were deferred until the maturity of the hedged transactions.
2. Foreign exchange forward contracts and foreign currency option contracts were utilized to hedge foreign exchange exposures in export sales and procurement from overseas suppliers. Trade receivables and payables denominated in foreign currencies were translated at contract rates if the forward contracts qualified for hedge accounting.

*Source*: OSG Annual Report (2005), http://www.osg-ir.com/english2/annual/.


## *Possible Hedging Methods Available*

Sonobe further explained to the board that in order to eliminate short term transaction exposure, defined as exposure of less than a year, a variety of hedging methods were available to the company at varying costs (see **Appendix 1**).

### 1. *Forward Contracts*

This was the only method that OSG was using for eliminating transaction exposure. For example, suppose OSG had sold its product to a US company under a sales contract that specified the payment of US$1 million in 90 days. OSG could eliminate its transaction exposure by selling US$1 million to its bank at a 90-day forward rate of ¥114.09/$. No matter what happened to the exchange rate over 90 days, OSG would be able to convert US$1 million into ¥114.09 million. If OSG had an account payable instead of a receivable, it could eliminate its transaction exposure by buying US dollars at the forward rate of ¥114.09/$.

**Exhibit 8**   OSG's Foreign Currency Account Receivables as of November 30, 2005

| | Book Value | | As of November 30, 2005 | | Foreign Exchange Profit and Loss |
|---|---|---|---|---|---|
| | **Foreign Currencies** | **Yen Equivalent** | **Spot Rate** | **Yen** | |
| $ (no forward contract) | $14,300,330.23 | ¥1,584,637,653 | ¥119.67/$ | ¥1,711,320,519 | ¥126,682,866 |
| € (no forward contract) | €1,773,506.08 | ¥233,760,667 | ¥140.94/€ | ¥249,957,947 | ¥16,197,280 |
| $ (forward contract) | $7,488,139.29 | ¥835,635,579 | | ¥835,218,153 | ¥ (417,426) |
| € (forward contract) | €3,500,000.00 | ¥460,032,423 | | ¥455,520,000 | ¥ (4,512,423) |
| Total | | ¥3,114,066,322 | | ¥3,252,016,619 | ¥137,950,297 |

*Source:* OSG, "Supplement to Annual Report, 2005 by Support Center Finance Group", April 25, 2006.

**Exhibit 9**   OSG'S Foreign Currency Account Payables as of November 30, 2005

| | Book Value | | As of November 30, 2005 | | Foreign Exchange Profit and Loss |
|---|---|---|---|---|---|
| | Foreign Currencies | Yen Equivalent | Spot Rate | Yen | |
| $ (no forward contract) | $279,946.86 | ¥31,501,003 | ¥119.67/$ | ¥33,501,137 | ¥2,000,134 |
| € (no forward contract) | €2,567,221.19 | ¥352,236,559 | ¥140.94/€ | ¥361,824,140 | ¥9,587,581 |
| £ (no forward contract) | £465.40 | ¥95,616 | ¥205.62/£ | ¥95,695 | ¥79.00 |
| Total | | ¥383,833,178 | | ¥395,420,972 | ¥11,587,794 |

*Source*: OSG, "Supplement to Annual Report, 2005 by Support Center Finance Group", April 25, 2006.

However, the transaction exposure was eliminated only if the US buyer paid its US$1 million obligation on or before the settlement date of the forward contract. If the US buyer defaulted on the payment, OSG would not be relieved of its obligation to deliver US$1 million to the bank in return for ¥114.09 million. Instead, OSG would have to buy US$1 million at the spot rate at that time.

Typically, banks refused to offer forward contracts to companies that were not creditworthy. However, all the banks associated with OSG were eager to offer forward it contracts due to its creditworthiness cultivated over years.

## 2. *Hedges Using the Money Market*

If it was not possible for OSG to form forward market hedges, or if it was not cost effective to do so, OSG could form money market hedges. This method entailed entering into a short term loan in the same currency as the account receivable that OSG wanted to hedge. This money would then be converted in the company's home currency, Japanese yen. The proceeds from the accounts receivable would be used to pay back the outstanding loan at the end of the loan period. Money market hedging was a method of matching an asset with a liability in the denominated currency.

If, for example, OSG was expected to receive US$1 million in 90 days from a US customer, OSG would enter into a money market hedge by borrowing an amount in US dollars and converting it into Japanese yen. Ninety days later, OSG would pay back the loan and the accrued interest in US dollars using the US$1 million receivable. The better the quality of the account receivable, which was used as the collateral for the loan, and the credit condition of the borrower, the lower the lending rate of the bank and thus the more attractive the money market hedge.

## 3. *Options*

As an alternative, OSG could also protect itself against an exposure of US$1 million because of a 90-day account receivable by buying an option. An American long currency option position gave the buyer the right (it is not an obligation) to buy (call option) or sell (put option) a certain amount of the denominated currency at a specific price (the strike price) on or before an agreed date after 90 days.[22] In case of protecting itself against an exposure because of an account receivable, OSG would buy a put option. This would enable the company to reduce losses caused by unfavorable exchange rate changes while preserving gains from favorable exchange rate changes. OSG would exercise the option only if it was profitable to do so. However, this flexibility had a cost.

Let's say, for example, OSG as an importer had to pay a US company US$1 million in 90 days. OSG was concerned about large losses that would be incurred if the US dollar appreciated against the yen before the obligation was paid. The spot rate was ¥115.03/$ on April 27, 2006. OSG could buy a three-month call option for US$1 million on that date, at an exercise price of ¥115.77/$. The company would then have to pay 1.29% per dollar premium, or US$12,900, to the writer of the call option. This premium was equal to ¥1,483,887 at the spot rate on April 27. The future value of the premium would be ¥1,502,435.50 at the WACC of 5%. If by July 27 the value of the dollar fell to ¥110/$, then OSG would discard the option and buy the US$1 million at the new spot rate for ¥110 million. The total cost to the company would be the earlier option premium plus the cost of US dollars for a total of ¥111,502,435.50.

If the value of the dollar rose above the exercise price, say ¥120/$, the company would exercise the call option and buy the US$1 million, the exercise price for ¥115,770,000, to satisfy the account payable. In this scenario, the total cost to OSG would never exceed the total of premium plus cost of buying US dollars for a total of ¥117,272,435.50.

If OSG had a dollar-denominated account receivable, it could purchase a dollar put option. The put option gave it the right to sell the dollar that it received to the writer of the put option at the exercise price specified in the option contract. Consequently, the company was guaranteed a minimum total yen amount in the future that was equal to the exercise value of the option, less the premium paid for the put option. If the value of the

---

[22] A European option can be exercised only on the expiration date. An American option has more flexibility as it can be exercised at any time before the expiration date.

dollar rose, the firm would discard the put option and receive yen value of the dollar receivable at that time, less the premium paid on the option.

Although an option hedge suggested a win–win situation for a company like OSG, the real benefits of the hedge were somewhat in question since buying options meant paying an option premium, which was not cheap. Nevertheless, the company replaced an unknown return that could potentially be a disastrous loss with a certain or better return.

### 4. *Unhedged*

OSG might decide to accept the transaction risk. If buying goods for US$1 million with a specified payment date 90 days in the future, OSG could wait 90 days, exchange yen for US dollars at that time, and make its payment. If OSG expected the spot rate in 90 days to be ¥116/$, the payment would cost ¥116,000,000. However, this cost would be uncertain since the spot rate in 90 days could be very different than expected.

The Support Center Finance Group concluded that although hedging reduced the variability of the cash flows, it did not increase the cash flow to the company since the costs of hedging would be a factor in lowering its cash flow. The Finance Group's position was that it was debatable whether OSG should hedge currency risk rigidly.

## Future Direction

After the presentation by the Support Center Finance Group, a heated discussion between the members of the board followed. They all knew that an increasing number of firms were actively hedging transaction exposure not only in the US but also in Japan. One argument was that currency risk was simply a part of doing business internationally, and therefore one should start the analysis of a company's transaction exposure from an unhedged baseline. The opposite argument was that currency risk was just unacceptable, starting their analysis from a full forward contract baseline. On the day of the meeting the board did not make a definitive decision to change their current hedging method; instead, they asked the Support Center Finance Group to conduct further studies in order to make a more informed decision on the hedging strategies to be employed by OSG.

However, through the discussions, the board reached a consensus on the following points:

1. The risk of currency exposure could be mitigated or even eliminated in its entirety by the techniques and instruments described by the Support Center Finance Group.
2. OSG, like most other international businesses, preferred the certainty of minimizing exposure, despite the increased transaction costs involved, in lieu of unquantifiable and potentially disastrous foreign exchange risk.
3. However, how much currency risk exposure should remain covered depended on the management's philosophy and decision. The policy that was currently in use by OSG did not intend to hedge transaction exposure perfectly and intended to leave it partially open to the market. The board needed to make a decision which specified how much hedging was required as a policy.
4. One director suggested that OSG's board should establish a transaction exposure limit for each individual currency, which specified the maximum level of uncovered exposure OSG could have to specific currencies.

Finally, Osawa told the board that many multinational companies in the US had established rather rigid risk management policies to transaction exposure which mandated proportional hedging, and that these policies generally required the use of forward contract hedges on a percentage of existing transaction exposure. He further said that the remaining portion of the exposure was then selectively hedged on the basis of the firm's risk tolerance, view of future exchange rate movements and confidence level on the forecasted currency values.

As an example, he introduced the board to an American company, S. Corporation. This company did away with selective hedging long ago. If the date of the transaction was known with certainty, all cash flow denominated in foreign currency had to adhere to a mandatory forward contract cover formula, with any remaining amount left uncovered at the

**Exhibit 10**    Account Receivables, Minimum Forward: Cover by a US Corporation

1. S. Corporation in the US did away with selective hedging. If the maturity of the transaction is known, all cash flow denominated in foreign currency must adhere to the forward contract cover formula determined by the company's board in advance. Remaining amounts, if any, may be left uncovered. The points, paying or receiving on the forward rate, are the forward rate's premium or discount defined by the formula in 2.

|  | Exposure Coverage Required | | |
|---|---|---|---|
|  | *Up to 90 days* | *90–180 days* | *180 days or longer* |
| "paying the points forward" | 75% | 45% | 50% |
| "receiving the points forward" | 100% | 90% | 60% |

2. Use the following formula to find the forward rate's premium or discount. The forward premium or discount is the percentage difference between the spot and forward exchange rate, stated in annual percentage terms. When the foreign currency price of the home currency (US dollar) is used as in this case of yen per dollar, the formula for the percent-per-annum premium or discount (denoted $f$ here for yen) becomes:[23]

$$ f^{¥} = \frac{\text{Spot} - \text{Forward}}{\text{Forward}} \times \frac{360}{\text{days to maturity}} \times 100 $$

discretion of the operations department (see **Exhibit 10**). Osawa had been given this formula by the president of S. Corporation to be used as a reference. At the end of the meeting, Osawa asked Sonobe to study whether OSG should undertake the same mandatory hedging policy as this American company.

## For Further Discussion

1. Explain non-hedging techniques for OSG to minimize transactions exposure, if any.

---

[23] For details of the formula, see Eiteman, D.K., Stonehill, A.I. and Moffett, M.H. (2007) *Multinational Business Finance*, 11th Edition, Massachusetts: Pearson, pp. 191–192.

2. What are the costs of alternatives for reducing short-term foreign currency risk?

   Assume OSG has an account receivable of US$1 million. Use the information provided in **Appendix 1** for this accounts payable case of US$1 million to a US company. Which of the possible hedging methods presented in the case should OSG use if they expect the dollar to depreciate versus the yen during the next three months (the spot will be ¥110/$)?

3. Suppose that OSG undertakes the same mandatory hedging policy as S. Corporation, the American company whose minimum forward-cover schedule is shown in **Exhibit 10**. Apply this schedule to the US$1 million account receivable case for OSG and find the expected total end-of-period value of the position taken by OSG. OSG expected to receive a US dollar (foreign currency) payment of US$1 million in three months. The spot rate was ¥115.03/$, and the forward rate ¥116.18/$ as shown in **Appendix 1**. Use **Exhibit 10** for minimum forward cover. Note that the yen is the home currency for OSG.

   1. What would be the amount of forward cover required?
   2. If the spot rate in three months were expected to be ¥110.00/$, what would be the amount in US dollars, covered and uncovered?
   3. What would be the expected total end-of-period yen value of the position taken in the above question? Suppose the spot rate in three months will be ¥115.00/$.

## Appendix 1  Financial and Market Information for the Currency Exposure Exercise

OSG makes the purchase of materials in US dollars at the end of April 2006, with payment due three months later in July 2006. Assume OSG's weighted average cost of capital is 5%. The accounting department collected the following information.

- Spot exchange rate: ¥115.03/$
- Three-month forward rate: ¥116.18/$
- Japan's three-month borrowing interest rate: 3% (or 0.75% per quarter)

- Japan's three-month investment interest rate: 2% (or 0.5% per quarter)
- US three-month borrowing interest rate: 4% (or 1% per quarter)
- US three-month investment interest rate: 3.3% (or 0.825% per quarter)
- July call option in the over-the-counter (bank) market for US$1 million: strike price ¥115.77/$; 1.29% premium for three months
- July put option in the over-the-counter (bank) market for US$1 million: strike price ¥115.77/$; 2.66% premium for three months

*Source*: *Nihon Keizai Shinbun*, April 25, 2006, p. 18.

# 10

# Bank of Japan's Meeting in March 2006: An End to the Quantitative Easing Policy?

As the Bank of Japan (BOJ) officials filed out of their 110-year-old head-quarters on March 8, 2006, the world was watching. That might not seem so odd given the attention paid to the US Federal Reserve or European Central Bank (ECB). Yet, it had been more than a decade since entire economies had been waiting anxiously for the outcome of monetary policy talks in Tokyo.

The main issue on the table was the BOJ's quantitative easing policy — a five-year-old, super loose monetary stance under which it had flooded the market with far greater amounts of liquidity than needed[1] (see **Exhibits 1** and **2**). The Japanese economy was improving and the core consumer price index (CPI) was showing steady growth after years of deflation, one of the predetermined conditions for lifting the policy. As such there was widespread speculation over the future of the policy. The BOJ policy board, which would convene on this and other matters for two days, would make the ultimate decision on the future of Japan's monetary policy. Would the current quantitative easing policy persist or would the BOJ return to a normal monetary stance that targeted interest rates?

---

[1] The BOJ had been flooding commercial banks with excess liquidity to promote private lending, leaving commercial banks with large stocks of excess reserves, and therefore little risk of a liquidity shortage. Together, these policies were commonly referred to as the BOJ's "quantitative easing" policy. For details, see Federal Reserve Bank of San Francisco, USA, Economic Research and Data, FRBSF Economic Letter, 2004-33, November 19, 2004, http://www.frbsf.org/publications/economics/letter/2004/el2004-33.html (accessed July 15, 2006).

**Exhibit 1**  Missions of the BOJ

The BOJ is the central bank of Japan. It is a juridical body based on the BOJ Law (hereafter, the Law), and is not a government agency or a private corporation.

The Law sets the Bank's objectives "to issue banknotes and to carry out currency and monetary control" and "to ensure smooth settlement of funds among banks and other financial institutions, thereby contributing to the maintenance of an orderly financial system".

The Law also stipulates the Bank's principle of currency and monetary control as follows: "currency and monetary control shall be aimed at, through the pursuit of price stability, contributing to the sound development of the national economy."

According to its charter, the missions of the BOJ are:

- Issuance and management of banknotes
- Implementation of monetary policy
- Providing settlement services and ensuring the stability of the financial system
- Treasury and government securities-related operations
- International activities
- Compilation of data, economic analyses and research activities

*Source*: BOJ's homepage, http://www.boj.or.jp/en/.

## History of the Super-Loose Monetary Policy

Even 12 years after the economic bubble burst in 1989, the situation still looked precarious. Banks were saddled with mounting bad loans that stood at ¥30 trillion;[2] many banks, including several major ones, went bankrupt, creating a fear of bank runs; corporate bankruptcies were rampant; unemployment rose to a record 5.5%; and consumer prices continued to fall significantly. The Japanese economy was viewed as teetering on the brink of breakdown. This prompted the BOJ to turn to the policy of seemingly limitless monetary abundance after its "zero interest policy", which was adopted in February 1999 and maintained until August 2000, looked insufficient to provide further monetary reassurance since interest rates could not go down any more.

The quantitative easing policy was implemented in March 2001 as an emergency measure with the intention of preserving Japan's

---

[2] US$1= ¥116.73 in 2006.

**Exhibit 2**   History of the BOJ

The BOJ was established under the BOJ Act (promulgated in June 1882) and began operating on October 10, 1882, as the nation's central bank. Like most modern Japanese institutions, the BOJ was born after the Meiji Restoration. Prior to the Restoration, Japan's feudal fiefs all issued their own money, *hansatsu*, in an array of incompatible denominations. The New Currency Act of Meiji 4 (1871) did away with these and established the yen as the new decimal currency. The former *han* (fiefs) became prefectures and their mints became private chartered banks, which initially retained the right to print money. For a time both the central government and these so-called "national" banks issued money. To bring an end to this situation the BOJ was founded in Meiji 15 (1882) and given a monopoly on controlling the money supply.

The BOJ issued its first banknotes on Meiji 18 (1885), and the run was largely successful. In 1897 Japan joined the gold standard and in 1899 the former "national" banknotes were formally rendered obsolete.

The Bank was reorganized on May 1, 1942 in conformity with the BOJ Law (hereafter, the Law of 1942), promulgated in February 1942. The Law of 1942 strongly reflected the wartime situation: for example, Article 1 stated the objectives of the Bank as "the regulation of the currency, control and facilitation of credit and finance, and the maintenance and fostering of the credit system, pursuant to 'national polity',[3] in order that the general economic activities of the nation might adequately be enhanced."

The BOJ has continued operating ever since, except for a brief post-WWII hiatus when the occupying allies issued military currency and restructured the bank into a more independent entity. The Law of 1942 was amended several times after World War II. Such amendments included the establishment of the Policy Board as the bank's highest decision-making body in June 1949.

However, despite a major 1997 rewrite of the BOJ Law intended to give it more independence, the BOJ has been criticized for lack of independence. A certain degree of dependence is enshrined in the Law itself, Article 4 of which states: "In recognition of the fact that currency and monetary control is a component of overall economic policy, the Bank of Japan shall always maintain close contact with the government and exchange views sufficiently, so that its currency and monetary control and the basic stance of the government's economic policy shall be mutually harmonious."

The Law of 1942 was revised completely in June 1997 under the two principles of "independence" and "transparency". The revised law (the Law) came into effect on April 1, 1998.

*Source*: BOJ's homepage, http://www.boj.or.jp/en/.

---

[3] National polity was the notion that all authority and privilege reside in the nation and the emperor. The national mobilization for war was heavily promoted through this notion of "national polity", and all citizens were pressured to fulfill their duty for national polity.

banking system and saving the Japanese economy from a deepening deflationary spiral in the aftermath of the burst of the bubble in 1989. Through the policy the central bank provided commercial banks with cash in great abundance — much more than they actually needed — in order to preclude any fear that a banking crisis might develop. Such a policy was unprecedented in the history of central banking in any country.

Since taking office in March 2003, BOJ Governor Toshihiko Fukui had been anxious to get out of this unusual situation and had been persistently driving for a policy change. Mounting signs of marked improvement in the Japanese economy, which by any measure had been in robust recovery since early 2004, convinced him that the time for exit from the emergency measure had arrived. A switch of policy by the BOJ would be taken as an official declaration that the Japanese economy had put the post-bubble lethargy and deflation behind it. However, a change in policy would raise the question of how a major change in the monetary climate would affect the actual economy and businesses themselves. The BOJ had to prevent unexpected turbulence from developing as a result of a possible policy change.

## Obstacles to the BOJ's Decision

It had become the norm throughout the world that monetary policy in pursuit of price stability be conducted by a central bank independent from the government. This was because it was easy for those conducting monetary policy to come under pressure to adopt inflationary policies. Looking at the history of central banks, there were many cases where an increase in issuance of currency to cover government spending such as war expenses sparked severe inflation. Moreover, central banks were often pressured to take measures to stimulate the economy in the short term since there was a lag before inflation actually occurred, even if the central bank had taken a looser monetary policy.

In the case of the quantitative easing policy, such pressure was mounting on the BOJ from outside. Some economists and certain political circles in particular were strongly opposed to an early dropping of the policy. Those economists opposed to the policy change warned that the Japanese economy was still vulnerable from lingering effects of the post-bubble weakness and that a hasty end to the quantitative easing could backfire. Many ruling party politicians, including Prime Minister Junichiro Koizumi, did not hide their displeasure at the central bank's inclination toward an early policy change, although in the end they said they would respect it. Politicians were concerned that a "premature" monetary policy change could hamper the economic recovery and subsequently their standing with voters. Koizumi was reportedly intent on making his own declaration of an end of deflation to maximize his political standing before he would step down in September 2006[4] (see **Exhibits 3** and **4**).

*The overall economy hasn't yet escaped deflation. We'll need to continue working with the central bank. BOJ is in a position to independently decide which way to go.*

— Sadakazu Tanigaki, finance minister of Japan[5]

On March 7, 2006, BOJ Governor Toshihiko Fukui expressed a willingness to make a policy shift just one day after Prime Minister Junichiro Koizumi urged the BOJ to exercise caution when making its decision on the future of the policy at its upcoming policy board meeting.[6]

*A failed lifting and a return to square one are inadmissible. I trust that a wise decision will be made. Needless to say, the Japanese economy should never again face the risk of deflation. There are signs of an impending end to deflation, but we cannot say that we have already escaped it. But the BOJ must make a decision independently.*

— Junichiro Koizumi, prime minister of Japan[7]

---

[4] *Nihon Keizai Shinbun*, March 3, 2006, http://www.nikkei.co.jp/news/main/20060303AT 2C0300C03032006.html Also see *Yomiuri Shinbun*, March 3, 2006, http://www.yomiuri. co.jp/atmoney/mnews/20060303mh14.htm.

[5] *Nihon Keizai Shinbun*, March 3, 2006, http://www.nikkei.co.jp/news/main/20060303AT 2C0300C03032006.html. Also see *Yomiuri Shinbun*, March 3, 2006, http://www.yomiuri. co.jp/atmoney/mnews/20060303mh14.htm.

[6] *Nihon Keizai Shinbun*, March 7, 2006, http://www.nikkei.co.jp/news/seiji/20060307AT 3S0700C07032006.html. Also see *Yomiuri Shinbun*, March 7, 2006, http://www.yomiuri. co.jp/atmoney/mnews/20060307mh08.htm.

[7] *Nihon Keizai Shinbun*, March 4, 2006, http://www.nikkei.co.jp/news/seiji/20060304AT 3S0302C03032006.html.

**Exhibit 3**  The Position of the Cabinet Office (for the Prime Minister) on the BOJ's Policy Change, Expressed at the Board Meeting on March 8, 2006 at the BOJ

1. The government considered that Japan's economy was recovering as stated in the Monthly Economic Report of February 2006, in which it made an upward revision of the assessment of the current state of the economy. However, deflation, albeit moderate, persisted, based on a comprehensive review of the underlying trend of prices. It was therefore vital to achieve the government's goal of overcoming deflation in fiscal 2006, as it had reiterated in such cabinet statements as "Basic Policies for Economic and Fiscal Management and Structural Reform", "Structural Reform and Medium-Term Economic and Fiscal Perspectives", and "Economic Outlook and Basic Stance for Economic and Fiscal Management".

2. The government would like to strongly request at this time that the bank continue its policy efforts to overcome deflation together with the government, taking fully into consideration consistency with the government's basic policy for the economy when it examined termination of the quantitative easing policy. Termination of the quantitative easing policy would mean that the commitment in terms of policy duration would be lost. The government therefore hoped that the bank would present a transparent framework of monetary policy that would ensure accountability to the public, making it easier for market participants and the public to form an economic outlook and stabilize their expectations.

*Source*: BOJ Minutes of the Monetary Policy, March 8 and 9, 2006, http://www.boj.or.jp/en/.

*The bank is fully aware that a crucial period is approaching regarding consumer prices. But we have no predetermined conclusions. We will carefully consider economic and consumer price conditions and make the appropriate decision*

— Toshihiko Fukui, governor of the BOJ[8]

Opinions were split in the private sector. On March 8, 2006, Hiroshi Okuda, chairman of Nippon Keidanren,[9] the nation's largest business

---

[8] *Nihon Keizai Shinbun*, March 5, 2006, http://www.nikkei.co.jp/news/keizai/20060305A T3S0400604032006.html.

[9] Keidanren is the Japan Business Federation. The organization is a general economic organization consisting of 1,623 companies and other organizations, which include 91 companies with foreign capital affiliations and 1,306 major representative Japanese companies. It is the strongest interest group in Japan that applies pressure on the government

**Exhibit 4**   The Position of Ministry of Finance (MOF) on the Chairman's Proposal to Change the Guideline for Money Market Operations on the Board Meeting on March 8 2006 at the BOJ

1. Japan's economy was recovering, as seen in the fact that the first preliminary estimate of real GDP for the October–December quarter of 2005 indicated quarter-on-quarter growth of 1.4%. Although moderate deflation persisted, a comprehensive review of the underlying trend of prices suggested that the price situation was improving gradually: for example, the year-on-year rate of change in the CPI (excluding fresh food, on a nationwide basis) was 0.5% in January 2006, registering 0% or higher for the fourth consecutive month. The government considered that it was necessary to ensure that this improvement continues.

2. The chairman had submitted proposals to terminate the quantitative easing policy and to introduce a new framework for the conduct of monetary policy. The government would like the bank to make a decision concerning termination of the quantitative easing policy based on careful consideration of the following points. First, it was necessary for the government together with the bank to firmly continue policy efforts to overcome deflation. Second, the current situation required that due consideration be given to the stability of the financial markets.

3. The government considered that, if the bank decided to terminate the quantitative easing policy at this meeting, it should firmly support the economy from the financial side by maintaining a zero interest rate environment in order to ensure the overcoming of deflation in a situation where there remained disparities in economic conditions among regions in terms of the real economy. Moreover, the government considered it necessary that the bank conduct monetary policy that would ensure market stability. Specifically, first, after termination of the quantitative easing policy, the bank should carry out money market operations appropriately to prevent the financial markets from becoming unstable by, for example, carefully lowering the outstanding balance of current accounts at the bank, taking into account developments in the market. Second, the bank should enhance the transparency of its communication concerning its thinking and the future course of its monetary policy, given that the financial markets could become unstable due to speculation. Third, the bank should make it clear that it would closely monitor developments in overall interest rates including long-term interest rates, and should continue its outright purchases of long-term Japanese government bonds at the current amounts.

4. The government would respect the bank's decision concerning termination of the quantitative easing policy, since the discussions and the policy proposals at this meeting showed that the bank shared the government's views. The government would like the bank to support the economy from the financial side responsibly to prevent the economy from weakening again, bearing in mind that ensuring the sustainability of the economic recovery and overcoming deflation were important policy tasks. The government hoped that the bank would continue to implement appropriate monetary policy consistent with the government's economic policy.

*Source*: BOJ, Minutes of the Monetary Policy, March 8 and 9, 2006, http://www.boj.or.jp/en/.

lobby, endorsed the Bank of Japan's possible ending of its quantitative monetary policy.

*Conditions are gradually falling into place. It is up to BOJ's policymakers to carefully evaluate a future economic outlook and make a judgment.*

— Hiroshi Okuda, chairman of Nippon Keidanren[10]

## The Bank of Japan Law

The new BOJ Law, passed in June 1997, established the BOJ's independence.[11] The law also called on monetary authorities to make their stance consistent with the government's overall economic policy.[12] Under the leadership of Fukui, the BOJ loosened its stance three times by raising the target amount of liquidity, although each time some members of the Policy Board opposed the step, claiming it was appropriate to leave the liquidity target unchanged pursuant to the economic conditions of the time.[13] These members considered that the conditions for the changes had not been met.

Stressing transparency of the board's decision-making process, Fukui said that the policy board would come to a conclusion on the future of the

---

as well as overseas organizations by collecting opinions from all corners of business communities on any important issues ranging from economic and industrial issues to labor issues urging speedy solutions. See the Keidanren' website, http://www.keidanren.or.jp/Japanese/profile/pro001.htm (accessed April 28, 2006).

[10] See his speaking at a news conference in the city of Fukuoka on March 6, 2006, http://www.nikkei.co.jp/news/main/20060308AT3S0800L08032006.html.

[11] The old Bank of Japan Law ("Law No. 67 dated February 24, 1942") was revised in June 1997 to give greater independence to the central bank. Under the old law, the Cabinet had the right to dismiss the governor and deputy governor of the BOJ. Moreover, the BOJ was subject to supervision by the minister of finance and the minister could issue specific orders to the BOJ. Under the new law, the BOJ was allowed to act on its own policy judgments, free from political interference, to meet the needs of deregulation and globalization of Japan's financial business. For details, see the BOJ homepage, http://www.boj.or.jp/type/exp/about/index.htm.

[12] *Nihon Keizai Shinbun*, March 13, 2006, http://www.nikkei.co.jp/news/main/20060313AT2C1300W13032006.html.

[13] Ibid.

quantitative easing process through consensus at the March 2006 meeting.[14] He feared that a postponement of the lifting would be interpreted by the market as a capitulation to government pressure and might lead to a loss of trust in the bank.[15] Although the BOJ could lift the easing policy later in April — a move that would appease the government — Fukui knew it would be difficult for the BOJ to do so given that the market had largely factored in a March lifting.[16]

On the other hand, if maintaining the policy would help ease concerns about the financial system and assist the corporate sector in cleaning up their excess debt, production capacity and labor, the BOJ would be doing the right thing in the context of the law if it decided to uphold the policy. The problem was that it was not clear whether the principal aim of the policy was to stabilize the financial system or shore up economic activities, raising concern that the BOJ might still be under the influence of the government as much as when it was under the old BOJ law (see **Exhibits 5** and **6**[17]). It was clear to everybody at that time that the government was implicitly urging the BOJ to act without regard for its autonomous obligations.

## Consumer Prices

After deflation took hold of Japan in July 1998, the price gauge posted negative growth for seven consecutive years through fiscal 2004.[18] After staying flat in October 2005 on a year-on-year basis, the core CPI edged up 0.1% during the following two months (see **Exhibit 7**).[19] In January 2006, the core nationwide rose 0.5% compared to the same month in the

---

[14] *Nihon Keizai Shinbun*, March 7, 2006, http://www.nikkei.co.jp/news/seiji/20060307AT 3S0700C07032006.html. Also see Yomiuri Shinbun, March 7, 2006, http://www.yomiuri. co.jp/atmoney/mnews/20060307mh08.htm.

[15] Ibid.

[16] Ibid.

[17] *Nihon Keizai Shinbun*, March 13th 2006, http://www.nikkei.co.jp/news/main/20060313AT 2C1300W13032006.html

[18] The Ministry of Foreign Affairs of Japan homepage, http://www.mofa.go.jp/mofaj/area/ ecodata/index.html.

[19] Ibid.

**Exhibit 5**    The BOJ's Independence

The BOJ Law states:

1. "The Bank of Japan's autonomy regarding currency and monetary control shall be respected." (Article 3, Paragraph 1)
2. "Due consideration shall be given to the autonomy of the Bank's business operations." (Article 5, Paragraph 2)
3. To ensure the independence of the bank, members of the Policy Board, which is the Bank's highest decision-making body, cannot be dismissed for holding opinions at variance with the government, and the government cannot order the bank to undertake any particular policy action or to conduct any particular business operation. (Article 14)
4. It is important that the bank's monetary policy be consistent with the government's basic economic policy framework, so it states that the bank shall "always maintain close contact with the government and exchange views sufficiently". (Article 4)
5. The BOJ Law also allows representatives of the government to attend monetary policy meetings of the policy board, to give their views and submit proposals, or request that the board postpone a vote on monetary policy measures until the next meeting. (Article 19)
6. The government representatives have no votes in the monetary policy decisions, and the decisions are made only by a majority vote of the nine members of the policy board. (Article 19)

*Source*: Bank of Japan Law, Law No. 89 of 1998, http://www.boj.or.jp/type/law/bojlaws/bojlaw1.htm.

previous year, marking the third straight month of gain and the steepest rise since March 1998.[20] The growth in the index — pushed up to 97.7 against the base of 100 for the year 2000 — was fuelled mainly by a hike in energy prices stemming from higher crude oil prices.[21] The hike in the price of petroleum products contributed 0.37 of a percentage point to the January growth figure.[22] The rise in the CPI showed that the economy was crawling out of its deflationary rut at a faster pace.

---

[20] Ibid.

[21] Ibid.

[22] The Ministry of Foreign Affairs of Japan homepage, http://www.mofa.go.jp/mofaj/area/ecodata/index.html.

**Exhibit 6**   Good Practices for Transparency in Monetary and Financial Policies for Central Banks by IMF Code

The IMF has developed a Code of Good Practices on Transparency in Monetary and Financial Policies for central banks and financial agencies. The Code was elaborated in cooperation with the Bank for International Settlements, and in consultation with a representative group of central banks, financial agencies, relevant international and regional organizations, and selected academic experts. It is premised on four broad principles:

1. **Clarity of Roles, Responsibilities, and Objectives**

   The objectives of the central bank for monetary policy should be clearly defined, publicly disclosed, and written into law. The institutional relationship between monetary and fiscal policies should be clearly defined, as should any agency roles performed by the central bank on behalf of the government. For financial agencies, their objectives and institutional framework should be clearly defined, preferably in relevant legislation or regulation, and the role of oversight agencies with regard to payment systems should be publicly disclosed.

2. **Open Process for Formulating and Reporting Policy Decisions**

   Central banks should publicly disclose and explain the framework, instruments, and targets, if any, which are used to achieve objectives. The structure of their decision-making bodies should be publicly disclosed and their decisions communicated in a timely manner. Periodic public statements should be made on progress towards achieving monetary policy objectives. The conduct of financial policies by financial agencies should be transparent and compatible with confidentiality considerations and the need to preserve effectiveness. Periodic progress reports on the pursuance of policy objectives should be issued.

3. **Public Availability of Information on Policies**

   For the central bank, information on monetary policy should be consistent with the IMF's standards for data dissemination and its balance sheet should be publicly available. The central bank should establish and maintain public information services. Financial agencies should issue periodic public reports on major developments in the financial system, report aggregate data on a timely and regular basis, make texts of regulations and directives readily available to the public, and publicly disclose special protections, such as deposit insurance schemes and consumer protection arrangements.

(*Continued*)

**Exhibit 6**   (*Continued*)

> **4. Accountability and Assurances of Integrity**
>
> Central bank officials should periodically appear before a designated public author-ity to explain the conduct and performance of their policy. The central bank should provide assurances of the integrity of operations and officials through the release of audited financial statements of its operations and the standards of conduct for its officials. The Code suggests similar practices to hold officials of financial agencies accountable for their actions.

*Source*: IMF Fact Sheet, April 2006, http://www.imf.org/external/np/exr/facts/mtransp.htm.

The Ministry of Internal Affairs and Communications was still cau-tious about the price trend, saying, "price movements could change in the months to come depending on crude oil prices."[23] However, the ministry's estimate for the comprehensive price index, excluding food and energy products, was up 0.1% in January 2006 from a year earlier, climbing for the second straight month.[24] This was a sign that the economy was gradu-ally becoming capable of beating deflation even without the effects of rising oil prices.

Consumer prices would be a key component of the decision on the quantitative easing policy. The recent growth in CPI could be interpreted as an indication that deflationary forces had disappeared.[25] However, the CPI's component items were scheduled to be reviewed in August, 2006. According to a central bank official, the review could produce up to a 0.3% fall in the index.[26]

## New Monetary Policies

The key price index had registered zero or positive year-on-year change for four straight months, fulfilling the primary condition the central bank

---

[23] Ibid.

[24] Ibid.

[25] Ibid.

[26] Ibid.

**Exhibit 7**   Charts on Japan

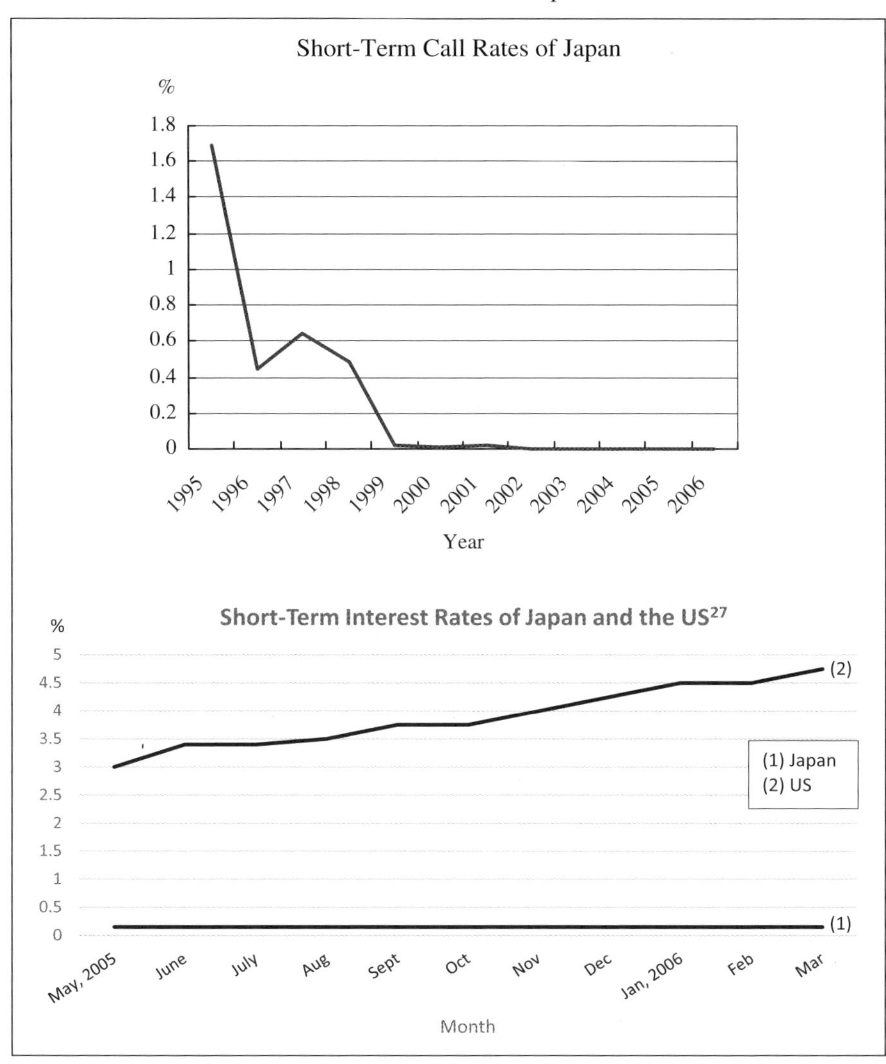



*(Continued)*

---

[27] Japan: Official Discount Rate; the US: Federal Fund Rate.

**Exhibit 7**   (*Continued*)

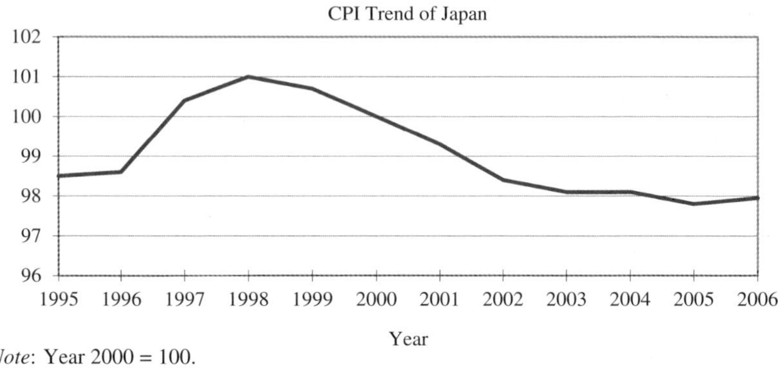

CPI Trend of Japan



*Note*: Year 2000 = 100.

CPI Change[28]



Yen/US$ Exchange Rate

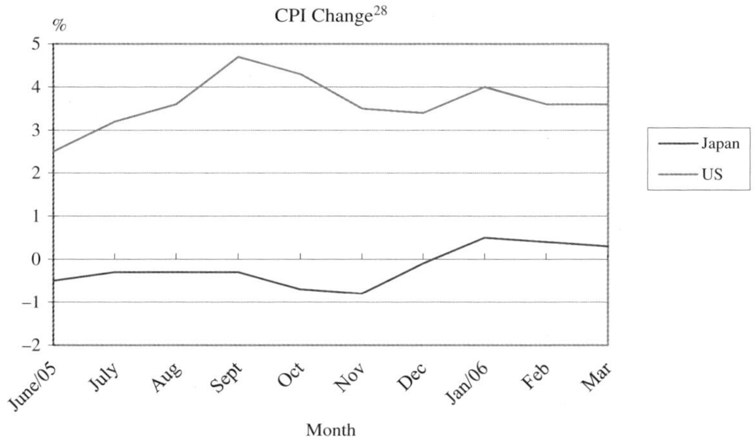

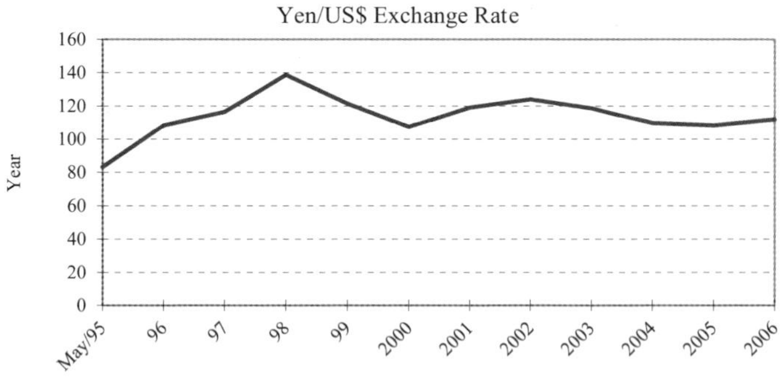

*Source*: The Ministry of Foreign  Affairs of Japan homepage, http://www.mofa.go.jp/mofaj/area/ecodata/index.html.

[28] Percentage change compounded with the same month of the previous year.

had set for ending its quantitative easing policy: a stable uptrend in consumer prices.[29]

Under the quantitative easing policy, the BOJ had been purchasing large amounts of government bonds from commercial banks, leaving them with ¥30–35 trillion in reserves.[30] If the BOJ decided to exit the extraordinary and unorthodox monetary expansion policy it had been using to defeat deflation, it needed to make clear the pace at which it was planning to draw down these excess reserve levels to the required amount of some ¥6 trillion.[31] It also needed to take steps to give a degree of transparency to its policy for raising short-term rates after lowering the reserve levels. In the short term, the BOJ was expected to maintain its monthly purchase of government bonds at the current level of ¥1.2 trillion to prevent a surge in long-term rates,[32] even if they decided to adopt a new monetary policy. Two policy actions (purchasing government bonds and lowering the reserve levels) associated with the decision were reducing the stock of excess reserves held by commercial banks in their BOJ current accounts and raising nominal short-term interest rates from the current zero levels.[33]

## Inflation Targeting Approach

If the BOJ decided to end the loose monetary policy, they were expected to adopt an inflation targeting approach instead. This would mean that the current policy yardstick (that the growth rate of the CPI remain steady and above zero) had to be replaced with a new benchmark. Some price reference values had emerged as a possible new monetary policy gauge.

As one such benchmark, certain government and ruling party policymakers were calling for an explicit numerical target for the CPI — an annual growth rate of around 2%.[34] One big problem with such an inflation

---

[29] *Nihon Keizai Shinbun*, March 3, 2006, http://www.nikkei.co.jp/news/main/20060303AT 2C0300C03032006.html. Also see *Yomiuri Shinbun*, March 3, 2006, http://www.yomiuri. co.jp/atmoney/mnews/20060303mh14.htm.

[30] Ibid.

[31] Ibid.

[32] Ibid.

[33] Ibid.

[34] The Ministry of Foreign Affairs of Japan homepage, http://www.mofa.go.jp/mofaj/area/ ecodata/index.html.

targeting approach would be that the central bank could not respond flexibly to sharp rises in asset prices when overall inflation remained benign, with the CPI below the target. Most BOJ policymakers took a dim view of such explicit targets and favored communicating its policy posture in verbal form as the US Federal Reserve had.[35] The BOJ expected that the new yardstick based upon the CPI, if adopted, suggested to the market that it would keep interest rates very low. However, some BOJ officials were concerned that the yardstick could restrain the central bank's free hand in monetary policy operations.[36]

The central bank had considered several means for indicating its policy direction, including increasing the frequency of announcements of the "Outlook and Risk Assessment of the Economy and Prices", which at the time was released twice a year, and publishing written explanations of the direction of monetary policy for market participants.[37] The idea of indicating numerical values had come up because the BOJ thought it would be difficult for the market to understand its policy unless some numerical values were presented.[38] The central bank would carefully consider whether it could stabilize the market with such explanations or if it needed to make public some numerical benchmarks that would not limit its maneverability in monetary policy.

Among the various possible numerical measures were "inflation reference values",[39] previously adopted by the ECB,[40] under which monetary policies were adjusted to meet the targets set for desirable consumer price growth rates. While the ECB's measure was intended to curb inflation, the numerical measure that had surfaced at the BOJ was aimed at maintaining low interest rates. The Japanese central bank was not considering "inflation targets", under which monetary policies were changed in relation to consumer price growth rates (see **Exhibit 8**).

---

[35] Ibid.

[36] *Nihon Keizai Shinbun*, March 2, 2006, http://www.nikkei.co.jp/news/keizai/20060302AT2C0103Z01032006.html.

[37] Ibid.

[38] Ibid.

[39] Ibid.

[40] Ibid.

**Exhibit 8**   Central Banks of the World

Most countries have a central bank. Central banks take many forms.

**1. The Bank of England**

One prototype can be seen in the Bank of England, which was founded in 1694 as a commercial bank conducting ordinary banking business. Over the course of the next century, the Bank of England earned a particularly important status among commercial banks, and following the financial crisis of 1825, other commercial banks deposited their reserves with the Bank of England, thereby effectively establishing a payment and settlement system centered on the Bank of England. The Bank Charter Act of 1844 designated the Bank of England's banknotes as legal tender. As the case of the Bank of England shows, a central bank is an institution that has developed naturally as a result of the concentration of currency issuance and inter-bank settlement at a single bank.

**2. The US Federal Reserve System**

Among central banks that developed later in other countries, most were established by law concerning central bank from the beginning. One example is the US Federal Reserve System consisting of: the Board of Governors of the Federal Reserve System, as one of the governmental agencies governing the Federal Reserve System; twelve regional Federal Reserve Banks conducting central bank services; and member commercial banks holding stocks in one of the 12 Federal Reserve Banks.

**3. The European Central Bank**

Another example established by law from the beginning is the ECB. The member states of the European Union drew up a treaty to establish the ECB and issue a single currency, the euro. The ECB sets the monetary policy direction, and the member central banks conduct their operations according to the direction.

As shown in the following table, BOJ was established very early in its history, compared with the world's other central banks.

| Year of foundation | Name | Country | (Currency) |
| --- | --- | --- | --- |
| 1668 (world's oldest) | Sveriges Riksbank | Sweden | (Krona) |
| 1694 | Bank of England | United Kingdom | (Pound Sterling) |
| 1882 | Bank of Japan | Japan | (Yen) |
| 1913 | Federal Reserve System | United States | (US Dollar) |
| 1998 | European Central Bank | EU member states | (Euro) |

*Source*: "Function and Operation of BOJ", http://www.boj.or.jp/en/type/exp/about/data/foboj03.pdf.

# Market Reactions

## *The Financial Market*

The stock market sharply rebounded on March 6, 2006, while the bond market fell only slightly. The Nikkei stock average was boosted by purchasing of exporter issues. Expectations of a future strengthening of the yen took a back seat.

In the bond market, the yield on newly issued 10-year government bonds, a benchmark for long-term interest rates, rose 1.5 basis points to 1.635%.[41] Market participants were increasingly taking a wait-and-see stance, but most expected only a limited immediate impact from the expected lifting of the quantitative easing policy.[42]

The BOJ mulled over moves to curb interest rates amid a possible policy shift. The central bank was expected to ensure that the uncollateralized overnight call rate did not exceed 0.1%, effectively keeping the key rate close to zero.[43] In a bid to prevent a sharp increase in short-term rates, the BOJ indicated it would continue to make outright purchases of ¥1.2 trillion in long-term government bonds each month.[44] When the quantitative easing policy was launched in March 2001, the BOJ initially purchased ¥400 billion in long-term government bonds each month. The balance was gradually increased.[45]

In the event that the key short-term rate showed signs of surpassing 0.1%, the BOJ was considering responding by slowing the pace for drawing down the current-account balance or conducting fund-supplying market operations.[46] The 0.1% figure was equivalent to the official discount rate at which the BOJ provided funds to financial institutions facing

---

[41] Ibid.

[42] *Nihon Keizai Shinbun*, March 2, 2006, http://www.nikkei.co.jp/news/keizai/20060302 AT2C0103Z01032006.html.

[43] *Nihon Keizai Shinbun*, March 1, 2006, http://www.nikkei.co.jp/news/keizai/20060301 AT1F2801F28022006.html. Also see *Yomiuri Shinbun*, March 1, 2006, http://www.yomiuri. co.jp/atmoney/mnews/20060301mh09.htm.

[44] Ibid.

[45] Ibid.

[46] Ibid.

liquidity constraints.[47] The BOJ also planned to outline post-policy goals to foster stability in the financial markets.

Some within the government were concerned that upward pressure on long-term rates stemming from a policy shift could have adverse effects on the economy.[48] Among these concerns were higher interest rates increasing debt-servicing costs, hampering efforts to reform the nation's finances.

## *The Foreign Exchange Market*

Expectations were growing in the foreign exchange market that an end to the BOJ's quantitative monetary easing policy would help boost interest rates and send the yen higher.

This expectation had translated into a higher demand for the Japanese yen by foreign parties, leading the yen to appreciate against the dollar to a high of 115.45 in Tokyo on March 8.[49] Since the start of 2006, the interest rate gap between Japan and the US had been a major factor in the dollar–yen exchange rate. There had been speculation that the US would soon bring its series of rate hikes to an end and that expansion in the interest rate differential would come to a halt. As a result, dollars were sold and the yen appreciated to ¥113 in mid-January.[50] But with Federal Reserve Board Chairman Ben Bernanke hinting in mid-February that rates could rise further, dollar buying took the upper hand and the yen plunged to ¥118.[51]

The reversal of fortunes came on February 23, 2006. On that day, BOJ Governor Fukui told the upper house's Committee on Financial Affairs that the central bank would like to end its loose monetary policy as soon as it determined that conditions for the termination had been met.[52] This sparked heightened speculation that a policy shift would be brought

---

[47] Ibid.

[48] Ibid.

[49] *Nihon Keizai Shinbun*, March 2, 2006, http://www.nikkei.co.jp/news/keizai/20060302 AT2C0103Z01032006.html.

[50] Ibid.

[51] Ibid.

[52] Ibid.

forward. On foreign exchange markets, yen buying had increased as even foreign parties were sensing a rise in yen interest rates on the heels of government remarks. If Japanese interest rates climbed, dollar-denominated investments would lose their attractiveness. Transactions that involved borrowing yen at low interest rates and investing in dollar-denominated assets would be subdued.

Expectations were that the bank would maintain its zero-interest rate policy for some time, even if the BOJ ended its quantitative easing, policy.[53] There was also a widespread view that the yen would not advance steadily against the dollar as long as the absolute interest rate gap between the US and Japan did not contract due to additional rate hikes in the US.[54]

## Coordination between the Government and the BOJ to Boost Investment

Showing a united front to the rest of the world by coordinating policy between Japan's government and central bank was important in order to improve the country's investment environment, especially with financial markets being more closely connected around the globe.

The recent confrontation between the government and the central bank over monetary policy had come about through their focus on normalizing the negative legacies of past fiscal and monetary policies. The government's fiscal deficit had become bloated due to a series of pump-priming measures, including lavish spending on public works projects and tax cuts. Given the steady progress in resuscitating the private sector, the country was unarguably in the second stage of structural reform, facing a new challenge of returning its fiscal and monetary policies to normalcy. The key issue, however, was how to co-ordinate the two policies in a balanced way.

Under the circumstances, the government, which is responsible for restoring the nation's fiscal health, had been pressuring the BOJ to keep yields on government bonds low to reduce its debt-servicing costs.

---

[53] Nihon Keizai Shinbun, March 2, 2006, http://www.nikkei.co.jp/news/keizai/20060302 AT2C0103Z01032006.html.

[54] Ibid.

But the government's excessive influence over monetary policy, if any, could add a new distortion to the economy. This was shown during the late 1980s, when the bubble economy was triggered by the yen's rapid appreciation against the dollar immediately after the 1985 Plaza Accord.[55]

The central bank was set to maintain zero interest rates for some time. However, if the policy was continued for too long, it would have the undesirable effect of inducing the flow of individual investors' funds into high-risk, high-return instruments such as foreign exchange margin trading from deposits and savings that yield near-zero rates. It would also give rise to speculative money games played out in some corners of the real estate and stock markets. To stabilize long-term interest rates, the Japanese government needed to show the market its determination to improve the fiscal balance without relying solely on the central bank.

The collaboration between US Treasury Secretary Robert Rubin and Federal Reserve Board Chairman Alan Greenspan was a successful example of the US achieving economic growth and fiscal reconstruction concurrently during the 1990s. At the time, there was a perfect harmony of the government's spending cuts and tax hikes initiatives and the Fed's flexible monetary policy. In the second phase of structural reform, Japan was expected to strike a similar balance between economic growth and changes in fiscal and monetary policies.

## The Decisions to be Made

On March 9, 2006, the central bank made the widely expected decision to lift the quantitative easing policy. The policy board judged that the conditions for ending the policy, including steady year-on-year growth in the core CPI, had been met. The BOJ also drew up a set of measures

---

[55] The Plaza Accord was an agreement made in August 1985 in which the finance ministers of the Group of five — the United States, Great Britain, France, Germany, and Japan — met to devalue the US Dollar in relation to the Japanese Yen and German Deutsche Mark by intervening in currency markets. The exchange rate value of the dollar versus the yen declined 51% over the two years after this agreement took place. For details, see "The Japan Paradox: A Booming and Unfit System", http://www.iht.com/articles/1991/08/09/ken_.php.

aimed at averting possible market turmoil that could result from lifting the policy.

On the same day the BOJ made its decision, the Japan Investment Council, a ministerial-level panel chaired by Prime Minister Junichiro Koizumi, agreed to set a target of doubling the amount of direct investment in Japan by overseas investors to 5% of gross domestic product over the next four years.[56] Achieving the goal would be possible only if foreign investors had confidence in Japan's monetary policy.

The Japanese economy was still a convalescent needing special care. Now that the Rubicon had been crossed, however, the real question was how the BOJ would steer monetary policy and keep the economy healthy. In order to prevent any overreaction from financial markets and businesses, such as a steep rise in commercial interest rates, BOJ Governor Fukui took pains to reassure that the rates set by the BOJ would remain where they were — virtually zero — for the foreseeable future, even though the central bank's decision base for monetary policy from then on would be interest rates rather than the quantity of money provided to commercial banks.

The BOJ was now faced with a few difficult questions (see **Exhibit 9**). The first key issue was when to move out of zero interest and restore a market mechanism based on interest rates. How long should the central bank continue to support the economic recovery by stressing its determination to stick to the zero interest policy? Being overly cautious could mean running the risk of allowing an asset bubble.

Secondly, the BOJ was now committed to setting a realistic inflation target. The BOJ's actual policy target appeared deliberately vague, with its statement saying that it would pursue its policy keeping in mind a consumer price rise in a range of 0% to 2%.

Finally, there was the issue of the bank's autonomy from the state. While the government should respect the central bank's independence, the BOJ needed to maintain good communications with the government in order to avoid negligent lapses. A central bank highly independent and trusted by the markets would be beneficial not only to the bank itself but

---

[56] *Nihon Keizai Shinbun*, March 13, 2006, http://www.nikkei.co.jp/news/main/20060313AT 2C1300W13032006.html.

**Exhibit 9**   The BOJ's Press Release on Change in the Guideline for Money Market Operations on March 9, 2006

The following four policy proposals submitted by the chairman were approved.

**1.  Change in the Guideline for Money Market Operations**

At the Monetary Policy Meeting held today, the BOJ decided to change the operating target of money market operations from the outstanding balance of current accounts at the Bank to the uncollateralized overnight call rate, and to set the following guideline for money market operations for the inter meeting period. The BOJ will encourage the uncollateralized overnight call rate to remain at effectively 0%.

**2.  Measures concerning Money Market Operations**

The outstanding balance of current accounts at the BOJ will be reduced towards a level in line with required reserves. Given that financial institutions have managed liquidity against the backdrop of large amounts of current account balances and extensive funds supplying operations by the Bank for a prolonged period since the adoption of the quantitative easing policy, the reduction in current account balance is expected to be carried out over a period of a few months, taking full account of conditions in the short-term money market. The process will be managed through short-term money market operations. With respect to the outright purchases of long-term interest-bearing Japanese government bonds, purchases will continue at the current amounts and frequency for some time, with due regard for future conditions of the balance sheet of the Bank. With respect to the complementary lending facility, the loan rate will remain at the current level. The temporary waiver of add-on rates for frequent users of the facility, in effect since March 2003, will also be maintained.

**3.  The Bank's View on Economic Activity and Prices**

Since March 2001, in view of preventing sustained decline in prices and preparing the basis for sustainable growth, the Bank of Japan has supplied extremely ample liquidity with current account balance at the Bank as the main operating target. The Bank also made a clear commitment to maintain the policy until the CPI (excluding fresh food, on a nationwide basis) registers stably 0% or an increase year-on-year. The Bank has since maintained the quantitative easing policy according to this commitment.

Currently, Japan's economy continues to recover steadily. Exports have continued to increase reflecting the expansion of overseas economies. With respect to domestic private demand, business-fixed investment has also continued to increase against the backdrop of high corporate profits. Robust corporate activity is positively influencing households, and private consumption has become solid. Looking ahead, the Bank expects a sustained recovery.

*(Continued)*

**Exhibit 9**　(*Continued*)

> Concerning prices, year-on-year changes in the CPI turned positive. Meanwhile, the output gap is gradually narrowing. Unit labor costs generally face weakening downward pressures as wages began to rise amid productivity gains. Furthermore, firms and households are shifting up their expectations for inflation. In this environment, year-on-year changes in the CPI are expected to remain positive. The Bank, therefore, judged that the conditions laid out in the commitment are fulfilled.
>
> **4. Current View on Monetary Policy**
>
> Given that the effects of the quantitative easing policy on economic activity and prices now mainly result from short-term interest rates being zero, there will be no abrupt change as a result of today's policy decision.
>
> Looking ahead, in considering the central scenario for economic activity and prices, there is a high probability of realizing sustainable growth under price stability. In the meantime, it should be noted that, over the medium- to long-term, there is a risk of swings in economic activity, as the stimulus from monetary policy is amplified against the backdrop of improving corporate profitability and a positive turn in price developments.
>
> On the future path of monetary policy, there will be a period in which the overnight call rate is at effectively 0%, followed by a gradual adjustment in the light of developments in economic activity and prices. In this process, if the risk mentioned above remains muted, in other words, if it is judged that inflationary pressures are restrained as the economy follows a balanced and sustainable growth path, an accommodative monetary environment ensuing from very low interest rates will probably be maintained for some time.

*Source*: BOJ, Minutes of the Monetary Policy, March 8 and 9, 2006, http://www.boj.or.jp/en/.

also to the Japanese people as a whole and that was what the BOJ should strive to become. How could the BOJ maintain a collaborative relationship with the government while maintaining its independence?

## For Further Discussion

1.  What might the discussion have been at the BOJ policy board meeting, held on March 8 and 9, 2006, before it was decided on whether to end the five-year, super-loose, monetary policy and return to a normal policy targeting interest rates?

2. What was the significance of the quantitative easing policy?
3. Even if it did work, the policy of quantitative easing was not much more than a psychological trick to give assurance of a safe guard to the market in Japan. Comment on this.
4. What kinds of unintended side effects could be expected after termination of the quantitative easing policy?
5. What were the factors that contributed to the creation of the Japanese economic bubble in the late 1980s?
6. Comment on the timing of the BOJ decision on March 9, 2006, to end its quantitative easing policy.

# 11

# World Co. Ltd., Japan:
# Why Go Private?

*Wholehearted creation and sharing of values — always strive to go beyond.*

— Hidezo Terai, President of World Co. Ltd.[1]

Early 2005 saw the first hostile takeover in Japan when Livedoor Co. Ltd. (Livedoor), an upstart internet company, took on Fuji Television Network Inc. (Fuji TV) in a battle to acquire Nippon Broadcasting System Inc. (NBS).[2] Financed by foreign capital, this takeover scared Japan's traditional business establishments who now feared that the threat of hostile takeovers had finally become a reality in Japan. In response, many companies scrambled to introduce anti-takeover defenses.[3] This, however, posed a challenge for these companies as the US institutional infrastructure supporting poison pills differed considerably from that of Japan.

Meanwhile, Japan also went through numerous accounting scandals in public companies and was seeing dramatic changes in the disclosure and corporate-governance rules and regulations governing issuers of publicly traded securities and their officers and directors. Concurrently, Mr. Hidezo Terai, president of World Co. Ltd., Japan (World), a publicly traded apparel company on the Tokyo and Osaka Stock Exchanges, considered "going private" and delisting it from both the stock exchanges.

---

[1] World Co. Ltd., "2006 nen no Me, World no Kigyoushokai (Eye 2006, Corporate Profile, World)" (privately published material), p. 5.

[2] See Case 5 "Hostile Takeover in Japan: Fuji TV vs. Livedoor for NBS" in this book.

[3] See Case 7 "Nireco Japan: Introduction of the Poison Pill" in this book.

It was reported[4] that this move was driven by a need to seek relief from the new disclosure and corporate-governance rules and regulations and to protect World from possible hostile takeovers.

World's top management believed that being a publicly listed company was more a burden than a blessing for a small company such as themselves. Returning the company to private status might be a cost efficient alternative to being listed and would alleviate the burdens that came with being a publicly traded company. However, there were business as well as legal considerations that had to be thoroughly evaluated before this decision could be taken. In early summer 2005, top executives at World conducted a study that would enable them to make the right decision for the company — whether to stay public or go private.

## World: Company Background

World was established in 1959 as a wholesaler of women's knitwear. Located in Kobe, the capital city of Hyōgo prefecture, the company went public in 1988 with a listing on the second section of the Tokyo Stock Exchange.[5] Over the years, World expanded its business and by 2005 it had branched out across the value chain, from dying yarn upstream to selling finished products through retail stores, mainly located in railroad stations, and their own direct-marketing magazine downstream (see **Exhibits 1**, **2**, and **5** for more information on World).

The company specialized in high class women's apparel and was starting to expand into men's apparel. By 2005 yearly sales figures were

---

[4] Despite World's denial that this move was not intended to be a poison pill against takeovers, that is the way the industry interpreted it. See "Koreha kyukyokuno Nottori Boueisakudearu (This is an Ultimate Measure against Takeovers)", *Nikkei* (*Japan Economic Journal*), July 26, 2005, p. 1. See also "Jihyo (Editorial, the fashion industry report)", "World no Touzen na Baishu Bouei (This is an excellent company and their move against takeovers is natural)", July 26, 2005, http://selgae.exblog.jp/1384523 (accessed November 26, 2007). Also, see another fashion industry report, Demand Works, "Fashion Ryutsu Gyoukai no Kannshinnji (Fashion Industry's interest; this move is to hedge against takeover risk", July 26, 2005, http://dwks.cocolog-nifty.com/fashion_column/2005/07/post_758c.html (accessed November 26, 2007).

[5] In 1999 the listing was transferred to the first section of the Tokyo Stock Exchange and the Osaka Securities Exchange.

**Exhibit 1**   World's Corporate Data

| Company Name | | World Co. Ltd. |
| --- | --- | --- |
| **Businesses** | | |
| World was originally a wholesale business of clothing for women, men and children. The development of their first total co-ordinated brand, World Co-Ordinate (currently, Cordier), overturned the then-prevailing industry norm of selling clothing on a single-item basis. The company subsequently added the Lui Chantant and Ville D'Azur brands, among others, and organized a support structure for specialty shops, including the introduction of VMD (visual merchandising — a specialized function for supporting the merchandizing of goods using a visual aspect, such as displays, interiors and sales promotions) and mid-season additional orders. In 1997, it launched a full-fledged structural reform of its wholesale business in response to the changing market environment. It reorganized its brands, revised transaction terms and conditions with specialty shops, and built the specialty shop platform as a wholesale business model by systematizing a series of processes, from exhibitions, order taking, and information support to recovery. Using this model as a baseline, it promoted WRS (World Rep System, which is one of the brands of the company), a system for distributing the distinctive brands of its partners, in addition to its own brands, thereby satisfying the diverse needs of specialty shops and customers. | | |
| **Kobe Head Office** | | 8-1, 6-Chome, Minatojima-Nakamachi Chuo-ku, Kobe 650-8585, Japan<br>Tel: +81 78 302 3111 |
| **Tokyo Office** | | Shiodome-Sumitomo Bldg. 19F, 9-2, 1-Chome, Higashi-Shinbashi, Minato-ku, Tokyo 105-8620, Japan |
| **Date of Establishment** | | January 13, 1959 |
| **Paid-In Capital** | | ¥18.7 billion[6] |
| **Executive Officers** | | |
| President and CEO | Hidezo Terai | |
| Senior managing executive officer and CFO | Keizo Koizumi | General manager, Management and Administration Division |
| Senior managing executive officer and COO | Yuichi Nakata | General manager, Sales, Marketing and Operations Division |
| Managing executive officer and CPO (Chief Personnel Officer) | Manabu Minamiyama | General manager, Human Resources Division |

(Continued)

---

[6] US$1 = ¥107.22 on March 31, 2005.

**Exhibit 1**   (*Continued*)

| Managing executive officer | Koichi Tanimura | General manager, Business Model Development Department |
| Managing executive officer | Masao Hibino | General manager, Store Development Administration Department |
| Managing executive officer | Atsushi Miyake | General manager, Management Planning Division |

| **Directors** | |
|---|---|
| Chairman | Shigeo Hatasaki |
| President | Hidezo Terai |
| Director | Keizo Koizumi |
| Director | Yuichi Nakata |
| Director | Hiroshi Watanabe |
| Director | Manabu Minamiyama |
| Director | Osamu Sudo |
| Director | Satoshi Yura |

| **Corporate Auditors** | |
|---|---|
| Standing corporate auditor | Sadaaki Kitagawa |
| Standing corporate auditor | Katsumi Tomoda |
| Corporate auditor | Yoshiharu Kurosawa |
| Corporate auditor | Kenzo Doi |
| **Number of Employees** | 1,780 |
| **Number of Group Employees** | 6,804 |

As of summer 2005

*Source*: World's website: http://www.world.co.jp/english/company/index.html.

growing at 4–5% per year, showing constant growth. It was one of the top five largest Japanese companies specializing in women's apparel.

World was financially healthy and performing well (see **Exhibit 3**). As of March 2005, the shareholders' equity ratio was 65.4%, which was higher than the average for listed companies. Shareholders' equity amounted to ¥131,516 million.[7] For fiscal year 2005,[8] net profit was ¥9,270

---

[7] US $1 = ¥111.59 on July 25, 2005.

[8] The company's fiscal year runs from April 1 to March 31.

**Exhibit 2**   World's History

| | |
|---|---|
| **1959** | Established in Kobe City with ¥2 million in capital. |
| **1967** | Developed and expanded the brand World Co-Ordinate (currently, Cordier). |
| **1977** | Introduced new corporate image through corporate identity program. |
| **1978** | Entered the men's clothing business. |
| **1980** | Created World Industry Co. Ltd. |
| **1982** | Opened the Ginza Liza shop. |
| **1984** | Established Le Monde Des Gourmet Inc. to enter the restaurant business. |
| **1987** | Created the joint venture Shanghai World Fashion Co. Ltd. in Shanghai. |
| **1988** | Established the subsidiary World Taiwan Fashion Co. Ltd. in Taipei. |
| **1989** | Set up a joint venture in knitwear production with Shanghai World Knitting Co. Ltd. in Shanghai. |
| **1992** | Announced the medium-term business plan, "The SPARCS Concept".[9] |
| **1993** | Launched Ozoc as the first SPA brand.[10] Listed on the second section of the Osaka Securities Exchange. Established Shanghai World United Garments Co. Ltd. by merging Shanghai World Fashion Co. Ltd. and Shanghai World Knitting Co. Ltd. |
| **1998** | Listed on the second section of the Tokyo Stock Exchange. |
| **1999** | Transferred listing to the first section of the Tokyo Stock Exchange and Osaka Securities Exchange. |
| **2000** | Merged the marketing subsidiaries to form World Store Partners Co. Ltd. |
| **2001** | Created the marketing subsidiary World Korea Co. Ltd. in Korea. |
| **2002** | Set up World Hong Kong Co. Ltd. in Hong Kong as the Asia Pacific headquarters overseeing South-East Asia. Established World Fashion (China) Co. Ltd. in Beijing, to which the sales operations of World United Fashion (Beijing) Co. Ltd. and Shanghai World United Garments Co. Ltd. were transferred. Consequently, World United Fashion (Beijing) Co. Ltd. was dissolved. |
| **2003** | Created World Business Brain Co. Ltd. for educational and consulting services. |
| **2004** | Established ITS'[11] Demo Co. Ltd. and World Business Support Co. Ltd. as spin-offs. |

*Source*: World's website: http://www.world.co.jp/english/company/history.html.

---

[9] SPARCS means Super Production Apparel Retail Customer Satisfaction. In 1992, the company introduced this system, a customer-centric system that unifies the entire business process from retail to production, thereby converting losses and inefficiencies into new value. Since then, the company has pursued various reforms to achieve maximum customer value and productivity. For details on the SPARCSs concept, see Hideo Terai, Message from the president, "Enhancing Long-Term Sustainable Corporate Value Based on Human-Centric Management", on World's web, http://www.world.co.jp/english/company/message/message_01.html (accessed November 26, 2007)

[10] The company developed their business as a SPA (Specialty store. retailer of Private label Apparel) chain. The company has positioned themselves uniquely and decisively in the fashion market due to this business model. For details, see World's web, http://world.jp/index.html (accessed November 26, 2007).

[11] ITS' Demo Co. Ltd. This is the name of the company but "Itsudemo" in Japanese means "always". The name of the company was taken from there.

**Exhibit 3**   World's Consolidated Financial Performance

Year Ended March 31, 2005

| Year | Sales | Operating Profits | Net Profits | Earnings per Share (EPS) | Return on Shareholders' Equity | Total Assets | Shareholders' Equity | Shareholders' Equity Ratio | Book Value per Share (BPS) |
|---|---|---|---|---|---|---|---|---|---|
| | million $ | million $ | million $ | $ | % | million $ | million $ | % | $ |
| 2002 | 2,068.5 | 142.5 | 47.1 | 0.92 | 3.9 | 1,881.2 | 1,243.2 | 66.1 | 23.98 |
| 2003 | 2,174.4 | 130.9 | 56.2 | 1.07 | 4.6 | 1,814.7 | 1,188.9 | 65.5 | 24.28 |
| 2004 | 2,203.2 | 164.7 | 67.8 | 1.39 | 5.7 | 1,140.4 | 1,140.4 | 66.3 | 25.54 |
| 2005 | 2,286.8 | 171.4 | 86.5 | 1.83 | 7.2 | 1,226.6 | 1,226.6 | 65.4 | 26.82 |

*Note*: US$1 = ¥107.22 on March 31, 2005.

*Source*: World's website: http://www.world.co.jp.

million (3.8% to the sales), earnings per share were ¥196.21 and total assets stood at ¥201,067 million.

On 25 July 2005, the total number of outstanding shares were 52.12 million; the stock price was ¥4,410. The market price of the company in terms of the stock price was ¥229,850 million, which meant that the market was evaluating the hidden asset value at ¥28,783 million (see **Exhibits 4** and **5**).[12]

## *Corporate Governance at World*

World's management believed that the top-priority management goal of the company was to be a value creation company within the fashion industry, continuously creating and delivering added value to satisfy its customers. They believed that this management goal could only be achieved by fulfilling their corporate social responsibilities towards all their stakeholders — customers, employees, business partners, shareholders, governments and society.[13]

To reinforce their efforts to promote a group-wide compliance system, the management enacted the World Code of Conduct, a list of principles outlining proper business conduct which each World director, officer and employee had to follow. World's Code of Conduct covered corporate ethics, social expectations, management philosophies (sincerity) as well as legal compliance and compliance with internal rules. It stipulated the company's business conduct principles for managing business with integrity, maintaining harmony with all stakeholders and improving World's corporate value.

The board of directors oversaw proper corporate governance to ensure efficiency of operations in accordance with this Code of Conduct (see **Exhibit 6** for ongoing improvement of World's corporate value). The board also contributed to maintaining a high level of transparency in management through measures including timely and appropriate information

---

[12] The hidden asset value is defined to be the market price minus total assets on the book. In this case it is ¥229,850 million – ¥201,067 million = ¥28,783 million.

[13] Hideo Terai, president of World. For details, see footnote no. 1, p. 33.

**Exhibit 4**   World's Shares

(As of March 31, 2005)

| | |
|---|---|
| Number of issued and outstanding shares | 52,119,512 |
| Number of shareholders | 7,472 |

**Breakdown of Shares by Type of Shareholder (As of March 31, 2005)**

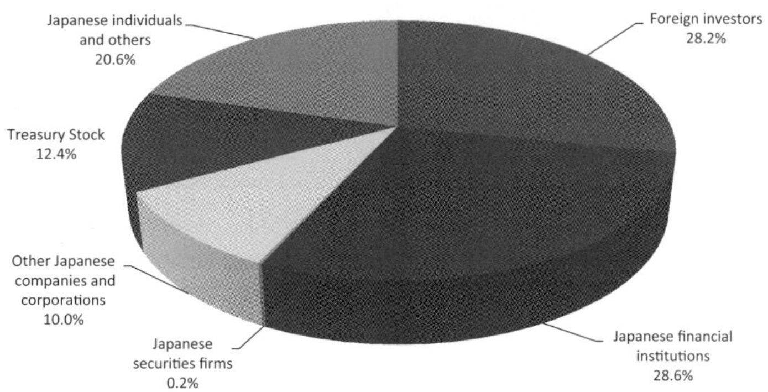


**Principal Shareholders (As of March 31, 2005)**

| | Number of Shares (Thousands) | Percentage of Total Shares in Issue |
|---|---|---|
| World Co. Ltd. (Treasury stock) | 6,460 | 12.39 |
| Master Trust Bank of Japan, Ltd. (Trust Account) | 4,535 | 8.70 |
| Hirotoshi Hatasaki | 4,356 | 8.35 |
| Japan Trustee Services Bank Ltd. (Trust Account) | 4,150 | 7.96 |
| Kiguchi Foundation | 2,250 | 4.31 |
| Nihon Sohken Co. Ltd. | 2,234 | 4.28 |
| Bank of New York Europe Ltd. Lux Branch Account Client | 2,079 | 3.99 |
| Calyon Paris Ordinary Account | 1,042 | 2.00 |
| BNP-Paribas Securities Services Luxembourg-Jasdec Securities | 841 | 1.61 |
| Japan Trustee Services Bank Ltd. | 791 | 1.51 |

*Source*: World's website: http://www.world.co.jp/english/ir/market.html#ss.

**Exhibit 5**   Stock Performance of World

In yen

Volume (× 1,000,000 shares)

*Source*: Yahoo Japan!, "fainansu (Finance)" January 5, 2006, http://quote.yahoo.co.jp/q?s=3596.
o&d=c&k=c3&a=v&p=m130,m260,s&t=5y&l=off&z=m&q=c&h=on (accessed January 5, 2006.
This is no longer available, since the company has delisted from the market.)

disclosure so that the company continued to be an enterprise worthy of society's trust.

# Japan's Rapidly Changing Business Environment

## *Japan's First Takeover Case*

The takeover battle for NBS between Livedoor and Fuji TV was a mile-stone in the history of Japanese corporate governance[14] because it had

---

[14] For details, see Case 5 in this book.

**Exhibit 6**  World's Business Conduct Principles

1. Conduct in Relation to Customers
2. Conduct in Relation to Employees
3. Conduct in Relation to Business Partners
4. Conduct in Relation to Shareholders
5. Conduct in Relation to Society and Governments
6. Conduct in Relation to the Environment
7. Conduct in Relation to the Company
8. Conduct in Relation to International Communities
9. Conduct in Relation to Crisis Management

*Source*: World Co. Ltd., "2006 nen no Me, World no Kigyoushokai (Eye 2006, Corporate Profile, World)" (privately published material), p. 33.

long been believed that hostile takeover bids would have little chance of success in Japan. This high-profile case attracted much media attention since it was the first domestic hostile takeover using American tactics in Japan. Its high visibility on the various media demonstrated that the threat of hostile takeovers had become a reality in Japan.

Despite World's announcement that it sought a delisting of its shares in order to maximize corporate value on a long-term basis, the business world, including investors, interpreted the move differently.[15] They took it to mean that World's top management thought Livedoor's hostile takeover bid would no doubt serve as a trigger for more hostile takeovers of Japanese companies by offshore companies, particularly US firms. Given that World's move was made in a tense corporate atmosphere where the fear of Japanese companies being swallowed up by foreign investors ran high, the business world assumed that World's management must have thought their company needed to introduce "poison pill" defenses as a means to counter hostile takeover bids.[16]

In the meantime, the Japanese business world had realized that Japanese companies faced a very big hurdle in setting up rational poison

---

[15] See footnote no. 4.

[16] Ibid. Also see, the company's announcement: World Co. Ltd. (March 14, 2005) "For the Plan to Improve the Corporate Value", http://www.nireco.co.jp/jap/# (accessed November 26, 2007).

pill defenses since the US institutional infrastructure supporting poison pills differed considerably from that in Japan.[17] Hence, they had come to believe that "going private" was perhaps the best defense available to any public company at risk of being taken over.

## New Conditions Concerning Mergers

Japan's Ministry of Justice had decided to create new conditions concerning mergers.[18] The law they were suggesting would let foreign companies buy Japanese businesses by merging the two to form Japan-based subsidiaries of themselves, using parent company stock to pay for the deal. As a result of this law, overseas companies would find it easier to take over Japanese companies.[19] The new law raised concerns with top management in Japanese companies regarding the possibility of a hostile takeover with foreign capital. The business establishment was especially concerned about what was known as "triangular mergers", namely, using shares listed offshore as counter values in merger deals (see **Exhibit 7**).

The Ministry of Justice planned to clarify the scope and condition of offshore shares that could be used after the bill was adopted by means of

**Exhibit 7**   Triangular Scheme of Using Offshore Shares for Payment

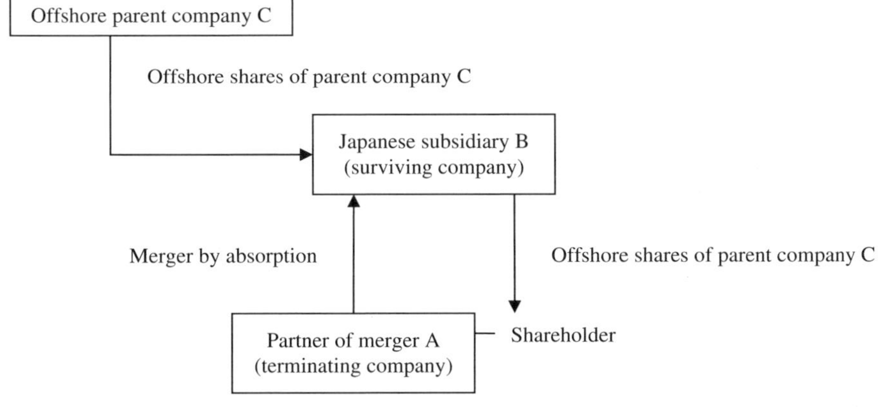


---

[17] For more information on this difference, see Case 7 in this book.

[18] The law was officially enacted on May 1, 2006.

[19] *Economist* (Japan) (April 1, 2005), "Sanbaku Gappei (Triangular Mergers)", p. 11.

a ministerial ordinance. Specifically, the Ministry would require the acquiring company to pass a special resolution in a general meeting, instead of an ordinary resolution as was the case with other types of mergers and acquisitions, for the purchase of a Japanese company through a triangular merger. One of the main differences between special resolutions and ordinary ones was that the former needed a two-thirds majority to pass rather than a simple majority. This would make triangular mergers harder to carry out, particularly in the case of a company with many individual shareholders.

One of the fears of Japanese corporations was that offshore shares provided as counter values may not be shares of European and US companies listed on mature securities markets. Considering the ease of cashability and the ease of obtaining information on these overseas companies and their shares, it was not unreasonable to set different requirements for merger resolutions. A particular concern was the possibility of shares being bought beforehand and then being used to "coerce" a triangular merger. It was speculated that the top management of World had to consider a possibility of such a case where a corporate raider with malice bought shares in advance to control a shareholders meeting and force an exchange with shares of a phantom corporation.[20]

## *The Court's Decision on the Use of Poison Pills*[21]

On March 14, 2005, Nireco Corporation, an industrial control equipment manufacturer, introduced Japan's first ever poison pill in the form of share warrants issued to current shareholders[22] as a counter-measure to possible future hostile takeovers. SFP Value Realization Master Fund Ltd. (SFP),[23]

---

[20] Although in March 2005 the government was contemplating implementing this new policy in April 2006, it decided to delay the implementation by a year after voices from the industry in Japan urged more caution.

[21] This section borrows heavily from Case 7 in this book.

[22] Nireco introduced a poison pill providing two share warrants to each shareholder free of charge at the end of March 2005. With these share warrants, each shareholder was eligible to acquire a new share at the price of ¥1 per share on June 16, 2005.

[23] A US investment fund located in Caymans Islands which held approximately 6.8% of Nireco shares requested an injunction against the issuance on May 9, 2005.

a major Nireco shareholder, filed a lawsuit seeking a court injunction against the proposed poison pill on May 9, 2005. It argued that the implementation of the scheme would adversely affect Nireco's shareholders. In response to SFP's lawsuit, the Tokyo District Court delivered an injunction against the issuance of the share warrants on June 2, 2005 on the grounds that "it corresponded to an extremely unfair issuance which the Commercial Law prohibited".[24]

The Tokyo District Court indicated three conditions in which a share warrant could be issued as a defensive measure in "peace time", i.e., when no battle existed for management rights. The court pointed out that primarily, share warrants could only be issued as a defense against a hostile takeover if it was decided upon in the shareholders' meeting. However, this requirement could be replaced with a decision of the board meeting if (1) there was a mechanism to reflect the opinion of the shareholders' meeting; (2) a willful activation of the defensive measure by the board meeting could be prevented; and (3) it did not cause any unexpected damages to shareholders.

The court judged that Nireco had not set up a mechanism to incorporate shareholders' opinions at the shareholders' meeting which was to be held at the end of June 2005, and that it was possible that the board of directors may not follow the recommendation of the special committee[25] regarding the exercising of share warrants. Thus, the court concluded that Nireco's introduction of the poison pill "could not be justified as a premeditated countermeasure against a hostile takeover", considering the fact that "there was a risk of existing shareholders incurring unexpected damages because of a dilution of stocks".

Nireco's case, in which the Tokyo District Court served an injunction order against the issuance of share warrants, was a poison pill of a special nature: share warrants were issued to shareholders prior to any announcement of a hostile takeover bid. The court raised two questions, which were

---

[24] This position was confirmed by a court judgement: Tokyo Higher Court (June 15, 2005) "Heisei 17 (Ra) No. 942", http://corporation.rikkyo.ac.jp/data/jp/39.pdf (accessed November 26, 2007)

[25] The board of Nireco appointed the special committee comprised outside experts to make recommendations to the board as to the actions to be taken, see footnote no. 19 for details.

related to securing and confirming the third party's positions[26] by the board members. One was whether there was any way by which the defensive measure could be suitably judged by highly independent, outside members. Although Nireco claimed that it would "observe the (third party) special committee's recommendations to the fullest extent", the district court pointed out that "there was room for the board of directors to not follow the recommendations".

The other question was under what circumstance the defensive measure would be activated. In the Livedoor case,[27] the Tokyo High Court gave examples of cases where the issuance of share warrants were considered appropriate, such as when the buyer asked the company to buy back shares at high prices or was about to dispose of the company's assets in order to obtain temporary profits. However, Nireco claimed that a defensive measure was justifiable for a case where the takeover was contrary to the benefits of stakeholders, e.g., employees, customers and suppliers, in addition to the conditions that the Tokyo High Court had indicated. In response to this claim, the Tokyo District Court ruled that "such a judgment standard was too broad and lacked clarity to be used as a means of preventing willful judgments of the board of directors". These rulings by the courts made the business world believe that World's top management would question the value of setting up poison pill defenses to ward off possible future hostile takeovers.

Japan's top management was of the opinion that the poison pill had worked in the US as it had been largely used to seek a better deal for the shareholders rather than simply to block a bid, and that independent directors, courts and active institutional investors had all come together in policing the use of the pill. Traditional Japanese corporate governance was not conducive to nurturing independent directors of the character that had proven so important in the instances where the poison pill was used in the US. Recent Commercial Code amendments allowed Japanese corporations to elect a US-style governance structure with outside directors staffing governance committees. However, the Japanese top management was sceptical of the impact of this change since Japanese corporate law did not require an "outside" director to be independent in the sense that that term was used in the US.

---

[26] Such as the special committee, which is specified in footnote no. 18.

[27] See Case 5 in this book.

## World's Reasons for Delisting

According to World, a significant reason to delist the stock was in order to maximize corporate value on a long-term sustainable basis toward realizing the ideal corporate structure.[28] The top management claimed that the primary reason for returning the company to its private status was the belief that they had to secure a management system for quick, flexible responses in the ever-changing fashion business. Such a management system would allow them to maximize World's enterprise value on a long-term, sustainable basis regardless of fluctuations in the company's short-term business performance.[29] They believed they should pursue a management style founded on human resources, which would realize sustainable growth and the return of profit to customers, employees and business partners. Although it was possible to do this as a listed company, World believed they would do better as an unlisted company.[30] Moreover, the company did not like it said that its delisting was just a defense against takeovers. Admitting that it was one of the main reasons, the company wanted to show that its aim was more forward looking — it was going to maximize corporate value by delisting. However, the business community did not take it that way.[31]

In the future, World looked to aggressively capitalize on the characteristic freedom and flexibility of a private company to realize the management's ideal vision of the apparel industry. From the medium- and long-term perspectives, it would therefore pursue ongoing strategic development of new business models and implement structural innovations in pursuit of an optimal holistic performance of the organization.[32]

## The Final Decision

World's study of the pros and cons of going public and private was reported to the board (for details, see **Exhibit 8**). After weighing the advantages and disadvantages of going private and the burdens of

---

[28] Hideo Terai, president of World. For details, see footnote no. 1, p. 33.

[29] Ibid.

[30] Ibid.

[31] See footnote no. 4.

[32] See footnote no. 1, p. 8.

Exhibit 8   Pros and Cons of Going Private

### 1. Advantage of Unlisted Companies

*Escape from Takeover Risk*

By being unlisted on the stock market, a corporation could avoid the risk of being bought out by surprise. A listed company carried the risk of being the target of a takeover bid at any time or having its stock bought out in the open market without its knowledge. In Japan, many companies had recently been the subject of takeover attempts by foreign investors, and so many of them were considering delisting their stocks.

*Reduction of Costs*

The cost of conforming to the duty of information disclosure to shareholders was becoming enormous. This included payments to professionals — such as lawyers and accountants — investor relations costs as a service to shareholders, and the cost of shareholders' meetings. Publicly traded corporations were also required to have some outside board members to ensure trustworthy corporate governance. A company also required a substantial number of employees to conduct information disclosure activities. All of these costs could be drastically reduced if a company went private.

*Management Resiliency*

In the case of an unlisted company, the management enjoyed more flexibility in the area of corporate governance. For example, there was no need to hold shareholders' meetings once a year; rather, shareholders could be summoned at short notice whenever necessary. It was even possible to make a corporate decision by issuing documents asking for the relevant parties' signatures of approval. Moreover, managers' compensations could be executed without any disclosure to shareholders and employees.

*Management Based on Long-Term Strategy*

A publicly held corporation was generally interested in maintaining a reputable level of, or increasing, dividend on a quarterly basis to keep shareholders happy. Therefore, these corporations were conservative when it came to capital investment, which was necessary on a long-term basis, but could cause a reduction of profits due to depreciation on a short-term basis. On the other hand, a privately held corporation possibly had less interest in short-term profits and was more interested in maximizing the value of the corporation from a long-term viewpoint. Thus, it was easier for a privately held corporation to invest in research and development based on a long-term strategy.

*Non-Disclosure of Confidential Information*

A publicly held corporation was generally required to disclose information for the benefit of its current and future shareholders. However, it was obviously undesirable to disclose certain information as competitors could then have access to it. Moreover, the

(Continued)

**Exhibit 8**   (*Continued*)

disclosure of corporate information tended to be very expensive, requiring a lot of time and money for analysis with the help of internal and external professionals. Managers of privately held companies had no such problems and could concentrate more on the essential management of the company.

### Free from Securities-Related Lawsuits

The duty of information disclosure was mandatory for a publicly traded company because of various laws related to securities. Managers were constantly under the risk of being sued by shareholders on account of securities fraud. Even if a manager followed proper disclosure guidelines, he or she could easily lose in a lawsuit on account of failure to disclose material information. Although being privately held did not guarantee managers a complete escape from similar suits, the probability of being sued by the shareholders was extremely low.

## 2. Advantage of Listed Companies

### Obtaining Finance Using Stock Market

In order to obtain finance, a corporation did not need to be listed on the stock market or to issue bonds; funds could be raised from banks. However, as a corporation grew and needed larger funds for a longer period, it would be easier to raise money through the stock market or bond market.

### Improvement of Corporate Image

A listed company enjoyed better recognition in society and better stability. This gave a corporation a better position in business competition and also helped to obtain more advantageous loan terms and conditions from banks. Vendors' and buyers' trust could improve as well.

### Securing Stock Fluidity

Managers and employees could easily encash their stocks if the company's stock was publicly traded, and if the prices and fairness of trading were guaranteed. If the company was not listed on the market, it would be difficult to find buyers and to determine fair prices.

### Easier to Access Mergers and Acquisitions

While being listed made a corporation a target for takeovers, it also meant that it was easier to attempt mergers and acquisitions of other companies. In other words, it was possible to acquire another company by exchanging treasury stocks the corporation held, making it unnecessary to fund the merger with cash.

remaining a public company in Japan's current economic climate, the time had come to make a final decision on the future status of World.

On July 25, 2005, World announced that it planned to go private through a management buyout (MBO) (see **Exhibit 9**). The management wanted to buy 67% of the outstanding shares offering ¥4,700 per share — 25.6% higher than the past half-year average performance (see **Exhibit 10**). The total MBO amount was ¥220,000 million, which made it the largest in the history of Japan.[33]

The market had the following to say on the decision by the top management of World.

*This unique management judgment by World is questioning the meaning of going public. Concerning the aim of the latest management buyout, president Terai has explained that they went private "for the sake of developing*

**Exhibit 9**　　Management Buyout

When the management of a company purchased a controlling interest in the company from existing shareholders, it would buy out all the outstanding shareholders and then privatize the company. It would make this move because it would feel it had the expertise to grow the business in a better way if it controlled the ownership. Quite often, management teamed up with a venture capitalist to acquire the business because it was a complicated process that required significant capital.

*Source*: Investopedia, The Investing Education Site, http://www.investopedia.com/terms/m/mbo.asp (accessed November 26, 2007).

**Exhibit 10**　　Basis of Tender Offer Price

The offer price of ¥4,700 per share had been determined by taking into account World's past share price trends, financial and operation conditions, and a purchase of more than 67% of World's stake with voting rights. The offer price was set at 25.6% over the arithmetic average (rounded down to ¥3,741) of the closing share prices of World shares at the Osaka Securities Exchange during the six-month period ending July 22, 2005, and it was above ¥4,410, the highest share price since January 6, 2003.

*Source*: World Co. Press Release, "Tender Offer no Tuuchi (Notice of Endorsement of Tender Offer)", July 25, 2005, http://world.jp/english/news/2005/0725.html (accessed November 26, 2007).

---

[33] World Co. Ltd. (July 25, 2005), Press Release, "Tender Offer no Tuuchi (Notice of Enforcement of Tender Offer)", http://world.jp/english/news/2005/0725.html (accessed November 26, 2007)

*the management strategy quickly". His move to call a declaration of intention by the company is based on the nature of the apparel industry where business fluctuation is extremely fast, and on the fact that the company would not likely be influenced in their business decisions by investors, who seek short-term profits. Going public has been good for many Japanese companies. They went public without closely examining the necessity of doing so, hurrying to raise funds from the market. In that sense, we can probably consider that the decision of the company is rich in suggestion. There is, however, some criticism. Going private may jeopardize the company image by showing the anti-transparency policy of the company, and by escaping obligation of information disclosure to the public. There is also a voice that says this is a strategy for the management to protect itself. If we assume that they don't have such an intention, then they have to explain what they intend to do for the shareholder and society. In any case, it is important for future managers to have the strategic skill to decide which of the two, going public or private, raises real company value.*[34]

## For Further Discussion

1. What are private companies? How are they different from public companies?
2. A does not need to go totally private. Is it possible to go partially private? This process is not yet standardised in Japan. Report on how the company can go partially private as a practical alternative based on US law and regulation.
3. It is said that more small public companies in the US are going private because of the stringent accounting and auditing standards required by law. At the same time, however, on witnessing the collapse of big public companies like Enron because of accounting skulduggery, small public companies are seeing that increased corporate governance resulting from compliance can enhance their reputations and growth opportunities in the US. The same trend may occur in Japan. Comment on this trend.

---

[34] Kobe Newspaper (July 29, 2005) "World; kubashiki Jyojyo ni Omoi Toikake (A Heavy Question Raised for IPO)", Editorial, http://www.kobe-np.co.jp/shasetsu/00024649ss200607290900.shtml (accessed November 26, 2007).

# 12

# J-COM: Share-Trade Irregularities on the Day of IPO

*Unfortunately, a "typing error" caused the trade to go off as selling 610,000 shares for one yen. Oops.*[1]

On December 8, 2005, the Tokyo Stock Exchange (TSE) was struck by an unbelievable transaction slip-up that triggered waves of speculative buying and selling, affecting a wide range of stocks. The shares of J-COM Co. Ltd. (J-Com) were at a limit-up[2] level of ¥772,000[3] during the afternoon's trading, having recovered from a brief plunge to ¥572,000 shortly after they debuted at ¥672,000. A giant sell order followed by a large number of buy orders had caused the plunge in J-Com's stock price during the morning session. It was not clear who was behind the sell order, which eclipsed the number of outstanding J-Com shares. The TSE said it was looking into details of the big movements in J-Com's stock price.

*We are investigating the cause of a possible trading error. Right now, we really have no idea what happened.*

— Yasuhiko Okamoto, president of J-Com[4]

---

[1] *Wall Street Journal*, December 8, 2005, "Oops", http://www.pearcec.com/rss/CrossingWallStreet_com/ (accessed April 11, 2007).

[2] The Tokyo Stock Exchange has set a daily price limit of around 5% up or down from the previous day's closing price. For details, see the TSE'S website: http://www.tse.or.jp/english/sr/compliance/monthly/e_cmr0307.pdf (accessed April 11, 2007).

[3] US$1 = ¥120.27 on December 8, 2005.

[4] *Nikkei* (*Japan Economic Journal*), December 8, 2005, http://markets.nikkei.co.jp/special/sp014.cfm?id=d2e0801l08&date=20051208 (accessed April 11, 2007).

What were the implications of the irregularities for the parties involved? Who should have been held responsible and what should have been done to make sure such a thing would not happen again?

## Confusion in the Tokyo Stock Market

The day-long turmoil on the day of the initial public offering (IPO) started when a broker placed an erroneous sales order for 610,000 shares of J-Com for ¥1 each, instead of an order to sell a single share of the staffing and multimedia start-up firm for ¥610,000. The erroneous order was sent to the stock market despite warning signals from the brokerage's order processing system, and it was subsequently executed because the steps the broker took to cancel the order did not follow the procedure set by the TSE. The brokerage rushed to buy back the shares it had wrongly sold.

Many market participants quickly realized that the sell order was a mistake and that the brokerage had intended to sell one share at ¥610,000. Dedicated online bulletin boards soon lit up with speculation about the unusual order. Betting that the brokerage that had placed the order would be forced to short-cover the shares, individual investors and others began snapping up the stock. After nose-diving on the massive sell order, J-Com's stock shot up on the buy-back. This eventually pushed up J-Com's share price to a limit-up level of ¥772,000 with the shares remaining bid-only[5] from this point onwards.

J-Com's topsy-turvy movements soon spread to the overall market. Investors who discovered the trading blunder scrambled to dump the stocks of securities firms that could sustain losses on the mistake and then jettisoned a broader range of shares on speculation that the brokerage which had made the error would sell some of its own shareholdings to cover the loss. All this speculative selling sent a number of stocks plunging. The Nikkei 225 Stock Average plunged 301.30 points, or suffered a 2% loss, to 15,183.36. This was its third largest fall measured in points

---

[5] Quotations are given as a bid and ask price (also referred to as offer). A bid is the price at which a dealer will buy and an ask is the price at which a dealer will sell. Bid-only describes a situation where there are only buy orders and no sell orders.

since the start of 2005. In the Topix index of the entire TSE, first section issues fell 29.86 points, or 1.9%, to 1568.73.

*The extent of the fall today was clearly to do with what happened at J-Com.*

Brand Ginsberg, co-head of equities at Nikko Citigroup, Tokyo[6]

Securities firms took a pummeling in the confusion. Shares in Nikko Cordial at one point slumped 8% but later rebounded to ¥1,755, a 3.3% loss, after the brokerage denied hearsay that it was behind the bungled trade and that any of its group companies, which included Nikko Citigroup, were responsible. E-Trade, which denied any connection to the J-Com order, also came under fire. It fell 5.3% to ¥727,000. Nomura Holdings also dropped 3.7% to ¥2,085,[7] while second-tier securities house Shinko Securities plunged 5.2% to ¥515.[8]

## History Repeats Itself

The debacle on December 8 was not the first time a brokerage had made such a huge error in the Tokyo market. In fact, the TSE had seen such big order errors in the recent past. In 2001, UBS Warburg (Japan) Ltd. placed an incorrect order for Dentsu Inc. shares, which had just debuted. Instead of the correct 16 shares at ¥610,000, the brokerage's order called for 610,000 shares at ¥16. The same year Deutsche Securities Ltd. erred when it put in an order to sell 90,000 shares of Isuzu Motors Ltd. as 90 million shares. Both errors were the result of brokerage employees punching in incorrect numbers and overlooking on-screen cautions. After the order errors in 2001, the TSE told its brokerage members to bolster their oversight structures. But the measures in place at brokerages to prevent errors

---

[6] Quoting Brandon Ginsberg, co-head of equities at Nikko Citigroup in Tokyo in *Nikkei* (*Japan Economic Journal*), December 8, 2005, http://markets.nikkei.co.jp/special/sp014.cfm?id=ds0iss1608&date=20051208 (accessed April 11, 2007).

[7] This was the spot price at the close of trading on the previous day.

[8] *Nikkei* (*Japan Economic Journal*), December 8, 2005, http://markets.nikkei.co.jp/special/sp014.cfm?id=ds0iss1608&date=20051208 (accessed April 11, 2007).

varied with the proprietary software systems being used and the level of error reporting set by the firms.[9]

## *Suspension of J-Com Shares Trading*

The TSE suspended trading of J-Com's shares in the morning of December 9, 2005, following the previous day's market turbulence. The TSE suspended transactions for J-Com shares to prevent the issue's lopsided supply–demand balance from adversely affecting overall stock price formation in the market.[10] It was quite rare for trading to be halted the day after an issue's debut on the exchange. The presence of these unexecuted contracts created market instability.

> *The bourse suspended trading of the J-Com shares because a sizable portion of the sales contracts concluded with investors by the brokerage on December 8, 2005 have not yet been honored.*
>
> — Kaoru Yosano, minister for financial services[11]

## J-Com Reacts

J-Com, which was listed on the TSE's Mothers market on December 8, 2005, was a company specializing in personnel services[12] (see **Exhibits 1** and **2**). On November 19, 2005, the company announced its IPO which was to take place on December 8, 2005. J-Com was to float 2,800 shares at an offering of ¥467,500, with a green shoe option for the sale of 200 additional shares. Total outstanding shares at that time were 14,500, of which 10,840 shares were owned by J-Com's founding family, Okamoto. The lead manager for the underwriters was Nikko Citigroup.[13]

---

[9] *Nikkei* (*Japan Economic Journal*), December 11, 2005, http://www.nikkei.co.jp/news/main/20051211NTE2INK0111122005.html (accessed April 11, 2007).

[10] *Nikkei* (*Japan Economic Journal*), December 8, 2005, http://markets.nikkei.co.jp/special/sp014.cfm?id=d3l0804m08&date=20051208 (accessed April 11, 2007).

[11] *Nikkei* (*Japan Economic Journal*), December 9, 2005, http://www.nikkei.co.jp/news/main/20051209AT3L0906Y09122005.html (accessed April 11, 2007).

[12] See J-Com's website: http://www.jcom.co.jp/english/index.

[13] *Nikkei* (*Japan Economic Journal*), December 8, 2005, http://company.nikkei.co.jp/index.cfm?scode=2462 (accessed April 9, 2008).

**Exhibit 1**  Basic Data of J-Com

| Name | J-Com Co. Ltd. |
|---|---|
| Address | 4-4-3 Minamisenba, Chuoku, Osaka, Japan 542-0081 |
| Established | September 22, 1993 |
| TSE Industry | Service |
| President | Yasuhiko Okamoto |
| Shares Outstanding | 14,500 |
| Accounting Term | May, each year |
| Listed | TSE (Mothers) |

*Source:* J-Com's website http://www.jcm.co.jp.

**Exhibit 2**  Basic Financial Data

Unit: ¥1,000

|  | May 2001 | May 2002 | May 2003 | May 2004 | May 2004 |
|---|---|---|---|---|---|
| Sales | 1,369,622 | 1,616,761 | 2,222,747 | 3,271,108 | 4,684,111 |
| Ordinary Income | 70,223 | 76,990 | 88,920 | 141,254 | 281,628 |
| Net Income | 34,644 | 40,248 | 45,521 | 56,005 | 152,503 |
| Net Income per Share | 4,277.84 | 3,354.04 | 3,793.45 | 4,667.16 | 12,639.40 |
| Net Asset per Share | 5,532.62 | 8,886.66 | 12,680.10 | 17,347.26 | 30,453.69 |

*Source:* J-Com's website http://www.jcm.co.jp.

On December 8, Yasuhiko Okamoto, president of J-Com, told the press that it was looking into possible irregularities in trading of its shares, shortly after they debuted on the Mothers market.[14]

*We are looking into the details of the big movements in J-Com's stock price.*

— Takuo Tsurushima, president of TSE[15]

---

[14] *Nikkei (Japan Economic Journal)*, December 8, 2005, http://markets.nikkei.co.jp/special/sp014.cfm?id=d2e0800808&date=20051208 (accessed April 11, 2007).

[15] Ibid.

Later on that same day, J-Com's president, Yasuhiko Okamoto, stated in a news conference that he was told by the TSE and Nikko Citigroup, its IPO underwriter, that one brokerage house mistakenly placed a massive sell order for J-Com shares and that neither the TSE nor the underwriter gave the name of the broker whose erroneous sell order caused J-Com shares to plummet earlier in the day. They told J-Com that a single sell order had been placed for 610,000 shares due to a data input error by the brokerage concerned.

*The mistaken order, which caused J-Com shares to plunge briefly and was partly to blame for the Tokyo share price decline today, was regrettable.*

— Yasuhiko Okamoto, president of J-Com[16]

*If a brokerage firm misplaced orders on J-Com, it could have incurred a tremendous loss and may need to unload its shareholdings to cover the loss. It could develop into a problem to shake the firm's management foundation.*

— Kenichi Azuma, equity strategist at Cosmo Securities Co.[17]

## Mizuho Securities

There are rogue traders, and then there are fat-fingered traders. Mizuho Securities Co. (Mizuho Sec), the brokerage arm of Mizuho Financial Group Inc., fell victim to the latter. On December 8, 2005 at 6 p.m. when the market had closed, Makoto Fukuda, president of Mizuho Sec, said the company had mistakenly placed a large sell order for J-Com shares, which debuted on the TSE's Mothers market earlier in the day. To add to the embarrassment, Mizuho Sec was one of the managers for the J-Com IPO, being invited by the lead manager, Nikko Citigroup.

*We deeply apologize for causing considerable trouble for those concerned. We are currently investigating the erroneously placed order and are in talks*

---

[16] *Nikkei* (*Japan Economic Journal*), December 8, 2005, http://markets.nikkei.co.jp/special/sp014.cfm?id=d2e0801108&date=20051208 (accessed April 11, 2007).

[17] *Nikkei* (*Japan Economic Journal*), December 8, 2005, http://www.nikkei.co.jp/news/sangyo/20051208AT2D0800W08122005.html (accessed April 11, 2007).

*with the Tokyo bourse on how to cope with the incident, which likely caused us a massive loss.*

— Makoto Fukuda, president of Mizuho Sec[18]

On December 9, 2005, Fukuda said that the company had suffered a ¥27 billion loss as a result of the erroneous order to sell 610,000 shares for at least ¥1 apiece. Because of market rules limiting price fluctuations, the shares could not be sold for ¥1 but may have been sold as cheaply as ¥572,000 per share. Furthermore, the brokerage had inadvertently placed a short-selling order because it did not have any J-Com shares on hand. And with the order attracting many eager buyers, the brokerage would be forced to hand over stock certificates to investors that placed buy orders.

When it realized its error, Mizuho Sec placed buy orders for J-Com shares, helping to push up the issue's price. It succeeded in covering short positions for about 514,000 shares but was unable to secure the 96,000 remaining shares — six times the amount of the total outstanding J-Com shares. On December 9, the brokerage had yet to complete the rest of the short-covering, a factor that could cause its losses to balloon. If Mizuho Sec was unable to make progress on this, market authorities such as the TSE were likely to take action.

According to Mizuho Sec, it would not have any problem with day-to-day funding as a result of the incident, with shareholder equity topping ¥380 billion as of September 30, 2005.[19] Mizuho Financial Group, Mizuho Sec's parent and Japan's second largest bank, stated that they would fully back the losses from the erroneous trades, which could wipe out Mizuho Sec's first quarter profit of ¥28 billion.[20]

---

[18] *Nikkei* (*Japan Economic Journal*), December 8, 2005, http://markets.nikkei.co.jp/special/sp014.cfm?id=d3l0807j08&date=20051208 (accessed April 11, 2007).

[19] Makoto Fukuda in *Nikkei* (*Japan Economic Journal*), December 8, 2005, http://markets.nikkei.co.jp/special/sp014.cfm?id=d2d0900p09&date=20051209 (accessed April 11, 2007).

[20] Business Law Prof Blog, December 9, 2005, "Botched Trade Costs Tokyo Brokerage Approximately $225M", http://lawprofessors.typepad.com/business_law/investing/index.html (accessed April 9, 2008).

## *The Rise of Mizuho Sec*

Since opening for business in October 2000, Mizuho Sec had rapidly broadened its business operations by tapping outside talent. The firm quickly rose to be one of the top bank-affiliated stock brokerages. However, internal control and compliance mechanisms might not have kept up with its fast-paced expansion. These top bank-affiliated stock brokerages tended to rely heavily on bond trading, but Mizuho Sec stood out because of its efforts to beef up earnings through stock transactions. Stocks accounted for 19% and bonds made up 42% of its net operating revenue on a non-consolidated basis for the year ending on March 31, 2003. Two years later, stocks represented 42% and bonds 29% of this figure.

Mizuho Sec's share of total trading value on the TSE stood at around 3% by December 2005, up from below 1% in the second half of fiscal 2000. The brokerage employed about 1,500 people, adding around 200 staff every year. As conditions warranted, it assigned outside recruits to core duties.


# Emergency Measures

*The bourse may take emergency steps, since we are concerned about a worst-case scenario in which Mizuho Sec will be forced to shoulder ever-growing costs to buy back J-Com shares.*

— Tomio Amano, managing director of TSE[21]


Directly after the market noticed a mistake had been made, the TSE started to consider taking emergency measures to prevent further market confusion. The steps included confirming the identities of all the traders involved and consulting with related organizations, including Japan Securities Clearing Corp. (JSCC), a company engaged in settling stock transactions.

The stock exchange also appeared to be mulling over Mizuho Sec giving cash, rather than certificates of J-Com stock, to investors who

---

[21] *Nikkei* (*Japan Economic Journal*), December 9, 2005, http://markets.nikkei.co.jp/special/sp014.cfm?id=de2ink0409&date=20051209 (accessed April 11, 2007).

placed buy orders for the newly listed shares. Mizuho Sec's president Makoto Fukuda told a press conference on December 9, 2005 that the firm was still unable to buy back about 100,000 shares.

The TSE and JSCC knew that Mizuho Sec would fail to secure enough J-Com shares to cover its short position. JSCC's rules stated that if a company was unable to execute a settlement due to such factors as natural disasters, extreme changes in the economic environment, or a stock certificate shortage, the settlement terms could be changed.[22] The TSE believed Mizuho Sec's case fell under the certificate shortage category. The provision could enable Mizuho Sec to make cash payments *in lieu* of the J-Com shares to investors who purchased the stock. In addition, the brokerage would be able to extend the settlement beyond December 13, 2005, the third business day after the transactions. However, the provision had never been enacted since the establishment of JSCC in 2002.

## Mizuho Sec's Options

Mizuho Sec had few options at its disposal as it braced for the settlement date of December 13, 2005. One possible scenario was J-Com's issuance of new shares to Mizuho Sec via a private placement. But this could sharply dilute the stock's value and wreak havoc on J-Com's capital procurement plans.[23] J-Com's founding family, including its president Yasuhiko Okamoto, owned 10,840 shares. They were restricted from selling the shares following the company's IPO, but Mizuho Sec could borrow the shares for the settlements.

A more likely option for Mizuho Sec might be to pay damages and fines to investors that had signed up to buy the J-Com shares and gradually cover the short positions over a period of time. Of the 610,000 J-Com shares that the brokerage accidentally short-sold on December 8, 2005, it needed 96,000 by December 13, 2005 for settlement purposes. To address this dilemma, the TSE and JSCC were eyeing plans to invoke an

---

[22] Ibid.

[23] *Nikkei* (*Japan Economic Journal*), December 9, 2005, http://www.nikkei.co.jp/news/kei zai/20051209AT3L0906909122005.html (accessed April 11, 2007).

emergency provision for settlements that would allow the brokerage to honor the sell order with cash payments instead of shares.

In such a scenario, the biggest focal point would be the settlement price. Mizuho Sec might face a tough time convincing investors to accept a given price because the price would not be shaped by the market. And because J-Com made its market debut on December 8, 2005, investors did not have past share prices to use for a reference. Price negotiations were also likely to be hampered by the number of buyers, which remained mostly unknown at this time. Mizuho Sec could opt to negotiate cash settlements with major institutional investors first and then deliver stocks to individual investors who purchased a smaller number of shares.

Other options available to the brokerage included an extension of the settlement date under the emergency provision for settlements. Mizuho Sec could also pay late fees to the investors and hand over J-Com shares that it had originally delivered to other investors and subsequently bought back. Such measures, however, were likely to take a considerable amount of time. And because the TSE suspended trading of J-Com shares until the settlements had been completed, Mizuho Sec's options were limited.

## Cash Settlement

JSCC publicly announced on December 12, 2005 that it would let Mizuho Sec pay cash to buyers of J-Com shares instead of delivering stock certificates to them to settle transactions resulting from the sell order it erroneously placed on December 8, 2005.[24] The clearing body set the settlement price at ¥912,000, which was determined by adding some consideration to the limit-up price of ¥772,000. This would mark the first time that a public third-party entity had stepped in to arrange a stock transaction settlement with cash. The TSE would also take disciplinary measures against Mizuho Sec for the market turmoil it caused.

Securities companies were obliged to follow decisions made by the nation's settlement body, which was jointly owned by Japan's six

---

[24] *Nikkei* (*Japan Economic Journal*), December 9, 2005, http://markets.nikkei.co.jp/special/sp014.cfm?id=d3l0906509&date=20051209 (accessed April 11, 2007).

exchanges.[25] The brokerage unit of Mizuho Financial Group Inc. was expected to buy J-Com shares from investors at ¥912,000 apiece on December 13, 2005.

*If it had not been for the erroneous order, it is highly likely that the issue would have opened at this price. The arrangement should be understood as a special measure to protect the infrastructure of settlements.*

— Yoshimasa Yamashita, president of Japan Securities Settlement and Custody, Inc.[26]

Mizuho Sec needed to buy 96,000 shares from J-Com stock buyers, with investors having bought each share at an average of roughly ¥595,000, according to the clearing body. The brokerage's losses, when it began buying back these shares, reached around ¥27 billion by December 12, 2005. With the settlement price set at ¥912,000 apiece, the brokerage's loss was expected to balloon to around ¥40 billion.

The TSE worked with brokerages to determine who bought the J-Com stock from Mizuho Sec. According to documents filed with the Finance Ministry's Tokyo Regional Office:

1. The UBS group owned a total of 38,198 J-Com shares. The number of shares was equivalent to 2.6 times J-Com's outstanding shares. The group accounted for about 40% of the 96,236 shares that Mizuho Sec was not able to buy back.
2. Morgan Stanley owned 4,522 shares and would pocket nearly ¥1.44 billion if Mizuho Sec settled the transaction at ¥912,000 a share as decided by JSCC.
3. The Lehman Brothers Japan group owned 3,150 shares and would get about ¥1 billion.
4. The Credit Suisse First Boston Securities (Japan) Ltd. group acquired 13,540 shares on December 8, 2005 but sold 10,651 of them, leaving

---

[25] Japan Securities Clearing Corporation, April 1, 2008, http://www.jscc.co.jp/english/about/index.html (accessed April 9, 2008).

[26] *Nikkei* (*Japan Economic Journal*), December 12, 2005, http://markets.nikkei.co.jp/special/sp014.cfm?id=d2d1200512&date=20051212 (accessed April 11, 2007).

it with 2,889, which were expected to provide it with a profit of more than ¥900 million.

5.  The Nikko Cordial Securities Inc. group owned 3,455 shares.
6.  Nomura Securities Co. was believed to have purchased 1,000 shares.[27]

> *As to the special measure made by Board of Directors at Japan Securities Clearing Corporation on the shares of J-Com, we recognize this to be a decisive, swift and appropriate action in terms of ensuring the stability of settlement in the securities market. In accordance with this decision, we are determined to follow the procedures without delay in co-operation with the relevant authorities and securities firms.*
>
> — Makoto Fukuda, president of Mizuho Sec[28]

On December 9, it was reported by the press that there were also a number of individual investors who had bought J-Com shares and the TSE was working on identifying these buyers and fleshing out settlement measures.[29] A 27-year-old man in Chiba Prefecture bought 7,100 J-Com shares and made about ¥2 billion from the settlement of Mizuho Sec's erroneous sell order, according to a report filed to the Tokyo Local Finance Bureau. Another 24-year-old company executive in Tokyo made a profit of ¥560 million. The man, who lived in the Roppongi district of Tokyo, bought 3,701 J-Com shares. While the Japan Securities Dealers' Association (JSDA) planned to ask its members to give up profits they earned on settlement, individual investors were not subject to this policy.[30]

---

[27] *Nikkei* (*Japan Economic Journal*), December 9, 2005, http://www.nikkei.co.jp/news/main/20051209AT3L0906509122005.html (accessed April 11, 2007).

[28] *Nikkei* (*Japan Economic Journal*), December 12, 2005, http://markets.nikkei.co.jp/special/sp014.cfm?id=d311205p12&date=20051212 (accessed April 11, 2007).

[29] *Nikkei* (*Japan Economic Journal*), December 9, 2005, http://markets.nikkei.co.jp/special/sp014.cfm?id=d310906509&date=20051209 (accessed April 11, 2007).

[30] *Sankei* (*Industrial and Economic Newspaper*), December 9, 2005, http://news.goo.ne.jp/topics/keizai/market/new_market/?fr=RSS (accessed April 9, 2008).

# The Trading System

Normally, trading systems employed by brokerages such as Mizuho Sec would stop an order in which prices deviated sharply from real prices or if it greatly exceeded the total number of outstanding shares. The Mizuho Sec employee who handled the order, however, was said to have ignored the warning signs and there were rumors that inadequate familiarity with both the trading system and communication channels by the employee(s) involved contributed to the debacle.[31] The Financial Services Agency planned to call on Mizuho Sec to submit a report on what had gone wrong on that specific day.

*The factors leading to the botched order were under investigation. We will do our utmost to work on the order settlements. We are also weighing such measures as employee training and system changes to prevent erroneous orders from occurring again. We will revamp its trading system structure to ensure that alarms work properly to warn of unusual orders. For my responsibility, I will continue to address my responsibility for the time being by working to quickly resolve the current turmoil.*

— Makoto Fukuda, president of Mizuho Sec[32]

*We must take action to prevent another mistake. I want people to think of measures not to repeat the same kind of mistake.*

— Junichiro Koizumi, prime minister[33]

*It was an extremely unfortunate situation. Mizuho Sec should make sure that settlements are carried out properly and that errors in orders do not recur.*

— Kaoru Yosano, minister for financial services[34]

---

[31] *Nikkei (Japan Economic Journal)*, December 8, 2005, http://www.nikkei.co.jp/news/main/20051208AT2Y0800I08122005.html (accessed April 11, 2007).

[32] *Nikkei (Japan Economic Journal)*, December 9, 2005, http://markets.nikkei.co.jp/special/sp014.cfm?id=d1f0901f09&date=20051209 (accessed April 11, 2007).

[33] Ibid.

[34] Ibid.

The TSE initially told the regulatory agency that there was no problem with its computer system, but on December 10, 2005 the stock exchange changed its opinion and told the regulator that there could have been a system failure, according to the Financial Services Agency. Takuo Tsurushima, president of the TSE, indicated on December 11, 2005 that he would resign to take responsibility for Thursday's market turbulence, after admitting that Mizuho Sec was unable to cancel its erroneous sell order for J-Com shares due to flaws in the bourse's computer system.[35]

*Mizuho Sec could have readily canceled the 1 yen order if the computer system of TSE had no defects.*

— Tomio Amano, managing director of TSE[36]

Because of these new developments, expectations were that Mizuho Sec would share these losses with the TSE.[37] The TSE and Fujitsu Ltd., developers of the system, were expected to flesh out measures to prevent a recurrence of similar glitches and would likely take four to five weeks to fix the existing problem. However, there was a voice in the market that Fujitsu Ltd. was also responsible for this happening. The computer system was built by Fujitsu Ltd. in May 2000. The TSE would conduct, together with Fujitsu Ltd., a thorough analysis of the cause of the system's failure.

*It is uncertain at the moment whether it had been checked in advance for the ability to cope with a botched trade of the kind that occurred.*

— Tomio Amano, managing director of TSE[38]

---

[35] *Nikkei* (*Japan Economic Journal*), December 12, 2005, http://markets.nikkei.co.jp/special/sp014.cfm?id=d311205k12&date=20051212 (accessed April 11, 2007).

[36] Ibid.

[37] Ibid.

[38] *Nikkei* (*Japan Economic Journal*), December 12, 2005, http://www.nni.nikkei.co.jp/AC/FEAT/mizuho/mizuho00022.html (accessed April 11, 2007).

## Trading Resumes

The TSE resumed J-Com's suspended trading on December 15, 2005 at a base price of ¥912,000 — the per-share price that JSCC had decided Mizuho Sec would pay for the settlement.[39]

On that day, investors eagerly greeted J-Com stock with a large number of buy orders. The shares, which made their market debut on December 8, 2005, remained bid-only through the day. At closing, available sell orders were allocated among buyers at ¥1.02 million — the limit-up level from its base price of ¥912,000. Total executed trades reached just 215 shares. Buy orders that went unexecuted stood at 19,293 shares, topping J-Com's 14,500 total outstanding shares (see **Exhibit 3**). The botched share order had made J-Com a household name.[40]

*Mizuho Sec's bungled sell order quickly boosted J-Com's name recognition. This then spurred buying interest among investors.*

— Tsutomu Yamada, market analyst at Kabu.com Securities Co.[41]

**Exhibit 3**   Stock Price of J-Com in December, 2005

| Date | Open | High | Low | Close | Volume (Shares) |
|---|---|---|---|---|---|
| December 15, 2005 | 1,220,000 | 1,220,000 | 1,220,000 | **1,220,000** | 346 |
| December 14, 2005 | 1,020,000 | 1,020,000 | 1,020,000 | **1,020,000** | 215 |
| December 8, 2005 | 672,000 | 772,000 | 572,000 | **772,000** | 708,124 |

*Source:* Yahoo Finance.

---

[39] *Nikkei* (*Japan Economic Journal*), December 12, 2005, http://markets.nikkei.co.jp/special/sp014.cfm?id=d311205i12&date=20051212 (accessed April 11, 2007).

[40] *Nikkei* (*Japan Economic Journal*), December 8, 2005, http://markets.nikkei.co.jp/special/sp014.cfm?id=d2e0801l08&date=20051208 (accessed April 11, 2007).

[41] *Nikkei* (*Japan Economic Journal*), December 14, 2005, http://markets.nikkei.co.jp/special/sp014.cfm?id=d2e1400514&date=20051214 (accessed April 11, 2007).

# Windfall for Investor Protection Funds

Brokerage houses that profited from the erroneous sell order for J-Com shares would voluntarily place the proceeds into an investor protection fund under a proposal backed by the JSDA.

The UBS AG group, Morgan Stanley, the Credit Suisse First Boston Securities group, the Nikko Cordial Securities Inc. group, Lehman Brothers Japan Inc. and Nomura Securities Co. each held at least 5% of J-Com shares after Mizuho's order on December 8, 2005, when the firm debuted on the TSE's Mothers market.

As a result of a cash settlement for the erroneous order, the six securities groups were said to have profited to the tune of ¥16.6 billion.

1. UBS announced on December 13, 2005 that it had no intention of keeping its reported ¥12 billion profit.
2. Lehman Brothers Japan also indicated plans to give up the nearly ¥1 billion in proceeds.
3. The Nikko Cordial group said it was leaning towards giving up the profit.
4. Nomura Securities expected to do the same.

It was thought that other brokerages had also acquired J-Com shares. The JSDA called on all securities firms to part with the proceeds from the mistaken order. In addition to the proposal for placing the proceeds in the Japan Investor Protection Fund, another plan called for creating a new fund. Whether the transfer of the proceeds would take the form of a donation remained unclear, given that details of the arrangement had yet to be finalized.[42]

It was possible that the JSDA would not win sweeping industry support for its proposal to have the brokerages contribute their proceeds to an investor protection fund. One official at a European brokerage firm was cautious about the proposal, saying that it was unclear how contributions to the fund would be taxed.

---

[42] *Nikkei (Japan Economic Journal)*, December 14, 2005, http://markets.nikkei.co.jp/special/sp014.cfm (accessed April 11, 2007).

In addition, brokerages that stopped buying J-Com shares upon learning of the slip-up would likely distance themselves from those that exploited it and question why they had to take part in a scheme apparently aimed at deflecting public criticism of an unethical pursuit of profit. Deutsche Securities Ltd.'s Tokyo branch stopped buying early in the morning after realizing that the order had been placed by mistake. Because of this, the brokerage was believed to have bought only a small number of J-Com shares. Lehman Brothers Japan Inc. made a ¥1 billion profit from the erroneous order, but could have made more had it not stopped. In contrast, the UBS group firms kept buying until the market closed, with dealers outside Japan leading the charge. The group made ¥12 billion as a result.[43]

*We stopped buying early because we thought it is socially unacceptable.*

— A high-ranking executive of Lehman Brothers Japan Inc.[44]

## Effects on J-Com

J-Com's president, Yasuhiko Okamoto, never forgot the day, December 8, 2005. On that day, he was watching J-Com's stock price go up in bid-only mode since morning, along with officials from Nikko Citigroup Ltd., the leading manager of the listing. That was when the sell order for more than 40 times the firm's outstanding shares was placed by Mizuho Sec. He voiced his frustration over a massive erroneous sell order that rained on the firm's debut that day on the TSE's Mothers market.

*I was confused because the sell order was for an impossible number of shares.*[45]

> *It was regrettable that a mistake made by a single brokerage dragged down the entire stock market. We don't know what impact that mistaken sell order will cause, but we'll consult the Tokyo Stock Exchange and the lead*

---

[43] Ibid.

[44] *Nikkei (Japan Economic Journal)*, December 12, 2005, http://markets.nikkei.co.jp/special/sp014.cfm?id=d311205i12&date=20051212 (accessed April 11, 2007).

[45] *Nikkei (Japan Economic Journal)*, December 9, 2005, http://markets.nikkei.co.jp/special/sp014.cfm?id=d2e0801l08&date=20051209 (accessed April 11, 2007).

*manager in formulating our response. We wanted the market to value our company properly under the normal conditions.*

— Yasuhiko Okamoto, president of J-Com[46]

*We can't pretend we're not displeased. We are not blaming the brokerage [USB, Morgan Stanley, Lehman Brothers etc] for making money, but what exasperates us is that they did so while some investors, who bought shares that they underwrote, were losing money.*

— Takashi Tanima, board member of J-Com[47]

The top executives of J-Com wanted the market to value their company properly under normal conditions on their IPO day.[48] They felt the mistaken order which caused J-Com shares to plunge briefly on that day was regrettable.[49] They had not expected the TSE to suspend trading of J-Com's shares on December 9, 2005, even though it did not come as a complete surprise. They knew it was quite rare for trading in an issue to be halted the day of its debut on the exchange.[50]

On December 9, 2005 the company announced that the management would be unaffected by this incident.[51] On December 12, 2005 the company announced that it was not involved in the decision by the clearing body which set the settlement price at ¥912,000 and it hoped the market would value the company properly under the normal conditions after the reopening.[52]

Overall, on December 15, 2005, J-Com's president, Yasuhiko Okamoto, wondered:

1. Did we lose or gain out of these unexpected happenings?
2. Is there anything we should recover for the sake of our shareholders if we lost something? If Mizuho Sec asks our company to issue new

---

[46] Ibid.

[47] *Nikkei* (*Japan Economic Journal*), December 9, 2005, http://www.topix.net/business?p=6009&co=1&s=LNK (accessed April 11, 2007).

[48] *Nikkei* (*Japan Economic Journal*), December 9, 2005, http://markets.nikkei.co.jp/special/sp014.cfm?id=d3l0903e09&date=20051209 (accessed April 11, 2007).

[49] Ibid.

[50] Ibid.

[51] See J-Com's press release of December 9, 2005 at J-Com's website http://www.jcm.co.jp/.

[52] See J-Com's press release of December 12, 2005 at J-Com's website http://www.jcm.co.jp/.

shares to solve the settlement issue, what should we say? This would dilute the stock's value. If Mizuho Sec asked the Okamoto family to lend the shares it owned, what should the Okamoto family say? Would it be good for the family?

3. Who was responsible for what parts of this botch-up?
4. Was there any possibility of legal action on our part?

He said to the public after seeing confusion on the IPO day, "We aren't considering taking any legal action against the broker at this time."[53]

## For Further Discussion

1. Could J-Com, the issuer, sue someone for damages?
2. Should these share transactions be honored? Shouldn't the exchange have caught this error?
3. Who was responsible for this unprecedented case? Comment on this old saying: To err is human, but to really screw things up, you needed a computerized system without proper controls. Isn't it true that typing is an underappreciated skill? Should the specific trader involved be allowed to continue trading on the exchange after this incident?
4. Comment on the following statement: Excessive computerization makes bourses much more vulnerable to technical glitches and basic human error.
5. After this incident, the TSE made some improvements to prevent cases like this from happening again. What could these improvements be?
6. What other important issues are not resolved, i.e., issues such as the tax issue, information access issue, and market capacity issue?
7. What lessons should the Tokyo market draw from J-Com's IPO troubles?

---

[53] *Nikkei* (*Japan Economic Journal*), December 8, 2005, http://markets.nikkei.co.jp/special/sp014.cfm?id=d2e0801108&date=20051208 (accessed April 11, 2007).

# 13

# Softbank's New Strategy: The Largest LBO in Japan

On March 17, 2006, Japanese Internet company Softbank Corp. (Softbank) announced that it had reached a final agreement with British cellular phone giant Vodafone Group Plc. (Vodafone) to buy its Japanese unit, Vodafone K.K. for ¥1.75 trillion.[1,2] Under the agreement, Softbank would acquire a 97.7% stake in Vodafone K.K. through a wholly owned subsidiary.[3] Markets said that, as part of the acquisition, Softbank would take over roughly ¥200 billion of the unit's interest-bearing debts.[4] To finance the largest business acquisition ever by a Japanese firm, Softbank intended to raise between ¥1.1 trillion and ¥1.2 trillion through leveraged-buyout (LBO) financing, using Vodafone K.K.'s assets as collateral.[5]

Founded by Masayoshi Son in 1981, Softbank was the second-largest broadband internet access provider in Japan, after Nippon Telegraph and Telephone Corp. (NTT). Its subsidiary, Yahoo, Japan Corp. (Yahoo Japan), operated the most popular web portal in the nation.[6] With 15 million customers, Vodafone K.K. was Japan's third-largest mobile operator.[7] With the acquisition of Vodafone K.K., Softbank aimed to build a multi-lateral communications business, integrating news, video and other online content with Vodafone's cellular and fixed-line services.[8]

---

[1] US$1= ¥115.89 on March 17, 2006.

[2] Softbank (March 17, 2006) "Press Release", http://www.softbank.co.jp/en/news/release/2006/060317_0001.html (accessed July 9, 2008).

[3] Ibid.

[4] Asia Pulse News, March 20, 2006, "Softbank signs US$15BLN deal to buy Vodafone's Japanese Unit".

[5] Ibid.

[6] Ibid.

[7] Ibid.

[8] Ibid.

Son felt that by signing the deal, he had laid the foundation for a business that would continue to expand. However, there was still a long way to go before he could rest on his laurels. Son and his management team had to decide on a course for the combined entity and ensure that the firm would maintain its ability to respond quickly and effectively to client needs throughout the anticipated period of rapid growth. Of more immediate concern was the fact that Softbank had to borrow between ¥1.1 trillion and ¥1.2 trillion to finance its purchase. The sum was the largest ever to be raised for a buyout by a single Japanese company. A study on financing alternatives including the all-in cost of the debt financing alternatives in terms of yen was required.

## The Players

### *Vodafone*

Vodafone (see **Exhibit 1**) was a public company incorporated in the UK in 1984.[9] It was the world's leading mobile telecommunications company, with a significant presence in Europe, the Middle East, Africa, Asia-Pacific and the US.[10] The group's mobile subsidiaries operated under the brand name Vodafone.[11] Except in the US, where the group's associated undertaking was Verizon Wireless.[12] Vodafone K.K. in Japan held a 100% interest in Japan Telecom Co. Ltd. (Japan Telecom) and had deepened its presence in Japan's mobile phone market through Japan Telecom's fast-growing local mobile network, J-Phone Communications Co. and its regional wireless operating companies.[13]

Japan's market was dominated by two domestic carriers, NTT (see **Exhibit 2**) and the KDDI Corporation (KDDI) (see **Exhibit 3**). Vodafone's unit, Vodafone K.K., was the third-largest carrier.[14] Vodafone trumpeted

---

[9] For details, see Vodafone's website: http://www.vodafone.com/hub_page.html.

[10] Ibid.

[11] Ibid.

[12] Ibid.

[13] Ibid.

[14] Fackler, M. (March 4, 2006) "Vodafone Says Japanese Unit Has a Suitor", *The New York Times*, http://www.nytimes.com/2006/03/04/business/worldbusiness/04vodafone.html (accessed July 9, 2008).

**Exhibit 1**   Vodafone K.K.

**Corporate Profile**

Vodafone K.K., formerly Vodafone Holdings K.K., is a leading mobile operator in Japan with over 15 million customers and is a subsidiary of Vodafone, the world's largest mobile community.

The Tokyo-based company is listed on the Tokyo Stock Exchange and the Osaka Securities Exchange, with Vodafone holding an indirect interest in the company of 97.7%.

Vodafone K.K. offers a wide range of sophisticated mobile voice and data services, including Vodafone Live!, which provides e-mail and internet access to 85% of its customers, and Sha-mail, the pioneering picture messaging service first introduced in November 2000, which now has over 12 million users.

In December 2002, Vodafone K.K. launched the world's first commercial 3G W-CDMA service based on 3GPP, the international standard. Vodafone K.K.'s 3G service offers its customers fast data speeds in Japan and roaming on 147 networks in 112 countries and regions as of December 31, 2004. Vodafone K.K. also owns 100% stakes in Japan System Solution Co. Ltd. and Telecom Express Co. Ltd.[15]

| | |
|---|---|
| Name | Vodafone K.K. |
| Representative Executive Officer, President | Bill Morrow |
| Headquarters | 2-5-1 Atago, Minato-ku, Tokyo 105-6205 |
| Start of Service | April 1, 1994 |
| Capital | ¥177.2512165 million |
| Employees | Approximately 2,700 |

**Financials (Consolidated, ¥ billion)**

**Profit/Loss Statement**

| Financial Year | 2005 | 2006 |
|---|---|---|
| Operating Revenue | 1,470.0 | 1,467.6 |
| Operating Cost | 1,312.0 | 1,391.3 |
| Operating Income | 158.0 | 76.3 |
| Ordinary Income | 153.4 | 74.4 |
| Net Income | 162.0 | 49.5 |
| Depreciation | 236.9 | 216.1 |

**Balance Sheet**

| | | |
|---|---|---|
| Total Assets | 1,364.4 | 1,355.8 |
| Interest-Bearing Debt | 371.5 | 296.1 |
| Shareholders' Equity | 710.3 | 757.8 |
| Total Number of Employees | 2,582 | 2,728 |

*Sources*: Vodafone's website: http://www.vodafone.com; Vodafone Japan's website: http://www.vodafone.jp.

---

[15] Vodafone website, http://www.vodafone.jp/english/company/ir/pdf/050126_kessantanshin_e.pdf.

**Exhibit 2   NTT**

**Corporate Profile**

NTT is Japan's largest telecom operator, with annual group sales of more than ¥10 trillion. It aimed to become a multimedia service provider. In 1999 the company was split into three entities — two handling regional business and one handling long distance — under a holding company. NTT was privatized in 1987, but the government still owns 53%.

| | |
|---|---|
| Industry Category | Telecommunications |
| Established | August 1, 1952 |
| President | Norio Wada |
| Website | http://www.ntt.co.jp/index_e.html |
| Head Office | 2-3-1, Otemachi, Chiyoda-ku, Tokyo |
| | Tel: 03-5205-5111 |

**Current Info**

NTT's is struggling:

- The market for fixed telephones continues to shrink.
- The profit spread of IP phones is hurting.[16]
- ADSL and other services are offsetting lower sales and revenue remains flat.
- Achieving goals for fiber-optics services may be difficult.
- The benefit of streamlining has temporarily ended and little room for cost-cutting remains.
- Group pretax profit will likely decline.
- Parent-only pretax profit is expected to be below the line for dividend resources, but the dividend will be maintained at ¥5,000 per share.

Capital spending:

- The company will maintain capital spending at ¥2 trillion.
- The company will place emphasis on fiber optics.

**Financials (Consolidated, ¥ million)**

**Profit/Loss Statement**

| Financial Year | 2005/03 | 2004/3 | 2003/3 |
|---|---|---|---|
| Sales | 10,805,868 | 11,095,537 | 10,923,146 |
| Operating Profit | 1,211,201 | 1,560,321 | 1,363,557 |
| Pretax Profit | 1,723,312 | 1,527,348 | 1,405,025 |
| Net Profit | 710,184 | 643,862 | 233,358 |
| Interest/Dividend Income | 26,288 | 26,661 | 26,321 |
| Interest Expense | N/A | N/A | 128,826 |
| Net Interest Balance | 26,288 | 26,661 | −102,505 |

**Balance Sheet**

| | 2005/03 | 2004/3 | 2003/3 |
|---|---|---|---|
| Total Assets | 19,098,584 | 19,434,873 | 19,783,600 |
| Shareholders' Equity | 6,768,603 | 6,397,972 | 5,637,595 |

*Source*: *Nihon Keizai Shimbun*, http://www.nni.nikkei.co.jp/CF/AC/CW/fininfo.cfm?scode=9432.

---

[16] An IP phone uses voice over internet protocol technologies allowing telephone calls to be made over an internet protocol network such as the internet instead of the ordinary public switched telephone network system.

**Exhibit 3**   KDDI

**Corporate Profile**

KDDI is a leading provider of telecommunications services. Born out of the merger of DDI, KDD and IDO in October 2000, the company counts Kyocera and Toyota Motor among its major shareholders. KDDI teamed up with China Unicom in the field of mobile communications and planned to open its communications network for EZweb mobile internet services to other firms.

| | |
|---|---|
| Industry Category | Telecommunications |
| Established | June 1, 1984 |
| President | Tadashi Onodera |
| Website | http://www.kddi.com/english/ |
| Head Office | 3-10-10, Idabashi, Chiyoda-ku, Tokyo |
| | Tel: 03-6678-0719 |

**Recent Info**

Profits are soaring:

- The company is working to cut sales commissions and other operating costs.
- The initial goal of a net gain of 1.85 million subscriptions to the Au Mobile Phone service will likely be revised upward.[17]
- Data communications fees are sharply higher thanks to the effect of 3G mobile phones.
- Despite costs of ¥77.5 billion to eliminate microwave transmission lines, net profit will likely expand.
- This will raise the dividend ¥305, to ¥2,400 per share.

Broadcast business:

- The company is planning to start a broadcast business in October 2008 using fiber-optic communication lines.

**Financials (Consolidated, ¥ million)**

**Profit/Loss Statement**

| Financial Year | 2005/03 | 2004/03 | 2003/03 |
|---|---|---|---|
| Sales | 2,920,039 | 2,846,097 | 2,785,343 |
| Operating Profit | 296,175 | 292,104 | 140,652 |
| Pretax Profit | 286,343 | 274,547 | 113,210 |
| Net Profit | 200,591 | 117,025 | 57,358 |
| Interest/Dividend Income | 700 | 722 | 1,462 |
| Interest Expense | 20,948 | 27,762 | 35,891 |
| Net Interest Balance | −20,248 | −27,040 | −34,429 |

**Balance Sheet**

| Total Assets | 2,472,322 | 2,639,580 | 2,782,038 |
|---|---|---|---|
| Shareholders' Equity | 1,162,191 | 1,009,390 | 894,710 |

*Source*: *Nihon Keizai Shimbun*, http://company.nikkei.co.jp/index.cfm?scode=9433.

---

[17] Au (pronounced *Ēyū*) , or Au by KDDI, is a mobile phone brand in Japan marketed by KDDI in Japan.

its entry into Japan in September 2001 as "giving it access to high-spending consumers and advanced handset technologies".[18] However, it lost customers when it rolled out its third-generation (3G) service in early 2005 before enough base stations were in place to handle the traffic volume, leading to disruptions.[19] A line up of unappealing handsets also turned off Japanese consumers.[20] In March 2006, "Vodafone had been struggling with its Japanese unit for some time and attempts to turn it around had so far met with limited success, frustrating Vodafone's management and investors."[21]

## *Softbank*

Since its establishment in September 1981, Softbank (see **Exhibit 4**) had aimed to be one step ahead of external change.[22] The company was constantly anticipating changes in its operational environment and had repeatedly expanded the scope of its operations from its original information technology (IT) distribution business to becoming an internet portal, engaging in content- and service-related business, developing broadband infrastructure, and fixed-line telecommunications.[23] In all its businesses, Softbank upheld its commitment to the creation of new lifestyles through the IT revolution.[24] As the company strived to increase the value of its infrastructure, portals, platforms, services and content, it continued working to leverage synergies and to enhance its enterprise value.[25] The success

---

[18] Ibid.

[19] 3G cellular technology brought wireless broadband data services to mobile phones, including browsing, streaming music and video, on-demand video programming, downloading, and videoconferencing. For details, see AT&T's website: http://www.wireless.att.com/learn/messaging-internet/media-entertainment/attvideoshare.jsp?WT.srch=1.

[20] Fackler, M. (March 4, 2006) "Vodafone Says Japanese Unit Has a Suitor", *The New York Times*, http://www.nytimes.com/2006/03/04/business/worldbusiness/04vodafone.html (accessed July 9, 2008).

[21] Ibid.

[22] Softbank (2007) "Annual Report".

[23] Ibid.

[24] Ibid.

[25] Ibid.

**Exhibit 4**   Softbank

---

**Corporate Profile**

Softbank is an IT-based holding company that focuses on telecommunications. It acquired Japan Telecom Co. as part of its plan to break into the mobile phone sector.

| | |
|---|---|
| Industry Category | Telecommunications |
| Established | September 3, 1981 |
| Chairman and CEO | Masayoshi Son |
| Website | http://www.softbank.co.jp/ |
| Head Office | 1-9-1, Higashishinbashi, Minato-ku, Tokyo. Tel: 03-6889-2000 |

**Recent Info**

2006 revenue as percent of sales (1st quarter)[26]:

| | |
|---|---|
| Fixed-line telecommunications | 30.9% |
| E-commerce | 24.7% |
| Broadband infrastructure | 23.5% |
| Internet culture | 13.6% |
| Other | 7.3% |

Softbanks operating losses continue:

- The cost burden from membership campaigns is heavy in the Yahoo! Broadband business.
- The growth in the number of Yahoo! Broadband subscribers is slowing.
- Unrealized gains on the stock portfolio are rising.
- The company is working to improve modem inventory turnover and taking other streamlining measures.
- Monthly usage fees are edging higher.
- The company is expecting an inflow of ¥100 billion in cash on the sale of Aozora Bank shares, but the company will record a loss on the sale.
- The company is planning to raise user fees by increasing ADSL speeds to 26 mega-bits per second.

**Financials (Consolidated, ¥ million)**

**Profit/Loss Statement**

| Financial Year | 2005/03 | 2004/03 | 2003/03 |
|---|---|---|---|
| Sales | 837,018 | 517,393 | 406,891 |
| Operating Profit | −25,359 | −54,893 | −91,997 |
| Pretax Profit | −45,248 | −71,901 | −109,808 |
| Net Profit | −59,871 | −107,094 | −99,989 |
| Interest/Dividend Income | 2,398 | 799 | 1,311 |

*(Continued)*

---

[26] Softbank (2006) "Annual Report".

**Exhibit 4**   *(Continued)*

| Interest Expense | 22,971 | 12,052 | 8,741 |
| Net Interest Balance | −20,573 | −11,253 | −7,430 |
| **Balance Sheet** | | | |
| Total Assets | 1,704,853 | 1,421,206 | 946,331 |
| Shareholders' Equity | 178,016 | 238,080 | 257,396 |

**Stock Price Trading Volume**

*Note*: Stock prices are average prices for each month, and trading volumes are average volumes for each month (retroactively adjusted).

**Soft Business Lines**

*Source*: Nihon Keizai Shimbun, http://www.nni.nikkei.co.jp/CF/AC/CW/compinfo.cfm?scode=9984.
*Source*: Softbank (2007) "Annual Report".

of its businesses was not achieved by simply increasing customer numbers, but by developing innovative services that truly added groundbreaking value for users and by improving customer satisfaction to increase per-user revenues.[27] What was most important in these endeavors was not the perspective of the operators or the industry, but what users considered to be added value and innovation.[28] It was this strategy and business model that had created a positive growth cycle, with stronger customer support leading to a larger customer base.

## *Son's Business Style*

Son's biggest bet at Softbank so far, the ¥1.75 trillion acquisition of Vodafone K.K. would transform the company he had founded 25 years before into a business empire with annual sales of more than ¥2 trillion.[29] However, many in the Japanese telecommunications industry questioned the wisdom of spending so much money on Vodafone K.K.[30]

> *I wonder if the investment will pay off, because Softbank will have to spend hundreds of billions of yen on cell phone network infrastructure amongst others, in addition to the acquisition cost.*
> — Norio Wada, president of NTT[31]

Son had repeatedly proved these critics wrong in the past through the success of his risky investments.[32] In 1995, when Softbank was still a personal computer software marketing venture with annual sales of less than ¥100 billion, Son embarked on acquisitions of two major US firms — publishing firm Ziff-Davis Inc. and trade show operator Comdex — for a sum of roughly ¥260 billion.[33] Among Softbank's string of acquisitions

---

[27] Ibid.

[28] Ibid.

[29] *Nihon Keizai Shimbun*, March 12, 2006, http://www.nikkei.co.jp/news/sangyo/2006031 2AT1D1101R11032006.html (accessed July 1, 2007).

[30] Ibid.

[31] Ibid.

[32] Ibid.

[33] Ibid.

**Exhibit 5**   Yahoo! Japan

**Corporate Profile**

Yahoo! is Japan's largest internet portal site operator. It is aggressive in mergers and acquisitions and has entered financial services businesses such as banking and securities brokering.

| | |
|---|---|
| Industry Category | Telecommunications |
| Established | January 31, 1996 |
| President | Masahiro Inoue |
| Website | http://www.yahoo.co.jp/ |
| Head Office | 6-10-1, Roppongi, Minato-ku, Tokyo |
| | Tel: 03-6440-6000 |

**Financials (Consolidated, ¥ million)**

**Profit/Loss Statement**

| Financial Year | 2005/03 | 2004/03 | 2003/03 |
|---|---|---|---|
| Sales | 117,779 | 75,776 | 59,095 |
| Operating Profit | 60,187 | 41,211 | 24,072 |
| Pretax Profit | 60,295 | 41,308 | 23,524 |
| Net Profit | 36,521 | 24,826 | 12,096 |
| Interest/Dividend Income | 707 | 479 | 22 |
| Interest Expense | 7 | 2 | 10 |
| Net Interest Balance | 700 | 477 | 12 |

**Balance Sheet**

| Total Assets | 130,244 | 82,410 | 47,774 |
|---|---|---|---|
| Shareholders' Equity | 96,059 | 59,806 | 30,482 |

*Source*: *Nihon Keizai Shimbun*, http://www.nni.nikkei.co.jp/CF/AC/CW/compinfo.cfm?scode=4689.

and investments, a major stake in Yahoo! Inc. and the establishment of Yahoo! Japan in 1996 had turned out to be major hits both financially and strategically (see **Exhibit 5**).[34]

## *Son's Vision for a Digital Revolution*

*The information industry started hundreds of years ago through the analog information providers — the newspapers, radio, TV, all of these information industries, even telephone. The big change has happened in the last fifteen*

---

[34] Softbank (2007) "Annual Report".

*years because of the arrival of digital information industries. In the earlier stages of the information industry, first technology providers succeed, then service providers come along and increase their market cap. Then, in the third stage, the digital information technology providers, such as Microsoft, Intel, and Cisco, become very successful in market cap. In the fourth stage, the "dot.com" company, the pure internet service company, becomes successful. People are realizing that a new economy, a new market is coming. It's an early stage of the great success that's going to come.*

— Mr. Son, chairman and CEO of Softbank [35]

By acquiring the Japanese unit of Vodafone, Softbank had not only gained immediate access to a mobile phone business, but also added a key piece to the overall structure of the company in line with the digital information revolution advocated by Son.[36] In addition, Softbank and Vodafone were planning to set up a joint venture in order to offer internet access services on cellular phones, both for Japan and for Vodafone group firms in other countries.

Softbank spent about ¥200 billion on capital investments for this acquisition and would continue to do so after the acquisition. Since the Softbank group already had an internet protocol (IP) backbone network, it could use this network to build a high-speed communications network without investing much more. Softbank would focus on bolstering all four weak points of Vodafone K.K.'s cellular phone business that Son had identified: the network, the management of the sales organization and branding, the service content and the handsets.

Son described a T-shaped business model, with a vertical structure in Japan encompassing everything from infrastructure to content, and a horizontal structure based on a digital platform providing content to cellular phones around the world. To this end, Son said Softbank would partner with Vodafone for mobile delivery.

---

[35] According to Son, the digital information revolution was soon approaching. See Son, M. (2000) "Accessing the Information Revolution", Speech from the Annual Meeting of the Trilateral Commission in Tokyo, http://www.trilateral.org/annmtgs/trialog/trlgtxts/t54/mas.htm (accessed July 1, 2007).

[36] *Nihon Keizai Shimbun*, March 17, 2006, http://www.nikkei.co.jp/news/main/im20060317AT3L1706M17032006.html (accessed July 1, 2007).

Son anticipated great synergy between mobile phones, fixed-line services and the internet, and would continue to add pieces to the structure of the business to accommodate his envisioned digital information revolution.

## Negotiating the Acquisition of Vodafone K.K.

Son's vision led him to approach the Tuka Celphone group in 2004 for a possible acquisition. However, KDDI, the group's mother company, declined Son's proposal in early 2005 (see **Exhibit 3**). Soon after that, Son set his sights on Vodafone.[37] Son knew Arun Sarin, Vodafone's chief executive, from their stints in the 1990s as outside directors[38] of leading US telecommunications equipment maker Cisco Systems Inc. Son kept in contact with Sarin, exchanging phone calls and e-mails.[39] When Bill Morrow arrived at Narita International Airport in March 2005 to take up the position of president of Vodafone K.K., he was handed a cell phone. The caller was Son. After the brief conversation, the two started meeting regularly, usually several times a month.[40]

In November 2005, Softbank acquired a mobile license from the Japanese government, but the company flinched at the prospect of having to spend trillions of yen to build the infrastructure for a mobile service from scratch. The company tried to lease facilities from Vodafone, but this proved to be more expensive than it had expected.[41]

Talks for an actual deal began to build momentum at the end of January 2006, when Son met with Sarin in London and informed him of Softbank's decision to invest in Vodafone K.K. In response, Sarin said he was willing to sell 85% of the Japanese subsidiary.[42]

---

[37] Ibid.

[38] In the US and UK, outside directors were commonly referred to as "non-executive directors".

[39] *Nihon Keizai Shimbun*, March 17, 2006, http://www.nikkei.co.jp/news/main/im20060317AT3L1706M17032006.html (accessed July 1, 2007).

[40] Ibid.

[41] Ibid.

[42] Ibid.

Son immediately instructed Softbank's planning department to report on the corporate value of Vodafone K.K. Son needed to know what price Softbank might be expected to pay to take over Vodafone K.K. After careful examination of all the relevant data and analyses, the study was presented to the top management of Softbank. The planning department reported that, at most, the value was ¥1.783 trillion as of January 2006 (see **Exhibit 1** and **Appendix 1**).

The gritty details involved in the painstaking process of negotiating a sale price started in February 2006. Sarin put the value of the Japanese unit far above ¥2 trillion, saying the number of subscribers would increase when the infrastructure for 3G services was enhanced.[43] Son countered that it was worth no more than ¥1.5 trillion, saying that the Vodafone subscriber base would shrink further when new rules came into force allowing number portability, which would allow cellular phone users to switch service providers without losing their existing phone numbers.[44] Son also demanded a 100% stake in the unit.[45] During the months leading up to the sale, Sarin had been under fire from shareholders because of his firm's lackluster performance.[46] Sarin nevertheless managed to take the lead in the negotiations because he knew how badly Son wanted Vodafone's Japanese assets.[47]

On March 3, 2006, Vodafone offered to sell all the shares of its Japanese business, and the two sides agreed to start discussing the details, setting the price range at ¥1.7 trillion to ¥2.0 trillion.[48] Around March 12, 2006, however, foreign media reported that a Western investment fund was considering a competing offer to acquire Vodafone K.K.[49] The news infuriated Son, who threatened to walk away from the negotiations if Vodafone talked with the investment fund. The report put huge pressure

---

[43] Ibid.

[44] Ibid.

[45] Ibid.

[46] Vodafone (March 17, 2006) "Press Release", http://www.vodafone.co.uk/ (accessed July 1, 2007).

[47] *Nihon Keizai Shimbun*, March 18, 2006, http://www.nikkei.co.jp/news/sangyo/2006031 8AT1D1708V17032006.html (accessed July 1, 2007).

[48] Ibid.

[49] Ibid.

on Softbank to thrash out a deal quickly.[50] When the deal was announced on March 17, the companies' chief executives had the following to say on the deal:

> *We thought we could develop business from a much bigger base than starting from scratch. We aim to develop a comprehensive digital business that delivers services and content sought by users, rather than developing an ordinary telecommunications business.*
>
> — Mr. Son, chairman and CEO of Softbank[51]

> *It has become increasingly clear that the greatest operational benefits come from strong local and regional scale. We seek to deploy capital only where we can generate superior returns for our shareholders in markets that offer a strong local position. In the case of Japan, we have been making progress on the turnaround in recent months. However given the relative competitive position of the business, the reduced prospects for superior long term returns and a good offer from SoftBank, the Board took the decision to sell.*
>
> — Mr. Sarin, chief executive of Vodafone[52]

## Competition among Telecommunications Service Providers in Japan

The agreement signed on March 16, 2006 to purchase Vodafone's Japanese unit transformed Softbank into the third-largest comprehensive telecommunications service provider in Japan.[53] The acquisition would bolster Softbank's group sales by about 150% to around ¥2.5 trillion, narrowing the gap between KDDI's roughly ¥3 trillion in group sales and NTT's group sales of approximately ¥11 trillion.[54]

---

[50] Ibid.

[51] *Nihon Keizai Shimbun*, March 17, 2006, http://it.nikkei.co.jp/internet/special/tele.aspx?n=MMITaa830717032006 (accessed July 9, 2008).

[52] Vodafone (March 17, 2006) "Press Release", http://www.vodafone.co.uk/ (accessed July 1, 2007).

[53] *Nihon Keizai Shimbun*, March 17, 2006, http://www.nikkei.co.jp/news/sangyo/2006031 7AT1D1702K17032006.html (accessed July 1, 2007).

[54] Ibid.

**Exhibit 6**   Number Portability

This service makes it possible for a telephone user to switch service providers while using the same telephone number in the same area. It also makes it possible to switch from a telephone on a fixed line to a wireless phone. However, if a user moves to another town, the same telephone number cannot be used.

"Number portability became globally popular with the advent of mobile telephones because, in most countries, different mobile operators provided different area codes and, without portability, changing one's operator would require changing one's number. Some operators, especially incumbent operators with large existing subscriber bases, have argued against portability on the grounds that providing this service incurs considerable overhead. Its supporters argue that it prevents lock-in and allows operators to compete fairly on price and service. Due to this conflict of interest, number portability is usually mandated for all operators by telecommunications regulatory authorities.

In the US, the Federal Communications Commission (FCC) has mandated number portability in order to increase competition among providers."[55] As of March 2006, "local number portability is required of all landline and wireless common carriers, so long as the number is being ported to the same geographical area or telephone exchange. Most cellular telephone companies still charge for this conversion as a regulatory cost recovery fee."[56]

With the upcoming introduction of number portability in the autumn of 2006 (see **Exhibit 6**), which would allow cellular phone users to switch service providers without losing their existing phone numbers, cellular phone service firms were expected to engage in a fierce battle to lure rivals' customers.[57] Many industry watchers predicted that Vodafone would be hard-pressed to avoid losing customers to KDDI and NTT groups once the system was introduced.[58] This service would incur considerable overhead and only big companies like KDDI and NTT could absorb such overhead.

---

[55] http://www.askmore.net/en/Local_number_portability.htm (accessed November 20, 2008).

[56] Ibid.

[57] Ibid.

[58] Ibid.

## *Fixed-line and Mobile Phone Services Converge*

Services based on integration of fixed-line and mobile phone networks, known as fixed-mobile convergence (FMC) services, were about to be launched in Japan following their introduction in the UK.[59] FMC was still loosely defined, and the services grouped under it ranged from the simple integration of billing for fixed-line and cellular phones to direct access to both fixed and cellular networks using a single mobile handset.[60] For phone companies, the FMC concept was a double-edged sword that could save their declining fixed-line businesses but could also trigger major industry reorganization because it required all-around capabilities to be competitive.[61]

Japanese phone companies were warming to FMC at a time when the number of fixed phone subscriptions had fallen by 5.4% from the 1970 peak to less than 60 million in the fiscal year 2004 and the cellular phone market neared saturation at 90 million subscribers.[62] Phone companies hoped to channel some of the heavy cellular phone traffic back to fixed phones. To customers and the telecom firms, FMC meant saving money. KDDI cellular phone subscribers paid ¥15.75 per minute to call fixed phones, but only ¥8.4 per three minutes for intra-prefectural calls on FMC if they used a wireless terminal connected to a fixed phone at the office.[63]

Because they owned infrastructure for both cellular and fixed phones, KDDI, NTT and now Softbank saw a need for balance so that both services could prosper without conflict. Customer enthusiasm was another factor pushing phone companies toward FMC. In a survey by Rakuten Research and Mitsubishi Research Institute Inc., 60%

---

[59] *Nihon Keizai Shimbun*, March 20, 2006, http://www.nni.nikkei.co.jp/AC/TNKS/Search/Nni20060320D20HH638.htm (accessed July 1, 2007).

[60] Ibid.

[61] Ibid.

[62] Ibid.

[63] Ibid.

of respondents said they wanted to use FMC when it became available.[64]

*We intend to reinforce ties between NTT Communications Corp. and NTT DoCoMo Inc. in the group's medium- and long-term plans, in which FMC is a priority.*

— Mr. Wada, president of NTT[65]

In March 2005, NTT DoCoMo and NTT West Corp. jointly began offering FMC service under the name One Phone (see **Exhibit 7**) to corporate customers. The service allowed NTT DoCoMo's 3G FOMA cellular phones to double as workplace extensions free of charge.[66] Osaka Gas Co., one of NTT's major customers, planned to issue One-Phones to 4,000 employees working in fields such as sales and construction by March 31, 2006.[67] The service would improve efficiency because calls directed to fixed phones could be received by cellular phones. Osaka Gas Co. was projecting annual cost savings of ¥450 million because of the One-Phone service.[68]

On January 23, 2006, KDDI introduced its Listen Mobile (LISMO) service (see **Exhibit 8**), which allowed cellular phones to work as portable digital players of music downloaded via the internet to personal computers.[69] At the time, KDDI anticipated having to compete not only with major players like NTT, but also with newcomers like Softbank, which had been planning to enter the cellular phone market for some years, adding to the landline service it offered through group company Japan Telecom Ltd.[70]

---

[64] Ibid.

[65] Ibid.

[66] Ibid.

[67] Ibid.

[68] Ibid.

[69] Ibid.

[70] Ibid.

**Exhibit 7**   One Phone Service

One Phone is a software application that enables service providers to deliver high-value mobility services to their customers. With One Phone, "providers can offer bundled FMC services that offer seamless handoffs of voice calls between cellular networks and WiFi networks".[71,72] It was the only approach available in January 2006 that was based on open SIP standards, and the only one that added value to FMC with "a compelling portfolio of revenue-generating personal mobility applications (PMAs)".[73,74]

One Phone's client-server software enables a dual-mode (WiFi and cellular) handset to support ubiquitous voice services across WiFi and cellular networks using a single phone number.[75] With it, users gain the combined power of mobility and advanced voice communications services, while service providers have an attractive managed service opportunity that can vastly improve their business models.[76] They also have an opportunity to bring a whole new category of services (e.g., PMAs) to the market that are optimized for converged networks.

One Phone delivers both voice and data services to subscribers "over a secure wireless local area network connection using WiFi whenever they are within range of a WiFi access point"[77] in their home, in a public hotspot, or on their enterprise WiFi networks. The application automatically and seamlessly logs the user on to a WiFi network. When out of the range of a WiFi network, it delivers the same set of advanced voice services over the cellular network, including advanced business features and PMAs.

*(Continued)*

---

[71] Business Wire (September 29, 2005) "Persona Software Introduces Major New Version of Persona OnePhone Solution for Fixed Mobile Convergence; Ready for Service Provider Deployments."

[72] In cellular telecommunications, the term handoff refers to the process of transferring an ongoing call or data session from one channel connected to the core network to another.

[73] Business Wire (September 29, 2005) "Persona Software Introduces Major New Version of Persona OnePhone Solution for Fixed Mobile Convergence; Ready for Service Provider Deployments."

[74] The session initiation protocol (SIP) is a signaling protocol, widely used for setting up and tearing down multimedia communication sessions such as voice and video calls over the Internet. Other feasible application examples include video conferencing, streaming multimedia distribution, instant messaging, presence information and online games.

[75] Business Wire (September 29, 2005) "Persona Software Introduces Major New Version of Persona OnePhone Solution for Fixed Mobile Convergence; Ready for Service Provider Deployments".

[76] Reed Business Information (September 2005) "Mobilizing for Mobility: Delivering the 'quadruple play' with Fixed Mobile Convergence".

[77] Ibid.

**Exhibit 7**   (*Continued*)

One Phone allows users to seamlessly roam between WiFi and cellular networks with a single identity, a single phone number and a transparent user experience.[78] With One Phone's managed mobility services, carriers can attract new customers, increase average revenue per user, reduce churn and minimize CAPEX.[79,80] Additionally, it keeps subscribers on a service provider's network and in its control, optimizing the provider's business model. It enables subscribers to reduce their cost and improve their wireless coverage, addressing two major issues that cause them to churn. It also increases subscribers' productivity and provides them with advanced voice applications across both WiFi and cellular networks.

One Phone provides continuous, ubiquitous access to services and content and advanced telephony features for mobile phones and IP PDAs.[81] Highly mobile consumers and businesses with highly mobile workforces, such as those in the healthcare, sales, professional services or manufacturing sectors, are attractive targets for it.[82]

## Softbank's Finances under Scrutiny

Softbank,[83] which needed to borrow between ¥1.1 trillion and ¥1.2 trillion to finance its purchase of Vodafone K.K., faced the challenge of dispelling market concerns about its financial health.[84] A syndicate of banks led by 7 banks including Mizuho Corporate Bank and Deutsche Bank[85] extended between ¥1.1 trillion and ¥1.2 trillion in bridge loans.[86] Softbank planned to replace the bridge financing by procuring funds through fixed-rate

---

[78] Users want value out of the experience and want to create the experience in a transparent way.

[79] Customer churn is the loss of customers you'd rather keep. Not the loss of unprofitable customers you're content to shed.

[80] Capital expenditures (CAPEX) are expenditures creating future benefits.

[81] IP (Internet Protocol) is the method or protocol by which data is sent from one computer to another on the Internet. PDA (a personal digital assistant) is a handheld computer also known as small or palmtop computers.

[82] For details, see NTT's website: http://www.ntt.com/release_e/letters/BK_is/05_aug/05_aug.pdf.

[83] For financing, Softbank used BB Mobile, a 100% subsidiary. For the details, see http://www.softbank.co.jp/news/release/2006/060427_0002.html (accessed July 1, 2007)

[84] *Nihon Keizai Shimbun*, March 17, 2006, http://www.nikkei.co.jp/news/main/im20060317AT3L1706M17032006.html (accessed July 1, 2007).

[85] For the details, see http://www.softbank.co.jp/news/release/2006/060427_0002.html (accessed July 1, 2007).

[86] Ibid.

**Exhibit 8**  KDDI's LISMO Service

In January 2006, KDDI announced the start of a new music service called LISMO. LISMO was integrated into the company's existing cell phones and would enable music-player phones to better compete with dedicated music players like Apple's Ipod. It did this by introducing PC based file-management and synchronization software, which had been absent from Japan's music-player phones till then.

KDDI opened an online music store and offered tracks that users could download, store, and play on their PC, in addition to their phone. Instead of a credit card, customers could just enter their phone numbers and a four-digit personal identification numbers to purchase songs. The purchase would then appear on the customer's monthly phone bill. KDDI had become the first carrier combining these features across all their new and future models. The combination of music-player phones with an online music store and management software for the PC, meant the wireless carrier had started to implement the same business model that Apple used, thus leading the way for direct competition with the iPod in Japan.

long-term instruments. Softbank also borrowed ¥100 billion from Vodafone, which wanted to help in order to entice Softbank to acquire their fledgling business in Japan.[87]

In addition, Softbank raised ¥420 billion through equity financing, with its cellular phone entity issuing ¥120 billion worth of preferred shares to Yahoo! Japan and ¥300 billion worth to Vodafone.[88] Because the transaction was to be made in cash instead of stock swaps, and because Softbank would depend on cash flow from its operations to recoup the investment, the profitability of its business would be scrutinized by the management of Softbank.[89]

The value of Softbank's stock declined after news of the acquisition broke.[90] The financial market factored in the expected deterioration of Softbank's financial health,[91] as the market had seen many unsuccessful

---

[87] Ibid.

[88] Ibid.

[89] Ibid.

[90] *Nihon Keizai Shimbun*, March 20, 2006, http://www.nni.nikkei.co.jp/AC/TNKS/Search/Nni20060320D20HH638.htm (accessed July 1, 2007).

[91] Softbank shares ended ¥120 lower at ¥3,430 on March 20, 2006 following news that the company had reached a basic agreement to purchase Vodafone K.K. For details see *Nihon Keizai Shimbun*, March 20, 2006, http://www.nni.nikkei.co.jp/AC/TNKS/Search/Nni20060130D30HH689.htm (accessed July 1, 2007).

large LBO acquisitions in the past.[92] On March 17, 2006, Japan Credit Rating Agency Ltd. said it would re-evaluate its rating for Softbank bonds.[93,94]

## Background of the LBO

There were two basic macroeconomic factors that made the big LBO possible (LBOs are defined in **Exhibit 9**).

First, there was Japan's monetary policy change. On March 9, 2006, the Bank of Japan (BOJ) announced that it was ending its longstanding Quantitative Easing Policy,[95] a decision that was generally seen as negative by corporations because it would push interest rates higher and affect earnings.[96] In the long term, however, the change would instill investment and strategic discipline in companies and enhance their international competitiveness.

The end of the zero-interest policy had encouraged companies to be more aggressive. LBOs such as that of Vodafone K.K. by Softbank were possible only when many banks happily lent with the anticipation that the low current interest rate was going up. To banks, such buyouts were high-return, high-risk deals because the loans used the assets of takeover targets as collateral. Nevertheless, leading banks were lining up to provide such loans because the end of deflation was on the horizon.[97]

---

[92] *Nihon Keizai Shimbun*, March 20, 2006, http://www.nni.nikkei.co.jp/AC/TNKS/Search/Nni20060130D30HH689.htm (accessed July 1, 2007).

[93] In fund raising for an acquisition, the borrower usually faced early debt repayment if the financial strength of an acquired company fell below certain standards.

[94] *Nihon Keizai Shimbun*, March 17, 2006, http://www.nikkei.co.jp/news/main/im20060317AT3L1706M17032006.html (accessed July 1, 2007).

[95] BOJ had been flooding commercial banks with excess liquidity to promote private lending, leaving commercial banks with large stocks of excess reserves and therefore little risk of a liquidity shortage. Together, these policies were commonly referred to as BOJ's Quantitative Easing Policy. For details, see Federal Reserve Bank of San Francisco (November 19, 2004) "Easing Out of the Bank of Japan's Monetary Easing Policy", Economic Research and Data, FRBSF Economic Letter, 2004-33, http://www.frbsf.org/publications/economics/letter/2004/el2004-33.html (accessed July 9, 2008).

[96] *Nihon Keizai Shimbun*, March 10, 2006, http://www.nni.nikkei.co.jp/AC/TNKS/Search/Nni20060310D10HH093.htm (accessed July 1, 2007).

[97] Ibid.

**Exhibit 9**    Leveraged Buyout Defined

"LBO is a strategy involving the acquisition of a company using a significant amount of borrowed money (bonds or loans) to meet the cost of acquisition. Often, the assets of the company being acquired are used as collateral for the loans in addition to the assets of the acquiring company. The purpose of LBOs is to allow companies to make large acquisitions without having to commit a lot of capital. In an LBO, there is usually a ratio of 90% debt to 10% equity.

LBOs have been notorious, especially in the 1980's when several buyouts led to the eventual bankruptcy of the acquired companies.[98] This was mainly due to the fact that the leverage ratios were nearly 100% and the interest payments were so large that the companies' operating cash flows were unable to meet the obligations. As of 2006, the largest LBO to date was the acquisition of RJR Nabisco in 1989 by Kohlberg Kravis Roberts & Co. for between US$25 billion and US$31 billion.

It is ironic that an acquired company's success in the form of cash on the balance sheet can be used against it as collateral by the hostile company that acquires it. For this reason, some regard LBOs as an especially ruthless predatory tactic."

*Source*: http://www1.investopedia.com/terms/l/leveragedbuyout.asp (accessed November 20, 2008).

Financial leverage, or the average debt-to-equity ratio among 30 core Tokyo Stock Price Index companies other than financial institutions, fell to 2.8 in 2004 from a 1995 peak of 3.4, meaning that Japanese companies had a lot of room to increase debt.[99] Even if interest rates rose over the long term, Japanese companies would continue increasing debt strategically. Because companies had sold off nonperforming assets and serviced their debts during deflationary times, they could live with more debt if rates rose gradually. BOJ's relaxation policy had been in place for a long time, and signs of economic recovery were finally appearing. BOJ might not raise rates immediately, but it would likely do so before corporate discipline slackened. The change in policy was an opportunity for corporations to pursue profitable investment strategies.

The second factor enabling the LBO was the trend of private firms urging NTT to open up its monopolies. In study groups hosted by the Ministry of Internal Affairs and Communications in January 2006, private-sector firms lashed out against NTT for the monopolies it held in

---

[98] Some LBOs in the 1980s in the US resulted in corporate bankruptcy, such as Robert Campeau's 1988 buyout of Federated Department Stores. The failure of the buyout was a result of excessive debt financing.

[99] Ibid.

the telecommunications sector.[100] To study competition in the telecommunications industry, the ministry held a meeting of industry experts and listened to the views of telecom companies.[101]

NTT had earlier announced a plan to create a fiber-optic network covering 30 million homes and offices by 2010.[102] The main point of the discussion was the handling of telecommunications lines. NTT had a near monopoly on access lines into homes and commercial enterprises.[103] Other private telecom firms offered their services to consumers by renting the lines from NTT.

*The NTT group still has powerful control over the market. NTT should spin off its access line segment, and KDDI is willing to invest in this spun-off entity.*

— Mr. Onodera, president of KDDI[104]

Son proposed that private-sector telecom firms and broadcasters establish a joint venture to lay fiber-optic access lines.[105]

*Because the price of 5,000 yen per month for the fee that NTT charges for use of its fiber-optic access line is too high, we are unable to compete. If the joint venture makes use of government-guaranteed bonds to create a network covering all households and assumes a depreciation period of 20 years, then the monthly fee can be lowered to 690 yen.*

— Mr. Son, chairman and CEO of Softbank[106]

---

[100] *Nihon Keizai Shimbun*, January 30, 2006, http://www.nni.nikkei.co.jp/AC/TNKS/Search/Nni20060130D30HH689.htm (accessed July 1, 2007).

[101] Ibid.

[102] Ibid.

[103] NTT was established in 1952 and succeeded telecommunication business from the government that had monopolized it by that time. NTT was a shareholding company established by the Law concerning NTT (Law No. 85. Dec/1984).

[104] *Nihon Keizai Shimbun*, January 30, 2006, http://www.nni.nikkei.co.jp/AC/TNKS/Search/Nni20060130D30HH689.htm (accessed July 1, 2007).

[105] The exchange telecommunications industry was transitioning from a narrowband network of circuit switches and copper cables to a broadband network of packet switches and fiber optics. This transition was expected to be largely completed between 2015 and 2020. For details, see NTT's website: http://www.ntt.co.jp/index_f.html.

[106] *Nihon Keizai Shimbun*, January 30, 2006, http://www.nni.nikkei.co.jp/AC/TNKS/Search/Nni20060130D30HH689.htm (accessed July 1, 2007).

*Even now, fiber-optic lines cost about 13,000 yen per line, so we are offering the service at a loss. A fee of 690 yen is unthinkable.*

— Mr. Wada, president of NTT[107]

## The Future

In November 2005, Softbank obtained the go-ahead from the Ministry of Internal Affairs and Communications to enter the cellular phone business. However, "it could take up to one and half years to build the necessary infrastructure for the service, not to mention a huge amount of money".[108]

Softbank's ¥340 billion purchase of Japan Telecom in 2004 had not contributed much to the group's earnings.[109] The question was whether the addition of Vodafone K.K.'s cellular phone service would likely enhance the value of Japan Telecom because the fixed-line phone service subsidiary would be a crucial ingredient in Softbank's transformation into a comprehensive telecommunications service provider.

Son felt satisfied that with the acquisition of Vodafone K.K., he had closed a big deal that would prove successful for both companies and allow him to build up a business base that would continue to expand. At the same time, he was fully aware of the pros and cons of the deal. He knew that some key questions had to be answered in order for Softbank to continue to be competitive.

First, in what direction should he take Softbank? Could Softbank maintain its culture, structure, and ability to respond quickly and effectively to client needs throughout the anticipated period of rapid growth? Should Son's strategy of growth through acquisition continue? If so, could Softbank raise the capital necessary to make such acquisitions?

Although one of the main issues of acquisition was valuation, the settlement of the deal, the obtainment of regulatory approval and post-acquisition management also had to be taken into account. Financial issues aside, what would be the role of developing human resources in Softbank's future success? The top management of Softbank would have

---

[107] Ibid.

[108] Ibid.

[109] Ibid.

to answer these questions clearly to outsiders, including the company's shareholders.

The immediate concern for the top management of Softbank was the financing of its purchase of Vodafone K.K. The top management instructed the planning department to conduct a study on the company's financing alternatives and calculate the all-in cost of yen, US dollar and British pound financing in terms of yen.

## For Further Discussion

1. What are reasons for a company such as Softbank to acquire another company?
2. What were Son's motivations for Softbank's acquisition of Vodafone K.K.?
3. What could be the pros and cons of this deal for Softbank?
4. Predict the future of Softbank after the deal.
5. In the US, LBOs of large public companies became common in the 1980s? Why?
6. Was all this takeover and LBO activity good for the US economy?
7. Prepare Vodafone KK's pro forma future cash flow statement for 2006–2008.
8. Estimate the future exchange rates between the US dollar, British pound and yen.
9. Estimate the all-in cost of the debt financing alternatives in terms of yen.
10. What are the key future trends in the worldwide telecommunications market?

## Appendix 1 Assumptions for Financial Projection for Valuation of Vodafone K.K.

The projection was constructed based upon the following attributes:

1. The Japanese corporate tax rate is 40%.
2. Net operating cash flow would stay at the level of 2005.
3. Depreciation would decrease at 3% per year.

4. The weighted average cost of capital (WACC) for Softbank is estimated at 7%. Softbank generally requires new investment to yield an additional 5% over the WACC for international projects. Thus, the discount rate for Vodafone K.K.'s cash flow should be 12%.
5. The terminal value was calculated as the present value of a perpetual net operating cash flow generated in the 3rd year.
6. Vodafone K.K.'s valuation was coordinated using the net present value (NPV), which is defined as follows:

$$NPV = \sum_{t=1}^{T} \frac{CF_t(1-\tau)}{(1+\bar{r})^t}$$

Where:

$\quad CF_t$ = expected before-tax cash flow in year t
$\quad \tau$ = tax rate
$\quad \bar{r}$ = weighted average cost of capital
$\quad T$ = life of the project

# Appendix 2 Assumptions for Calculating the All-in Cost of the Debt Financing Alternatives in Terms of Yen

1. The future *currency* value over the five-year loan period can be forecasted, based upon purchasing power parity. We use the following formula:

$$\frac{F}{S} = \frac{1+\pi^{\yen}}{1+\pi^{\$}}$$

Where:

$\quad F$ = Future spot rates
$\quad S$ = Current spot rates
$\quad \pi^{\yen}$ = Yen's inflation rate
$\quad \pi^{\$}$ = US dollar's inflation rate

The following data was provided on March 22, 2006:

    (1)  Spot rate[110]: ¥116.72/US\$, £0.571984/US\$, ¥204.062/£

    (2)  Inflation rate[111]: Japan −0.1% p.a. US 2.8% p.a., UK 1.9% p.a.

2.  All-in cost in yen is calculated as the internal rate of return (IRR) of the complete series of cash flows in yen (yen associated with the borrowings, including proceeds net of the fees and complete repayment of principal and interest).

For the calculation, assume:

— Interest Rates (fixed, five-year treasury yields, p.a.)[112]: Japan 1.01%, US 4.69%, and UK 4.26%
— The national amounts: ¥1 million equivalent
— The maturities: five years
— The up-front fees: 2% for all the borrowings.

3.  The internal rate of return is defined as the value of IRR in the following equation:

$$C_0 = \sum_{t=1}^{T} \frac{CF_t(1-\tau)}{(1 + IRR)^t}$$

Where:

    $C_0$ = initial investment

    $CF^t$ = expected before-tax cash flow in year $t$

    $\tau$ = tax rate

    $t$ = life of the project

---

[110] For exchange rates, see BOJ's website: http://www.boj.or.jp/.

[111] For inflation rates, see the International Monetary Fund's website: http://www.imf.org/external/country/index.htm.

[112] For interest rates, see the Japan Ministry of Finance's website: http://www.mof.go.jp/english/.

**14**

# Keidanren: Foreign Political Contributions in Japan

*Economics and politics are inseparable. I want to keep my lines of communication open to politicians so I can have in-depth discussions with them.*

— Fujio Mitarai, chairman of Keidanren[1]

On May 23, 2006, Fujio Mitarai was appointed chairman of the Japanese Federation of Economic Organizations (Keidanren). Keidanren was regarded by many as the strongest interest group in Japan. It applied pressure on both the government and overseas organizations on economic, industrial and labor issues facing Japan's business community. At the time of Mitarai's inauguration as chairman, Japan's corporate sector was facing a number of urgent issues. Chief amongst these was the dwindling competitiveness of Japanese companies.

Mitarai believed that technological innovation was not enough, and that social and economic reform were required to increase the competitiveness of Japanese companies. Japan had long been closed to foreign businesses, and by 2006, foreign companies still didn't have equal access to Japan's economy. Public-sector contracts were typically awarded to Japanese companies. By opening up the economy to foreign companies, Mitarai aimed to increase the competitiveness of domestic firms.

The first step towards opening up the economy would be to give foreign companies a voice in the political process. Politicians and political parties in Japan depended on donations from companies and individuals to finance their political activities. By law, foreigners, foreign companies and companies with

---

[1] Mitarai, F. (May 10, 2006) Press Conference on May 9, 2006, http://japundit.com/archives/2006/03/10/2086/ (accessed April 28, 2008).

335

foreign capital affiliations of over 30% of total capital were barred from making political donations. Although there had been a number of high-profile scandals involving political donations by Japanese companies and their executives, the organization had continued supporting the system of political donations. As the new chairman, should Mitarai press for a change in the law so foreign companies would be allowed to make political donations?

## Political Donations in Japan

*We should continue to work closely together in political and economic areas to create a better society.*

— Junichiro Koizumi, prime minister of Japan[2]

Political activities often required substantial funds, and the situation in Japan was no different. In Japan, a large share of the money spent on political campaigns came from corporations and their executives. In the 1990s and early 2000s, such donations were at the center of scandals that rocked the nation. Challenges to the Liberal Democratic Party (LDP), which had ruled Japan since the party's founding in 1955, and the broader political crisis[3] revolved around a series of scandals involving payments to politicians to cover their huge election expenses. This led to increased scrutiny of companies' general participation in the political process and political campaign contributions in particular. New restrictions on companies' political giving were put in place and greater disclosure of campaign contributions was required (see **Exhibits 1–3**).

---

[2] Koizumi, J. (May 24, 2006) Speech given at the May 2006 General Meeting of Nippon Keidanren, http://www.nni.nikkei.co.jp/AC/TNKS/Search/Nni20060525D25HH461.htm (accessed April 28, 2008).

[3] Between 1955 and 1990, land prices in Japan appreciated by 70 times and stocks increased 100 times over. Investors may have realized the looming bubble, but many believed that the high level of collusion between the government and business could sustain the growth. But an inverted growth cycle perpetuated itself. The prosperity of Japan proved to be its undoing and corruption began to spread throughout the political and business realms. This was when Japanese politics faced the real crisis.

**Exhibit 1**  Political Donation System in Japan

Recipient: Individual Politician (through the creation of a Fund Raising Group)

| Donor | Allowed to Donate to Recipient? | Limit |
|---|---|---|
| Individual | Yes | ¥10 million[4] |
| Political Party | Yes | ¥10 million |
| Corporation | No | N/A |

Recipient: Political Party and/or Fund Raising Group

| Donor | Allowed to Donate to Recipient? | Limit |
|---|---|---|
| Individual | Yes | ¥20 million[5] |
| Corporation | Yes | ¥7.5 million[6]– ¥1 billion[7] (depending on the amount of capital the corporation has) |

**Exhibit 2**  Government Regulation of Political Donations in Japan

Companies' political donations in Japan, and also their overall involvement in the political process, are now under increasing scrutiny by shareholders. More and more, shareholders are seeking companies' transparency in their political donations and in other types of political involvement, such as lobbying. Many criticisms have been raised over the issue of transparency and the method of enforcing the related laws.

**A. Contribution Limits**

The Political Donation Control Law sets quantitative controls through Articles 21 and 22.[8] Article 3 of the Political Donation Control Law deals with the contributor and recipient aspects of donations: the contributors and recipients are categorized into separate groups, and the quantitative limits placed on the different types of contributors and recipients vary significantly, as described below.[9]

*(Continued)*

---

[4] US$88,449 at US$1 = ¥113.06 in May 2006.

[5] US$176,897 at US$1 = ¥113.06 in May 2006.

[6] US$66,336 at US$1 = ¥113.06 in May 2006.

[7] US$8,844,861 at US$1 = ¥113.06 in May 2006.

[8] Seijishikin Kisei Hō (Political Donation Control Law), Law No. 194 of 1948.

[9] Ibid.

**Exhibit 2**   (*Continued*)

---

**Case 1: For Individual Politicians**

Individuals can make political contributions of up to ¥1.5 million each year to individual politicians.[10] The limit on individual donations through fundraising groups set up by individual politicians is ¥10 million each year.[11] Companies and labor unions are prohibited from donating to individual politicians, even through fundraising groups set up by individual politicians.[12] Political parties, however, are an exception, and can make contributions to individual politicians, with no specific time limit on their contributions.[13]

**Case 2: For Political Parties**

Individuals, companies and labor unions are permitted to donate to political parties and political fund groups established by political parties, subject to certain limitations.[14] Individuals may contribute a maximum of ¥20 million;[15] and companies and labor unions can contribute from ¥7.5 million to ¥100 million, depending on the company's capitalization.[16] The flow of money originating from political organizations, especially political parties, is least restricted.[17] Only during an election period are individuals allowed to donate to individual politicians without going through a single fundraising group.[18] However, regardless of whether the contribution is made during election time, political parties may contribute to individual politicians and other political organizations, including individual fundraising groups.[19] This is because political parties are treated differently in a rigidly regulated regime.[20] This special treatment is currently one of the most serious flaws of the regulatory regime because political parties are now able to appoint only one fundraising political organization and must register it at the Ministry of Internal Affairs and Communications.[21] There are only a few qualitative control restrictions on who can give political donations, and they are minor. For example, under the present regulatory regime, foreign companies and companies that are in deficit or receiving government subsidies are prohibited from making political

---

(*Continued*)

---

[10] Ibid., Article 21.

[11] Ibid., Article 21-3.

[12] Ibid., Article 21.

[13] Ibid., Article 21-3.

[14] Ibid., Article 21-3.

[15] Ibid., Article 21-3(1)(i).

[16] Ibid., Article 21-3(1)(ii)(iii)(iv) and Article 21-3(2).

[17] Ibid., Article 3.

[18] Ibid., Article 19.

[19] Ibid., Article 21-2.

[20] Ibid., Article 21-2(2).

[21] Ibid., Article 6-2.

**Exhibit 2**   (*Continued*)

donations.[22] Section 22 of the Political Donation Control Law also specifies that political donations cannot be made under the name of someone else or anonymously.[23]

**B. Disclosure**

Articles 9 and 10 of the Political Donation Control Law set out the procedures for disclosing financial statements relating to political contributions.[24] Individual politicians are not required to file financial statements detailing political contributions they have received, invested or used.[25] But Section 12(1)(i)(c) of the Political Donation Control Law makes it mandatory for political organizations to prepare an annual report listing the names and addresses of everyone who donated over ¥50,000 that year and the names and addresses of everyone to whom the organization gave over ¥50,000 that year. They are also required to list various assets, such as movable property, savings, valuable securities, loans and debts exceeding ¥1 million.[26] The Political Donation Control Law states that political organizations are required to file a formatted report detailing the proceeds earned through fundraising events.[27] Article 12 stipulates that the names and addresses of anyone who made a payment greater than ¥200,000 for services at a certain event must be disclosed.[28] Article 20-2 of the Political Donation Control Law states that the significant points of political organizations' annual financial statements must be made public, either in the public register (Kanpō) or the prefectural bulletin (Kōhō).[29] Section 20 also states that these statements must be in public view at the prefectural election administration committee (Senkyo Kanri Iinkai) or at the Ministry of Home Affairs for a duration of three years.[30] With the enactment of the Administrative Information Disclosure Act, the right to view these financial statements now includes the right to photocopy them.[31] Criticisms have been raised, however, that these reporting requirements are inconsistent and insufficient. The major criticism has been the difficulty in confirming

(*Continued*)

---

[22] Ibid., Article 22-3, Article 22-4 and Article 22-5.

[23] Seijishikin Kisei Hō (Political Donation Control Law), Law No. 194 of 1948.

[24] Ibid.

[25] Ibid.

[26] Ibid., Article 12(1)(i)(c).

[27] Ibid., Article 12.

[28] Ibid., Article 12(1)(i)(g).

[29] Ibid., Article 20.

[30] Ibid., Article 20-2(2).

[31] Gyoseikikan No Hoyusuru Jyoho No Koukai Nikansuru Houritsu (Administrative Information Disclosure Act), Law No. 102 of 2005, Article 14.

**Exhibit 2**   (*Continued*)

the accuracy of reported numbers.[32] Under the current law, politicians are not required to disclose the acceptance of contributions from a single corporation if the sum given to the politician's political organization totals less than ¥50,000 that year for each group.[33] Under the same law, a political organization files different contribution reports for politicians in different prefectures, and multiple reports with the Ministry of Home Affairs, depending on where the contributions came from and how the contributions are used.[34] This makes it difficult for a third party to reconstruct a complete picture of the flow of money. Many politicians have reportedly tried to hide money received from companies by asking each company to pay in small amounts so that none of the sums require disclosure to the Ministry of Home Affairs.[35] This method, whereby corporations make contributions in small amounts to a number of political and fundraising organizations, all for a single politician, is a standard Japanese political practice.[36]

**Exhibit 3**   Regulations for Political Financing in the US

Over the past decade, the US has placed new restraints on companies' political donations and has demanded greater transparency of these contributions.[37]

In the US, the first attempts at nationally regulating campaign contributions started in the 1970s, although there were attempts to regulate this through legislation as early as 1867.[38] The Federal Election Campaign Act of 1971 (FECA) required

(*Continued*)

---

[32] The list of criticisms includes those presented by the Democratic Party of Japan, http://www.dpj.or.jp/news/dpjnews.cgi?indication=dp&num=10179 (accessed November 13, 2007); New Kōmei Party, http://www.komei.or.jp/ (accessed November 13, 2007). To secure transparency, both parties are claiming that the names of the recipients to whom the organization made a payment of more than ¥1 must be disclosed. *Sanyo Shimbun*, September 20, 2007, http://www.sanyo.oni.co.jp/newsk/2007/09/20/20070920010007201.html (accessed April 28, 2008).

[33] Seijishikin Kisei Hō (Political Donation Control Law), Law No. 194 of 1948, Article 12.

[34] Ibid.

[35] *Sanyo Shimbun*, November 3, 2007, "Debate on Political Donations, Transparency Needed".

[36] *Asahi Shimbun*, September 24, 1993, "Political Donation — Keidanren's Position Goes Against the Times", p. 2.

[37] In the US, "campaign finance reform" refers to the political effort to change the involvement of money in political campaigns. For further details, see "Campaign Finance Reform", http://www.opensecrets.org/news/campaignfinance/index.asp (accessed April 28, 2008).

[38] The Naval Appropriations Bill 1867 was the first federal legislature regulating campaign finance. This bill prohibited officers and employees of the government from soliciting money from workers at naval yards. For details, see "Campaign Finance History", http://www.campaignfinancesite.org/history.html.

**Exhibit 3**   (*Continued*)

candidates to disclose the sources and applications of campaign contributions.[39] In 1974, the act was amended so that legal limits on contributions were introduced and the Federal Election Commission (FEC) was established.[40]

The US government adopted two sets of campaign-contribution legislation in 2000 and 2002.

The 2000 legislation required tax-exempt organizations under Section 527 of the Internal Revenue Code that raise and use funds through political activities to disclose the sources and applications of donations.

The Bipartisan Campaign Reform Act of 2002 (often referred to as the McCain–Feingold Law)[41] banned companies, unions, and other groups from giving "soft money" donations to national political parties; increased the caps on "hard money" donations that individuals can donate to candidates; and put limits on advertisements pertaining to certain issues. The act is considered the most aggressive change ever to the US political contributions system.

In 2003, the US Supreme Court upheld the following provisions of the McCain–Feingold Law[42]:

1. The ban on national parties and officeholders who are raising and spending "soft money" (i.e., unlimited contributions to parties from companies, unions and individuals).
2. The limit on state parties spending soft money that may affect federal elections.
3. The new definition of campaign ads subject to campaign contribution regulation and disclosure: Any broadcast ad aired before an election (60 days before a general election or 30 days before a primary election) that depicts a federal candidate and targets that candidate's constituency (so-called "electioneering communications").
4. The requirement that special interest groups use only regulated "hard money" (i.e., contributions from individuals or political action committees, subject to the limits

(*Continued*)

---

[39] The text of the FECA of 1971, as amended; the Presidential Election Campaign Fund Act, as amended; and the Presidential Primary Matching Payment Account Act, as amended, contained in Titles 2 and 26 of the US Code.

[40] Ibid.

[41] The Bipartisan Campaign Reform Act of 2002, Public Law 107–155 was signed by the president and enacted on March 27, 2002. The law capped a seven-year effort by its congressional sponsors to change federal campaign law and marked the most significant amendment to the FECA in more than one-quarter century.

[42] McConnell v. FEC, No. 02-1674 (December 10, 2003).

**Exhibit 3**   (*Continued*)

and disclosure requirements) to pay for electioneering communications and that they disclose the source of the money.

5. The mandate that broadcast stations compile a public record of political ads and their sources.[43]

## Contribution Limits

In the US, FECA[44] provides the legal framework that guides corporate donations. Companies, contractors for the federal government, and foreign individuals may not make contributions or spend money to influence federal elections that call for the direct election or defeat of any specific candidate.[45] Rather, companies must primarily focus on party-building activities, (i.e., soft money).[46] Companies may form political action committees, which are subject to federal guidelines.[47] Political action committees may give contributions as explained in the following table.

|  | To candidate or local and state party | To national party |
| --- | --- | --- |
| Multicandidate political action committees[48] | No more than US$5,000 each | No more than US$15,000 |
| Non-multicandidate political action committees | No more than US$1,000 to a candidate and no more than US$5,000 to a local and state party | No more than US$20,000 |

## Disclosure Requirements

Companies, candidate committees, party committees and political action committees must file reports periodically, disclosing the sources and applications of funds they raised.[49] Companies must disclose all in-kind and other non-monetary contributions

(Continued)

---

[43] Ibid.

[44] See the Democratic Party of Japan, http://www.dpj.or.jp/news/dpjnews.cgi?indication=dp&num=10179 (accessed November 13, 2007), New Kōmei Party, http://www.komei.or.jp/ (accessed November 13, 2007) and *Sanyo Shimbun*, September 20, 2007, http://www.sanyo.oni.co.jp/newsk/2007/09/20/20070920010007201.html (accessed April 28, 2008).

[45] The Federal Election Campaign Act of 1971, 2 US Code §441.

[46] Ibid.

[47] Ibid.

[48] Multicandidate political action committees are those that have been registered for six months, have more than 50 candidates and contribute at least five federal candidates.

[49] 2 US Code §§432, 433, 434.

**Exhibit 3**  (*Continued*)

and campaign support.[50] A company can ask its employees or restricted class, which is made up of its stockholders, executives and administrative personnel and their families, to vote for or against a particular candidate and permit candidates to use facilities for campaign activities if its employees are attending.[51] Companies may not collect contributions for the candidate, but the candidate may solicit and accept contributions from attending employees.[52] Companies may permit candidates to use their offices and equipment if the candidate reimburses the company for the cost. Corporate lawyers, certified public accountants and other professionals may donate their time to help candidates' campaigns, and companies may continue to pay their salaries.[53]

At the same time, shareholders were starting to hold companies accountable for their campaign contributions.

## *Lawsuits Brought by Shareholders*

In 2003, political parties and political organizations accumulated a total of ¥319.6 billion, most of which came from corporations. The lack of transparency and the ineffectiveness of enforcement mechanisms led to many lawsuits, the most important of which were the Yawata Steel Shareholders' Derivative Suit in 1970[54] and the Kumagaigumi Shareholders' Derivative Suit in 2003.[55] Both cases addressed a continuing legal question in Japan: whether a company was entitled to freely undertake political activities (see **Exhibit 4**) and more specifically whether the donation of political funds was one aspect of this entitlement, even if such donations would influence political trends.

---

[50] Ibid.

[51] Ibid.

[52] In 2003, Yoshihiko Tsuchiya, president of the House of Councilors from 1988 to 1991, was suspected of violating the Political Donation Control Law. Muneo Suzuki was the deputy chief cabinet secretary to Prime Minister Obuchi who pressured the Foreign Ministry to fund the Japanese–Russia Friendship House, which became a scandal in 2002. For the details, see Hanson, R. (June 20, 2002) "Suzuki Arrest Offers Welcome Sideshow", *Online Asia Times*, http://www.atimes.com/japanecon/DF20Dh02.html (accessed April 28, 2008).

[53] Japan Policy & Politics (August 4, 2003) "Ex-Saitama Gov. Escapes Indictment, Daughter Charged", http://findarticles.com/p/articles/mi_m0XPQ/is_2003_August_4/ai_106218800 (accessed April 28, 2008).

[54] Arita v. Yawata Steel, 330 Hanrei Jihō 29 (Tokyo District Court, April 5, 1960).

[55] Kumagaigumi Kabunushi Daihyō Soshō (Kumagaigumi Shareholders' Derivative Suit), Hanrei Jihō No. 1814, p. 151 (Fukui District Court, February 12, 2003).

**Exhibit 4**   Academic Debate in Japan Concerning Corporate
Political Donations

There are various academic opinions in Japan as to whether political donations by corporation are legal and just. The two opposing theories are: that political donation is lawful and within the right capacity of a corporation; and that political donation is outside a company's business objective, so therefore it is inappropriate as it is outside the right capacity of a corporation.

**Theories Upholding Corporate Donation**

Among the theories based on Civil Law and Commercial Law, the prevailing theory is one that approves corporate political donations from the standpoint of advantages such as usability and efficiency for business purposes.[56] A view that approves corporate political donation stressing the social existence and real existence of a corporation is exemplified by the second trial decision and the Supreme Court's decision in the Yahata Steel political donation case, as well as the second trial decision of the Kumagaigumi case, which identifies corporate political donations as necessary and useful for the business purposes of a corporation based on the general position of profitability, such that it does not constitute any violation of directors' responsibility.[57]

The typical opinion among them concludes that violation of directors' responsibilities cannot be proven on recognition that political donations are, from a macro perspective, useful actions necessary for the profitability of a corporation.[58] In other words, "approval of a corporate political donation should be based on whether its economic effect is useful for the execution of the business, which is the purpose of the corporation".[59]

Another view that supports political donations, the juristic person's real existence theory, defines the essence of a juristic person as "a thing that owns a social value suitable to be a subject of right capacity" similar to a natural person, and so it is quite "impossible" to prove that "corporate political donation is outside of the scope of the objective of a corporation".[60]

**Theories Opposing Corporate Donation**

There is a theory that denies a corporation's right to make political donations on the ground that it is against the public order and morality specified in Article 90 of the Civil

*(Continued)*

---

[56] Mitsueda, K. (1990) "Political Donations by Corporations", *Houritsu Ronsou*, 63(2), p. 31.
[57] See *supra* n. 27.
[58] Suzuki, T. (1971) "Political Donations by Corporations", *Yuhikaku*, p. 301.
[59] Ibid.
[60] Wagatsuma, S. (1966) "Regarding the Court's Decisions on Corporate Donations", *Jurist*, 341, p. 10.

**Exhibit 4**   (*Continued*)

Law.[61] A recent theory states: "The logic of the Supreme Court was specifically intended to establish the legality of corporation's political donations. However, it should agree with the viewpoint that it is already invalid at the stage of the Constitution and the Civil Law prior to the Commercial Law unless a corporation's donation is made after a unanimous decision by all the shareholders. It is based on a theory that such a donation should be made according to a citizen's own selection as a natural person and it is against such a theory for any director to use the corporation's assets, which are not the director's assets, for political purposes, as can be found in the Supreme Court's own statement that a political donation can 'affect the political trends' and 'affect the formation of the political opinions of the public.'"[62]

A typical constitutional law theory states that it is "too far-fetched and inappropriate to consider an act that has nothing to do with the objectives of a corporation under its articles of incorporation, in particular, of a corporation (especially a huge organization that is otherwise considered a social power) having an enormous economic power and socially influencing capability, as an act responding to 'expectations and requests (for the corporation) within the boundary of socially accepted notions' or 'an expected act of a social being,' and consider that the Constitution approves unlimited freedom for corporation's political actions similar to that of a natural person."[63] It is undeniable that a large donation not only can affect the outcome of an election but also enormously affect an "individual citizen's exercise of its voting right and other political suffrage".[64]

The view that denies the legality of political donation is exemplified by the first trial decision of the Yahata Steel case[65] and the first trial decision of the Kumagaigumi case,[66] in which the corporation's actions are divided, based on the corporation's profitability, into trading actions (profit-making actions) and non-trading actions (non-profit-making actions), the latter being considered actions unrelated to the objectives of the corporation, including a tolerated exception for a "social obligation action" to which an agreement of all the shareholders can be expected. Because the political donations in question do not fit the above exception, the directors' liabilities for damages were sought in both cases. One can see the theory opposing political donation developed most systematically and precisely in the arguments of these cases.

(*Continued*)

---

[61] It provides that a juristic act that has for its object such matters as are contrary to public or good morals is null and void.

[62] Kawamoto, I. (1999) "Modern Corporation, Eighth Edition", *Shouji Houmu Kenkyuukai*, p. 72.

[63] Ashizawa, S. (1995) "Corporation and Human Rights", *Keibundo*, p. 33.

[64] Ibid.

[65] See *supra* n. 21.

[66] See *supra* n. 22.

**Exhibit 4** *(Continued)*

> Popular theories these days often describe political donations as duplicitous "in that they are first considered to be within the scope of the corporation's objective, but then after further examination of appropriateness after making a judgment on social appropriateness" it is found that "they are not after all within the scope of the business objective".[67] "What happens to the money is not an essential matter; in other words, which political party to be supported and to which political party the money is to be donated are something to be judged by an individual, so that robbing the privilege of such a choice is a violation of Article 90",[68] and that corporate political donations are considered violations of public order and morality, which essentially take them outside the scope of a corporation's objectives.[69] The argument refers to an "individual's political suffrage" and a possibility of it being "OK if every shareholder agrees", but it quickly criticizes such a possibility as something that is totally unrealistic because it is an impossible legal fiction[70] to obtain political agreement of all the shareholders in a large corporation such as Yahata Steel.

## *The Yawata Steel Decision*

By May 2006, the leading case in Japan concerning the issue of a corporation's political donations was a lawsuit brought by shareholders against the directors of Yawata Steel under Commercial Law, Article 267 (Shōhō, Law No. 48 of 1890). A group of shareholders of Yawata Steel[71] claimed that the directors acted outside the business purpose specified in the articles of incorporation and violated their fiduciary duty as defined in Commercial Law, Article 254-2 (now Article 254-3).[72]

The defense claimed that the political donation was in accordance with the purpose of the corporation stated in the articles of incorporation and was socially appropriate, and hence it did not constitute any violation of the directors' duty.[73] The plaintiff won the case at the first trial, as the judge decided that the defendants' action was a violation of his fiduciary

---

[67] Shinomiya, K. (1966) "Legal Issues on Corporate Political Donations", *Jurist*, 343, p. 36.

[68] Ibid.

[69] Ibid.

[70] Ibid.

[71] Yawata Steel merged with Fuji Steel in 1981 to form Shin Nippon Steel.

[72] Arita v. Yawata Steel, 330 Hanrei Jihō 29 (Tokyo District Court, April 5, 1960).

[73] Ibid.

duty because the defendant's action was basically not a profit-making act and was a violation of the articles of incorporation, recognizing the defendant's liabilities.[74] However, an upper court of appeal accepted the defendant's claim and rejected the complaint,[75] which was also dismissed by the Supreme Court.[76]

The case established a new theory that corporations can act within the bounds of socially accepted objectives, even if a certain act seems unrelated to its articles of incorporation. Because of this, corporate management garnered more flexibility to make political donations.

## *The Kumagaigumi Decision*

The Kumagaigumi decision exposed the cozy relationship between politicians and businesses, particularly public works contractors.[77] In this case, a group of shareholders of Kumagaigumi brought a shareholders' lawsuit based on Commercial Law, claiming that under Article 267,[78] Kumagaigumi's

---

[74] Ibid.

[75] Arita v. Yawata Steel, Tokyo High Court, January 31, 1963. 1966(ne) No. 791, Hanji No. 433, p. 9.

[76] Arita v. Yawata Steel, Grand Court, Supreme Court, June 24, 1970. Minshuu No. 24-6, p. 625 and Hanji No. 596, p. 3.

[77] Kumagaigumi Kabunushi Daihyō Soshō (Kumagaigumi Shareholders' Derivative Suit), Hanrei Jihō No. 1814, p. 151 (Fukui District Court, February 12, 2003).

[78] It provided:

(1) Any shareholder who has held a share continuously at least for the last six months may demand, in writing, of the company to institute an action to enforce the liability of directors.

(2) In case the company has failed to institute such action within 30 days from the date on which the demand mentioned in the preceding paragraph may institute such action on behalf of the company.

(3) In case irreparable damage may be caused to the company by the expiration of the period provided for in the preceding paragraph, the shareholder mentioned in Paragraph 1 may immediately institute the action mentioned in the preceding paragraph, notwithstanding the provisions of the preceding two paragraphs.

(4) When shareholder has instituted an action mentioned in the preceding two paragraphs, the Court may, at the request of the defendant, order him to furnish adequate security.

(5) The provisions of Article 106 Paragraph 2 shall apply *mutatis mutandis* to the request mentioned in the preceding paragraph.

donations to the People's Political Association (Kokumin Seiji Kyōkai),[79] a political funding group,[80] were: against public order and morality; outside the boundary of the purpose of the corporation; a violation of the Public Office Election Law[81] (Article 199, Section 1);[82] a violation of the Political Donation Control Law[83] (Article 22-4, Section 1);[84] and a violation of the fiduciary duty of care as good managers under Article 298[85] of the Civil Code.[86] The plaintiffs demanded damages in accordance with Commercial Law, Article 266, Sections 1–5 and an injunction of the political donations based on Commercial Law, Article 272.[87] The five issues facing the Fukui District Court on February 12, 2003 were:

---

[79] This was the organization receiving political donations for the LDP. For details, see the website: http://www.kokuseikyo.or.jp/jimin/ (accessed November 7, 2007).

[80] Seijishikin Kisei Hō (Political Donation Control Law), Law No. 194 of 1948, Articles 21 and 22.

[81] Kōshoku Senkyo Hō (Public Office Election Law), Law No. 100 of 1950.

[82] The article provides that donations from companies competing for or receiving public works orders must be banned.

[83] Seijishikin Kisei Hō (Political Donation Control Law), Law No. 194 of 1948.

[84] The article prohibited donations from companies that had run deficits for three or more consecutive years.

[85] It provided:

(1) A person having a right of retention shall keep the thing retained with the care of a good manager.

(2) A person having a right of retention may not, without the consent of the obligor, use or lease the thing retained or give it as security: however, this shall not apply to such use of the thing as is necessary for its preservation.

(3) If a person having a right of retention contravenes the provisions of the preceding two paragraphs, the obligor may demand the extinction of the right of retention.

[86] Minpō (Civil Code), Law No. 89 of 1896, Article 298.

[87] It provided: When a director performs an act that is not within the scope of the objectives of the company, or an act against any law or ordinance or the articles of incorporation, and thereby gives rise to fear of irreparable damages done to the company, any shareholder who has held a share continuously for at least the last six months may demand the director to stop such an act on behalf of the company. The section of Corporation in the Commercial Law was amended in June 2005 and the new Companies Act was enacted on July 26, 2005 (Law No. 77). Article 272 of Commercial Law became Article 360 under the new Companies Act. Kumagaigumi Kabunushi Daihyō Soshō (Kumagaigumi Shareholders' Derivative Suit), Hanrei Jihō No. 1814, p. 151 (Fukui District Court, February 12, 2003).

- Was the political donation in question against public order and morality?[88]
- Did the political donation in question reside within the objects of the articles of incorporation?[89]
- Did the political donation in question violate the Public Office Election Law?[90]
- Did the political donation in question violate the Political Donation Control Law?[91]
- Did the political donation in question violate the fiduciary duties of the directors?[92]

The court decided that, because the political donations in question had been executed without the company rigorously examining the appropriateness, scope, amount, timing and effect on current financial losses of the donation, and without considering the alternate benefits of paying out the donation as dividends to the shareholders, the directors of Kumagaigumi violated their fiduciary duties, by making the wanton decision to make the political donation.[93]

The judgment by the Fukui District Court was notable because it was the first decision to find such a donation illegal since the Yawata Steel decision in 1970. The decision that the management wantonly made political donations and that by doing so violated their fiduciary duties is important because it went against the findings of the Yawata Steel case that said it was permissible and useful for a corporation to donate to a political party. The holding did not, however, explicitly refute the Yawata Steel judgment.

The Fukui District Court decision was overturned by an appeals court (the Kanazawa branch of Nagoya High Court).[94] Explaining the appeals

---

[88] Kumagaigumi Kabunushi Daihyō Soshō (Kumagaigumi Shareholders' Derivative Suit), Hanrei Jihō No. 1814, p. 151 (Fukui District Court, February 12, 2003).

[89] Ibid.

[90] Ibid.

[91] Ibid.

[92] Ibid.

[93] Ibid.

[94] Kumagaigumi Kabunushi Daihyō Soshō Kōsoshin (Kumagaigumi Shareholders' Derivative Suit], Hanrei Jihō No. 1814, p. 151 (Nagoya District Court, January 11, 2006).

court's decision, one of the judges noted: "The directors were trying to improve the management and financial status of the company."[95] Discussing the violation of the fiduciary duty of care by the directors, the judge stated: "[T]here was a danger that, unless they accommodate the donation request by the industry association, the company would have lost the trust of the market and the stock price could have plummeted. The amount of the donation was within a reasonable range judging from the sales and the operating performance of Kumagaigumi."[96] While the decision by the Nagoya Appeals Court overturned the first trial decision by the Fukui District Court, the case was significant because it highlighted the arguments against political donations by corporations.[97] Critics of political donations in Japan relied on the decision by the Fukui District Court in Kumagaigumi as the legal basis for their claims, ignoring the appellate decision.[98]

## Laws Governing Political Donations in Japan

By 2006, the Japanese regulatory regime relevant to political contribution consisted of three laws: the Political Donation Control Law;[99] the Political Party Subsidy Law;[100] and the Public Office Election Law.[101] The most important was the Political Donation Control Law, which placed various limitations on political donations and mandated compulsory disclosure of campaign contributions.[102] The Political Party Subsidy Law outlined the

---

[95] Ibid.

[96] Ibid. The defendants had taken the case to the Supreme Court on January 13, 2006. The case was still pending. For details, see *Mainichi Shimbun*, January 14, 2006, "Kumagaigumi Case Jōkoku", p. 1.

[97] Kumagaigumi Kabunushi Daihyō Soshō Kōsoshin (Kumagaigumi Shareholders' Derivative Suit], Hanrei Jihō No. 1814, p. 151 (Nagoya District Court, January 11, 2006).

[98] Ibid.

[99] Seijishikin Kisei Hō (Political Donation Control Law], Law No. 194 of 1948, Articles 3, 21 and 22-6.

[100] Seitō Josei Hō (Political Party Subsidy Law], Law No. 5 of 1994.

[101] Kōshoku Senkyo Hō (Public Office Election Law), Law No. 100 of 1950.

[102] Seijishikin Kisei Hō (Political Donation Control Law), Law No. 194 of 1948.

process of political donations.[103] The Public Office Election Law helped to regulate the use of political funds during election periods.[104]

# Keidanren

Keidanren consisted of 1,623 companies and other organizations, including 91 companies with foreign capital affiliations[105] and 1,306 representative Japanese companies. It was the strongest interest group in Japan and applied pressure on both the government and overseas organizations by collecting opinions from throughout the business community on economic, industrial and labor issues, among others.[106] On May 23, 2006, Mitarai, Chairman of Canon Inc., was appointed chairman of Keidanren. Mitarai inherited the course charted by outgoing chairman Hiroshi Okuda (who was also chairman of Toyota Motor Corp.) and planned to push for structural reforms under private-sector leadership as well as economic interchange with the rest of Asia.[107] The keywords in Mitarai's philosophy were "reform" and "competition". His thinking was that not only was technological innovation necessary, but so was reform of economic and social systems, and that Japan, with its aging population and dwindling birthrate, should be revitalized. He believed that the foundation for Japan's revitalization should be free competition.

*The ideal society is one in which anyone can obtain the opportunity to participate in competition and even people who are unsuccessful can undertake this challenge again any number of times.*

— Fujio Mitarai, chairman of Keidanren[108]

---

[103] Seitō Josei Hō (Political Party Subsidy Law), Law No. 5 of 1994.

[104] Kōshoku Senkyo Hō (Public Office Election Law), Law No. 100 of 1950.

[105] This included companies with foreign capital comprising over 30% of total capital.

[106] For details, see Keidanren's website: http://www.keidanren.or.jp.

[107] *Nikkei (Japan Economic Journal)*, May 25, 2006, http://www.nni.nikkei.co.jp/AC/TNKS/Search/Nni20060525D25HH450.htm (accessed April 28, 2008).

[108] Mitarai, F. (May 10, 2006) Press Conference on May 9, 2006, http://japundit.com/archives/2006/03/10/2086/ (accessed April 28, 2008).

In terms of concrete policy demands, Keidanren was approaching a turning point. Among the themes that would be given priority, strengthening corporate ethics would be vital. Outgoing chairman Okuda had listed a series of scandals, including collusion among member companies, as one of the regrets he had about his tenure.[109] Mitarai's favorite theory was that "adherence to the law hinges on the ethical view of a company's top executives" and thus he demanded a high code of ethics from representatives of member companies.[110] If the public perceived Keidanren as going easy on insiders, the degree of public support its policy suggestions garnered would diminish. Mitarai felt it was also important that he not become overly intimate with politicians but that he instead maintain a healthy sense of separation from them.

In May 2006, at the start of Mitarai's term as chairman of Keidanren, the senior managers of Keidanren were busy preparing its new policy statements. Among others, they pondered whether Keidanren should clearly express its policy on promoting voluntary political donations by corporations in Japan. In particular, they were considering whether or not Keidanren should express its opinion on donations by companies marked as foreign companies.[111] Foreign companies included companies such as Canon, a famous Japanese brand headquartered in Tokyo, with the majority of its shares held by foreigners. By law, foreigners, foreign companies and organizations primarily composed of foreigners were not allowed to make political donations. The Political Donation Control Law stipulated that political organizations were "not allowed to receive donations intended for their political activities from foreigners or organizations or other institutions based in other countries"[112] in order to prevent Japanese politics and elections from being influenced by foreign countries. The Ministry of Internal Affairs and Communications acknowledged that the

---

[109] *Nikkei* (*Japan Economic Journal*), May 25, 2006, http://www.nni.nikkei.co.jp/AC/TNKS/Search/Nni20060525D25HH450.htm (accessed April 28, 2008).

[110] Ibid.

[111] According to the Ministry of Internal Affairs and Communications, foreign companies included legal entities, 50% of whose shares were owned by foreigners.

[112] Seijishikin Kisei Hō (Political Donation Control Law), Law No. 194 of 1948, Article 22-5.

legal entities whose shares are more than 50% owned by foreigners are subjected to this restriction.[113]

# Keidanren's Stance on Political Donations

*We should continue to work closely together in political and economic areas to create a better society.*

— Junichiro Koizumi, prime minister of Japan[114]

Keidanren, Japan's influential champion of the corporate sector, promoted political donations as a means to strengthen participatory democracy. It did so despite the existence of strong public criticism of political donations by corporations in Japan.[115] The public was perceived to be seeking to increase the transparency of political funding, and journalists were supporting these efforts.[116] Critics called the donations a form of bribery (see **Exhibit 5**). Keidanren underlined its stance on political donations on May 12, 2003 in a statement, "Seisakuhoni no Seijinimuketa Kigyō to Dantai Kifu no Sokushin Nitsuite" ("Promotion of Donations by Corporations/Organisations Keyed Toward Policy-Oriented Politics").[117] In the statement, Keidanren expressed its policy on promoting voluntary political donations by corporations and organizations based on their own evaluations of the policies of political parties.

---

[113] Acknowledged on December 13, 2006. Minutes of Ad Hoc Committee on the Establishment of Political Ethics and the Change of the Public Election Law, No. 5, December 1, 2006, http://kokkai.ndl.go.jp/SENTAKU/syugiin/165/0071/1651201007100 5c.html (accessed June 1, 2009).

[114] Koizumi, J. (May 24, 2006) Speech given at the May 2006 General Meeting of Keidanren, http://www.nni.nikkei.co.jp/AC/TNKS/Search/Nni20060525D25HH461.htm (accessed April 28, 2008).

[115] Political Donation Ombudsman (October 27, 2004) "Criticism against Amendment of PDCL by the Party in Office: Corporate Donations should be Ended", http://homepage2. nifty.com/~matsuyama/0041.html (accessed April 28, 2008).

[116] Ibid.

[117] Keidanren (May 12, 2003) "Promotion of Donations by Corporations/Organizations Keyed Toward Policy-Oriented Politics", http://www.keidanren.or.jp/japanese/policy/ 2003/040.html (accessed April 28, 2008).

**Exhibit 5**   Political Corruption in Japan

There has been a spate of political corruption cases in Japan over the past two decades, some of which have involved senior politicians.[118] This problem highlights the close and sticky relationship between politicians and the construction industry with regard to public works projects. The following case studies exemplify this corruption and help define the current and central problems of the laws, regulations and court decisions on this issue.

In 2003, Yoshihiko Tsuchiya, president of the House of Councilors (the upper house of the Diet) from 1988 to 1991 and governor of Saitama Prefecture from 1992 to 2003, was suspected of violating the Political Donation Control Law. He escaped indictment, but his daughter, who was in charge of his political-fund management organization, was arrested and pled guilty to misappropriating ¥116 million from the organization to prop up her own failing businesses. She also had sought, if not extorted, millions of yen from local firms, such as construction firms, and often tried to hide it by requesting that the donations be given in units smaller than the ¥50,000 limit.[119] Although Tsuchiya claimed to have known nothing of his daughter's activities, he resigned his position as governor.[120] In 1999, Suzuki interfered in a construction project for a public lodging facility (the Japan–Russia Friendship House, commonly known as "Muneo House") on Kunashiri Island, one of the Russian-held islands known as the Northern Territories.[121] He asked the ministry to only accept tender offers from companies from his constituency, Hokkaidō's Nemuro district.[122] The ministry opted to restrict eligible bidders to "those who have building experience in the Nemuro district".[123] This was decided through consultation with the Assistance Committee, the implementing body for aid projects in the Northern Territories, but Suzuki was also greatly involved in deciding bidding qualifications.[124] In 2004, he was sentenced to two years in jail for accepting bribes from two Hokkaido companies. His secretary, Akira Miyano, was charged with

*(Continued)*

---

[118] Ibid.

[119] Japan Policy & Politics (August 4, 2003) "Ex-Saitama Gov. Escapes Indictment, Daughter Charged", http://findarticles.com/p/articles/mi_m0XPQ/is_2003_August_4/ai_106218800 (accessed April 28, 2008); Japan Policy & Politics (July 22, 2003) "Saitama Gov. Tsuchiya Resigns, Election Set for Aug. 31", http://findarticles.com/p/articles/mi_m0XPQ/is_2003_July_22/ai_105676145 (accessed April 28, 2008).

[120] Ibid.

[121] Ibid.

[122] *Japan Times*, March 6, 2002, "Shady Politico-Bureaucratic Ties", http://search.japantimes.co.jp/cgi-bin/ed20020306a1.html (accessed April 28, 2008); Wijers-Hasegawa, Y. (November 6, 2004) "Suzuki Fined, Handed Two-Year Term", *Japan Times*, http://search.japantimes.co.jp/cgi-bin/nn20041106a1.html (accessed April 28, 2008).

[123] Ibid.

[124] Ibid.

**Exhibit 5**   (*Continued*)

bribery in July 2003 and given an 18-month suspended jail sentence for violating the Political Donation Control Law by not reporting ¥100 million in donations.[125] Suzuki and Miyano also helped fix ¥400 million in multiple public-works projects for construction firms.[126]

In 1988, the Recruit corruption scandal led to the forced resignation of many prominent Japanese politicians.[127] Recruit is a telecommunications and real-estate company located in Tokyo. The founder and chairman was Hiromasa Ezoe, who offered a substantial number of shares of Cosmos, one of Recruit's subsidiaries, to politicians and business executives just before Cosmos was listed on the Tokyo stock exchange in 1986. Cosmos's share price skyrocketed after the initial public offering, and the individuals who were offered the shares profited on average by approximately ¥66 million.[128] Initially, 17 members of the Diet were in this scheme and later another 30 were found to have been involved in insider trading.[129] Noboru Takeshita, who was prime minister of Japan at the time, was also involved in this scandal.[130] Due to their involvement in this scandal, Takeshita's cabinet had to resign.[131] After 13 years, the Tokyo District Court finally made its decision in 2003, giving Ezoe, the former Recruit chairman, a 3-year suspended prison term.[132] These incidents reveal that the existing Japanese laws and regulations concerning the regulation of political contribution are not effective.

Keidanren followed up this statement with an opinion paper, "Yūsenkadai to Kigyōseijikenkin no Jūyōsei" ("On Preferential Policy Matters and the Significance of Political Donations by Corporations"),

---

[125] Ibid.

[126] Ibid.

[127] Japan Policy & Politics (October 25, 1999) "Top Court Rejects Lawmaker's Appeal in Bribery Case", http://www.findarticles.com/p/articles/mi_m0XPQ/is_1999_Oct_25/ai_57163161 (accessed April 28, 2008). The politicians involved in the scandal were Prime Minister Noboru Takeshita, former Prime Minister Yasuhiro Nakasone and Chief Cabinet Secretary Takao Fujinami. See Doerner, W.R. (April 24, 1989) "Japan: A Scandal That Will Not Die", *Time*, http://www.time.com/time/magazine/article/0,9171,957517,00.html (accessed April 28, 2008).

[128] Japan Policy & Politics (October 25, 1999) "Top Court Rejects Lawmaker's Appeal in Bribery Case", http://www.findarticles.com/p/articles/mi_m0XPQ/is_1999_Oct_25/ai_57163161 (accessed April 28, 2008).

[129] Ibid.

[130] Ibid.

[131] Ibid.

[132] Ibid.

published on September 25, 2003.[133] This paper included a list of policies Keidanren regarded as necessary for realizing an autonomous economic society led by the private sector. Keidanren wanted companies to use these policies to evaluate political parties on their own and then act accordingly.[134] Also included in the paper was an evaluation of political donations based on opinion polls conducted with 1,600 major Japanese corporations as well as independent professionals, and thus represented the most widely-held opinions of Japanese economic circles.[135] The polls revealed that political donations by corporations were regarded as being extremely important in the following three ways.

## *Policy-Oriented Politics*

As the process of globalization continued, industries were strenuously trying to strengthen their international competitiveness. Meanwhile, institutional reforms such as regulatory reform, tax reform and foreign-trade agreements needed to be implemented by politicians to provide incentives to private industries. Corporate donations and contributions based on policy evaluations increased the competition among political parties and contributed to the realization of politics based on the selection of policies.

## *Healthy Development of Parliamentary Democracy*

Parliamentary democracy was a cost-effective system that funneled people's ideas through a broad communication channel, with the private sector bearing the cost. This applied especially to corporations, which were expected to bear a reasonable share of this social responsibility as good corporate citizens. Since the induction of the public-funding system for political parties, most parties expected more from public funding. Corporations needed to remember that donations from the private sector, including corporations, helped secure the independence and autonomy of political parties, two rights which formed the basis of democracy.

---

[133] Keidanren (January 10, 2007) "The Keidanren Vision 2007: The Land of Hope", http://www.keidanren.or.jp/english/policy/2007/vision.pdf (accessed April 28, 2008).
[134] Ibid.
[135] Keidanren (May 12, 2003) "Promotion of Donations by Corporations/Organizations Keyed toward Policy-Oriented Politics", http://www.keidanren.or.jp/japanese/policy/2003/040.html (accessed April 28, 2008).

## *Maintaining Transparency of Political Funds*

Donations to political parties that did not induce individual profit were considered the most transparent among all of the sources of funding for political parties. Enrichment of such donations could contribute to the transparency of the entirety of a political party's funding. This could be further improved by asking that corporations' political donations be used specifically for the planning and promotion of policies.[136]

> *The ideal society is one in which anyone can obtain the opportunity to participate in competition and even people who are unsuccessful can undertake this challenge again any number of times.*

> — Fujio Mitarai, chairman of Keidanren[137]


# Current Campaign Finance Issue

Whether foreign corporations such as Canon — for which Mitarai had been the chairman until May 25, 2006 — could make political donations was a major issue in Japan. There was a move toward legalization of political donation by foreign sources. The LDP planned to submit a bill containing amendments to the Political Donation Control Law to the future Diet session so that foreign-held Japanese companies would be allowed to make political contributions. The bill proposed that, as long as a Japanese company was listed on a Japanese stock exchange (i.e., Tokyo, Osaka or Nagoya), the company could make political contributions, regardless of its percentage of foreign-held shares.[138]

---

[136] Ibid.

[137] Mitarai, F. (May 10, 2006) Press Conference on May 9, 2006, http://japundit.com/archives/2006/03/10/2086/ (accessed April 28, 2008).

[138] *Nishinippon Newspaper*, February 15, 2006, "LDP wa Gaishi no Kenkin Kanwa Kentō, Seisakueno Kenen Hirogaru" (LDP Plans to Change Law to Enable Political Donations from Foreign Capital, Spread Concerns], p. 2, http://www.nishinippon.co.jp/news/wordbox/display/3617/ (accessed April 28, 2008); *Kochi Newspaper*, December 19, 2006, "Gaishi Kisei Kanwa, Uraganai to Ieruka?" (Foreign Capital Can Make Political Donations, What is the Real Intent?), p. 2, http://www.kochinews.co.jp/0612/061219editor.htm (accessed April 28, 2008).

## *Decision Time*

Due to the internationalization of the Japanese economy, it was likely that an increasing number of foreign companies would enter the Japanese market. However, foreign access to the Japanese market remained difficult. In particular, participating in large public-works bidding processes was very difficult for foreign firms (see **Exhibit 6** for major issues affecting foreign firms in Japan).

Behind the move toward legalization of political donations by foreign entities were the hopes of both the LDP, which sought to increase political donations,[139] and the foreign business establishment in Japan, which wanted a greater voice in Japanese national politics and also better market access.[140] However, critics were concerned that a political party might change its political stance and policies concerning the national interest after receiving political contributions from foreign-held companies.[141]

---

[139] *Nishinippon Newspaper*, May 15, 2006, "LDP wa Gaishi no Kenkin Kanwa Kentō, Seisakueno Kenen Hirogaru" (LDP Plans to Change Law to Enable Political Donations from Foreign Capital, Spread Concerns], p. 2, http://www.nishinippon.co.jp/news/wordbox/display/3617/ (accessed April 28, 2008).

[140] Behind the move toward legalization of political donations by foreign entities was Keidanren's intention to beef up its influence on the political scene through donations. When Mitarai was officially elected as the new chairman of Keidanren in January 2006, he stated: "Canon, whose foreign investors own more than 50% is prevented from legally making any political contributions under the current law" and "such a law logically contradicts the trend of the times." See *Yomiuri Shimbun*, November 8, 2005, "Mitarai is to Be the Next Chairman for Keidanren", http://www.yomiuri.co.jp/atmoney/mnews/20051108mh10.htm (accessed April 28, 2008).

[141] *Nishinippon Newspaper*, February 15, 2006, "LDP wa Gaishi no Kenkin Kanwa Kentō, Seisakueno Kenen Hirogaru" (LDP Plans to Change Law to Enable Political Donations from Foreign Capital, Spread Concerns), p. 2, http://www.nishinippon.co.jp/news/wordbox/display/3617/ (accessed April 28, 2008).

**Exhibit 6**   Foreign Corporations' Priority Issues in Japan

Keidanren recommends the following reforms to the business climate for the benefit of foreign companies, encouraging new entrants to the Japanese market.[142]

**1. Extensive Reform of the Foreign Access Zone System**

The July 1992 Law on Extraordinary Measures for the Promotion of Imports and Facilitation of Inward Investment allows for Foreign Access Zones (FAZs) to be established in Japan. As of now, however, the FAZ system only accommodates for the establishment of facilities related to import. Comprehensive incentives for import and investment companies are needed since the Law's intent is to promote imports and foreign direct investment in Japan.

**2. Taxation**

To boost foreign direct investment, it is necessary that Japan's high cost structure be reformed. The tax burden in Japan is greater than in many other countries, and should be reduced. It is of the utmost importance that there be a cut in the corporate tax rate, as well as that a consolidated tax return system be concurrently introduced.

**3. Treaties Covering Portable Pensions**

The double payment of premiums for public pension plans could be avoided through treaty agreements on pension payments. As of now, however, no such agreement has been reached. The Japanese Government should quickly reach portable pension agreements with major countries.

**4. Lifting the Ban Against Holding Companies**

In its Deregulation Action Plan, the Government lays out a 3-year period during which it will contemplate lifting the ban against holding companies. It would be best if this ban were to be lifted — doing so is in keeping with the legislation of other countries, would further corporate restructuring, along with persuading foreign companies to invest in Japan. In another area, a consolidated tax return system is vital.

**5. Unifying Registration Procedures for Businesses Participating in Government Procurement Plans**

The "Outline of External Economic Reform Measures," which was issued in March 1994, was one of several official statements that established plans to renovate the Japanese Government's procurement system. None of the statements in the measure

*(Continued)*

---

[142] Keidanren (June 12, 1995) "The Promotion of Foreign Direct Investment and Imports to Japan", http://www.keidanren.or.jp/english/policy/pol023.html.

**Exhibit 6**   (*Continued*)

alluded to reform of procedures requiring that businesses register at a number of different ministries and agencies. The Japanese Government should create a "one-stop shop" system, unifying its registration procedures for businesses participating in government procurement plans.

**6. Liberalization of the Private Employment Agency Sector, Permitting Paid Services**

Foreign companies investing in Japan have trouble attracting suitable personnel. If Japan's labor market continues to lacks fluidity, this situation will persist. The Government should create suitable conditions (e.g., the granting of permits) to make it possible for the private sector to run employment agencies; this could help settle Japan's employment problems and also help secure personnel for foreign companies.

**7. Relaxation of Regulations Controlling the Liquidity of Lease and Credit Loans**

Provisions of the Jurisdiction of the Business Asset Securitization Law monitor lease and credit loans. The Deregulation Action Plan details that, after required measures are drawn up during FY1995, there will be the establishment of a system providing for asset-backed securities to act as collateral for lease and credit loans. This measure should be implemented swiftly, in order to facilitate easy and effective access to capital.

Since May 2003, the following criticisms had made Keidanren's decisions to promote foreign corporate donations more difficult:

- The role Japanese politicians played in the decision-making process in Japanese administrations and politics was not easy for foreign companies to understand. Consequently, they did not understand how to effectively direct their political donations.[143]
- Japanese politicians focused on representing their constituencies and rarely established an international profile.[144]
- Aviation, oil and energy, and defense were key industries in which political donations were most numerous. These industries were either strongly regulated or were completely closed to foreign firms.[145]

---

[143] Ibid.

[144] Ibid.

[145] Ibid.

In May 2006, Mitarai, as the chairman of Keidanren, had to declare the organization's stance on foreign corporate donations. Careful consideration had to be given to various political, legal and economic factors surrounding this sensitive issue.

## For Further Discussion

1. Political donations are classified by donor into two groups: corporate donations and personal donations. Should they be treated differently? Should both types of contributions be prohibited?
2. There are differing views on what types of corporate donations to politicians and political parties are acceptable or even legal. What do you think of corporate political donations? Are they justified?
3. Some consider Japan's rules on corporate political donations, even with the proposed revision regarding foreign political contributions, to be restrictive in light of the internationalization of Japan's economy and politics. What is your opinion?

# 15

# Tokyo Disneyland (3): New Strategies Needed for Sluggish Demand

On May 9, 2005, Oriental Land Co. Ltd. (OL) announced changes in the company's top management: Toshio Kagami, President, would be Chairman and CEO and Yoshiro Fukushima, Senior Executive Management Director, would be the new president and COO. The company indicated that this organizational change was needed to strengthen the company's business management. OL, which was the operator for Tokyo Disneyland Park and Tokyo DisneySea Park, revealed the total combined attendance for both parks to be at 25.021 million guests, 98.2% of the previous year's attendance.[1] This was the fifth time in the past 20 years that the company had experienced a decline in visitors compared to the previous year (see **Exhibit 1**). The new executive management team immediately felt the heat as summer began.

## Possible Explanations for the Decline

The company's research department attributed the current decline in visitors to the following:[2]

*Since the previous fiscal year had the advantage of various events related to the Tokyo Disneyland 20th Anniversary celebration, a decrease in the combined attendance of the two parks for this fiscal year was expected. Furthermore, the record-breaking heat wave and the record number of*

---

[1] See the press interview with Yoshiro Fukushima, the new president of OL, *Nikkei* (*Japan Economic Journal*), November 27, 2005, p. 7.

[2] OLC's website, http://www.olc.co.jp/en/company/index.html.

*typhoons hitting the country during the summer season and more snowfall than the average year were additional contributing factors for the decrease in attendance this fiscal year.*

However, the newly appointed executive management was concerned that the decrease in attendance this time might be different from in

**Exhibit 1**    Increases in Visitor Attendance

### Attendence per fiscal year

| year | Attendance |
|------|------------|
| 1983 | 9,933,000[1] |
| 1984 | 10,013,000 |
| 1985 | 10,675,000 |
| 1986 | 10,665,000 |
| 1987 | 11,975,000 |
| 1988 | 13,382,000 |
| 1989 | 14,752,000 |
| 1990 | 15,876,000 |
| 1991 | 16,139,000 |
| 1992 | 15,815,000 |
| 1993 | 16,030,000 |
| 1994 | 15,509,000 |
| 1995 | 16,986,000 |
| 1996 | 17,368,000 |
| 1997 | 16,658,000 |
| 1998 | 17,459,000 |
| 1999 | 16,507,000 |
| 2000 | 17,300,000 |
| 2001 | 22,047,000[2,3] |
| 2002 | 24,820,000 |
| 2003 | 25,473,000 |
| 2004 | 25,021,000 |

Note: 1. From Appril 15, 1983.
2. Two parks conbined starting 2001.
3. September 4 to May 31, 2001 for Tokyo Disneey Sea.

(*Continued*)

**Exhibit 1**   (*Continued*)

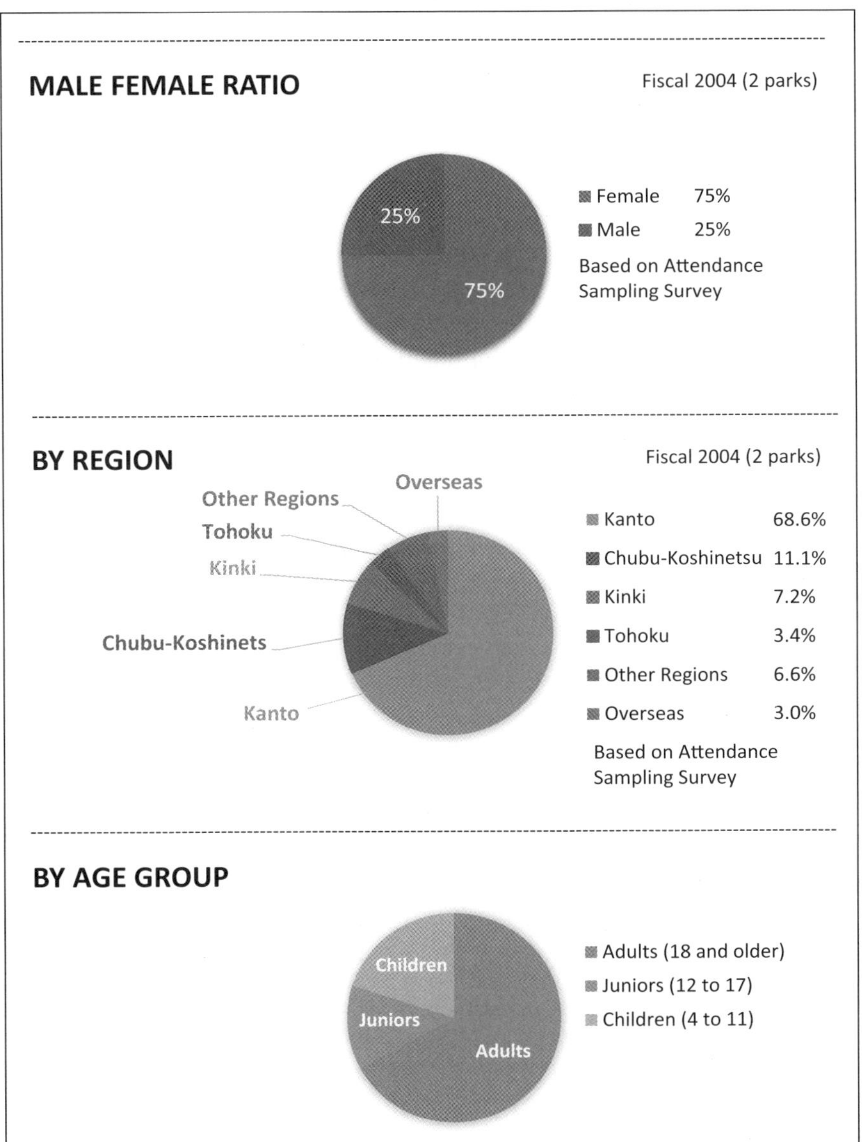


*Source*: OLC's website, http://www.olc.co.jp/en/company/guest/index.htm.

previous years. The highly successful theme park operator had regularly introduced new attractions to attract visitors. The income was used to develop new attractions and improve existing facilities. This formula, which had made Tokyo Disneyland an overwhelming success in Japan's theme park market, was beginning to see its limits. Secondly, the market was becoming saturated and the number of visitors would ultimately diminish. Of OL's customers, 90% were repeat visitors.[3] Would the customers come back for a fourth time after two or three visits? OL's management was concerned that customers would eventually get bored with the existing attractions and facilities, resulting in a decline in the number of visitors. Thirdly, Tokyo Disneyland had intense competition: domestically there was Universal Studios, Japan (USJ), and regionally there was Hong Kong Disneyland. The company's management was fully aware of the need to revamp the park's business operations.

Now at a turning point, management planned to make some fundamental changes in the company's policies on short- and long-term bases to fuel growth and enhance the company's earning capability[4] (see **Exhibits 2** and **3**).


## Tokyo Disney Resort[5]

Tokyo Disney Resort was an integrated entertainment destination that expanded the concept of a theme park to a theme resort. Located on some 200 hectares of land, Tokyo Disney Resort was Japan's first "theme resort" and encompassed a number of distinct facilities, each providing a unique brand of themed entertainment. Guests visiting the resort would enjoy a thrilling environment filled with high-quality amenities, hospitality and entertainment.

Before the establishment of Tokyo Disney Resort, there was Tokyo Disneyland Park, the first Disney Park to be built outside the United States. Opened in April 1983, Tokyo Disneyland brought the dreams and magic of Disney family entertainment to Japan.

---

[3] OL (2006) "Annual Report", http://www.olc.co.jp/en/.

[4] For details, see OL's press release dated October 3, 2005, http://www.olc.co.jp/news. cgi?home_f.

[5] Tokyo Disney Resort, http://www.olc.co.jp/en/company/resort/index.html.

**Exhibit 2**   OL's past financial data as of 2005

(¥ million)

| Year | No. of Visitors (thousands) | Sales Revenue | Operating Costs | Depreciation | Administrative Expenses | Interest Paid | Ordinary Income | Income Before Tax | Taxes (35%) | Income After Tax | New Investment | Fixed Assets | Total Assets |
|---|---|---|---|---|---|---|---|---|---|---|---|---|---|
| 2001 | 17,300 | 182,877 | 145,448 | 13,395 | 14,827 | 4,158 | 14,771 | 13,117 | 4,595 | 8,522 | 183,022 | 460,950 | 633,846 |
| 2002 | 22,047 | 250,246 | 204,697 | 29,550 | 15,485 | 4,610 | 23,292 | 21,475 | 9,017 | 12,458 | 346,317 | 616,396 | 683,396 |
| 2003 | 24,820 | 275,787 | 231,587 | 37,749 | 15,032 | 4,664 | 27,406 | 27,264 | 11,561 | 15,703 | 11,181 | 585,477 | 675,785 |
| 2004 | 25,473 | 276,898 | 233,893 | 36,790 | 13,812 | 4,090 | 29,680 | 28,765 | 10,729 | 18,036 | 25,324 | 573,451 | 645,578 |
| 2005 | 25,021 | 271,435 | 230,215 | 36,904 | 13,921 | 3,821 | 30,780 | 29,707 | 9,896 | 19,811 | 42,698 | 573,224 | 654,511 |

*Note*: Each year ends at the end of March.

*Source*: Yukashoken Houkokusho (Annual Reports), Oriental Land Corp. 1996–2001, http://www.olc.co.jp/en/ir/ir.html.

**Exhibit 3**  OL's financial performance

| Year Ended | 03/2000 | 03/2001 | 03/2002 | 03/2003 | 03/2004 | 03/2005 |
|---|---|---|---|---|---|---|
| Return on Equity (%) | 3.1 | 1.5 | 3.8 | 5.5 | 5.1 | 4.5 |
| Return on Assets (%) | 1.9 | 0.8 | 1.9 | 2.7 | 2.8 | 2.6 |
| Operating Margin (%) | 14.6 | 11.1 | 12.0 | 11.5 | 11.5 | 10.4 |
| Ordinary Margin (%) | 10.8 | 6.0 | 8.5 | 10.2 | 10.2 | 9.3 |
| Return on Sales (%) | 5.7 | 2.4 | 4.5 | 5.7 | 5.5 | 5.2 |
| Price Earnings Ratio (Times) | 113.34 | 165.81 | 64.83 | 29.27 | 40.17 | 40.89 |
| Net Income per Share (Yen) | 98.99 | 47.34 | 127.11 | 188.24 | 184.23 | 171.19 |
| Stockholders' Equity per Share (Yen) | 3,237.83 | 3,272.28 | 3,381.21 | 3,543.92 | 3,732.22 | 3,890.51 |
| Dividends per Share (Yen) | 14.00 | 14.00 | 19.00 | 24.00 | 29.00 | 35.00 |

*Source*: OLC's website, http://www.olc.co.jp/en/ir/ir.html.

Just outside JR East[6] Maihama Station was Ikspiari, which opened on July 7, 2000. Featuring nine unique themed zones of shopping, dining and entertainment, including some 130 shops and restaurants, Ikspiari was also the location of AMC Ikspiari 16, a state-of-the-art cinema complex with 16 screens, and Camp Nepos, a children's play and care center specially designed to stimulate creativity.

Disney Ambassador Hotel, the first Disney-branded hotel in Japan, also opened on July 7, 2000. This elegantly designed resort hotel featured 1930s American art deco design and special Disney-themed amenities. Guests were greeted by Disney characters while they dined. Couples planning to get married could host ceremonies in the hotel's Rose Chapel as part of Disney's Fairy Tale Weddings package.

Tokyo DisneySea Park and the in-park Tokyo DisneySea Hotel MiraCosta were opened on September 4, 2001. Tokyo DisneySea was comprised of seven themed ports. The luxurious Tokyo DisneySea Hotel

---

[6] "JR East" stood for East Japan Railway Company. This was the largest passenger railway company in the world and one of the seven Japan Railways Group companies. The company name was officially abbreviated as "JR East" in English. For details, see http://www.jreast.co.jp/e/investor/factsheet/index.html.

MiraCosta offered accommodations with impressive views of the park's major waterway and Tokyo Bay.

The Disney Resort Line monorail system began operations on July 27, 2001. The system connected the various resort facilities, providing guests with a convenient means of transportation around the resort.


## A Brief History of Oriental Land[7]

OL was founded in July 1960 with the aim of reclaiming land on Chiba Prefecture's Urayasu coast and developing leisure facilities that would contribute to the cultural life of the nation and the welfare of the citizens. In April 1983, OL opened Tokyo Disneyland in Maihama, in Urayasu City, Chiba Prefecture, a mere 10 kilometers east of central Tokyo. Initial investment was ¥180 billion.[8] Over the next two decades after its opening, Tokyo Disneyland had contributed significantly to the expansion of Japan's amusement and leisure park industry while enabling OL to leverage its competitive advantages and establish a solid market position in the Japanese theme park industry. In September 2001, OL opened its second theme park, Tokyo DisneySea, together with new Disney hotels and a commercial complex, linked by the new Disney monorail. Soon the Maihama area evolved into the Tokyo Disney Resort (see **Exhibits 4** and **5**). While OL worked to further develop Tokyo Disney Resort, new business areas outside the Maihama area were under consideration for further development, with a special emphasis on businesses that "Power Your Heart with Happiness".

*Our corporate mission is to "provide enjoyment and create magic, inspired by imagination and a sense of adventure, and guided by a desire to fulfill dreams." This mission is intended to offer today's individuals the dreams that may be dwelling at the bottom of their hearts, refreshing impressions, and enjoyment and real peace of mind that rejuvenate people.[9]*

---

[7] Business Growth, http://olc.netir-wsp.com/BusinessGrowthU,locale,en_US.html.

[8] US$1 = ¥232.90 in 1983.

[9] OLC's website, http://www.olc.co.jp/en/ir/ir.html.

**Exhibit 4**   About OL

| Date of Establishment | July 11, 1960 |
|---|---|
| Capital | 63,201,127,000 (yen) |
| Representative | Chairman and CEO Toshio Kagami<br>President and COO Yoshiro Fukushima |
| Major Shareholders | Keisei Electric Railway Co. Ltd.<br>Mitsui Fudosan Co. Ltd.<br>Chiba Prefecture<br>The Master Trust Bank of Japan (Trust Account)<br>Mizuho Trust and Banking Co. Ltd. (Employee Retirement Benefit Trust, of Keisei Electric Railway Co. Ltd.)<br>Japan Trustee Service Bank, Ltd. (Trust Accounts)<br>State Street Bank and Trust Company<br>Keisei Kaihatsu Co. Ltd.<br>The Dai-ichi Mutual Life Insurance Company<br>Trust & Custody Services Bank, Ltd. (Mizuho Corporate Bank, Limited Retirement Benefit Trust Account re-entrusted by Mizuho Trust and Banking Co. Ltd.)<br><br>(as of March 31, 2005) |
| Board of Directors | 13 members (as of June 29, 2005) |
| Number of Employees | Regular employees 2,179 (as of April 1, 2005)<br>Part-time employees 17,390 (as of April 1, 2005) |
| Corporate Headquarters | 1-1 Maihama, Urayasu-shi, Chiba-ken, 279-8511 Japan |
| Nature of Operations | Operation and management of theme parks, land development, etc. |
| Subsidiary | Maihama Corporation Co. Ltd.<br>Maihama Resort Hotels Co. Ltd.<br>Maihama Resort Line Co. Ltd.<br>Green And Arts Co. Ltd.<br>Photoworks Co. Ltd.<br>Design Factory Co. Ltd.<br>Bay Food Service Co. Ltd.<br>Maihama Business Service Co. Ltd.<br>Ikspiari Co. Ltd.<br>Resort Cleaning Service Co. Ltd.<br>Maihama Building Maintenance Co. Ltd.<br>OLC Kitchen Techno Co. Ltd.<br>Retail Networks Co. Ltd.<br>E Production Co. Ltd.<br>OLC/Rights Entertainment Inc.<br>(The above 15 subsidiaries are wholly owned by Oriental Land Co. Ltd.)<br>RC Japan Co. Ltd. |

**Exhibit 5**   Chronology of OL

| July 1960 | Oriental Land Co. Ltd., was established with the aim of reclaiming land off the coast of Urayasu, developing commercial and residential land and constructing a major leisure facility, thereby contributing to the cultural life of the nation and the welfare of its citizens. (Capital: 250 million yen) |
|---|---|
| July 1962 | Oriental Land and Chiba Prefecture concluded the Urayasu District Land Reclamation Agreement, permitting Oriental Land to reclaim land off the coast of Urayasu and purchase the land for development. |
| September 1964 | Reclamation work began off the coast of Urayasu. |
| March 1970 | Chiba Prefecture began dividing reclaimed land into lots for sale to Oriental Land for construction of leisure facilities and houses. |
| December 1972 | Oriental Land began sales of the residential section of the reclaimed land purchased from Chiba Prefecture. |
| November 1975 | Reclamation work was completed. |
| April 1979 | Oriental Land and Walt Disney Productions (currently Disney Enterprises, Inc.) concluded an agreement concerning the licensing, design, construction and operation of Tokyo Disneyland park. |
| December 1980 | Construction of Tokyo Disneyland park began in the Maihama district of the town of Urayasu (now the city of Urayasu). |
| April 1983 | Tokyo Disneyland opened. |
| April 1996 | Oriental Land and Disney Enterprises concluded an agreement concerning the licensing, design, construction and operation of a new Disney theme park, Tokyo DisneySea, and the Tokyo DisneySea Hotel (now Tokyo DisneySea Hotel MiraCosta). |
| June 1996 | Wholly owned subsidiary Maihama Resort Hotels Co. Ltd. was established for management and operation of hotels. |
| December 1996 | Oriental Land listed its shares on the First Section of the Tokyo Stock Exchange. |
| April 1997 | Wholly owned subsidiary Maihama Resort Line Co. Ltd. was established for management and operation of a monorail. |

*(Continued)*

**Exhibit 5**   (*Continued*)

| | |
|---|---|
| August 1998 | Construction of Maihama Station Area Development Project (IKSPIARI and Disney Ambassador Hotel) began in Maihama. |
| September 1998 | Oriental Land and Disney Enterprises, Inc., concluded an agreement concerning the licensing, construction and operation of Disney Ambassador Hotel. |
| October 1998 | Oriental Land and Disney Enterprises, Inc., concluded an agreement concerning the licensing, design, construction and operation of Disney Resort Line. Maihama Resort Line began construction of Disney Resort Line in Maihama. Construction of Tokyo DisneySea and Tokyo DisneySea Hotel MiraCosta began in Maihama. |
| February 1999 | Wholly owned subsidiary Maihama Business Services Co. Ltd. was established. |
| October 1999 | Consolidated subsidiary RC Japan Co. Ltd. was established for management and operation of themed restaurants. |
| July 2000 | Ikspiari and Disney Ambassador Hotel opened. |
| October 2000 | Wholly owned subsidiary Resort Cleaning Services Co. Ltd. was established for cleaning services. |
| June 2001 | Wholly owned subsidiary Maihama Building Maintenance Co. Ltd. was established for building maintenance service and OLC Kitchen Techno Co. Ltd. was established for sales and maintenance of kitchen units. |
| July 2001 | Disney Resort Line opened. |
| September 2001 | Tokyo DisneySea and Tokyo DisneySea Hotel MiraCosta opened. |
| April 2002 | OLC acquired all issued shares of wholly owned WDIJ subsidiary Retail Networks Co. Ltd., and started operation of The Disney Store shops in Japan. |
| December 2002 | Wholly owned subsidiary E Production Co. Ltd. was established for management of entertainers. |
| May 2003 | Wholly owned subsidiary OLC/Rights Entertainment Inc. was established for management of copyrights. |
| July 2005 | Wholly owned subsidiary M TECH Co. Ltd. was established for maintenance of theme park attractions, including ride vehicles and other attraction components. |

*Source*: OLC's website, http://www.olc.co.jp/en/company/history/index.html.

**Exhibit 6**  The OL Group Continues to Grow.

*Source*: OLC's website, http://www.olc.co.jp/en/company/guest/index.html.

By November 2002, cumulative attendance at the two parks had topped 300 million. Based on the strong brand power of Tokyo Disney Resort, OL had created a business model that maximized synergy to generate robust growth throughout the OL Group (see **Exhibit 6**).

In addition to its initial investment in Tokyo Disneyland, OL had invested approximately ¥500 billion in Tokyo Disney Resort. Investments at Tokyo Disneyland would focus on replacing and enhancing existing attractions, while those at Tokyo DisneySea would seek to make use of available space to build new attractions, thereby increasing both the appeal and the capacity of the park. OL also had ample space to develop parking lots and real estate holdings in the Maihama area so that the company might continue to invest in the development of new facilities to ensure growth going forward.

As part of its corporate growth strategy, OL was also broadening its operations outside of the Maihama area. In April 2002, the company acquired Retail Networks Co. Ltd., and assumed operation and management of Disney Stores throughout Japan. New original merchandise from the Disney/Pixar film *The Incredibles*, in addition to the Disney Pals figurine series featuring uniquely shaped Disney characters, were sold at the stores. Under OL's new store management, it strategically opened three new stores and closed one existing store. Existing stores were revitalized through renewing store designs and concepts. In July 2005, Disney Mall, Disney's official Internet shopping site, started selling Disney merchandise online.

OL entered into the intellectual property business by establishing OLC/Rights Entertainment Inc. In May 2003, the company presented the OL Group's original Nepos Napos characters and characters bought from overseas. While increasing the recognition of these characters, OLC/Rights Entertainment secured new licensees to further develop this business through television programmes and other channels.

To lay the foundation for new businesses, in December 2003 the company built an alliance with Japan Post.[10] In accordance with the Central Government Reform, Japan Post was established on April 1, 2003, with the objective of comprehensively and efficiently carrying out a range of business activities, including Postal Service, Postal Savings, Money Order, Giro and Postal Life Insurance Services, provided through the nationwide post office network of approximately 24,700 post offices.[11]

OL's accommodations-only hotel, opened in the spring of 2005 in the Shin-Urayasu area near Maihama, would be called the Palm & Fountain Terrace Hotel. This hotel would consist of two buildings: Palm Terrace Hotel, which would be lined with palm trees, and Fountain Terrace Hotel, which would feature a courtyard fountain. As a hotel designed for overnight accommodation for families, it would offer four beds per room with reasonable rates.

At Tokyo Disneyland and Tokyo DisneySea, OL continued to create a series of new, large-scale attractions and entertainment. During the fiscal year ending in March 2005, the new Buzz Lightyear Astro Blasters attraction was opened at Tokyo Disneyland on April 15, 2004, and the new night-time entertainment BraviSEAmo!, with a theme of fire and water,

---

[10] See OL's press release dated December 3, 2003, http://www.japanpost.jp/pressrelease/japanese/sonota/031203j901.html.

[11] See the website of Japan Post, http://www.japanpost.jp/top/profile/english/2.html.

was introduced at Tokyo DisneySea on July 17, 2004. Tokyo DisneySea planned to open major new attractions in two consecutive years: a roller coaster-type attraction on July 21, 2005, and the Tower of Terror attraction in the fiscal year ending in March 2007.

In the years ahead, OL would continue to develop and expand its business in line with its corporate philosophy:

*Inspired by imagination and a sense of adventure, and guided by a desire to fulfill dreams, provide enjoyment and create magic.*[12]

## Emergence of a Competitor: Hong Kong Disneyland

In October 2005, the 310-acre Hong Kong Disneyland opened to high hopes. The park was intended to polish Hong Kong's image, draw tourists from mainland China and boost the local economy. The park was built on land reclaimed from the harbor on the sparsely developed Lantau Island, near Hong Kong's seven-year-old airport. It was the smallest of Disney's five locations around the globe.

As Hong Kong struggled to recover from the Asian financial crisis of the late 1990s, the government agreed in 1999 to invest US$2.9 billion (including infrastructure improvements and loans) and took a 57% stake in the project; Disney owned 43%. The government estimated that the construction of the theme park created 30,000 jobs and the park would draw 5.6 million visitors in 2005 and add US$19 billion to the territory's economic growth over the next four decades.[13]

Added to the various challenges to the top management of OL, the emergence of the new competitor in the Asian market was one of the reasons that they thought the sluggishness of visitor numbers to Tokyo Disneyland might not be temporary but structural.[14] OL was no longer the

---

[12] OLC's website, http://www.olc.co.jp/en/company/index.html.

[13] Wiseman, P. (November 9, 2005) "Miscues Mar Opening of Hong Kong Disney", *USA Today*, http://www.usatoday.com/money/companies/2005-11-09-hong-kong-disney-usat_x.htm?

[14] See the press interview with Yoshiro Fukushima, the new president of OL, *Nikkei* (*Japan Economic Journal*), November 27, 2005, p. 7.

only company selling these services to a closed market. OL had been enjoying receiving many visitors from overseas, especially from Asia. In 2004, 3% of all visitors were from overseas, which, as the top management of OL was worried about, could have been very much affected downward by the opening of Hong Kong Disneyland (see **Exhibit 1**).

## New Pricing Policy

Due to factors such as slackening consumer spending and demographic changes, OL's top management believed that a study was needed to determine whether OL could diversify its income sources. OL's management was quite confident that OL had a potential capability to draw 26 million visitors (it drew 25 million in 2004).[15] The question was how to get more visitors. They specifically wanted to know whether the then current pricing policy was effective or not and how changes in pricing to visitors, if necessary, would affect the company's revenue in the future.

OL's top management asked the planning department to study the following scenarios:

- Case 1: If the company raised admission prices by 5% in 2006, the number of visitors would decrease by 1% a year for five years.
- Case 2: If the company lowered admission prices by 5% in 2006, the number of visitors would increase by 1% a year for five years.

The price elasticity of demand by the visitors to the company's services was fundamental to the new pricing strategy. OL's top management asked the planning department to use net present value (NPV) methods (see **Exhibit 7**) to evaluate the two alternatives for a duration of five years. Moreover, these evaluations would incorporate the company's established long-term strategies, which would use the borrowed funds of ¥31 billion for investments in 2006 (see **Exhibit 8** for other specific instructions given by the top management to the planning department for these evaluations). The planning department was able to project financial data for 2006–2010 based on data from 2000–2005 (see **Exhibit 2**).

---

[15] Ibid.

**Exhibit 7**    Formulas for NPV and IRR

NPV was defined as follows:

$$NPV = -C_0 + \sum_{t=1}^{T} \frac{CF_t(1-\tau)}{(1+\bar{r})^t}$$

$C_0$ = initial investment
$CF_t$ = expected before-tax cash flow in year $t$
$\tau$ = tax rate
$\bar{r}$ = weighted average cost of capital
T = life of the project

The internal rate of return was defined as the value of IRR in the following equation:

$$C_0 = \sum_{t=1}^{T} \frac{CF_t(1-\tau)}{(1+IRR)^t}$$

**Exhibit 8**    Bases and Assumptions for Projection of OL's Financial Data

1. The average admission fee per person was ¥10,848 in 2005.
2. Suppose a capital investment for long-term strategies of ¥31.0 billion will be made in 2006. The borrowings for ¥31.0 billion above were made in 2005. For those borrowings, the long the interest rate was 3% p.a., which is to be paid each year. With regard to their long-term targets, top management expects revenues of ¥296 billion and ordinary income of ¥33.9 billion by the fiscal year ending March 31, 2010.
3. Operating costs other than depreciation (71.2% of the sales, 2005 data), and administrative expenses (5.1% of the sales, 2005 data), would increase proportionately with the increase in sales.
4. Assume depreciation of ¥36.904 billion for the existing fixed assets will continue. Use the straight-line method over 20 years for the new investment of ¥31.0 billion in 2006.
5. The Japanese rate of taxation is 35%.
6. Assume the cash flows generated from OL use a discount rate of 8% (a weighted average cost of capital of 4% + the hurdle rate of 4%).

## Decision Time

The planning department finally presented the results of the study to OL's top management, after carefully examining all the relevant data and analyses. The department calculated the NPV for three potential plans:

- Base case: If the company did not raise admission prices for five years from 2006, the number of visitors would decrease by 1% a year for five years.
- Case 1: If the company raised admission prices by 5% in 2006, the number of visitors would decrease by 1% a year for five years.
- Case 2: If the company lowered admission prices by 5% in 2006, the number of visitors would increase by 1% a year for five years.

OL tried to make the most viable strategic decision on how to best cope with the new structural problems. To address the issues more articulately, the top management asked the planning department to conduct a sensitivity analysis for the following Cases 3 and 4, based on different projections of growth and decline in numbers of visitors, price increase and decrease, cost structures, profitability ratios, and interest rate levels:

- Case 3: If the company raised admission prices by 5% in 2006 and additionally it raised prices to visitors by 2% a year for 2007–2010 to cope with inflation, the number of visitors would increase by 1% a year for five years.
- Case 4: If the company lowered admission prices by 5% in 2006 and additionally it raised prices to visitors by 2% a year for 2007–2010 to cope with inflation, the number of visitors would increase by 1% a year for five years.

The results of the planning department's NPV study of the five cases were presented to the board (see **Exhibit 9**). The key points to consider were:

1. The target of at least a 1% increase of visitors per year would need to be maintained in the coming future.

**Exhibit 9**   NPV Analysis — Annual Cash Flow

The results of the initial analysis were as follows:

Unit: ¥1 million

|  | **Base Case** | **Case 1** | **Case 2** |
|---|---|---|---|
| 2006 | 57,550 | 57,921 | 56,383 |
| 2007 | 59,500 | 59,268 | 58,112 |
| 2008 | 61,452 | 60,622 | 59,850 |
| 2009 | 63,413 | 62,032 | 61,538 |
| 2010 | 65,316 | 63,320 | 63,328 |
| NPV at 8% | 244,144.70 | 241,257.77 | 237,871.25 |

The results of the sensitivity analysis were as follows:

Unit: ¥1 million

|  | **Base Case** | **Case 3** | **Case 4** |
|---|---|---|---|
| 2006 | 57,550 | 58,310 | 56,740 |
| 2007 | 59,500 | 59,654 | 58,290 |
| 2008 | 61,452 | 60,941 | 60,024 |
| 2009 | 63,413 | 62,411 | 61,902 |
| 2010 | 65,316 | 63,693 | 63,701 |
| NPV at 10% | 231,259.56 | 230,271.69 | 226,685.50 |

2.  The reasons for the decline of visitors in amusement parks and leisure attractions in Japan were:

    (1) Decline in customer interest as the various establishments began offering similar services and activities.
    (2) A prolonged recession and growing inflation.

3.  The total number of visitors may have declined if no action was taken.
4.  Senior executives of OL were wary of the risks in raising prices when the general economy was not good.
5.  Reduction in prices to entice customers was difficult from the company's perspective because of the high initial and maintenance investment.

## Implementation of the New Pricing Policy

The board members had differing opinions. Some said that raising prices was risky when the demand was sluggish. Some said that raising prices was necessary and lowering prices was not realistic to recover the high initial and maintenance investment to maintain the then current number of visitors. OL's objective was to overcome sluggish demand while maintaining its status as the leader of the leisure industry in Asia.

The final decision of the board was to undertake Case 1; the company raised admission prices by 5% in 2006 and the company took the risk of a decrease of the number of visitors by 1% a year for five years. The board expected that the decrease of the number of visitors by 1% a year for five years might not happen if the domestic strong competitor, USJ, followed suit to raise prices. In that case, the top management of OL was confident that the number of visitors would not decrease even with the price hike.

On May 9, 2006, the ticket price hike was announced by OL.[16] The ticket prices at Tokyo Disneyland Park and Tokyo DisneySea went up as of September 1, 2006. This was the first ticket price change since September 2000. The price for a One Day Passport for an adult for all facilities went up from ¥5,500 to ¥5,800 (a 5.45% increase). The price of a One Day Ticket for young adults (middle school and high school students) went up from ¥4,800 to ¥5,000 (a 4.17% increase). The price of a One Day Ticket for small children (4–11 years old) went up from ¥3,700 to ¥3,900 (a 5.40% increase). Two Day Tickets for all classes increased by ¥200. The prices of the annual passport and group discount tickets were also raised. The reason given for increasing the prices was that the value of the theme park as a whole had risen due to introductions of several new attractions. The price increases were about 5% on average.

---

[16] *Nikkei* (*Japan Economic Journal*), May 9, 2006, http://www.nikkei.co.jp/news/main/20060509AT2F0903609052006.html.

On June 23, 2006, the theme park USJ, OL's competitor in Japan, raised its ticket prices as of July 20, 2006.[17] The price of a Studio Pass (One Day Ticket), which was good for any facilities for a full day, would go up ¥100–300. This was the first ticket price increase since the theme park opened in 2001. The price of a Studio Pass for children would go from ¥3,700 to ¥3,900 (a 5.4% increase), while the price of the same pass for adults would go from ¥5,500 to ¥5,800 (a 5.5% increase). The price of a Two Day Studio Pass and the group discount ticket price increased by ¥130 and ¥500 respectively. The price increases were about 5% on average, which was about the same as at Tokyo Disneyland. USJ's president, Mr. Gumpel, explained the price hike by saying that "the price hike was needed to improve the attractiveness of the theme park by introducing new attractions".

## Conclusion

OL's decision to raise prices by 5% in 2006 was a great success. The number of visitors did not decrease by 1% as the analysis assumed (see **Exhibit 10**). Rather, the number increased 0.72% on average for five years from 2006 to 2010, although it decreased by 1.6% in 2006, by 1.5% in 2008 and by 5.2% in 2010. With the 5% price increase in 2006, sales increased 2.62% on average for five years from 2006 to 2010, although it decreased by 0.3% in 2008 and by 4.1% in 2010.

The cash flow of ¥56.7 billion in 2005 increased to the level of ¥62.0 billion in 2010. This success could be attributed to the following reasons:

1. The domestic strong competitor, USJ, followed suit with a 5% price increase, and Tokyo Disneyland did not lose any competitive edge.
2. New attractions drew visitors from all over the world to visit Tokyo Disneyland. The hotels nearby, directly run by OL, factored in additional contributions to revenues. The concern that repeat visitors might not return was unnecessary, and they came back even for a fourth time.

---

[17] *Nikkei (Japan Economic Journal)*, May 23, 2006, http://www.nikkei.co.jp/news/sangyo/20060523AT1D2307923052006.html.

**Exhibit 10**   OL's Past Financial Data After 2005

Unit: ¥1 million

| | No. of Visitors (1000) | Sales | Income After Tax | Depreciation | Cash Flow |
|---|---|---|---|---|---|
| 2005 | 25,021 | 271,435 | 19,811 | 36,904 | 56,715 |
| 2006 | 24,766 (−1.0%) | 272,039 (+0.2%) | 16,680 | 36,697 | 53,377 |
| 2007 | 25,816 (+4.2%) | 284,528 (+4.6%) | 14,790 | 37,112 | 51,902 |
| 2008 | 25,424 (−1.5%) | 282,525 (−0.3%) | 12,187 | 37,864 | 50,051 |
| 2009 | 27,211 (+7.1%) | 318,467 (+12.7) | 12,629 | 43,016 | 55,645 |
| 2010 | 25,818 (−5.2%) | 305,425 (−4.1%) | 21,931 | 40,049 | 61,980 |
| Average | +0.72% | +2.62% | | | |

*Notes*: (1)  Each year ends at the end of March.
(2)  Cash Flow = Income after Tax + Depreciation.

3.  The management noticed that for Tokyo Disneyland, price elasticity of demand was relatively "inelastic".[18] This meant that the numbers of visitors were unresponsive to price changes for this period.[19]

---

[18] The concept of *price elasticity of demand* was useful when determining the price change. The own-price elasticity of demand for any product was the percentage change in quantity of the product demanded as a result of the percentage change in the product's own price:

$$\text{Price elasticity of demand} = e_p = \frac{\%\Delta Q_d}{\%\Delta P}$$

where $Q_d$ was quantity demanded and P was product price. If the absolute value of $e_p$ was less than 1.0, the good was relatively "inelastic", and greater than 1.0 indicated a relatively "elastic" good.

[19] For the five years of 2006–2010, the number of visitors increased 0.36% vs. the price increase of 5%. This meant that the numbers of visitors was unresponsive to price changes for this period. Considering this 0.36% was almost equal to 0%, the price elasticity of demand for this case was zero and very "inelastic".

Except in the year 2010, profits were relatively low as a result of heavy depreciation resulting from the initial and maintenance investments, although cost control measures like curbing personnel costs were showing results. At the same time, cash flow (depreciation plus profit) each year after 2006 increased due to high depreciation figures.

## For Further Discussion

1. Prepare OL's *pro forma* future financial data for the new project for the year, 2006–2010. The format for the past data of the company is shown in **Exhibit 5**. Use the assumptions given in **Exhibit 7** of the case.
2. Prepare the Case 1 projections of the net present value of the future cash flows for the 5 years form 2006–2010, based upon certain assumptions in **Exhibit 7**. Prepare the Case 2 projections of the net present value of the future cash flows for the 5 years from 2006–2010, based upon certain assumptions in **Exhibit 7**.
3. Evaluate the results of the projections of the net present values of the future cash flows. Do you recommend the short-term pricing strategies to increase or decrease the current price for the visitors?
4. Conduct sensitivity analysis under a variety of assumptions. The planning department assumed that the inflation rate for Japan would be zero and the weighted average cost of capital for OL was 8% for the 5 years to come. What if these assumptions are changed?
5. In what ways do you think Tokyo Disneyland can sustain growth from here in the future? How do you evaluate OL's strategic alliance with the Japan Post?

# 16

# Licensing Arrangement or Joint Venture (4): An *Ex Post* Case Study of Tokyo Disneyland

When a multinational enterprise (MNE) is expanding its business with a local company in a foreign country, how does it decide whether to select a licensing arrangement or a joint venture? Which of these choices would give it the most benefits?

For Tokyo Disneyland, there were severe conflicts as to the possible form of cooperation between the two partners at the offset; the Oriental Land Corp. (OL) (see **Exhibit 1**) of Japan and Walt Disney (WD) of the United States. OL preferred a joint venture mode,[1] and WD preferred a licensing arrangement. With both companies holding on to their own agendas, it was a tough job for both sides to resolve the differences and clear the obstacles in order to arrive at a mutually beneficial agreement. After lengthy and difficult negotiations, a licensing mode was selected.

OL and WD finally came to an agreement on April 30, 1979.[2] Although the partnership between OL and WD was a prominent success story of foreign investments in Japan by a US company, the partnership floundered as differences in management philosophies and decision-making techniques created tensions, resulting in mixed feelings towards the project.

---

[1] See, Takahashi, M. (July 17, 1999), an excerpt from "Watashi no Rirekisho (My Personal History)" series, *Nikkei* (*Japan Economic Journal*), 16, p. 40. Takahashi was OL's second president. Also see, Arima, T. (July 1, 2001) "Disneyland Story", *Nikkei Business Bunko*, pp. 137–138.

[2] For details, see Takahashi, M. (July 26, 1999), an excerpt from "Watashi no Rirekisho (My Personal History)" series, *Nikkei* (*Japan Economic Journal*), 25, p. 40.

**Exhibit 1**  Basic Oriental Land Data (as of March 31, 2010)

| Name | Oriental Land Co. Ltd. |
|---|---|
| Date of Establishment | July 11, 1960 |
| Paid-in Capital | ¥63,201 million |
| Sales | ¥389,242 million |
| Net Income | ¥18,089 million |
| President | Kyoichiro Uenishi |
| Employees | 2,196 |
| Address | 1-1, Maihama, Urayasushi, Chiba-ken, Japan |
| Main Banks | Mizuho Corporate Bank (Industrial Bank of Japan) |
|  | Chuo Mitsui Trust (Mitsui Trust Bank) |
| Major Shareholders | Keisei Electric Railway Corp. 19.08% |
|  | Mitsui Real Estate Corp. 15.95% |
| Tie-up Company | Disney Enterprises Inc. (US) |

*Source*: Yukashoken Houkokusho (Annual Reports), Oriental Land Corp. 2010.
See also www.olc.co.jp/en/company/profile/index.html (accessed October 30, 2010).

# Negotiations of Tokyo Disneyland

The negotiations to bring Disneyland to Japan, which started in December 1974, took four years and five months to complete. Initially, OL's parent company Mitsui Real Estate Corp. and other stakeholders objected to the terms and conditions. They strongly resisted WD's traditional licensing fee format, thinking that it was unfair to pay royalties each year while WD took no risks and used the land for free. As the two sides came to see each other as indispensable partners, hard-edged negotiations softened to more agreeable discussions. OL relied on WD's brand name and its marketability. WD relied on OL's resources as the risk absorber. OL and WD finally came to an agreement on April 30, 1979.[3] According to the agreement, OL would pay a license fee equivalent to 10% of the gate receipts and 5% of other sales (averaged to about 7% of the total annual revenue).[4]

---

[3] Ibid.

[4] WD originally demanded a 10% license fee, to which OL's parent company Mitsui Real Estate Corp. strongly objected. OL's management group asked WD to lower the royalty to 5% in accordance with the intention of Mr. Tsuboi (president of Mitsui Real Estate Corp), which infuriated WD and caused mistrust. For details, see Takahashi, M. (July 17, 1999), an excerpt from "Watashi no Rirekisho (My Personal History)" series, *Nikkei* (*Japan Economic Journal*), 16, p. 40. For the details of the royalty, see Arima, T. (July 1, 2001) "Disneyland Story", *Nikkei Business Bunko*, pp. 136–141.

## *WD's Position*

Although WD favored Urayasu as a Disneyland location, its offer in 1979 was simply to provide know-how without shouldering any risk.[5] WD was not willing to pay anything for the construction of the park, yet it sought 10% royalties on both admission fees and food and beverage sales.[6] OL balked at this proposal. Its board of directors commented, "We have never seen such a lopsided contract condition and high royalty."[7]

At the time of the negotiations, WD's financial position was weak.[8] Disneyland and Walt Disney World were attracting only 10 million people each year, and WD could not raise entrance fees to increase income. Additionally, the movie and television production division was floundering. Under these conditions, generating a new revenue source with minimal involvement was an attractive option for WD. Should it find a Japanese partner capable of building a Disneyland park to its stringent quality standards, WD would eagerly close the deal.[9]

## The Positions of Stakeholders of OL

### *Mitsui Real Estate Group as the Major Shareholder*

The Mitsui Real Estate Group (MREG), OL's parent company, owned 48% of OL's shares. Since the initial negotiations started in 1974, MREG had been very critical of all the deals with WD. The first issue was the period of the contract. During a meeting between the WD and Japanese parties (OL, MREG and other related parties) in November 1978, Hajime Tsuboi, MREG's president, objected to the contract that WD offered.[10] He said:

*While it is such a violently moving time that we have no way of knowing what is going to happen 10 years ahead, how come we can have a contract*

---

[5] Ibid.

[6] Ibid.

[7] Ibid.

[8] See Arima, T. (July 1, 2001) "Disneyland Story", *Nikkei Business Bunko*, pp. 146–147.

[9] Ibid.

[10] Finally they agreed on 20 years as the basic term with five extensions of five years. For details, see Takahashi, M. (July 26, 1999), an excerpt from "Watashi no Rirekisho (My Personal History)" series, *Nikkei (Japan Economic Journal)*, 25, p. 40.

*for as long as 50 years. Doing so makes it something similar to the US-Japan Trade Agreement of the Edo Period [some 100 years ago]. We will never be able to accept such a servile agreement.*[11]

— Hajime Tsuboi, president of Mitsui Real Estate Corp.

The second problem involved license fees. WD originally demanded 10% license fees, to which MREG strongly objected.

*Disneyland is a remnant of the previous century. The Japanese would soon be bored of it. There is no way to be profitable if we paid 10% royalty to the US side.*

— Hajime Tsuboi, president of Mitsui Real Estate Corp.[12]

WD was infuriated when OL's management requested 5% royalty fees, in accordance with Hajime Tsuboi's position. WD's fury in turn caused the Japanese parties to mistrust WD.[13]

The third issue was risk sharing. From the start of the project in 1978, MREG had agreed to guarantee project borrowing for up to 48% of its investment, but not higher. The remaining balance would have to be borne by WD. Hajime Tsuboi had the following to say about this issue:

*The matter is decided by our board meeting, [it is] not my personal decision. This is such a humiliating contract and we, as a company of the proud Mitsui Group, cannot accept it. If you really wish to do it, do it on your own.*

— Hajime Tsuboi, president of Mitsui Real Estate Corp.[14]

---

[11]Takahashi, M. (July 23, 1999), an excerpt from "Watashi no Rirekisho (My Personal History)" series, *Nikkei* (*Japan Economic Journal*), 22, p. 36.

[12]Takahashi, M. (July 20, 1999), an excerpt from "Watashi no Rirekisho (My Personal History)" series, *Nikkei* (*Japan Economic Journal*), 19, p. 36.

[13]Takahashi, M. (July 21, 1999), an excerpt from "Watashi no Rirekisho (My Personal History)" series, *Nikkei* (*Japan Economic Journal*), 20, p. 36.

[14]Takahashi, M. (July 24, 1999), an excerpt from "Watashi no Rirekisho (My Personal History)" series, *Nikkei* (*Japan Economic Journal*), 23, p. 40.

## *The Main Bank*

Tokyo Disneyland was financed by a group of 22 banks. The group was headed by the Industrial Bank of Japan (IBJ), and Mitsui Trust Bank was the second largest partner. WD's position of demanding fees without risk caused much commotion among the Japanese banks. Kisaburo Ikeura, IBJ's president, who called this policy "very strange", stated:

> *WD's position was that they don't offer any land or money, take no risk; you must construct as we tell you to do, and we collect 10% license fee for entrance fees and 5% license fee for beverages and novelty goods; such a policy was never heard of in Japan.*

— Kisaburo Ikeura, president of IBJ[15]

IBJ, due to its history of success, was often called the "Morgan Guaranty Trust Bank" of Japan. It dealt with many large Japanese corporations in a variety of complex and delicate transactions. However, even with decades of experience, lending money to OL for the Tokyo Disneyland project was something of a new proposition. As a former government-owned bank, IBJ lent money in accordance with government policies that favored those traditional companies in the heavy industries sector, such as steel, ships and machinery, that had supported the recovery of the Japanese economy after the Second World War. IBJ's top management, however, believed that Japanese businesses would shift towards service-related industries based on software and technology, in addition to becoming more internationalized through joint ventures and export.[16] With that macroeconomic view, IBJ was therefore quite willing to lend to OL. The group of banks decided in August 1979 to lend ¥65 billion (US$550 million) to OL.[17] By 1997, when DiseySea Park was being

---

[15] Arima, T. (July 1, 2001) "Disneyland Story", *Nikkei Business Bunko*, pp. 136–138.

[16] See Takahashi, M. (July 25, 1999), an excerpt from "Watashi no Rirekisho (My Personal History)" series, *Nikkei (Japan Economic Journal)*, 24, p. 40.

[17] See Arima, T. (July 1, 2001) "Disneyland Story", *Nikkei Business Bunko*, pp. 161–166.

discussed, the total bank loans amounted to ¥195 billion (US$1.65 billion), indicating the group's strong commitment to the project.

In Japan, banks were closely involved with the client companies' internal affairs, both in cross-ownership[18] and as a prime lender. OL and IBJ maintained a very close relationship. Mitsuaki Mori, a high-ranking officer of IBJ, succeeded Masatomo Takahashi as the second president of OL in 1988.

## *Landlord*

OL was granted a vast plot of reclaimed land by the Japanese government, with the condition that it could be taken back if it was not used for its agreed purpose of developing the theme park, or if it was not used within a certain time frame.[19] In March 1962, Chiharu Kawasaki, president of Keisei Electric Railway Co., one of OL's largest shareholders, asked Masatomo Takahashi to approach Chiba prefecture and negotiate a grant of 1 million tsubo (1 tsubo = 3.3 m$^2$) of reclaimed land to OL.[20] Chiba responded:

> *We hear that even the Disneyland in Los Angeles is only 90,000 tsubo (73 acres). We've never heard of an amusement park as large as 1 million tsubo, which is 10 times that.*
>
> — Chiba government office[21]

Eventually, OL got 750,000 tsubo. Kawasaki later told Takahashi the reason he wanted such a large piece of land.

---

[18] Cross-ownership was a method of reinforcing business relationships by owning stock in the companies with which a given company did business. In Japan, cross-ownership of shares was a major part of the business culture and it was commonly seen between banks and companies. It was criticized for: (1) stagnating the economy, (2) wasting capital that could be used to improve productivity and (3) expanding economic downturns by preventing reallocation of capital. Positives were: (1) it tied closely each business to the economic destiny of its business partners and (2) it promoted a slow rate of economic change.

[19] Takahashi, M. (July 14, 1999), an excerpt from "Watashi no Rirekisho (My Personal History)" series, *Nikkei (Japan Economic Journal)*, 13, p. 40.

[20] Ibid.

[21] Ibid.

*If you go to Disneyland in Los Angeles, you will learn that by the time the company wanted to build a few hotels close to the park as the business was booming, all the adjacent lands had been bought up by others. I didn't want to see the same thing happen to us.*

— Chiharu Kawasaki, former president of Keisei Electric Railway Co.[22]

In his autobiography, Takahashi noted Kawasaki's foresight in suggesting the acquisition of such a large piece of real estate to accommodate any future expansion.[23]

With the opening of Maihama station on the Keiyo line in 1988, a 43 km railroad between Tokyo and Soga, the number of entrants to Disneyland increased tremendously, topping 13 million that year.[24] OL's top management remembered that the plot of land was reclaimed from the sea, causing many fishermen to lose their jobs and way of life; they felt obligated to help those affected.[25]

## *Government Intervention*

Before finalizing a deal with WD, OL needed to obtain permission from the Japanese government as a legal requirement.[26] OL consulted with the Ministry of Finance (MOF) and the Ministry of International Trade and Industry (MITI) to decide whether it should license the relevant technologies from WD or form a joint venture with WD. (For the legal base of the government intervention, see **Appendix 1**.) The Japanese government reviewed the case and advised as follows:

1. WD was a large company with huge capital and OL was a relatively small company, so a joint venture was not recommended. Even if the joint venture started out at 50/50, WD would eventually take over.

---

[22] Ibid.

[23] Ibid.

[24] Ibid.

[25] Ibid.

[26] Foreign Exchange and Foreign Trade Act (Act No. 228 of December 1, 1949) (FEFTA), Article 1.

2.  It was better for OL to purchase all the necessary technologies under the licensing agreement even though it was expensive.

3.  The new Tokyo Disneyland would attract a lot of children as visitors. The cultural influence on them would be tremendous. It was recommended to build a Japanese Disneyland rather than a direct American Disneyland. The park should have elements of both American and Japanese culture. Under this context, the licensing agreement would be better.

4.  The only concern about the licensing arrangement was the expensive fee. OL should negotiate with WD to get a lower fee.[27]

The Japanese government recommended a licensing agreement between WD and OL, contrary to OL's preference.

OL acted as "contrarian" to a consensus of stakeholders (except the government). The majority of stakeholders preferred a joint venture, but OL selected a licensing arrangement (see **Appendix 2**).

## *Ex Post* Empirical Comparison of Licensing versus Joint Venture for Tokyo Disneyland

OL was able to make the project profitable in four years, despite hefty licensing fees that were, on average, 7% of sales. An increase in customer spending on food, beverages and novelty goods rather than an increase in the number of entrants accounted for this profitability. OL preferred a joint venture mode, and WD preferred a licensing arrangement. Although a licensing arrangement was selected for this project, Tokyo Disneyland was operated very profitably. The question still remained which mode was more profitable as a project and for both parties.

OL listed shares on the Tokyo Stock Exchange in 1993. Since then, financial data had been available (see **Exhibit 2**). Based on the data of the past performance of Tokyo Disneyland, the two arrangements — licensing vs. joint venture — were empirically compared. The study estimated the

---

[27] Internal document dated March 1, 1975 and held at the IBJ, which was a main bank for OL and was informed of this decision by the government (MITI). OL didn't have disclosed the matter related to government approval.

**Exhibit 2**   Financial Figures of Oriental Land for the Period of 1993–2010

| Year | Sales (¥ million) | Net Income (¥ million) | Paid Capital (¥ million) | Net Asset (¥ million) | Dividend Paid (¥ million) | Payout Ratio (%) | Highest Stock Price (¥) | ¥/$ (end of the year) |
|---|---|---|---|---|---|---|---|---|
| 1993 | 150,557 | 8,359 | 18,831 | 67,612 | 498 | 5.95 | | 111.35 |
| 1994 | 156,272 | 9,558 | 18,831 | 105,679 | 498 | 5.21 | | 100.37 |
| 1995 | 153,923 | 13,123 | 18,831 | 118,229 | 498 | 3.79 | | 102.87 |
| 1996 | 171,502 | 14,690 | 18,831 | 132,346 | 665 | 4.52 | | 116.13 |
| 1997 | 180,965 | 15,902 | 63,201 | 287,595 | 1,201 | 7.55 | 9,030 | 130.30 |
| 1998 | 175,471 | 14,292 | 63,201 | 300,401 | 1,402 | 9.81 | 8,490 | 115.88 |
| 1999 | 187,772 | 15,068 | 63,201 | 313,983 | 1,402 | 9.30 | 6,200 | 102.19 |
| 2000 | 174,184 | 9,911 | 63,201 | 324,179 | 1,402 | 14.15 | 12,980 | 114.62 |
| 2001 | 200,191 | 4,740 | 63,201 | 327,628 | 1,402 | 29.58 | 9,930 | 131.30 |
| 2002 | 281,081 | 12,726 | 63,201 | 338,533 | 1,402 | 11.01 | 9,150 | 119.92 |
| 2003 | 331,753 | 18,931 | 63,201 | 354,908 | 2,403 | 15.11 | 7,250 | 107.18 |
| 2004 | 276,898 | 18,530 | 63,201 | 373,759 | 2,603 | 13.96 | 7,730 | 103.13 |
| 2005 | 271,435 | 17,224 | 63,201 | 389,606 | 3,003 | 21.00 | 7,140 | 117.62 |
| 2006 | 332,885 | 15,703 | 63,201 | 375,832 | 3,887 | 24.75 | 7,020 | 118.95 |
| 2007 | 344,682 | 16,309 | 63,201 | 385,000 | 4,732 | 24.51 | 7,180 | 112.93 |
| 2008 | 342,421 | 14,730 | 63,201 | 388,180 | 5,707 | 38.66 | 7,500 | 90.65 |
| 2009 | 389,242 | 18,089 | 63,201 | 375,352 | 5,581 | 30.94 | 7,450 | 91.53 |
| 2010 | 371,414 | 25,427 | 63,201 | 367,430 | 7,273 | 28.54 | 7,080 | 89.22 |

*Notes:* (1) Each year ends at the end of March.

(2) The stocks were first listed in December 1996.

(3) OL disclosed consolidated figures after 1999.

*Source:* OL's Annual Reports, 1993–2010.

total value of the venture for WD in terms of the net present value (NPV)[28] of WD's investment in the Tokyo Disneyland project. A foreign investor's assessment of a project's return depended on the actual cash flows that were returned in its own currency. For WD, this meant that the return must be analyzed in terms of US dollar cash inflows. The NPVs of WD's investment share for the following two cases were calculated on the basis of the entire 18 years after OL listed the shares and the data was made available for public consumption.

Case 1 (License Method) — This was the actual case. A 7% license fee was paid for the entire project. We calculated the NPV of what WD had received as licensing fees for the period of 1993 to 2010. The

---

[28] In a capital budgeting approach, NPV was determined by the present value of expected future cash inflows, discounted by an appropriate opportunity cost, which was subtracted from the present value of outflows. This was to determine whether or not investment in long-lived assets, or projects, was viable.

NPV was defined as follows:

$$\text{NPV} = C_0 + \sum_{t=1}^{T} \frac{CF_t}{(1+\bar{r})^t}$$

$C_0$ = initial investment
$CF_t$ = expected, after-tax cash flow in year $t$
$\bar{r}$ = weighted average cost of capital
$T$ = life of the project

In this study, the same theory was applied to determine NPV, based on the past actual data. To determine the NPV, the past data was compounded with an appropriate opportunity cost.

NPV was defined as follows:

$$\text{NPV} = -C_0 + \sum_{t=1}^{T} CF_t(1+\bar{r})^t$$

$C_0$ = initial investment
$CF_t$ = expected, after-tax cash flow in year $t$
$\bar{r}$ = weighted average cost of capital
$T$ = life of the project

Then NPVs of the two different modes were compared — joint venture vs. licensing arrangement. This was to determine which mode was more profitable. The past data was compounded with an appropriate opportunity cost.

licensing fees paid in the past were compounded back to the present value based on the compound interest rate.

Case 2 (Joint Venture Method) — This was a hypothetical case. We assumed the formation of a 50–50 basis joint venture. We calculated the NPV of the venture for WD's 50% share. The accumulated dividends paid in the past were compounded back to the present based on the compound interest. Because the available financial data represented the value after the 7% licensing fee had already been deducted, we added back all the licensing fees to calculate the real, total corporate value of Tokyo Disneyland. Then we subtracted the initial 50% investment by WD.

## *Data*

The main source of company data was the annual reports submitted to the MOF. **Exhibit 2** was compiled based on this data. Information for OL sales, net income, paid capital, net asset, dividend paid, payout ratio, stock price of the company (highest of the year) and exchange rate of yen/$ at the end of year are shown in **Exhibit 2** and also in **Figure 1**.

## **The Models**

For a list of notations and their meanings, refer to **Exhibit 3.**
The model of Case 1 (License Method):

$$Sn \times 0.07 = Ln$$

where "*Sn*" was sales of year "*n*" and "*Ln*" was the licensing fee (7%) paid in year "*n*".

$$\text{NPVWD(¥)} = \sum_{t=1}^{n} Lt(1+r)^t$$

where NPVWD (yen) was the NPV of WD's investment in yen, *Lt* was the licensing fee paid from OL to WD at time "*t*", and "*r*" was a compound interest rate of yen. For "*r*", there was a difference between a relatively riskless royalty payment and risky potential joint venture cash flows.

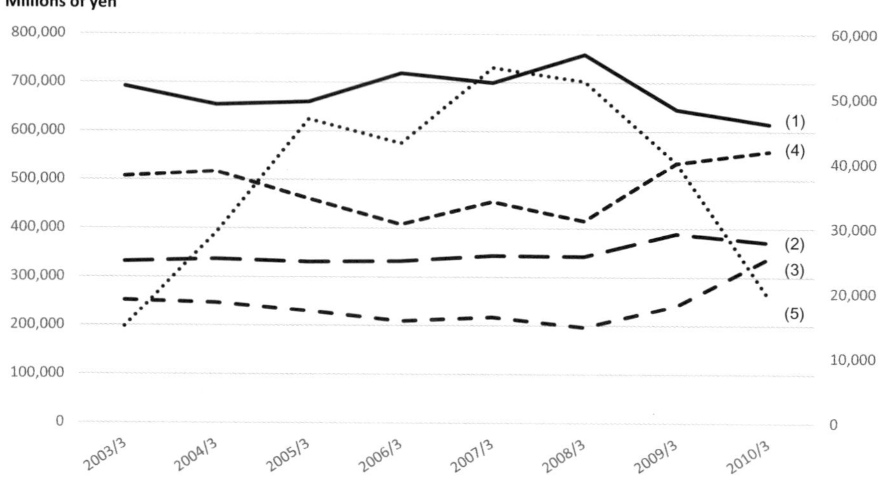



**Figure 1**   Past 18 Years of Tokyo Disneyland

*Note*: The left y-axis is for lines (1) and (2), and the right y-axis is for lines (3), (4), and (5).

     (1) shows Total Assets;

     (2) shows Revenues;

     (3) shows Net Income;

     (4) shows Operating Income;

     (5) shows Capital Expenditures.

*Source*: OL's Annual Reports, 2003–2010.

**Exhibit 3**   Definitions of Parameters, Variables, and Functions

| NPVWD | NPV of WD's Investment |
|---|---|
| S | Sales |
| L | Licensing fee |
| D | Dividend |
| IO | Initial Investment |
| CI | Capital Increase |
| TI | Total Investment |
| CV | Corporate Value |
| t | Time Period |
| n | Project's life; 1993–2010 (18 years) |
| r | Compound interest rate of yen, 3% |
| W | Weighted average cost of capital of OL, 10% |
| E | Exchange rate, ¥/$ |

Since *ex ante* these two cash flows had different risk profiles, implying a different discount rate for each of them, this *ex post* study made use of the different compound rate — 4% for royalty payments and 3% for joint venture cash flows.

Since management culture and target market preferences in Japan were different from the rest of world, the foreign company's management may not have been able to appraise the needs of the local market in their decision making and may have preferred relatively riskless royalty payments. Therefore, it was important to have different compound rates as a form of control for such factors that the foreign company's management may not have been able to appraise.

$$\text{NPVWD (\$)} = \text{NPVWD (¥)}/E$$

where "NPVWD (\$)" was the NPV of WD's investment in US dollars and "E" was the exchange rate, "¥/\$".

The model of Case 2 (Joint Venture Method):

$$\text{NPVWD (\$)} = \sum_{t=1}^{n} D_t (1+r)^t + 0.5$$

$$\times \left( \text{CV in 2010} + \sum_{t=1}^{n} Lt(1+r)^t - \text{IO}(1+r)^n \right)$$

where "NPVWD (\$)" was the NPV of WD's investment in US dollars, "$D_t$" was a dividend paid by OL to WD at time "$t$", "CV in 2010" was the corporate value of Tokyo Disneyland in 2010, "$Lt$" was the licensing fee paid at time "$t$" and "IO" was initial investment at "$r$". Total licensing fees paid by OL to WD were added back to the present corporate value. For CV, the recaptured licensing fees and IO, WD's portion was 50%.

For finding CV in 2010, we used three methods: (1) the current stock price, (2) the highest stock price and (3) Terminal Value Theory.


## *Calculations*

Case 1 — The result of the calculation for licensing fee payments compounded by interest rate, r, indicated an NPV of \$4,055.1 million (see **Exhibit 4**).

**Exhibit 4**  NPT of Licensing Fees Paid by WD for the Period of 1993–2010

| Year | Sales = A (¥ million) | Licensing Fees = B (¥ million) | B = C ($ million) | Compound Factor = $(1+r)^t$ = D | C × D ($ million) |
|---|---|---|---|---|---|
| 1993 | 150,557 | 10,538.99 | 94.65 | 2.2058 | 208.78 |
| 1994 | 156,272 | 10,939.04 | 109.06 | 1.9479 | 212.44 |
| 1995 | 153,923 | 10,774.61 | 104.73 | 1.8730 | 196.16 |
| 1996 | 171,502 | 12,005.14 | 103.38 | 1.8009 | 186.18 |
| 1997 | 180,965 | 12,667.55 | 97.21 | 1.7317 | 160.55 |
| 1998 | 175,471 | 12,282.97 | 105.99 | 1.6651 | 176.48 |
| 1999 | 187,772 | 13,144.04 | 128.62 | 1.6010 | 205.92 |
| 2000 | 174,184 | 12,192.88 | 106.37 | 1.5396 | 163.77 |
| 2001 | 200,191 | 14,013.37 | 106.73 | 1.4802 | 157.98 |
| 2002 | 281,081 | 19,675.67 | 164.08 | 1.4243 | 233.70 |
| 2003 | 331,753 | 23,222.71 | 216.66 | 1.3686 | 296.52 |
| 2004 | 336,516 | 23,556.12 | 228.34 | 1.3159 | 300.47 |
| 2005 | 331,094 | 23,176.58 | 197.04 | 1.2653 | 249.95 |
| 2006 | 332,885 | 23,301.95 | 195.89 | 1.2167 | 238.34 |
| 2007 | 344,082 | 24,085.74 | 213.27 | 1.1699 | 249.51 |
| 2008 | 342,421 | 23,969.47 | 264.41 | 1.1249 | 297.43 |
| 2009 | 389,242 | 27,246.94 | 297.67 | 1.0816 | 321.96 |
| 2010 | 371,414 | 26,208.98 | 293.75 | 1.0400 | 305.50 |
| | | | | Total | 4,161.64 |

*Note:* (1) Licensing fee = 0.07 × Sales

(2) $r = 0.04$.

Then,

$$\text{NPV} = \sum_{t=1}^{n} C_t(1+r)^t = \$4,161.64 \text{ million}$$

*Source*: OL's Annual Reports, 1993–2010.

Case 2 — First, accumulated dividend payments compounded by interest rate, r, indicated an NPV of $261.5 million (see **Exhibit 5**).

Second, corporate value, CV, was estimated by:

1. Using stock prices:

    (a) Current stock price of Tokyo Disneyland was ¥7,080 (as of June 8, 2010).

**Exhibit 5**   NPV of Dividends Paid by WD for the Period of 1993–2010

| Year | Dividends = A (¥ million) | A × 0.5 = B (¥ million) | B = C (¥ million) | Compound Factor = $(1+r)^t$ = D | C × D ($ million) |
|---|---|---|---|---|---|
| 1993 | 498 | 249 | 2.24 | 1.7024 | 3.81 |
| 1994 | 498 | 249 | 2.48 | 1.6528 | 4.10 |
| 1995 | 498 | 249 | 2.42 | 1.6047 | 3.88 |
| 1996 | 665 | 333 | 2.87 | 1.5580 | 4.47 |
| 1997 | 1,201 | 601 | 4.61 | 1.5126 | 6.97 |
| 1998 | 1,402 | 701 | 6.05 | 1.4685 | 8.88 |
| 1999 | 1,402 | 701 | 6.86 | 1.4258 | 9.78 |
| 2000 | 1,402 | 701 | 6.12 | 1.3842 | 8.47 |
| 2001 | 1,402 | 701 | 5.34 | 1.3439 | 7.18 |
| 2002 | 1,402 | 701 | 5.85 | 1.3048 | 7.63 |
| 2003 | 2,403 | 1,202 | 11.21 | 1.2668 | 14.20 |
| 2004 | 2,587 | 1,294 | 12.55 | 1.2299 | 15.44 |
| 2005 | 3,088 | 1,544 | 13.13 | 1.1941 | 15.68 |
| 2006 | 3,887 | 1,944 | 16.38 | 1.1593 | 18.99 |
| 2007 | 4,732 | 2,366 | 20.95 | 1.1255 | 23.58 |
| 2008 | 5,694 | 2,847 | 31.37 | 1.0927 | 34.28 |
| 2009 | 5,596 | 2,798 | 30.57 | 1.0609 | 32.43 |
| 2010 | 7,258 | 3,629 | 40.67 | 1.0300 | 42.13 |
|  |  |  |  | Total | 261.9 |

*Notes*: (1) WD's Share of the Dividends Paid = 50%

(2) $r = 0.03$.

Then,

$$\text{NPV} = \sum_{t=1}^{n} D_t (1+r)^t = \$261.90 \text{ million}$$

*Source*: OL's Annual Reports, 1993–2010.

CV¥ = Stock price × Shares = ¥7,080 × 90,922,540 shares = ¥643,731 million

CV\$ = CV¥ (at ¥89.22/\$) = \$7,215.1 million

An NPV of \$4,161.6 million of the licensing fees was added back because they would not be paid in a joint venture scenario.

Then, WD's share = 50% of (\$7,215.1 million + \$4,161.6 million) = \$5,688.4 million

(b) The highest stock price of ¥9,930 (as of July 1, 2001) was used.

CV¥ = Stock price × Shares = ¥9,930 × 90,922,540 shares = ¥902,860 million

CV$ = CV¥ (at ¥89.22/$) = $10,119 million

An NPV of $4,161.6 million of licensing fees was added back because they would not be paid in a joint venture scenario.

Then, WD's share = 50% of ($10,119 million + $4,161.6 million) = $7,140.3 million

2. Using Terminal Value Theory in capital budgeting:[29]

CV¥ = Net Operating Cash Flow in 2010/W (Weighted Cost of Capital)

Net Operating Cash Flow in 2010 = Net Income in 2010 + Depreciation in 2010 = ¥23,427 million + ¥46,694 million = ¥72,121 million = $808.4 million (at ¥89.22/$).

CV$ = ($808.4 million)/0.1 = $8,084.0 million

An NPV of $4,055.1 million of licensing fees was added back because they would not be paid in a joint venture scenario.

Then, WD's share = 50% of ($8,084.0 million + $4,055.1 million) = $6,069.6 million

Third, total investment (TI) was estimated. TI was the initial investment (IO) plus additional capital invested (CI).

1. IO in 1993 = ¥18,831 million

Suppose 50% paid by WD (i.e., ¥9,415.50 million), which was $84.55 million (at ¥111.35/$ in 1993).

An NPV of $84.55 million (compounded by 3%) = $84.55 million × 1.7024 = $143.95 million

2. CI in 1997 = ¥44,370 million

Suppose 50% paid by WD (i.e., ¥22,185 million), which was $170.26 million (at ¥130.30/$ in 1997).

An NPV of $170.26 million (compounded by 3%) = $170.26 million × 1.5126 = $257.54 million

Then, WD's share = 50% of TI $(1+r)^n$ = $143.95 million + $257.54 million = $401.5 million

---

[29] Terminal Value = (Net Operating Cash Flow)/(Weighted Cost of Capital). For details, see Eiteman, D., Stonehill, A.L. and Moffett, M.H. (2010) *Multinational Business Finance*, 12th Edition, Prentice Hall: Boston, p. 496.

We combined the following US dollar positive cash flows with the US dollar negative cash flows to determine the NPV of WD's investment for Case 2, using:

$$\text{NPVWD \$} = \sum_{t=1}^{n} D_t(1+r)^t + 0.5 \times \left( \text{CV in } 2010 + \sum_{t=1}^{n} Lt(1+r)^t - \text{IO}(1+r)^n \right)$$

The results of the different methods of NPV calculation for WD's investment in Case 2 were as follows:

For corporate value estimation, if we used:

the current stock price: $261.5 million + $5,688.4 million − $401.5 million = $5,548.4 million

the highest stock price: $261.5 million + $7,140.3 million − $401.5 million = $7,000.3 million.

If Terminal Value Theory was used for corporate value estimation:

$261.5 million + $6,069.6 million − $401.5 million = $5,929.6 million

Then, we compared the results of NPVs in Case 1 and Case 2.

Additionally, we determined what kind of arrangement offered higher combined returns/value for the project.


## *Results*

NPVWD:

Case 1 (Licensing) $4,055.1 million
Case 2 (Joint venture)

(a)  With current stock price: $5,548.4 million
(b)  With highest stock price: $7,000.3 million
(c)  With Terminal Value Theory: $5,929.6 million

We concluded that OL made a good decision. WD's selection of a licensing agreement, on the other hand, was not a good decision. Had WD entered into a joint venture, its NPV could have been as high as $7,000.3 million, nearly 68% higher than the $4,055.1 million that it obtained through its licensing arrangement. This did not escape WD's notice, and when similar situations arose in the development of Euro Disney[30] and Hong Kong Disneyland,[31] WD strove to obtain maximum profits through joint ventures.[32]

Now we could find what kind of arrangement offers higher combined returns/value for the project.

1. Under licensing, we could adopt the current corporate value, since this was the result of payments of licensing fees.

   (a) With current stock price: $7,215 million
   (b) With highest stock price: $10,119 million
   (c) With Terminal Value Theory: $8,084 million

2. Under a joint venture, the licensing fees were added back because they would not be paid in a joint venture scenario and instead dividends were to be paid. Then,

   Combined value of the project =

   $$\text{CV in } 2010 + \sum_{t=1}^{n} Lt(1+r)^t - \sum_{t=1}^{n} D_t(1+r)^t$$

   (a) With current stock price: $7,215 million + $4,055.1 million − $261.5 million = $11,008.6 million
   (b) With highest stock price: $10,119 million + $4,055.1 million − $261.5 million = $13,912.6 million

---

[30] Disneyland Paris was operated by French company Euro Disney S.C.A., a public company of which 39.78% of its stock was held by WD, 10% by the Saudi Prince Alwaleed and 50.22% by other shareholders. For details, see Euro Disney's website, http://corporate.disneylandparis.com/index.xhtml (accessed December 1, 2011).

[31] At the start, the Hong Kong government held a 57% stake, while WD held 43%. But after the expansion plans were announced in 2009, when WD invested HK$3.63 billion (US$465 million), the Hong Kong government's holdings were reduced to 52% while WD's shares increased to 48%. For details, see Hong Kong Disneyland's website, http://hkcorporate.hongkongdisneyland.com/hkdlcorp/en_US/home/home?name=HomePage (accessed December 1, 2011).

[32] See Arima, T. (July 1, 2001) "Disneyland Story", *Nikkei Business Bunko*, pp. 172–173.

   (c) With Terminal Value Theory: \$8,084 million + \$4,055.1 million − \$261.5 million = \$11,877.6 million

Now we found that a joint venture arrangement could offer higher combined returns/value for the project. This was expected, since a licensing arrangement resulted in a huge cash outflow from corporate value.

## For Further Discussion

1. What are the concepts and definitions of licensing and joint venture? Describe the pros and cons for the investing company and the host company.
2. How do you evaluate the importance of *ex post* case study?
3. What kinds of expansions to further study are expected out of this study?
4. This study offers a complete analysis for any MNE that may be considering foreign investments. What do you consider Walt Disney study most out of the experience with Tokyo Disneyland.
5. Conduct a sensitivity study by calculating NPV for licensing fee payments compounded by interest rate of 5%.

   (1) Use the same numbers in **Exhibit 4** in the main text except r. For $r$, use 0.05.
   (2) Note that Licensing fee = 0.07 × Sales.

6. Conduct a sensitivity study by calculating NPV for accumulated dividend payments compounded by interest rate of 4%.

   (1) Use the same numbers in **Exhibit 5** in the main text, except $r$. For $r$, use 0.04.
   (2) WD's Share of the Dividends Paid = 50%

7. Evaluate the government intervention in foreign investment decisions in the private sector.
8. This case of Tokyo Disneyland revealed an interesting and noteworthy principle as the basis of its success, which was the position of contrarian. "Contrarian" denotes someone who moves in opposition to others. What did you study out of OL's performance as a contrarian?

# Appendix 1 Government Intervention Under the Foreign Exchange and Foreign Trade Act in Japan

The Foreign Exchange and Foreign Trade Act (FEFTA) in Japan stated:

*The purpose of this Act is, on the basis of the freedom of foreign exchange, foreign trade and other foreign transactions, to enable proper expansion of foreign transactions and the maintenance of peace and security in Japan and in the international community through the minimum necessary control or coordination of foreign transactions, and thereby to ensure equilibrium of the international balance of trade and stability of currency as well as to contribute to the sound development of the Japanese economy.*[33]

Based on FEFTA, the Japanese government intervened in the negotiation between the OL (see **Exhibit 1**) of Japan and WD of the United States as to the possible form of cooperation. One of the main points of negotiation was deciding on a licensing arrangement or a joint venture. WD, in 1979, proposed a licensing agreement to provide only the know-how of creating a Disneyland theme park without shouldering any risk. OL and its stakeholders in Japan desired to have a joint venture. The Japanese government recommended a licensing arrangement, based on FEFTA. Thirty-eight years later, it was worthwhile to examine the validity of their decisions, which benefited the project and the partners most. This case study presented *ex post* empirical evidence for this discussion. The efficacy and effectiveness of the law that allowed the Japanese government to intervene were also questioned.

After the Second World War, the Japanese government did not approve any direct investment applications from the US automobile industry under the infant-industry theory, which asserted that emerging domestic industries should be protected until they become stable and mature. Proponents of the infant-industry theory argued that governments should use tariffs, quotas and duty taxes to keep international competitors from ruining the domestic "infant" industries. The Japanese government, subscribing to this school of thought, had already given similar advice in the

---

[33]FEFTA, Article 1.

1950s when it recommended that the Japanese auto industry get technology information from the US auto industry rather than enter into partnerships. We needed only look at how Toyota, Nissan and other Japanese auto companies were prospering, while the US auto industry was suffering from financial difficulties, to see that the Japanese government's counsel was wise. Nonetheless, the Japanese government's decision had been globally criticized as selfish and the MITI had become notorious. After World War II, the Japanese government took the same infant-industry approach for the steel, electric and computer industries. Because of this, Japan was often referred to as "Japan Inc", meaning that the government and private sector worked very closely together.

A more recent example of the application of FEFTA was the prohibition of foreign investment in Japanese companies. In May 2008, the MOF and the MITI, acting pursuant to FEFTA,[34] ordered the Children's Investment Master Fund (TCI) of the United States to halt further acquisition of electric power wholesaler Electric Power Development (J-Power) shares. Both the MOF and the MITI based their rulings on the grounds that J-Power management might be affected should TCI continue to acquire shares. This change in management could then affect the stable supply of electric power and Japan's nuclear and nuclear fuel cycle-related policies.

When making an investment in a Japanese company (whether listed on a stock exchange or not), it was essential for foreign investors to have an understanding of the many regulations regarding inward direct investments by foreign investors. For example, in the case of a joint venture with a foreign company, FEFTA stated:

*When MOF finds that capital transactions by a resident or non-resident are conducted without any restrictions, it will cause a situation that prevents Japan from sincerely fulfilling obligations under treaties and other international agreements Japan has signed or from making its contribution to international efforts for achieving international peace, which will make it difficult to achieve the purpose of this Act, or when a cabinet decision has been made, he/she may impose, pursuant to the provisions of Cabinet Order, on a resident or non-resident who intends to commit the capital transactions, the obligation to obtain permission for implementation of the capital transactions.*[35]

---

[34] FEFTA, Article 1.
[35] FEFTA, Article 21.

FEFTA also stated:

> *When a foreign investor intends to make an inward direct investment, he/she shall notify in advance, pursuant to the provisions of Cabinet Order, MOF and the minister having jurisdiction over the business of the business purpose, amount, time of making the investment, and the like and other matters specified by Cabinet Order in regard to the inward direct investment.*[36]

Furthermore:

> *When MOF and the minister having jurisdiction over the business have received a notification it examines whether or not inward direct investment falls under any of the following inward direct investments and makes recommendation of change of content pertaining to inward direct investment or discontinuance of inward direct investment.*
>
> > a. *National security is impaired, the maintenance of public order is disturbed, or the protection of public safety is hindered.*
> > b. *Significant adverse effect is brought to the smooth management of the Japanese economy.*[37]

Based on this, OL needed to obtain permission from the Japanese government if it intended to enter into a joint venture with WD.

For a licensing agreement, FEFTA provided:

> *When a resident intends to commit acts of concluding or renewing, with a non-resident, a contract pertaining to the transfer of industrial property rights or other rights related to technology, establishment of the right to use these rights or guidance on technology related to business management conducted by the non-resident, or acts of making changes in the provision of such a contract, he/she shall notify in advance, MOF and the minister having jurisdiction over the business of the provisions of the contract.*[38]

FEFTA also provided:

> *When MOF and the minister having jurisdiction over the business have received a notification it examines whether or not the Conclusion of a*

---

[36] FEFTA, Article 27.
[37] FEFTA, Article 24.
[38] FEFTA, Article 30.

*Technology Introduction Contract falls under any of the following contracts and makes recommendations of change of content pertaining to the contracts or discontinuance of the contracts.*

> a.  *National security is impaired, the maintenance of public order is disturbed, or the protection of public safety is hindered.*
> b.  *Significant adverse effect is brought to the smooth management of the Japanese economy.*[39]

Based on this, OL needed to obtain permission from the Japanese government if it intended to enter into a licensing agreement with WD.

# Appendix 2  A Contrarian Example from Our Ordinary Lives

You were driving on the expressway and you came to a fork in the road. On Side A, the traffic light was crowded, and on Side B, the traffic light was not crowded. Which way would you have chosen? Most people would have chosen Side B, but a contrarian would have chosen Side A, counting on the fact that most other people would select Side B so that Side B would become more crowded and Side A would become less crowded (see below).

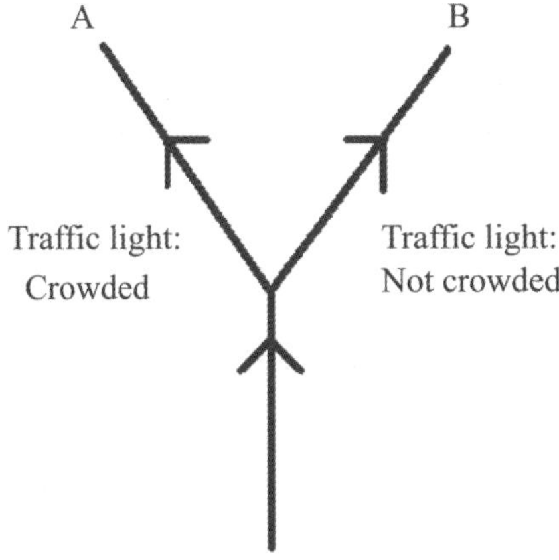


---

[39] Ibid.

# 17

# Ina Food Industry (2):
# Marketing Strategies
# in a Deflationary Environment

Ina Food Industry Co. Ltd. (Ina Food)[1] was situated in the city of Ina, Nagano Prefecture, and surrounded by the soaring mountains of the Japanese Alps. Hiroshi Tsukakoshi, Ina Food's 75-year-old chairman, had led the company through an incredible 55 years of continuous revenue and profit growth. Ina Food was a leading manufacturer of powdered agar,[2] a traditional gelatin product derived from seaweed. Ina Food was producing healthy products that were used in cooking. The main product, Kanten Papa, was easy to use and was the very basis that mothers used in cooking at home and preparing family meals. As Japanese people worried about preserving their family life, easy-to-use ingredients became all the more significant in preparing family meals. By upgrading its refining process, Ina Food had found a new application for agar in the field of fine chemicals and medical products. Ina Food was pushing the frontier of biotechnology.

In the summer of 2012, Tsukakoshi was looking through the windows of his office in Ina City, Japan. He was thinking about how he aimed for his company to be a corporation that was conscious of the global environment. He felt he had done a good job so far. The business had prospered and did not pose any urgent problems. But he also felt that he should not simply sit back and savor his success. He was facing his retirement and had concerns about the long-term growth of the company. He thought it might be the right time to introduce some new marketing strategies for the company. There was a reason for his concern: the Japanese deflation of the previous 20 years. He was interested in increasing sales volume and profit

---

[1] See **Exhibit 1** for information about Ina Food.
[2] See **Exhibit 1** for information about Agar.

by raising prices when most other companies were lowering prices under deflation. To him, maintaining the current prices meant also price increases under deflation, since the general trend was towards price decreases.

## Growth Strategy

Ina Food (see **Exhibits 1** and **2**) strove for perpetual existence. It sought stable, as opposed to quick and explosive, growth. The company's policy had been a 2–3% increase in both sales and profit. Tsukakoshi believed that if a business grew too fast, backlash would undoubtedly occur. Tsukakoshi believed that clients generally became aggravated when the price of an identical item swung violently up and down. This company had so far used a meticulously controlled pricing policy for each product category. Company personnel continually reviewed and changed the individual prices of over 100 products to maximize sales and profit on the whole.

Shareholders always asked for a short-term return. Management tended to let the company grow fast in all possible ways, such as sharp price increases, bigger production capacity, or more output by overwork. Or the huge demand might come all of a sudden. For example, the year 2005 was a special year for the company. The business boom for Ina Food was caused by a notion promoted on national TV that agar was good for health. In response to this broadcast, the company began receiving a flood of orders for agar. At first, management felt that it should not fulfill the orders. This rather counterintuitive decision came from the company's motto, "Those who plan for the distant future would be rich and those who plan for the near future would be poor," taken from Sontoku Ninomiya (1787–1856)[3], who was highly respected in Japan for his work on ethics and benevolence.

---

[3] Sontoku Ninomiya was a farm technologist and the leading agricultural philosopher of the late Edo period (1600–1868). His practical and moral teachings, which urged cultivators to raise output and pay their taxes, helped strengthen the economic basis of Tokugawa rule. For this he was later praised as a paragon of virtue in the national ethics textbooks of the 1930s. Ninomiya taught farmers to improve themselves through *hotoku* ("repaying virtue"), the idea that benefits received from heaven, man, and earth should be repaid, and that doing so would create a "true society" of peacefulness and prosperity. To the familiar Confucian virtues of sincerity, diligence, and thrift, Ninomiya added cooperation with others to his code of ethics. See Kodansha (1983) *Kodansha Encyclopedia of Japan*, Tokyo: Kodansha, Vol. 6, p. 7.

**Exhibit 1**   Company Profile

| | |
|---|---|
| Company name | Ina Food Industry Co. Ltd. |
| Chairman and CEO | Hiroshi Tsukakoshi |
| President and COO | Osamu Inoue |
| Date established | June 18, 1958 |
| Capital | ¥96.8 million |
| Annual sales | ¥17,449 million (2012) |
| Operating income | ¥2,291 million (2012) |
| Head office address | 5074 Nishiharuchika, Ina-City, Nagano, Japan |
| Plants | Sawando Plant, Kitaoka Plant, Fujisawa Plant, Inosawa Plant |
| Branches | Tokyo, Nagoya, Osaka |
| Business offices | Sapporo, Sendai, Nagano, Fukuoka, Okayama |
| Number of employees | 423 (2012) |

Ina Food Industry Co. Ltd. was established in 1958 to produce agar. This natural gelatin was originally developed as an important ingredient and used in traditional Japanese confectionery. Its manufacture was the product of a cottage industry by farmers, who used the natural cold during the coldest three months of the year for its production. As a consequence of (a) production being confined to only the three winter months of the year when the farmers were free, (b) the quantity and quality not being stable or reliable, (c) it appearing in both bars and a fibrous state, and (d) it being the victim of a seasonally fluctuating market, use of the product was avoided by large industry.

Ina Food therefore concentrated on producing powdered agar, developed sources from which the raw material could be imported and stored throughout the year, and through the consolidation of production into a highly efficient process, achieved a stable market that eliminated fluctuating prices to develop a stronger demand. The history of the company was actually the history of the development of powdered agar in Japan.

Recently, with the discovery of the cancer-resistant properties of oligosaccharides in agar, agar's effectiveness as a deterrent of constipation, its use in meals for the aged, etc., distinctively effective uses of agar had been on the increase.

*Source*: Annual Report Ina Food Industry, 2013.

After a few months of operating at full capacity in 2005, the employees started showing signs of strain. Tsukakoshi believed they could not continue production at this breakneck pace and he decided instead to decrease production. Consequently, he began to think that the company

**Exhibit 2**    Sales, Operating Income, and Number of Employees for INA Food for the Past 10 Years

| | 1996 | 1997 | 1998 | 1999 | 2000 | 2001 | 2002 | 2003 | 2004 | 2005 | 2006 | 2007 | 2008 | 2009 | 2010 | 2011 | 2012 |
|---|---|---|---|---|---|---|---|---|---|---|---|---|---|---|---|---|---|
| sales | 9,344 | 9,757 | 9,843 | 10,630 | 10,910 | 11,787 | 12,422 | 13,317 | 14,411 | 20,074 | 17,468 | 16,522 | 15,937 | 15,906 | 17,135 | 17,398 | 17,449 |
| Operating Income | 822 | 705 | 834 | 1,123 | 1,085 | 1,325 | 1,603 | 2,025 | 2,373 | 3,819 | 2,602 | 1,857 | 1,597 | 1,885 | 2,356 | 2,404 | 2,291 |
| Number of Employees | 241 | 249 | 259 | 264 | 277 | 286 | 302 | 304 | 329 | 345 | 378 | 385 | 385 | 387 | 393 | 409 | 423 |

*Source*: Annual Report Ina Food Industry, 2013.

did not exist for the management or even for itself; rather, it existed for the happiness of the employees. If all the employees were happy and had a high morale, the communities they lived in would improve, thus making a contribution to society.[4]

> *A company exists for its employees. Happiness and steady growth makes it possible for the company to grow forever.*

> — Hiroshi Tsukakoshi, chairman of Ina Food[5]

## Deflation

Since December 29, 1989, when the Japanese stock market reached a historical all-time high, ¥38,915, the Japanese economy had lost two decades to economic stagnation (see **Exhibit 3**). During this period,

---

[4] Tsukakoshi, H. (2005) "Iikaisha wo Tsukurimashou" (Let Us Build a Good Company), *Bunya Publishing Company*, Seventh Edition, pp. 11–213.
[5] Ibid.

Japan had also suffered from chronic deflation. Deflation[6] was caused by a shift in the supply-and-demand curve for goods and services,

**Exhibit 3**   Japan Consumer Price Index (January 1985–April 2013)

The Consumer Price Index (CPI) in Japan decreased to 99.50 index points in January 2013 from 99.60 index points in December 2012. The CPI in Japan was reported by the Statistics Bureau of Japan. Historically, from 1985 until 2013, the CPI averaged 99.13 index points, reaching an all-time high of 104.90 index points in November 1998 and a record low of 89.10 index points in February 1985. In Japan, the CPI measured changes in the prices paid by consumers for a basket of goods and services. This page includes a chart with historical data for the CPI.

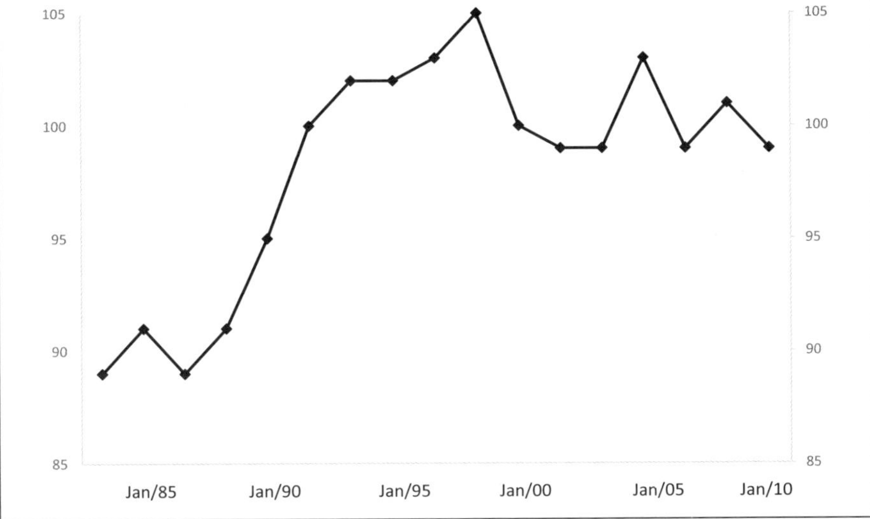


*Source*: Statistics Bureau of Japan Consumer Price Index (www.stat.go.jp/english/data/cpi)(accessed July 30, 2013).

---

[6] The opposite of inflation, deflation meant a general decline in prices, often caused by a reduction in the supply of money or credit. Declining prices, if they persisted, generally created a vicious spiral of negatives, such as falling profits, closing factories, shrinking employment and incomes, and increasing defaults on loans by companies and individuals. It could be caused also by a decrease in government, personal, or investment spending. It had the side effect of increased unemployment since there was a lower level of demand in the economy, which could lead to an economic depression. To counter deflation, central banks attempted to use monetary policy to increase the money supply and deliberately induce rising prices, causing inflation. Rising prices provided an essential lubricant for any sustained recovery because businesses increased profits and took some of the depressive pressures off wages and debtors of every kind.

particularly a fall in the aggregate level of demand, leading consumers to have an incentive to delay purchases and consumption until prices fell further, which in turn reduced overall economic activity. Consumers were clever; they reasoned that "tomorrow's price would be lower than today's". Because this idled productive capacity, investment also fell, leading to further reductions in aggregate demand. This phenomenon was known as the deflationary spiral. To counter these alarming trends, Japan enacted a zero-interest-rate policy, but so far it had not fostered sufficient expansion to induce recovery. Neither had the most recent expansion of the monetary base. Changing expectations of deflation to expectations of inflation in consumers was not easy. This was the path that the Japanese economy had walked in the previous 20 years, and Tsukakoshi was concerned that even his company could not continue to grow under deflation.

During a deflationary period, consumers were reticent to spend. Companies selling a good or service had to make adjustments in order to continue earning profits, attempt to break even, or sometimes even lose as little money as possible in the hopes of staying afloat until the deflationary period ended. Of course, with any decision as drastic as this, it was important to carefully judge how it would affect every facet of the company — bottom line, brand, customers' perceptions, and anticipated position once the deflationary period ended, to name a few. A common first move by companies navigating this difficult situation was to explore changing their pricing strategy. Price decreases, including predatory-pricing strategies to combat decreased market share and insufficient demand, were popular choices among these companies.

On this occasion, Tsukakoshi explored the relationship between consumers and price. It had been well established that consumers used price as a guide in consumption decisions. Price information could be accumulated passively through prior knowledge and experience, or actively sought through comparative shopping.[7] Consumers viewed price as an

---

[7] Mazumdar, T. and Papatla, P. (2000) "An Investigation of Reference Price Segments", *Journal of Marketing Research*, 37(2), pp. 246–258.

indicator of quality.[8] The connection was further explored, finding a positive correlation between reference price and consumers' opinions of quality.[9] Even though a high-priced product required financial sacrifice on the part of the consumer, so too did the higher-priced product garner more esteem. Therefore, perceived value was a trade-off between perceived sacrifice and perceived prestige. Given this, it implied to Tsukakoshi that companies could use pricing as a tool to influence consumer behavior.

## Price Decrease or Increase

Tsukakoshi further considered price decreases. For a company caught in an economy in recession, simply decreasing supply might not have been enough to offset the decrease in consumer demand. If that was the case, prices might have needed to be adjusted downward, which often caused cutthroat price competition. The rationale was that weaker companies, unable to stay afloat during the difficult times, would withdraw from the market. In general, resource-poor or less established companies were forced to join the price-cutting competition. Resource-abundant or more established companies, however, were more likely to have a choice. Common rationale dictated that resource-rich companies would have the infrastructure and holdings to survive a drought, but it was less clear whether or not simply surviving the drought was the best choice. The fact was highlighted that overuse of price as a promotional tool might have damaged the prestige of a brand.[10] The issue was explored further that consumers perceived such

---

[8] Teas, K. R. and Agarwal, S. (2000) "The Effects of Extrinsic Product Cues on Consumers' Perceptions of Quality, Sacrifice, and Value", *Journal of the Academy of Marketing Science*, 28(2), pp. 278–290; Yoo, B., Donthu, N. and Lee, S. (2000) "An Examination of Selected Marketing Mix Elements and Brand Equity", *Journal of the Academy of Marketing Science*, 28(2), pp. 195–211.

[9] Chapman, J. and Wahlers, R. (1999) "A Revision and Empirical Test of the Extended Price-Perceived Quality Model", *Journal of Marketing Theory and Practice*, 7(3), pp. 53–64.

[10] Ibid.

price cuts as an admission of product quality reduction, reducing previously high brand associations and awareness.[11] Recent studies agreed with traditional brand management beliefs, which stated that preferences for a certain brand were easily damaged, or forgotten, after price promotion.[12] In a study on sustainable pricing strategies, it was urged that companies should consider both internal and external influences.[13]

Though it might have seemed that larger and more established companies, with more abundant resources and experience, would be better equipped to handle recessionary periods, Tsukakoshi knew this was not always the case. In fact, it was found that small companies sometimes had better survival rates than large companies.[14] It was much easier for small companies to shift to a new or niche market, as well as imitate their larger competitors' actions and perform new pricing and promotional actions more quickly; they were strategically nimble.[15]

## Price Elasticity of Demand

The price elasticity of demand (see **Exhibit 4**) for Ina Food's goods was generally low. Raw agar was made of seaweed and there was no competition as a healthy product. Agar was considered to be life-saving, as it contained lots of vegetable fiber and was effective in preventing obesity, high blood pressure, hyperlipidemia, and diabetes.

---

[11] Yoo, B., Donthu, N. and Lee, S. (2000) "An Examination of Selected Marketing Mix Elements and Brand Equity", *Journal of the Academy of Marketing Science*, 28(2), pp. 195–211.

[12] Guadagni, P.M. and Little, J.D.C. (1983) "A Logit Model of Brand Choice Calibrated on Scanner Data," *Marketing Science*, 2(3), pp. 203–238; Scott, C.A. and Yalch, R.F. (1980) "Consumer Response to Initial Product Trial: A Bayesian Analysis", *Journal of Consumer Research*, 7(1), pp. 32–41.

[13] Chou, T. and Chen, F. (2004) "Retail Pricing Strategies in Recession Economies: The Case of Taiwan", *Journal of International Marketing*, 12(1), pp. 82–102.

[14] Duncan, J.W. and Handler, D.P. (1994) "The Misunderstood Role of Small Business", *Business Economics*, 29(3), pp. 7–12.

[15] Grinyer, P.H. and Yasai-Ardekani, M. (1981) "Strategy, Structure, Size and Bureaucracy", *Academy of Management Journal*, 24(3), pp. 471–486; Stasch, S.F., Lonsdale, R.T., Ward, J.L. and Harris, D.A. (1999) "Characteristics of Share-Gaining Marketing Strategies for Smaller-Share Firms: Literature Review and Synthesis", *Journal of Marketing Theory and Practice*, 7(2), pp. 54–67.

**Exhibit 4**   Price Elasticity of Demand

The price elasticity of demand (commonly known as just price elasticity) measures the rate of response of quantity demanded due to a price change. The formula for the price elasticity of demand is:

$$\text{Price Elasticity of Demand (PED)} = \frac{\%\ \text{change in Quality}}{\%\ \text{change in price}} = \frac{\%\ \Delta\ Q}{\%\ \Delta\ P}$$

1. Given the following data, let us calculate the price elasticity of demand (PED).

Price (OLD) = 9
Price (NEW) = 10
Quantity of Demand (OLD) = 150
Quantity of Demand (NEW) = 110

Then, Percentage Change in Quantity Demanded = −0.2667
[110 − 150]/150 = (−40/150) = −0.2667

Percentage Change in Price = 0.1111
[10 − 9]/9 = (1/9) = 0.1111

Then, PED = (% Change in Quantity Demanded)/(% Change in Price)

We can now fill in the two percentages in this equation using the figures we calculated earlier. PED = (−0.2667)/(0.1111) = −2.4005

When we analyze *price* elasticity we are concerned with their absolute value, so we ignore the negative value. PED is always positive. We conclude that the price elasticity of demand when the price increases from $9 to $10 is 2.4005.

2. Interpretation of Price Elasticity of Demand

In the case of price elasticity of demand, it is used to see how sensitive the demand for a good is to a price change. The higher the price elasticity, the more sensitive consumers are to price changes. A very high price elasticity suggests that when the price of a good goes up, consumers will buy a great deal less of it, and when the price of that good goes down, consumers will buy a great deal more. A very low price elasticity implies just the opposite, that changes in price have little influence on demand.

If PED > 1 then Demand is Price Elastic (demand is sensitive to price changes)

If PED = 1 then Demand is Unit Elastic

If PED < 1 then Demand is Price Inelastic (demand is not sensitive to price changes)

In the case of the good above, we calculated the price elasticity of demand to be 2.4005, so our good is price elastic and thus demand is very sensitive to price changes.

The following were characteristics of Ina Food's goods with low price elasticity:

1. Goods with differentiations that had no competition in the market.
2. Goods that were selling for reasons other than price, which consumers thought were cheap compared to alternative merchandise.
3. Goods without clear alternatives, merchandise for which the manufacturers always found order backlogs, or those whose demand always exceeded supply.

## Factors Supporting Price Increase under Deflation

Tsukakoshi believed that, in essence, as long as a company was confident in its products' competitiveness, there were always methods to raise prices and increase profits smoothly. The key was raising the prices of merchandise and services in a way that the customers could accept the price changes. Not all companies could do it, though. These consumers might not have noticed the price increase in short periods of time, but over a year or more they would become obvious as the increased prices started to constrain consumer budgets. Then the consumers would stop buying that product. Why could Ina Food do it? The consumers would not stop buying its product even after they noticed the price increases. Tsukakoshi thought Ina Food could do it because of the seven good business practices below.

### 1. *Be a good company.*

Tsukakoshi believed that increasing hedonic value[16] could increase consumer loyalty to the brand and thus allow for greater price increases.[17] Tsukakoshi had made it a priority that the company maintain a meaningful

---

[16] Hedonic value was defined as the degree of happiness or sadness felt by the decision maker at the moment of an outcome's announcement. For details, see Bagai, J.P. (1999) "Hedonic Value and Choice", PhD Dissertation, University of Pennsylvania, Paper AAI9926093, http://repository.upenn.edu/dissertations/AAI9926093 (accessed July 23, 2013).

[17] Chaudhuri, A. (1999) "Does Brand Loyalty Mediate Brand Equity Outcomes?" *Journal of Marketing Theory and Practice*, 7(2), pp. 136–146; Chaudhuri, A. and Holbrook, M.B.

presence, constantly striving to be a corporate entity lauded and appreciated by its stakeholders. He considered that in its quest to seek better profits and efficiency, the company must have been careful not to inconvenience its customers and suppliers, not to discard its regard for the environment, and not to force sacrifices upon its employees.

## 2. *Be a company conscious of progress and not of trends.*

Tsukakoshi believed that there was an axis of progress and an axis of trend in human society. The axis of progress was a straight line that led to an ideal society. The axis of trend was a movement of society that swung constantly to the left and right, perpendicular to the axis of progress. He felt that the axis of trend should be accounted for, but warned against misunderstanding it as the path to follow. According to Tsukakoshi, American-style management, which paid disproportionate attention to shareholders' profits, was merely a trend. If one wanted stability and long-term existence of a company, one should not have been influenced by trends. To move steadily along the axis of progress with a thorough understanding of the optimum growth rate, while keeping an eye on trends, was the ideal mix for the company.

## 3. *Stabilize materials costs.*

In order to store more agar, the company built four additional bays of storage buildings, using the profits earned from a price hike. At the same time, the production facilities and the factory were enlarged to increase production capacity. Furthermore, Tsukakoshi and other members of top management visited various countries to secure suppliers of raw materials needed in the production of agar in order to stabilize flow inputs. They visited approximately 20 countries, including Chile, the Portuguese Azores Islands in the Atlantic Ocean, Morocco, China, South Korea, and Vietnam, in search of partner companies. The company signed partnership agreements with suppliers from three countries: Chile, Morocco, and

---

(2001) "The Chain of Effects from Brand Trust and Brand Affect to Brand Performance: The Role of Brand Loyalty", *Journal of Marketing*, 65(2), pp. 81–93.

South Korea. As a result of its new and stable supplies and its increased storage capacity, the company was able to maintain constant price increases. Recently the company had published an opinion advertisement in an industry paper declaring, "Agar is no longer a market-driven flamboyant merchandise."

## 4. *Maintain strong research and development.*

Tsukakoshi believed that the survival of an enterprise rested on its research and development (R&D) capabilities and that R&D should be a mainstay of any company. Based on this conviction, it had been a company rule to always engage 10% of its workforce in the R&D of materials and production technologies. Agar, which was mostly dietary fiber of very low calorific value, presented limitless possibilities for development. The company was pushing the frontier of biotechnology. This attitude supported its task of exploring new possibilities for agar. By upgrading its refining process, it had found a new application for agar in the field of fine chemicals. Research at the company was not only for making profits, but also allowed excited young researchers to pursue their dreams.

## 5. *Present the proposed uses.*

Tsukakoshi believed that presentation determined demand. New types of agar developed from basic R&D augmented the benefits for Ina Food's customers. The company was fully equipped with the necessary facilities to conduct conclusive experiments. The research department regularly took newly developed materials to exhibitions of other industries, such as high-tech materials, and showed them around, asking for possible uses in new products or processes.

## 6. *Discover new uses.*

In one discovery, the research department noted an agar that could not be solidified. Such a product, while obviously unsuitable for normal usage, could have some use if Ina Food could develop a technology to produce it in a stable manner. A use was found: a soft agar for elderly patients who had difficulty swallowing. The company then produced soft foods made of agar by adding water and cooked food chopped into small pieces, which made it easier for elderly people to swallow. The technology to produce unsolidified agar was patented and was also used to produce agar juices, lipsticks, and cosmetic foundations.

## 7. *Maintain close communication with customers.*

To serve customers, Ina Food set up a mail order department, which had 500,000 regular customers. This allowed for an ideal relationship with clients. As soon as it received a complaint or a thank you letter, it sent back a handwritten letter to the client. Although it sold the products through the internet as well, relationships with clients were such that when an employee handling client communications got married, he or she received numerous gifts from clients congratulating him or her on the marriage.

## Contrarian Theory

Contrarian Theory suggested that for a company caught in an economy in recession, simply decreasing supply might not be enough to offset the decrease in consumer demand and prices might need to be adjusted downward. Tsukakoshi knew that raising the price under deflation was contrary to this theory. When the economy faced serious difficulties, the company had obtained successful results in marketing, producing, financing, and allocating resources. Tsukakoshi thought it might have to act the role of "contrarian" as the basis of success. A "contrarian" acted in opposition to others, or rejected popular opinion. The company's position as a contrarian was supported by the following reasons:

1. Traditionally, it had been believed that a high demand for a product was a clue to raise prices and that there was a negative correlation between price level and willingness to buy. But if the consumer perceived that a product was harmonious with certain of his or her key needs and values, he or she would continue to purchase it despite price increases.

2. Price itself could be used as a tool to control consumer behavior. A wanted hedonic value ascribed to merchandise could increase loyalty to the brand, enabling companies to be more fluid with price changes.[18]

3. Price, in some instances, might actually have played a subordinate role to product worthiness in the consumer's decision-making process. This could be put in terms of price elasticity of demand. In this case the demand for a good was inelastic and a consequence of this was that price change had a relatively small effect on the quantity of good demanded.

## Decision Time for the Future

Tsukakoshi was thinking that a new pricing strategy had to be explored to maintain successful performance despite deflation. Under long-lasting deflation, Tsukakoshi was thinking that it was high time for him to make a decision on the new pricing strategy. He had to make decisions in a dynamic environment of deflation and evaluate various options:

1. Decrease the price as other companies had.
2. Stay as is, which was a *de facto* price increase under deflation.
3. Increase the price as a contrarian.

Raising prices in a difficult economic climate was a risky decision. Many studies had pointed out that the overuse of price as a promotional tool could damage the prestige of a brand.[19] It was risky for companies to rush into price competition without considering the possible side effects.

The company would be successful in increasing sales and profits even while the economy at large faced deflation. If the gross margin of

---

[18] Chaudhuri, A. and Holbrook, M.B. (2001) "The Chain of Effects from Brand Trust and Brand Affect to Brand Performance: The Role of Brand Loyalty", *Journal of Marketing*, 65(2), pp. 81–93.

[19] Chapman, J. and Wahlers, R. (1999) "A Revision and Empirical Test of the Extended Price-Perceived Quality Model", *Journal of Marketing Theory and Practice*, 7(3), pp. 53–64.

a product was 30%, it could be increased by as much as 17% through simply raising the price 5% if the cost was not changed. In general the gross margin would drop as the number of units sold dropped when the price was raised, but Ina Food had merchandise whose sales quantities were less sensitive to price increase than average merchandise.

Tsukakoshi asked the marketing department to create a list of the pricing strategies for the future.

1. Introducing a new and similar product in a higher price range. By introducing it well, through good advertisement, the company enticed consumers from existing products to the new one. Once the new product was available for consumption, it terminated existing products.

2. Blaming a price increase on the increase of a constituent raw material, the change of a materials supply source, the rise in cost of imported materials due to yen depreciation, etc. The company could have begged the pardon of consumers, appealing to their understanding through public relations efforts. It was essential that it was careful not to cause the customers to feel like the company was using the situation to its advantage.

3. Implementing the price range by changing the product line up. There were three grades of merchandise for a particular kind of product — lower, middle, and upper class — and they were priced at ¥110, ¥140, and ¥170, respectively. Ina Food had established that customers tended to choose the middle-class product, that is, the product sold at ¥140. This type of consumer psychology was best exemplified in a sushi bar where clients tended to choose the better if there were three classes of sushi: best, better, and good. The company then introduced a new product line, which had the upper-class price of ¥200. Customers were made to feel, through advertising, that the ¥170 and ¥200 products shared some basic quality, causing them to flock to the ¥170 product. This resulted in a price increase by shifting the demand for the ¥140 product to the ¥170 product. The company could terminate the ¥110 product with proper timing, thus smoothly completing the price increase campaign with little resistance (see **Exhibit 5**).

**Exhibit 5**  Price Increase by Adding the Higher Price

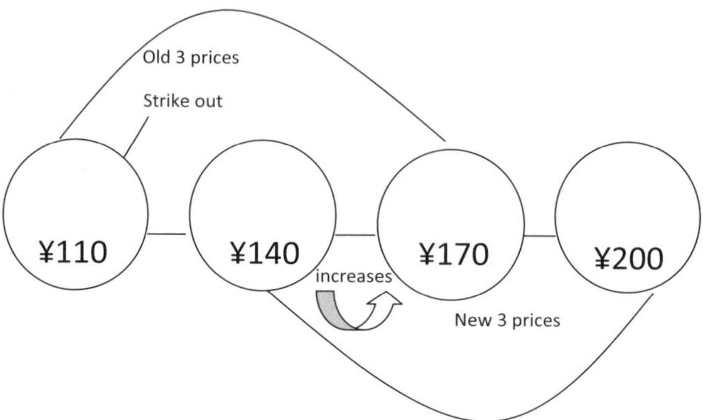


4. Shifting the price range in one blow by changing the product name. In one discovery, the research department noted that it sometimes created agar that could not be solidified. A new use was found: a soft agar for elderly patients who had difficulty swallowing. Ina Food changed the name of the product and raised the price.

5. Transferring the cost of services that used to be free, such as wrapping and delivery, to the consumer, making them available only for a fee.

Top management had to make a decision about whether the company should adopt these techniques if it decided to raise the prices. The decision had to be made based on Tsukakoshi's management philosophy that Ina Food should be a good company.

*Let us build a good company. I hope to make it a company not just with good management indices, but a company that people would call a good company* (**Exhibit 6**).

— Hiroshi Tsukakoshi, chairman of Ina Food[20]

---

[20]Tsukakoshi, H. (2005) "Iikaisha wo Tsukurimashou" (Let Us Build a Good Company), *Bunya Publishing Company*, Seventh Edition, pp. 11–213.

**Exhibit 6**   Ina Food Industry's Picture in the Autumn

Photo courtesy of Hiroshi Tsukakoshi, chairman of Ina Food.

# For Further Discussion

1. In the main text, it is said, "If the gross margin a product is 30%, it can be increased by as much as 17% through simply raising the price 5% if the cost is not changed." Explain this mathematics.

2. Takekoshi believes that as long as a company is confident in its products' competitiveness, there are always methods to raise prices and increase profits smoothly. Then why other companies can do it under deflation?

3. Actually top management raised prices and this decision was rational in if viewed on an ex post basis. However, it did not have the benefit of clairvoyance during the process. The case of the company shows that a company that modifies its price strategy appropriately can maintain or improve the performance in times of deflation. It is said widely that Ina Food revealed an interesting and noteworthy principle as the basis of the success — it played the role of "contrarian." Comment on "contrarian", taking this case as the base.

4. Would larger companies be better equipped to handle deflationary periods? Or smaller companies would do better?
5. Given the following data, calculate the price elasticity of demand. Is this good price elastic or inelastic?
6. Takekoshi decided to raise the prices. But if he decided to lower the prices as other companies were doing under deflation, what would have happened for the company?

# 18

# Bank of Japan (2): The Meeting on April 4, 2013 (Doubling Japan's Monetary Base via Government Bond Purchases)

On April 4, 2013, the Japanese parliament approved Haruhiko Kuroda[1] for a full, five-year term as the Bank of Japan's (BOJ) governor. He officially replaced his predecessor Masaaski Shirakawa, who stepped down on March 19 before his official term was expected to end on April 8.[2]

The new BOJ under Kuroda decided on the same day that it planned to double the monetary base over two years, primarily through a massive increase in Japanese government bond (JGB) buying.[3] Kuroda intended to establish a policy target for a 2% annual rate of inflation as a big step in the first round of Prime Minister Shinzō Abe's policy push and to induce the wealth effect with aggressive easy money strategies. With this he intended to encourage real demand to buoy corporate investment and consumer spending so that Japan could overcome deflation.

---

[1] Haruhiko Kuroda (born on October 25, 1944), was the 31st governor of the Bank of Japan. He was formerly the president of the Asian Development Bank from February 1, 2005 to March 18, 2013. Kuroda assumed the BOJ position in late March 2013, immediately discussing bond buying and a two-year target of 2% inflation as goals. Education: 1967, B.A. in Law, The University of Tokyo; 1971, M.Phil. in Economics, University of Oxford; 1967, joined Japan's Ministry of Finance; 1999, Vice Minister of Finance for International Affairs; 2003, Special Advisor to the Cabinet and Professor, Graduate School of Economics, Hitotsubashi University, Japan.

[2] *Nikkei* (*Japan Economic Journal*), April 5, 2013, "Parliament Approves Full 5-year Term For BOJ Gov.", http://e.nikkei.com/e/fr/tnks/Nni20130405D05JF455.htm (accessed May 1, 2013).

[3] *Nikkei* (*Japan Economic Journal*), April 5, 2013, "BOJ-Kuroda Color", http://www.nikkei.com/article/DGXNASGC0401O_U3A400C1EE1000/?df=2 (accessed May 1, 2013).

The BOJ launched an aggressive easing program in what markets said were surprisingly bold first steps by Kuroda as he began his campaign to rid the economy of over 20 years of deflation (see **Exhibit 1**). Nearly all of Kuroda's proposals were adopted by unanimous approval on April 4, 2013, at his first policy board meeting. Prior to the meeting, Kuroda told staffers that half measures would not work. He rejected the status quo of ramping up easing incrementally, weighing the benefits and side effects of each step.[4] By taking every conceivable measure at once, he drove home

**Exhibit 1**   Japan Consumer Price Index (CPI) (January 1985–April 2013)

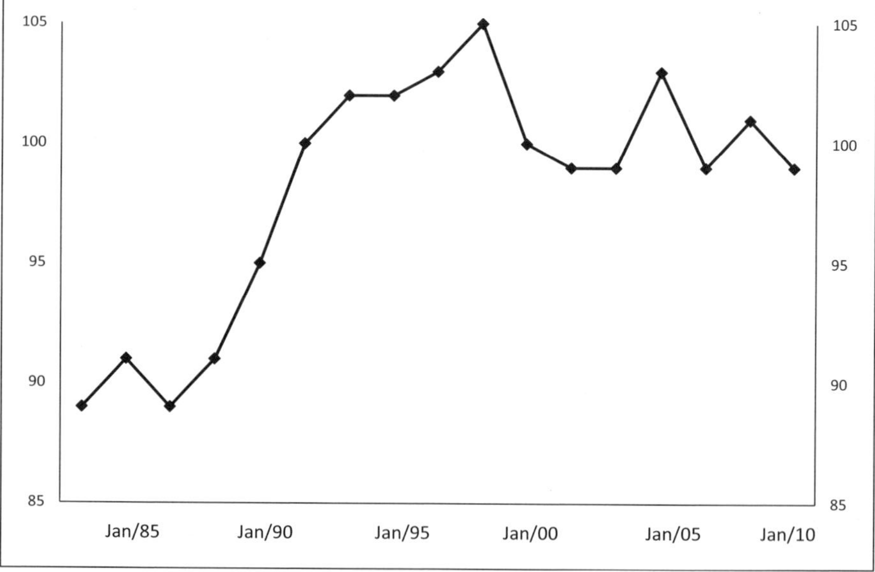

The CPI in Japan was reported by the Statistics Bureau of Japan. In Japan, CPI measured changes in the prices paid by consumers for a basket of goods and services. It decreased to 99.50 Index Points in January 2013 from 99.60 Index Points in December 2012. Historically, from 1985 until 2013, it averaged 99.13 Index Points, reaching an all-time high of 104.90 Index Points in November 1998 and a record low of 89.10 Index Points in February 1985.



*Source*: Statistics Bureau of Japan, Consumer Price Index (www.stat.go.jp/english/data/cpi/) (accessed July 30, 2013).

---

[4] *Nikkei* (*Japan Economic Journal*), April 4, 2013, "Haruhiko Kuroda, Bank of Japan governor, pulled off a neat trick", (http://www.nikkei.com/article/DGXDASFS0402N_U3A400C1MM8000/) (accessed May 1, 2013).

the point that the central bank's monetary easing had entered a new dimension. The BOJ policy board had thus agreed to a 2% price-rise target at the earliest possible time, with a time horizon of about two years.[5] With this, the BOJ had cut off its own retreat.

The BOJ's intent could be summed up in two words: raising expectations. The BOJ's policy statement played up the word "double" — double the monetary base, double the purchases of government bonds and exchange-traded funds. The emphasis on "double" the easing was meant to plant the idea of a bolder central bank in the markets.

The monetary base consisted of financial institutions' current-account deposits at the BOJ and cash circulating in the market. The central bank aimed to expand this base by stepping up purchases of banks' JGB holdings, expecting the increased funds in the current-account deposits to eventually find their way into businesses and households. Under this new easy money policy, the BOJ planned to guide financial markets so that monetary supply would grow at the pace of 60–70 trillion yen a year. This meant the monetary base in Japan, which stood at 138 trillion yen as of the end of 2012, would climb to 200 trillion yen at the end of 2013 and 270 trillion yen a year later (see **Exhibit 2**).

1. The BOJ had decided to expand the scope of government debt purchases to all JGBs, including the longest 40-year instruments. Under the previous policy, bond buying was limited to those maturing between one to three years. The new policy would extend the average remaining maturity of the BOJ's JGB holdings to roughly seven years from slightly less than three years.
2. The qualitative aspect of the new policy had to do with the fact that the BOJ planned to push down long-term interest rates by buying more bonds with longer terms to maturity. Under previous governor Masaaki Shirakawa, the focus was on lowering interest rates on bonds maturing in less than three years. By bringing down long-term rates, the BOJ

---

[5] *Nikkei* (*Japan Economic Journal*), April 4, 2013, "Monetary Base Hits Record High For 2nd", http://www.nikkei.com/article/DGXDASFS0303Y_T00C13A4MM8001/ (accessed May 1, 2013).

**Exhibit 2**    Monetary Base Target and the BOJ's Balance Sheet Projection

(trillion yen)

| | End of 2012 (actual) | End of 2013 (projected) | End of 2014 (projected) |
|---|---|---|---|
| **Monetary base** | 138 | 200 | 270 |
| Breakdown of BOJ's balance sheet | | | |
| JGBs | 89 | 140 | 190 |
| CP | 2.1 | 2.2 | 2.2 |
| Corporate bonds | 2.9 | 3.2 | 3.2 |
| Exchange-traded funds (ETFs) | 1.5 | 2.5 | 3.5 |
| Japan real estate investment trusts (J-REITs) | 0.11 | 0.14 | 0.17 |
| Loan Support Program | 3.3 | 13 | 18 |
| Total assets (including others) | 158 | 220 | 290 |
| Banknotes | 87 | 88 | 90 |
| Current deposits | 47 | 107 | 175 |
| Total liabilities and net assets (including others) | 158 | 220 | 290 |

*Source*: *Nikkei* (*Japan Economic Journal*), April 5, 2013, "Monetary Base Target and the BOJ's Balance Sheet Projections", http://e.nikkei.com/e/ac/TNKS/Nni20130405D0404A12.htm?NS-query=BOJ (accessed May 1, 2013).

hoped to encourage individuals to take out mortgages and businesses to make capital investments.

3. Furthermore, the BOJ had decided to boost holdings of exchange-traded funds by 1 trillion yen a year. The bank also had decided to buy real estate investment trusts. It hoped these efforts would raise stock and property prices and create the so-called wealth effect to spur consumer spending and business investments.

# The BOJ Played to the Various Markets

The BOJ's all-out monetary easing reverberated in the financial markets on April 5, 2013, after the policy was announced, with the stock, bond, and currency markets all swinging wildly. Long-term interest rates sank as bond dealers and other participants snapped up holdings in response to the BOJ's plan to increase purchases of long-term JGBs. The 10-year JGB yield briefly fell 14 basis points on the day to 0.315%. The Nikkei Stock Average at one point shot up 591 points to climb above 13,000. And the trading volume on the Tokyo Stock Exchange's first section surged to a record 6.44 billion shares, while turnover hit 4.86 trillion yen, the highest in five years and eight months. Hopes for an escape from deflation sent real estate stocks sharply higher.

But in afternoon trading, the tone abruptly reversed. Government bond futures trading was briefly suspended twice after hitting single-day price drop limits. Market observers attributed the steep declines to overseas investors unloading their holdings to lock in profits, along with selling by some major banks. The wild ride in the bond futures market triggered selling in cash bonds, briefly lifting the 10-year yield to 0.62%.

*I've observed this market for a long time, but the single-day volatility was unprecedented.*

— Daisuke Uno,
chief strategist at Sumitomo Mitsui Banking Corp.[6]

The bond market's wide fluctuations eventually spread to the stock market, where investors turned to selling. The Nikkei average ended up 199.10 points, or 1.58%, at 12,833.64, shedding nearly 400 points from its intraday high. The yen sank to its weakest level in 44 months in morning trading, with the dollar reaching 97 yen. But the yen reversed course in the afternoon, pushing the dollar to the upper 95-yen level as the roller-coaster ride in the bond market sparked yen-buying among investors seeking the currency's relative safety.

---

[6] *Nikkei (Japan Economic Journal)*, April 5, 2013, "BOJ Acts As Long Rates March Ever Higher", http://www.nikkei.com/article/DGXNASFS05059_V00C13A4MM8000/ (accessed May 1, 2013).

**Exhibit 3**   The Trend of Yen/$ for the Past Five Years: April 2008–April 2013

*Source*: Yahoo Finance, April 1, 2013, http://info.finance.yahoo.co.jp/exchange/ (accessed July 30, 2013).

Kuroda seemed to have carefully weighed the potential for new monetary easing to bring about a further downward correction in the yen. Currency market watchers were interested in how much funds provision the BOJ would commit.[7] The answer was enough to raise the monetary base by 60–70 trillion yen a year. Such considerations seemed to have factored into the yen's decline against the dollar on April 5, 2013. The move into the upper 90s would surely be what the BOJ had intended, as a weaker yen was crucial for stimulating corporate activity (see **Exhibit 3**).

*Overseas investors now view the yen differently.*

— Yunosuke Ikeda, chief foreign exchange strategist
at Nomura Securities Co.[8]

---

[7] Based on this, Junichi Makino, chief economist at SMBC Nikko Securities Inc., reckoned the dollar would be worth 95 yen in one year and 105–110 yen at the end of 2014. See *Nikkei* (*Japan Economic Journal*), April 5, 2013, "BOJ's Dilemma: How Far To Bend For Market", http://www.nikkei.com/article/DGXNASDC0400R_U3A400C1EA1000/ (accessed May 1, 2013).

[8] *Nikkei* (*Japan Economic Journal*), April 6, 2013, "BOJ Scrambles To Curb Long-Term Rates' Upward", http://www.nikkei.com/article/DGXDASFS05059_V00C13A4MM8000/ (accessed May 1, 2013).

# Concerns in the Markets

"Working on expectations" alone could not change some things. There were many concerns in the markets.

1. The biggest concern was a rise in consumption of foreign energy, the effect of having most nuclear power plants offline. Energy imports were up by several trillion yen a year compared with before the March 2011 disaster,[9] and as the yen softened further, this flow would only increase in value terms. In turn, Japan's trade deficits had become chronic, and the current-account surplus was shrinking. A weak yen would bolster exports, but until this support took hold, Japan would walk an economic tightrope. This would give a fickle market cause to worry (see **Appendix 1** for yen devaluation).
2. In the stock market in Tokyo, the Nikkei Stock Average topped 13,109.58 yen after surging 475.04 points, or 3.76% (on BOJ easing steps and the yen's decline on April 5, 2013, see **Exhibit 4**).[10] The Tokyo market was boosted by stocks of property developers and

**Exhibit 4**   Ten Years' Trend of Japanese Stocks (April 2004–April 2013)

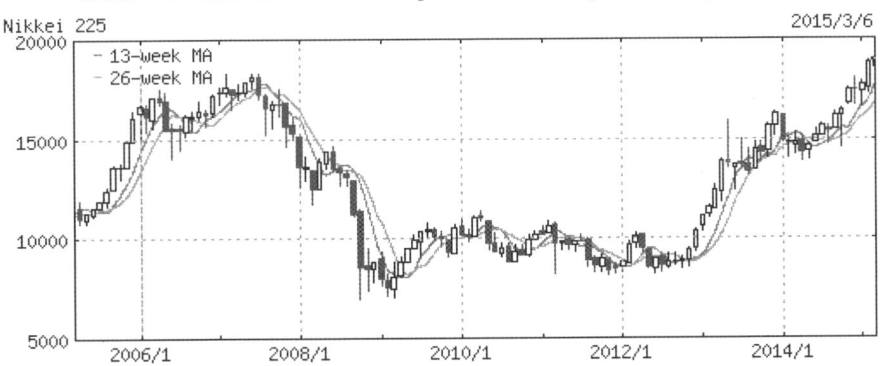


*Source*: Yahoo Finance, April 1, 2013, http//stocks.finance.yahoo.co.jp/stocks/detail/?998407 (accessed July 30, 2013).

---

[9] Ibid.

[10] *Nikkei* (*Japan Economic Journal*), April 5, 2013, "BOJ Market Magic Fades, But Econ Looks Up", http://e.nikkei.com/e/fr/tnks/Nni20130405D05SS446.htm (accessed May 1, 2013).

financial institutions, which were bought aggressively. The yen's fall prompted buying of blue chip exporters, which hit a year-to-date high. The investment money procured because of lower interest rates flew into the stock market. Many expected at this time the BOJ's bold monetary easing to spur on further rises in share prices.[11] The central bank's plan to increase purchases of risk assets might have fueled hopes for still higher stock and real estate prices. A weaker yen could also have enhanced the export competitiveness of Japanese manufacturers. This could have helped stimulate consumer spending. The inverters were concerned about how long this good trend would continue.

3. The outlook for the government bond market, however, appeared uncertain. The 10-year yield swung around as market participants continued to digest the BOJ's plan to buy 7 trillion yen-plus of bonds every month. The BOJ's purchases could have decreased trading in Japan. Since investors were concerned that the volume of bonds circulating in the market might decrease as a result of the BOJ's purchases, they might have decided to leave the domestic bond market.

> *Until the BOJ's specific bond-buying plans become clear, the market may stay volatile.*
>
> — Makoto Yamashita,
> chief rates strategist at Deutsche Securities Inc.[12]

4. Companies had appeared unconvinced by the currency's dramatic depreciation since November 2012. As of March 2013, with the yen-dollar rate in the mid-90s, big manufacturers were forecasting a rate of only a little more than 85 yen for fiscal 2013, the BOJ's latest survey showed.[13] This was apparent in the cautiousness of their outlooks for

---

[11] Ibid.

[12] *Nikkei* (*Japan Economic Journal*), April 6, 2013, "All Eyes On BOJ Policy Board, But Change Unlikely", http://www.nikkei.com/article/DGXNASDF0500K_V00C13A4EE8000/ (accessed May 1, 2013).

[13] *Nikkei* (*Japan Economic Journal*), April 4, 2013, "The BOJ's Tankan (short-term observation) Survey", http://www.nikkei.com/article/DGXDASDF0500M_V00C13A4EA1000/ (accessed May 1, 2013).

the future. Among large manufacturers, planned investments were down slightly from the previous year, according to the report. Big companies overall were expecting pretax profit gains of just 6%.[14] An outpouring of such tepid forecasts in the coming earnings season could have cooled the stock market. The BOJ expected firms to act by ensuring the yen stayed weak. Since the market had moved in the direction the BOJ wanted, it would be looking for changes in corporate outlooks for investment and earnings. There was growing recognition that the yen would be in a long-term weakening trend. But the yen's slide may have halted at that threshold as the US economic recovery lagged, and woes in Europe lingered, thereby enhancing the yen's role as a safe-haven currency.

## Abenomics: Relentless Pressure on the BOJ

Prime Minister Abe had been promoting various economic stimulus measures since taking office in December 2012. So far, his relentless pressure on the BOJ to further ease its monetary policy had had some impact on the markets. The economic policies advocated by Abe were dubbed "Abenomics". This was a portmanteau of *Abe* and *economics*. Abenomics was a combination of monetary relaxation, heavy fiscal spending, and targeted growth strategies. The detailed policies included inflation targeting at a 2% annual rate, correction of the excessive yen appreciation, radical quantitative easing, expansion of public investment, buying operations of JGB by the BOJ, and revision of the BOJ Act. The markets had taken the BOJ's recent decision to set a 2% inflation target as the last big step in the first round of Abe's policy push.

> *Government interference and pressure on the BOJ endangers their independence.*
>
> — Jens Weidmann, policymaker at European Central Bank[15]

---

[14] Ibid.

[15] *Reuters*, January 21, 2013, "ECB's Weidmann: Pressure on Central Banks Risks FX Competition", http://www.reuters.com/article/2013/01/21/ecb-weidmann-currency-idUSL6N0AQCMF20130121 (accessed May 1, 2013).

Concerns were being raised that even if these new economic policies being implemented by Abe lifted Japan out of deflation, an even more formidable challenge might have awaited the government.

1.   Higher Interest Rates

It was extremely difficult to simultaneously pursue a 2% target and maintain low interest rates. There was concern that stock and land prices would rise if the BOJ continued its "open-ended" easing, because investors would pull their money out of JGBs to buy stocks and real estate. As a result, JGB prices would decline and interest rates would go up. It would make it difficult for the government to pay high interest on its debt — JGBs. A sharp drop in JGB prices might have forced some financial institutions that held large amounts of JGB to take unreasonable risks to avoid earnings erosion and this could have jeopardized stability in the financial system (see **Appendix 2**).

2.   Currency War Fears

A weaker yen helped Japan regain its export competitiveness but made other countries nervous, as it could have cut into the market shares of domestic firms. Russia had recently expressed concern that the weakening of the yen could trigger a "currency war".

> *Other countries might follow suit and engage in destabilizing devaluations.*
>
> — Alexei Ulyukayev, Russian central banker[16]

Besides Japan's monetary policy, there were many external factors that could have promoted yen-selling. Many investors believed that the yen-selling would stretch over a protracted period, pointing to Japan's energy import increases, a growing trade deficit, signs of a US economic recovery, and the easing impact of the euro-zone sovereign debt crisis. There was a chance that a new round of yen-selling would begin and continue. Yen might have gone too low with more yen-selling ahead (see **Appendix 2**).

---

[16] Ibid.

3.   Appearance of the Economic Bubble

Historically reflationary policies had carried grave risks. The concern was a reappearance of the economic bubble that blew up in the latter half of the 1980s in Japan. The government was moving toward monetization of the debt. Monetization was when a central bank printed money to buy government bonds, thereby covering the government's fiscal deficit. But the effects of government spending were temporary. In effect, the country was spending future income in the present to keep the economy moving. Once the effects wore off, the BOJ would have to make huge purchases of government bonds for each additional round of fiscal stimulus.

Increased spending by the government to take advantage of extremely low interest rates could have loosened fiscal discipline.

History showed the risks of this strategy. In the 18th century, John Law, a Scottish economist, created the world's first fiat money system — that was, not backed by a hard asset such as gold — to end deflation in France. Law established France's first central bank to issue notes and create credit to stimulate the economy. He also set up the Company of the West, which became the Mississippi Company and later the Company of the Indies, which had a monopoly on trade in North America. The company drew in speculators who bid up the price of its shares, resulting in the "Mississippi Bubble."[17] The bubble soon burst, as the company's business was not backed by hard assets, such as commodities or natural resources. Because the company was designed to exchange government debt for shares in a debt-equity swap, Law's fiscal rehabilitation scheme collapsed, along with the company's share price.

---

[17] In the 1720s, France was experiencing a bubble, known as the "Mississippi Bubble". It was brought on by government debt and the advice of the head of the finance ministry, John Law, to create paper money and to invest in his Mississippi Company. Over a three-year period (1718–1720), things went very wrong and too much money was printed. In a 2008 *Financial Times* article, "How the French Invented Subprime in 1719" (http://journalisted.com/article/7txk, accessed May 1, 2013), James MacDonald compared the Mississippi Bubble with the 2008 financial crisis. He cited six major similarities, including significant public debt, a charismatic financial wizard (Law), and the power of securitization. The American writer Emerson Hough wrote a best-selling historical novel in 1902 entitled *The Mississippi Bubble* (http://books.google.com/books?id=9bMcAAAAMAAJ, (accessed May 1, 2013).

The lesson from the Mississippi Bubble was that it was important to balance monetary and economic growth if reflationary policies were to work. While reflationary policy was effective if the balance was maintained, as in the case of Japan in the 1960s, the risk of an economic bubble rose if the sources of growth were insufficient.

## The Time for the BOJ to Make More Decisions: Could the BOJ Deftly Manage Never-Ending Expectations?

When the BOJ announced the easing measures on April 5, 2013, Kuroda made clear that it had deployed every policy tool at its disposal and had no intention of adopting additional steps for about one year. The BOJ temporarily turned a blind eye on the risks posed by bold monetary easing in its laser-beam focus on beating deflation, but achieving that goal would not be easy.

1. An expectation gap appeared to be emerging between the BOJ and the markets, which were already looking ahead to what steps might come next. If Kuroda's BOJ failed to deliver and the markets' raised expectations fizzled, the just-announced bold easing could lose its efficacy. Private-sector research institutes reckoned the 2% target would be difficult to achieve in two years.[18] The consumer price index (CPI), excluding perishables, fell 0.3% in February 2013. The Japan Center for Economic Research estimated that for prices to rise 2% in two years, Japan would need to achieve real gross domestic product growth of 4%, a pace akin to emerging markets.[19] The success of the BOJ's bold attempt would hinge on whether real demand emerged to buoy corporate investment and consumer spending.

---

[18] *Nikkei* (*Japan Economic Journal*), April 5, 2013, "BOJ Puts Optimistic Spin on Inflation Forecast", http://www.nikkei.com/article/DGXNASGC0500G_V00C13A4MM0000/ (accessed May 1, 2013).

[19] Ibid.

The markets had not shied away in the past from showing their disappointment toward the BOJ's actions. When the BOJ unexpectedly loosened monetary policy in February 2012, the move helped reverse the tide of yen strength that had pushed the dollar to the 77-yen level. Market participants and the business community welcomed the BOJ's more aggressive stance. But the BOJ skipped additional offerings between March and early April of 2012, sparking market disappointment. In just two and a half months, the yen strengthened from the 80s range against the dollar back to the 70s. The last lesson was that it was important to hint at second and third steps to continue buoying market expectations.

2. When should this aggressive monetary easing have been ended? To underscore the support for aggressive monetary easing, Kuroda asserted it was premature to discuss an exit strategy from the policy. But the BOJ's plan to sharply increase government bond purchases actually raised the hurdles for ending such a policy. If the economy escaped deflation and interest rates jumped up, the BOJ could have sustained hefty losses. Kuroda said greater consideration of the financial system would need to be taken into account in ending the policy in the future, as spikes in bond yields could damage the financial soundness of the BOJ and private financial institutions.

3. The 2% inflation target was evident in the BOJ's decision to include bulk purchases of risk assets and long-term government bonds in its strategy. Re-energizing the economy would have required making the most of the BOJ's actions, but the BOJ also needed to pay close attention to possible side effects. It would need to remain flexible in implementing the new policy to avoid overshooting the inflation target, and be disciplined in its purchases of government bonds so that the measure was not seen as an attempt to plug Japan's huge budget hole.

While the BOJ's using these measures to help spur growth in the Japanese economy was fine, it raised the concern that assets held by the BOJ would pile up if prices did not rise as targeted. Then bubbles could be formed. But Kuroda played down concerns over asset bubbles. He made the comments below amid a steep rally in the Tokyo stock market and a weakening of the yen following the BOJ's decision on April 3, 2013, to introduce a series of unprecedented easing steps.

> *Financial markets aren't yet in a "bubble," and are unlikely to be so soon, but the direction of markets needs to be carefully watched as the central bank proceeds with its bold monetary policy.*
>
> — Haruhiko Kuroda, governor of BOJ[20]

Kuroda explained further that the BOJ would stick to the policy if a rise in the consumer-price index looked "temporary and not sustainable." But he indicated that the BOJ would adjust its policy if the index looked set to keep rising above 2%.[21]

4. Japan's trade deficit widened in April 2013 as the boost to exporters from a weaker yen was outweighed by rising prices for imports. Japan posted a deficit of 879 billion yen in its trade balance in March 2013, almost 70% wider than a year earlier, as rising shipments of cars and iron and steel products were offset by much higher bills for fuel, food, clothing, and semiconductors.[22] These figures were consistent with what was called the "J-curve effect" (see **Appendix 1** for yen devaluation). A weaker currency improved a country's trade balance over time, but in the short term it might have actually boosted a deficit because it could take several months for customers overseas to switch suppliers. A weaker yen had been a key element of the economic revitalization program of Shinzō Abe, Japan's prime minister, but the BOJ had to be very careful to watch the trend of Japan's trade deficit.

5. Kuroda had placed an emphasis on communicating with the markets, as evidenced by the BOJ's decision to meet with a large group of

---

[20] *Nikkei* (*Japan Economic Journal*), April 5, 2013, "Monetary Base Hits Record High", http://www.nikkei.com/article/DGXDZO53613820V00C13A4EE2000/ (accessed May 1, 2013).

[21] Ibid.

[22] *Wall Street Journal*, May 22, 2013, "Japan Posts 10th Straight Trade Deficit", http://online.wsj.com/article/SB10001424127887324787004578497812964033312.html (accessed June 1, 2013).

economists on the same day as the policy announcement.[23] But meeting the market's never-ending expectations at every stage might have proven a formidable task even for Kuroda. The markets were always reading the future, so Kuroda's approach risked placing the BOJ in a reactive position.

The Federal Reserve (Fed) of the United States turned to quantitative easing after the financial crisis in 2008. In 2013, the United States was in round three of quantitative easing, the formal term for the Fed injecting $85 billion in bonds a month into the economy by purchasing longer-term assets like Treasury bonds. There were dangerous signs of pre-bubble activity in the United States: overvalued stocks and real estate and junk bond yields at record lows. The Fed was starting to look for a way out. About the same time in 2013, similar strategies were being carried out in Japan. The difference between the United States and Japan was that the Fed made quantitative easing on a step-by-step basis (QE1, QE2 and QE3),[24] but the BOJ rejected the status quo of ramping up easing incrementally, weighing the benefits and side effects of each step, and took every conceivable measure at once.

The BOJ was finally starting a full-fledged battle against deflation. How long until its inflation target came within sight? Given how high the markets' expectations had risen, they would easily crumble into disappointment unless the bank could produce results. To sustain the momentum, it had to maintain a dialogue with the markets. Kuroda's predecessor, Masaaki Shirakawa, who warned at his final news conference of the danger of trying "to move the markets with words," came across at best as honest, at worst as naive. Fellow Western central bankers had used a combination of verbal pressure and actions to convince markets.[25]

6. The BOJ had shown that it could deliver the bold measures that had been sought by Prime Minister Abe. Now the question was whether the BOJ could deftly manage expectations down the road. The BOJ's dramatic

---

[23] *Nikkei* (*Japan Economic Journal*), April 5, 2013, "All Eyes On BOJ Policy Board, But Change Unlikely", http://www.nikkei.com/article/DGXDASFS0401T_U3A400C1MM8000/ (accessed May 1, 2013).

[24] QE1 stood for quantitative easing round/phase 1.

[25] *Nikkei* (*Japan Economic Journal*), April 4, 2013, "Monetary Base Hits Record High For 2nd", http://www.nikkei.com/article/DGXDASFS0303Y_T00C13A4MM8001/ (accessed May 1, 2013).

conversion to Federal Reserve-style unlimited monetary easing lifted share prices, weakened the yen, and sent the 10-year government bond yield plunging. There was still cause for concern, however. Since taking office, Kuroda had sought to remind the government to keep its side of the bargain by pursuing fiscal sustainability. Runaway government spending abetted by ultra-loose monetary easing could bring about the long-predicted crash in JGBs. If the political leadership shunned the heavy lifting of regulatory reforms while indulging in deficit spending, the BOJ would come across as merely picking up the tab. The Japanese government had to work as one with the BOJ, and with equal determination, to break deflation's nearly 20-year hold on Japan. The Japanese government and the BOJ had to bear in mind that there was the issue of the central bank's autonomy from the state. While the BOJ needed to maintain good communications with the government in order to avoid negligent lapses, the government had to respect the central bank's independence.

7. The BOJ raced ahead to an ultra-loose monetary policy. After a piecemeal and seemingly halfhearted pursuit of monetary easing, Japan had finally caught up with the advanced economies pushing loose credit to the extremes. This drastically changed where Japan stood in relation to both the United States and Europe, as well as emerging economies. International opposition to the BOJ's new monetary policy was relatively light. With a debate on winding down easing going on in the United States, the BOJ's stance would look looser by comparison.

> *Parallel campaigns of monetary easing in advanced economies are "enrich-thy-neighbor actions," rather than the more familiar beggar-thy-neighbor kind.*
>
> — Ben Bernanke, chairman of US Federal Reserve[26]

> *The ECB will do whatever it takes to preserve the euro and stands ready to act.*
>
> — Mario Draghi, president of European Central Bank[27]

---

[26] Ibid.

[27] Ibid.

Many questions remained unanswered. Would concerns about Japan's fiscal health grow? Could Japan escape from deflation? The BOJ would have to address such doubts persistently. The appropriateness of the BOJ's decision on April 4, 2013, doubling the monetary base via government bond purchases, would be studied internationally on an *ex post* basis in the future.

## For Further Discussion

1. Do you think deflation will go away due to the BOJ's quantitative easing policy?
2. Will the new easing initiatives of Japan put the BOJ on a par with its American and European counterparts?
3. How do you evaluate the risks and side effects of the BOJ's new monetary easing?
4. Do you think that the BOJ alone can end deflation?
5. Is the BOJ's independence defined as operational rather than absolute?
6. It is widely said that global economies are now facing an age of deflation. Comment on this.
7. Money and foreign exchange markets in Tokyo and New York are very efficient. The following information is available on April 1, 2013:

|  | Tokyo | New York |
| --- | --- | --- |
| Spot exchange rate | ¥85.00/$ | — |
| One-year treasury bill rate | 1.00% | 3.00% |
| Expected inflation rate | unknown | 3.00% |

(a) What do the financial markets suggest for inflation in Japan next year? If the BOJ's 2% inflation target can be achieved, what happens to Japanese interest rates?

(b) What do the financial markets suggest for the exchange rate after one year, if the BOJ's 2% inflation target can be achieved?

# Appendix 1  Yen Devaluation

## Japanese Trade

Per the BOJ's extremely easy monetary policy, the Japanese yen was devalued substantially from ¥80/$ to ¥99/$ in a three-month period in 2013. The devalued yen would make Japanese exports more price-competitive on world markets. The devaluation of the new Taiwan dollar in 1997 during the Asian financial crisis was believed to have been one such competitive devaluation. What were the logic and the likely results of intentionally devaluing the domestic currency to improve the trade balance? These competitive devaluations were considered to be self-destructive, as they also made imports relatively more expensive. These competitive devaluations would invite other countries' countermeasures of devaluation. The result would be "devaluation war."

## The J-Curve Adjustment Path

The trade balance adjustment process occurred in three stages[28]:

(1) the currency contract period;
(2) the pass-through period; and
(3) the quantity adjustment period.

(See **Exhibit 4** for the three stages, and the resulting time-adjustment path of the trade balance.)

The path of adjustment took on the shape of a flattened "j".

Suppose  $P_x^{¥}$ = the price of exports
$P_M^{fc}$ = the price of imports
$Q_x$ = the quantity of exports
$Q_M$ = the quantity of imports
$S^{¥/fc}$ = the spot exchange rate

---

[28] Eiteman, D.K., Stonehill, A.I. and Moffett, M.H. (2012) *Multinational Business Finance*, 13th Edition, New York: Pearson Series in Finance.

Then, the Japanese trade balance, expressed in yen, could then be expressed as follows:

$$\text{Japanese trade balance} = (P_x^{\yen}Q_x) - (S^{\yen/\text{fc}}P_M^{\text{fc}}Q_M)$$

A devaluation of the yen would first result in a deterioration in the trade balance (currency contract period $= t_1$). After the then-current contracts, new prices reflecting pass-through had been instituted and improvements in the trade balance would have been evident (pass-through period $= t_2$). Finally, the price elasticity of demand would take effect (quantity adjustment period $= t_3$) and the trade balance would rise above where it started.

The J-Curve Trade Balance Adjustment to Exchange Rate Changes

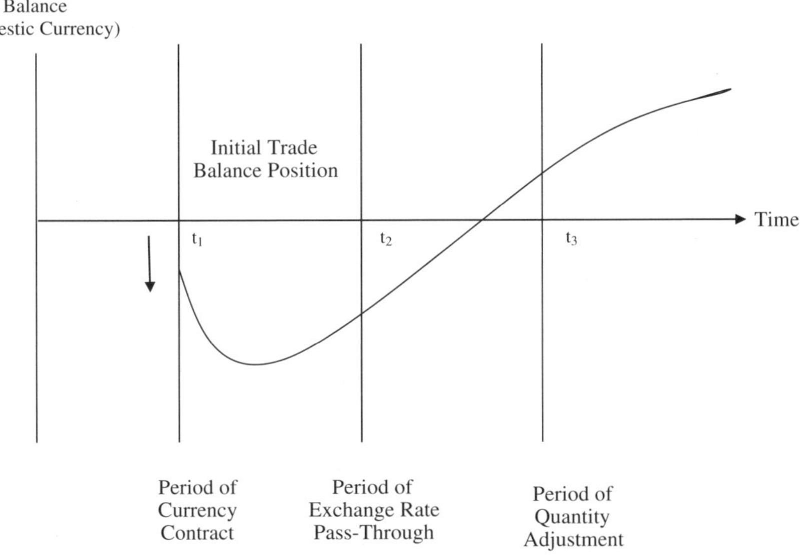

# Appendix 2  International Party Conditions in Equilibrium: Related Formulas[29]

Suppose:

$S$ = the spot exchange rate (a direct quote on ¥ is, for example, ¥/$) at the beginning of the period ($S_1$) and the end of the period ($S_2$)

$i^¥$ = the Japanese interest rate

$i^$ = the US interest rate

$\pi^¥$ = the Japanese interest rate

$\pi^$ = the Japanese interest rate

Home currency = ¥

## 1.  $\Delta\%$ change in S

In direct quotation when the home currency price for a foreign currency is used, the formula becomes:

$$\Delta\%\text{Change} = \frac{(S_2 - S_1)}{S_1}$$

## 2.  Purchasing Power Parity (PPP)

According to the relative PPP, the relative change in prices between two countries over a period of time determines the change in the exchange rate over that period. The formula becomes:

$$S_2 = S_1 \times \frac{1 + \pi^¥}{1 + \pi^S}$$

The figure below shows a general case of relative PPP. The vertical axis shows the % change in S for foreign currency, and the horizontal axis shows the % difference in rates of inflation (foreign relative to home country). The diagonal parity line shows the equilibrium position between a change in the exchange rate and inflation rates.

---

[29] Ibid.

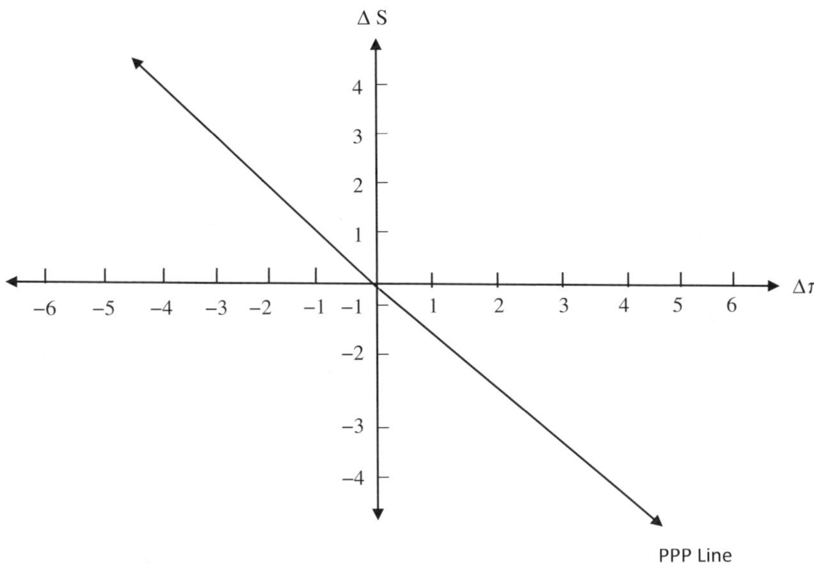


## 3. The International Fisher Effect

The forecast change in the spot exchange rate is equal to, but opposite in sign to, the differential between nominal interest rates. The relationship between the % change in S over time and the differential between interest rates in different markets is known as the international Fisher effect.

The formula becomes:

$$\frac{(S_2 - S_1)}{S_1} = (i^{¥} - i^{\$})$$

## 4. The Fisher Effect

The real rate of return ($r$) is the nominal rate of interest ($i$) less the expected rate of inflation ($\pi$). Assuming efficient and open markets, the real rates of return should be equal across currencies.

The formula is: $r = i - \pi$

## 5. Prices, Interest Rates, and Exchange Rates in Equilibrium

The figure below illustrates all of the fundamental parity relations in equilibrium, using the $ and the ¥.

**International Party Conditions in Equilibrium**

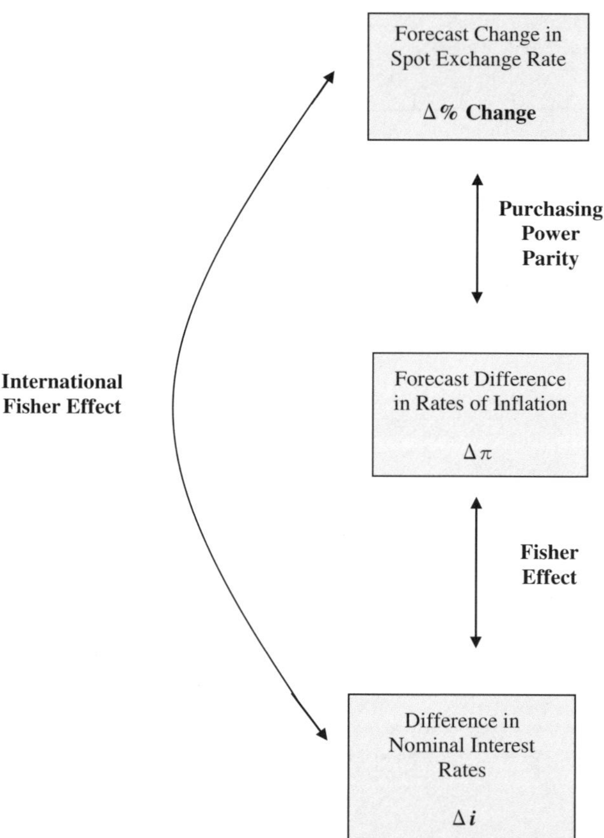

# 19

# Abenomics of Japan: What Was It? Could This Conquer Japan's Decade-Long Deflation?

The economic policies advocated by Prime Minister Shinzo Abe of Japan, dubbed Abenomics, had weakened the yen and given new life to Japan's stock market. Abe called for the "three arrows" to conquer Japan's more than decade-long deflation (see **Exhibit 1**), along with aggressive monetary easing and large-scale public works projects. There were three components of Abenomics: monetary easing, fiscal spending, and growth strategies.[1] But the third component, growth strategies, was among the key policies.

---

[1] To better explain its "third arrow" of economic policy worldwide, Prime Minister Abe's government dispatched top advisers to New York and other foreign cities to hold seminars. With the financial markets on a wild ride at the time, the government provided more information about its strategy for growth, which, along with monetary easing and stimulus spending, was designed to pull Japan out of its extended economic funk. Cabinet adviser Koichi Hamada, Yale University professor emeritus of economics, and Cabinet Office Senior Vice-Minister Yasutoshi Nishimura held a seminar at the Japan Society in New York on June 28, 2013 for local investors. Hamada was a key adviser to Abe on monetary policy, while Nishimura and others were core architects of the government's growth strategy. They explained the aims of Abenomics as well as their approaches toward the growth strategy and fiscal consolidation. Similar events were scheduled for Hong Kong and Singapore to present information to investors there. Stock prices in Japan had declined sharply, and the government aimed to dampen volatility in equities and interest rates by encouraging inflows of overseas money. For details, see *Nikkei* (*Japan Economic Journal*), June 18, 2013, "Investor Relations, Abe-Style", http://e.nikkei.com/e/ac/TNKS/Nni20130 617D1706A08.htm?NS-query=abenomics (accessed July 27, 2013).

**Exhibit 1**   Japan Consumer Price Index (January 1985–April 2013)

The CPI in Japan is reported by the Statistics Bureau of Japan. In Japan, CPI measures changes in the prices paid by consumers for a basket of goods and services. It decreased to 99.50 Index Points in January 2013 from 99.60 Index Points in December 2012. Historically, from 1985 until 2013, it averaged 99.13 Index Points, reaching an all-time high of 104.90 Index Points in November 1998 and a record low of 89.10 Index Points in February 1985.

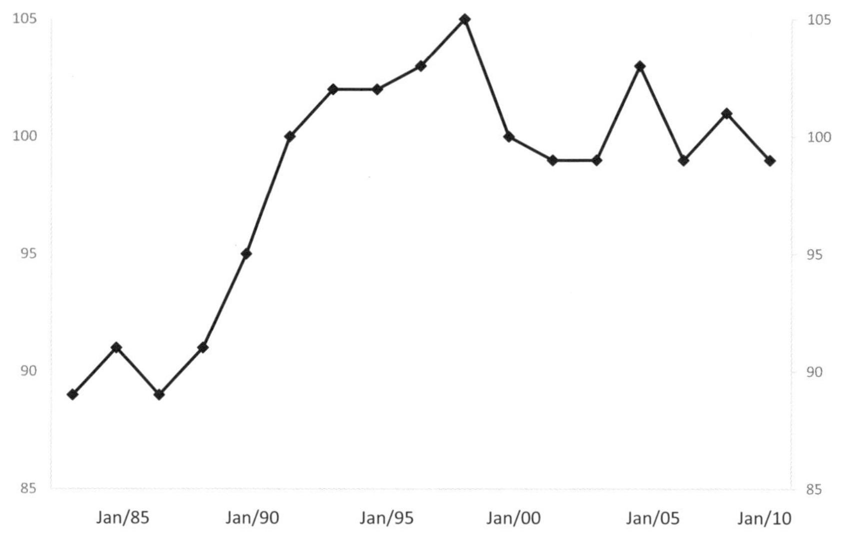


*Source*: Statistics Bureau of Japan, Consumer Price Index, Historical Data, http://www.stat.go.jp/english/data/cpi/ (accessed July 30, 2013).

# Japan Market Boom Meant Little Without Growth Strategy

The economy-boosting effects of Abenomics and the Bank of Japan's (BOJ's) bold monetary easing policy were stirring up considerable global interest in Japan. Without plans for keeping the growth momentum alive, however, the excitement might have all been for nothing.

This sudden interest in Japan was being driven by three main factors:

1. The extraordinary size of the BOJ's easing caught many overseas investors by surprise. The central bank planned to double the

monetary base to 270 trillion yen[2] in two years, a far cry from the previous policy of incremental easing.

2. Corporate profits were rising more quickly than expected. Earnings per share at firms listed on the first section of the Tokyo Stock Exchange were expected to jump 54% on the year in fiscal 2013 and 23% the following year.[3]

3. The trend stood out as a bright spot amid the global economic gloom. A recent World Economic Outlook report by the International Monetary Fund was downgraded from January 2013, but Japan was an exception.[4] This caused many who had long overlooked Japan to view the country in a fresh light.

But these expectations could be lofty.

1. Along with this renewed interest in Japan came some bloated expectations for Tokyo, such as that "Japan money," including investment in foreign bonds, would begin circulating strongly again; that investment would shift from Japanese bonds to Japanese stocks; and that Japanese companies would increasingly focus on domestic production and investment.

2. As for a recovery in investment in foreign bonds, Japanese investors continued to be net sellers. Given that Japan regularly posted a trade deficit and its current-account surplus was shrinking, the outflow of capital from the country was also decreasing. Regarding the allocation of assets to stocks and bonds, a flight of funds to bonds was still present. This was largely due to capital-adequacy rules for banks and other mechanisms that worked to funnel money into government bonds.

3. When it came to the repatriation of production and investment, Japanese firms had been burned before. Even amid a weaker-yen trend that lasted until 2007, there was a push to focus more on domestic manufacturing, and companies stepped up their capital investment.

---

[2] US$2.87 trillion at ¥94.16/$ of April 1, 2013.

[3] *Nikkei* (*Japan Economic Journal*), April 23, 2013, "BOJ Puts Optimistic Spin on Inflation Forecast", http://e.nikkei.com/e/ac/TNKS/Nni20130423D22HH025.htm?NS-query= Abenomics (accessed July 25, 2013).

[4] Ibid.

But just as that was happening, the global financial crisis erupted, triggering the yen's ascent. Even though the strong yen had been tamed, Japanese firms still had to deal with internationally high tax rates and surging energy costs.

But maintaining the momentum was important. The boost given by Prime Minister Abe's policy mix and the BOJ would mean little if the growth could not be sustained. To help the nascent recovery in consumption spread to corporate production and investment, moves to support companies needed to be studied, such as tax breaks for capital spending. It was also important for shareholders to put more pressure on firms to put their internal reserves to use.

Another key to unlocking the economy was restarting the nation's idled nuclear power plants. The Nuclear Regulation Authority, which was tasked with deciding which plants were allowed to reopen, was understaffed. The organization urgently needed more man power so that the plant-screening process did not get stuck in limbo.

## Painful Reform Had to Be Part of the Abenomics Formula

Of the three components of Abenomics, monetary easing and fiscal spending were unlikely to inflict much pain on the public, apart from the fact that younger generations would be forced to pay back the debt the government was rapidly incurring. But the third component, growth strategies, could only be effective when addressing regulatory issues that had long been left untouched.

In announcing the first batch of his growth strategies at a press conference on April 20, 2013, Abe touted plans to take Japanese technologies to the global market.[5] He promised to be the top salesperson to peddle medical technologies and related know-how to Russia and Middle Eastern countries.

---

[5] *Nikkei (Japan Economic Journal)*, April 20, 2013, "Painful Reform Needed for Abenomics", http://e.nikkei.com/e/ac/TNKS/Nni20130423D22HH025.htm?NS-query=Abenomics (accessed July 25, 2013).

In Japan, the government aimed to help people stay healthy longer by promoting regenerative medicine and streamlining the screening of new drugs. To curb declines in the birth rate, the government would provide subsidies to a broader range of child-care facilities and urge companies to grant longer parental leaves.

All of these measures were long overdue, but they were mostly government-led initiatives. What Japan needed most was regulatory and structural reform — painful, drastic reforms that would shuffle the deck for protected businesses. While structural reforms almost always inflicted pain on vested interests protected by regulatory walls, creative initiatives by newcomers benefited consumers and helped to revitalize the economy.

As Japan prepared to join the Trans-Pacific free trade pact,[6] for example, relaxation of a farmland law would be essential to consolidating farms into large-scale operators. This type of regulatory reform would likely gain broad support from consumers, even if the government would lose support from those that would be hurt by it.

## Abe was Eager to Set Up Special Economic Zones to Spur the Economy

Abe expressed eagerness on April 12, 2013, to establish special economic zones in the nation's three major metropolitan areas, aiming to spur the economy by boosting investment and attracting foreign businesses to Japan.[7] His remarks came as private-sector members of the panel, such as scholars and company executives, called for creating "Abenomics strategic special zones" in Tokyo as well as Osaka and Aichi prefectures. The panel intended to include the measures in the government's economic growth strategies to be put forward in June 2013. The members also urged Abe to

---

[6] See ibid. The United States and 11 Pacific Rim nations — Australia, Brunei Darussalam, Canada, Chile, Malaysia, Mexico, New Zealand, Peru, Singapore and Vietnam — were negotiating the 2005 Trans-Pacific Partnership (TPP) Free Trade Agreement in 2013. Japan had expressed its desire to become a negotiating partner in the TPP in 2013.

[7] *Nikkei* (*Japan Economic Journal*), April 18, 2013, "Abe Eager Sets up Special Economic Zones", http://e.nikkei.com/e/ac/TNKS/Nni20130417D1704F01.htm?NS-query=Abenomics (accessed July 21, 2013).

drastically lower corporate taxes in the zones to invigorate investment, but it was unclear whether the request was feasible, as the government would have to look for alternative sources of revenues should the tax cuts be carried out.

Among other proposals by these nongovernment members was allowing private organizations to operate infrastructure, including water supply and sewerage systems, airports, and toll roads, which had been mainly managed by the public sector. In Britain, for example, the number of users at Bristol Airport, which was sold to the private sector in 2001, tripled in 2008 compared with the pre-acquisition level as it launched new routes and expanded commercial space.[8]

The private-sector members also asked the government to take steps to invite top universities overseas to set up facilities in Japan and increase the number of hospitals providing medical services in English to improve the living environment for foreigners. Direct investment in Japan by foreigners as a percentage of gross domestic product was lower than in the United Kingdom, the United States, and South Korea, partly because of difficulties English-speaking people faced when living in Japan. The idea was to improve the working environment for foreigners and encourage more overseas companies to establish their Asian headquarters in Japan, which would lead to job creation. And accepting more engineers and other skilled foreigners was seen as leading to better personnel training and higher technological levels.

Central to this push would be easing restrictions on firing.[9] Proposals included letting companies fire as long as they paid re-employment benefits and allowing firms based in the special zones to follow the same rules elsewhere in Japan. Another idea was to make it easier to extend contract workers' terms. Under the existing rules, employers were required to have

---

[8] Ibid.

[9] It was a big issue to fire people in Japan, since Japan still basically enjoyed a lifetime employment system. In Japan, large companies hired regular employees right out of college and kept them until retirement. They were considered the company's assets to be trained, cultivated, and assigned to positions in the company's best interests. These employees were expected to serve the company loyally and not try to leave for a better position. This system worked well during Japan's long period of post-war economic growth, but in the 1990s, this system had begun to break down slightly during a prolonged economic recession.

offered contract workers full-time jobs after five years. A proposal for a so-called white-collar exemption to the legally mandated eight-hour workday and 40-hour workweek would also be discussed. This would lower the burden of overtime pay on employers. Greater flexibility to hire, fire, and pay would make the labor market more dynamic. The corporate sector was eager to see such changes happen, but critics said workers would be the ones to suffer. Other proposed reforms included easing Japanese-language requirements for foreign guest-worker nurses and child-care workers.

The second phase would bring a bigger wave of deregulation later. The Cabinet Office was considering some 130 potential items in such areas as employment, health care, farming, energy, urban redevelopment, and cultural initiatives.[10]

*Special zones will become a bridgehead that will allow us to create the world's friendliest business environment.*

— Shinzo Abe, prime minister of Japan[11]

## Japan Had to Specify Concrete Steps to Restore Fiscal Health

The Organisation for Economic Co-operation and Development (OECD)[12] put pressure on Japan in its policy proposal issued on April 23, 2013, to specify concrete measures to restore the country's precarious fiscal health, considered the worst among major developed economies.[13]

As for drastic monetary easing by the BOJ aimed at achieving its 2% inflation target within two years, a pillar of Japan's Abenomics, the OECD

---

[10] Ibid.

[11] Ibid.

[12] The OECD (www.oecd.org) was a Paris-based group of 34 economically advanced nations. Its mission was to promote policies that would improve the economic and social well-being of people around the world. For more information, see OECD (n.d.) "About the OECD," www.oecd.org/about (accessed August 1, 2013).

[13] *Nikkei* (*Japan Economic Journal*), April 23, 2013, "Japan Has to Specify Steps for Fiscal Health", http://e.nikkei.com/e/ac/TNKS/Nni20130423D23JF165.htm?NS-query=Abenomics (accessed July 25, 2013).

said what the central bank called quantitative and qualitative monetary easing was welcome.[14]

*The new government's resolve to revitalize the economy through a three-pronged strategy combining bold monetary policy, flexible fiscal policy and a growth strategy is most encouraging, But, given the size and duration of fiscal consolidation, Japan faces the risk of a marked rise in interest rates, threatening a banking system that is highly exposed to Japanese government debt.*

— Angel Gurria, secretary general of OECD[15]

Japan should "set out a detailed and credible plan, including spending goals by category and a timetable for tax hikes" to attain its globally pledged goal of budget deficit reduction, the OECD said in the first annual report released after the government of Prime Minister Abe was formed on December 26, 2013.[16]

Tokyo aimed to cut its primary balance deficit to 3.2% of the country's gross domestic product by fiscal 2015, or half the level of fiscal 2010, and turn the balance into a surplus by fiscal 2020. A deficit in the balance meant the nation could not finance government spending without issuing new bonds. The latest estimates, however, suggested the goals were almost infeasible, as Japan's fiscal health had shown little sign of improving. The Cabinet Office said in February 2013 that Japan could log a deficit of 33.9 trillion yen, or 6.9% to nominal GDP, in fiscal 2013 through March 2014, worsening from 25.4 trillion yen, or 5.2%, calculated in August 2013. Abe, who had promised to implement large-scale public works projects to bolster domestic demand, would likely need to quickly hammer out a plan for putting Japan's fiscal house in order.

Japan's public debt ratio had risen steadily for two decades to over 200% of GDP, as the country fell into recession for the third time in five years against a backdrop of the global financial crisis in the late 2000s and the devastating quake-tsunami disaster of March 2011. Japan's fiscal

---

[14] Ibid.

[15] Ibid.

[16] Ibid.

deterioration could have affected international economic growth. Japan, the world's third-largest economy, was planning to double its 5% sales tax rate in two stages by 2015, as scheduled, and to reform its social security system to curb public spending amid the rapid aging of its population. Increasing the sales tax rate was essential to stabilizing public debt in Japan, but its effect on low-income earners would need to be mitigated with an earned income tax credit. Some Japanese lawmakers had proposed lowering the sales tax rate on daily goods, such as food, to reduce the impact of the tax hike on low-income earners. To maintain social cohesion, the tax needed to be raised equally across all goods and services with no exceptions, no exemptions, no holes, and no preferential treatment.

The OECD pointed out that Japan first needed to make efforts to beat the nation's more than decade-long deflation and boost its growth potential to pave the way for its strong and protracted fiscal rehabilitation.[17] As part of the growth strategy, Japan needed to make use of its untapped human capital, including women in the workforce. Raising the pension eligibility age in Japan was also needed to reflect workers' long average life expectancy. As it stood, public pensions were paid in stages to those aged 60 or older.

## Inflation Rate Expected to Keep Rising — The BOJ's Position

The market's expected inflation rate (see **Appendix 1** and **Exhibit 2**) continued to rise. The trend of the expected inflation rate had a high correlation with those of the exchange rate and stock prices. It was important that the BOJ had pledged to achieve a 2% price growth in two years by bold monetary easing. Once expectations for a 2% increase spread within the market, real interest rates — or the nominal rate minus the expected inflation rate — would decline (see **Appendix 2**). This would bolster the psychological impact of encouraging borrowing and help buoy capital spending and housing investment for economic growth (for the GDP component, see **Appendix 3**). As for recent adjustments in stock prices and

---

[17] Ibid.

the dollar–yen rate, the markets had become susceptible to volatility since the expanded monetary easing measures were rolled out in April 2013.

In accordance with the BOJ's extremely easy monetary policy, the Japanese yen was devalued substantially from ¥80/$ to ¥99/$ in the three-month periods from November 1, 2012 to March 1, 2013. The devalued yen would make Japanese exports more price-competitive on world markets. What were the logic and likely results of intentionally devaluing the domestic currency to improve the trade balance? These competitive devaluations were considered self-destructive, as they also made imports relatively more expensive. These competitive devaluations would invite other countries' countermeasures of devaluation. The result would be devaluation war. While the weaker yen helped major Japanese exporting

**Exhibit 2**   Inflation Expectations (BEIR), Nikkei Stock Index, Yen Exchange Rate, and Bond Yields in Japan

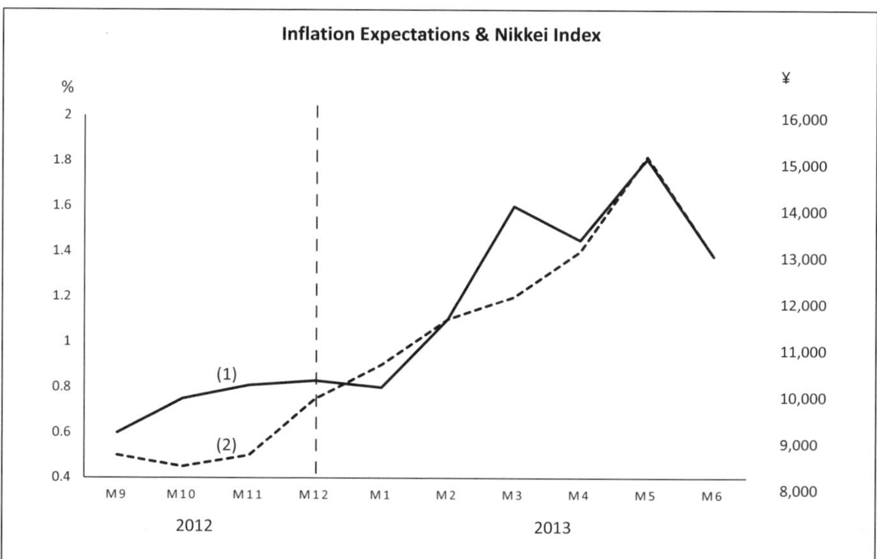


*Note*: (1) I.E. = Inflation expectation rate (BEIR) (%),
        (2) Nikkei = Nikkei stock price (yen).

*Source*: *Nikkei* (*Japan Economic Journal*), June 25, 2013, "Expected Inflation Rate Is Rising", http://e.nikkei.com/e/ac/tnks/Nni20130624D2406F01.htm (accessed July 25, 2013).

(*Continued*)

**Exhibit 2**   (*Continued*)

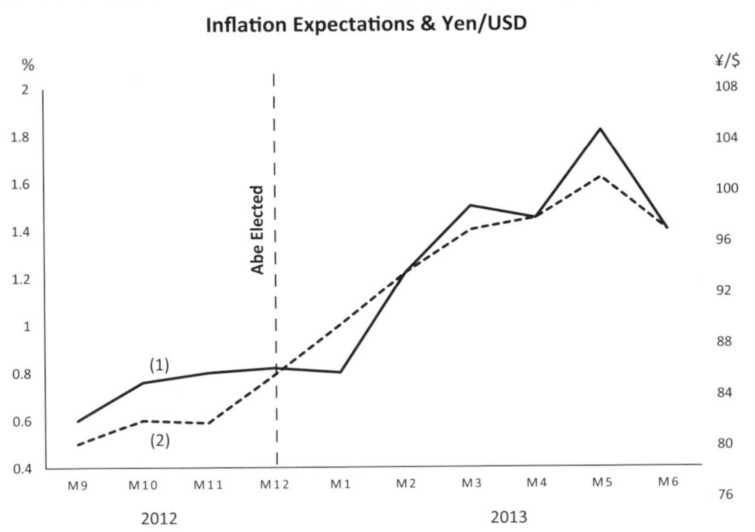



*Note*: (1) I.E. = Inflation expectation rate (BEIR) (%),

(2) FX = Yen/$ (yen).

*Source*: *Nikkei* (*Japan Economic Journal*), June 25, 2013, "Expected Inflation Rate Is Rising", http://e.nikkei.com/e/ac/tnks/Nni20130624D2406F01.htm (accessed July 25, 2013).

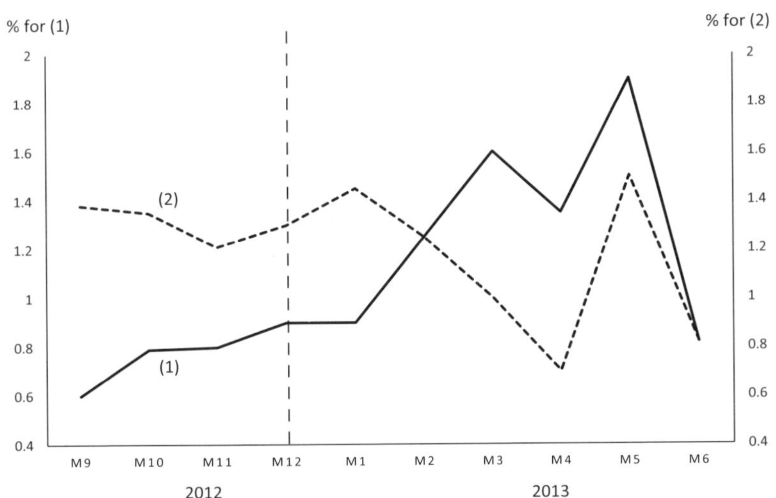



*Note*: (1) I.E. = Inflation expectation rate (BEIR) (%),

(2) 10 year Bond = Yield of 10-year government bond.

*Source*: *Nikkei* (*Japan Economic Journal*), June 25, 2013, "Expected Inflation Rate Is Rising", http://e.nikkei.com/e/ac/tnks/Nni20130624D2406F01.htm (accessed July 25, 2013).

companies book solid earnings, Japan's trade balance became a deficit of 181 billion yen in June 2013. Exports increased 7.4%, while imports surged 11.8%. Japanese imports increased for eight consecutive months, as yen depreciation was making foreign products more expensive (see **Appendices 4** and **5**).

Furthermore, the market held varying views about whether Japan's 2% inflation target was within reach or far off. The markets were also highly susceptible to turbulence amid discussions about a US exit from loose monetary policy. The brief spike in Japanese long-term interest rates after easing measures were expanded was attributed to the BOJ's pledge to boost the expected inflation rate. The BOJ's policy entailed large purchases of government bonds, or the capability to lower nominal interest rates, and once the impact of easing became more widespread, interest rate volatility was expected to subside.

The BOJ estimated that the impact of the easing was equivalent to necessary funding volumes assuming nominal 3% growth and 2% inflation.[18] The BOJ would not dole out small-bore easing initiatives, shelving additional steps for the time being. The BOJ was indicating a flexible stance for policy management and that it would take appropriate action when the existing policy became inadequate.

## Structural Reforms and Growth Strategies were Needed

A debate was sparked between reflationists, who supported bold monetary easing, and anti-reflationary forces, which advocated structural reforms first. More jobs and higher wages could help speed Japan toward its 2% price growth target. The fastest way to attain that goal might have been to get the two forces of monetary easing and structural reforms to work as one.

The BOJ's expanded monetary easing helped lift market expectations, but structural reforms had to accompany such measures to sustain prices and economic growth. Share prices rallied and the yen retreated after the December 2012 launch of Prime Minister Abe's government-fueled plans

---

[18] *Nikkei* (*Japan Economic Journal*), June 25, 2013, "Expected Inflation Rate Is Rising", http://e.nikkei.com/e/ac/tnks/Nni20130624D2406F01.htm (accessed July 25, 2013).

for bold monetary easing. The BOJ delivered in April 2013 by rolling out major easing steps, accelerating stock gains and the yen's depreciation. But expectations alone could not change reality. Mortgage rates, which had a direct impact on housing investment, had risen since the BOJ easing. The Nikkei Stock Average briefly surged past 15,000, but had since fallen back to its pre-easing level. Such trends highlighted the limits of relying on expectations alone.

The effects of quantitative easing were still unknown as well. The BOJ contended that a 10% rise in the balance of current accounts that financial institutions had deposited there would lift the expected inflation rate by 0.44 percentage point.[19] The current-account balance stood at 83 trillion yen, doubling in six months. But the expected inflation rate remained flat.

The economy was showing signs of a virtuous cycle, with stock price gains spurring consumer spending. But for companies to increase capital spending and hiring, anticipated price gains needed to be transformed into hopes for economic growth. To achieve that, the government needed to liberalize trade and offer growth strategies, such as tax breaks for capital investment, before the virtuous cycle lost steam.

## Sustained Growth Required a New Policy Dimension

The cabinet of Prime Minister Abe was set to lay out its plans for the next phase of its economic growth package, which it hoped would spur a sustained recovery. Abe unveiled the second phase of his growth strategy in May 2013. He said the cabinet was putting policies in place to achieve an economic recovery of a new dimension.[20] The same day, the Cabinet Office released preliminary data showing Japan's gross domestic product grew at an annualized 3.5% on the year in January–March 2013. That was much

---

[19] *Nikkei* (*Japan Economic Journal*), June 25, 2013, "Structural Reforms Are Needed with Growth Strategies", http://www.nikkei.com/article/DGXNASGC2401W_U3A620C1000000/ (accessed July 26, 2013).

[20] *Nikkei* (*Japan Economic Journal*), May 23, 2013, "Abe's Investment Attraction Strategy Fails to Impress", http://e.nikkei.com/e/ac/TNKS/Nni20130523D23HH746.htm?NS-query= abenomics (accessed July 29, 2013).

higher than the country's estimated potential growth rate of about 0.5%. This economic data seemed to bear out that optimism. The prospects were good for the economy to pick up steam, helped by Abe's expansionary economic policies, a weakening yen, higher stock prices, and a global economic recovery.

There were still several hurdles to jump, however, before declaring the arrival of a full-fledged recovery. A virtuous circle of higher exports and production, stronger corporate earnings, increased capital investment, higher wages and employment, and rising personal spending were needed. Some of the challenges included the following:

1. One potential bottleneck was capital investment. The GDP data showed that capital investment fell 0.7% year-on-year in real terms in January–March 2013, the fifth straight quarter of contraction. This pointed to lingering caution among Japanese companies about the prospects for recovery, which was holding back new investment. Abe appeared aware of the problem. He said that it was time to shoot the third arrow to stimulate corporate investment and called for the next three years to be an intensive period for spurring investment, saying the government would try to boost nominal corporate capital spending from 63 trillion yen per year to 70 trillion yen by fiscal 2016.[21] To reach that goal, capital spending needed to grow by 3.8% annually. That pace would not be easy. Growth in Japan's nominal corporate spending exceeded 3.8% in only three of the last 15 years: 1997, 2005, and 2006.

2. Although Abenomics had the potential to raise companies' growth expectations, it was uncertain whether the government would be able to spur domestic investment by major industries, many of which had been shifting production overseas. This could have been a major obstacle to shifting the economy into high gear.

3. Wages were another problem. According to data from the Japanese Trade Union Confederation,[22] the average annual wage increase for

---

[21] Ibid.

[22] The Japanese Trade Union Confederation (RENGO) was the largest national trade union center in Japan, with over six million members as of 2013. For more information, see RENGO (February 24, 2010) "Role & Function", www.jtuc-rengo.org/about/index.html (accessed August 11, 2013).

members of its 3,143 affiliated unions came to 1.77% following the 2013 spring wage negotiations, little changed from the previous year's 1.75% rise.[23] So far, Abe's call for big wage increases appeared to have fallen on deaf ears.

4.  Export growth was seen stalling as Asian shipments fell in the short run (see **Appendices 1, 3, 4** and **5**). Japanese overall exports would continue to rise in the long run thanks to the weaker yen and recovery in the global economy, including in the United States. But the economic slowdown in China and elsewhere could weigh on Japanese exports. The Chinese economy was still growing, but the growth rate could soon fall below 7.5%, which was the government's target rate for 2013.[24] The government would lower interest rates and the reserve requirement ratio to spur the economy.

Actually, Japanese exports were being weighed down by sluggish shipments to Asia, even while exports to Europe recovered. The trade deficit came to 1.02 trillion yen in July 2013, up 93.7% from a year earlier and a record for the month, according to data by the Finance Ministry. Imports exceeded exports for the 13th straight month.[25] The decline of the yen and higher resource prices pushed up the import values of crude oil and liquefied natural gas. Imports increased 19.6% to 6.98 trillion yen, while exports rose just 12.2%. Seasonally adjusted exports in July 2013 dropped 1.8% from June to 5.78 trillion yen, marking the first decline in eight months.[26] Without the impact of fluctuations in currency rates and commodity prices, exports shrank 3.2% on the month in real terms on the same basis. Exports to Asia, which accounted for half the overall total in value terms, fell by 5.7% on a price-adjusted basis.[27] This was due to a Chinese policy of curbing excess capital investment.

---

[23] *Nikkei* (*Japan Economic Journal*), August 20, 2013, "Japanese Export Growth Stalling as Asian Shipments Fall", http://e.nikkei.com/e/ac/TNKS/Nni20130819D1908A15.htm?NS-query=chinese%20economy%20and%20japan (accessed July 25, 2013).

[24] Ibid.

[25] Ibid.

[26] Ibid.

[27] Ibid.

The government had already fired its monetary and fiscal arrows. That made it all the more important for the Abe government to ready its economic and regulatory reform arrow, due out in June, to reinvigorate corporate and personal spending. It planned to include measures aimed at encouraging leasing of plant and equipment to bolster capital spending, and deregulation aimed at spurring the development of regenerative medicine. That was unlikely to be enough. Abe appeared reluctant to take other steps, such as lowering corporate tax rates and lifting the ban on combining insured and uninsured medical care. But an incomplete economic strategy was unlikely to produce results, even if the policy direction was correct. More work was needed to make sure Abe's third arrow hit home.

## Decision Time

Since coming to power in December 2012, Abe had continuously promised to reduce regulatory burdens and improve the business climate. So far, he had not delivered enough.

## The Government's Growth Strategy Needed Work

The government's growth strategy, the third arrow of Abenomics, was supposed to deliver a kill shot to deflation by spurring private-sector investment and otherwise reinvigorating businesses. But for Japan, which had been beset by falling prices for two decades, the deregulation and reform measures included in the plan were not powerful enough. Abe's growth strategy was still a limply fired arrow. His work here was just beginning. The road to steady growth had to be paved with serious reforms.

The growth strategy was not short on targets. It called for increasing per-capita gross national income by over 1.5 million yen ($15,300) in 10 years. It aimed to triple infrastructure exports and private finance initiatives. Foreign direct investment in Japan and Japanese exports of farm products were to be doubled. The government said it set these targets to ensure that policies based on the strategy led to tangible results. The Abe administration had come up with some promising ideas, such as creating special deregulated zones that would serve as international-business-friendly ecosystems. Formally lifting a ban on online sales of over-the-counter drugs was another step in the right direction.

Reasonable as that may have sounded, targets were not enough to constitute the core of a growth strategy. What was needed were concrete policy instruments. The strategy was lacking in well-defined, potent measures. It was particularly unfortunate that the administration stopped short of promising a cut in the effective corporate tax rate. Also missing was a reform to allow patients to receive both publicly insured and uninsured medical treatments without voiding coverage for the former.

To develop a truly effective approach, Abe needed to create a policy-making system that could overcome the silo mentality of bureaucrats and the vested interests of powerful lobby groups. Only strong, integrated leadership would do the trick. Meeting expectations for reform, both at home and abroad, might have been the Japanese government's best bet for bringing calm.

## No Painful Reforms in the Fiscal Plan Either

Abe endorsed the strategy on June 14, 2013, and approved longer-term economic and fiscal policy blueprints, setting a new goal of reducing the ratio of public debt to gross domestic product in a stable manner, starting in fiscal 2021.[28] Japan began to draw up a medium-term fiscal consolidation plan that could be called the fourth arrow of Abenomics, but so far, there was no sign of entitlement benefit cuts or other painful spending reforms.

The point of the plan was to allow for natural growth in social security costs by squeezing other parts of the budget. Policy spending, which excluded debt-servicing costs but included social security, was to be kept at the fiscal 2013 level through fiscal 2015.

The government intended to wait until fiscal 2015 to come up with a plan for achieving a primary balance surplus by fiscal 2020. But the view

---

[28] *Nikkei* (*Japan Economic Journal*), June 17, 2013, "Japan Inc. Tested for Resolve to Engage in Global Mega-Competition," http://e.nikkei.com/e/ac/20130617/tnw/Nni2013 0617FP7CABI1.htm (accessed July 27, 2013).

from the financial markets was that Japan needed to practice more stringent fiscal discipline by curbing natural growth in social security costs.[29] German Chancellor Angela Merkel called attention to Japan's enormous budget deficit. The message was that Japan could not rely on monetary easing alone, and that failing to make progress on fiscal rebalancing would threaten the global economic recovery.[30] With Abenomics, Abe had stressed unconventional policies for beating deflation. The question was whether his commitment to fiscal reform would also be cast from a different mold.

In May 2013, the OECD urged Japan to map out a credible fiscal rehabilitation plan, warning that a lack of such a plan would erode the credibility of government bonds and trigger a spike in long-term interest rates, which could weigh on the economy ahead.[31]

## *More Government-Level Communication Needed*

The government of Prime Minister Shinzo Abe had begun earnestly seeking to strengthen its communication with the markets for concrete support measures. The government should have been eager to bring the markets, which had responded well to the premier's so-called Abenomics economic

---

[29]The cabinet approved a goal of cutting the primary deficit to 3.2% of gross domestic product in fiscal 2015 — half the fiscal 2010 level. This would require a roughly 17 trillion yen improvement over two years. For details, see *Nikkei* (*Japan Economic Journal*), May 29, 2013, "OECD Raises Japan Growth Forecasts, Calls for Fiscal Reform", http://e. nikkei.com/e/ac/TNKS/Nni20130529D2805A01.htm?NS-query=abenomics (accessed August 1, 2013).

[30]*Nikkei* (*Japan Economic Journal*), June 20, 2013, "Abe Govt. Must Continue Strong Economic Reform Drive", http://e.nikkei.com/e/ac/TNKS/Nni20130619D1906A15. htm?NS-query=abenomics (accessed July 27, 2013).

[31] Since the BOJ embarked on a new course of monetary easing in April 2013, the yield on 10-year government bonds had bucked wildly, touching a 14-month high of 1% in May 2013. Escaping deflation and achieving medium-term growth would entail controlling spending on health care and other nondiscretionary budget items, as well as expenditures by local governments. For details, see *Nikkei* (*Japan Economic Journal*), May 29, 2013, "OECD Raises Japan Growth Forecasts, Calls for Fiscal Reform", http://e.nikkei.com/e/ ac/TNKS/Nni20130529D2805A01.htm?NS-query=abenomics (accessed August 1, 2013).

policy mix, to its side. Market players were trying to guess what stock-price and yen-rate levels the government would use as the triggers for taking action to push them in a favorable direction.

Since May 2013, market players worldwide had been trying to figure out the relationship between Japanese stock-price volatility and Abenomics. The government was considering preparing a growth-strategy package and pushing forward with work on tax system reform, among other measures, to reinforce its policy. Under such changing circumstances, there was a growing need in Japan for policy contests among legislators in the financial market arena. The expression "Bernanke put" was heard on Wall Street. While the term "put" referred to the right to sell a financial derivative, in the latest sense it referred to the belief that US Federal Reserve Chairman Ben Bernanke would do whatever was necessary to keep markets from falling. Perhaps an "Abe put" was around the corner.

## For Further Discussion

1. Haruhiko Kuroda, the BOJ governor, pulled off a "neat trick" in April, 2013 but is there danger in leading people to expect a "miracle"? Could the goal be reached in two years?
2. How do you think that the BOJ under Kuroda has targeted the monetary base?
3. How about the risk of the BOJ's new policies triggering harmful inflation? Will a weaker yen help the BOJ toward its goal?
4. Comment on Abenomics, Prime Minister Shinzo Abe's three-pronged attack on deflation and economic growth.
5. Why Japan is urged to map out a credible fiscal rehabilitation plan to escape deflation and achieve medium-term growth?
6. Calculate Break-Even Inflation Rate (BEIR) for the data given below. Interpret what it means.

Nominal 5-Year Certified Deposit Rate (R) = 4%

Real 5-Year Inflation-Linked Yield ($r$) = 1%

7. It Is Said That New BOJ Policy Is Not Achieving Desired Results After Two Months. Why

# Appendix 1 Expected Inflation Rate and its Measurement

For Japan, the consumer price index (CPI) had been negative since 1994 and it was widely believed that *expectations* of future inflation had been persistently negative. This means that ongoing deflation was expected.

On April 4, the BOJ announced a program (Quantitative and Qualitative Monetary Easing), which was a pledge to drastically ramp up asset purchases to increase the monetary base, and to extend the duration of assets held on the Bank's balance sheet. This policy action by the BOJ had shown a spotlight on Japanese inflation expectations. An important measure of success for this monetary policy was the BOJ's ability to anchor inflation expectations, since inflation expectations influenced actual inflation and the achievement of a given inflation goal. The BOJ recently announced a 2% price stability target. How to measure inflation expectations? It is the consensus that there is no single reliable measure. There are three market methods:

1. A commonly used market-based gauge of the inflation expectations rate is the break-even inflation rate (BEIR), which is the difference between the nominal yield on a fixed-rate investment (R) and the real yield on an inflation-linked investment ($r$) of similar maturity and credit quality. In Japan, it is the difference between the nominal yield on Treasury Bonds and the real rate for Treasury Inflation-Protected Bonds (inflation-protected government bonds, called JGBi). Using the following simplified formula, the data in the chart below are calculated based on the JGBi's Closing Prices (**JGBi breakeven, 5 years**, in **Appendix 1-1**).

$$\text{BEIR} = (R - r)/(1 + r) \doteq R - r$$

2. Analogous measures come from over-the-counter derivatives called inflation swaps (**Inflation swap breakeven, 10 years** in **Appendix 1-1**). In Japan, the market for this swap is very thinly traded in recent years. There is doubt about the ability of these swap prices to convey reliable information about inflation expectations.

3. Alternative measures are available from surveys of households, investors, and professional forecasters (**Bank of Japan household survey — 5 years** and **Nikkei Quick survey — 10 years** in the chart below). However, survey responses may be formed in a backward-looking manner, making them more responsive to actual inflation than predictive of the future.

## *Appendix* **1-1** *Various Trends of BEIR in Japan for January 2010–April 2013*

**Existing Measures of Japanese Inflation Expectations**

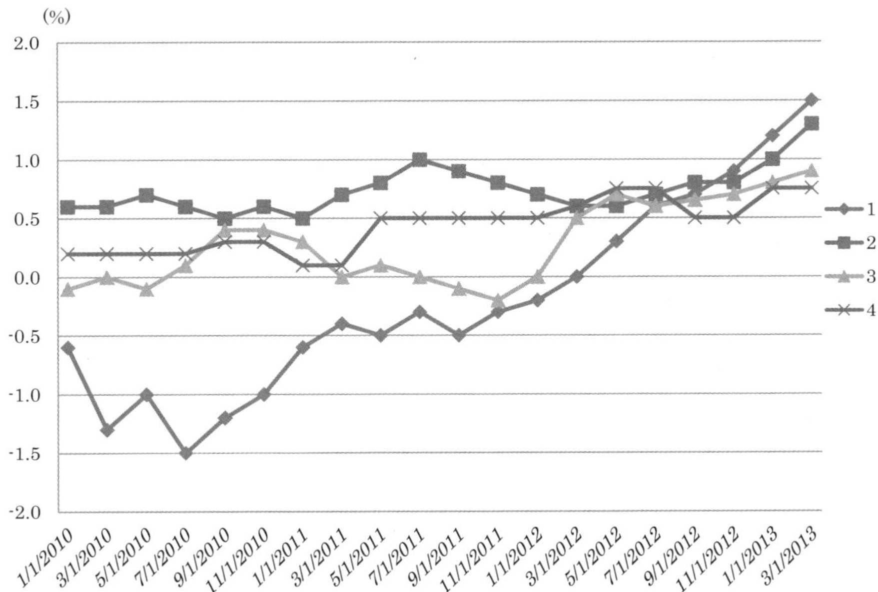


*Notes*: 1 shows Nikkei Quick survey (10-year);
2 shows Bank of Japan household survey (5-year);
3 shows Inflation swap breakeven (10-year);
4 shows JGBi breakeven (5-year).

*Source*: Bloomberg L.P.; Bank of Japan; Barclays Live, Quick; Nomura.

## *Appendix 1-2  Trend of BEIR in Japan for March 2005–March 2012*

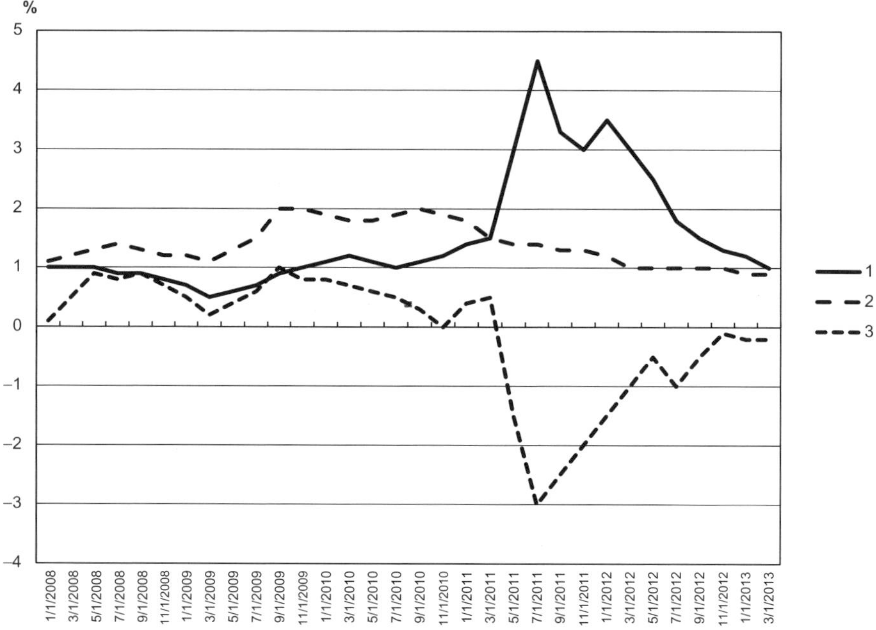


*Notes*: 1 shows yield on 10-year JGBi (compound);
2 shows yield on 10-year Government Bond (compound);
3 shows BEIR.

*Source*: *Nikkei* (*Japan Economic Journal*), June 25, 2013. "Expected Inflation Rate is Rising".

## Appendix 2  International Party Conditions in Equilibrium: Related Formulas[32]

Suppose:

$S$ = the spot exchange rate (a direct quote on ¥ is, for example, ¥/\$) at the beginning of the period ($S_1$) and the end of the period ($S_2$).

$i^¥$ = the Japanese interest rate

$i^\$$ = the U.S. interest rate

---

[32] Eiteman, D.K., Stonehill, A.I., and Moffett, M.H. (2012) *Multinational Business Finance*, 13th Edition, New York: Pearson Series in Finance, pp. 203–204.

$\pi^{¥}$ = the Japanese interest rate
$\pi^{\$}$ = the Japanese interest rate
Home currency = ¥

## 1. Δ% change in S

In direct quotation when the home currency price for a foreign currency is used, the formula becomes:

$$\Delta\%\text{Change} = \frac{(S_2 - S_1)}{S_1}$$

## 2. Purchasing Power Parity

According to the relative purchasing power parity, the relative change in prices between two countries over a period of time determines the change in the exchange rate over that period.

The formula becomes:

$$S_2 = S_1 \times \frac{1 + \pi^{¥}}{1 + \pi^{\$}}$$

## 3. The International Fisher Effect

The forecast change in the spot exchange rate is equal to, but opposite in sign to, the differential between nominal interest rates. The relationship between the percentage change in S over time and the differential between interest rates in different markets is known as the international Fisher effect.

The formula becomes:

$$\frac{(S_2 - S_1)}{S_1} = (i^{¥} - i^{\$})$$

## 4. The Fisher Effect

The real rate of return (r) is the nominal rate of interest (i) less the expected rate of inflation ($\pi$). Assuming efficient and open markets, the real rates of return should be equal across currencies.

The formula is: $r = i - \pi$

## Appendix 3  GDP Components

In a static (accounting) sense, a nation's GDP can be represented by the following equation[33]:

$$GDP = C + I + G + X - M$$

where:

| | |
|---|---|
| C | = consumption spending |
| I | = capital investment spending |
| G | = government spending |
| X | = exports of goods and services |
| M | = imports of goods and services |
| X − M | = the balance on current account (when including current income and transfers) |

Thus, a positive current account balance (surplus) contributes directly to increasing the measure of GDP, but a negative current account balance (deficit) decreases GDP.

In a dynamic (cash flow) sense, an increase or decrease in GDP contributes to the current account deficit or surplus. As GDP grows, so does disposable income and capital investment. Increased disposable income leads to more consumption, a portion of which is supplied by more imports. Increased consumption eventually leads to more capital investment.

Growth in GDP also should eventually lead to higher rates of employment. However, some of that theoretical increase in employment may be blunted by foreign sourcing (i.e., the purchase of goods and services from other enterprises located in other countries).

*Supply chain management* has increasingly focused on cost reduction through imports from less costly (e.g., lower wages) foreign locations. There imports can be from foreign-owned firms or from foreign subsidiaries of the parent firm. In the latter case, foreign subsidiaries tend to buy components and intellectual property from their parent firms, thus increasing exports. Although outsourcing has always been a factor in determining where to locate or procure manufactured goods and

---

[33] Eiteman, D.K., Stonehill, A.I. and Moffett, M.H. (2012) *Multinational Business Finance*, 13th Edition, New York: Pearson Series in Finance, pp. 102–106.

commodities, during the past decade an increasing amount of high-tech goods and services have been sourced from abroad. Foreign sourcing from the United States and Western Europe has been to countries such as India (software and call centers), China, Eastern Europe, Mexico, and the Philippines. This has caused a loss of some white-collar jobs in the United States and Western Europe and a corresponding increase elsewhere.

## Appendix 4 Yen Devaluation — The J-Curve Adjustment Path

The trade balance adjustment process occurred in three stages[34]:

1. the currency contract period;
2. the pass-through period; and
3. the quantity adjustment period

The three stages and the resulting time-adjustment path of the trade balance are illustrated below. The path of adjustment takes on the shape of a flattened "*j*."

Suppose    $P_x^{\yen}$ = the price of exports

$P_M^{\text{fc}}$ = the price of imports

$Q_x$ = the quantity of exports

$Q_M$ = the quantity of imports

$S^{\yen/\text{fc}}$ = the spot exchange rate

Then, the Japanese trade balance is expressed in yen as follows:

$$\text{Japanese trade balance} = (P_x^{\yen}Q_x) - (S^{\yen/\text{fc}}P_M^{\text{fc}}Q_M)$$

A devaluation of the yen would first result in a deterioration in the trade balance (currency contract period = $t_1$). After the current contracts, new prices reflecting pass-through would have been instituted and improvements in the trade balance would have been evident (pass-through period = $t_2$). Finally, the price elasticity of demand would take effect

---

[34] Ibid.

(quantity adjustment period $= t_3$) and the trade balance would rise above where it started.

### *Appendix 4-1  The J-Curve Trade Balance Adjustment to the Exchange Rate[35]*

Trade Balance

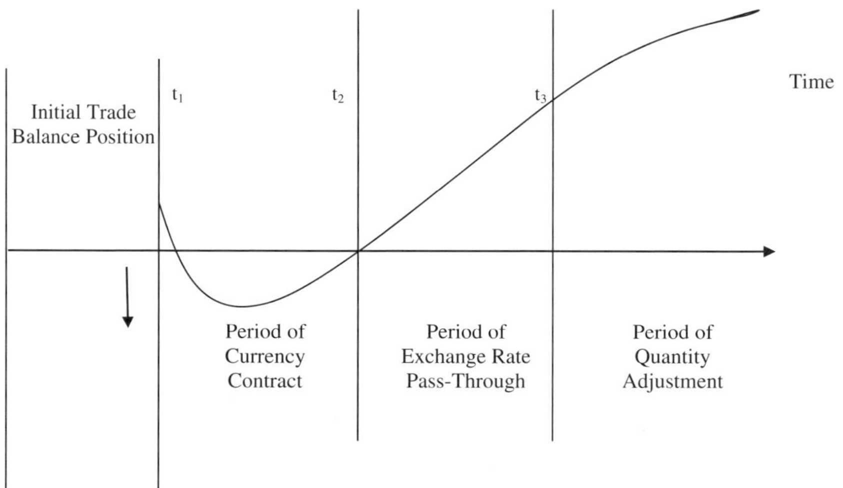


## Appendix 5  Balance of Payment and Exchange Rates

A country's balance of payment (BOP) can have a significant impact on the level of its exchange rate and vice versa, depending on that country's exchange-rate regime. The relationship between the BOP and exchange rates can be illustrated by use of a simplified equation that summarizes BOP data[36]:

|  *Current*  |  *Capital*  |  *Financial*  |  *Reserve*  |  *Balance*  |
| :---: | :---: | :---: | :---: | :---: |
|  *Account*  |  *Account*  |  *Account*  |  *Account*  |  *of Payment*  |

$$(X - M) + (CI - CO) + (FI - FO) + FXB = BOP$$

---

[35] Ibid.

[36] Ibid.

where:

| | | |
|---|---|---|
| X | = | exports of goods and services |
| M | = | imports of goods and services |
| CI | = | capital inflows |
| CO | = | capital outflows |
| FI | = | financial inflows |
| FO | = | financial outflows |
| FXB | = | official monetary reserves such as foreign exchange and gold |

The effect of an imbalance in the BOP of a country works somewhat differently depending on whether that country has fixed exchange rates, floating exchange rates, or a managed exchange rate system.

Under a floating exchange rate system, the government of a country has no responsibility to peg its foreign exchange rate. The fact that the current and capital account balances do not sum to zero will automatically alter the exchange rate in the direction necessary to obtain a BOP near zero. For example, a country running a sizable current account deficit, with a capital and financial accounts balance of zero, will have a net BOP of deficit. An excess supply of the domestic currency will appear on world markets. Like all goods in excess supply, the market will rid itself of the imbalance by lowering the price. Thus the domestic currency will fall in value, and the BOP will move back toward zero. Exchange rate markets do not always follow this theory, particularly in the short to immediate term. This delay is known as the *J-curve effect*. The deficit gets worse in the short run but moves back toward equilibrium in the long term.

# 20

# Saizeriya and the Use of Foreign Currency Coupon Swaps: Was This for Hedging or Speculation?

On December 9, 2008, Yasuhiko Shogaki, president of Saizeriya Co. Ltd. (Saizeriya) made a public announcement as to losses caused by the use of foreign currency coupon swaps. Saizeriya announced that on December 10, 2008 it terminated its Forex[1] reference-type Australian dollars (A\$) currency coupon swap contracts with BNP Paribas Securities (Japan), Ltd. (BNP Paribas), which caused a substantial potential valuation loss.

Saizeriya's management determined that the effects of the volatile fluctuation in the exchange rate could produce major instability in the future, and it was necessary to dissolve them immediately. The costs of termination amounted to ¥15 billion[2] and would be financed with the company's own money and bank loans.

The company imposed remuneration reductions on its directors as part of their director responsibilities concerning the occurrence of losses from the derivative transactions; the president and the representative director received a 70% reduction for 12 months, the financial director a 50% reduction for three months, and other directors a 10–30% reduction for three months.[3] Shogaki pledged to the public that the company would endeavor to strengthen its analysis and control of risks in order to avoid a recurrence of the case.[4]

---

[1] "Forex" meant the foreign exchange market. This was a technical term commonly used in the market.

[2] A\$0.24 billion at the rate of A\$62/¥ on December 9, 2008.

[3] Saizeriya's public release, see Saizeriya's website (http://www.saizeriya.co.jp/ir_info/jp/release.html) (accessed January 5, 2013).

[4] Ibid.

**Exhibit 1**    Corporate Data (as of November 30, 2010)

**Corporate Name:** Saizeriya Co., Ltd.
**Head Office:** 2-5 Asahi, Yoshikawa-city, Saitama 342-0008, Japan
**Established:** May 1, 1973
**Common Stock:** 8,612,500,000
**Number of Shares Issued:** 52,272,000 shares (including treasury stock)
**Fiscal Year-end:** August 31
**Securities Code Number:** 7581 (T.S.E., 1st Sec.)
**Business Lines:** Italian-style restaurant chain
**Number of Employees:** 2,200 (as of August 31, 2010)
**Board of Directors and Auditors:**
Chairman Yasuhiko Shogaki
President Issei Horino
Director Nobuyuki Masuoka
Director Hideharu Matsutani
Director Noboru Nagaoka
Director Minoru Orido
Standing Corporate Auditor Sakae Abe
Corporate Auditor Tsutomu Okada
Corporate Auditor Yoshiaki Miyaza

*Source*: Saizeriya (2010) "Saizeriya Data File 2010", http://www.saizeriya.co.jp/PDF/
irpdf000039.pdf (accessed January 5, 2013).

Saizeriya was a company involved in the restaurant business. It focused on providing healthy and tasty Italian meals at affordable prices to its customers (see **Exhibit 1**).[5] Aiming to achieve higher quality at lower prices, the company established a uniform production and sales system that covered everything from the procurement of ingredients to service at its 775 chain restaurants throughout Japan.[6] Hoping to offer richer and more varied food to more customers around the world, the company opened its first overseas restaurant in China in 2003, and by 2013 it operated a total of 24 restaurants in Shanghai, Guangzhou, Beijing and Taiwan.[7] On the domestic front, the company also launched the

---

[5] Ibid.

[6] Ibid.

[7] Ibid.

fast-food-style restaurants Saizeriya Express and Eat Run, in order to meet the tastes and needs of its customers, who were becoming more diverse.[8] The company was established in 1973 and employed 2,200 employees throughout Asia in 2013. Its annual sales totaled ¥84,949 million (US$791.84 million)[9] (see **Exhibits 2** and **3**).

> *From soil to tables, the company will continue to provide tasty food while meeting the new tastes and needs of outlets operating under direct production.*
>
> — Yasuhiko Shogaki, president of Saizeriya[10]

## Loss on the Coupon Swap Contracts

Also on December 9, 2008, Shogaki further announced that due to such transactions as derivatives meant to hedge against foreign exchange risks, Saizeriya might fall into the red in terms of group net earnings for that fiscal year through August 2009, although its initial projection called for a net profit of 4.2 billion yen (see **Exhibits 2** and **3**).[11] He said Saizeriya signed derivatives deals with BNP Paribas in October 2007 and February 2008 to procure Australian dollars needed to import food from Australia.[12]

Under the deals, he said Saizeriya was to receive A$1 million (US$646,400)[13] every month, payments of which started in September 2008.[14] If the yen weakened below the level set in the contract, Saizeriya was entitled to buy the Australian dollars at a discount (see **Appendix 1** and **Exhibit 4**). But if the yen appreciated beyond that threshold, the purchase price rose.[15] According to Shogaki, Saizeriya faced a 500 million

---

[8] Ibid.

[9] At the rate of ¥107.28/US$ on September 9, 2008.

[10] Saizeriya (2008) "Annual Report", http://www.saizeriya.co.jp/ir_info/jp/release.html (accessed January 5, 2013).

[11] *Nikkei* (*Japan Economic Journal*), December 1, 2008, http://www.nni.nikkei.co.jp/AC/20081201/TNW/Nni20081201IV5SAIZE.htm (accessed January 5, 2013).

[12] Ibid.

[13] At the rate of US$0.6464/A$ on September 9, 2008.

[14] Ibid.

[15] Ibid.

**Exhibit 2**   Saizeriya's Balance Sheets

(¥ Million)

|  | 2008/8 | 2009/8 | 2010/8 |
|---|---|---|---|
| **Assets** | | | |
| Current assets: | 21,700 | 25,772 | 29,929 |
| Cash and deposits with banks | 5,245 | 14,681 | 22,654 |
| Accounts receivable-tenants | 603 | 526 | 679 |
| Inventories | 3,370 | — | — |
| Merchandise and finished goods | — | 2,854 | 3,147 |
| Raw materials and supplies | — | 619 | 536 |
| Deferred tax assets | 648 | 3,748 | 975 |
| Income taxes receivable | — | 1,432 | — |
| Other current assets | 1,833 | 1,908 | 1,935 |
| Fixed assets: | 42,251 | 42,596 | 44,172 |
| Tangible fixed assets | 26,884 | 26,741 | 28,038 |
| Buildings and structures | 17,651 | 17,502 | 18,249 |
| Machinery, vehicle and equipment | 2,599 | 2,292 | 2,132 |
| Tools, furniture and fixtures | 1,069 | 1,458 | 1,975 |
| Land | 5,400 | 5,363 | 5,357 |
| Lease assets | — | — | 169 |
| Construction in progress | 163 | 124 | 154 |
| Intangible fixed assets | 264 | 234 | 208 |
| Investments and other assets | 15,102 | 15,621 | 15,924 |
| Total assets | 63,951 | 68,369 | 74,102 |
| **Liabilities** | | | |
| Current liabilities: | 9,494 | 14,033 | 18,403 |
| Accounts payable-trade | 3,450 | 3,315 | 3,473 |
| Current portion of long-term borrowings | — | 5,442 | 5,442 |
| Lease obligations | — | — | 7 |
| Corporation and inhabitants tax payable | 1,598 | 264 | 3,152 |
| Accrued bonuses | 701 | 759 | 1,205 |

(*Continued*)

**Exhibit 2**   (*Continued*)

|  | 2008/8 | 2009/8 | 2010/8 |
|---|---|---|---|
| Allowance for special benefit for shareholders | 224 | 213 | 207 |
| Derivative liabilities | — | 737 | 782 |
| Other current liabilities | 3,520 | 3,301 | 4,132 |
| Long-term liabilities: | 102 | 7,091 | 1,792 |
| Long-term borrowing | — | 6,930 | 1,488 |
| Lease obligations | — | — | 164 |
| Deferred tax liabilities | 43 | 21 | 7 |
| Other long-term liabilities | 58 | 140 | 131 |
| Total liabilities | 9,596 | 21,125 | 20,195 |
| **Net assets** | | | |
| Shareholders' equity: | 52,232 | 46,358 | 53,278 |
| Capital stock | 8,612 | 8,612 | 8,612 |
| Capital surplus | 9,007 | 9,007 | 9,007 |
| Retained earnings | 35,883 | 30,011 | 36,933 |
| Treasury stock | −1,270 | −1,272 | −1,274 |
| Valuation and translation adjustments: | 2,122 | 885 | 606 |
| Unrealized loss on marketable securities | −66 | −86 | −80 |
| Translation adjustments | 2,189 | 972 | 686 |
| Subscription rights to shares | — | — | 21 |
| Total net assets | 54,354 | 47,244 | 53,906 |
| Total liabilities and net assets | 63,951 | 68,369 | 74,102 |

*Source*: Saizeriya (2010) "Saizeriya Data File 2010", http://www.saizeriya.co.jp/PDF/irpdf000039.pdf (accessed January 5, 2013).

yen (A$8.66 million)[16] loss every time the Australian dollar slipped by 1 yen.[17] The loss it announced for the quarter was, according to him, an estimate based on an exchange rate of 65 yen to the A$ (see **Exhibit 5**).[18]

---

[16] At the rate of A$62/¥ on December 9, 2008.

[17] Ibid.

[18] Ibid.

**Exhibit 3**   Saizeriya's Income Statement

(¥ million)

|                                          | 2006/8 | 2007/8 | 2008/8 | 2009/8 | 2010/8 |
|------------------------------------------|--------|--------|--------|--------|--------|
| Net sales                                | 78,976 | 82,866 | 84,949 | 88,323 | 99,459 |
| Increase rate (%)                        | 5.9    | 4.9    | 2.5    | 4.0    | 12.6   |
| Ordinary income (loss)                   | 6,722  | 8,298  | 7,853  | −6,929 | 14,022 |
| Ordinary income (loss) to net sales (%)  | 8.5    | 10.0   | 9.2    | −7.8   | 14.1   |
| Net income (loss)                        | 3,563  | 4,411  | 4,011  | −4,896 | 7,842  |
| Net income (loss) to net sales (%)       | 4.5    | 5.3    | 4.7    | −5.5   | 7.9    |
| Total net assets                         | 49,267 | 53,156 | 54,354 | 47,244 | 53,906 |
| Shareholders' equity ratio (%)           | 82.3   | 84.9   | 85.0   | 69.1   | 72.7   |

*Source*: Saizeriya (2010) "Saizeriya Data File 2010", http://www.saizeriya.co.jp/PDF/irpdf000039.pdf, (accessed January 5, 2013).

**Exhibit 4**   Australian Dollar to Japanese Yen Exchange Rate (August 2007 – August 2010)

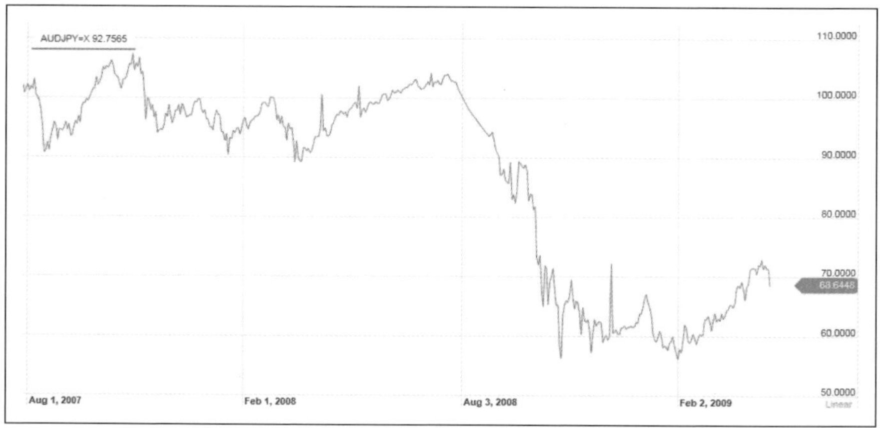


*Source*: Yahoo Finance (n.d.) "Currency Converter", http://finance.yahoo.com/currency-converter/#from=USD;to=EUR;amt=1, (accessed January 5, 2013).

Those contracts were taken out in an attempt to reduce risks stemming from exchange rate fluctuations between the yen and the A\$. Saizeriya would suffer losses once the A\$ fell below 78 yen to the dollar.[32] The

---

[32] Ibid.

**Exhibit 5**   Analysis of Swap at ¥65/A$

| Date | Amount | Spot (¥/A$) | Effective Rate Due to the Contract (¥/A$) | Profit/Loss (¥) |
|---|---|---|---|---|
| 2008/12/1 | 1,000,000 | 65 | 78 | −13,000,000[19] |
| 2009/1/1 | 1,000,000 | 65 | 93.6[20] | −28,600,000 |
| 2009/2/1 | 1,000,000 | 65 | 112.3[21] | −47,300,000 |
| 2009/3/1 | 1,000,000 | 65 | 134.8[22] | −69,800,000 |
| 2009/4/1 | 1,000,000 | 65 | 161.7[23] | −96,700,000 |
| 2009/5/1 | 1,000,000 | 65 | 194.0[24] | −129,000,000 |
| 2009/6/1 | 1,000,000 | 65 | 232.9[25] | −167,900,000 |
| 2009/7/1 | 1,000,000 | 65 | 279.5[26] | −214,500,000 |
| 2009/8/1 | 1,000,000 | 65 | 335.4[27] | −270,400,000 |
| 2009/9/1 | 1,000,000 | 65 | 402.5[28] | −337,500,000 |
| 2009/10/1 | 1,000,000 | 65 | 483.0[29] | −418,000,000 |
| 2009/11/1 | 1,000,000 | 65 | 579.6[30] | −514,600,000 |
| 2009/12/1 | 1,000,000 | 65 | 600[31] | −535,000,000 |
| 2010/1/1 | 1,000,000 | 65 | 600 | −535,000,000 |
| 2010/2/1 | 1,000,000 | 65 | 600 | −535,000,000 |
| 2010/3/1 | 1,000,000 | 65 | 600 | −535,000,000 |
| 2010/4/1 | 1,000,000 | 65 | 600 | −535,000,000 |
| 2010/5/1 | 1,000,000 | 65 | 600 | −535,000,000 |
| 2010/6/1 | 1,000,000 | 65 | 600 | −535,000,000 |
| 2010/7/1 | 1,000,000 | 65 | 600 | −535,000,000 |
| 2010/8/1 | 1,000,000 | 65 | 600 | −535,000,000 |
| 2010/9/1 | 1,000,000 | 65 | 600 | −535,000,000 |
| 2010/10/1 | 1,000,000 | 65 | 600 | −535,000,000 |
| 2010/11/1 | 1,000,000 | 65 | 600 | −535,000,000 |
| Total | | | | −8,727,300,000 |

*Note*: This table was developed by the author. The company did not disclose these data to the public.

---

[19] $(65 \times 1{,}000{,}000) - (78 \times 1{,}000{,}000) = -13{,}000{,}000$.

[20] $78 \times 78/65 = 78 \times 1.2 = 93.6$.

[21] $93.6 \times 78/65 = 93.6 \times 1.2 = 112.3$.

[22] $112.3 \times 1.2 = 134.8$.

[23] $134.8 \times 1.2 = 161.7$.

[24] $161.7 \times 1.2 = 194.0$.

[25] $194.0 \times 1.2 = 232.9$.

[26] $232.9 \times 1.2 = 279.5$.

[27] $279.5 \times 1.2 = 334.5$.

[28] $334.5 \times 1.2 = 402.5$.

[29] $402.5 \times 1.2 = 483.0$.

[30] $483.0 \times 1.2 = 579.6$.

[31] $579.6 \times 1.2 = 695.5$ (since the maximum in the contract was 600, 600 was taken). 600 was applied for the remaining years.

actual total loss might end up being larger, depending on how the exchange rate panned out. The A$ was hovering around 62 yen at that time.[33] The total loss over two years that the company would incur due to this particular transaction was ¥10,031 million at ¥60/A$. Given that the A$ had weakened to below 60 yen, the company's loss might have ballooned.[34] The company's net income in 2008, the previous year, was ¥4,001 million (see **Exhibit 3**). The loss due to this particular transaction could easily have wiped out all the income of 1 year. The company's net assets in 2008 were ¥52,232 million (see **Exhibit 2**). With this substantial loss due to this particular transaction, Saizeriya either had to sell off business units or was facing bankruptcy as worst-case scenarios. Saizeriya decided to terminate the contract at a cost of ¥15,000 million, which Shogaki believed saved the company.

*We understood the risks, but the yen appreciated faster than expected.*

— Shogaki, president of Saizeriya at a news conference
on December 10, 2008[35]

## Press Conference with Shogaki

On December 21, 2008, Shogaki held a press conference:[36]

*Q: At your shareholders meeting that concluded on November 27, 2008, how did stockholders react to news of the large derivatives loss?*

*A: Some within our company were reluctant to disclose the loss, but I decided to proceed with the disclosure. I think that our transparency was appreciated by our shareholders. We intended to determine the total amount of the loss soon so that we could decide what measures to take. I would also make clear where the responsibility lay. As for the derivatives*

---

[33] Ibid.

[34] Ibid.

[35] *Nikkei* (*Japan Economic Journal*), December 10, 2008, http://www.nni.nikkei.co.jp/AC/TNKS/Search/Nni20081210D10JF950.htm, (accessed January 5, 2013).

[36] Ibid.

*deals, I intended to cancel them when the loss would be the smallest possible by keeping an eye on the foreign exchange markets.*

*Q: How would the loss impact your fiscal 2009 results?*

*A: We initially expected 4.2 billion yen in profits, but now an overall loss was unavoidable. On the other hand, our operating profits were solid, as we were able to keep input costs low thanks to the strong yen.*

*Q: Saizeriya imported one third of its food materials from Australia. You suffered a large loss on your hedging of the Australian dollar. Did you feel that you depend too much on that country for procurement?*

*A: We planned to construct a new food processing plant in Singapore and open it in 2010. The plant would produce such foods as white sauce, an ingredient for rice casserole. This would reduce our dependence on Australia and spread our foreign exchange risk. Our Southeast Asian operations would be centered on this new plant. With the yen's value so high, we cannot miss this opportunity to go abroad.*

The Tokyo rules required key information to be published just once a year in principle, and it was not very clear what was subject to disclosure. Whether the risks were unique or not, one thing was certain: companies needed to step up the disclosure of information that was useful to investors (see **Exhibit 6**).[37] Shogaki also studied the US case of derivatives disclosure, and the US requirements encouraged him to proceed with the disclosure of the loss due to derivatives (see **Exhibit 7**).

## Analysis of the Coupon Swap Contracts

This was the first case in which the buyer of derivatives like the coupon swap contracts had disclosed the terms and conditions in detail so that not only the shareholders but also the public could understand the details of the deals and the risks involved on the part of the buyer. However, Shogaki thought that these terms and conditions were difficult for ordinary people to understand and that the real risks were not clear to them without being fully analyzed by professionals. Soon after the public disclosure of the

---

[37] Ibid.

**Exhibit 6**   Recent Japanese Cases of Nondisclosure of Material Facts

While 26 listed companies had gone bust since April 2008, 12 of them did not disclose information in advance on matters that caused their bankruptcies. The shortcomings of the disclosure rules were particularly noticeable in the case of Oriental Shiraishi Corp., a midsize construction firm that filed for bankruptcy on November 26, 2008 as a result of a liquidity crunch.

In its last financial statement, Oriental Shiraishi mentioned five key issues that affected its business, such as its heavy reliance on public works projects, but made no reference to a liquidity crunch.

Said an angry supplier, "The company placed a 30 million yen order with us for construction materials the day before announcing its failure." Because the sudden squeeze in bank credit in the summer of 2008 was behind Oriental Shiraishi's fate, once-a-year disclosure proved incapable of giving concerned parties time to prepare for the company's failure.

According to information disclosed by the top 100 nonfinancial companies in terms of market capitalization as of the end of March 2008, about 1,160 different risk factors were cited in fiscal 2007, up about 30% from fiscal 2003, and 91% of them referred to the "impact of interest rates and exchange rates" and "competition and changes in demand." A substantial 61% of the firms, including Toyota Motor Corp., cited "higher materials prices" as a risk factor.

*Source*: *Nikkei* (*Japan Economic Journal*), December 11, 2008, http://www.nni.nikkei.co.jp/e/ac/TNKS/Nni20081211D11HH986.htm.


loss, Shogaki asked an accounting firm to analyze the loss and prepare a report (see **Appendix 2**).

The derivatives here were currency swaps, in which a firm like Saizeriya and a swap dealer like BNP Paribas agreed to exchange an equivalent amount of two different currencies, such as yen and A$, for a specified period of time. Currency swaps could be negotiated for a wide range of maturities up to at least 10 years, although the deal here were intended to cover two years. The swap dealer acted as a middleman in setting up the swap agreement. Swap dealers arranged most swaps on a blind basis, meaning that the initiating firm (e.g., Saizeriya) did not know who was on the other side of the swap arrangement — the counterparty. So Saizeriya viewed the dealer as its counterparty. The dealer could generally arrange for the currency, amount and timing of the desired swap. The swap markets were dominated by the major money center banks worldwide, such as BNP Paribas. After being introduced on a global scale in the

**Exhibit 7**   US Disclosure Requirements for Derivatives

Many suffered significant financial losses caused by derivatives. Congress, the Securities and Exchange Commission, businesses and other groups became highly concerned about derivative products. These groups have called upon the Financial Accounting Standards Board (FASB) to improve its disclosure requirements regarding derivative financial products.

FASB's pronouncements comprised Statements of Financial Accounting Standards, Statements of Financial Accounting Concepts, Interpretations, Technical Bulletins, and Staff Positions; constituted rules and guidelines in preparing, presenting, and reporting financial statements within the US according to; and comprised a substantial part of the body of generally accepted accounting principles (GAAP) in the United States.

The Board agreed that more disclosure was necessary because of the escalating size of the derivatives market and their importance to the business community. They also felt that many investors and creditors did not fully understand these complex financial arrangements. The Board intended to help financial statement readers understand why the companies used and how the companies accounted for derivatives. FASB had issued the following instructions:

- In March 1990, FASB No. 105 was issued for Disclosure of Information about Financial Instruments with Off-Balance-Sheet Risk and Financial Instruments with Concentrations of Credit Risk.
- In December 1991, FASB No. 107 was issued for Disclosures about Fair Value of Financial Instruments.
- In October 1994, FASB No. 119 was issued for Disclosure about Derivative Financial Instruments and Fair Value of Financial Instruments.

Statement 105 required that the disclosure of information regarding derivative financial instruments be provided by class of financial instrument. Statement No. 119 allowed disclosure by category as optional. Disclosure could be disaggregated by any category that was in conformity with managing those instruments. If disaggregation was not by category of financial product, the company had to furnish a description of the types of financial instruments by category.

Statement No. 107 allowed companies to disclose the fair value information in their financial statements any way they felt was appropriate. These fair value disclosures were difficult to understand and isolate because they were mixed throughout the financial statements' footnotes.

For the purpose of FASB No. 119, the Board considered a derivative financial instrument as a future, forward, swap, or option contract or other financial instrument with similar characteristics of options.

*(Continued)*

**Exhibit 7**   (*Continued*)

> Disclosures were needed when derivative financial products were held or issued as hedges towards expected transactions, such as firm commitments and forecasted transactions having firm commitment. The Board determined that the then current hedge-related disclosures were mostly aimed at exchange-related futures contracts. However, such derivative financial instruments commonly used for hedging, such as interest rate swaps and forward contracts, were not fully covered by any disclosure statement. The Board concluded that additional information was needed that would allow financial statement users to determine if a company was successful in its hedging activities. The new disclosures were: (1) a description of the expected transactions, including their time periods; (2) a description of the types of derivative financial products used for hedging purposes; (3) the deferred hedging gains and losses; and (4) a description of the events that would arise in recognizing gains or losses of the amounts deferred in the income statement.

*Source*: FASB, "Statements of Financial Accounting Standards", "Statements of Financial Accounting Concepts", "Interpretations", "Technical Bulletins", and "Staff Positions", http://www.fasb.org/home, (accessed January 5, 2013).

early 1980s, currency swaps had grown to be one of the largest financial derivative markets in the world.

When Saizeriya concluded the currency swap (see **Appendix 1** and **Exhibit 8**) with BNP Paribas, the exchange rate was ¥105.83/A\$ as of the end of October 2007. Saizeriya had A\$-denominated accounts payable and was required to make A\$ payments at a future date for securing materials. Saizeriya would do well if the yen appreciated versus the A\$ and management was concerned about the possibility that the yen would fall. Anticipating that the exchange rate would follow the trend of yen depreciation against the A\$ in the future, Saizeriya arranged these currency swaps at the effective rate of ¥78/A\$, which was 35.7% appreciation against the then exchange rate of ¥105.83/A\$ at the end of October 2007. Saizeriya speculated on the potential for depreciation of the yen in the future, but what actually happened was the yen appreciated versus A\$ over the two-year period of the arrangement (see **Exhibit 4**). Unfortunately, if Saizeriya had not arranged any currency swaps, the company could have enjoyed the benefits of the yen's appreciation in its A\$-denominated payments.

**Exhibit 8**   Original Contracts of Derivative Transactions Between Saizeriya and BNP Paribas

Saizeriya informed the public that it anticipated the valuation loss on derivative transactions for the first quarter of the fiscal year ending August 2009 (September 1, 2008 to August 31, 2009).[38]

**Reason for Potential Valuation Loss on Derivative Transactions**

The company ascertained that huge valuation losses on derivative transactions were anticipated as non-operating expenses on a non-consolidated basis. The reason was that sharp appreciation of the yen was anticipated at the end of November 2008, in comparison to the level at fiscal year ended August 31, 2008, which was caused by the volatile fluctuation in the exchange rate resulting from the unprecedented financial crisis.

**Amount of Potential Valuation Loss on Derivative Transactions**

The amount of potential valuation loss was approximately 13 billion yen (A$0.21 billion at the rate of ¥62/A$ on December 9, 2008).

**Principal Terms and Conditions of the Derivative Agreements**

The counterparty was BNP Paribas Securities (Japan) Limited.

**FX (Foreign Exchange) Reference Type A$ (Australian Dollar) Currency Coupon Swap**

The amount of potential valuation loss was 8.73 billion yen (A$0.14 billion at the rate of ¥62/A$ on December 9, 2008), which was based on the estimated rate of ¥65.00/A$.

1. Agreed date: October 22, 2007.
2. Middle rate as of the last date of agreed month (the end of October 2007) = ¥105.83/A$.
3. Payment dates: On the first day of each month during the term from December 1, 2008 to November 1, 2010.
4. Agreed amount in Australian dollars: A$1,000,000.
5. Agreed rate: First agreed rate: ¥78.00/A$.
   If the yen became stronger below ¥78.00/A$ in the FX rate, the agreed rate thereafter would be recalculated in the following manner:
   [Previous agreed rate] × [78.00/FX] = the agreed rate (¥/A$)
   Minimum = ¥78.00/A$, Maximum = ¥600.00/A$
6. FX above = Middle rate of ¥/A$ exchange rate at 3 p.m. (Tokyo time) on each foreign exchange reference date.
7. Foreign exchange reference date above was the business day that was five business days before each payment date.

---

[38] Saizeriya's public release, see Saizeriya's website http://www.saizeriya.co.jp/ir_info/jp/release.html (accessed January 5, 2013).

**Exhibit 9**   Agreed Rates ($F_n$) Due to the Swap Contract Based on ¥65/A\$ AS the Spot Rate

600
579.6
483
402.5
335.4
279.5
232.9
194
161.7
134.8
112.3
93.6
78
600 600 600 600 600 600 600 600 600 600 600 600
12/1/2008
1/1/2009
2/1/2009
3/1/2009
4/1/2009
5/1/2009
6/1/2009
7/1/2009
8/1/2009
9/1/2009
10/1/2009
11/1/2009
12/1/2009
1/1/2010
2/1/2010
3/1/2010
4/1/2010
5/1/2010
6/1/2010
7/1/2010
8/1/2010
9/1/2010
10/1/2010
11/1/2010
0
100
200
300
400
500
600

Saizeriya's mistake had severe consequences for the company. The contract stipulated that if the yen appreciated, the effective rate would be an extremely depreciated yen as ¥500/A\$ or ¥600/A\$ (see **Exhibit 9**). The company's profits and losses due to the currency swap were as follows (see also **Appendix 2** for relevant mathematical models).

Saizeriya's two-year profits and losses at different exchange rates were as follows (see **Exhibits 10** and **11**):

At ¥60/A\$, loss of ¥10,031 million.
At ¥65/A\$, loss of ¥8,667 million.
At ¥78/A\$, breakeven.
At ¥88/A\$, profit of ¥240.0 million.
At ¥110/A\$, profit of ¥768.0 million.
At ¥120/A\$, profit of ¥1,008.0 million.

The payoff amounts from Saizeriya to BNP Paribas at the different exchange rates were as follows (see **Exhibit 10**):

At ¥60/A\$, ¥11,471 million.
At ¥65/A\$, ¥10,227 million.
At ¥78/A\$, ¥1,872 million.
At ¥88/A\$, ¥1,872 million.
At ¥110/A\$, ¥1,872 million.
At ¥120/A\$, ¥1,872 million.

**Exhibit 10**  Yen for Accounts Payable (A), P/L Due to Swap (B) and Payoff (C) for A$1 Million/Month for the 2 years, December 1, 2008 to November 1, 2010

(Unit ¥ million)

| | **Yen for Account Payable (A)[1]** | **P/L Due to Swap (B)[2]** | **Payoff (C = A + B)[3]** |
|---|---|---|---|
| at ¥60/A$ | 1440[4] | 10031 | 11471[5] |
| at ¥65/A$ | 1560 | 8727 | 10287 |
| at ¥78/A$ | 1872 | 0 | 1872 |
| at ¥88/A$ | 2112 | −240 | 1872 |
| at ¥110/A$ | 2640 | −768 | 1872 |
| at ¥120/A$ | 2880 | −1008 | 1872 |

*Notes*: (1) A = Monthly Yen Paid by Saizeriya to BNP Paribas for A$1 million of Account Payable Payment, baased on the Current Spot Rate.
(2) B = Profit/Loss due to Swap.
(3) C = A + B = Payoff by Saizeriya to BNP Paribas for A$1 million.
(4) A$1 million × 24 months × ¥60/A$ = ¥1440 million.
(5) ¥1440 million + ¥10031 million = ¥11471 million.

**Exhibit 11**  Graph of Exhibit 13



If the yen had fallen below ¥78/A$, the currency swap would have functioned as a hedge. Saizeriya would have received A$1 million from BNP Paribas for two years, which it would have used to pay the Australian companies. Saizeriya's total payoff amounts to BNP Paribas, so that Saizeriya would receive A$1 million from BNP Paribas, would have been ¥1,872 million only, and would have leveled off at this amount, if the exchange rates had continued the trend of yen depreciation against the A$ past ¥78/A$ (see **Exhibits 10** and **11**). However, the yen appreciated versus the A$, to levels near ¥60/A$ or ¥65/A$ over the two-year period. Therefore, Saizeriya incurred substantial losses near ¥8,667 million (the payoff amount was ¥10,227 million) at ¥65/A$ and ¥10,031 million (the payoff amount was ¥11,471 million) at ¥60/A$ (see **Exhibits 12–14**).

For this currency swap, the main problem was the following clause in the contract:

Agreed rate: First agreed rate ¥78.00/A$. If Yen becomes stronger below ¥78.00/A$ in the FX rate, the agreed rate thereafter will be re-calculated in the following manner:

$$[\text{Previous agreed rate}] \times [78.00/\text{FX rate}] = \text{the agreed rate (¥/A\$)}$$
$$\text{Minimum} = \text{¥78.00/A\$ and Maximum} = \text{¥600.00/A\$}$$

This maximum rate of ¥600/A$ was too expensive for the currency swap buyer, that is, Saizeriya. The underlying transaction of the currency swap was the exchange of A$1 million and the equivalent yen amount at the market rate. But this currency swap contract was settled through cash payments of profits or losses based on the formula in the contract. The value of the derivative part was dependent on the value of the underlying asset at a specific point in time before the expiration date, a deliberate design feature intended to include the cash payments of profit and loss between the buyer and the seller for final settlement as payoff (see **Appendix 1**). For this currency swap, if the yen appreciated versus the A$ beyond the level of ¥78/A$ (the breakeven point), to ¥60/A$ or ¥65/A$ over the two-year period, Saizeriya incurred substantial losses and this amount of loss was paid to BNP Paribas.

## Saizeriya's Shares Fell Sharply on News of the Swap Losses

Saizeriya's stock price went limit-down on December 10, 2008 as investors rushed to dump the stock, following the disclosure that the major Italian restaurant chain operator would likely rack up roughly 13 billion yen

**Exhibit 12**    Analysis of Swap at ¥60/A$

| Date | Amount | Spot (¥/A$) | Effective Rate Due to the Contract (¥/A$) | Profit/Loss (¥) |
|---|---|---|---|---|
| 2008/12/1 | 1,000,000 | 60 | 78 | −18,000,000[39] |
| 2009/1/1 | 1,000,000 | 60 | 101.4[40] | −52,400,000 |
| 2009/2/1 | 1,000,000 | 60 | 131.8[41] | −71,800,000 |
| 2009/3/1 | 1,000,000 | 60 | 171.3[42] | −111,300,000 |
| 2009/4/1 | 1,000,000 | 60 | 222.7[43] | −162,700,000 |
| 2009/5/1 | 1,000,000 | 60 | 289.5[44] | −229,500,000 |
| 2009/6/1 | 1,000,000 | 60 | 376.4[45] | −316,400,000 |
| 2009/7/1 | 1,000,000 | 60 | 489.2[46] | −429,200,000 |
| 2009/8/1 | 1,000,000 | 60 | 600[47] | −540,000,000 |
| 2009/9/1 | 1,000,000 | 60 | 600 | −540,000,000 |
| 2009/10/1 | 1,000,000 | 60 | 600 | −540,000,000 |
| 2009/11/1 | 1,000,000 | 60 | 600 | −540,000,000 |
| 2009/12/1 | 1,000,000 | 60 | 600 | −540,000,000 |
| 2010/1/1 | 1,000,000 | 60 | 600 | −540,000,000 |
| 2010/2/1 | 1,000,000 | 60 | 600 | −540,000,000 |
| 2010/3/1 | 1,000,000 | 60 | 600 | −540,000,000 |
| 2010/4/1 | 1,000,000 | 60 | 600 | −540,000,000 |
| 2010/5/1 | 1,000,000 | 60 | 600 | −540,000,000 |
| 2010/6/1 | 1,000,000 | 60 | 600 | −540,000,000 |
| 2010/7/1 | 1,000,000 | 60 | 600 | −540,000,000 |
| 2010/8/1 | 1,000,000 | 60 | 600 | −540,000,000 |
| 2010/9/1 | 1,000,000 | 60 | 600 | −540,000,000 |
| 2010/10/1 | 1,000,000 | 60 | 600 | −540,000,000 |
| 2010/11/1 | 1,000,000 | 60 | 600 | −540,000,000 |
| Total | | | | −10,031,300,000 |

*Note*: This table was developed by the author. The company did not disclose these data to the public.

---

[39] $(60 \times 1{,}000{,}000) - (78 \times 1{,}000{,}000) = -18{,}000{,}000$.

[40] $78 \times 78/60 = 78 \times 1.3 = 101.4$.

[41] $101.4 \times 78/60 = 101.4 \times 1.3 = 131.8$.

[42] $131.8 \times 1.3 = 171.3$.

[43] $171.3 \times 1.3 = 222.7$.

[44] $222.7 \times 1.3 = 289.5$.

[45] $289.5 \times 1.3 = 376.4$.

[46] $376.4 \times 1.3 = 489.2$.

[47] $489.2 \times 1.3 = 636.0$ (since the maximum in the contract was 600, 600 was taken). 600 was applied for the remaining years.

**Exhibit 13**   Analysis of SWAP at ¥110/A$

| Date | Amount | Spot (¥/A$) | Effective Rate Due to the Contract (¥/A$) | Profit/Loss (¥) |
|---|---|---|---|---|
| 2008/12/1 | 1,000,000 | 110 | 78 | 32,000,000[48] |
| 2009/1/1 | 1,000,000 | 110 | 78[49] | 32,000,000 |
| 2009/2/1 | 1,000,000 | 110 | 78 | 32,000,000 |
| 2009/3/1 | 1,000,000 | 110 | 78 | 32,000,000 |
| 2009/4/1 | 1,000,000 | 110 | 78 | 32,000,000 |
| 2009/5/1 | 1,000,000 | 110 | 78 | 32,000,000 |
| 2009/6/1 | 1,000,000 | 110 | 78 | 32,000,000 |
| 2009/7/1 | 1,000,000 | 110 | 78 | 32,000,000 |
| 2009/8/1 | 1,000,000 | 110 | 78 | 32,000,000 |
| 2009/9/1 | 1,000,000 | 110 | 78 | 32,000,000 |
| 2009/10/1 | 1,000,000 | 110 | 78 | 32,000,000 |
| 2009/11/1 | 1,000,000 | 110 | 78 | 32,000,000 |
| 2009/12/1 | 1,000,000 | 110 | 78 | 32,000,000 |
| 2010/1/1 | 1,000,000 | 110 | 78 | 32,000,000 |
| 2010/2/1 | 1,000,000 | 110 | 78 | 32,000,000 |
| 2010/3/1 | 1,000,000 | 110 | 78 | 32,000,000 |
| 2010/4/1 | 1,000,000 | 110 | 78 | 32,000,000 |
| 2010/5/1 | 1,000,000 | 110 | 78 | 32,000,000 |
| 2010/6/1 | 1,000,000 | 110 | 78 | 32,000,000 |
| 2010/7/1 | 1,000,000 | 110 | 78 | 32,000,000 |
| 2010/8/1 | 1,000,000 | 110 | 78 | 32,000,000 |
| 2010/9/1 | 1,000,000 | 110 | 78 | 32,000,000 |
| 2010/10/1 | 1,000,000 | 110 | 78 | 32,000,000 |
| 2010/11/1 | 1,000,000 | 110 | 78 | 32,000,000 |
| Total | | | | +768,000,000 |

*Note*: This table was developed by the author. The company did not disclose these data to the public.

---

[48] $(110 \times 1,000,000) - (78 \times 1,000,000) = 10,000,000$.

[49] 78 (the previous agreed rate on December 1, 2008) $\times$ (78/110) = 55.3. But the minimum rate was 78 and this was used on January 1, 2009. The same rule was applied for the following years.

**Exhibit 14**   Analysis of Swap at ¥120/A$

| Date | Amount | Spot (¥/A$) | Effective Rate Due to the Contract (¥/A$) | Profit/Loss (¥) |
|---|---|---|---|---|
| 2008/12/1 | 1,000,000 | 120 | 78 | 42,000,000[50] |
| 2009/1/1 | 1,000,000 | 120 | 78[51] | 42,000,000 |
| 2009/2/1 | 1,000,000 | 120 | 78 | 42,000,000 |
| 2009/3/1 | 1,000,000 | 120 | 78 | 42,000,000 |
| 2009/4/1 | 1,000,000 | 120 | 78 | 42,000,000 |
| 2009/5/1 | 1,000,000 | 120 | 78 | 42,000,000 |
| 2009/6/1 | 1,000,000 | 120 | 78 | 42,000,000 |
| 2009/7/1 | 1,000,000 | 120 | 78 | 42,000,000 |
| 2009/8/1 | 1,000,000 | 120 | 78 | 42,000,000 |
| 2009/9/1 | 1,000,000 | 120 | 78 | 42,000,000 |
| 2009/10/1 | 1,000,000 | 120 | 78 | 42,000,000 |
| 2009/11/1 | 1,000,000 | 120 | 78 | 42,000,000 |
| 2009/12/1 | 1,000,000 | 120 | 78 | 42,000,000 |
| 2010/1/1 | 1,000,000 | 120 | 78 | 42,000,000 |
| 2010/2/1 | 1,000,000 | 120 | 78 | 42,000,000 |
| 2010/3/1 | 1,000,000 | 120 | 78 | 42,000,000 |
| 2010/4/1 | 1,000,000 | 120 | 78 | 42,000,000 |
| 2010/5/1 | 1,000,000 | 120 | 78 | 42,000,000 |
| 2010/6/1 | 1,000,000 | 120 | 78 | 42,000,000 |
| 2010/7/1 | 1,000,000 | 120 | 78 | 42,000,000 |
| 2010/8/1 | 1,000,000 | 120 | 78 | 42,000,000 |
| 2010/9/1 | 1,000,000 | 120 | 78 | 42,000,000 |
| 2010/10/1 | 1,000,000 | 120 | 78 | 42,000,000 |
| 2010/11/1 | 1,000,000 | 120 | 78 | 42,000,000 |
| Total | | | | +1,008,000,000 |

*Note*: This table was developed by the author. The company did not disclose these data to the public.

---

[50] $(120 \times 1{,}000{,}000) - (78 \times 1{,}000{,}000) = 42{,}000{,}000$.

[51] 78 (the previous agreed rate on December 1, 2008) × (78/120) = 50.7. But the minimum rate specified in the contract was 78 and this was used on January 1, 2009. The same rule was applied for the following years.

**Exhibit 15**　Saizeriya's Stock Prices of Last 10 Years

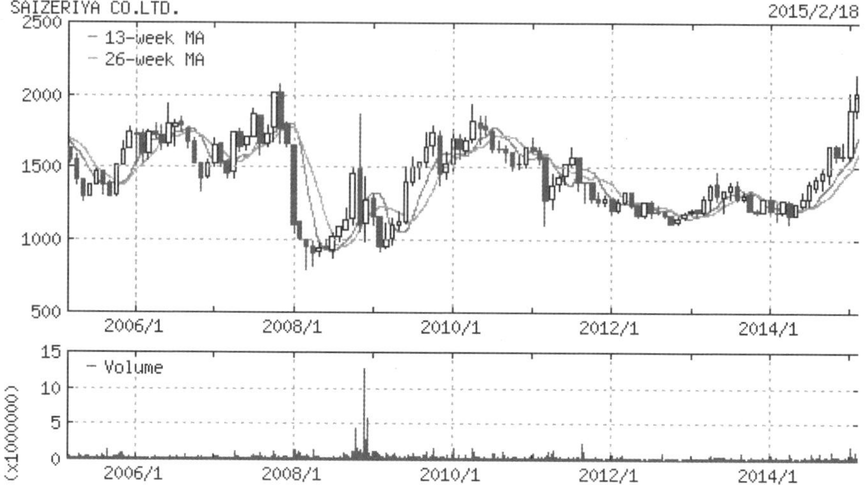


*Source*: Yahoo Finance, "Currency Converter", http://finance.yahoo.com/ (accessed January 5, 2013).

(A\$210 million at the rate of A\$62/¥ on December 9, 2008) in derivative losses in the period of September to November 2008 (see **Exhibit 15**).[52]

After gradually falling in the morning, the stock hit the limit-down trigger level of 1,485 yen, down 300 yen, or 16.8%, from the closing price in the previous trading session. About 70,500 shares changed hands, and sell orders totaling roughly 9 million shares went unfulfilled at the day's end.[53]

Insufficient, or even nonexistent, corporate disclosure of risk factors that could have a negative impact on business were having serious repercussions for investors and business partners.[54] Saizeriya announced six days before its general shareholders' meeting in November 2008 that it would likely incur an appraisal loss of 13 billion yen on derivatives contracts in the September–November period.[55] The loss eventually increased to 15 billion yen (A\$240 million at the rate of A\$62/¥ on December 9,

---

[52] *Nikkei* (*Japan Economic Journal*), November 25, 2008, http://www.nni.nikkei.co.jp/AC/TNKS/Search/Nni20081125D25JFA20.htm (accessed January 5, 2013).

[53] Ibid.

[54] *Nikkei* (*Japan Economic Journal*), December 11, 2008, http://www.nni.nikkei.co.jp/e/ac/TNKS/Nni20081211D11HH986.h (accessed January 5, 2013).

[55] *Nikkei* (*Japan Economic Journal*), June 9, 2008, http://www.nni.nikkei.co.jp/AC/TNW/Search/Nni20080609FR0CONSU.htm (accessed January 5, 2013).

2008) due to the cancellation of the contracts.[56] The restaurant chain operator, which relied on Australia for one-third of its ingredients, concluded regular hedging contracts to procure Australian dollars for food imports and avoid foreign-exchange risks.[57] In October 2007, Saizeriya changed the contracts to those for high-risk, high-return derivatives designed to enable the firm to earn a profit if the yen was weaker than 78 to the Australian dollar.[58]

Though Saizeriya revealed previously the total value of the contracts in its earnings report for the six months through August 2008, it did not mention the contracts' terms and other details.[59] Because the yen was quoted at around 100 against the Australian dollar at that time, Shogaki said that he did not feel there was any risk.[60] In a financial statement released a week after the earnings announcement, Saizeriya added information about the possible appraisal loss.[61]

*I never imagined that two years' worth of pre-tax profit would be wiped out instantly by derivatives trading.*

— Shogaki, president of Saizeriya at the general shareholders' meeting on November 27, 2008[62]

## Situations Surrounding Saizeriya at That Time

As president, Shogaki had to be aware that the company operated on relatively narrow margins and the competition in the industry was getting more intense. Saizeriya had to continue to import lots of its food materials from foreign countries. The company had to attempt to reduce risks stemming from exchange rate fluctuations. The following were the issues the company was facing at that time.[63] These factors were important to know

---

[56] Ibid.

[57] Ibid.

[58] Ibid.

[59] Ibid.

[60] Ibid.

[61] Ibid.

[62] Ibid.

[63] Ibid.

in order to understand why this company relied on such risky derivatives for hedging.

## *Rising Prices Dampened Spending*

In 2007–2008, the Japanese economy remained lethargic and consumers were cutting back on spending as prices of gasoline and food continued to race upward while wage growth remained stagnant.[64] Weaker sales were seen as the byproduct of household spending cuts stemming from a combination of low wage growth and soaring prices for food and other essential items.

That was bad news for Saizeriya, a major family restaurant chain, which in May 2008 suffered its eighth consecutive year-on-year decline in same-restaurant sales — 2.9% from a year earlier.[65] For those who drove, expenses grew on June 1, 2008 when gas prices jumped, with signs showing some service stations charging more than 170 yen ($1.63 at the exchange rate of ¥104.30/$ on August 31, 2008) per liter.[66] People used their cars for work, so they needed to drive even when gasoline was expensive; they cut spending on food and other items instead.[67]

## *Competition*

The year ended August 31, 2008 was marked by the beginning of a period of severe culling in restaurant chains, with companies intensifying competition to attract customers.[68] Market conditions were also severe for Saizeriya, where sales at existing restaurants declined for the ninth consecutive month in comparison with the previous year.[69] In the face of slowing consumer spending, the competitors tried to attract customers

---

[64] Saizeriya (2008) "Annual Report", http://www.saizeriya.co.jp/ir_info/jp/release.html (accessed January 5, 2013).

[65] Ibid.

[66] Ibid.

[67] Ibid.

[68] Ibid.

[69] Ibid.

through advertising and promotional campaigns, aiming to guarantee their sales. Saizeriya put effort into enhancing its competitiveness by further improving the vertical direct-to-consumer production and sales systems that were unique to the company, such as by refining its core products, strengthening outlet operations, and promoting efficient production and logistics systems.[70]As a result, the company booked consolidated net sales of ¥84,949 million in 2008, up 2.5% from the previous year; ordinary income of ¥7,853 million, down 5.4%; and net income of ¥4,011 million, down 9.1% (see **Exhibit 3**).[71]

## *Enhancement of Core Products*

Amid intensifying competition in the dining-out industry, the competitors tried to attract customers through advertising and marketing campaigns, such as TV commercials and discount cards. Saizeriya considered it most important to create products that were priced reasonably enough for the customers to be genuinely willing to choose them.[72] From this viewpoint, the company worked on creating core products through refining the products.[73] The company's efforts to improve the quality of its products by further refining popular products and narrowing down targeted items were well underway, and the sales at the existing restaurants had picked up on a year-on-year basis.[74] The company expected that per-customer spending, the number of customers and sales would slowly grow together in and after the following fiscal term.[75]

## *Responding to Surges in the Prices of Ingredients*

Saizeriya procured most of its ingredients by itself and employed vertical merchandising from production up to the point at which food

---

[70] Ibid.

[71] Ibid.

[72] Ibid.

[73] Ibid.

[74] Ibid.

[75] Ibid.

was consumed by customers.[76] If ingredients were purchased from other companies, the main effect of surges in material costs was an increase in menu prices. In contrast, the direct-to-consumer production and sales system operated by the company allowed for numerous improvements at every stage of the process, such as enhancing productivity by focusing product lines at plants and curbing shipping costs by improving transport efficiency and transportation methods. Given this, Saizeriya believed that it was able to hammer out its own reform and improvement measures, as it employed a more vertical, direct-to-customer production and sales system than any other food service provider.[77] Despite shortages of ingredients due to surges in prices, Saizeriya strived to offer its products at unchanged prices by taking full advantage of its direct-to-customer production and sales system, as well as absorbing the increasing cost of ingredients by streamlining the entire process.[78]

## *Overseas Operations and the Future Outlook for the Domestic Market*

Saizeriya's overseas operations, primarily in cities across China, performed well.[79] Thanks to strong business performance in Shanghai, where Saizeriya had 20 restaurants, the company opened new restaurants in Guangzhou, Beijing and Taiwan in 2008.[80] In 2009, the company strived to further enhance its restaurant management, lower costs and improve productivity.[81] The company expected to achieve an increase in per-customer sales by improving the side-dish items that complemented its popular products.[82] It was hoped that the refinement of core products would improve productivity at plants, as well as increase gross profits.[83]

---

[76] Ibid.

[77] Ibid.

[78] Ibid.

[79] Ibid.

[80] Ibid.

[81] Ibid.

[82] Ibid.

[83] Ibid.

# Other Alternatives for Hedging
# and Currency Swaps

Shogaki asked the planning department to determine what hedging strategies other than the currency swaps were available on October 22, 2007 when the currency swaps were made. The planning department presented an analysis using other hedging strategies: forward exchange rates, money market hedging and currency options. The planning department used the market information provided in **Exhibit 16**, which was available on October 22, 2007, for an accounts payable case of A$1 million to be paid to an Australian company. Saizeriya expected the yen to depreciate versus the Australian dollar during the next one to two years and predicted that the spot rate would be ¥110–120/$ for this period. Since Saizeriya wanted to eliminate transaction exposure, there were a variety of hedging instruments available for the accounts payable case at varying costs to the company for the payment one year ahead (see **Appendix 3** for detailed analysis of various hedging alternatives; see **Exhibits 17** and **18** for a summary of three hedging strategies: forward contract, money market and call option).

If Saizeriya's management was willing to consider all alternatives, the company's view of likely exchange rate changes aided the hedging choice. As shown in **Exhibit 18**, if the exchange rate was expected to move against Saizeriya, to the right of ¥120/A$, the option hedge was the clearly preferred alternative, the money market hedge was the second best, the forward contract hedge was the third and staying unhedged was the fourth. If the exchange rate was expected to move for Saizeriya, to the left of ¥65/A$, remaining unhedged was the best alternative, the option hedge was the second best, the money market hedge was the third and the forward contract hedge was the fourth.

The accounting firm's report compared all possible hedging alternatives, including the currency swap at various exchange rates. It included a comparison to see the total payoff amount for A$1 million for each month for a year for the currency swap, since other alternatives were performed on a one-year basis. The total A$ amount to be hedged needed to be A$12 million for one year (see **Appendix 3**).

**Exhibit 16**    Market Data on Exchange Rates and Interest Rates Between Australia and Japan on October 22, 2007

Spot and Forward Quotations for the Japanese Yen (¥) and the Australian Dollar (A$)

| Spot | | ¥105.83/A$ |
|---|---|---|
| Forward | 1 month | 106.12 |
| | 2 months | 106.38 |
| | 3 months | 106.91 |
| | 6 months | 107.00 |
| | 9 months | 107.30 |
| | 1 year | 107.50 |

360-Day Australian Dollar Option Quotation (¥/A$)

| Option | Strike price | Premium |
|---|---|---|
| put on A$ | ¥85/A$ | 1.5% |
| call on A$ | ¥85/A$ | 1.0% |

Interest Rates of Japan and Australia

Japan's 1 year borrowing interest rate: 0.03%

Japan's 1 year investment interest rate: 0.02%

Australia's 1 year borrowing interest rate: 4.25%

Australia's 1 year investment interest rate: 3.50%

Saizeriya's 1 year weighted average cost of capital: 1.2%

*Source*: Compiled from Bank of Japan, http://www.boj.or.jp/en/ (accessed January 5, 2013).

**Exhibit 17**    Money Market Hedging

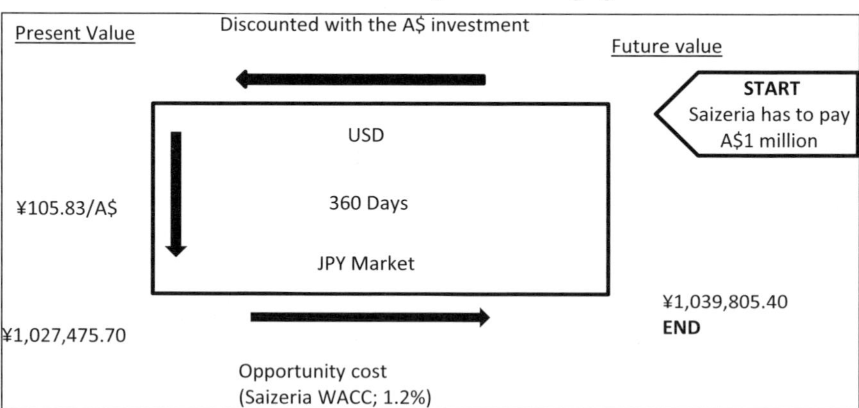

## At the Exchange Rate of ¥65/A$

In December 2008, the exchange rate was hovering at around ¥62/A$. The basis was the unhedged position. The total A$ amount needed to be A$12 million for one year: A$12 million × ¥65/A$ = ¥780 million. The total yen amount for A$12 million for the first year was ¥1,296 million (= ¥108 million × 12) under a forward contract, ¥1,248 million (= ¥104 million × 12) under a money market hedge, ¥1,032 million (= ¥86 million × 12) under an option contract and ¥792 million (= ¥66 million × 12) under the un-hedged position (see **Exhibit 18**). The total payoff for the currency swaps at ¥65/A$ was ¥10,287 million for two years (see **Exhibit 13**). For one year, 50% of it was ¥5,144 million. The total payoff amount for the currency swaps was exceptionally high. It was much better if the company did not hedge. Hedging under an option contract worked very well, since the total amount was almost the same as the unhedged position.

## At the Exchange Rate of ¥120/A$ or Weaker

In the currency swap, the total payoff was ¥936 million for the first year (= ¥1,872 million × 0.5) (see **Exhibit 10**). At ¥120/A$, the total yen amount for A$12 million for the first year was ¥1,296 million (= ¥108 million × 12) under a forward contract, which was the same at ¥65/A$, ¥1,248 million (= ¥104 million × 12) under a money market hedge, which was the same at ¥65/A$, ¥1,032 million (= ¥86 million × 12) under an option contract, which was the same at ¥65/A$ and ¥1,440 million (= ¥120 million × 12) under the unhedged position (see **Exhibit 18**). It was clear that the currency swap worked very well as a hedging technique when the yen was very weak against the A$, such as an exchange rate of ¥120/A$. It was the smallest yen needed among all of the alternatives. It was much better than the unhedged position, since the buyer could make money using a currency swap.

In order to caution buyers of currency swaps to consider the costs and benefits of any type of hedging trade, the currency swap coupon contract was compared with the forward markets, money market methods and options. The report concluded:

1.  The currency swap in this case did not work as a hedging technique for the buyers when the yen was exceptionally high against the A$,

**Exhibit 18**   Valuation of Cash Flow Under Various Hedging Alternatives, Including Swaps

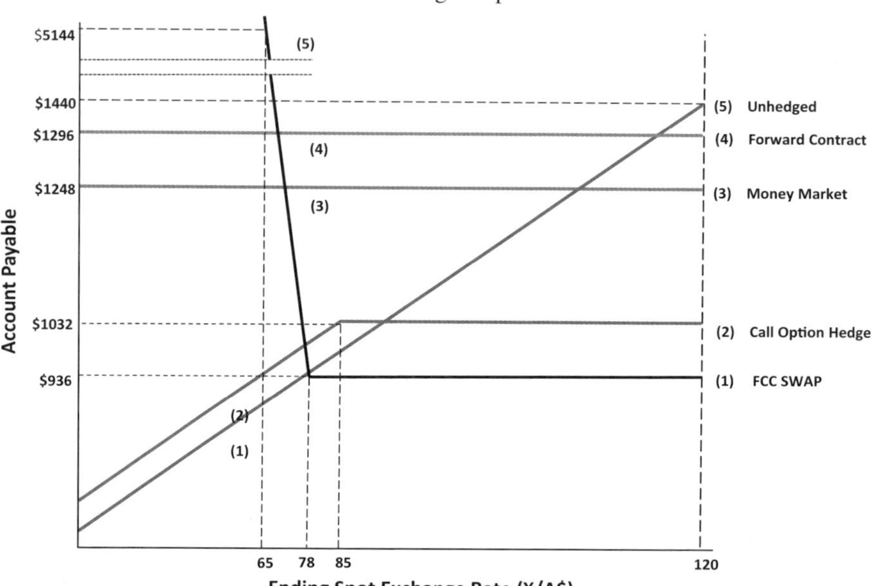


although other alternatives worked as hedging techniques for the buyers, regardless of the yen position against the A$. This difference was due to the fact that the currency swap was designed asymmetrically for the advantage of the seller. These instruments were designed so that the maximum agreed rate was ¥600/A$, far from the average spot rate, and the minimum agreed rate was ¥78/A$, near to the average spot rate. This currency swap should have been considered a speculation instrument and not a hedging alternative.

2.   There were two groups of derivative contracts. One was privately traded over-the-counter (OTC) derivatives, such as swaps that did not go through an exchange. The swaps here were OTC products between a bank and its customers and were very costly and hard to unwind. The other group was exchange-traded derivative (ETD) contracts that were traded through specialized derivatives exchanges or other exchanges. Common hedging strategies, such as forward exchange rates, money market hedging, and currency options, belonged to the ETD group.

3. The characteristics of an OTC swap with a bank as a counterparty could be structured to meet the needs of either party, buyer and seller, when compared to ETD straight hedges with options or forwards. These ETD derivatives could be structured to meet the concept of "fairness" without being designed asymmetrically for the advantage of the seller when compared to other hedging vehicles. Another point was that the other hedging vehicles also were offered by banks to their customers as OTC forwards or options. The seller would "price" these instruments to its advantage, but the range of mispricing was probably narrower. Also, exchange-traded products, such as forward exchange rates and options, had the benefits of daily market to market, no counterparty risk, and sufficient liquidity to help keep prices aligned.

## Decision Time

Some directors and shareholders questioned Saizeriya's disclosure. Saizeriya's stock price plummeted following the disclosure. The Japanese rules were not clear regarding what was subject to disclosure (see **Appendix 4**). But Shogaki was confident that he had done the right thing and believed that the transparency would eventually be appreciated by the shareholders.

But Shogaki had to decide whether the company should continue hedging, such as with the currency swaps with which Saizeriya had suffered huge losses this time.[84] If Saizeriya did not arrange any currency

---

[84] A survey by the Financial Services Agency (FSA), part of the Japanese government, in January 2011 showed that the number of small and midsize companies holding currency derivatives contracts, which inflicted huge losses following the yen's sharp appreciation against the dollar, totaled some 19,000 in Japan. For details, see http://www.fsa.go.jp/news/22/syouken/20100913-1/01.pdf (accessed January 5, 2013).

International banks have sold currency derivatives contracts in other countries too. For example, these derivatives were sold to several companies in India, and this caused substantial losses to Indian companies. Some companies even sold off business units or faced bankruptcy due to the derivative losses. For details, see Gupta, n.d. (April 3, 2010) "Banks Can't Ignore Their Fiduciary Responsibility to Customers", http://www.dnaindia.com/money/1366708/comment-banks-can-t-ignore-their-fiduciary-responsibility-to-customers (accessed March 1, 2013).

hedging, the company could enjoy the benefits of yen appreciation for the payments in A$. Hedging or unhedging was really the issue for Shogaki. He fully understood the accounting firm's and the planning department's reports as to the risks involved in the currency swaps as well as the availability of other traditional hedging alternatives (see **Appendices 2** and **3**).

Saizeriya possessed a multitude of positive and negative cash flows that were sensitive to changes in exchange rates. As president, Shogaki knew that these kinds of financial risks were the subject of the growing field of financial risk management. He knew that many firms believed that currency risk was simply a part of doing business internationally and therefore their basic position was an unhedged baseline. These companies operated under the assumption that multilateral netting of various currencies' payments and receivables should work to reduce the risks of changes in exchange rates.

One of Shogaki's motivations to hedge was driven by accounting reasons. He knew that Saizeriya would be criticized severely by shareholders for incurring foreign exchange losses in the financial statements and that incurring hedging cash costs in avoiding the foreign exchange losses was acceptable to them. The hedging costs were buried in operating expenses.

Even if the company continued hedging, Shogaki would need to be more careful in selecting hedging techniques. He thought Saizeriya would never use currency swaps and should resort only to normal contractual hedging instruments, such as simple forward contracts and plain vanilla options, which the planning department presented in detail and which Shogaki understood fully. He wondered if these contractual hedging instruments would be more appropriate for Saizeriya's way of doing business, since they would be less speculative.

Shogaki assumed that buyers had to be sophisticated enough to pick the best hedging vehicle that met their "utility" function for risk and return. He believed that companies should act with caution, rather than blindly believing what they were told. What he learned from this incident was that corporate management needed to know the real risks of the financial products involved before buying. He believed that companies needed to continuously assess and manage their risks. It was clear that a "hedge and forget" approach proved to be very costly and reckless. He decided that it was a good idea to create middle-management offices or risk management teams that quantitatively assessed derivative transactions and fully reviewed them before trading occurred, in an effort to comply with company policies in terms of criteria established by the board. He also decided that using independent evaluations of the derivatives by outside investment advisors and independent appraisers was a way of assessing and reducing the risks involved.

Shogaki also knew that diversification of operations in foreign countries would help because Saizeriya's dependence on one currency, such as the Australian dollar, would be reduced. The company planned to construct a new food processing plant in Singapore and open it in 2010 as its Southeast Asian operations. With the yen's high value, this was a good opportunity for the company to make foreign investments.

Finally, Shogaki asked Saizeriya's legal counsel to study whether the company could sue the seller of this derivative for the damages the company suffered.[85]

## For Further Discussion

1.  What did you study from this case?
2.  President Shogaki considered this case was material facts and disclosed it to the public. But stock prices dropped sharply due to this disclosure and some shareholders didn't welcome this disclosure. President Shogaki's decision of disclosure was right?
3.  For companies, what are the reasons to hedge?
4.  For companies, what are the reasons not to hedge?
5.  Do the following sensitivity study on this currency coupon SWAP (1) for the amount of potential valuation loss or profit in the same way shown Exhibits 5 and 6 in the main text.

    Case 1: based on at the estimated rate @¥60.00/A\$.
    Teaching Note Exhibit 1

---

[85] Saizeriya filed civil suits against BNP Paribas Securities that sought damages of ¥16.8 billion at Tokyo District Court on July 3, 2012. For details see *Asahi Shimbun*, July 4, 2012, http://www.asahi.com/national/update/0704/TKY201207030768.html. Many other companies in Japan filed similar civil suits against their respective banks. The banks' legal responsibility was questioned in the courts.

Case 2: based on at the estimated rate @¥88.00/A$.

Teaching Note Exhibit 2

These two cases show the sensitivity as follows:

If yen was appreciated but only up to ¥88.00/A$, the swap produced the profit of ¥240 million. If yen was appreciated much further up to ¥60.00/A$, this swap would produce the loss of ¥10 billion. The break–even spot was ¥78.00/A$ due to the contract.

When this swap was arranged on October 22, 2007, the rate was ¥105.83/A$.

6. Judging from the sensitivity study, how do you evaluate the real problem of this currency coupon swap (1) for Sazeriya.

7. To understand contractual hedging techniques; forward market hedge, money market hedge and option market hedge, study the case of accounts receivable, which is the opposite situation Saizeria faced; the case of accounts payable.

8. Is the bank who sold this Swap responsible?

## Appendix 1　Monthly Transaction of Forex Derivatives (Swaps) for the Month of December 2008

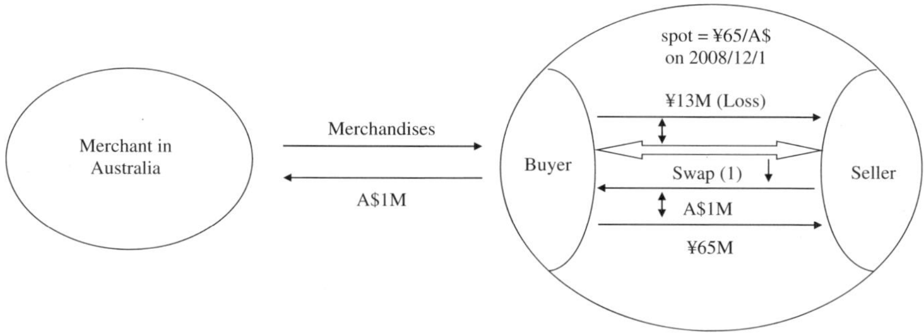


*Note*: M = million

# Appendix 2  Mathematical Analysis of Foreign Currency Coupon Swaps

This study was conducted by an accounting firm at the request of Saizeriya. Under the terms and conditions of the specific foreign currency coupon swaps for Saizeriya, the company was to receive A$1 million every month, starting in September 2008. If the yen were to weaken below a certain threshold level, provided in the contract, the company would be entitled to buy the Australian dollars at a discount (see **Exhibit 4**). If the yen were to appreciate beyond that threshold level, however, the purchase price of the Australian dollars would rise.

The contract (see **Exhibit 8**) had an article stating that if the yen appreciated, the effective rate would be an extremely depreciated yen — as low as ¥500/A$ or ¥600/A$. According to the contract, the currency swap for the company was calculated as follows:

First, the accounting firm provided the following definitions:

$P$ = Principal amount (A$1 million)

$S$ = Current spot rate (¥/A$)

$n$ = The currency swap's life (24 months from December 1, 2008 to November 1, 2010)

$F_1$ = First month's agreed rate (¥78/A$ set by the contract)

$F_n$ = n month's agreed rate = ¥78/A$ × (Fn – 1)/S (set by the contract)

$F_{n.max}$ = Maximum allowable agreed rate = ¥600/A$ (set by the contract)

$F_{n.min}$ = Minimum allowable agreed rate = ¥78/A$ (set by the contract)

$P/L_n$ = Profit or loss in a month = $P(F_n – S)$

TL = Aggregating currency swap losses for all valuation dates

$V(S, P, F_n)$ = Payoff amount (¥) for nth month

TV = Aggregating currency swap payoffs for all valuation dates

### Saizeriya's Profits and Losses

The accounting firm took the then current spot rate to be ¥65/A\$, which was the spot rate on December 9, 2008, when Saizeriya publicly announced its losses (see **Exhibit 5**).

1. On December 1, 2008 (the first month), the loss was calculated as below. According to the contract, the first agreed rate, $F_1 = ¥78/A\$$. $L_1 = P(F_1 - S) = A\$1$ million $\times (¥78/A\$ - ¥65/A\$) = ¥13,000,000$.

2. On January 1, 2009 (the second month), the loss was calculated as below. The contract stated that if the yen fell below ¥78.00/A\$ in the spot rate, the agreed rate thereafter would be recalculated in the following manner: [Previous agreed rate] $\times$ [78.00/FX rate] = the agreed rate (¥/A\$). But Minimum = ¥78.00/A\$ and Maximum = ¥600.00/A\$]. Then, $F_2 =$ second month's agreed rate $= ¥78/A\$ \times (F_1)/S = ¥78/A\$ \times (78.00/65.00) = 93.60$ (¥/A\$), since the previous month's agreed rate $(F_1)$ on December 1, 2008 was ¥78/A\$. $L_2 = P(F_2-S) = A\$1$ million $\times (¥93.60/A\$ - ¥65/A\$) = ¥28,600,000$.

3. On December 1, 2009 (the 13th month), the loss was calculated as below (the period from March 1, 2009 to November 1, 2009 was omitted, since the same formula worked): Now, $F_{13} = $ 13th month's agreed rate $= ¥78/A\$ \times (F_{12})/S = ¥78/A\$ \times (579.60/65.00) = 695.50$ (¥/A\$), since the previous month's agreed rate $(F_{12})$ on November 1, 2009 (the 12th month) was ¥579.60/A\$. But, due to the contract, Max. $F_n = ¥600/A\$$. Then, $= ¥600/A\$$ (Max). $L_{13} = P(F_{13} - S) = A\$1$ million $\times (¥600/A\$ - ¥65/A\$) = ¥535,000,000$.

4. From the nth month after December 1, 2009 (the 13th month) to November 1, 2010 (the 24th month), the loss was calculated as follows: $F_n = $ nth month agreed rate $= ¥78/A\$ \times (F_{n-1})/S = ¥600/A\$$ (Max). Then, $L_n = P(F_n - S) = A\$1$ million $\times (¥600/A\$ - ¥65/A\$) = ¥535,000,000$.

5. Aggregating currency swap losses for all valuation dates (TL), the accounting firm obtained the total swap losses, as below. (See **Exhibit 9** for a graph showing the trend of $F_n$, the nth month agreed rate on each month after December 1, 2008 (the first month), due to the swap based on ¥65/A\$.)

$$P/L_n = (F_n \times P) - (S \times P) = P(F_n - S)$$

$$TL = \sum_{t=1}^{n} L^t$$

## The Payoff to Be Made by Saizeriya

The accounting firm took the then current spot rate to be ¥65/A\$, which was the spot rate on December 9, 2008, when Saizeriya publicly announced its losses.

Based on the then current spot rate, Saizeriya must have paid A\$1 million yen to BNP Paribas monthly. In general terms, this could be expressed as $P \times S \ (= A)$.

In general terms, the profit and loss each month could be expressed as $P \ (F_n - S) \ (= B)$.

Therefore, the payoff amount for a particular month (C) was:

$$C = A + B = (P \times S) + P \ (F_n - S) = P \times F_n$$

1. On December 1, 2008 (the first month), the payoff was calculated as follows: $V_1 = P \times S + P \ (F_1 - S) = ¥65,000,000 \ (¥65/A\$ \times A\$1 \ \text{million}) + ¥13,000,000 \ ((¥78/A\$ - ¥65/A\$) \times A\$1 \ \text{million}) = ¥78,000,000$.
2. On January 1, 2009 (the second month), the payoff was calculated as follows: $V_2 = P \times S + P(F_2 - S) = ¥65,000,000 + ¥28,600,000 = ¥93,600,000$.
3. On December 1, 2009 (the 13th month), the payoff was calculated as follows (the period from March 1, 2009 to November 1, 2009 was omitted, since the same formula worked): $V_{13} = P \times S + P \ (F_{13} - S) = ¥65,000,000 + ¥535,000,000 = ¥600,000,000$.
4. From the nth month after December 1, 2009 (the 13th month) to November 1, 2010 (the 24th month), the payoff was calculated as follows: $V_n = P \times S + P \ (F_n - S) = P \times F_n$.
5. Aggregating payoff amounts for all valuation dates (TV), the accounting firm obtained the total swap losses, as below.

$$TV = \sum_{t=1}^{n} V^t$$

## General Equation for Payoff

The currency swap payoff, $V(S,P,F_n)$ for a notional amount of A$1 million at each valuation date, was formally expressed as:

$$V(S,P,F_n) = \begin{cases} PS + P(F_{n.\min} - S); & F_n \leq 78 \\ PF_n; & 78 < F_n < 600 \\ PS + P(F_{n.\max} - S); & F_n \geq 600 \end{cases}$$

where $P$ = Principal amount (A$1 million)

$V(S,P,F_n)$ = Payoff amount (¥) for nth month

$S$ = Current spot rate (¥/A$)

$n$ = The currency swap's life (24 months from December 1, 2008 to November 1, 2010)

$F_1$ = First month's agreed rate (¥78/A$ set by the contract)

$F_n$ = nth month's agreed rate = ¥78/A$ × $(F_{n-1})$/S

$F_{n.\max}$ = Maximum allowable agreed rate = ¥600/A$

$F_{n.\min}$ = Minimum allowable agreed rate = ¥78/A$

The preceding equation could be represented by the following general equation:

$$V(S,P,F_n) = \begin{cases} PS + P(F_{n.\min} - S); & F_n \leq F_{n.\min} \\ PF_n; & F_{n.\min} < F_n < F_{n.\max} \\ PS + P(F_{n.\max} - S); & F_n \geq F_{n.\max} \end{cases}$$

This could be further simplified to:

$$V(S,P,F_n) = \begin{cases} PF_{n.\min}; & F_n \leq F_{n.\min} \\ PF_n; & F_{n.\min} < F_n < F_{n.\max} \\ PF_{n.\max}; & F_n \geq F_{n.\max} \end{cases}$$

Aggregating the currency swap payoffs for all valuation dates (TV), the accounting firm obtained the total Swap payoff:

$$\text{TV} = \sum_{t=1}^{n} V(S,P,F_n)^t$$

# Summary

Using these formulas, the accounting firm calculated Saizeriya's profits or losses at different, constant, two-year exchange rate values. At an exchange rate of ¥65/A$ for two years, Saizeriya's losses totaled ¥8,667 million by contract's end (November 1, 2010) (see **Exhibit 5** for the losses by month). At an exchange rate of ¥60/A$, Saizeriya's losses were even bigger, at ¥10,031 million (see **Exhibit 12**). At exchange rates of ¥110/A$ and ¥120/A$, Saizeriya's profits were ¥1,768 million and ¥1,008 million (see **Exhibits 13** and **14**).

Saizeriya's two-year profits or losses at different exchange rates were as follows (see **Exhibits 13** and **14**):

At ¥60/A$, loss of ¥10,031 million.
At ¥65/A$, loss of ¥8,667 million.
At ¥78/A$, breakeven.
At ¥88/A$, profit of ¥240.0 million.
At ¥110/A$, profit of ¥768.0 million.
At ¥120/A$, profit of ¥1,008.0 million.

Then, the payoff for Saizeriya at the different exchange rates were as follows (see **Exhibits 13** and **14**):

At ¥60/A$, ¥11,471 million.
At ¥65/A$, ¥10,227 million.
At ¥78/A$, ¥1,872 million.
At ¥88/A$, ¥1,872 million.
At ¥110/A$, ¥1,872 million.
At ¥120/A$, ¥1,872 million.

# Appendix 3 Analysis of Various Hedging Alternatives

First, the planning department conducted a comparative study of various hedging methods: forward hedges, money market hedges, and options market hedges.

### Forward Hedges

The most direct and popular way to hedge currency risk was a currency forward contract: buy the A$1 million forward at ¥107.50/A$ (one year

forward rate) for a guaranteed payment of ¥107.50 million (A$1 million ×
107.50), regardless of what happened to the spot rate after one year.

If the yen appreciated to ¥65.00/A$, Saizeriya would pay ¥65 million
(A$1million × ¥65.00/A$), but the forward loss was ¥42.5 million (= ¥65
million − ¥107.50 million). If the yen depreciated to ¥120.00/A$,
Saizeriya would pay ¥120 million, which Saizeriya was concerned about,
and would earn a profit of ¥12.5 million (= ¥120 million − ¥107.50 million) on the forward contract. No matter what happened to the spot rate in
the future, Saizeriya would be able to lock in the exchange rate at
¥107.50/A$.

**Money Market Hedges** (see **Exhibit 17**)

To implement a money market hedge, Saizeriya would exchange Japanese
yen spot and invest them for one year in an Australian dollars-denominated
interest-bearing account. The principal and interest in Australian dollars at
the end of the one-year period would be used to pay A$1 million.

In order to ensure that the principal and interest exactly equaled the
A$1 million due in one year, Saizeriya would discount the A$1 million by
the Australian dollar investment interest rate of 3.5% per annum for
360 days in order to determine the Australian dollars needed today:

$$A\$1{,}000{,}000/1.03 = A\$970{,}873.78$$

This A$970,873.78 needed today would require ¥102,747,570 at the then
current spot rate of ¥105.83/$:

$$A\$970{,}873.78 \times ¥105.83/A\$ = ¥102{,}747{,}570$$

Finally, in order to compare the money market hedge outcome with the
other hedging alternatives, the ¥102,747,570 (the then present value) cost
today must have been carried forward 360 days to the same future date as
the other hedge choices. If the then current yen cost was carried forward
at Saizeriya's one-year weighted average cost of capital (WACC) of 1.2%,
the total future value cost of the money market hedge was ¥103,980,540.

$$¥102{,}747{,}570 \times 1.012\% = ¥103{,}980{,}540$$

## Options Market Hedges

One disadvantage of a complete hedge, using a forward or money market hedge, was that it eliminated all currency risk, even the favorable exchange rate changes that could increase profits by lowering costs or raising revenues in the home currency. If the spot rate went to ¥65/A$, Saizeriya would pay ¥65 million instead of ¥103,980,540 (money market hedge) and would save ¥38,980,540. In other words, hedging would cost Saizeriya ¥38,980,540 on an *ex-post* basis. Saizeriya might have regretted hedging if the yen appreciated.

Currency options provided a solution to limit the upside risk of the yen depreciating while preserving the downside profit potential of the yen appreciating if Saizeriya bought a dollar call option. Suppose that dollar call options were selling for 1.00% for A$1 million, with a strike price of ¥85/$, and an expiration of 360 days. Saizeriya could buy A$1 million worth of call options for ¥1,058,300.00 (A$1 million × 1.00% × ¥105.83/A$), giving it the right to buy A$1 million at ¥85/A$ for ¥85,000,000.

Suppose the option premium had become due. So considering the time value of money, the future yen cost (360 days) of the call options, ¥1,058,300.00 would be ¥1,070,999.60 (using 1.2% WACC for Saizeriya for 360 days). Suppose the spot rate would be ¥120/A$ in 360 days. Saizeriya could exercise the option and pay ¥85,000,000 at the strike price in gross proceeds for the AS$1 million and ¥86,070,999.60 after the premium (the effective exchange rate was ¥86.07/A$). If the yen appreciated significantly, this call option would be allowed to expire and A$1 million for the payable would be purchased on the spot market. Suppose the spot rate would be ¥65/A$ in 360 days. A$1 million for the payable would be purchased on the spot market and would be ¥65,000,000.00. Adding ¥1,070,999.60 as the premium paid, the total payments would be ¥66,070,999.60. The call premium was like buying an insurance policy for ¥1,070,999.60 that would guarantee that Saizeriya would pay a maximum of ¥86,070,999.60 in 360 days.

# Appendix 4  Responsibility of Corporations for Disclosure of Important Matters Listed by the Financial Services Agency in Japan[86]

## Nonconsolidated Basis

- In case primary offering of securities was made overseas.
- Granting of equity warrant as a stock option.
- Change in personnel of parent company or subsidiary as well as major shareholders.
- Happening of significant accident.
- In case a specific kind of lawsuit was filed or solved.
- Conclusion of agreement concerning stock-exchange.
- In case there was a resolution of the shareholders' meeting concerning stock transfer.
- In case an agreement was concluded concerning transfer or acquisition of sales or business.
- Conclusion of an agreement concerning a merger.
- Conclusion of an agreement concerning transfer of sales.
- Change of representative director.
- Filing of a petition of bankruptcy.
- In case an uncollectable claim or delayed collectable claim developed.
- In case a circumstance that severely affected financial status or operating performances occurred.
- Occurrence or change of information related to stock offering.

## Consolidated Basis

- Happening of significant accident at a consolidated subsidiary.
- In case a specific kind of lawsuit was filed or solved for a consolidated subsidiary.
- Conclusion of agreement concerning stock-exchange for a consolidated subsidiary.
- In case there was a resolution of the shareholders' meeting concerning stock transfer at a consolidated subsidiary.

---

[86] The FSA (December 2002) "Responsibility of Corporations for Disclosure of Important Matters", http://www.fsa.go.jp/inter/ios/press04.pdf (accessed January 5, 2013).

- In case an agreement was concluded concerning transfer or acquisition of sales or business at a consolidated subsidiary.
- Conclusion of an agreement concerning a merger of a consolidated subsidiary.
- Conclusion of an agreement concerning transfer of sales of a consolidated subsidiary.
- Filing of a petition of bankruptcy, etc. related to a consolidated subsidiary.
- In case an uncollectable claim or delayed collectable claim developed at a consolidated subsidiary.
- In case a circumstance that severely affected financial status or operating performances occurred.
- Occurrence or change of information related to stock offering (maximum of ¥86,070,999.60 in 360 days).

# Appendix



**Table 1**  Largest Users of Author's Cases in the Past Six Years (2009–2014)

|  | Countries | Copies |
|---|---|---|
| **Universities in the US** | | |
| Harvard Business School (MBA) | | 1,453 |
| MIT | | 445 |
| Northwestern University | | 363 |
| University of Washington | | 269 |
| USC | | 158 |
| University of Maryland | | 129 |
| Wharton, University of Pennsylvania | | 110 |
| University of North Carolina-Chapel Hills | | 85 |
| Cornell University | | 78 |
| Willamette University | | 72 |

*(Continued)*

**Table 1**   (*Continued*)

|  | Countries | Copies |
|---|---|---|
| **Foreign Universities** | | |
| SDA Bacconi School of Management<br>(Ranked 5th for its MBA program in Europe and 15th<br>   in the world by the *Financial Times*) | Italy | 509 |
| Monash University<br>(The 69th university in the world according to the<br>   2013/2014 QS World University Rankings) | Australia | 470 |
| Instituto De Empresa, Business<br>(Ranked as the best business school in Europe by<br>   the *Financial Times* in 2013) | Spain | 328 |
| Narsee Monjee Institute of Management Studies<br>(India's leading business school; ranked 4th best<br>   business school in India) | India | 315 |
| Graduate School of Management, GLOBIS<br>(As the largest and fastest-growing business school in<br>   Japan, ranked 1st among Japanese MBA schools<br>   by *Nikkei Career Magazine* for 2012 in terms<br>   of student satisfaction) | Japan | 292 |
| Asian Institute of Management, Makati City<br>(Established in partnership with Harvard Business<br>   School and uses the Harvard Business School<br>   case study teaching methodology. One of the<br>   few business schools in Asia to be internationally<br>   accredited with the AACSB) | Philippines | 273 |
| National University of Singapore<br>(The *Financial Times* placed NUS at 26th in the world<br>   and 2nd in Asia. Yale–NUS College is a liberal arts<br>   college in Singapore, opened in August 2013, as a<br>   joint project of Yale University, and NUS) | Singapore | 235 |
| Concordia University<br>(The university's John Molson School of Business is<br>   consistently ranked within the top 10 Canadian<br>   business schools, and within the top 100 worldwide) | Canada | 149 |
| University of Haifa<br>(Ranked 5th best university in Israel) | Israel | 126 |

*(Continued)*

**Table 1**   (*Continued*)

| | Countries | Copies |
|---|---|---|
| Lund University<br>(One of the most renowned institutions of higher<br>   learning in the Nordic countries; ranked 1st among<br>   comprehensive universities in Scandinavia and<br>   123rd in the world by the Financial Times in 2013) | Sweden | 116 |
| TiasNimbas Business School<br>(The *Financial Times* ranked the MBA program of the<br>   school 2nd in the BeNeLux region — Belgium/<br>   Netherlands/Luxemburg — and 20th in Europe) | Netherlands | 116 |
| University of Melbourne | Australia | 113 |
| SP Jain School of Global Management | India | 113 |
| Educomp Raffles Higher Education | India | 80 |
| **Companies** | | |
| International Professional Managers Association (IPMA) | UK | 151 |
| Stormont Consulting Firm | USA | 23 |
| Boston Consulting Group International | USA | 21 |
| Nichibei Kaiwa Gakuin | Japan | 15 |
| Bain & Company, Inc. | USA | 14 |
| Management Association of Japan | Japan | 10 |
| **Others** | | **6,058** |
| **Total** | | **12,689** |

**Table 2**   List of Large and Prestigious Users in the Past Six Years (2009–2014)

**Universities in the US**

Harvard MBA
Thunderbird
MIT
University of Pennsylvania (Wharton)
Columbia University
Dartmouth College
Northwestern University
USC
University of Michigan
University of Chicago
Cornell University

(*Continued*)

**Table 2**   (*Continued*)

Duke University
New York University
University of Washington
University of Illinois
Michigan State University
Georgetown University
Johns Hopkins University
University of Georgia
Indiana University
University of Maryland
University of Texas at Austin
University of Texas at Dallas
Florida State University
Arizona State University
Louisiana State University
Virginia Tech
Purdue University
University of North Carolina-Chapel Hill
University of South Carolina
Oregon State University
Colorado State University
College of William & Mary
US Military Academy
Boston University
University of Notre Dame
State University of New York
Temple University (Fox School of Business)
University of Hawaii
Boston University (Halt International Business School)
Nova Southeastern University
University of Rochester
University of Buffalo
University of Connecticut
Loyola University
Tufts University

**Foreign Universities**

**UK**
University of Oxford

(*Continued*)

| **Table 2**  (*Continued*) |
| --- |

London Business School
Salford Business School
International Professional Managers Association (IPMA)

**Spain**
ESADE
IE Business School
Instituto De Empresa Business

**Italy**
SDA BOCCONI School of Management

**Denmark**
Copenhagen Business School

**France**
ESSEC Business School

**Ireland**
University College Dublin (UCD) (College of Business & Law)
UCD Michael Smurfit School of Business

**Sweden**
Lund University, University of Gothenburg

**Germany**
Universitat Duisburg-Essen
University of Applied Sciences Trier (Fachhochschule Trier)

**Netherlands**
TiasNimbas Business School

**Portugal**
University of Porto — Faculty of Economics

**Belgium**
University of Liege

**Poland**
Kozminski University

**Canada**
University of British Columbia
Concordia University

*(Continued)*

**Table 2**   (*Continued*)

**Japan**
Hitotsubashi University
Keio University
Waseda University
Aoyama Gakuin University
Kyushu University
Hosei University
Rikkyo University
Nagoya City University
Ritsumeikan University
Nichibei Kwansei Gakuin Daigaku
Nomura Advanced Management
Globis University (MBA)
Senshu University

**Korea**
Yonsei University
Korea Advanced Institute of Science & Technology
SKK School of Business

**Singapore**
Singapore Management University
Nanyang Technological University
National University of Singapore

**Australia**
Monash University
University of Melbourne
Univ. of New South Wales

**China**
China Europe Int. Business School
Zhejiang University

**India**
Indian Institute of Management Ahmedabad (IIMA)
Narsee Monjee Institute of Management Studies
SP Jain School of Global Management
Educomp Raffles Higher Education
KJ Somaiya Institute of Management
Symbiosis Institute of Business
India Institute of Technology
International Management Institute

(*Continued*)

Table 2   (Continued)

**Pakistan**
Lahore University of Management

**Hong Kong;**
City University of Hong Kong
The University of Hong Kong

**Philippine**
Asian Institute of Management, Makati City

**Thailand**
Sasin Graduate Institute of Business

**Taiwan**
National Chengchi University
National Taiwan University of Science

**Israel**
University of Haifa

**Brazil**
Coppead/Ufrj
Federal University of Rio De Janeiro

**Columbia**
CESA (Colegio de Estudios Superiores de Administracio)

**United Arab Emirates**
Institute of Mgt Technology

**Companies**
Dow Chemical, Walt Disney, Pepsico, IBM, Chrysler, NTT (Japan), Management
Association of Japan

**Investment Banks and Consulting Firms**
Goldman Sachs, Mckinsey, Citigroup, Boozallen Hamilton, Boston Consulting Group,
Bain & Company, KPMG, Merrill Lynch, Morgan Stanley Dean Witter, Deutsche Bank,
Blackstone group

**Table 3**   List of Main Users in 2014

| | Countries | Copies |
| --- | --- | --- |
| **Universities in the US** | | |
| Northwestern University | | 68 |
| Nova Southeastern University | | 66 |
| University of Washington | | 53 |
| Bethel University | | 43 |
| Northeastern University | | 39 |
| NYU | | 32 |
| Tulane University | | 31 |
| Brandeis University | | 28 |
| University of Texas | | 25 |
| George Mason University | | 23 |
| University of Rochester | | 21 |
| University of Buffalo | | 20 |
| Columbia University | | 17 |
| University of Connecticut | | 16 |
| Loyola University | | 14 |
| Harvard University | | 10 |
| Tufts University | | 11 |
| **Firms in the US** | | |
| Stormont Consulting Firm | | 23 |
| **Foreign Universities** | | |
| Monash University | Australia | 224 |
| National University of Singapore | Singapore | 152 |
| Graduate School of Management, GLOBIS | Japan | 146 |
| Instituto De Empresa, Business | Spain | 133 |
| SP Jain School of Global Management | India | 113 |
| University of Melbourne | Australia | 113 |
| Educomp Raffles Higher Education | India | 80 |
| Concordia University | Canada | 66 |
| Institute of Management Technology | United Arab Emirates | 60 |
| KJ Somaiya Institute of Management | India | 60 |

(Continued)

**Table 3**   (*Continued*)

|  | Countries | Copies |
|---|---|---|
| Korea Advanced Institute of Technology (KAIST) | Korea | 59 |
| SDA Bocconi School of Management | Italy | 55 |
| University College Dublin (UCD) | Ireland | 54 |
| ESADE — Barcelona | Spain | 54 |
| Symbiosis Institute of Business | India | 42 |
| India Institute of Technology | India | 30 |
| Zhejiang University | China | 29 |
| Senshu University | Japan | 28 |
| City University of Hong Kong | Hong Kong | 28 |
| National Taiwan University of Science | Taiwan | 26 |
| Lahore University of Management | Pakistan | 25 |
| Sasin Graduate Institute of Business | Thailand | 25 |
| University of New South Wales | Australia | 25 |
| Nanyang Technological University | Singapore | 23 |
| Asian Institute of Management, Makati City | Philippines | 17 |
| Lund University | Sweden | 16 |
| Rikkyo University | Japan | 16 |
| International Management Institute | India | 15 |
| Narsee Monjee Institute of Management Studies | India | 15 |
| **Others** |  | **509** |
| **Total** |  | **2,778** |

**Table 4**   List of Main Users in 2013

|  | Countries | Copies |
|---|---|---|
| **Universities in the US** |  |  |
| Nova Southeastern University |  | 141 |
| Hult International Business School — Boston |  | 140 |
| MIT |  | 120 |
| State University of NY |  | 61 |
| Northwestern University |  | 60 |

(*Continued*)

**Table 4**  (*Continued*)

| | Countries | Copies |
|---|---|---:|
| **Universities in the US** | | |
| Hawaii Pacific University | | 25 |
| Hofstra University | | 14 |
| Northeastern University | | 11 |
| University of Washington | | 10 |
| New York University | | 1 |
| Harvard University (Kennedy School of Government) | | 1 |
| **Foreign Universities** | | |
| Monash University | Australia | 246 |
| University of Melbourne | Australia | 180 |
| Graduate School of Management, Globis | Japan | 146 |
| Asian Institute of Management | Philippines | 131 |
| SDA Bacconi School of Management | Italy | 83 |
| Rikkyou University | Japan | 82 |
| China Europe International Business School | China | 65 |
| International University of Singapore | Singapore | 63 |
| ESSEC Business School | France | 30 |
| Indian Institute of Management | India | 24 |
| City University of Hong Kong | Hong Kong | 12 |
| Nagoya City University | Japan | 2 |
| Aoyama Gakuin University | Japan | 2 |
| **Consulting Companies** | | |
| Boston Consulting Group Int. | USA | 21 |
| Bain & Company, Inc. | USA | 14 |
| Contents Works | Japan | 3 |
| **Others** | | 887 |
| **Total** | | **2,575** |

**Table 5**   List of Main Users in 2012

|  | Countries | Copies |
| --- | --- | --- |
| **Universities in the US** | | |
| Wharton, University of Pennsylvania (Nomura Advanced Management, Japan) | | 50 |
| Indiana University | | 21 |
| Fox School of Business, Temple University | | 26 |
| Northwestern University | | 59 |
| Hawaii Pacific University | | 59 |
| State University of New York | | 30 |
| University of Maryland | | 5 |
| **Foreign Universities** | | |
| Asian Institute of Management, Makati City | Philippines | 143 |
| SDA Bocconi School of Management | Italy | 88 |
| National University of Singapore | Singapore | 83 |
| Concordia University | Canada | 83 |
| Instituto De Empresa Business | Spain | 68 |
| University College Dublin (UCD) College of Business & Law | Ireland | 62 |
| Korean Advanced Institute of Science and Technology | Korea | 60 |
| Department of Business Administration, Lund University | Sweden | 50 |
| University of Haifa | Israel | 50 |
| Globis Management School | Japan | 48 |
| Waseda University | Japan | 14 |
| **Others** | | **894** |
| **Total** | | **1,798** |

**Table 6**   List of Main Users in 2011

| **Universities in the US** | **Copies** |
| --- | --- |
| MIT | 182 |
| Northwestern University | 140 |
| Boston University | 55 |
| Cornell University | 32 |
| Indiana University | 32 |

(Continued)

**Table 6**   (*Continued*)

| Universities in the US | | Copies |
|---|---|---|
| Virginia Tech | | 31 |
| University of Maryland | | 22 |
| **Foreign Universities** | | |
| Instituto De Empresa | Spain | 125 |
| SDA Bocconi School of Management | Italy | 97 |
| UNIVERSITY OF HAIFA | Israel | 73 |
| COPPEAD/UFRJ | Brazil | 72 |
| University of British Columbia | Canada | 59 |
| Lund University | Sweden | 50 |
| The University of Hong Kong | Hong Kong | 45 |
| **Others** | | **477** |
| **Total** | | **1,492** |

**Table 7**   List of Main Users in 2010

| | Copies |
|---|---|
| **Universities in the US** | |
| Harvard Business School (MBA) | 1,063 |
| MIT | 185 |
| USC | 130 |
| University of Maryland | 102 |
| Northwestern University | 72 |
| Wharton, University of Pennsylvania<br>   (Nomura Advanced Management, Japan) | 61 |
| Cornell University | 46 |
| University of Texas-Dallas | 38 |
| Boston University | 35 |
| Brigham Young University | 29 |
| Gannon University | 25 |
| Loyola University | 16 |
| Willamette University | 8 |
| Purdue University | 7 |

(*Continued*)

**Table 7** (*Continued*)

|  |  | Copies |
|---|---|---|
| **Foreign Universities** |  |  |
| SDA Bocconi School of Mgt | Italy | 92 |
| Lund University | Sweden | 50 |
| Lund University | Spain | 36 |
| Nanyang Technological University | Singapore | 33 |
| National Chengchi University | Taiwan | 21 |
| Singapore Management University | Singapore | 19 |
| Universitat Duisburg-Essen | Germany | 16 |
| Salford Business School, University of Salford | UK | 11 |
| Federal University of Rio De Janeiro | Brazil | 11 |
| CESA — Colegio de Estudios Superiores de Administracio | Columbia | 10 |
| Asian Institute of Management | Philippines | 10 |
| University of Gothenburg | Sweden | 5 |
| Hitotsubashi University | Japan | 5 |
| **Company** |  |  |
| Contents Works Inc. |  | 2 |
| **Others** |  | **14** |
| **Total** |  | **2,151** |

**Table 8** List of Main Users in 2009

|  | Countries | Copies |
|---|---|---|
| **Universities in the US** |  |  |
| University of North Carolina-Chapel Hill |  | 85 |
| Harvard Business School |  | 80 |
| Willamette University |  | 72 |
| University of Washington |  | 59 |
| University of Texas at Dallas |  | 53 |
| Hawaii Pacific University |  | 47 |
| Northwestern University |  | 45 |
| University of Georgia |  | 40 |

(*Continued*)

**Table 8**  (*Continued*)

|  | Countries | Copies |
|---|---|---|
| University of Hartford |  | 40 |
| USC |  | 28 |
| **Universities in the US** |  |  |
| Central Connecticut State University |  | 28 |
| NY Institute of Technology |  | 19 |
| Gannon University |  | 15 |
| College of William & Mary |  | 15 |
| University of North Florida |  | 15 |
| Boston University |  | 6 |
| MIT |  | 1 |
| **Foreign Universities** |  |  |
| Narsee Monjee Institute of Management Studies (India) | UK | 300 |
| International Professional Managers Association (IPMA) | Netherlands | 151 |
| TiasNimbas Business School | Italy | 115 |
| SDA Bocconi School of Management | Ireland | 55 |
| UCD Michael Smurfit School of Business | Singapore | 45 |
| Nanyang Technological University | Japan | 37 |
| Hitotsubashi University | Singapore | 33 |
| Singapore Management University | Portugal | 24 |
| University of Porto — Faculty of Economics | India | 21 |
| Indian Institute of Management Ahmedabad (IIMA) | Belgium | 20 |
| University of Liege | Germany | 13 |
| University of Applied Sciences Trier | UK | 12 |
| **Others** |  | **377** |
| **Total** |  | **1,895** |

**Table 9** Sales Records of Misawa's Cases by Harvard Business Publishing (HBS), the European Case Clearing House (ECCH) and the Asian Case Research Center, University of Hong Kong (ACRC) in the Past Eight Years (2007–2014)

| | | | |
|---|---|---|---|
| 2007 | 1. Through HBSP | 1,567 copies | |
| | 2. Through ECCH | 483 | |
| | 3. Through ACRC | 10 | Total 2,060 |
| 2008 | 1. Through HBSP | 960 copies | |
| | 2. Through ECCH | 334 | |
| | 3. Through ACRC | 261 | Total 1,555 |
| 2009 | 1. Through HBSP | 1,455 copies | |
| | 2. Through ECCH | 435 | |
| | 3. Through ACRC | 5 | Total 1,895 |
| 2010 | 1. Through HBSP | 2,075 copies | |
| | 2. Through ECCH | 63 | |
| | 3. Through ACRC | 13 | Total 2,151 |
| 2011 | 1. Through HBSP | 1,226 copies | |
| | 2. Through ECCH | 220 | |
| | 3. Through ACRC | 46 | Total 1,492 |
| 2012 | 1. Through HBSP | 1,423 copies | |
| | 2. Through ECCH | 215 | |
| | 3. Through ACRC | 169 | Total 1,798 |
| 2013 | 1. Through HBSP | 2,219 copies | |
| | 2. Through ECCH | 162 | |
| | 3. Through ACRC | 194 | Total 2,575 |
| 2014 | 1. Through HBSP | 2,398 copies | |
| | 2. Through ECCH | 192 | |
| | 3. Through ACRC | 188 | Total 2,778 |
| **Total for the past eight years** | | | **16,304 copies** |

**Table 10**   Author's Most Popular Cases in 2014

|  | Copies |
|---|---|
| 1. Tokyo Disneyland and the DisneySea Park(2): Corporate Governance and Differences in Capital Budgeting Concepts and Methods between American and Japanese Companies | 598 |
| 2. OSG Corporation: Risk Hedging against Transaction Exposures | 531 |
| 3. Tokyo Disneyland (3): New Pricing Policy Needed for Sluggish Demand | 331 |
| 4. Ina Food Industry: A New Management Philosophy for Japanese Businesses | 266 |
| 5. Livedoor: The Rise and Fall of a Market Maverick | 245 |
| 6. Abenomics of Japan: What Was It? Could This Conquer Japan's Decade-Long Deflation? | 174 |
| 7. Softbank's New Strategy: The Largest LBO in Japan | 134 |
| 8. Hostile Takeover Battle in Japan: Fuji TV vs. Livedoor for NBS | 112 |
| 9. A Rogue Trader at Daiwa Bank (A): Management Responsibility under Different Jurisprudential Systems, Practices and Cultures A Rogue Trader at Daiwa Bank (B): The Board Meeting on September 25th 1995 in Japan | 72 |
| 10. Tokyo Disneyland: Licensing vs. Joint Venture (1) | 66 |
| 11. World Co., Ltd., Japan: Why Go Private? | 54 |
| 12. Ina Food Industry (2): Marketing Strategies in a Deflationary Environment | 46 |
| 13. Nireco Co., Japan: Introduction of the Poison Pill | 44 |
| 14. Saizeriya and the Use of Foreign Currency Coupon Swaps: Was this for Hedging or Speculation? | 27 |
| 15. Licensing Arrangement or Joint Venture (4): An *Ex Post* Case Study of Tokyo Disneyland | 20 |
| 16. Keidanre: Foreign Political Contributions in Japan | 12 |
| 17. Bank of Japan (2): The Meeting of April 4, 2013 (Doubling Japan's Monetary Base via Government Bond Purchases) | 5 |
| **Total** | **2,778** |

**Table 11**   Author's Most Popular Cases in 2013

|  | Copies |
|---|---|
| 1. OSG Corporation: Risk Hedging against Transaction Exposures | 481 |
| 2. Tokyo Disneyland and the DisneySea Park: Corporate Governance and Differences in Capital Budgeting Concepts and Methods between American and Japanese Companies | 468 |
| 3. Tokyo Disneyland (3): New Pricing Policy Needed for Sluggish Demand | 410 |
| 4. Livedoor: The Rise and Fall of a Market Maverick | 309 |
| 5. Ina Food Industry: A New Management Philosophy for Japanese Businesses | 300 |
| 6. Softbank's New Strategy: The Largest LBO in Japan | 133 |
| 7. A Rogue Trader at Daiwa Bank (A): Management Responsibility under Different Jurisprudential Systems, Practices and Cultures | 105 |
| 8. Bank of Japan's Meeting in March 2006: An End to the Quantitative Easing Policy | 63 |
| 9. Nireco Co., Japan: Introduction of the Poison Pill | 59 |
| 10. World Co. Ltd., Japan: Why Go Private? | 59 |
| 11. A Rogue Trader at Daiwa Bank (B): The Board Meeting on September 25th 1995 in Japan | 55 |
| 12. Abenomics of Japan: What Was It? Could This Conquer Japan's Decade-Long Deflation? | 45 |
| 13. Licensing Arrangement or Joint Venture (4): An *Ex Post* Case Study of Tokyo Disneyland | 35 |
| 14. Tokyo Disneyland: Licensing vs. Joint Venture | 27 |
| **Total** | **2,575** |

**Table 12**   Author's Most Popular Cases in 2012

|  | Copies |
|---|---|
| 1. Tokyo Disneyland and the Disney Sea Park: Corporate Governance and Differences in Capital Budgeting Concepts and Methods between American and Japanese Companies (and other 3 cases) | 619 |
| 2. Softbank's New Strategy: The Largest LBO in Japan | 325 |
| 3. OSG Corporation: Risk Hedging against Transaction Exposures | 255 |
| 4. Ina Food Industry: A New Management Philosophy for Japanese Businesses | 206 |

*(Continued)*

**Table 12**   (*Continued*)

| | Copies |
|---|---|
| 5. A Rogue Trader at Daiwa Bank: Management Responsibility under Different Jurisprudential Systems, Practices and Cultures | 100 |
| 6. Nireco Co., Japan: Introduction of the Poison Pill | 84 |
| 7. Bank of Japan's Meeting in March 2006: An End to The Quantitative Easing Policy? | 78 |
| 8. Others | 131 |
| **Total** | **1,798** |

**Table 13**   Author's Most Popular Cases in 2011

| | Copies |
|---|---|
| 1. Tokyo Disneyland and the Disney Sea Park: Corporate Governance and Differences in Capital Budgeting Concepts and Methods between American and Japanese Company | 343 |
| 2. OSG Corporation: Risk Hedging against Transaction Exposures | 303 |
| 3. Ina Food Industry: A New Management Philosophy for Japanese Businesses | 143 |
| 4. Nireco Co., Japan: Introduction of the Poison Pill | 139 |
| 5. Softbank's New Strategy: The Largest LBO in Japan | 128 |
| 6. Tokyo Disneyland: Licensing vs. Joint Venture | 88 |
| 7. A Rogue Trader at Daiwa Bank (A): Management Responsibility under Different Jurisprudential Systems, Practices and Cultures | 78 |
| 8. A Rogue Trader at Daiwa Bank (B): The Board Meeting on September 25, 1995 in Japan | 71 |
| 9. Hostile Takeover Battle in Japan: Fuji TV vs Livedoor for NBS | 68 |
| 10. World Co. Ltd., Japan: Why Go Private? | 65 |
| 11. Keidanren: Foreign Political Contributions in Japan | 42 |
| 12. Livedoor: The Rise and Fall of a Market Maverick | 22 |
| 13. J-COM: Share-Trade Irregularities on the Day of IPO | 2 |
| **Total** | **1,492** |

**Table 14**   Author's Cases Used in World Top Universities in 2010–2014

| | Copies |
|---|---|
| **1. Harvard Business School (MBA)** | |
| 1. OSG Corporation: Hedging Transaction Exposure | 968 |
| 2. A Rogue Trader At Daiwa Bank: Management Responsibility Under Different Jurisprudential Systems, Practices And Cultures | 69 |
| 3. Tokyo Disneyland and the DisneySea Park: Corporate Governance and Difference in Capital Budgeting Concepts and Methods Between American and Japanese Companies | 26 |
| 4. Abenomics of Japan: What Was It? Could This Conquer Japan's Decade-Long Deflation? | 8 |
| **2. MIT** | |
| 1. Nireco Japan: Introduction of the Poison Pill | 153 |
| 2. World Co. Ltd., Japan: Why Go Private? | 151 |
| 3. Tokyo Disneyland and the DisneySea Park: Corporate Governance and Difference in Capital Budgeting Concepts and Methods Between American and Japanese Companies | 100 |
| 4. Bank of Japan's Meeting in March 2006: An End to the Quantitative Easing Policy | 66 |
| 5. SOFTBANK's New Strategy: The Largest LBO in Japan | 14 |
| 6. Keidanren: Foreign Political Contributions in Japan | 1 |
| **3. Northwestern University** | |
| 1. A Rogue Trader at Daiwa Bank: Management Responsibility Under Different Jurisprudential Systems, Practices and Cultures | 239 |
| **4. USC** | |
| 1. Tokyo Disneyland — Joint Venture vs. Licensing | 100 |
| 2. Tokyo Disneyland and the DisneySea Park: Corporate Governance and Differences in Capital Budgeting Concepts and Methods Between American and Japanese Companies | 30 |
| **5. Boston University** | |
| 1. Ina Food Industry: A New Management Philosophy for Japanese Businesses | 108 |
| 2. Keidanren: Foreign Contributions in Japan | 16 |
| **6. University of Maryland** | |
| 1. Tokyo Disneyland — Joint Venture vs. Licensing | 122 |

*(Continued)*

**Table 14**   *(Continued)*

| | Copies |
|---|---|
| **7. Wharton (Nomura School of Advanced Management)** | |
| 1. OSG Corporation: Hedging Transaction Exposure (in English and in Japanese; used by Professor John Percival and Professor Alen at the Wharton School of the University of Pennsylvania) | 120 |
| **8. Cornell University** | |
| 1. Tokyo Disneyland and the DisneySea Park: Corporate Governance and Differences in Capital Budgeting Concepts and Methods Between American and Japanese Companies | 62 |
| 2. Tokyo Disneyland — Joint Venture vs. Licensing | 49 |
| **9. University of Washington** | |
| 1. Tokyo Disneyland and the DisneySea Park: Corporate Governance and Differences in Capital Budgeting Concepts and Methods Between American and Japanese Companies | 86 |
| 2. Abenomics of Japan: What Was It? Could This Conquer Japan's Decade-Long Deflation? | 26 |
| **10. University of Texas** | |
| 1. Tokyo Disneyland and the DisneySea Park: Corporate Governance and Differences in Capital Budgeting Concepts and Methods Between American and Japanese Companies | 78 |
| 2. OSG Corporation: Hedging Transaction Exposure | 38 |
| **11. University of North Carolina** | |
| 1. OSG Corporation: Hedging Transaction Exposure | 72 |
| 2. World Co., Ltd., Japan: Why Go Private? | 7 |
| 3. J-Com: Share-Trade Irregularities on the Day of IPO | 5 |
| **12. NYU** | |
| 1. Abenomics of Japan: What Was It? Could This Conquer Japan's Decade-Long Deflation? | 21 |
| 2. Ina Food Industry (2): Marketing Strategies in a Deflationary Environment | 12 |
| 3. Livedoor: The Rise and Fall of a Market Maverick | 3 |
| **13. University of Rochester** | |
| 1. OSG Corporation: Hedging Transaction Exposure | 21 |

*(Continued)*

**Table 14** (*Continued*)

| | Copies |
|---|---:|
| **14. Columbia University** | |
|   1. Tokyo Disneyland and the DisneySea Park: Corporate Governance an Differences in Capital Budgeting Concepts and Methods Between American and Japanese Companies | 17 |
| **15. Tufts University** | |
|   1. Ina Food Industry: A New Management Philosophy for Japanese Businesses | 11 |
| **16. Bocconi (Italy)** | |
|   1. Tokyo Disneyland and the DisneySea Park: Corporate Governance an Differences in Capital Budgeting Concepts and Methods Between American and Japanese Companies | 234 |
| **17. Instituto de Empresa (Spain)** | |
|   1. OSG Corporation: Hedging Transaction Exposure | 68 |
|   2. Tokyo Disneyland — Joint Venture vs. Licensing | 53 |
|   3. A Rogue Trader at Daiwa Bank: Management Responsibility Under Different Jurisprudential Systems, Practices and Cultures | 36 |

# Index